SUSANNA DE VRIES is an international author and former lecturer at the Queensland University of Technology. She writes full time but gives occasional study days as part of the '*Travel and Destinations*' programme run by the Continuing Education Dept of the University of Queensland. She also lectures to branches of the Australian Fine and Decorative Art Society.

Born in London, Susanna attended boarding school at Ascot and then went to study at the Sorbonne University in Paris and won a scholarship to study Art History in Madrid. She speaks fluent Spanish and French and has lived and worked in London, Edinburgh, Berlin, Florence, Barcelona and Sydney. She came to Australia in 1975 and now lives in Brisbane.

Susanna's fourteen books have won her literary awards in Ireland and Britain, and she was made a member of the Order of Australia in 1975 for services to art and literature. She has twice been short-listed for the Queensland Premier's Non-Fiction awards. Many of her books, including *Great Australian Women and Blue Ribbons, Bitter Bread* are now Australian classics.

For further details, see www.susannadevries.com

Edna:
I hope you enjoy
this as much as I did.
Love Maureen Q
June 18-2011.

THE COMPLETE BOOK OF HEROIC AUSTRALIAN WOMEN

TWENTY-ONE EXTRAORDINARY WOMEN WHOSE STORIES CHANGED HISTORY

SUSANNA DE VRIES

HarperCollins*Publishers*

This book contains the text and photos of *Great Pioneer Women of the Outback* and *Great Australian Women in War* by Susanna de Vries.

HarperCollins*Publishers*

Heroic Australian Women in War was first published in 2004 by HarperCollins*Publishers* Pty Limited and *Great Pioneer Women of the Outback* was first published in 2005 by HarperCollins*Publishers* Pty Limited
ABN 36 009 913 517
A member of the HarperCollins*Publishers* (Australia) Pty Limited Group
harpercollins.com.au

HarperCollins*Publishers*
25 Ryde Road, Pymble, Sydney, NSW 2073, Australia
31 View Road, Glenfield, Auckland 0627, New Zealand
A 53, Sector 57, Noida, UP, India
77–85 Fulham Palace Road, London, W6 8JB, United Kingdom
2 Bloor Street East, 20th floor, Toronto, Ontario M4W 1A8, Canada
10 East 53rd Street, New York NY 10022, USA

National Library of Australia Cataloguing-in-Publication entry:

De Vries, Susanna.
    The complete book of heroic Australian
    women / Susanna de Vries.
    ISBN 978 0 7322 9006 1 (pbk.)
    Includes index.
    Women–Australia.
    Women–Australia–Biography.
    Australia–Social conditions.
305.40994

Front cover: main image Vivian Bullwinkel; top right, Joyce Tweddell; (back and) centre right,
Myrtle Rose White; bottom right, Jeannie Gunn (courtesy State Library of South Australia,
B27404/7).
Unless otherwise stated, all photographs are from private collections.
Cover design by Greendot Design
Maps by Jake de Vries
Typeset in 12/15.5pt Bembo by Letter Spaced
Printed and bound in Australia by Griffin Press
70gsm Classic used by HarperCollins*Publishers* is a natural, recyclable product made from wood
grown in sustainable forests. The manufacturing processes conform to the environmental regulations
in the country of origin, Finland.

6 5 4 3 2   10 11 12 13

CONTENTS

About the Author   1

PART 1: GREAT PIONEER WOMEN OF THE
         OUTBACK

Foreword by Terry Underwood   9

Introduction   13

1   Farming Fresh Fields   17
    Georgiana Molloy
    Frances ('Fanny') Bussell
    Elizabeth ('Bessie') Bussell
    Charlotte Cookworthy Bussell

2   The Spinifex Pioneer Who Became the
    'Mother of the North-west'   87
    Emma Mary Withnell

3   Mothering Seven Little Australians at Alice Springs
    Atlanta Hope Bradshaw   119

4   The Story Behind *We of the Never-Never*
    Jeannie Gunn, OBE   165

5   An English Rose in the Outback
    Evelyn Maunsell   217

6   On the Desert Fringe
    Catherine Langloh Parker
    Myrtle Rose White   259

PART 2: HEROIC AUSTRALIAN WOMEN IN WAR

Introduction   305

7   Olive May Kelso King   319

8   Dr Agnes Elizabeth Lloyd Bennett   389
     and Dr Lilian Violet Cooper

9   Sister Alice Elizabeth Kitchen   415

10   Joice NanKivell Loch   475

11   Sister Sylvia Muir, Sister Vivian   517
     Bullwinkel, Sister Joyce Tweddell,
     Sister Betty Jeffrey and other
     'Paradise Road' Nurses

12   Mavis Parkinson and Sister Frances
     May Hayman   573

Acknowledgements   597

Endnotes   601

Index   621

PART 1

GREAT PIONEER
WOMEN OF THE OUTBACK

Facing hardship, danger and deprivation

To Dame Elisabeth Murdoch,
whose life of outstanding generosity to worthy causes
that have touched her heart is an inspiration to
all Australian women today.

And in memory of all those women
who, like Georgiana Molloy, died in the outback
giving birth to children but who lack gravestones or
memorials and whose names have been forgotten.

FOREWORD

ℓℓ ℓℓ ℓℓ

by Terry Underwood

As a modern pioneer woman, I followed my man to the back of beyond. It was 1963 and I was an eighteen-year-old trainee nurse at St Vincent's Hospital, Sydney, when I nursed the patient who broke his back to meet me. After a five-year courtship by correspondence, the strapping young stockman from way up north and his city nurse were married in St Mary's Cathedral in Sydney. We took to the road in a red Bedford truck, loaded with six tea chests of wedding presents, and drove for days — and days and days — to our new home, a bough shed on the banks of a dry creekbed. My journey from the big smoke to one of the most remote locations in the Northern Territory, Australia, the world, was just the beginning of a lifetime of unimaginable adventure.

How could there have been any signposts for the new bride? There wasn't a coil of wire, let alone a fence, no building, no herd of cattle. The nearest hospital and shops were 600 kilometres away. But knowing that our love would make all things possible, I remained undaunted by the challenges of building from scratch our own cattle station in the middle of nowhere, as indeed it was.

How I empathise with my soul mates of yesteryear. The passage of time has done little to dissipate many of the parallels in our lives. The 1960s heralded an era when roadtrains were replacing drovers, but telephones and televisions were just dreams of the future. My new homeland, the last frontier, was considered still to be no place for a woman, just as it was two centuries ago, when opportunities and incentives lured new settlers to our undeveloped lands.

Everyone knew that 'ladies' did not go outback. But this was also an era when wives were duty-bound to follow their husbands wherever the men went. Hard-working, ambitious husbands reassured their loyal wives that the primitive conditions and services would improve in time.

With limited resources but unlimited determination, pioneer women carved out an existence for their families. Of necessity they adopted the roles of teacher, cook, seamstress, storekeeper, gardener, hostess, nurse and midwife. They worked beside their men to clear land, erect shelters and fences, as well as tend livestock. With strength of spirit and dogged persistence, they battled the scourges of the bush.

As each of the stories in this book unfolds, Susanna de Vries faithfully documents the effects of droughts and sandstorms, cyclones and floods in lands blanketed by isolation. We feel the blazing sun, scorching temperatures and drying winds that burn deep, as we traverse the kilometres of bush and desert travelled by the women in buggies or on horseback.

We marvel at the unwavering stoicism of our women forebears. Reliable doctors, medical supplies and fresh food were scarce. As mothers mourned their dead babies, they prepared to fight another round. Somehow courage, commitment and endurance became the pillars of their survival.

Interwoven throughout these stories is an aching loneliness. It is not coincidental that tender friendships with Aboriginal women were developed in nearly each case here. Women of different languages and cultures embraced the unspoken reality that they needed each other, thereby exchanging skills and information. With conflict on many fronts, while the original inhabitants of Australia and the new settlers adjusted to each other, the women from both worlds demonstrated that they could live in great harmony.

It has been said by some that colonial life was boring, tiring and repellent. In an era when females too often failed to realise their worth, these women stood proud. They learned to appreciate and interpret the vibrant colours and raw beauty of their rugged inhospitable terrains, the purity of the air and the fascinating plant life. What astonishing historians were our pioneer women as they collated, documented and wrote now priceless journals and stories! Perhaps one of the most cherished is the Australian classic *We of the Never-Never*, by Jeannie Gunn.

Today the ancient land that has claimed my family remains stunningly beautiful, totally demanding, and still treacherous and unforgiving. The Aboriginal families who have lived and worked beside us at Riveren have demonstrated their unique brand of loyalty and friendship. We all remain inextricably linked by our empathy with the land. Inevitable stumblings at mountainous hurdles and at times sheer unadulterated terror have left us counting more thankfully and frequently than ever all of our blessings.

In the midst of worldwide fear and uncertainty, it has never been more important to pay tribute to the endurance of the land and its people. Complex issues continue to confront us, as the wheels of life spin out of control for too many. At a time when bush people feel abandoned and undervalued, the cry 'go west' has become a hoarse whisper. Yet people everywhere reach out for grass-roots reassurance and inspiration.

Over the decades I have been driven by a very real passion and sense of responsibility to showcase who we are and what we do. Wife, mother, cattlewoman, nurse, cook, teacher, gardener, photographer, author and counsellor are amongst the roles I still juggle each day on our now thriving 3000-square-kilometre cattle station. The vagaries of nature continue to haunt and taunt those who provide vital food to the cities. Yet this city convert remains overwhelmed by the majesty of our timeless country, and the dedication and diverse skills of those who live in harmony with their land, livestock and each other.

I applaud and uphold the legacy of our great pioneer women of the outback. They made it possible for others to follow in their footprints. This superb book rightfully acknowledges their contribution to the development of Australia.

Terry Underwood
Riveren, Northern Territory, 2005

Terry Underwood is the author of the bestselling autobiographies *In the Middle of Nowhere* and *Riveren, My Home, Our Country.* She and her husband run Riveren, a successful Northern Territory cattle station, 600 kilometres south-west of Katherine.

INTRODUCTION

The remarkable stories of ten pioneer women whose lives touch our hearts today illustrate the diversity of women's experiences in many different parts of colonial Australia. These brave women made long, hazardous journeys by ship, buckboard, buggy and horseback to reach remote outback stations.

Travel by horseback, buckboard or buggy was uncomfortable. Pioneer women were forced by Victorian prudery to wear long cumbersome skirts and corsets — uncorseted women being deemed of dubious morality and possibly 'loose women'.

Atlanta Bradshaw was injured when she was thrown from a jolting buggy and fell under the horses' hoofs. She managed to save the baby she was nursing by throwing her to the side. Myrtle Rose White's account of days travelling to take a sick child to hospital was so poignant that the Reverend John Flynn would read it out to audiences from whom he was trying to raise money for the new Flying Doctor Service.

Those who began their journey by steamer or sailing ship faced other hazards: seasickness, stormy weather and shipwreck. Emma Withnell not only saw her family's stock and possessions swept overboard in a storm, but was deposited unceremoniously on an unknown beach along the isolated north-west coast of Western Australia after their ship ran aground.

The women featured in this book can be divided into two categories: those who followed husbands whose work took them temporarily to the outback; and those who went there intending to take up land and settle.

Among the first group was Atlanta Bradshaw, wife of the superintendent of the Alice Springs Telegraph Station, a woman with young children to worry about and no doctor for hundreds of miles. Also in this group were Jeannie Gunn, Evelyn Maunsell and Myrtle White, whose husbands were station managers working on other people's properties.

Women who went to the outback with the idea of taking up their own land and settling permanently included Georgiana Molloy, the Bussell sisters, Emma Withnell and Katie Langloh Parker.

In the outback all these resourceful women faced isolation, danger and tragedy — the classic example being Jeannie Gunn whose husband died from malarial dysentery. For Evelyn Maunsell on Mount Mulgrave Station in Queensland, the isolation was complete during the Big Wet, when the area flooded and became a malaria-ridden hell hole. One of the most emotive stories is that of delicately nurtured Evelyn, living in a manager's house which was little more than a tin shed and nearly dying of malaria while miscarrying when her husband was away at a remote corner of the property.

In the nineteenth century and the early years of the twentieth century, scores of outback children died in childbirth. Georgiana Molloy lost a baby nine days after the birth and later lost a precious toddler by drowning. Each birth and childhood illness in the outback was an anxious and dangerous experience.

Injury, disease and the lack of medical facilities were ever-present. Housing was frequently basic. Floors were often just dirt or ant-bed; walls were usually timber lined with newspaper. Primitive kitchens were separate from the main house with an improvised kerosene tin for a sink, and a wood-fired stove — for which women lacking domestic staff had to chop the wood. There was no glass in the windows, just rough wooden shutters, and no screens to avoid malarial mosquitoes. Summer was hellish, not only due to the heat, but because flies swarmed over eyes and mouths and infected food.

Another terror for these women in a predominantly male world was rape: when husbands were away they feared the swagmen who came to their doors asking for a meal in return for work. Some women were raped or murdered by white swagmen or by Aborigines who bore a grudge against Europeans who had shot their relatives or given them flour laced with strychnine. None of the women featured here recorded a rape (perhaps for reasons of delicacy), but they endured some life-threatening episodes.

Men often remarked that the outback was 'no place for a woman'. This was not only for the amount of drinking and trading of Aboriginal girls that went on, but because there were no proper lavatories. Stockmen and station hands urinated and defecated wherever they wanted. Latrines were open pits with a couple of saplings laid across them to act as a seat; or the lid of a 44-gallon drum with a hole cut in it might be placed across the pit. Most 'dinkum dunnies' lacked a door, so there was scant privacy for women. Victorian prudery prevented most pioneer women writing about this in their journals.

By the 1920s and 1930s, some houses or homesteads had the luxury of a 'thunder box' with a wooden seat and a door that locked — plus a few huge spiders and even a snake or two.

A number of these pioneer women went to live in some of the harshest places on earth and watched creeks and waterholes vanish in the Dry. Myrtle White decried the never-ending dust and sand of north-eastern South Australia. Both she and Katie Langloh Parker endured two of the most severe droughts on record and watched their animals starve and die as crows pecked out their eyes.

Amid this life of hardship, it is heartening to learn that many of these pioneer women developed loving, affectionate relationships with some of their station Aborigines. Atlanta Bradshaw, Katie Langloh Parker and Jeannie Gunn informally fostered part-Aboriginal children, usually girls they saw as neglected or orphaned. They may well have been aware that these girls were at risk from stockmen and telegraph linesmen, who bartered alcohol and tobacco with elders for a bit of 'black velvet'. The father of little Bett-Bett (Dolly Cummings) — Jeannie Gunn's Little Black Princess — for example, was a Scottish telegraph linesman, something Jeannie Gunn never revealed in her writings. In far north Queensland, Mary, a girl from the Coleman River tribe married Albert, who worked for Charlie and Evelyn Maunsell on Mount Mulgrave. Albert and Mary were devoted to Evelyn Maunsell and insisted on staying with her and Charlie even after the family left Mount Mulgrave and started up their own dairy farm on the Darling Downs.

The stories of the European women who pioneered the outback are extraordinary and heartbreaking. In several cases the harshness of the outback triumphed. Drought meant that Myrtle White and Katie Langloh Parker walked away from their properties with nothing to show for decades of hard work. Jeannie Gunn left the Elsey Station grieving and depressed after her husband died of malarial dysentery. Although some women hated and feared Aborigines, it is clear from their writings that Jeannie Gunn, Katie Langloh Parker, Atlanta Bradshaw, Evelyn Maunsell and Emma Withnell took a genuine interest in the welfare of the Aboriginal women they employed and their families, when many settlers were either uninterested or actively taking steps to remove Aborigines from their land.

The voices of these women show us an Australia which was very different from the one we inhabit today — just as articles in the *Bulletin* published in the colonial era reflect a totally different ethos about the land, its Aboriginal inhabitants, the British Empire and the role of women from that of today.

These pioneer women (some of whom had been city dwellers) were all intelligent, adaptable and resourceful. They found themselves keeping a pastoral station, ordering stores, nursing dying men and sick children, planting gardens, sometimes feeding hens, pigs and nursing sick lambs, working harder than they could ever have imagined. They coped bravely with a life that few would put up with today.

With stories from many different areas of Australia placed together for the first time, this book forms an important record for anyone seeking an understanding of Australia's complex past and the day-to-day life of outback women.

CHAPTER 1

Georgiana Molloy
1805 – 1843

Frances ('Fanny')
Bussell
1806 – 1881

Elizabeth ('Bessie')
Bussell
1812 – ?

Charlotte
Cookworthy Bussell
1808 – 1899

She was, of course, far too good for him: but as nobody ever minds having what is too good for them, so he was steady . . . in his pursuit of such a blessing.

JANE AUSTEN, *MANSFIELD PARK*, 1814

FARMING FRESH FIELDS

In the summer of 1829 the engagement was announced between Miss Georgiana Kennedy, eldest daughter of the late Mr David Kennedy and Mrs Mary Kennedy, formerly of Crosby Lodge, Cumberland, and Captain Jack Molloy of the 95th Rifle Regiment. The wedding was to take place later that summer in Scotland before the couple departed for Western Australia.[1]

Georgiana Kennedy resembled one of those pretty girls in white muslin dresses who feature in novels like *Emma, Mansfield Park* and *Pride and Prejudice*; they lose their dowries but still manage to marry the handsome hero. The premature death of Georgiana's father in a hunting accident meant her mother had to sell the family home with its beautiful flower garden and park, dismiss the servants and take her children to live in genteel poverty in the midland town of Rugby, where Georgiana's youngest brother, George Kennedy, attended Rugby School.

In that era, girls were intended to be 'the angels of hearth and home' and sacrifice themselves for their brothers and husbands. Selling handsome Crosby Lodge and moving to a smaller, less expensive house ensured that there was enough money to buy Georgiana's eldest brother, David Dalton Kennedy (known as

Dalton to his family) a commission in the prestigious 95th Regiment, and keep her younger brother at school — but there would be no money left to provide dowries for the daughters.

The shock of their father's death and the move from their ancestral home affected the whole Kennedy family. Georgiana's mother's health deteriorated, Georgiana turned to religion for comfort, and her two younger sisters set about finding husbands to support them.

Georgiana was considered the most attractive of the three Kennedy girls. Her portrait shows a magnolia complexion, large intelligent blue-grey eyes under long lashes, and long fair hair which framed her face with ringlets. She was gentle and reflective by nature, and loved poetry, reading and playing the piano.

The Kennedy sisters, like the Bennett sisters in *Pride and Prejudice*, knew that without dowries they were at a disadvantage in finding husbands. Marriage in that era meant that, while a husband gained a wife and housekeeper, a wife gained lifelong security and status, depending on the husband's income and occupation. Marrying an 'eligible man' was one of women's chief preoccupations, and essential when they were denied access to university or the right to careers or even bank accounts.

Unlike her giddy but mercenary younger sister Mary, Georgiana did not think endlessly of ball gowns, cotillions and weddings. Intelligent but pious, Georgiana was happiest when gardening, playing the piano or reading. She enjoyed 'botanising', which entailed pressing specimens of flowers and seeds between the heavy pages of a large album called a *hortus siccus*, or herbarium, finding their Latin names and noting their habitats and characteristics.

Knowing how unhappy Georgiana was with town life and her reduced circumstances in the cramped little house in Rugby with her quarrelsome sisters, Georgiana's best friend, Helen ('Nellie') Dunlop, invited her to spend time with the Dunlop family at Keppoch House, a Georgian mansion in the south-west of Scotland. Helen Dunlop, her sisters Maggie and Mary, and the rest of the family were Presbyterian followers of Edward Irving, an emotional evangelist whose message warned of the nearness of judgement day. Helen was at the time preparing to marry an evangelical clergyman who was also drawn to Irving.

The era following the Napoleonic Wars was one of high unemployment and those with a strong social conscience, like the Dunlops, were moved to do something to help. They saw doing good works in the Lord's name as a way to counter the evils of slum housing, alcoholism and the lack of schools for the children of the poor and unemployed. The Dunlops of Keppoch House embraced evangelical Christianity with fervour. They involved themselves in setting up 'ragged-schools' for the poor, studied the Bible each day, and soon converted Georgiana to their way of thinking, which required a total commitment to the faith.

Georgiana came to believe that God had a plan for her life. She attended church with the Dunlops twice on Sundays and studied a passage from her Bible each day. She was certain God would make 'the right man' cross her path at the appropriate moment.

Georgiana returned to her mother's home in Rugby, where she tried to impose her religious beliefs on her sisters, causing more conflict between them. With her mind in turmoil, Georgiana wrote to Helen, by now married to the Reverend Robert Story and living in the south-east of Scotland, asking if she could come and stay with her again.

Helen wrote back to say she and Robert would be delighted to have her with them at Rosneath Manse. Georgiana travelled north and found Helen happily living in an attractive old stone manse in a picturesque lakeside vicarage on the Rosneath Peninsula. Here in this tranquil place with its magnificent garden, she felt at peace.

Helen Story and her clergyman husband worked together for the good of their parishioners and seemed utterly content in doing so. Georgiana enjoyed helping Helen visit the sick and the elderly, arranging flowers from the garden in the church, teaching the local children at Sunday school — and making periodic visits to her family.

Georgiana had by this time come to the notice of a handsome man with money, Captain Jack Molloy, hero of Waterloo and senior officer in her brother's regiment. Molloy was reputed to have Royal connections by way of being the illegitimate son of Frederick, Duke of York, one of the many dissolute sons of King George III. What is known for sure is that Jack Molloy had been adopted by a raffish former sea captain who had been court-martialled for cowardice and left penniless. Lending credence to the rumour about his real father being the Duke of York was the fact that Jack's fees for the exclusive Harrow private school and Oxford University had reputedly been paid by lawyers acting on behalf of the Royal family. Molloy also bore a striking resemblance to Frederick 'the military Duke', who had supposedly paid for Jack's commission in the exclusive 95th Regiment.[2]

Jack Molloy was tall and broad-shouldered and more than twice Georgiana's age — a strikingly handsome man who looked far younger than his years. His alleged Royal connections meant he had a certain cachet with women, but he had up till now resisted matrimony. As Captain Molloy and Lieutenant Dalton Kennedy were in the same regiment, it seems likely that this is how he came to meet the Kennedy girls. It may be supposed that Georgiana's sisters, Mary and Elizabeth, did their best to arouse the interest of the captain, simpering and fluttering around him, but it was the much quieter but highly intelligent Georgiana who interested the captain as a potential wife, and he maintained a correspondence with her while he was away with his regiment.

Most of the letters between them have been lost, although a letter from Georgiana dated 11 December 1828 shows them on friendly terms, with Georgiana pleased to hear Captain Molloy's regiment was not travelling to Canada as had been generally believed. By the next year, at the age of forty-eight and with further promotion unlikely, Captain Molloy was planning to forsake military life in favour of opportunities as a civilian.

The economic recession of the post-Napoleonic era had seen great interest in emigration among army and naval officers, who realised their chances of promotion were now very restricted. Captain Molloy had been present at a speech on the advantages of the new colony of Western Australia given by fellow officer Captain James Stirling on his visit to England in 1828. Stirling, who had briefly explored the Swan River area, claimed that Western Australia was highly suitable for settlement and promoted the new colony enthusiastically among army and naval officers.

With the prospect of emigrating to a land where there were few single girls, Jack Molloy badly needed an energetic and resourceful wife and companion. Who better than the beautiful, virtuous Miss Georgiana Kennedy?

Molloy was obviously not put off by any attempts Georgiana might have made to convert him to evangelical Christianity. Her letters discussing religion and its importance to her may indeed have made him keener to make her his wife. Like many men who have led a rakish life, Captain Molloy was probably determined to marry a virgin. It is quite likely that one of Georgiana's attractions for the gallant captain was her purity, sincerity and total innocence of the darker side of life.

In July 1829, he wrote to her proposing marriage and outlining his plans for emigration. Georgiana received Molloy's letter at Rosneath. She must have found 'Handsome Jack', as he was known in his regiment, attractive. For middle-class girls of this period options were limited. They could marry or remain that despised entity a 'spinster' or 'old maid'. But she was a prudent, cautious girl, unsure about the rightness of marrying a man who was not an evangelical Christian.

Doubtless Georgiana spent a long time discussing Jack Molloy's proposal of marriage with Helen. One can imagine Georgiana would have prayed a great deal about what course of action to follow and perhaps read and comforted herself with the redemptive passage in the Bible describing the joy God felt over 'a sinner that repenteth'. The more Georgiana prayed, the more she might have reflected that God intended her to marry Jack Molloy, convert him to her brand of evangelical Christianity and save his soul.

Georgiana was now twenty-four; most girls of her background were married by the time they turned twenty-one. She knew she could not continue to stay forever with Helen Story at Rosneath or with the Dunlop family at Keppoch House. And marriage to Captain Molloy and life in warm, sunny Australia must have seemed far more attractive than either remaining at the house in Rugby or becoming a poorly paid governess.

Georgiana must have convinced herself that she was doing God's will by accepting Captain Molloy and making a new life with him in the Antipodes. She wrote to him accepting his offer, then to her mother telling of her decision to marry and explaining that after a quiet wedding at Rosneath she and her husband would sail ten thousand miles and set up a farming enterprise in Western Australia.

It must have been galling for Georgiana's sisters to think that such an eligible bachelor as Captain Molloy had chosen their high-minded sister in preference to them. Elizabeth had only succeeded in attracting the attentions of a humourless clergyman-turned-librarian; she would soon become the wife of boring Mr Besley, a poorly paid curate.

Captain Molloy was risking his entire capital in this emigration venture and placed a great deal of trust in Captain Stirling's support of the Swan River settlement scheme. He had no idea that the promoters of the Swan River Association were financially dubious and that the area was nothing like the fertile, productive land Stirling had promised them.

In 1826 Captain Stirling, accompanied by the government botanist and sixteen men, had explored the Swan River region on a brief seventeen-day expedition. After only a cursory examination, Stirling had declared the area ideal for settlement and spent a good deal of energy promoting the region. In producing this over-optimistic version of the truth, Stirling may have been encouraged by his father-in-law, wealthy James Mangles, whose interests in the East India Company gave him reason to wish to see a trading port established on the west coast of Australia.

Stirling had duties that kept him in Australia until 1828. He then returned to Britain to personally take up his campaign for free settlement of the Swan River region — as he saw it, before the French took possession. Although the British Government was disinclined at first to fund another colony, Stirling allied himself with a group of investors who had formed the Swan River Association to 'market' a settlement scheme, and he continued lobbying.

One of the original investors of the Swan River Association was Thomas Peel, a woolly-headed idealist and a distant relative of the distinguished statesman Sir Robert Peel, whose name was used to lend the scheme a veneer of respectability. When his associates pulled out of the scheme, Peel teamed up with a silent financial backer, a dubious ex-convict from Sydney named Solomon Levey, and several others.[3]

The Association proposed a scheme by which it would attract and convey free settlers to the Swan River in return for extensive first-choice grants there to Peel and his silent backer. Only people with a certain amount of capital, stock and equipment would be eligible for the scheme, and settlers would be allocated land according to the capital they brought to the colony.

By the end of 1828 the government was persuaded of the need to claim Western Australia for the Crown. After rejecting Peel's initial proposals, it agreed to grant him 250,000 acres, once he had 400 settlers in the new colony. Stirling received a grant of 100,000 acres and was appointed commander of the colony. Regulations were drawn up describing the terms for grants.

Publication of the generous terms for land caused much interest in emigration. This was fanned by entrepreneurs who saw commercial opportunities in the mass migration of wealthy middle-class people and their belongings. Leaflets were widely distributed, offering investor-settlers hundreds of acres of land 'free of charge', just as long as they bought their livestock and provisions and sailed on ships chartered by the promoter. Indeed, land around the Swan River had 'every attraction that a Country in the State of Nature can possess and [was] highly suitable for settlement . . . Emigrants [would] not have to wage hopeless and ruinous war with interminable forests but be given acres of land . . . to which they will be heirs forever'.[4]

Stirling left for Western Australia with a detachment of the 63rd Regiment in February 1829, and arrived there in June. By August, the first free settlers had landed in the new colony, quickly followed by more. By September, with most land still not surveyed nor grants allocated, about 200 migrants were camped on the beach at Fremantle trying to feed families, tend stock and salvage belongings.

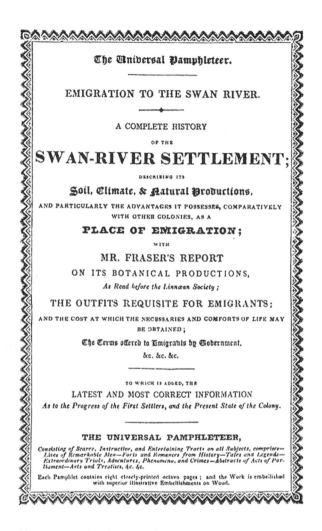

The Universal Pamphleteer.

EMIGRATION TO THE SWAN RIVER.

A COMPLETE HISTORY

OF THE

SWAN-RIVER SETTLEMENT;

DESCRIBING ITS

Soil, Climate, & Natural Productions,

AND PARTICULARLY THE ADVANTAGES IT POSSESSES, COMPARATIVELY
WITH OTHER COLONIES, AS A

PLACE OF EMIGRATION;

WITH

MR. FRASER'S REPORT

ON ITS BOTANICAL PRODUCTIONS,

As Read before the Linnæan Society ;

THE OUTFITS REQUISITE FOR EMIGRANTS;

AND THE COST AT WHICH THE NECESSARIES AND COMFORTS OF LIFE MAY
BE OBTAINED ;

The Terms offered to Emigrants by Government,

&c. &c. &c.

TO WHICH IS ADDED, THE

LATEST AND MOST CORRECT INFORMATION

As to the Progress of the First Settlers, and the Present State of the Colony.

THE UNIVERSAL PAMPHLETEER,

Consisting of Scarce, Instructive, and Entertaining Tracts on all Subjects, comprises—
Lives of Remarkable Men—Facts and Romances from History—Tales and Legends—
Extraordinary Trials, Adventures, Phenomena, and Crimes—Abstracts of Acts of Par-
liament—Arts and Treatises, &c. &c.

Each Pamphlet contains eight closely-printed octavo pages ; and the Work is embellished
with superior illustrative Embellishments on Wood.

Pamphlet setting out the advantages of emigrating to the Swan River settlement.

Around that time in Scotland, Miss Georgiana Kennedy and
Captain John Molloy were married at Rosneath by the Reverend
Robert Story — on 6 August 1829. At the reception at Rosneath
Manse, guests wished the bride and groom good luck and happiness
in their new lives as pioneers. Finally, came the sad moment when
Georgiana had to say goodbye to Helen Story and Maggie and
Mary Dunlop, her dearest friends. Tears flowed as the four young
women embraced, knowing they might never see one another
again. The colony of Western Australia was ten thousand miles
(16,000 kilometres) away.

The newlyweds stopped off at Rugby to see Georgiana's mother, who presented her daughter with seeds of flowers from her garden and bulbs of the tall, white yucca lilies that Georgiana loved.

From Rugby, the couple went to London, where Georgiana went shopping for her new life. She knew that the clothes she took with her to the isolated colony would have to last her for many years. Sensibly, she bought herself plain serviceable dresses which would not show marks and would wash and wear well.

In London, Jack Molloy commissioned a portrait of his new wife. The artist painted her in a low-cut gown, her long blonde hair piled high and falling around her face in fashionable ringlets. This was to be the last time she would ever have her hair styled professionally, although she would not have realised it at the time.

Her adoring husband bought expensive tickets to the opera at Covent Garden and the theatre at Drury Lane. However, the dire poverty Georgiana saw around her in London disturbed her. She was shocked and saddened by the sight of undernourished beggars in the streets, and girls soliciting outside Covent Garden Opera House.

Molloy had already purchased sight unseen two cows, twelve merino sheep, five lambs, twelve pigs, a dozen or so hens and ducks, a dozen fruit trees, two ploughs, two harrows, assorted building tools, horseshoes, and a crate of nails to build their new house and barns. Georgiana now busied herself buying household equipment and supplies. The couple also bought additional provisions for their first months at the Swan River.

Georgiana carefully listed the provisions that were to be loaded in London — whole sides of salt beef and pork, sacks of rice and split peas, twenty-five gallons of vinegar, 600 bottles of wine and 233 gallons of brandy. Jack Molloy was delighted by the capable way his young wife handled their business affairs.

Under the settlement scheme, each settler who sponsored an indentured servant to remain with them for a term of three (or five) years was to receive an additional 200 acres (500 hectares) of land. To receive the maximum land grant possible, and since there were many unemployed men who were happy to volunteer for a chance at a new and better life, Molloy engaged sixteen servants, some married, some single.

For Molloy, who had never handled a plough in his life, the idea of owning hundreds of acres of virgin land seemed an attractive proposition. He had spent a large sum, convinced he would become one of the biggest landowners in the new colony and a man of some importance as the West Australian settlement developed.

Although the Molloys and many other investor-settlers were ready to leave, the departure date of the *Warrior*, the ship that was to transport them was constantly being postponed, as the charterer, Hamilton Semphill, endeavoured to get more passengers for the vessel. With the extended delay and the living in London expensive, the Molloys had to find different accommodation, and they moved to Gosport near Southampton where lodgings were much cheaper. Not only did they need accommodation for themselves and their staff but also barns to store their fruit trees, tools and livestock.

The long delay in sailing also meant that the number of servants engaged by the Molloys dwindled away until the only ones to remain were Captain Molloy's former batman, Elijah Dawson, and his wife, neither of whom had farming experience; Robert Heppingstone and his wife and children; and Staples, an unmarried gardener.

Meanwhile in Gosport, the Molloys met other emigrants, people like themselves, former officers with capital, who were facing redundancy from the army. They, too, were bringing as many servants and animals as possible with them as a way of gaining more land. One of these was Captain Francis Byrne, whose indentured servant William Withnell would become the father-in-law of Emma Withnell (see chapter two).

Finally notice arrived that the ship was to sail and the passengers began loading their possessions. Although Captain Molloy had paid for first-class accommodation, the Molloys were disappointed when they were shown to a dark, cramped cabin underneath the poop deck. This was at least better than steerage class passengers' accommodation, which was located below the deck that held the settlers' horses and cows tethered in their stalls, and hens and roosters clucking away in coops. What no one had foreseen was that excrement and urine from the livestock would drip through the boards to the deck below, causing a terrible reek, while the thud of horses' hoofs drumming on the deck kept many a passenger awake at night.

The *Warrior* sailed on 22 October 1829 with the decks piled high with bales of hay, sacks of dried peas and beans and crates of building materials purchased by the settlers. Initially Georgiana suffered from seasickness, compounded by the fact that she was now in the early stages of pregnancy. The cramped and unsanitary conditions on the ship did little to relieve things, nor did the meals which, even for first-class passengers, were unappetising and in short supply. Semphill had scrimped and loaded insufficient food aboard. In steerage class it was worse; there passengers lived on ship's biscuits and salt beef or pork.

Once she gained her sea legs and ventured out of her cabin, Georgiana made the acquaintance of several families of quality. Among the other passengers was a man Captain Molloy had met six months earlier, a penniless 26-year-old divinity student just down from Oxford. His name was John Garrett Bussell. John had renounced the idea of entering the Anglican Church, but had been unsure of what to do instead. He wanted to marry his sweetheart Sophie Hayward but lacked the capital to do so. Captain Molloy had encouraged John to consider emigrating to Western Australia and given him some leaflets put out by the Swan River Association.

When John's father, the Reverend William Marchant Bussell, died, his widow, Mrs Frances Bussell, had been left with six boys and three girls to raise on a tiny pension. Lack of money meant the Bussell family was forced to move out of their comfortable rectory, and emigration seemed like a suitable solution to their financial problems.

It was agreed that the second boy, William, a medical student, would stay behind in England with his widowed mother and sisters Fanny, Bessie and Mary, and their youngest brother, Lenox, who was only twelve. The other four boys, including John, would emigrate. Once a home was prepared for the family and William had qualified as a doctor, the rest would sail out to Western Australia. It was also agreed that once the Bussell boys were financially secure, John would return to England to marry Sophie Hayward and bring her out to Western Australia.

Aboard the *Warrior,* Molloy made contact with John and his three younger brothers, who were travelling in steerage to save money. He introduced his wife to dark-haired John Bussell and his brothers, nineteen-year-old Charles, sixteen-year-old Alfred and fourteen-year-old Vernon.

Of the four Bussell boys, Charles, who stammered badly, was the most susceptible to feminine charms. He was impressed by the beauty of Mrs Molloy and described her as having 'the air of a lady well born and well bred without having mixed much in the world . . . inclined to the romantic.'[5] He was right: Georgiana's head was still filled with romantic ideas about the joys of pioneering.

The Molloys also met a builder named James Turner, who was a good amateur artist. At the relatively late age of forty-nine (like Jack Molloy), Turner was emigrating with his wife and eight children in search of a better life. Although wealthy, the Turners were of a very different social standing from the Molloys and, despite the awful shipboard conditions, as optimistic as everyone else setting out on the *Warrior.*

Georgiana was excited by the prospect of a new life. She was also very proud of her handsome husband, whom she referred to in a letter to Helen Story as 'dear Molloy'. She was still deeply imbued with a sense of religious mission, sometimes offending her fellow passengers with her efforts to convert them or censure them for impropriety. It soon became apparent that although John Bussell and Georgiana were both religious, they held widely differing views.

Throughout the long and arduous voyage Georgiana insisted that her husband and their servants attended morning and evening prayers. The gallant captain, not known for his religious fervour, seems to have accepted this as the price of a virtuous and dutiful wife.

When finally they arrived at Cape Town, Georgiana and Captain Molloy went ashore so that Georgiana could purchase materials for baby clothes, and Captain Molloy could replace those hens and sheep which had died or been swept overboard in stormy seas.

It was here that the unsuspecting Molloys received their first intimation that the Swan River colony was in trouble.

The British Government had failed to fulfil its promises to the settlers, including Thomas Peel, who had been promised a huge tract of land for his Swan River Association along the southern banks of the Swan River. Instead it had allocated most of the fertile land to those officers and migrants who had arrived earlier in the colony than Peel. Solomon Levey, the official dry goods supplier and hidden promoter of the Swan River Scheme, would never receive his land grant on Cockburn Sound. Unfortunately for Peel's settlers, Levey's ship bearing sacks of flour and other dry goods for members of the Association sank on the way to the Swan River. It was not good news for those coming in their wake.

Georgiana was also advised by friends in Cape Town to have her first child there so she could receive assistance from an experienced doctor or midwife. But her husband was determined that they should continue on to the Swan River, fearing that all good land would be allocated before they arrived. Georgiana agreed with him, something she may have come to regret later.

However, at the time, Georgiana could write to Helen Story from Cape Town, telling her how happy she was in her marriage:

> If [other married friends] are as happy as Jack and I they
> cannot wish for more conjugal affection. Molloy is a dear
> creature and I would not exchange him for ten thousand
> pounds per annum and a mansion in a civilized country.[6]

Further unforeseen delays meant that Georgiana was more than halfway through her pregnancy by the time the *Warrior* eventually sailed from Cape Town bound for the Swan River. On 30 March 1830, five months after leaving England, the *Warrior* arrived at the new colony and anchored off Gage Roads, between the mouth of the Swan River and Rottnest Island.

The following day the ship moved to the area that would eventually become the port of Fremantle. Here the Molloys caught their first sight of what they had been told was a land of milk and honey. They had been expecting a few streets lined with buildings, but all they could see were dense forests reaching down to the water's edge and white sandy beaches stretching away as far as the eye could see. On the beaches were rows of tents surrounded by crates, boxes, furniture and livestock, all jumbled together.

There were no jetties or wharves and no dockworkers to help settlers unload their goods. The arrivals had to load their farm tools, provisions and livestock onto flimsy rafts, and some of their precious cows and hens fell overboard and drowned. The sailors held the settlers to ransom, demanding extra money to carry their belongings ashore from the rafts before throwing the goods higgledy-piggledy on the beach, leaving the settlers to wade ashore as best they could.

The prospect that faced the Molloys and other settlers was described by a young woman named Mary Anne Friend, who accompanied her husband, naval officer, Captain Matthew Friend, to the Swan River in 1830. The Friends had arrived three months before the Molloys with a view to settling but decided not to stay and sailed on to Tasmania. In her journal Mary Anne complained about the blowflies, fleas and mosquitoes at the Swan River. She also noted that polluted water gave the settlers dysentery and that some feared they and their children might eventually starve to death. She wrote that '. . . dread is felt lest there should be a scarcity of provisions. I have never slept in such a miserable place; everything so dirty and such quantities of mosquitoes and fleas'.[7]

An engraved watercolour of the Swan River by Mary Anne Friend shows families camping amid sand dunes with their trunks, grand pianos, bookcases and crates of books, alongside hen coops and tethered calves. It also shows a settler's wife doing her best to cope with the difficulties of cooking over an open fire.

Captain Molloy had been notified that he could select a grant of 12,813 acres based on the considerable sum of money he had outlaid. But this was a hollow promise. The Swan River colony was now in trouble. What little fertile land there was had already been allocated to Captain Stirling's relatives and cronies. Meanwhile hundreds of new settlers were debating whether to go or stay in the hope things would improve. Most of those with money to spare were booking their passage home to Britain.

Engraved watercolour of a camp at the Swan River by Mary Anne Friend (1830).

Some settlers had spent all their money and could no longer continue paying their servants; some of these took to the bottle. Unmarried servant girls, desperate to escape what they feared could be a winter of starvation, had become sailors' molls in the hope of a free passage back to England with their new paramours.

Many of the indentured servants were angry they had been persuaded to travel 16,000 kilometres by sea to face a sandy wilderness. In revenge they did as little as possible for their employers.

For the brief time the Molloys were forced to camp on the beach, Georgiana was excruciatingly uncomfortable. She found their tent hot and stuffy and suffered badly from the heat and infected flea bites. Thousands of fleas lurked in the sand and at night her ankles were black with them. To add to her misery, her stomach was now so swollen she had difficulty walking through the soft sand.

Captain Molloy took careful stock of their situation and how much of his money remained. There was no question of returning. He decided almost immediately that they should make for Perth, the administrative centre of the new colony, where settlers registered before taking up a land grant. With this in mind he paid an exorbitant fee to boatmen to row himself, Georgiana, their servants, and their goods and livestock the twenty-two kilometres upriver to Perth in long boats. Before they even left Fremantle,

Captain Molloy was held to ransom by the greedy boatmen who demanded a premium because the current was so strong.

Yet the journey was a pleasant one — sunlight sparkling on the waters of the river and black swans and pelicans swimming in small bays fringed with reeds. Finally, the Swan widened out into a broad shallow area, and after disembarking the Molloys felt the passage money had been well spent. Perth was a most attractive place. They made their way to St Georges Terrace and asked for Governor Stirling's office. They were directed to a large tent where they learned Captain James Stirling was down south, exploring new land to colonise.

On hearing of Captain Molloy's military credentials and the fact that he had a personal letter of introduction to the Lieutenant Governor, Stirling's staff billeted the Molloys in a series of officers' houses. Mrs Ellen Stirling had remained in Perth, so Georgiana went to leave a calling card on the Governor's wife, as was customary. She found Ellen Stirling to be young, pretty and highly intelligent. The former Miss Ellen Mangles had married James Stirling straight out of the schoolroom and, although quite intrepid, was worried by the situation she now found herself in, like Georgiana expecting her first child in a place with few medical facilities. The two young women discovered they had much in common and had struck up a friendship before Captain Stirling returned from his expedition to the Leschenault and Vasse River estuaries. With his usual optimism, Stirling announced that both areas were suitable for agriculture.

Lieutenant Governor Stirling seemed delighted to meet Captain Molloy. The two men had mutual friends and shared a common background, both being used to command and regarding themselves as aristocrats. Despite the fact that Stirling had made rash promises over land, he was still enthusiastic about the new colony, and Captain Molloy was keen to get whatever advantage he could.

Mrs Stirling told her husband she was impressed with Mrs Molloy's poise and charm under extremely difficult circumstances and this may have been the reason they received a formal invitation to an official reception hosted by the Stirlings.

On the day of the reception, those who had secured invitations

— people with family connections and government posts — unpacked their best clothes from their trunks. The guests assembled in the huge Government tent where refreshments were served. Conversation was polite, stilted and formal. Plans for literary and musical societies, lending libraries and schools were discussed. On a platform draped with the Union Jack, Lieutenant Governor Stirling made a brave but fulsome speech to the new settlers, most of whom knew little or nothing about farming under harsh Australian conditions. He urged those who had not yet taken up their land to sail south to where it was cooler. They would find better land for their crops and livestock there, he said.

Georgiana found Perth beautiful but she suffered badly in the stifling heat. Once she learned the weather would be cooler there, she was keen to go south. Trusting the advice of Stirling, the Molloys, along with the Bussell brothers and James Turner and his family, whom they had remet, prepared to take up land in the south-western corner of the new colony.

Although he had never visited it, Stirling had, on the basis of reports from seal-hunters, sung the praises of the area that he had named Augusta, between Cape Leeuwin and Flinders Bay. All three families would have their main land grant for housing close to the beach between Seine and Flinders Bays and they would be given additional grazing land in the interior.

Since there were no roads to take them south, the settlers agreed to share the costs of chartering a ship. Just like the boatmen on the Swan River, the captain of the transport vessel *Emily Taylor* charged them a highly inflated fare.

By now, due to so many unforeseen expenses, Jack Molloy's funds were dwindling and he feared they would be left penniless. He was very relieved when Governor Stirling appointed him resident magistrate at Augusta for which he would be paid a small but regular salary. James Stirling also agreed to make up the balance of the money owing for the ship's charter from government funds on condition that the ship would transport the government surveyor, Captain Kellam, and a group of British soldiers — and then announced that he would accompany them also.

As soon as the *Emily Taylor* was ready, the Molloys and their servants, the Bussells and Pearce, their indentured servant, the Turner family, a labourer named John Herring, who was paying his own way, and half a dozen soldiers loaded all their goods and livestock aboard the ship. The weather was fine as they sailed down the coast and rounded Cape Leeuwin. They must have felt they were true pioneers, the first white settlers in the largely unknown frontier.

On 2 May 1830 the ship arrived off Flinders Bay. Over the following four days Captain Molloy and the other men made trips from the ship to explore the land. Satisfied, they decided to begin the slow process of disembarking. When Georgiana finally reached shore, she found herself facing a strip of white sandy beach fringed by forests of huge jarrah trees which grew nearly down to the water's edge. Between them was dense undergrowth made up of small shrubs, groundcovers and creepers. For Georgiana, the prospect of giving birth to her first child at such a remote spot with no medical help or midwife on hand must have been a nightmare.

Satisfied or not, having come so far and spent so much money to get to Flinders Bay, the pioneers had little choice but to unload their goods. Once again they pitched their tents on the beach.

Stirling, possibly embarrassed that his enthusiastic reports on the suitability of the Swan River area had caused the settlers to take up hundreds of acres of infertile land, immediately made each of the pioneer families their small land grant at Augusta so they could start building. He allotted James Turner twenty acres; Captain Molloy fifteen acres, the Bussell brothers ten acres and John Herring likewise. Stirling promised that further acreage would become available once the surveying was completed. His promise meant that the indentured servants thought only of breaking their indentures and trying to obtain land of their own.

Before sailing back to Perth, Stirling left Captain Kellam in charge of the survey, which would take over a year to complete, together with a few soldiers commanded by Lieutenant Richard Dawson. Surrounded by vast jarrah forest, the settlers were now completely on their own. To make matters worse the winter rains started to pour down.

The men set about cutting down the jarrah trees to clear the land. It took six men three days of hard work to cut down a single tree, as the timber was so hard. Then they had to grub out the stumps before their primitive ploughs could work the land and prepare it for planting. The settlers had believed such magnificent trees must mean the soil was fertile but this also turned out to be a fallacy.

Heavily pregnant Georgiana confined herself to the area on shore near their tent. In the intervals when the rain ceased, she attempted to stew the wild fowl her husband and their servant Elijah Dawson had shot; the only vegetables available in this wilderness were the split peas they had brought with them in sacks from England.

Once her labour pains came on, Georgiana lay in her leaky tent on the small strip of sandy beach with an umbrella over her bed to keep the rain off her. With no doctor or midwife to help, on 24 May 1830, after twelve hours of agonising labour, Georgiana's first child was born. The only assistance Georgiana received was from Ann Dawson, who probably knew little about midwifery, but was at least able to cut the umbilical cord.

The Molloys named their much-wanted baby Elizabeth Mary after both of Georgiana's sisters. The baby was weak, had difficulty breastfeeding and kept bringing up her food. There was no doctor to consult, and no remedies offered to help the baby keep down her mother's milk.

Despite Georgiana's loving care, nine days after her birth, Elizabeth died, causing intense grief to both of her parents. That evening they buried their baby girl in a tiny plot. Georgiana scattered wild flowers over the grave. Leaving the tiny corpse in the damp soil was the hardest thing poor Georgiana had ever done.

The horror of burying her first child under such harsh circumstances scarred Georgiana

Tents for Travellers & Emigrants

BENJAMIN EDGINGTON,
Marquee, Tent, Rickcloth & Flag Manufacturer

Georgiana Molloy would have given birth to her first child in a tent like this on the beach at Augusta.

deeply. She struggled to find religious meaning and comfort in the tragedy. Possibly she regretted continuing with her husband to Augusta instead of remaining in Cape Town and giving birth there. Years later Georgiana unburdened her still palpable grief to Helen Story. The trigger to do so was the receipt of a letter from Helen informing her that she and her husband, Robert, had also lost a much-wanted baby. Helen's letter seemed to have acted as a catharsis: all Georgiana's pent-up sorrow broke down. Doubtless she shed a few tears as she replied to her dear 'Nellie':

> I was indeed grieved my dear Nellie, to hear of the poor
> infant's demise for your sakes . . . I could truly sympathize
> with you, for language refuses to utter what I experienced
> when mine died in my arms in this dreary land with no
> one but Molloy near me . . . I know I have not made use of
> those afflictions God designed . . . I thought I might have
> had one little bright object left to solace all the hardships
> and privations I endured and have still to go through. [8]

As newly created resident magistrate, Jack Molloy had been empowered by Lieutenant Governor Stirling to provide certain services to the Swan River colony. His area of jurisdiction was Augusta, and later the Vasse and Leschenault, and his official duties included exercising a general superintendence over all the district, acting as justice of the peace when required, inspecting roads, buildings and other works, and receiving and forwarding all requests for land grants. He was to keep salary and cash accounts on the usual forms, transmit them every month, keep an account of all persons residing in his district and render an accurate report on them at the close of each year. [9]

This meant a great deal of paperwork for which Molloy needed Georgiana's help. However grim the conditions, the Molloys could not give up. Having burned his boats and left the army, Captain Molloy still clung grimly to his hopes of a good future if they worked hard enough. A man used to duty and command, he was proud to have been appointed representative of the young Queen Victoria.

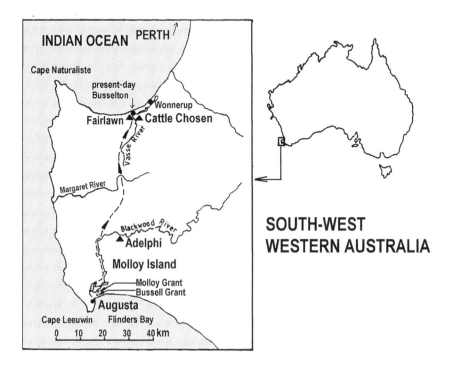

Even though her husband had not yet selected his land, Georgiana set about establishing a garden at Augusta. Near her tent, she sowed the mignonette and other seeds she had brought with her from England, the yucca lily bulbs her mother had given her, and peach stones and grape pips she had brought from Cape Town.

The felled trunks of the jarrah were turned into boards and slowly the Molloys' small timber house took shape. It had a veranda, a separate kitchen and scullery to reduce fire risk, a thatched roof and an outside bathroom with a bucket shower. There were separate living quarters for Elijah and Ann Dawson, the only servants to live with the Molloys. By the end of August 1830, the Molloys were able to camp in the shell of their future home.

The Molloys found fish were plentiful and easy to catch; ducks, herons and swans provided meat. Swan, cockatoo and parrot pies became delicacies, as did kangaroo tail soup. None of the settlers along the Blackwood River went hungry to begin with, but they begrudged the time spent hunting and fishing when there was so much land clearing and building to be done.

It soon became apparent that the pioneering life favoured brawn and those with building skills over those with a classical education. James Turner, the semi-literate builder with four strapping sons, had the necessary resources to build himself a large, solid house with stone foundations, which he patriotically named Albion.

Before long Captain Molloy had received applications for land grants from fifteen more settlers. They came from a wide spectrum of society and included the Molloys' former servant Robert Heppingstone (who had bought himself out of his indenture), and free settlers George Layman and John Cook, as well as the surveyor Captain Kellam and his brother Henry. Kellam soon resigned his commission and was replaced by surveyor Edwards.

The community slowly grew with the arrival by ship of another detachment of soldiers sent there by Captain Stirling, who may have feared that the indigenous Wardandi-Bibbulmun might try to attack the settlers. They included Dr Charles Simmons, a young medical officer, whose arrival must have been welcomed by Georgiana, who was soon pregnant again. But more disappointment was in store, and Georgiana miscarried early in the pregnancy. In a sign of how things would be for her at Augusta, she went into labour alone and unattended, with her husband and Dr Simmons away.

By now the busy Bussell boys had built themselves a small wooden house they named Datchet, after a hamlet in southern England. Around the house they planted beds of potatoes which, to their dismay, would not grow and remained as small as marbles. Only after a disastrous farming season did it become apparent that the soil of Augusta was unsuited to agriculture. Jarrah trees were the only thing that grew well.

On the north of the settlement of Augusta, along the line of what was officially known as Osnaburgh Street, now stood the houses of James Turner, the Bussells and the Molloys, all facing out over Seine Bay, with Flinders Bay and the landing place to their left.

As the Augusta settlement developed, Sunday services were held on the Molloys' veranda. But Georgiana was very lonely, missing her adopted sisters Maggie and Mary Dunlop and Helen Story. She had now lost two babies, and pined for someone at Augusta with whom she could replicate the close female friendships she had enjoyed in Scotland. She wrote to Helen telling her how homesick and isolated she was, and added that the soldiers and their wives were a rowdy, drunken crowd. Their drunkenness was made worse by the fact the men were issued with a daily allowance of rum, supplied by the army quartermaster on the orders of the British Government. Rather than joining in with the drinking parties, both the Molloys and the Bussells spent their evenings separately, reading by candlelight.

Georgiana comforted herself with the thought that the Bussell sisters, when they finally arrived, might bring her the company she craved, and by daydreaming about beautiful gardens, including those of Rosneath Manse and the Dunlops' garden at Keppoch House.

The Bussell boys had their own problems: they were running short of money. They had been awaiting a transfer from their mother in England, which should have reached them in the final months of 1830. But the Bussells seemed to be dogged by bad luck, and the transfer went astray, leaving the boys practically penniless. Exacerbating their situation, because the crops had delivered a poor yield, food had to be ordered in quantity and sent down from Perth by cutter.

With their money running low and anxious about their future, John Bussell set about making exploratory trips along the Blackwood River. He reached the conclusion that they would do better further up the Blackwood on a promontory he named the Adelphi, which was surrounded on three sides by water rendering it safer from attack by the Wardandi-Bibbulmun. The Bussells applied for and received an additional land grant there.

Eventually the transfer of money did arrive but it was an anxious time for the Bussells, during which Jack Molloy was both kind and generous to them. As he had been the one to persuade John Bussell to emigrate, possibly the captain felt some responsibility for them. He lent them seed corn to plant and agreed to temporarily employ their manservant Pearce, which would mean one less mouth for the Bussells to feed.

He also tried to find Charles a government job, so they would at least have one salary coming in, and persuaded Lieutenant Governor Stirling to let Charles Bussell act as government storekeeper at Augusta. By September 1831 Charles was earning a salary and the Bussells could afford to take Pearce back so he could help them finish the two small houses they were building for their mother and sisters, to be ready when they arrived.

Possibly anxiety over money may have caused differences of opinion between the Molloys and the Bussells, but relations between the two families began to deteriorate from about this time. The Bussell boys and Georgiana differed sharply in their approach to the Wardandi, a clan of the large Bibbulmun-speaking group whose territory stretched south from Perth down as far as Flinders and Geographe Bay.

When the British newcomers had first waded ashore and pitched their tents at Augusta, it was the beginning of the wet season and the Wardandi had moved inland to avoid the rain. When they returned in the drier months and found strangers on their land, the Wardandi interpreted the white-skinned men and women as ghosts of their long-dead ancestors whom they referred to as *djanga*. The trusting Wardandi hospitably showed the new arrivals springs of fresh water. They also indicated that there were grassy plains further north on the Vasse River which flowed into another bay (Geographe Bay), larger than the one at Augusta. The Wardandi's tribal lands, made rich in supplies of food through their fire-stick farming methods, seemed abundant and they had no qualms about sharing their game and fish.

For their part, with very different ideas about property and ownership, most of the settlers saw the Aboriginal people as a threat to their wealth creation and certainly not with rights of their own. The hardworking Bussell boys were dismissive of the Wardandi because to their eyes they did not farm or improve the land.

In contrast, Georgiana, who was principally concerned with laying out and planting the garden around her house, came to admire the Wardandi for their knowledge about the native plants she was just beginning to appreciate, and she attempted to learn a few words of their language so she could converse with them.

In early 1831, Georgiana discovered she was pregnant for the third time. She decided to rest as much as possible this time, determined not to lose this baby. With the Heppingstones, the best of the servants whom the Molloys had brought out with them, gone to take up their own land, Jack Molloy was left with only Staples the gardener and Elijah Dawson to perform the farm work. Georgiana had the increasingly unwilling Ann Dawson, who was also pregnant, to help her with their primitive arrangements for washing, cooking and carting water from the nearby Blackwood River. House cleaning seemed endless and the floors were often coated with fine sand as they were so near the beach.

Jack Molloy was busy morning, noon and night, either supervising the increasingly wider area he was responsible for or visiting the administration in Perth to meet some official request or other. Georgiana had to double as housewife and resident magistrate's wife, and in his absence to attend some of his duties. Her husband's returns home were occasions for great rejoicing.

On 2 November 1831, Governor and Mrs Stirling arrived for an overnight stay at Augusta. Despite the fact that Georgiana was only a week away from giving birth, it seemed she managed to prepare an excellent dinner for the Stirlings and provided a host of delicacies, duck and a variety of fish. The Stirlings greatly admired the large garden Georgiana had designed and planted.

For Georgiana the educated conversation of Ellen Stirling must have been a pleasure. It is likely that the festive meal took place by candlelight rather than in the gloom of the evil-smelling slush lamps they normally used. Conversation around the dinner table presumably ranged over subjects such as whether Perth would go ahead as the capital of the new colony, the planned balls and other entertainments of the settlers, and the exciting overall prospects for the new settlers. At some stage in the visit Georgiana must have mentioned to Ellen Stirling that she was collecting seeds from native plants, writing down details of their habitat, flowering season and the names by which the Wardandi-Bibbulmun called them.

Possibly at this juncture, Ellen Stirling may have mentioned her bachelor cousin, Captain James Mangles, a retired naval officer and a fellow of the prestigious Royal Geographical and Royal Societies. Mangles was passionately keen in cataloguing rare plants and collecting their seeds. He had made a trip out to Western Australia earlier that year and taken home with him the seeds of some native plants. Possibly Ellen Stirling said nothing to Georgiana but thought to herself that she would write and tell her cousin he had at Augusta a fellow enthusiast for his 'botanising' studies. In any case, it would be a letter from Ellen Stirling's cousin, Captain Mangles, which would alter Georgiana's life considerably.

The Stirlings stayed overnight in a vacant house and then with their entourage boarded their ship and headed north to Perth. Five days after the Stirlings departed, on 7 November 1831, Georgiana gave birth to a strong, healthy girl. They named her Sabina Dunlop Molloy, after Georgiana's best friends, the Dunlops of Keppoch House.

In view of the lack of medical help at Augusta, it was fortunate that Sabina turned out to be a healthy and contented baby. Georgiana found she greatly enjoyed the business of mothering, but with a baby to breastfeed and care for and none of the labour-saving devices we take for granted today, housework and mothering were time-consuming and tiring.

There was mending, sewing, carting water, boiling it up, washing, cleaning, cooking and salting down of meat, as well as hours of food preparation, with no frozen or tinned foods to rely on. It was the task of every housewife to make slush lamps or candles to light the house. Georgiana also had to run the dairy and look after their farm whenever her husband was away. All this work she had never imagined herself doing with a child to raise, let alone under such primitive conditions. By now Ann Dawson had turned sulky, did as little work as possible and dreamed only of the day when she and her husband, Elijah, would be free of their indentures and could work their own land.

In November 1831, John Bussell accompanied surveyor Edwards on an overland expedition northwards to Geographe Bay. There they found the 'fine grassy plains' the Wardandi had indicated, and local people who kindly showed them good waterholes. The Vasse River area seemed far better suited to agriculture than the heavily timbered country around Augusta and the Blackwood River.

John Bussell wrote a long report on their expedition. He handed it to Captain Molloy, who invited John to the house to discuss making an application to exchange part of their extensive land grants at Augusta for better grazing land at the Vasse. It was remarkable that these two men were considering moving their operations after expending such huge efforts to settle at Augusta. Government Resident Magistrate Molloy had just named the streets of Augusta,[10] and taken out a further land grant on a site he called Molloy Island in the Blackwood River.

But the Augusta settlement was far from flourishing. By February 1832, supplies of flour in the government store were running short and the price of flour had soared in Perth as well. The settlers were eating wild spinach, parrot pie and pigweed stew, and shooting kangaroos to survive. Finally, at the end of May, a transport ship called the *Sulphur* arrived, bringing the hungry settlers fresh supplies at reasonable prices.

With Jack Molloy's eyes also now resting firmly on the Vasse, the following November he sailed for Perth to apply for over 12,000 acres of land there for himself, leaving Georgiana and Sabina to fend for themselves yet again. Feeling depressed, lonely and overworked so near Christmas, Georgiana wrote a long and revealing letter to Maggie Dunlop. She told of her delight in little Sabina but indicated strained relations with their neighbours over a wandering cow that the Bussells had shot:

> This life is too much both for dear Molloy and myself . . .
> I have all the clothes to put away from the wash; a baby
> to put to bed; make tea and drink it without milk as they
> shot our cow for trespass; read prayers and go to bed
> besides sending off this tableful of letters.

She discussed their prospects, but obviously found it hard to see beyond the workload she was burdened with. She also confided in Maggie about things which she could not tell anyone else at Augusta where she had to keep up appearances as resident magistrate's wife, representative of the Queen and Governor in the area.

She told Maggie how:

> Molloy again went last Monday to view his large grant of land at the Vasse — a most pleasing country and answering with truth to the description given of its park-like appearance, with long waving grass, and abounding also in kangaroos.
>
> In the interim a vessel has been in, which has given me not only my own, but Jack's letters to write — which I am unable to do — as at the beginning of the week I was confined to my bed from over-exertion . . . I must unbosom myself to you, my dear girl . . . I am, of necessity, my own nursery-maid . . . I told you how it would be: I should have to take in washing and Jack carry home the clean clothes in a swill [a tub to hold pig-food]. The last of this has not yet happened, but between ourselves, dear Maggie, the first is no uncommon occurrence . . .
>
> I wish I had you here to help me. What golden dreams we used to have about your coming to stay with me! How would you like to be three years in a place without a female of your own rank to speak to or be with you whatever happened?

At one point in her letter Georgiana, once acknowledged as the prettiest girl in Cumberland, jokingly refers to herself as 'poor worn-out Mrs Molloy'. Missing Maggie, Mary and Helen very much, she signed the letter to Maggie 'With unabated affection from your sincerely attached sister'.[11]

ℓℓ ℓℓ ℓℓ

The settlers hoped that in 1833 life would be easier. The Bussell boys looked forward to the arrival of two of their sisters early in the year.

They were a close-knit family and perhaps they also expected that the women would make their domestic situation less messy and chaotic.

On 26 January 1833, 26-year-old Frances ('Fanny'), only one year younger than Georgiana, and high-spirited 20-year-old Elizabeth ('Bessie') Bussell arrived in Perth, with their youngest brother, Lenox, their former nurse, Phoebe Bower, and another servant, Emma Mould. The girls spent six happy weeks in Perth being entertained left, right and centre.

Like their brothers, the Bussell girls had boundless stores of energy. There were at that time few attractive single women in Perth, so the girls were deluged with invitations, including several to functions at Government House. Had the sisters stayed in Perth they would doubtless have received proposals of marriage. But the Bussell girls had a strong sense of family and were determined to sail south to Augusta and keep house for their bachelor brothers.

Directly he heard his sisters had arrived, John boarded the colonial schooner *Ellen* in Flinders Bay and sailed north to Perth, to escort his sisters down the coast.

Georgiana was excited at the thought of some female company at last. She had insisted that the girls should not begin life at Augusta in the rough bachelor quarters of their brothers and went to great pains to prepare for them the empty house of Lieutenant Dawson, which was often used as a guest house.

Fanny, a great chatterbox, and the spirited, vivacious Bessie were surprised by John's bushwhacker appearance when he arrived in Perth wearing 'canvas trousers made by his own hands . . . hair and beard both long . . . and moustaches enough to give a bandit look'.[12]

John and his sisters left Perth aboard the *Cygnet* in mid-April, arriving at Augusta on 20 April 1833. The following day Fanny wrote to her mother and told her that Captain Rolleston, the *Cygnet*'s captain, had been very attentive and they had dined with him frequently. Their trunks had arrived in good order, and both she and Bessie were well and thrilled to see their brothers, 'our own darlings', after such a long and anxious separation.

Their ship had landed them at sunset about a kilometre away from the three most important houses in Augusta — those of the

Molloys, the Bussells and the Turners — and Fanny described how they had followed a winding footpath lined by peppermint trees and with the unfamiliar scent of wild rosemary and pelargoniums. The path was bordered by low sandhills which muffled the sound of the waves, and the sky slowly faded from red to pink and pale lemon. They passed the farm labourers' allotments, with their little wooden cottages, until they reached the Blackwood River.

John and Alfred Bussell carried the luggage and Fanny was escorted by the current surgeon, Mr Green, although she had been warned by John that Mr Green was still yearning unrequitedly after Ann Turner, the daughter of James Turner, who had married the previous year. It was almost dark by now but Fanny saw that 'the river was broad and beautiful and the country more richly wooded than the English imagination can conceive'. She continued:

> Mrs Molloy came out to receive us with her little Sabina in her arms, looking so youthful and interesting. Her home is very comfortable and she is so active. We are to stay here for a few days, but as she has not accommodation for us she has fitted up one of Mr Dawson's houses so nicely, a French bed and all sorts of land comforts. A vase of sweet mignonette upon the table . . . and a large wood fire blazing on the hearth cast a cheerful light around. We spent a very pleasant evening, dear Charley [brother Charles] and Mr Green being of the party, though I must say that all [word indecipherable] with respect to him are futile, so let there be no speculations.[13]

(Clearly Mrs Bussell was as keen as Georgiana's mother had been to marry off her daughters.)

Georgiana did not describe the Bussell sisters in her letters but we know from a watercolour made of the Bussell family before they left for Australia that the girls were slim and attractive with dark curly hair and dark eyes.

Fanny and Bessie were too excited to sleep and walked over to see the boys' house. They were shocked to see how thin their brothers had become through working hard to establish themselves on the land and living off the very simple things they could cook for themselves. They found their brothers had only had very rudimentary help from Pearce. Their little wooden house was filthy and 'resembled a bandits' cave' with hammocks suspended from the ceiling. Casks and barrels of all description lay around. They found young Alfred and Vernon eating rashers of salt pork and pancakes without the help of knives, plates or forks. Dirty clothes and dishes were piled everywhere.

The brothers and sisters embraced, laughed and talked, fired off questions and hardly listened to the answers. By now the moon was rising, far larger than in the northern hemisphere, so they all went for a walk on the beach. Fanny wrote to her mother that she was thrilled 'by the wildness and grandeur' of their new surroundings.

The following day the Bussell sisters set to with a will to clean up the mess. It was even worse than the girls had thought. Fleas and bugs infested the boys' bedding. Washing dirty clothes was a difficult job without running water, and they had to cart buckets of water to the kitchen and heat it on the wood-fired stove. Fanny and Bessie could manage cleaning very well but had to learn from Phoebe Bower, who was too old to do heavy work, exactly how to bake bread and starch and iron clothes.

They cleaned up the mess the boys were living in but the sheer amount of housework would eventually get Fanny down. After a few weeks she burst into tears thinking that without any running water washday would last from 'Monday till Saturday'.

The Bussell girls, daughters from a vicarage, now had to learn a complete new range of skills — how to ride horses, groom them and harness them to the plough and how to row the boat which their brothers had constructed to cross the river. But the girls were young, strong and healthy and found they loved outdoor life. They were proud of the way they tackled the vegetable garden and planted neat rows of potatoes and other vegetables, and looked forward to harvesting them.

Though she found them pleasant enough, Georgiana did not forge the close friendships she hoped she would with the Bussell sisters. Besides the fact that they were busy attending to their brothers and the farm, it appears Georgiana had little in common with them.

Georgiana enjoyed playing and listening to classical music on the piano. Fanny also played the piano but preferred popular songs, while Bessie loved books but had little ear for music. Georgiana enjoyed cultivating flowers and reading poetry and religious tracts. The Bussell girls were far less intellectual. They enjoyed books but had very different tastes in literature from Georgiana.

Fanny and Bessie were to prove better suited to outback life than Georgiana. By now Pearce had served his indenture and had had enough of pioneering and running short of rations. When another whaling ship came into Flinders Bay he sought employment as a deckhand and departed on it. The girls pitched in to do farm chores as well as housework, and even helped their brothers build post and rail fences. Their good health and high spirits meant they could work all day from dawn to dusk, sharing the housekeeping, the butter and cheese-making, feeding the turkeys, ducks and hens, and working in the large vegetable garden. Their many cheerful hands making light work must have made the loneliness Georgiana and little Sabina suffered even more difficult to bear.

In May, however, the household split up. Bessie went upriver with Emma Mould and many of the household goods to live at the little wooden cottage the boys had built at the Adelphi. John, Vernon, Alfred and Lenox were often at the Vasse. Chatterbox Fanny stayed behind to look after Charles at Augusta.

≈ ≈ ≈

For all her hardship and loneliness, Georgiana was beginning to appreciate her new surroundings. A few months before her bitter letter to Maggie Dunlop, she had written to her sister Elizabeth not only of the 'heavenly clime' she was now living in, but in some detail about the brightly coloured birds that surrounded her and the flowers and leaves of the native plants she had observed. Georgiana loved the warmth and the sunlight and described in a letter to Helen Story how she would sit on her veranda surrounded by the sweet scents of her flowers and shrubs.

While she was most interested in her flowers, Georgiana also turned her expertise to the Molloys' crops. Their first wheat crop at

Georgiana Molloy and the Bussell women would have used irons like these. Those on the top row were heated on the stove. Those on the lower shelf were filled with hot coals. None had any temperature control.

Augusta had been ruined by the fungal disease known as rust. To avoid this happening again, before their second crop was sown in 1833, Georgiana organised for the gardener, Staples, to soak all their seed corn in salt water then dry it off. The result in June was the best harvest at Augusta.

That year, due to a fire at Kitty Ludlow's home, Georgiana was able to obtain the resident services of crippled Kitty Ludlow who also suffered from epilepsy. Kitty was the wife of a labourer who had an alcohol problem. Although her help was limited, Kitty was able to provide baby-sitting assistance and do dressmaking for Georgiana. She was also company for Georgiana when Jack Molloy was away.

Each afternoon Georgiana left Sabina in Kitty Ludlow's charge and the little girl would sit on Kitty's lap by the fireplace. One day, a mud-brick wall beside the fireplace collapsed following a prolonged rainstorm. Fortunately Sabina, who was about to run to the fireplace where Kitty was sitting, had instead stayed with her mother. Upset but relieved, Georgiana suffered the realisation that she could have lost another beloved child if the wall had fallen on Sabina.

Georgiana was now pregnant for the fourth time and grateful for the help Kitty could provide, but it was not to last. Kitty became increasingly subject to epileptic fits. She foamed at the mouth, rolled on the floor and her weakening condition alarmed and distressed Georgiana. Each fit left her worse than before. Kitty's mental processes gradually clouded and her physical condition weakened until she was condemned to Molloy Island where she died early in 1834, raving and insane.

As was so often the case, Captain Molloy was away and it fell to Georgiana to organise the burial of Kitty's decomposing body one night with a couple of farm labourers present. Burning torches on sticks illuminated the pathetic scene. Georgiana read the burial service aloud in a clear steady voice. The torchlight in the darkness of the surrounding bush accentuated the remoteness of their tiny outback settlement and the deep silence that surrounded them.

⁂

The story of the first European settlers at Augusta and the Vasse is one of determination, resourcefulness and resilience to the blows of fate. Unfortunately for the Bussells, who continued to be dogged by bad luck, on 5 November 1833 their thatched cottage at the Adelphi caught fire. 'The kitchen chimney was blazing fiercely and the ridge-post on fire. It was no use to try water,' wrote Bessie later that night to Fanny, explaining what had happened.

Risking her own life, Bessie had remained inside the blazing building and threw everything she could lay hands on out of the windows before fire destroyed it. She wrote to reassure Fanny that she had managed to save her precious books, diaries and clothes, but her underclothes and corsets (which 'nice' girls of the period wore even in the heat) and her boots, all irreplaceable in the outback, had been lost.

> Ally [Alfred] and Len [Lenox] pulled out the piano, tables and chairs. I ran to look after my crockery . . . I was endowed with unnatural strength, took your [Fanny's] mattress, my own and your bedding and rushed out of the room . . . Ally got into the loft through the ceiling and . . . threw down the boxes helter skelter. All [the] needles, tapes, bonnets, ribbons, pins are lost. All your shoes are safe. I have not a pair left, nor a bonnet . . . Len saved the medicine chest . . . All the Bibles and the Byron are safe . . . The piano got very hot after it was out. The music [is] safe, desks and workbox . . . The looking glasses are safe. I wish it was daylight. It is the longest night I ever knew.[14]

After the fire destroyed their thatched cottage, the Bussells left the charred ruins and removed most of their remaining possessions by boat. They rowed back to join Fanny and Charles at Datchet, still expecting their mother and sister Mary to join them from England later that year. Their misfortune provided one pleasure for Georgiana — they lent her their piano, one of the few generous acts Georgiana ever received from the Bussells.

ee ee ee

The local Wardandi women admired Sabina's blonde hair and chubby features and Georgiana sometimes let Sabina play with their children. However, Georgiana still faced the occasional problem with the Wardandi. As the settlers continued to shoot the wallabies and kangaroos the Wardandi relied on for food, tensions rose about supplies. Early in February 1834, in Captain Molloy's absence twenty Bibbulmun-speaking people from further south arrived at the Molloys' home. The men were naked, except for cloaks of kangaroo skin, and armed with spears and waddies, and they aggressively demanded potatoes from Georgiana's garden.

Georgiana described in a letter to Helen Story how she had been too afraid to show her fear. Masking it well, she smiled brightly at them as though she did not have a care in the world:

> The tall man, perceiving that I was not intimidated, cut
> the air close to my head with his wallabee stick. I stood it
> all, taking it as play but I heard the whizzing stick and
> expected Dawson, the child or I should be struck. He then
> . . . drew a piece of broken glass bottle close to my cheek.
> I smiled and trembled, and said 'Dirilia' or glass, meaning
> that I knew they used it for sharpening their spears.[15] He
> rubbed his fore-finger in his hair until it was covered with
> the fat and red earth with which they rub themselves and
> poked it right into my face. Yarner, a great thief, pointed to
> the potatoes and wanted Dawson to give him some.[16]

Elijah Dawson refused to give away their precious supply of potatoes. The Aborigines were clearly annoyed they had not been given any and refused to leave. The same man who had threatened Georgiana took hold of little Sabina by the leg and seemed about to drag her away with them. Georgiana was terrified for her daughter but realised it was safer if she continued to hide her fear. She had learned a little of the Bibbulmun language and said very firmly, '*Ben-o-wai*' (Be gone).

Georgiana then tried to retreat, but the tall man turned and followed her. She knew that by now the Bibbulmun were afraid of firearms, and while Elijah Dawson drew some water for them, Georgiana managed to locate her husband's pistol. Without saying a word she laid it on a table 'where they could see it'. This had the desired effect of making the men leave.

They moved to the next house to try to intimidate the Bussell sisters into giving them potatoes, since they knew the Bussell boys were away at the Vasse River.

Fanny and Bessie had planted their precious potatoes with their own hands and refused to give any away. Georgiana had meanwhile sent Elijah Dawson over to Datchet. When they saw him, the Bibbulmun took a few salt cellars (so they could use the glass to tip their spears) and departed. Fanny and Bessie quickly reported the theft to Georgiana, who sent soldiers after them. The salt cellars were retrieved under threat of bayonet and returned to the Bussells.

Two days later the same Wardandi–Bibbulmun returned with smiles and a freshly killed wallaby which they gave to Georgiana and the Bussell sisters as a peace offering.

ℓℓ ℓℓ ℓℓ

On 13 April 1834, John Bussell and his younger brothers loaded everything they could in the way of farm equipment aboard the schooner *Ellen* at Flinders Bay, which was to sail them round to Geographe Bay and a new life at the Vasse. The boys left Fanny and Bessie at Augusta, and took Phoebe Bower with them to do the housekeeping and, by agreement with Captain Molloy, Elijah Dawson accompanied them to help with ploughing.

John had planned things so a second shipment of valuable household and farm goods from Perth would arrive at Geographe

Bay while they were there. Many of these were irreplaceable in Western Australia. They included goods Mrs Bussell had sent out from England to Perth as she packed up their belongings in preparation for her own long trip out. She had then organised for the cargo, once it arrived at Fremantle, to be loaded onto the *Cumberland*, a coastal trader ship bound for Augusta. The leaky old vessel sank off the West Australian coast without trace in a storm, drowning several crew members. Under this further blow the family now had to start pioneering at the Vasse, living in the same minimal way they had done at Augusta.

Georgiana gladly gave the Bussells certain items to compensate for the loss of their household goods aboard the *Cumberland*. However, she was disappointed that the Bussells seemed unwilling to give anything in return for all the help she and her husband had provided. She commented that she found the Bussells 'close-fisted' and mean. Perhaps the damage had been done when they had first met and the Molloys had travelled in first class and the Bussell boys in steerage class — creating the impression that the Molloys were wealthy and could afford to be generous, and that the Bussells had no need to give anything in return. (Ironically enough, because the pioneering life was easier with a large and healthy family, and a sound sense for grasping opportunity, and because Captain Molloy expended much of his time and energy on government business in return for a minute salary, the Bussells would eventually become far wealthier than the Molloys.)

Georgiana puzzled over the Bussells' meanness. Like them she had once been affluent but had lost money and status after her father died. But she had a warm and generous nature and would not allow genteel poverty to make her any less generous to those in need.

⚜ ⚜ ⚜

From the first moment in 1834 when young Mary Bussell arrived with her mother in Perth she disliked colonial life. Mary had been fretting over a failed love affair in England and was also resentful that Patrick Taylor, a tall, dour Scot she had met on board the *James*

Pattison on the voyage to Perth, was not regarded as 'eligible' by her mother, who did her best to discourage their shipboard romance.

Mary Bussell and her mother finally arrived at Augusta aboard the *Ellen*. Mary, annoyed at having been made to leave Perth, found that she hated the isolation of Augusta, and the constant round of hard physical work, and complained incessantly to anyone who would listen.

Georgiana was unimpressed by the Bussell family matriarch, thinking Mrs Bussell foolish to have consigned the family's goods to such an ancient and unseaworthy vessel as the *Cumberland*. No wonder it had sunk on the way to Augusta. She was also upset that her generous loans of replacement items and her offers of friendship had met with so little response from the Bussells. She described in a letter to her mother how the Bussells accepted everything she gave or loaned them and added 'you will hardly believe they have made no return; nor have Molloy or myself ever broken their bread'. Disillusioned by her neighbours' apparent parsimony and lack of gratitude, Georgiana described the Bussells 'as perfectly selfish and inconsiderate as any people I ever knew', a judgment which seems to have been borne out by subsequent events.[17]

While his brothers toiled at the Vasse, Charles Bussell, still earning good money as storekeeper, remained in Augusta with Bessie, Fanny, his mother and Mary, along with the servant Emma Mould. In spite of his pronounced stammer Charles managed to seduce Emma, and after discovering she was pregnant Emma begged him to marry her. But Charles Bussell saw himself as a gentleman and never had any intention of marrying a servant. He denied he was the father. Emma had previously announced she was pregnant to another settler which turned out to be false. This time it was true. The Bussell family was extremely unsympathetic and blamed Emma for her plight. Since there were no welfare payments for single mothers, Emma's position was bleak.

Mrs Bussell, the clergyman's widow, showing a distinct lack of Christian charity, called Emma 'a most abandoned creature' who 'had violated every commandment'. The bossy matriarch turned penniless Emma out of the house when she was eight months pregnant and had nowhere else to go.

In the end it was Georgiana who showed true Christian charity by taking in the pregnant Emma Mould and helping her give birth to a baby whom Emma named Henry John. Although Charles Bussell continued to deny paternity, oddly enough the family demanded to keep Emma's baby. As soon as she recovered from the birth, however, Emma moved away to Perth where she got a job in a private house, eventually marrying a settler named Thomas Sweetman.

⚮ ⚮ ⚮

The arrival of Mary Bussell and her dragon of a mother in Augusta in October 1834 came only four months after Georgiana herself gave birth to another daughter, whom she named Mary Dorothea. Like her sister Sabina, Mary was a healthy, robust baby, and thrived in her mother's care.

Georgiana delighted in her new child, but she was soon tragically reminded of her isolation and distance from her family in England. In September she received a letter with the tragic news that her sister Elizabeth Besley had died.

News of her sister's premature death shocked evangelical Georgiana deeply, and her religious nature worried that Elizabeth, although married to an Anglican curate, had not been sufficiently pious. She wrote to Helen Story grieving for Elizabeth and the state of her soul, and hoping her unmarried sister Mary and her mother would change their ways before her mother died as well.

With two children to care for, Georgiana was also finding that she was no longer as strong as she had been. Carrying a heavy baby around made her lower back ache and she had sleepless nights when Mary Dorothea suffered teething problems. However, she managed to retain some sense of humour and wrote of her rapid weight loss that 'I have every day expected to see some bone poking through my epidermis'.[18]

While Georgiana tended to her growing family, the Bussells began the exodus from Augusta to the Vasse. In September 1835, the adventurous Bessie Bussell set out on horseback with John, Alfred, Vernon and Lenox, to take up residence at the Vasse in the rudimentary shelters they had so far constructed. The brothers had made frequent return visits to Augusta from the Vasse River and must have fired Bessie's enthusiasm for hard pioneering.

But even someone of Bessie's spirit and determination might have quailed a little as she set off on the 100-kilometre journey on horseback into the unknown.

The young men and Bessie camped out in mosquito-infested country. Bessie dealt with hordes of flies that swarmed over her eyes and lips by wearing a veil over her sunhat. They rode with 'the dogs frolicking around their horses' feet', dined under the stars and slept rough for the night.[19]

Crossing deep creeks in long skirts presented a problem but Bessie took it all in her stride. She wrote how 'I was sent into the bush while [the boys] changed their trousers'. In those days 'nice' girls could not wear trousers, for fear of being thought immoral, so Bessie had to ride side-saddle and wade across the creek in her long skirt which sopped up water like a sponge. She had to traverse swamps where the horses were in danger of being 'completely sucked into the mud'.

When Bessie's horse stumbled and nearly threw her, her brothers had to come to her rescue. Worse was the fact that her pale skin became badly sunburnt, despite her hat and veil. She described her face as 'burned to the red of a Virginia creeper in August'. But her brothers were proud of Bessie's courage and determination, and of the fact that their sister, who had never had anything to do with horses in England, had taught herself to ride so well in such a short time.

The Bussells kept themselves cheerful by singing, laughing and telling stories. They slept under the stars, cooked a breakfast of freshly caught fish and pancakes, which Bessie ate with her fingers from a saucepan lid instead of a plate.

Later, when writing about her big adventure to her wealthy cousin Capel Carter in England, Bessie seemed to take a delight in telling Capel how she was living the sort of life that would have been impossible for a girl of her class and background in England, milking their cow, churning butter and caring for farm animals.[20]

On the second and last night of their overland trek, Bessie was forced to sleep with her back propped against a tree, as by now she was so stiff, saddle-sore and sunburnt that the pain prevented her lying flat.

Eventually the group arrived at the place the Wardandi-Bibbulmun called Windelup (place of the digging sticks — implements carried by the women), where they would finally settle. The Bussells' land had been named Cattle Chosen by John Bussell, because Yulika, one of their best milking cows, having been lost for almost a year, was found there in 1834 accompanied by a valuable calf. Yulika was grazing contentedly in a pretty spot near a bend in the river.

The brothers had been working Cattle Chosen for more than a year now. John had decided they should build a main house for the family, with a smaller house for himself and Sophie Hayward, the girl he hoped to marry in England.

In January 1836, the houses were ready for the remainder of the family to move into from Augusta. The wattle-and-daub walls were fully plastered (Alfred by now having become proficient at plastering) and the furniture was installed. Books stood on shelves down the length of the room and the precious piano, retrieved from Georgiana Molloy, stood under the window. One long window overlooked the river; from the other they could watch their 'beautiful sleek cattle, horses and goats'. Mrs Bussell had her own room while the sisters shared a dormitory, as did some of the boys in this experiment in communal living. In her journal, written as a family history, Bessie described how:

> The great bell erected just before our windows awakens us
> from our slumbers just before daylight. Breakfast is
> prepared. After breakfast the boys separate to different
> duties; John and Len to carpentry and building, Vernon to
> the garden, Alfred to the cows. Bessie prepares vegetables
> for dinner. Mary clears away the breakfast and arranges the
> sitting room and Fanny goes to the boys' rooms to make
> their beds and look after the fleas, which we are gradually
> exterminating. Our duties are divided into three

departments, cook, housemaid and chambermaid; offices we change monthly. Bessie's bell summons us from our work and the dinner-hour is a welcome break. Then comes feeding the turkeys and the ducks and hens. Plates and dishes are washed and put away and then there is a little rest with a book, which often falls from a tired hand.[21]

The girls' afternoons were spent helping Phoebe to wash and fold the clothes and churn the butter made from their cows' milk:

We work until the setting sun calls in our animals to be fed and settled for the night. The boys come in and soon our last meal is in progress. The cows are all milked, the horses praised and petted and then we sit down to our bread and milk supper.[22]

By the end of their first year at Cattle Chosen, the Bussells owned thirteen cows, eight goats, and four horses as well as numerous hens, ducks and pigs. Surplus butter, potatoes and cheese was sent by boat to the Swan River settlement, where it brought good prices in the market. The Bussells also traded their produce with American whalers who put into Geographe Bay in search of fresh water.

The Bussells could reflect with satisfaction on their fortune now, but they identified one major obstacle to their advancement: the Wardandi-Bibbulmun whose land they were exploiting. For an initial period at Augusta the Bussells had enjoyed reasonably harmonious relationships with the Wardandi. They made them presents of flour and potatoes and showed them how to make damper and bake the potatoes in the ashes of a camp fire. But once the Wardandi found game in the area less plentiful, they turned to other food sources — the settlers' cattle and crops. The response of the Bussells was to shoot at the 'heathen natives'.

Although they were happy to use the local knowledge of the Wardandi people and take over grassland that had been produced by their burning off, the Bussells made no effort at all to understand Aboriginal customs, folklore or beliefs. They were offended by the Wardandi's nakedness and by their odour — the

Wardandi rarely washed, and greased their bodies with animal fat to keep warm and daubed their matted hair with red ochre. The Bussells mistrusted 'the natives', and, with labour in such short supply, were put out that the Wardandi refused to work in return for food. Along with many newcomers, the Bussells regarded the indigenous people as little better than animals.

The Bussells' limited tolerance for the Wardandi was also tested by the fact that the grassy Vasse (Windelup) area where they had established Cattle Chosen attracted large numbers of Bibbulmun-speaking people from near and far, who would make camp and hold noisy corroborees close to the Bussells' house. All night long the family could be kept awake by the noise of the clapsticks, the drone of the didgeridoo and the thumping of bare feet accompanied by wails and cries. It made the Bussell women very nervous indeed.

One night, when most of the family was away, Bessie noted in her diary, 'The natives nearly drive me out of my mind ... The noise they make puts conversation out of the question ... [the word 'native'] is fraught with fatigue, fear and anxiety.'[23]

In December 1836, the schooner *Champion* arrived at the Vasse with Lieutenant Henry Bunbury on board in charge of a group of soldiers. Bunbury, who had shot and killed Aboriginal men in the Avon district east of Perth, supported the Bussells in their increasingly violent stance against the Wardandi. For their part, the Wardandi-Bibbulmun could not understand the concept of owning land and regarded food sources as communal. Clashes were inevitable and would end in the demise of all clans of the Bibbulmun.

Enmity between the locals and the settlers escalated into open conflict when Leonard Chapman, another Vasse settler, found one of his calves missing. Chapman and the soldiers shot and killed nine Wardandi men and wounded two more without having any evidence that the Wardandi men were guilty.

Having employed Phoebe Bower and Emma Mould, the Bussells did not need to employ Aboriginal house girls. Had they done so, and got to know them as individuals, they might have developed a much warmer relationship with and appreciation of

Aboriginal people, as was the case with Emma Withnell, Jeannie Gunn, Evelyn Maunsell and Atlanta Bradshaw. But instead conflict escalated: soon the Bussell boys and Bessie came to see themselves as waging a war on the Wardandi. The brothers were convinced that killing some of them would teach the rest a lesson. And the aim of war is death to the enemy.

On 2 July 1837 Bessie remarked in her journal, 'The natives announced that a hostile tribe [probably another group of Bibbulmun] is making a descent on us. How will all these wars and rumours end?' Faced with the danger of an attack, those young hot heads, Charles, Alfred and Lenox, assembled a range of guns and ammunition and Lenox even attempted to build a cannon using ball cartridges. However, the cannon exploded into pieces when Lenox tried it out for the first time.

On 30 July the Bussell boys took the 'war' one step further. They and other settlers went out on a punitive raid and shot dead five Bibbulmun men and women whom they feared were about to attack them. They also left many more Aborigines badly injured.

♯ ♯ ♯

Back at Augusta Georgiana's life continued in her ceaseless round of cooking, cleaning, washing and ironing, feeding hens and what she described as 'the odious drudgery of cheese and butter making'. Georgiana was worked off her feet from dawn to dusk without domestic help. In addition to household and farm chores, without the services of a governess she had to find the time to give young Sabina, now a very active little girl, reading and writing lessons. If Georgiana took time off to write to Helen Story or Maggie Dunlop or to her own family, the sewing and mending piled up beside her work basket. She told Helen:

> I must either leave writing alone or some needlework
> undone . . . I never open a book and if I read a chapter
> on Sunday, it is quite a treat to have so much leisure . . .
> I have not a cap to put on my child's head.[24]

Now thirty years of age, pregnant again and working harder than she had worked in her life, Georgiana complained that she had no time to make baby clothes. Each new pregnancy sapped her strength and brought her more work. And always with her was the anxiety of something happening to her children.

To Georgiana's horror, in November 1835, two months before the Bussells left for Cattle Chosen, Sabina had developed convulsions and fever. Georgiana nursed her little daughter devotedly day and night until she recovered. But she lost faith in Mr Green, the inept surgeon who diagnosed that Sabina was suffering from sunstroke. Georgiana must have wished desperately there was a competent medical practitioner within reach.

Captain Molloy's frequent absences on resident magistrate's business coupled with Georgiana's pregnancies meant the Molloys were much slower to set up a new farm at the Vasse than the Bussells and other settlers. Whenever he could, Captain Molloy would travel to the Vasse property where he was building a homestead for the family, some five kilometres away from the sea, overlooking the Vasse River.

As more Augusta residents left for the Vasse, Georgiana's isolation and loneliness increased. The few visitors who arrived by ship were generally poorly educated and talked about nothing more stimulating than 'grubbing out stumps, whaling and harpooning'.

Her main comfort, besides her children, was still her flower garden. The seeds and the yucca lilies Georgiana had brought with her flowered abundantly, giving the effect of an English cottage garden. Flowering creepers climbed in profusion over walls and verandas, as did vines grown from the seeds she had brought from Cape Town, and the peach trees which she had grown from stones she had brought with her flourished. She sent new seeds home to her mother to show her what had become of those wedding presents of seeds and bulbs, and described her West Australian garden with pride.

Sometimes in the evening Georgiana took her children to the beach. While they played, she sat and daydreamed about happy days at Helen Story's stone manse at Rosneath, and listened to the sound of the waves of the great Southern Ocean pounding over the sandbar.

In April 1836 a much-wanted boy — heir to the Molloys' hard-won acres of land — was born. The Molloys were thrilled and named him John after his father. Little John grew into a handsome, fair-haired toddler — their pride and joy. They talked about how he would eventually inherit the land they were wearing themselves out clearing and cultivating.

Georgiana's life was also about to gain another new absorbing interest. One day in November 1836 she received a letter, with a box of English seeds, sent by Captain James Mangles, the cousin of Mrs Stirling. Ellen Stirling had forwarded the captain's letter in which he asked if she would be kind enough to collect and send to him in England some seeds from native plants for his plant collection, together with her notes on them, and he would pass some on to other leading collectors.

Captain Mangles had inherited a vast annual income from his father, who, like Ellen Stirling's father, was also a director of the prosperous East India Company. Mangles no longer needed to work and could afford to spend his time writing books on plants from exotic locations and importing specimens. He also owned a large and beautiful garden near London and corresponded regularly with other garden owners and horticulturalists. His hobby had put Captain Mangles in touch with the curators of major botanical gardens around Britain.

Before making his trip to Australia in 1831, Captain Mangles had offered to obtain new and exotic specimens for the collections of the Royal Horticultural Society, for various English botanical gardens and for the home of the Duke of Devonshire, Chatsworth in Derby, the gardens of which were run by the noted horticulturalist and garden designer Joseph Paxton. Mangles had been fascinated by Western Australia's profusion of wild flowers but had not had time to travel further south to collect additional specimens.

Now Captain Mangles had sent out by ship a box, a *hortus siccus* album and the letter in which he very politely asked Mrs Molloy to fill the box with the seeds and pressed flowers of her local plants and write notes on them. He would pay the cost of shipping them to England.

Georgiana took Captain Mangles' request very seriously indeed. For the next six years she would follow his instructions and, in doing so, gradually develop an encyclopaedic knowledge of the flowers and plants of the south-west of Western Australia. She was happy to think she was contributing in some small way to the process of scientific exchange.

Although her free time was limited with three children to care for and teach, and her household and farm duties to attend to, she took the job on with enthusiasm. She packaged and labelled seeds in small muslin bags and, whenever possible, added pressed leaves and flowers of each specimen with her notes on the plant and its medicinal properties, if known. She would also add the native name, which members of the Wardandi, who were always very helpful, would tell her.

Georgiana had found an outlet for her enthusiasm for Australian native plants. She had made no real friends at Augusta and found no one who shared her religious preoccupations. Now at last she had someone as fascinated as herself to communicate with about native plants of the area — an expert with access to a vast library of horticultural reference books. Captain Mangles, a man of roughly the same age as her husband, in touch with Britain's major botanical gardens and horticulturalists, could supply her with additional horticultural knowledge.

By March 1837 she had collected enough specimens to fill a small box. She sent them off to Mangles with a letter full of thanks for the seeds he had sent out, and humility in accepting the job he proposed. Georgiana was not to know that this first shipment would go astray and never reached Mangles.

In the months following Captain Mangles' letter requesting her help, Georgiana became absorbed in her new interest. She sewed more little muslin bags for next year's seeds, and found and tagged the plants whose seeds she and her children would collect once they had ripened. Georgiana's children helped her on her rounds of inspection, because, as she later wrote to Captain Mangles, their eyes were so much closer to the ground they often found samples she had missed.

By this time Georgiana was employing young Charlotte Heppingstone, which gave her more time to get out and 'botanise' than during the whole of the previous six years. Georgiana was aware of the need to pack seeds carefully to survive the long sea journey and still be useful for propagation. It was this careful preparation and handling that would impress Captain Mangles when he received her first shipment. He had already received packages and boxes from other collectors at the Swan River in very poor condition but would be delighted with those sent by Mrs Molloy and the quality of the information that she provided when he eventually received some.

Captain Mangles and his vast store of botanical knowledge became Georgiana's connection to the outside world: they offered her the chance of a new and more fulfilling life.

The Molloys' move to the Vasse was scheduled for 1838 and Georgiana was determined to send Captain Mangles as many seeds and research notes from Augusta as possible before starting to collect and annotate the plants of the Vasse region. She had been told by several of the settlers that the vegetation and the climate were very different at the Vasse. She was looking forward to a new challenge but had grown to love the mild climate and the beauty of Augusta and was sorry to be leaving them.

And then, in November 1837, without warning, when beloved little John was nineteen months old, came the tragedy of Georgiana's life.

One morning after breakfast, the family and Charlotte had dispersed to their various household duties. Georgiana went to the outside kitchen to bake and to churn the butter. Suddenly she noticed that little John was nowhere to be seen. Worried that he might wander into the bush and get lost she had fastened a little bell to his belt but she could not hear its ringing.

Desperate with fear, Georgiana checked to see if John was with Charlotte or with her husband. They told her they had not seen him since breakfast. Georgiana's mind turned to the well, a stone's throw from the house. 'Do not frighten yourself, he never goes there!' her husband tried to reassure her. But John *had* gone there and fallen down, and all their attempts to revive their little boy were in vain.

The shock of John's death brought on a deep depression in Georgiana, who by now was pregnant once more. She was unable to eat or sleep, endlessly reproaching herself for her only son's fate. She stayed inside the house and brooded on her baby's death. Everywhere she went in the house she saw her lovely little boy. There was no clergyman to absolve her from the terrible pain she took upon herself; her suffering was so profound she could not even write about it to her family.

The herbariums and the big collecting boxes stood empty for weeks. Slowly Georgiana regained some vigour and resumed her family duties, but little John's death was never far from her mind. It was a couple of months before she began a letter to Captain Mangles apologising for lack of communication. In the course of the preceding twelve months, Georgiana had composed one letter to Mangles, accepting his request. Now, in the aftermath of the tragedy, she was able to describe the painful details of little John's death to him, a stranger, more easily than she could to her sister or to Helen Story:

> We have recently been overwhelmed with the most bitter
> loss of our darling infant and only son of 19 months by
> the aggravated death of drowning. Painful as it is to
> record — distance of time and space compels me . . .
> Charlotte going to the well . . . pulled out that darling
> precious child, lifeless, his flaxen curls all dripping, his
> little countenance so placid, he looked fast asleep but not
> dead; and we do not believe he really was so until some
> minutes after . . . We tried every means of restoration, but
> to no effect. And that lovely, healthy child, who had never
> known pain or sickness and who had been all mirth and
> joyousness the last time we beheld him together, was now
> a stiff corpse, but beautiful and lovely even in death.[25]

Possibly writing about her dead child acted as a catharsis for Georgiana and unburdening herself to Captain Mangles allowed her to begin 'botanising' again. It was as though subconsciously she turned away from death in favour of life, represented by the flowers and seeds she was once more passionately collecting and documenting.

From now onwards her letters contained no more pious statements on spiritual questions and instead she concentrated on 'botanising'. She visited her chosen collecting grounds with her daughters up to several times in a single week, waiting for the ripening seed pods to burst, so that she could harvest the seeds at their peak. Mindful of how many children had been lost in the bush and starved to death, Georgiana never let her beloved little girls go seed collecting without her.

Georgiana asked her husband to bring new plant specimens back when overseeing the clearing of their land at the Vasse and the building of their new house. She also persuaded soldiers from the garrison to collect seeds for her, and tackled her collecting with precision, dedication and professionalism. She documented various medicinal plants, along with the uses to which the Wardandi put them. Several types of berries and roots were used to cure sore eyes, others healed skin rashes and fevers.

With Georgiana's pregnancy advancing, the Molloys' plans to move to the Vasse had to be delayed again. The family's continuing stay in Augusta near the graves of her dead children was some compensation for Georgiana, who was still losing her neighbours. The garden she had planted so carefully with her English seeds and her yucca lilies was by now at its best.

To provide much-needed entertainment in the outback for her husband and children on summer evenings they would move the little piano-organ she had brought with her out onto the grass. There she would play classical or religious music to her family in the moonlight with the broad sweep of the Blackwood River, fringed by the cream-coloured trunks of peppermint trees, gliding past in front of her. Her music was occasionally punctuated by the harsh call of black swans overhead, while the night air was heavy with the scent of her English garden flowers.

In June 1838 Georgiana gave birth to another daughter, her fourth baby to survive. The labour was a difficult one and did not produce the son she had hoped for, but a beautiful and healthy little girl, whom they named Amelia.

Georgiana was delighted that Sabina could now read and keep herself amused. By the end of winter she had also managed to teach four-year-old Mary Dorothea to read. But she worried that no ships were coming into Flinders Bay to collect the annotated specimens she had packed with such care for Captain Mangles in England. She was eager to hear his opinion of her collecting work and her research notes and to know to which botanical gardens he had sent the seeds.

As spring advanced Georgiana's health improved. She could not resist taking the children seed and flower collecting once more in the bush where, she told Captain Mangles, they 'ran like butterflies from flower to flower'.

It was months since Georgiana had begun her long letter to Captain Mangles following John's death, and packed her boxes and *hortus sicci*, and still no ship had called to pick them up. Finally, in November 1838, Georgiana consigned Captain Mangles' two precious collecting boxes to Ellen Stirling for onward shipment to her cousin in England. They would not reach him until early 1839. He was delighted by their carefully packed contents of seeds, pressed flowers and leaves and by Georgiana's annotations.

ll ll ll

In May 1839 the Molloys finally made the move from Augusta to the Vasse. A few days before the family's departure (some five years after the Bussells had gone there in April 1834), Georgiana planted a red rose on her beloved son's grave. She uprooted her favourite plants and put them in a saddle bag so she could take them with her by row boat and then on horseback. She was sad to leave the magnificent Blackwood River with its pelicans and the tall peppermints overhanging the dark water which mirrored their reflections. She was also reluctant to leave her first matrimonial home, her beautiful garden and the graves of her dead children.

It took a day for the crew of a visiting whaler to row them some fifty kilometres up the Blackwood River. They camped overnight and cooked a meal over a camp fire. The girls found it very amusing, although Georgiana had a heavy heart as she nursed her baby.

Captain Molloy had arranged for them to be met by horses and soldiers stationed at the Vasse who would escort them the 100 kilometres to their new home. With two young children and a baby, their progress was slow. Georgiana carried little Amelia in a wicker pannier attached to one side of the saddle, with her precious plants in a pannier on the opposite side. Sabina and Mary Dorothea rode donkeys. They spent two more nights camping in the bush and Georgiana and the children were totally exhausted by the time they reached the Vasse River on 10 May.

The new house which Georgiana named Fairlawn proved a big disappointment. Captain Molloy, it seemed, was a better soldier and magistrate than an architect. Although Georgiana's family was now much larger than when they had built the first house at Augusta, their new home was roughly the same size as the old one and had fewer windows. None of the small windows were fitted with glass, as Molloy had been unable to obtain any, so insects swarmed in.

The temperatures were much hotter during the day and colder at night than at Augusta and she missed the sea views. Georgiana found the surrounding countryside of the Vasse, with its flat grassy plains, uninteresting. While the Bussell boys had seen acres of rolling pastures, which would bring them wealth by fattening cattle, to Georgiana's eyes the semi-stagnant Vasse River was a poor substitute for the broad, sweeping expanse of the Blackwood and those magnificent stands of jarrah at Hardy's Inlet.

Her first thought on arrival was to find moist soil where she could bed the plants taken from her beloved garden at Augusta. Slowly she grew used to living in the colder climate of the Vasse. In spring she was thrilled by the profusion of wild flowers, which she thought even lovelier than those at Augusta. And in time she made friends with a Wardandi man named Calgood and gave him food in return for his help in collecting Vasse plants and seeds for her.

By now the Bussells were doing very well at the Vasse. As the district grew, so their income increased and they were able to employ labourers. They started thinking of more ways to make money from their land, and eventually came up with the idea of breeding and shipping horses to India for the British Army, a venture which would prove highly profitable.

But white settlement and land clearing meant diminishing food supplies for the Wardandi. As Europeans shot and killed the kangaroos and wallabies they relied on, so they continued to raid the settlers' stores in search of flour, tea and sugar, which provided them with an easy source of nourishment.

In February 1842, members of the Wardandi-Bibbulmun stole flour from the Bussells' flour mill, along with several goats. A warrant was issued by John Bussell for the arrest of the suspects. They were taken prisoner but escaped, with the Bussell brothers in pursuit. Charles shot and killed a Wardandi man named Erigedung but was acquitted of any wrong doing at a magisterial inquiry.

A month later, on 10 March, while investigating the theft of six kilograms of Bussell flour, Charles stated how, in order to frighten a seven-year-old girl called Cummangoot, who had been turned in by another tribesman, into confessing the crime, he had pointed a gun at her. The gun discharged and Charles shot her in the stomach. The unfortunate little girl died the following day. Charles was indicted and tried for manslaughter in Perth but was let off with a fine of only one shilling. He expressed no remorse for his actions.[26]

The callousness of the Bussells towards the Wardandi-Bibbulmun distressed Georgiana. She was one of the few pioneers of the Vasse who tried to understand Aboriginal culture with its richness of legends and ceremonies and their use of native plants for medicinal purposes.

Strangely enough, in view of the fact that Georgiana and John Bussell were opposed in many of their views, Georgiana gained a good friend in John's wife, Charlotte Cookworthy Bussell. In 1837 John had returned to England intending to marry Sophie Hayward, the young heiress with whom he had had an understanding since childhood and with whom he had kept up a correspondence. But unknown to him, Sophie was having second thoughts about migrating to Western Australia to live under the same roof as bossy

Mrs Bussell. In his letters John had insisted that, even when they married, his mother would be in charge of their communal living arrangements, and that Sophie must consult Mrs Bussell on every aspect of their domestic life. John's attitude says a great deal about Mrs Bussell's firm hold over her sons.

John had been distressed to arrive in England and learn that mutual friends accused him in front of Sophie of being a fortune-hunter. He broke off the engagement, desperately hurt by such accusations. Miserable and depressed, he also feared that, with the shortage of suitable single girls in Western Australia, his chances of finding a wife who would undertake the hardships of pioneering the outback were limited.

While recovering from his broken engagement in England, John met an attractive, intelligent and practical young widow, Charlotte Cookworthy, who had recently suffered a great deal herself. Charlotte proved a sympathetic confidante. Perhaps because she had been married before, Charlotte considered the prospect of a demanding matriarch at Cattle Chosen less intimidating than young Sophie Hayward had, or perhaps she was prepared to take more risks to improve her circumstances.

Within three weeks of their first meeting in August 1838 Charlotte and John had married — but not without difficulty and drama. After the death of her first husband, Charlotte had become a member of the Plymouth Brethren, who then ex-communicated her for marrying John, an outsider to the sect. Complications ensued when the Plymouth Brethren refused to release Charlotte's three children, intending to raise them themselves. John and Charlotte were forced to kidnap her children from the sect before they took a ship for Western Australia.

Charlotte's arrival at Cattle Chosen brought an end to Georgiana's terrible loneliness and led to something of a rapprochement between the Molloys and the Bussells. As there was as yet no bridge across the Vasse River, Charlotte, who lived on the opposite side to the Molloys' house, rowed across the narrow river to pay Georgiana a visit. The two women, one fair and one dark, embraced each other and began a friendship which was to enrich both their lives.

Charlotte commented in her diary on Georgiana's delicate complexion and the fact that on the table Georgiana had placed a beautiful bunch of wild flowers. When Charlotte complimented her on the beauty of the floral arrangements, Georgiana said that she could not 'bear to be without flowers in the room'.

~~*~*

The year before the Molloys moved to the Vasse, Bessie Bussell had married, but remained living at Cattle Chosen. Her husband was a young surveyor named Henry Ommanney, nephew of Rear-Admiral Sir John Ommanney on his father's side, while Captain

Lithographed drawing of Cattle Chosen at the Vasse River showing the Bussells' vegetable garden and home.

James Mangles was his maternal uncle. Henry was there to survey the districts of Leschenault and the Vasse River. In a case of instant attraction, Henry married vivacious, capable Bessie only a few months after their first meeting.

Georgiana must have been told of the match by her husband when he went on one of his trips to the Vasse and she conveyed the news to Captain Mangles.

In December 1839, Georgiana received Captain Mangles' first reply, congratulating her on the excellence of her collecting and assembling of the specimens. He told her how pleased curators at the Royal Botanical Gardens at Kew and Chelsea had been with the seeds she had packed so carefully, and mentioned that he had sent some seeds to Joseph Paxton, as well as other major British horticulturalists, who had been delighted with them.

In appreciation, Captain Mangles sent toys for the girls, books, some scented soap and other valued gifts the isolated settlers in their far-flung colony could never have bought. Georgiana did not want financial reward and did not expect academic credit for her research. She was happy that at last she had a friend and collaborator who shared her interests. She wrote humbly, thanking Captain Mangles for his 'disinterested liberality and kindness to those you have never seen, and who are not able to make you any return'.[27] Like most women of her era, Georgiana still failed to realise her own worth and worried whether she was able to do a capable enough job of documenting all the new species to satisfy Captain Mangles.

Georgiana was now impatient to start sending more Vasse dried flowers and seeds to Captain Mangles. She had an enormous box made up measuring one metre long by sixteen centimetres deep to export her specimens.

But an interruption to her collecting routine and to the creation of a handsome new garden at Fairlawn came in March 1840, when Georgiana's sister Mary Kennedy arrived. Georgiana had not seen her sister for ten years. As a visit to the family in England was out of the question, she had been imploring Mary to make the long trip out to the Vasse to stay with her. Now at last Mary had done so.

New arrivals were always fascinating in such a restricted society and Mary was invited to visit the Bussells, where Fanny and Mrs Bussell found Georgiana's mercenary sister 'far more congenial than Mrs Molloy'. But Mary remained unimpressed by the Bussells and their way of life. She ignored the remarkable beauty and tranquillity of the Vasse and its rich flora and fauna.

Mary told her older sister she was foolish to work like a slave for her husband and live in the wilds without entertainment or amenities, especially as she was now pregnant again. Even so, Miss

Kennedy searched in vain for a wealthy husband, possibly hoping she might find one at the Vasse — despite its primitive way of life and her claim that colonial life was boring and aged women prematurely.

In May 1840, the cook Georgiana had secured to provide meals for the farm labourers and the family, left, lured away to work for the Bussells. Captain Molloy was, as usual, away on government business when Georgiana went into labour. Doubtless not wanting to involve the alcoholic army surgeon Mr Green, Georgiana was assisted by her unmarried sister, who knew practically nothing about childbirth, and Ann McDermott (nee Turner), who had also recently arrived at the Vasse. Neither of them appreciated that a germ-free delivery was vital, something not understood generally before the work of Dr Ignaz Semmelweiss and Joseph Lister into asepsis.[28] With their help Georgiana gave birth to her sixth child, a healthy baby girl whom she named Flora, the Latin for flower.

The birth, once again without benefit of antiseptic conditions, good antenatal and post-partum care, left Georgiana with a debilitating uterine infection known as puerperal (childbed) fever. For a month she lay sick and exhausted, attended by Mary. As Georgiana's temperature soared, Fanny Bussell left her own work at Cattle Chosen and her sister Bessie, now Mrs Ommanney, who was also on the point of giving birth, to provide some nursing assistance to Mary Kennedy. Georgiana began haemorrhaging. With no medical help, and amateur nursing, Georgiana's recovery was very slow.

Even in her delirium, Georgiana had worried about her collecting, especially the seeds of the *Nuytsia floribunda*, or Christmas tree, which were just ripening. As the pods burst and scattered the seeds very quickly, they had to be collected at the right moment: Georgiana had been hoping to send specimens to Captain Mangles and had placed muslin bags around the pods to catch them. She now hoped the friendly Wardandi would harvest them for her.

In June 1840, while she was still recovering, Georgiana heard from Captain Mangles again. Impressed by the seeds and detailed research notes Georgiana had already sent him, he had forwarded out by sea a magnificent gift of two microscopes and a telescope. She was delighted that Captain Mangles was also commissioning from her an article about the flora of Western Australia for *The Floral Calendar*, a British horticultural magazine he edited. Georgiana felt honoured by his request, especially since at that time women were rarely invited to contribute to academic journals and were banned from joining most learned societies.

Modest as ever, she replied to Captain Mangles, telling him:

> I shall with unfeigned pleasure attempt to gratify you in writing in the 'Floral Calendar', but really feel you have over-rated my poor exertions . . . But I will glean all I can, and pray my health may permit of my making those much enjoyed floral excursions.[29]

With no wealthy husband in sight, Mary Kennedy had had quite enough of nursing, child care and deprivation in the outback. As soon as Georgiana showed signs of improvement, she packed her trunk and sailed back to England.

Race relations in the Vasse area continued to decline. The hot-headed and impulsive Vasse settler George Layman became involved in a dispute over stolen damper with Gaywal, an Aboriginal elder whose daughter had been raped by a settler. Gaywal was seen as a trouble maker and had already been accused by the Bussell brothers of spearing their cattle. The argument between Layman and Gaywal turned into a fight in which Layman was speared and died of his wounds.

The causes of the argument, of course, lay far deeper than the mere theft of some damper. No doubt Gaywal was a trouble maker but he was also seething with anger over the rape of his daughter by one of the settlers and the fact that his son-in-law was in gaol awaiting a charge of killing another settler for the rape of another Aboriginal woman.

The response of the settlers was brutal. Led by Captain Molloy and the Bussells, a search party located an Aboriginal camp where they shot dead seven of the Wardandi. Gaywal escaped but was later hunted down and also shot dead.

Captain Molloy was made guardian of the four Layman children, which meant even more work for the harassed Georgiana. She consoled Layman's widow and her children, and once more showed her generosity by inviting them to stay as her guests at Fairlawn for several months. Mrs Layman and her children were far too scared of Wardandi vengeance to stay in their own house.

Women were still greatly outnumbered by men at the Vasse, as they were at other West Australian settlements. Widowed Mary Layman was courted by young Robert Heppingstone, son of the former servant of the Molloys. Eight years younger than Mary and from a very different background, he nevertheless married Mary and she left Georgiana's home and moved into her own house with her new husband.

♧ ♧ ♧

Governor James Stirling had left Western Australia in mid-1839 with his wife. His replacement was Governor John Hutt, who had previously served with the East India Company. In November 1839 Governor Hutt had made his first official visit to the Vasse River, staying with the Government Resident Molloy and his wife.

As hostess at dinner Georgiana had had time to talk to Governor Hutt and discovered that he was also interested in the wild flowers of the district. Before long, Georgiana had received an introduction from Governor Hutt to a Mr Ludwig Preiss, a visiting German botanist. She hoped to learn a great deal from him and so she invited Preiss to stay. Unfortunately he turned out to be pompous and self-important, unlike Georgiana who underestimated the value of her own contributions to horticulture. In the event, Preiss learned a great deal more from Georgiana than she did from him. He failed to keep his promise to send her specimens of seeds and plants, but he took eagerly all those she offered him.

In December 1841 Governor Hutt, his valet and three accompanying soldiers revisited the Molloys in their somewhat primitive accommodation at the same time as the Reverend John Wollaston was staying with them.

The Reverend Wollaston, clergyman to another struggling settlement of south-west Western Australia called Australind, was also a keen amateur botanist. In the course of his three days with the Molloys, Wollaston noted in his journal that he would have liked to have them as neighbours — he wrote that they were 'uncommonly generous and motivated by less self-interest than anyone else in the colony'.[30]

Wollaston and his son John were also drawn to Georgiana by their common passion for botany. They admired her greatly for her botanical knowledge and dedication to collecting and studying plants.

Wollaston felt sorry for Georgiana who, since Charlotte had left to get married, was working harder than a maid servant. As Georgiana had no domestic help she had to cook a dinner suitable for a governor on a wood stove helped by her nine-year-old daughter. She also had to play the role of elegant hostess at table and keep the conversation flowing. Then later that night she had to heat the water and help the governor's valet wash and dry the dishes and greasy pans. Wollaston noted in his journal how:

> I could not help remarking to the Governor one
> morning, as Mrs Molloy passed in our view from the
> house to the kitchen, with the dinner dishes in one hand
> and her youngest daughter without shoes or stockings, in
> the other, how distressing and laborious must be the
> female emigrant's lot, who has in her native country been
> used to the common comforts and plain cleanliness of
> genteel life . . .
>
> . . . The Molloys are at present without servant of any
> kind, and if it had not been for the loan of the steward of
> one of the ships in the bay and the Governor's servant,
> they must have done everything for us themselves. As it
> was, Mrs Molloy, assisted by her little girl, only nine years
> old, had to attend to everything in the cooking way.
> Although the dining room has a clay floor and opens into
> the dairy, the thatch appears overhead and there is not a

single pane of glass on the premises . . . yet our
entertainment, the style and manners of our host and
hostess, their dress and conversation, all conspired to show
that genuine good breeding and gentlemanly deportment
are not always lost sight of among English emigrants.[31]

As there was still no church at the Vasse, the Reverend Wollaston held a service at the Bussells' home, Cattle Chosen, where he baptised the Molloys' youngest daughter. In his journal he remarked that 'Mrs Molloy was a perfect botanical dictionary'. Indeed, by that time Georgiana knew a large amount about the wild flowers of the region. Yet she was still eager to learn more whenever she could tear herself away from her exhausting and unending round of household chores.

Georgiana soon made contact with the captain of a British whaling ship at Geographe Bay, which was heading to England. The captain agreed to transport the precious collecting boxes containing seeds and notes addressed to Captain Mangles, who would pay the freight when they reached England.

By now, however, Georgiana's husband was becoming less supportive of her hobby. He suggested gently she should spend more time on domestic affairs and less time collecting flowers and seeds for Captain Mangles.

Despite her husband's lack of enthusiasm, Georgiana persisted. She kept watch on the precious seeds of the beautiful golden-orange flowers of the *Nuytsia floribunda* and began daily collecting trips in order to be there when the seeds ripened in April or May. Some she saved for Captain Mangles and with pride planted a few in her own garden at the Vasse, which was developing nicely.

In March 1842 Georgiana discovered that she was pregnant again. It seems clear that no doctor had warned Jack Molloy of the danger to his wife of bearing a seventh baby. She was dismayed but hoped that this time she would have a male child. She became tired and listless, and suffered severe bouts of morning sickness, but she continued to collect seeds for Captain Mangles.

'I should like nothing better than to kindle a fire and stay out all night . . . as I should be ready for my work early in the morning . . . but the natives are much greater than white people in flower seed hunting,' she wrote to Captain Mangles early that winter.[32]

It was mid-winter before Georgiana managed to pack and send her final shipment of seeds and pressed flowers, along with her notes on them. This shipment contained over 100 different specimens of seed, all neatly sorted, labelled and tied with pink tape around tiny brown muslin bags, together with notes describing them and their habitat, in the hope they would be officially classified.

It seemed that Captain Mangles had mentioned Georgiana's name to some English botanists and moves were already afoot to name a flower species after Mrs Georgiana Molloy, the woman who had done so much to enrich the botanical gardens of Europe and who had not received due credit for her work. It was proposed by the West Australian botanist James Drummond to name a species of grevillea *Grevillea molloyae* to honour her research and collecting work but this never eventuated. However, the naming of the tall, fragrant *Boronia molloyae* secured Georgiana a measure of botanical immortality.

By November 1842 Fairlawn deserved its name. Following Georgiana's design, a grassy lawn reached down to the river's edge, and vines and fig trees had been planted. In her final letter to Captain Mangles she wrote proudly, 'I believe I have sent you everything worth sending.'

Three weeks before Christmas, Georgiana's seventh child, another girl named Georgiana, was born.

When his wife went into labour, Captain Molloy, desperately woried, sent for Mr Green, the local medic, who arrived dead drunk. As was the custom at this period, he probably made a vaginal examination without first washing his hands with antiseptic. Once again the birth was difficult and the prolonged labour exhausting for the mother. Once again Mr Green proved so incapable that Captain Molloy begged Alfred Bussell to fetch another doctor. Alfred galloped on horseback to Leschenault but both the doctors there had too many urgent cases to be able to leave them.

Not until the following day did Alfred return with a third doctor, Dr Henry Allen, who dismissed the alcoholic and incompetent surgeon Green and treated Georgiana himself. However, by now it was too late. Georgiana was skeletally thin and her condition improved only marginally while her childbed fever continued throughout the month of January 1843. Before the discovery of antibiotics there was no sure way to heal childbed fever which grew steadily worse.

When the Reverend Wollaston visited the Vasse in January, he was alarmed by Mrs Molloy's condition. As the days grew hotter Georgiana suffered even more. Her temperature soared. From then on, Georgiana, weak and exhausted, realised she was dying. She worried as to who would rear her young daughters. She begged her husband to see that Mary Layman, now Mrs Heppingstone, her nearest neighbour, would care for the baby once Georgiana was dead.

Georgiana hung on in this condition for weeks. The Reverend Wollaston visited Fairlawn again on 27 March 1843 and noted in his journal that 'Mrs Molloy will lose her life for want of nursing', although the real damage had been inflicted by the doctor who delivered her baby, but Wollaston did not realise this. His own mood was bleak. Wollaston's wife was also 'weak and worn', and she and his two daughters were starting to suffer from the effects of ophthalmia from too much sunlight on their eyes. He added a warning note that around the Vasse region and further afield many of the Bibbulmun were dying from imported diseases, in particular from influenza.

John Ferguson, a West Australian settler and a former surgeon and carpenter, was sent for and arrived at the Vasse only to find poor Mrs Molloy's back covered in ulcerated bedsores and one of her legs paralysed from a blood clot. He and Jack Molloy attempted to make her a water bed out of a water trough covered with an old mackintosh coat to ease the pressure, and for a short time Georgiana had some relief.

Skilled medical care could have saved Georgiana. But there was none. She never blamed her husband for the fact that her final pregnancy was responsible for her childbed fever at a time when about sixteen per cent of all mothers died in childbirth. Even in her last days she loved him deeply and no doubt believed that her short life had been lived to the full through her family and her botanical work.

By now Wollaston was so alarmed by her condition, he reminded the dying Georgiana that she should 'set her house in order', by which he meant she should confess her sins and be administered the Last Sacrament. After doing this Wollaston returned to his home at Picton, where his own wife was sickly, saddened by the fact he would never see Mrs Molloy again and worried about the fate of her daughters.

As Georgiana's fever increased, she slipped into unconsciousness and died on 8 April 1843. She was only thirty-seven. She was buried in a paddock close to her beloved garden at Fairlawn, her grave surrounded by the tall, white yucca lilies she had loved.

Gentle, scholarly Georgiana Molloy was a martyr to medical mismanagement in the pioneering era. She could have had a splendid future as a botanist of international repute had women been more respected as scientific researchers — and had Captain Mangles given her credit for her research and collecting skills. Had Georgiana survived the birth of her last child, she would have learned that the seeds and information she had sent in her detailed letters and notes to Captain Mangles were greatly valued in plant nurseries and botanical gardens at Kew, Chelsea, Edinburgh and Dublin, as well as in other major botanical gardens in Europe and North America. Unfortunately only a few curators were told that these seeds had been collected by a woman botanist — most believed mistakenly that Captain Mangles himself had collected and annotated them.

Neither Captain Mangles nor Professor John Lindley, Professor of Botany at London University and Secretary of the Royal Horticultural Society, bothered to acknowledge her name in their publications.

Based on Georgiana's work from her first shipment of seeds and plants but still omitting any mention of her name, Professor Lindley wrote 'Sketch of the Vegetation of the Swan River Colony', which was published in London to great interest as an Appendix to Edward's *Botanical Register* in 1839. Lindley knew of Georgiana's existence and in a letter to Captain Mangles described how 'Your friend Mrs Molloy is really the most charming person . . . and you the most fortunate man to have such a correspondent. That many of the plants are beautiful you can see for yourself.'[33]

Because she was female, Lindley never mentioned her name once in his book, yet he published her work. The great Joseph Paxton at Chatsworth was sent Mrs Molloy's seeds but probably never knew her name.[34]

After Georgiana's death, the pioneer women of the Vasse cared for her children. Mary Heppingstone, widow of George Layman, was extremely supportive, and she and her husband, young Robert Heppingstone, virtually adopted little Georgiana during the early years of her life.

Once she was old enough, Georgiana's daughter and namesake went back to live at Fairlawn and acted as housekeeper to her widowed father. She became engaged but her fiance, J.K. Panter, nephew of a governor of Western Australia, was killed by Aborigines while exploring the Roebuck Bay area. Georgiana's last child never married and remained at Fairlawn looking after her father. She died in 1874.

Georgiana's closest friend, Charlotte Bussell, looked after the elder girls and did her best to be a surrogate mother to them. All her daughters had Georgiana's peaches-and-cream complexion and her blue-grey eyes, and were described as 'five daughters who . . . possess a grace and dignity and ease of manner which would do honour to the most refined society', by Archdeacon Matthew Hale. She would have been proud of all of them.

The Archdeacon visited the Vasse River in November 1848 and fell in love with Sabina Molloy. A strikingly handsome man, he proposed to young Sabina and she accepted him. They were married from the home of Charlotte Bussell and moved to Perth, where Hale eventually became Bishop of Perth.

Mary Dorothea Molloy married an aristocratic Englishman named Edmund DuCane and accompanied him to England, becoming Lady Mary Dorothea DuCane after her husband was knighted.

Amelia Molloy married William Bunbury, son of Lady Richardson Bunbury, and lived at Beechlands, about five kilometres from Busselton. Their descendants remained at the Vasse on a property named Marybrook on land that was once part of Captain Molloy's grant. Flora Molloy married William Brockman, a member of one of Western Australia's leading pioneer families.

The Bussell boys eventually achieved their aims and became financially secure, and by 1914, the start of the Great War, the Wardandi-Bibbulmun were seen no more. The neighbouring town of Busselton is named after the busy Bussells.

Fanny Bussell refused a proposal of marriage in Perth and returned to help her brothers at Cattle Chosen, where she managed the dairy on a profit-sharing basis. She married, relatively late in life, settler Henry Charles Sutherland and went to live at Crawley, now the site of the University of Western Australia. Her husband died four years later and she returned to end her days at Cattle Chosen. Bessie Ommanney remained at Cattle Chosen, had five children and a long and happy life.

The erratic Lenox Bussell who had built the cannon to kill the Wardandi became an alcoholic and died the same year as his mother, in 1845. Lenox's alcoholism may have explained his unstable behaviour and his violent treatment of the local Wardandi, two of whom he killed merely for stealing flour. Charles Bussell worked in Perth as a storekeeper and died in 1856.

John and Charlotte Bussell spent long and happy lives at Cattle Chosen. John died at the age of seventy-two. His grieving widow, Charlotte, could not bear to remain at the Vasse without him, so left widowed Mary Bussell in charge and sailed back to Europe. She spent her final years in Paris. Today descendents of Charlotte and John Bussell occupy Cattle Chosen, a historic property.

Jack Molloy never remarried. He extended Fairlawn and built a cottage in the grounds so his children and grandchildren could visit. In 1850 he made the long sea voyage back to London, where he was received cordially by the Duke of Wellington at Apsley House on Hyde Park Corner (known as No. 1, Piccadilly), which a grateful British nation had given the Iron Duke. The Duke presented Captain Jack Molloy with a Peninsula Medal in addition to his Waterloo Medal and asked him if farming in Western Australia had made him rich. Captain Molloy replied that unfortunately it had not. The captain also called on Sir James Stirling, the man mainly responsible for the Swan River disaster, but there is no record of their conversation.

When Captain Molloy returned to the Vasse, he found Western Australia experiencing a recession and a run on the banks. Due to repeated requests for help from the colonists who complained of the shortage of labour, in 1856 the British Government sent out shipments of convicts to be used on road works and public buildings, but with the promise that equal numbers of free settlers would also be sent out to the struggling colony.

Aged eighty-seven, Captain Molloy died the year after the first shipment of convicts and free settlers arrived in Western Australia. Jack Molloy had the sadness of seeing his wife and two of his children die before him but at least had the satisfaction of seeing the colony, which he and Georgiana had struggled so hard to pioneer, starting to prosper.

Out of all of these diverse characters and their achievements, it is Georgiana Molloy who arouses the most interest. Her fame has increased in recent years as more attention is paid to women's achievements in science. Georgiana's most striking epitaph as a botanist came from the noted British horticulturalist George Hailes, who had grown magnificent show specimens of West Australian flowers and native trees from the seeds Georgiana had collected and annotated in her years of botanising. In a letter of condolence to Captain Molloy, Hailes wrote with admiration:

> Not one in ten thousand who go out into distant lands
> has done what she did for the Gardens in her Native
> Country.

CHAPTER

Emma Mary Withnell

1842 – 1928

THE SPINIFEX PIONEER WHO BECAME THE 'MOTHER OF THE NORTH-WEST'

On 24 March 1864 the sailing ship *Sea Ripple* took Emma and John Withnell and their two children on a dangerous journey from Fremantle to the north-west of Western Australia to take up a land grant of 100,000 acres (40,500 hectares). With them were Emma's elder brother John Hancock, her sixteen-year-old sister Fanny, John's younger brother Robert Withnell and three farm labourers. They had packed on board a large quantity of farm equipment, household items, enough tea and sugar to last for six months and Emma's precious medicine chest, which would prove invaluable. Also on board were 650 sheep, and cows, poultry, sheep dogs and horses, including John Withnell's pride and joy — his Clydesdale stallion, which had cost him £300 (about the equivalent of the price of a luxury car today).[1]

Twenty-one-year-old Emma was pregnant with her third child but was delighted they were finally on their way to the De Grey River plains which her cousin, the famous explorer Francis Gregory, had promoted as 'fertile land suitable for pioneering'. A steady breeze filled the sails and the *Sea Ripple* made a speed of over six knots. The captain of this three-masted barque the Withnells had chartered for their family and their livestock reckoned they would reach their destination in a fortnight. Little did he — or the Withnells — realise that disaster was about to strike. They would never reach the De Grey plains or the river of the same name (today the area around thriving Port Hedland).

※ ※ ※

George Hancock and Sophia Gregory, Emma Withnell's parents, had been among the diverse group of free settlers who emigrated to the Swan River in the early 1830s aboard the British sailing ship *Warrior*, one of many specially chartered vessels to bring 2290 free settlers to Western Australia from different parts of the British Isles. George and Sophia met for the first time on board ship. George was eighteen years old while Sophia was only seven. Like the Molloys who were also aboard (see chapter one), the Gregorys had paid good money for stock in return for grants of land along the Swan River.

Some of the more prosperous Swan River migrants, like the Gregorys, had brought with them luxury items such as pianos, oil paintings, porcelain dinner services and silver cutlery — unaware that what they needed most as pioneer farmers were ploughs, harrows, spades, seeds and livestock.

Arriving at Fremantle the unfortunate migrants had been forced to camp on the beach, as there was no accommodation. In a desperate search for fertile land, many, like the Molloys, took up grants in other parts of Western Australia. The Gregory family, however, stayed around the Swan River, eventually receiving a grant in the Avon Valley.

The Hancocks were not so illustrious. George's father, John, came out on the *Warrior* as an indentured carpenter to retired soldier Captain Francis Byrne.[2] Like the Gregorys, Captain Byrne also obtained land in the Swan River district and the Avon Valley.

After working out his indenture John Hancock became licensee of the Mermaid Hotel and also worked with his sons in his own sawmill. He too was eventually granted land, some of which he also took up in the Avon Valley.

John Withnell's father, William, was a stonemason by trade. His wife, Martha, earned a little extra money by weaving. The Withnells came from a social strata much lower than that of the Gregorys. They had run a few cows on their land in Lancashire — their ancestors had been yeoman farmers for centuries — but the Industrial Revolution had adversely affected their modest way of life. The Napoleonic Wars had brought inflation and unemployment in their wake and the future seemed depressing to this hardworking couple who were ambitious but lacked capital. Emigrating to Western Australia must have seemed a solution to their problems.

In the autumn of 1829 William and Martha Withnell boarded the emigrant ship *Nancy* with their two children, six-year-old John and five-year-old Mary Ann. Martha was expecting another child when the Withnells sailed from Plymouth. On 9 January 1830 their ship dropped anchor in Cockburn Sound, Western Australia. They were rowed ashore and took shelter in a cave where Martha gave birth to another son, whom they named Robert.

After a great deal of hardship the Withnells took up land in the York area. Due to their limited finances, their eldest son, John, did not attend school but worked for his father, helping him establish their farm. When John was only sixteen his father died, and he had to support his widowed mother and run the farm as best he could. He gained practical experience in farming but as he could not read or write, his expectations were modest. Certainly he moved in very different spheres from the parents of the girl with whom he would fall in love.

෴ ෴ ෴

George Hancock and Sophia Gregory had married in 1839, nine years after they'd first met on board the *Warrior*. Sixteen months later, their son John Frederick Hancock was born. On 19 December 1842 their first daughter was born and named Emma Mary. The family grew until eventually George and Sophia had five sons and six daughters and a prosperous farm near Beverley.

Emma developed into a tall, long-legged teenager with pleasant rather than beautiful features. She wore her long blonde hair pinned in a knot on top of her head. Highly intelligent, hardworking, resourceful and responsible, she had been taught history, geography and science by her educated mother and had inherited her love of books and reading. She enjoyed caring for others and whenever her younger siblings fell sick, she helped nurse them through childhood ailments, such as whooping cough, mumps and measles.

By the time Emma was sixteen, the Hancocks were running Boyadine, a large farm near the West Australian settlement of York. Burly John Withnell owned a much smaller adjacent farm called Hillside. He enjoyed visiting Boyadine and became good friends with Emma's older brother John. On his visits to Boyadine, John was introduced to Emma, whom he thought very attractive. He knew her parents might not approve but, fascinated by this delightful, lively girl, was unable to keep away.

If George Hancock noticed that John Withnell seemed to spend a great deal of time talking to his eldest daughter, the fact that she had mentioned she thought John attractive would have worried him even more. George did not enjoy the thought of his clever young daughter marrying an illiterate man almost twice her age. George had worked hard to make something of himself and was now a considerable landowner. He hoped that Emma would marry well, as he himself had done. Although George had no objection to John as a friend for his son, he could not see him as a worthy son-in-law.

Emma was aware that her parents looked down on the Withnells, but that did not stop her from being attracted to John. She recognised him as hardworking and highly intelligent. When John eventually found the courage to ask her for her hand she accepted him, announcing to her father, 'When you have seven daughters and they are all as plain as me, you should be grateful for an honest man, even if he *is* poor, to take one of them off your hands,'[3] — rather cleverly playing on the fact that daughters cost money.

Emma was by no means plain but neither was she a raving beauty. Perhaps her father tried to talk Emma out of what he believed was potentially a disastrous marriage to a man unworthy of her. Doubtless he told her she was not nearly as plain as she made out and could do far better for herself. Maybe tempers flared and harsh words were exchanged. But Emma's mind was made up. She wanted John Withnell for a husband and nothing would change that.

Emma and John were married on 10 May 1859, when Emma was only seventeen. The newlyweds moved to Hillside into a single-storey stone and mud-brick cottage with a thatched roof, which John had built himself. They worked hard to develop their land and make their new home attractive. But Emma was frequently left alone, with John having taken up more land to clear and cultivate some distance away from Hillside. They were ambitious and were prepared to work extremely hard to achieve their goals.

By the early 1860s, large pastoral leases for riverside land in the area that came to be known as the Pilbara, about 1200 kilometres (as the crow flies) north of Perth, were available to applicants who could stock the land with sufficient cattle and sheep. To induce them to move to virgin territory, settlers were offered their first year free of rent. Settlement had begun after the publication of a very favourable report on these areas by the Royal Geographical Society of London. This initial report, which included a detailed map of the area, was made by Emma Withnell's cousin, the distinguished explorer Francis Gregory (later knighted for his work). In his report, Gregory stated that the area had good water and fertile soil and was highly suitable for grazing sheep. There were also possibilities for a pearl-diving industry on the coast.

The north-west region of Western Australia that was opened up for settlement encompassed more than 400,000 square kilometres[4] and eight-year grazing leases for vast acreages were offered on easy terms — *provided* intending settlers were prepared to stock their land and build a house on it immediately.

Emma, whose parents had been sent a copy of Gregory's report, read from cover to cover her cousin's account of the area. Her interest aroused, she made enquiries and learned about the favourable terms the West Australian Government was offering.

As the water supply at Hillside was poor and the Withnells were struggling to make John's farm pay, Emma thought it would be an excellent idea to sell Hillside, invest the money in livestock and sail north to set up a new farm there. Acreage in the north-west was to be granted proportionately to the amount of stock the settler possessed, so the fact that the Withnells owned a quantity of livestock would give them the right to take up a large tract of fertile, well-watered land on the De Grey River plains, an area specially praised in the Gregory report.

John Withnell may not have been able to read but he had a good grasp of finance and quickly saw the merits of his wife's idea to improve their lot without the outlay of large sums of capital. He started to make plans. They, with their two children and a large quantity of sheep and farming equipment, would charter a ship and sail north to virgin territory and establish a large farm there.

After four difficult years of hard work trying to make Hillside pay, with Emma's enthusiastic support John sold the farm. The Withnells invested practically all their capital in cattle, sheep and horses for their new farming venture. Emma was only twenty-one, full of energy and ideas and prepared to brave the unknown, even though she realised she might be the only European woman in a large area with no doctor near at hand. But she was convinced she could cope, and excited by the prospect of a new and more productive life with the man she loved.

John had earned enough to pay £650 (a great deal of money at that time) to charter the 187-ton *Sea Ripple* for the perilous voyage north and invest the remaining profits from the sale of Hillside in their pioneering venture.

Stocking up for the long sea voyage to Port Walcott took some time. By the time the *Sea Ripple* was ready to sail, Emma was six months pregnant. Her worried parents begged her to wait until after the baby was born and join John later, once he had established a home. Emma refused to listen to their fears, convinced that 'the Good Lord would look after her'.

The chartered vessel had restricted space and with so many farm animals in the hold, the atmosphere soon became foetid and smelly.

Engraving of the Sea Ripple, *the ship on which the Withnells sailed to Nickol Bay.*

But the ship made good headway in the steady breeze and at first everything went well. However, ten days after its departure from Fremantle the *Sea Ripple* was becalmed near the port of Cossack (then known as Tien Tsin, after a Chinese ship that had been wrecked there). For days they floated over calm water without making any progress. The stench of the animals in the hold increased and the burning hot sun made life on board uncomfortable.

At last dark clouds appeared on the horizon. Minutes later a gust of wind rippled the surface of the sea, the sails bulged again and the ship started to move. But the wind rapidly became a gale. Soon the sea became a boiling cauldron, tossing the *Sea Ripple* around like a walnut shell.

In panic the crew reefed in the sails, battened down the hatches and ordered passengers to remain in their cabins. While the wind howled around the rigging, the helmsman struggled to hold the ship steady. There was chaos on deck and much of the Withnells' precious cargo was swept overboard. For hours the gale whipped the waves into giant peaks and troughs, terrifying the children.

Finally, the helmsman lost control of the rudder. The *Sea Ripple* was blown in a north-easterly direction towards the shore, about 140 kilometres beyond Cossack on Nickol Bay. John and Emma watched in horror as the ship drifted towards a reef which suddenly emerged in front of the bow. Then, with a crushing sound and a violent shudder, the ship struck the reef. Water flooded into the hold through a gaping hole in the hull. The animals panicked and some were trampled to death.

The gale abated as quickly as it had blown up. While the crew tried to establish order on deck, the tide went out and the ship became lodged on the reef and would not budge. As the sea level dropped, so the ship gradually started to lean to one side. Eventually, the deck was sloping at such a steep angle that it was impossible to walk on it. The petrified sheep in the hold slid into a heap on the lower side, and many suffocated under the weight of those that lay on top. Others broke down the hatches and managed to escape, some plunged headlong overboard and drowned or became engulfed in the slimy mud and suffocated.

In haste, the crew lowered one of the tenders and seven months pregnant Emma, Fanny and the children were rowed to the nearby

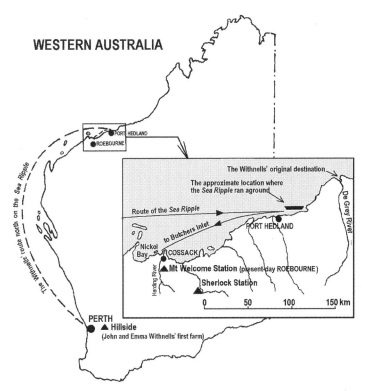

WESTERN AUSTRALIA

The Withnells' route north on the Sea Ripple

PORT HEDLAND
ROEBOURNE

The Withnells' original destination

The approximate location where the Sea Ripple ran aground

Route of the Sea Ripple

De Grey River

to Butchers Inlet

PORT HEDLAND

Nickol Bay

COSSACK

Harding River

Mt Welcome Station (present-day ROEBOURNE)

Sherlock Station

0   50   100   150 km

PERTH
▲ Hillside
(John and Emma Withnells' first farm)

shore. Treacherous mud flats, extending for hundreds of metres from the shore, had to be crossed on foot to reach higher ground. Black sticky mud oozed through the women's shoes as they carried the children to a small island surrounded by mangroves and still more mud — but to their dismay it was impossible to reach the mainland from that point.

They sheltered from the fierce heat under a canopy they rigged from a tarpaulin supported by driftwood. Before long they were bitten by hundreds of tiny sandflies.

The surviving stock was taken from the ship to the edge of the mud flats, but more sheep stuck fast in the black sticky morass and perished. Many of those that managed to make it to the island wandered off again and drowned in the incoming tide. It was agonising for John and Emma to watch the animals they had worked so hard to raise perish before their eyes.

The men helped to fix the hole in the ship's hull but the work could only be done at low tide. As a temporary measure the captain decided to fother a spare sail with tar and cover the hole with it. He wanted to get his damaged ship back to Fremantle for repairs as soon as possible, but was forced to wait for the next spring tide to be able to get her afloat again and unfairly blamed the Withnells for his predicament.

In the meantime, Emma, Fanny and the children remained on the island.[5] Mattresses, blankets, food and water were brought over from the ship. The sun was so fierce that their drinking water, kept in a wooden keg, became so hot it was almost undrinkable. At night, swarms of mosquitoes descended upon them.

After a couple of days, the stench from rotting carcasses became so overwhelming that the women and children could hardly bear it. Finally, on a spring tide, the men managed to get the ship afloat.

Emma and John realised they were less than thirty kilometres south of their destination, the De Grey River, but the captain, angry over the damage to his ship, refused to take them further north. After some deliberation and payment of another £100 he agreed to take his passengers 140 kilometres south to Cossack, which lay on his route back to Fremantle.

After three days of sailing into the wind, the *Sea Ripple* finally arrived at Nickol Bay — then known as Butchers Inlet. Late in the afternoon of 14 April they anchored in deep water a few kilometres offshore.

The following day John Withnell and the other men went ashore in one of the ship's tenders to inspect the area. The remaining stock, including John's precious stallion, were loaded into the second tender and taken ashore as well. Emma, Fanny and the children remained on board and waited for John's return.

While the others looked after the greatly depleted flock of sheep, John walked on ahead to assess the possibility of settling in that area, which seemed to grow nothing but spinifex. Towards the end of the day he arrived at a nearby sheep station, managed by William Shakespeare Hall, known locally as Shaky. Shaky was an eccentric but kind-hearted man with a bushy black beard. He knew the region well, having been a member of Francis Gregory's exploring party in 1861. Shaky kept a journal in order to keep his employer, the wealthy landowner John Wellard, informed about the events on his station. His diary entry for 15 April 1864 reads:

> Withnell arrived at Station about 7 p.m. Heard one gun
> from *Sea Ripple* at 8 p.m. previous night and would have
> gone down had there been a second.[6]

The following morning Withnell and Shaky went down to the shore. Shaky instructed two of his men to follow them in a bullock dray containing a dinghy and an eight-gallon (thirty-six litre) barrel full of drinking water. John and Shaky returned to the *Sea Ripple* in the dinghy while the other men remained to look after the Withnells' horses, bullocks and other livestock.

The next day all the passengers and what was left of their goods were taken ashore. They disembarked on a strip of beach, called Upper Landing, which was separated from *terra firma* by a large swamp. This time the women were saved from having to wade through murky water and mud because Shaky had arranged for two horses to be waiting for them on the beach.

On 17 April Shaky recorded in his diary:

> Two boats came on there [the beach called Upper
> Landing], one with Mrs. Withnell and children, without
> breakfast or a drop of water and in the blazing hot sun,
> and the poor little children crying for some [water].
>   I told Mrs Withnell the bullock dray was at the head of
> the marsh with 8 gallons of water waiting for her . . .
> I put Mrs Withnell's sister on one horse, with one child,
> carried the other and gave Mrs Withnell my horse
> [loaded] with bundles on to lead, so off we went with
> men following with such little things as they could carry.

Most of their goods were left on the beach inside a timber and canvas enclosure the men had built, believing it was above the high-tide level. Fortunately the most important items like tents, bedding and food were carried across the swamp by the horses and men.

After crossing the swamp they quenched their thirst and placed their luggage on top of the waiting dray. Shaky then led the party to Dig Down, an isolated spot about ten kilometres from their landing place, near the mouth of the Harding River. There they found shade trees and a waterhole containing drinking water. Tents were pitched which would be their living quarters for the next five weeks.

A few days later, John Withnell, John Hancock and one of Shaky's labourers rode back to near where they had been shipwrecked, in the hope of finding some of the missing sheep and horses. Frequently they needed to consult their copy of the map drawn by Francis Gregory. In the meantime Emma, Fanny and the Withnell children stayed at their camping spot. Shaky kept an eye on them and, on one occasion, led the whole family to his house to shelter them from a deluge of rain.

Three weeks later John Withnell and his companions returned with the sad news that they had been unable to find any trace of their lost stock. But John also had good news. They had found an excellent spot for permanent settlement about sixteen kilometres further along the Harding River beside a deep natural pool in the river.

When they did a final head count of the remaining stock, John found to his dismay that only eighty-four ewes, two rams, one horse and one cow had survived, plus a few chickens and ducks. Luckily, their sheep dogs were still alive and Emma's medicine chest was intact.

ℓℓ ℓℓ ℓℓ

With the help of Shaky, who by now had become a good friend, the Withnells and Hancocks moved camp upstream from Dig Down to a place called Yeeramukadoo pool (place of the wild fig) by the Ngarluma Aborigines whose hunting grounds it was.

On arrival Emma saw a green hill on the skyline and named it Mount Welcome, claiming, 'it gave us shelter, peace and rest at last'. She made them all kneel and thank God for saving them from the shipwreck. So Yeeramukadoo became the site of the Withnells' first home, which they named Mount Welcome Station.

They had to camp for many more weeks until John could build them a house on their site. Emma was now too near to giving birth to be able to assist. They had very little furniture left, so John fashioned a strong chair out of whale jawbones, which he had found on the shore.[7] Their shoes wore out and could not be replaced so Emma's resourceful husband made a variety of clogs using straps of sheepskin nailed to the upper side of wooden soles. He also made a baby's cradle out of half a water barrel.

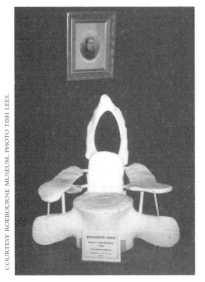

COURTESY ROEBOURNE MUSEUM. PHOTO TISH LEES.

Emma Withnell's whalebone chair made by her husband, John.

On 1 June 1864, only a week after their arrival at the Harding River, Emma and John's third son was born, the first European child to be born in the north-west of Australia. Unfortunately for Emma, John was not a great help — all he knew about birth was pulling calves out of cows with a rope.

Accordingly, Emma's younger sister, Fanny, who was only sixteen, helped deliver the baby by following Emma's instructions. Although the little boy was born under primitive conditions, the remarkable and stoic Emma remained calm and brave throughout and their child, whom they named Robert Harding DeWitt Withnell, arrived safely.

In mid-June the men returned to the landing spot on the beach to retrieve the rest of the goods. They found another gale had blown up since they left and had swamped the enclosure. The heavier items — crates with farm equipment, tools and some of their household goods — still remained on the beach, but they were horrified to find that the remaining possessions, including the children's clothes and all those for the new baby, had been washed away by an exceptionally high tide. Most of the stores Emma had chosen so carefully had also disappeared into the sea. They managed only to salvage some of the flour and sugar. 'We kept the sugar for the children and fortunately the cow had calved so at least we had fresh milk,' wrote Emma.[8] Unfortunately the flour turned out to be full of weevils.

John, aware that he had lost most of their money in the shipwreck, now worried that no matter how hard they worked they would *never* recover their capital. He became depressed, saw himself as a failure and even thought of giving up and going back to Perth. Emma restored her husband's self-confidence by insisting she trusted him completely and saying she knew they would do well. The resilient Emma insisted they must continue with their original plan of setting up a farm with their eighty-four remaining sheep. She was determined they would not return home to her parents as failures.[9]

With Emma's encouragement, John continued building their new house. It was a very basic structure, made from locally available materials — walls of stone, held together with river clay. Cajuput trees, which grew along the river, were used to make posts and roof-framing. The roof was thatched with the ubiquitous spinifex. Later, once the roof started to leak, wooden shingles were installed instead of the spinifex.

In September 1864, they sheared their sheep amid great rejoicing. The following month their precious hand-washed wool was sent to

Perth aboard a vessel called the *Stag*. Emma's sister Fanny, her brother John Hancock, and Robert Withnell returned home aboard the same ship. Two of their farm hands, having complained that Mount Welcome was too isolated, also returned to Fremantle.

The Withnells and their one remaining labourer were now alone in the vast undeveloped region. Emma felt desperately lonely — and found it was hard work running the farm and caring for three young children without the help of her younger sister. She described how in the outback, 'There is always the awful loneliness. It must be hard for newcomers for the work is hard and the lonesomeness at times terrible.'[10]

From the start Emma was determined to maintain friendly relationships with the local indigenous people known as the Ngarluma. Two of the women, Nungerdie and Thoodoo, became her devoted helpers in the house and came to love the children.

For her part Emma respected the Ngarluma women when she saw how many miles they had to walk to find edible roots, tubers, berries and seeds to pound into a paste. They turned the paste into a kind of flour and made small cakes or patties from it, which they roasted on the fire to supplement the game the men had caught. When she had been at Mount Welcome for some time, Emma could see why the Ngarluma women appreciated the occasional gift of flour from her as it saved them many hours of hard work. And she understood why they were sometimes tempted to take food or bulbs from her garden which they regarded as a communal resource.

Whenever Ngarluma women came to visit Emma and her new baby she gave them presents of tea and sugar. They were happy to help care for her children in return. Often the Ngarluma women would ask Emma to take out the pins and let her hair down and they would touch it, admiring its softness and pale golden colour.

The Ngarluma women took Emma to swim in the river. They also invited her to attend food-increase ceremonies or women's corroborees. In return, Emma frequently treated their sores with ointments from her medicine chest and bathed sore eyes with borax, earning the reputation of 'Medicine Woman' in the process.

Emma and her husband were also known as 'Boorong' and 'Banaker' which, in the Ngarluma language, were terms of great respect.

Although Emma loved her husband dearly, cherished her children and had great respect for the Ngarluma women, she longed for another European woman to talk to. Since that was impossible, she coped with loneliness and isolation by working extremely hard. She rose early each day to avoid the worst of the heat. There were all the farm duties to attend to as well as the usual household chores. With no shops handy or workers available, clothes, household items, farm equipment, fences, and so on had to be made by hand.

Mutton was their staple diet, and fruit and vegetables were scarce or non-existent. Ships bringing them fresh supplies and seeds for a vegetable garden took a long time to make their way up the coast. On one occasion, the supplies of dried goods, tea and sugar Emma had ordered from Perth were lost.

In the long evenings by candlelight, Emma taught her husband how to read and write. At first John found it difficult but persevered and eventually was able to write his own business letters.

There were, however, consolations for living in one of the most isolated regions of Australia. The wild flowers were beautiful, the soil around their house was fertile and Emma cultivated a fine ornamental garden. But she had less success with her vegetable garden; as soon as she planted seeds or bulbs the Ngarluma dug them up and ate them.

The Withnells had been 'squatting' (occupying without government permission) on the land along the Harding River for nearly six months when John became anxious to have the lease of his selection formalised. With Emma's help he submitted an application for lease of 10,000 acres (4000 hectares) and applied for the lease of 100,000 additional acres (40,500 hectares) on the Sherlock River. Emma's brother John had promised to take the necessary action to expedite the lease on behalf of his brother-in-law, as soon as he arrived back in Perth. On 20 July 1865, a lease in the name of John and Emma Withnell for 10,000 acres of land fronting the Harding River was approved.

Emma was confident they would obtain a lease on the land on the Sherlock River as well and was impatient to look at the area. She and John loaded their children and camping gear onto a dray and travelled the fifty kilometres to view their prospective property. Emma was delighted to see that it was both beautiful and fertile, with the Sherlock River running through the centre. Hoping that one day they would go and live there, she selected the spot where she wanted a homestead to be built.

A few months later their second lease was granted and John put a large flock of wethers (castrated rams) on the vast property, sunk a well and made plans to build a dwelling there as soon as they had enough capital to do so.

Hard as Emma and John worked, it became apparent that building up their farm could take years. So John decided to diversify his interests.

Collecting valuable pearl shells from the beaches and the seabed of Nickol Bay appealed to him. Although he hated being separated from his family, John now spent a lot of time at Nickol Bay where he started his own pearling operation, leaving Emma to manage the station.

Employing the Ngarluma as divers, he collected pearl shells and when there were enough shipped them to Fremantle. Occasionally John found a precious pearl in one of the shells which provided him with extra income. On his visits home to Mount Welcome, John brought some of the most beautiful shells with him and gave them to Emma. Gradually her collection grew and eventually she became an expert on pearls and pearl shells.

John, being a farmer at heart, longed to work his land rather than collect pearl shells. Leaving one of his labourers in charge of the pearling operation, he returned to Mount Welcome. He found that under Emma's capable management the farm had done well. Their flock was gradually increasing due to successful breeding and through Emma buying additional stock when she had the money to do so.

During the 1860s more settlers came to the area. Several development schemes were started but most of them foundered, with the new colonists taking the first ship south to Fremantle or returning to England, saying the land was impossibly harsh.

The Denison Plains Association was one such scheme, which had been formed by Melbourne investors in order to take up huge tracts of virgin land at the head of the Victoria River (East Kimberley) and further north at Roebuck Bay (the future site of Broome). Under its resettlement plan, in May 1865 a party of British settlers arrived in Fremantle by the sailing ship *Warrior*. They were told the grim news of failures of other pioneering ventures at Roebuck Bay, but were determined to sail northwards all the same.

This group included a surveyor by the name of Wedge, his wife and five children, and it may well have been their salvation that their ship was blown into Nickol Bay. Short of drinking water, the passengers decided to land and settle there instead of proceeding to Roebuck Bay.

The arrival of a ship was related to Emma by the Ngarluma women. She had now been in the isolated north-west for thirteen months and when she heard that women and children were camping on the shore she insisted that they all be brought to Mount Welcome to rest and recover. It had been so long since Emma had seen a European woman, she was thrown into confusion and worried that she had no suitable clothes in which to receive her guests. Normally she wore old working clothes, pulled her hair back and plaited it into a pigtail. Now she realised she could not greet total strangers like this; they would think her eccentric. She must play the role of gracious hostess as her mother would have done.

Emma pulled her shipping trunk out from under the bed, rummaged in it and brought out her best outfit, which had survived the shipwreck. She held up a faded silk dress with a lace collar that had been fashionable when she left Perth, all those years ago. She found the hooped crinoline which went under it, and some frilled petticoats, put them on and slipped the silk dress over her head. She pinned on a brooch which her mother had given her; it had belonged to her English grandmother and she comforted herself with the thought that if the new arrivals were 'gentlefolk' they would recognise that she too came from a similar milieu.

Emma untied her long hair, brushed it out and did her best to put it up in an elegant chignon. She longed for a woman friend and knew that this first meeting with the strangers could be important in making friends. And so, dressed in a gown that had been the height of fashion over a decade earlier, Emma laid the table with her few remaining pieces of good china and awaited her visitors.

When she heard Shaky's bullock team pull up in the yard, she watched eagerly as a pleasant-looking woman with five children and a young governess descended from the dray. Emma was so excited that she burst into tears of joy. Rather than playing the grand lady and waiting to be introduced, impulsively she ran out of the house and hugged Mrs Wedge and her children. She was overjoyed when they returned her embraces and seemed equally pleased to see her.

She ushered them all inside, sat them down and poured out cups of tea all round. She discovered that, like her, Mrs Wedge had endured a terrifying sea voyage and been through a severe storm. The two small Wedge boys played with the Withnell children. When the Ngarluma children approached giggling nervously, they were invited by the boys to join in their games.

Emma was delighted when the Wedges settled at Roebourne and the two families became good friends.

In 1864, a year before the Wedges arrived, a party of eighty-four people had drifted into Camden Harbour north of Roebuck Bay. They were quickly followed by a resident magistrate named Robert J. Sholl, who was accompanied by a staff of surveyors and police. Like many others in the north-west, this settlement also failed for lack of water and harsh conditions and was abandoned in 1865. Sholl was ordered south to Nickol Bay.

Sholl and his family arrived from Camden Harbour at Nickol Bay that same year. The Sholls had to take an exhausting fifteen-kilometre walk along the hot and dusty road to the new settlement at Roebourne where they decided to visit the Withnells before pitching their tents.

Sholl wrote to the Colonial Secretary in Perth, reporting his arrival and giving his impressions of Mrs Withnell as a kind and efficient woman:

> I landed at once with some of the passengers and set forth on foot in the direction of Mr. Withnell's station on the Harding, about 10 miles from the beach. We were kindly received by Mrs Withnell, her husband being absent from home at the time.
>
> I landed horses and stores at Butcher's Inlet beach [Nickol Bay]. As we were frightened of the tide, Mr. Gall carted our stores to high ground. The natives are a fine lot of men, their conduct is good and from the first settlement until now, have been able to help the settlers.[11]

An official residence was built for the Sholls, only a few hundred metres away from the Withnells' house.

The Withnells were a constant source of help and companionship to Magistrate Sholl and were frequently mentioned in his journal:

> December 5 1865: Withnell with two drays came bringing wool and water.

> December 15: Withnell cleansed and deepened the well. There is sufficient for shepherding the flock and water at a hole two miles away. This morning he started off with his bullock dray. Withnell is a most indefatigable man and took the bullock and horse teams to the landing for goods.

> December 28: Spoke to Withnell [to ascertain] if he would oblige us with meat from his station.

> April 2 1866: Kind Mrs Withnell sent cooked fish, the natives had caught a large one.

It is significant that in Sholl's records the ladylike Emma is referred to as 'Mrs Withnell' while John is not dignified by the title 'Mr' but is simply 'Withnell'.

With the influx of settlers to the Nickol Bay area, the town of Roebourne was formally established in 1866, and the district of Nickol Bay gazetted in 1871.

Mount Welcome Station presented a problem for those, including Robert Sholl, who were required to draw up the town allotments. The part of the property where John Withnell had built both his homestead and other outbuildings was right in the middle of the proposed new town. The solution found was to grant the Withnells six acres (three hectares) on which their buildings sat as a town allotment and compensate them for the loss to their run by granting them another lease on land adjoining Sherlock Station. The Withnells were now owners of a suburban lot.

With the approach from sea to the new town of Roebourne so difficult, John Withnell saw a new opportunity for business. On arrival ships had to put up with the inconvenience for passengers of having to anchor in deep water several kilometres offshore. Passengers and their luggage had to be rowed in a dinghy to the beach. Then they had to cross marshes before making the long walk to the settlement. Entrepreneurial John Withnell saw the possibilities for earning income by building a flat-bottomed lighter. For a fee, he would convey new arrivals and their luggage directly from the ship along the Harding River to the fledgling town of Roebourne.

While the lighter brought in some income, it was not enough and John saw other opportunities in the developing town. With Emma's approval and assistance, he opened a butcher's shop-cum-general store which could supply not only the new settlers to the area, but the increasing number of pearlers and other itinerant workers.

The influx of people to the Roebourne area, including Malays who participated in the fledgling pearling industry, also brought disease, and tragically for the Ngarluma, smallpox. In 1866 a smallpox epidemic broke out amongst the Ngarluma. Emma did whatever she could to reduce their suffering, including vaccinating many against the disease.[12] Nevertheless hundreds of workers and tribespeople died. Their rotting corpses were found on beaches and among the mangroves and Emma feared cholera or typhoid would result. She managed to persuade the Ngarluma *not* to follow their normal practice of mummifying corpses by exposing them to sunlight, but to bury them immediately, in order to reduce the possibility of more disease.

❦ ❦ ❦

A welcome event for Emma the following year, 1867, was the return of her sister Fanny and her brother John Hancock. Fanny, now Mrs George Fisher, already had one child and came north to join her husband, owner of Mount Fisher Station. Because there was as yet no home for them on Mount Fisher, Fanny and her husband lived in a cottage at Roebourne. It pleased Emma very much to have their company. Emma's brother John by now also had a wife and two daughters. He had come north to manage a property which he called Woodbrook.

On 10 February 1867, Emma's first daughter was born, a most welcome addition to a family with three sons. They called their beautiful baby Emily Ellen. Emma felt weak and ill after the birth and it took a long time for her to recover, partly because of a shortage of fresh vegetables leading to vitamin deficiency. The Withnells had had little success with their vegetable garden and orchard, and the settlement was still dependent for many supplies on trading vessels arriving from Fremantle.

The year 1867, however, was a disastrous one for coastal shipping. Seven ships were lost in the treacherous and uncharted waters along the coast of Western Australia. The most tragic loss for the Withnells was that of the 117-ton *Emma* (named after Emma Withnell by its owner Walter Padbury). Forty-two people perished aboard, many of them from Roebourne including young Treverton Sholl, much-loved son of Magistrate Robert Sholl.

As well as losing several close friends in the wreck of the *Emma*, the Withnells also suffered considerable financial loss. Golden sovereigns to the value of £148 (all the earnings from the Withnells' sales of meat Magistrate Sholl had bought for government staff and increasing numbers of prisoners in the local gaol) and their entire wool clip for that year sank to the bottom of the sea. Several bags of valuable pearl shells also went down with the ship.[13]

With the loss of such an amount of money as well as potential sales, the Withnells were forced to sell their store. They grieved with the Sholls and the other Roebourne families for their lost relatives but the continual round of farm and home duties kept them occupied.

On top of this, from 1868 to 1872 severe droughts devastated the Roebourne district and water reserves dried up. The Harding River virtually stopped running, and only a few muddy waterholes remained. Many sheep and cattle died of thirst or for lack of food, while the condition of the remaining livestock became pitiable. The Ngarluma also suffered from the shortage of drinking water and from assorted ailments which Emma nursed as best she could.

By the end of 1868 Emma was pregnant again and pleased that her sister Sophia had arrived in Roebourne and would be there to help with the birth. Sophia was also a great comfort to the Sholls, becoming firm friends with Robert Sholl's daughter Penelope. The two took many rides together and visited each other often.

On 25 August 1869 Emma gave birth to another boy. If the start of a new life gave her hope that their fortunes might turn, she was mistaken. With another mouth to feed and a larger family to care for there were more demands than ever on her time. Then the forces of nature hit with a vengeance.

In 1869 the area suffered from a cyclone, bringing much needed rain, but also causing havoc. Warned by the friendly Ngarluma, who instinctively knew that a 'willy-willy' was on its way, the settlers battened down. They put heavy chains across their roofs and attached these to boulders, a precaution that saved many structures and lives.

The cyclonic rain brought only a short reprieve from the drought. In the cycle of life and death, death seemed to be pre-eminent. In February 1871, Emma's younger sister Sophia fell ill from hepatitis and died on 10 April. She was only twenty-one. Not until 1875 would a doctor come to work in the area. Sophia's death was followed by another shock for Emma — the death of her father down south.

Then on 20 March 1872 the most devastating cyclone ever to strike Roebourne and the surrounding areas occurred. Again the pioneer settlers took all possible precautions, but this time they were to no avail. The whole town was virtually flattened and left a ruin.

Outside the Withnells' house the wind roared, uprooting trees and tossing them around like matchsticks. Emma, who was in the last months of another pregnancy, told her children to lie under the beds and the dining table. They were to wait for the cyclone to pass. It was a long time doing so. There was a brief silence as the eye of the cyclone passed overhead. Emma urged little Emily Ellen and the boys to escape to the only outbuilding that was still standing. In despair and mounting terror she discovered that her baby son was missing.

After the lull the wind began to howl again, this time even stronger than before. Fortunately the wooden outbuilding withstood the onslaught.

After a few hours the cyclone passed. Panic-stricken Emma and John went to look for the missing toddler. Finally they found their baby boy wedged tight between two rocks, where the gale-force wind had blown him. Miraculously, neither the baby nor any of the other children was seriously hurt, but Emma had received a deep gash on her wrist from a flying piece of wood.

Emma's sister, Fanny Fisher, who had three children by now, was not so lucky. After the cyclone destroyed the Fishers' cottage and the roof had collapsed, Fanny was found lying unconscious, her baby dead in her arms. In fact, poor Fanny suffered another terrible blow when, a few months later, she lost her other two children through a water-borne disease which may have been typhoid or blackwater fever. The final blow came seven years later when Fanny's husband, George, sailing home from Perth was shipwrecked and lost his life.

After the storm, Magistrate Sholl, still grieving for his dead son, found his recently completed house also in ruins. Like other Roebourne people, he had to resort to living in a tent until his house was rebuilt.

The Harding River, normally a sluggish stream, had changed into a torrent of murky brown water and was overflowing into the adjoining pastures. When John and Emma went to inspect the damage to their property they discovered many of their precious sheep that had managed to survive the drought had been drowned. In addition, some 600 valuable wethers had been lost from Sherlock Station. Once again Emma and John showed courage and resilience in overcoming their setbacks. With dogged determination they started to rebuild everything that had been ruined by the cyclone, replenished their stock and continued farming. Emma's medicine chest remained safe and she was able to go on treating her own children and those of other settlers.

Four months after the cyclone Emma gave birth to twin boys, Horace and Ernest. Their house was still not completed and it is almost beyond belief that 29-year-old Emma was able to look after and feed two babies and five other children without a proper roof over her head.

But despite the hardships and the setbacks Emma managed to maintain her faith in the future and her keen sense of humour. She was always able to laugh at her own mistakes. Once, when John was away on a pearling expedition, she saw lurking in the twilight what appeared to be the menacing figure of a man. She picked up her rifle and called out, 'Who's there?'

Receiving no reply, Emma took aim and fired — and hit one of her own long-skirted dresses which was swinging in the breeze on the clothesline.

With the continuing arrival of settlers at Roebourne, John Withnell recognised the dangers European men posed to Aboriginal women. John placed the Ngarluma camp at Mount Welcome out of bounds to Europeans at night and insisted that anyone who raided the camp for girls or tried to barter them for alcohol would be punished according to Ngarluma custom.[14]

The Ngarluma women came to respect the Withnells for doing their best to protect them but some of the new settlers experienced deteriorating relations with the local Aborigines. The newcomers complained that the Ngarluma were pilfering from them and sought retribution from the magistrate. On one occasion Sholl's men went to investigate but found that the settlers' complaints were unfounded. Like elsewhere in Australia, the Aborigines felt that as the settlers were shooting their kangaroos and other game, they had a right to take food in return. Nevertheless, the Withnells found themselves caught in the middle when one Aboriginal man was charged and locked up in John's wool press in the period before the prison was built in 1866.

Emma was deeply concerned about the condition of the Ngarluma, especially the Aboriginal pearl divers. Extremely good underwater swimmers, they were being exploited and forced to stay too long below the surface, placing their lives at risk to bring more profit to the owners of the pearling luggers. Emma suggested to Sholl that legislation should be brought in to limit this. Sholl agreed. Acting on information supplied by the Withnells, the now retired magistrate drafted a proposal that led to the passing of the 1873 Pearl Shell Fishery Regulation Act to protect Aboriginal and Malay divers.

Two more sons were born to the Withnells during their busy years at Mount Welcome Station and to the chores of cooking, sewing, mending and midwifery with which she was helped by her faithful house girls, Nungerdie and Thoodoo, Emma now added the duties of teaching, using old newspapers instead of textbooks to instruct the children to read. She described in a letter to her parents how 'I brought my children up in Christian faith and without most of the refinements of civilised life'.

By 1879 Emma had been the matriarch of Mount Welcome Station for fifteen years, bearing nine children and running their farm with her usual efficiency and good humour. She had endured cyclone, drought, epidemics and, in 1878, a fire which destroyed many wooden structures on the Withnells' property and once again necessitated an extensive rebuilding program. Now their homestead was surrounded by dozens of houses — in effect, their six acres were now in Roebourne itself and they felt hemmed in. Roebourne had become a sprawling, noisy town — no longer was Mount Welcome Station the quiet and peaceful spot where the family had settled fifteen years ago. During the day, bullock drays rattled over rugged stony roads; at night brawling and loud laughter at Roebourne's public houses kept Emma and the children awake.

Emma and John decided it was time to move away from the area. They sold their now flourishing property on the Harding River to their friend Robert Sholl and moved to the much larger Sherlock Station. In anticipation of the move, a large homestead had been completed on the spot Emma had selected years earlier.

By this time Emma and John's land holdings had dramatically increased from the original lease of 100,000 acres to 307,000 acres (124,000 hectares), which would provide sufficient land for their sons to farm as well. At Sherlock Station, named for the river which watered the property,[15] Emma developed beautiful gardens. Both she and John were happy to be away from the hustle and bustle of the town of Roebourne, now known as the 'capital of the north'.

In time Emma bore two more children. Of her eleven children only the first two had been born with the help of a doctor. Her others were delivered by Emma herself directing Fanny or Sophia, or more often her husband, who was assisted by her devoted Ngarluma house girls, Nungerdie and Thoodoo.

Emma and John remained at Sherlock Station for nine years, by which time their eldest sons were well capable of running the farm under their father's supervision.

Despite many setbacks from the harsh climate and the occasional cyclone, they enjoyed pioneering the vast north-west area which they and Walter Padbury, who started a sheep station in 1863, and John Wellard, had been the first to settle and develop. They had set off for the north with 650 healthy sheep but due to the shipwreck had been left with only eighty-four ewes, two rams, a horse and a cow. But they had never lost hope in the future — and now thanks to a great deal of hard work, courage and determination they possessed 20,000 sheep, 130 horses and 150 head of cattle and were regarded as very successful pioneers.[16]

The Withnells had seen many changes to the area and by 1885 isolation from civilisation was no longer such a problem. The Overland Telegraph Line now linked Roebourne, Geraldton and Perth, and many more people would arrive once gold was discovered in the Pilbara in 1888.

By that year, however, John's health had started to fail. He was now sixty-five and suffering from asthma. His right leg had been badly damaged in a fall and he had been advised he needed to live close to a hospital. He was now happy to hand over the running of the property to several of his sons and his capable son-in-law, John Meares.

At forty-five Emma was still healthy. However, she was concerned about her husband's health and was also anxious to have good schools for her younger children and opportunities for them to take up careers other than farming.

In September 1888, John and Emma finally left their beautiful Sherlock Station homestead. They said goodbye to the local Aborigines, who gathered around the homestead, keening and mourning for the departure of the children they had come to love. Emma embraced her two faithful helpers, Thoodoo and Nungerdie, who gave her a beautifully woven dilly bag as a present. When they passed through Yeeramukadoo — the place of the wild fig — now Roebourne, they also said goodbye to their Ngarluma friends, who wailed a mournful farewell to the much-loved Boorong and Banaker.

As their ship drew away, the wharf at Nickol Bay was crowded with settlers who had come to wave goodbye to Emma Withnell, 'the mother of the north-west', her husband and the younger children, Herbert, William, Lilla and Grace.

ℓℓ ℓℓ ℓℓ

Emma and John settled in the Perth suburb of Guildford. Through hard work they had made enough money to retire in comfort, although Emma would continue to assist those in need and help deliver babies free of charge whenever she was asked to do so.

Most of their elder children remained in the north, eventually marrying and providing the couple with grandchildren.

Karratha Station near Port Hedland, formerly owned by the Withnells.

Their eldest son, George, who had come north with them on that fateful boat trip in 1864, remained single. At thirty-four he married a Guildford girl named Ellen Amelia Worth, of whom Emma had become very fond. To celebrate the marriage of their first born, Emma and John gave a splendid ball at Guildford Town Hall.

John Withnell died in May 1898 in his seventy-fifth year. The following year Emma, always a shrewd investor, bought a half share in Karratha Station on the Maitland River (near today's Port Hedland), together with three of her sons. The property had been originally selected for their eldest daughter, Emily Ellen, who in 1886 had married pastoralist John Meares and given Emma and John their first grandchild. Eventually the widowed Emma rented out her Guildford residence and built herself a delightful new and smaller house, called Esselmont, at Northam.

For the next thirty years Emma divided her time between staying with her sons and daughters in the north-west, in her own house at Northam or with relatives in Perth. She joined the Karakatta Club and became an excellent public speaker. She was interviewed by journalists and historians who wanted to know what outback life had been like in the early days of the Pilbara.

Emma was one of the first women to be appointed a justice of the peace in Western Australia and was praised by the Premier, Sir James Mitchell, for her role in pioneering the region.[17] The Withnell family developed a total of eleven pastoral properties and Emma's descendants still run some of these stations.

In spite of their initial difficulties, Emma and John Withnell founded a dynasty which spread out across the rapidly developing state of Western Australia. Sons, daughters, grandsons and granddaughters all inherited the determination, enterprise and energy of Emma and her husband. Emma was proud of her eleven children and considered their successes in life ample repayment for her care and affection.

℮ ℮ ℮

In May 1928 Emma died of cholecystitis at the Mount Lawley home of her eldest son. She was buried in the Anglican cemetery at Guildford beside her husband. Nine of her children attended her funeral. Premier Sir James Mitchell gave the eulogy and said: 'Emma Withnell has been placed amongst the state makers of Western Australia in appreciation of the work she has done for her homeland.'

All her life Emma had been an imaginative yet supremely practical woman. She helped her husband in their many enterprises with determination and foresight. She was a woman in advance of her time — in an era when relations between Europeans and Aborigines were often hostile, she believed in establishing friendship with the local indigenous people and saved the lives of many Ngarluma during an epidemic of smallpox.

All those who have profited from the pearling industry around Broome and the vast mining wealth of the Pilbara area (which now exports one-eighth of the world's iron ore) owe Emma Withnell a debt of gratitude. Indeed, it was one of Emma's sons, James Withnell, who, in 1888, discovered the gold-bearing lode which started the Pilbara gold rush and eventually led to other mineral discoveries in the area. Another son ran an iron foundry as a sideline.

The name Withnell appears on street names and in small parks in many parts of the north-west of Western Australia — at Withnell

Emma Withnell's granddaughter Judith Stove standing beside the memorial to Emma near Roebourne.

Hill, Withnell Bay, and at Karratha and the more modern mining towns of Dampier and Port Hedland. It also appears on a plaque set amid a cairn of stones near Roebourne that acts as a memorial to Emma. The cairn was erected by the Country Women's Association, an organisation which has been of immense benefit to women in remote areas, and with which Emma Withnell was associated in her later years.

Due to the 'tyranny of distance', very few people in the eastern seaboard of Australia know the name Emma Withnell, although she was one of our greatest female pioneers, an entrepreneurial, enterprising and determined woman, as well as a dedicated humanitarian and a generous human being.

The plaque in Roebourne commemorates 'the mother of the north-west' who dared to take on the challenge of developing that formerly wild and remote region which has brought economic success and prosperity to the thriving state of Western Australia.

CHAPTER 3

Atlanta 'Attie' Hope Bradshaw

1866 – 1929

MOTHERING 'SEVEN LITTLE AUSTRALIANS' AT ALICE SPRINGS

In 1899 33-year-old Atlanta Bradshaw and her children undertook a hazardous journey from Adelaide across the red desert at the heart of Australia to take up residence at Alice Springs Telegraph Station.[1] Atlanta's husband, Thomas Bradshaw, had been appointed superintendent of the telegraph line as well as its postmaster. He was replacing Irish-born Francis Gillen who had been at the telegraph station for seven years and left to work on a book about Aboriginal desert peoples.

The Overland Telegraph Line was considered a technological marvel for its time. Alice Springs Telegraph Station played a vital role in transmitting the latest news from London, via undersea cable, to Australia. From Darwin (then known as Port Darwin), messages were passed through stations at Pine Creek, Katherine, Daly Waters, Powell Creek, Tennant Creek, Barrow Creek, Alice Springs, Charlotte Waters, Oodnadatta and several more stations to the head office at Adelaide, where Thomas Bradshaw had been employed as night superintendent.

As a boy Thomas Bradshaw had migrated to Australia with his family from southern England to the Portland area in Victoria,

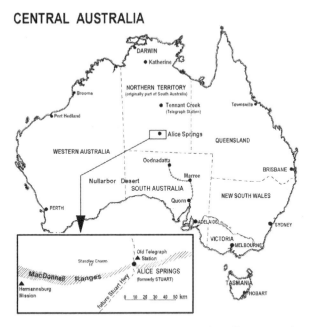

CENTRAL AUSTRALIA

where he grew up and joined the telegraph office.[2] He later moved to Adelaide and worked as a telegraphist at the General Post Office rising to the position of night supervisor.

In 1887, aged twenty-eight, Thomas married tall, raven-haired Atlanta Allchurch, a capable, resilient and hard-working 21-year-old, with a mind of her own. Atlanta enjoyed cooking and loved children. Soon she had four of her own, becoming a loving and devoted mother.

Perhaps in wanting a large family Atlanta was compensating for her lonely childhood. Her sea captain father was often away from home for long periods. In fact, Atlanta had been born at sea off the Cape of Good Hope. Her mother had been accompanying her husband, captain of the SS *Atlanta,* on its way to South Australia, and Atlanta was named after the ship.

Atlanta and Thomas eventually set up home in Halifax Street in Adelaide; however, late in 1898, feeling the toll of working at nights, Thomas decided on a career change. To Atlanta's dismay, he signed a contract to run the Alice Springs Overland Telegraph Station.

Once appointed Thomas had to set out almost immediately. In March 1899 he left by train for Terowie, farewelled by his wife and children — clever dark-haired Winifred Doris (Doris); plump little Katherine Constance ('Consie'); lively Edmund Mortimer ('Mort'), and cuddly Jack (christened Eric Ivan), the baby of the family.

At Terowie, Thomas had to change trains and go on to Oodnadatta. As there was no road across the desert beyond Oodnadatta he was to go by horse and buggy through rough country to Alice Springs. This leg of the journey would take Thomas five or six weeks, camping out every night. Once he arrived he had to prepare suitable accommodation for his family who were to make the same journey at a later date.

The idea of camping for weeks in the desert with a baby, a toddler and two lively elder children did not exactly enchant Atlanta. But she loved Thomas and lived in an era when the duty of a good wife was to follow her husband wherever he went, so she was determined to make the best of their situation at the telegraph station. She may also have remembered the times when her father was away for long periods at sea, and determined *her* children would not have an absentee father.

Atlanta's neighbours in Adelaide were horrified to learn she was off to the outback. Her parents were also extremely concerned. At that time 'ladies' did not go to the outback. But Atlanta shrugged off their fears. Perhaps she thought that if Francis Gillen's wife Amelia ('Minnie') had been able to stick it out, then so could she.

But the more she heard about the dangers and hardships of the outback, the more worried Attie Bradshaw must have felt. Wives of Thomas's former colleagues whispered about poisonous snakes and polluted water and told her the story of Carl Kraegen, the first superintendent at the telegraph station who had died of thirst on the journey out to Alice Springs to start operations. They also told her about poor Superintendent Flint, who died of rheumatic fever.[3] Nor could she have helped worrying that there would be no doctor or midwife for hundreds of miles.

Thomas had sought to calm his wife's fears by telling her they would have the very latest medical textbooks and that a doctor could be consulted over the line if the children fell sick. He would transmit messages to the doctor in Morse code and wait for his reply, or he could contact the nurses at the new hospital at Port Darwin.

Atlanta had reminded Thomas there was schooling for their children to consider. In those days no one ever dreamed of a School of the Air. Women in the outback had to educate their own children or, if they could afford it, employ a governess. To pacify Atlanta, Thomas had promised they too would employ a governess. Although they could not afford to pay her very much, Atlanta succeeded in engaging Bertha Easom, an enthusiastic and attractive young woman in her early twenties who wanted a change from working in an office.

Thomas was also aware that Atlanta had a soft spot for her younger brother Ernest, who had had trouble settling down to a steady job. So he promised he would find the young man a job with the telegraph station and he too could live with them. That thought cheered Atlanta up. She loved Ernest, her boisterous handsome young brother, and hoped he would soon settle down to a regular career and get married.

Eventually the sad day came when Atlanta had to leave her parents and her dear sister Emily. Bertha joined them on the station platform. With four children under the age of eight, Atlanta must have been relieved to have some help on the long and harrowing journey ahead of her.

The first leg of their journey from Adelaide took them to hot, dusty Terowie. Here they boarded the narrow-gauge train called the Ghan, named for the Afghan camel drivers who had opened up the outback and continued to deliver goods there by camel train. The Ghan was pulled by a steam engine that belched out smoke and soot. Cups of tea were made en route from the boiling water of the engine and passed down the train.[4] Legend had it that if ever the engine packed up and food ran out, passengers lived off whatever game the engine driver was able to shoot.

Along their way, the train stopped overnight at Quorn and at Hergott Springs, where thankfully they all piled off into hotels for the night. (Hergott Springs, named after a German settler, would in World War I be renamed Marree.)

Finally, after four days' travel, they reached the terminus at Oodnadatta. Oodnadatta was a bleak, dusty place, consisting of a combined telegraph station and post office, a campsite of Afghans, Hindus and smelly camels, a bush pub and a tented mosque.[5] The sandhill countryside around the town was monotonous and arid, consisting of spinifex grass, saltbush and small rocks called gibbers.

Atlanta was delighted to see the tall figure of her husband waiting for them at Oodnadatta railway station. He was accompanied by Bob Crann and George Hablett, two telegraph station employees, as well as two vehicles: a buggy drawn by five horses and a buckboard drawn by four. There was also a team of spare horses to pull the vehicles in shifts as the going was so rough it exhausted the animals.

George Hablett's eyes opened wide at the sight of pretty young Bertha. He searched around to see if she had any girlfriends, demanding plaintively, 'What's the use of only bringing one? You should've brought a cartload and let 'em loose up here.'[6]

They managed to purchase some freshly baked bread and stowed it away in the tucker box, a contraption of which Thomas was very proud. He had had it fitted out specially with separate compartments for salt beef, butter and other supplies for the journey. The buckboard was a flimsy open cart with a hard wooden seat across the front and a full-width shelf underneath it designed to take the heavier luggage, the tents they would pitch each night, their valises, Atlanta's steamer trunk, the tucker box, their cooking utensils and the blanket rolls on which they would sleep. The buggy was more substantial. It had springless horsehair seats and took several passengers. Objects such as canvas water bags and gridirons for grilling food over the camp fire were strung underneath.

It was some 500 kilometres of desert to Alice Springs. Atlanta sat in the buggy beside the driver, Bob Crann, with baby Jack on her knee. Mort, Consie, Doris and Bertha squashed together in the back. There was no canopy to protect them from the burning sun so Atlanta and the children wore hats which they had to hold fast to their heads when the wind blew. Thomas rode on the buckboard beside George Hablett and an Aboriginal groom, with the line of packhorses and spare horses following behind.

The eighteen-day journey, rattling and bouncing over uneven and stony ground in a buggy with steel-framed wheels and bad springs, was extremely tiring for all of them. Space in the overcrowded vehicle was at a premium. There were no shops to buy food so they had to make do with their meagre supplies, and nor could they carry fodder for the horses. Finding fodder and water for the horses was the priority for every camp, and each evening it would take a long time to feed, water and hobble them, and then erect the tents and start the cooking. The process had to be reversed each morning.

Each day they drove until dusk by which time the horses were exhausted. Their first camp was at a place called the Swallow. Alas, their dinner was vile — salt beef and bread — and would only get worse as the butter melted and turned rancid and the bread bought in Oodnadatta turned stale and rock hard, like the seats of the buggy. Atlanta spent an uncomfortable night on the blanket roll, the ground hard and unresisting as she lay worrying about the baby beside her. To cap it all she lost a brooch which friends had given her as a farewell present. She could have wept with vexation but

A buckboard or produce wagon, designed to be pulled by two horses. It had an unsprung seat and was a most uncomfortable vehicle.

bit back her tears and continued with unloading and loading the luggage, feeding the baby with condensed milk and checking the children.

In spite of Atlanta's efforts, as the journey continued the meals grew almost inedible. The children, bored and weary, grizzled that the food was horrible, with Doris refusing to eat a thing.

At first the ground was the colour of ochre and very monotonous. The closer they came to the original Alice Spring discovered by John Ross in the dry river bed of the Todd, the more varied the landscape became. Soon there were no more gibber rocks. Spinifex, grey-green mulga and eucalypts dominated the rich deep red of the earth, sometimes enlivened by the dark green feathery foliage of the desert oak. Bob Crann explained that this strange tree, unlike anything Atlanta had seen in Adelaide, had only one long single taproot which served to make the tree drought-proof. Aboriginal women would dig around it for ants after rain when the insects became engorged with a honey-like fluid. The women killed the ants by snapping off the heads then drank the sweet fluid in the bodies.

On the morning of 23 May, Atlanta felt anxious when she realised she had forgotten to send a card from Oodnadatta for her sister Emily's birthday. It was too late now to rectify the oversight. 'I wish I could send her a telegram,' she said ruefully.

'Go on,' Thomas said. 'You want to send a telegram — all right, I'll send it for you.'[7]

Atlanta thought her husband must be suffering from delusions brought on by sunstroke. But she decided to humour him and wrote out a loving message. Thomas took the piece of paper, went to one of the saddles on the packhorses and returned with linesmen's clamps — two curved pieces of metal which he fixed around his boots. Putting Atlanta's message in his pocket he straddled the nearest telegraph pole and proceeded to climb it like a monkey, much to the amazement of his children.

Reaching the top of the pole, Thomas took some tools from his pocket and, hanging on for grim death, did what he had seen other linesmen do — tap into the wire. Clinging on by his foot clamps he managed to send the telegram to Emily, care of the Adelaide Telegraph Office. Atlanta was astounded and said so once Thomas had descended from the telegraph pole looking pleased with himself.

As the journey continued they traversed ninety kilometres of dangerous sandhills, furrowed by the wind into regular patterns. In this country summer temperatures could reach as high as 50 degrees Celsius in the shade and many men had died of thirst. The horses plodded on with an occasional drink from the canvas water bags, but supplies were dwindling fast. Bob Crann warned them that there was a danger the water at isolated Alice Well and Deep Well might be polluted by dead animals, and this could lead to typhoid and dysentery.

As the water supplies decreased, Atlanta had to ration them. She did her best with the spoiled food from the tucker box but there was no denying the meals were unpalatable. The only thing she and the children enjoyed eating were the crisply baked hot Johnny cakes (small round dampers) that George Hablett made out of flour, water and salt, and cooked in the ashes of the fire rather than in the awkward camp oven. As the outer layer of the Johnny cakes tended to be crusted with charcoal, George filed the burned bits off with a rasp he kept for the horses' hoofs. Atlanta was delighted to see the children eating something with pleasure rather than with groans and grimaces.

Eventually they came through the sandhills and to deep-red rocks which marked the entrance to canyons and ravines. At the family-owned Alice Well Cattle Station they stopped to rest the horses. Here they were given a meal of salt beef and freshly baked bread by the pioneer graziers William Hayes and his wife. Atlanta was amazed by the primitive living conditions of the Hayes family. She had assumed they must be wealthy as they owned large mobs of cattle, but she was surprised to see dirt floors and their dining-room walls papered with yellowed, fading old newspapers. So this was life in the Never-Never.

After a short break, it was back on the road again. The children were delighted by the mobs of red and grey kangaroos, which bounded away from them in a series of leaps. Their little convoy passed through Heavitree Gap where two white policemen and six Aboriginal constables were stationed, near the camps of the gold and ruby miners who were starting to flood into the area. It would not be long before the miners realised that the 'rubies' they found were only garnets, worth very little. In spite of this, the rumour persisted that where there were garnets there *must* be gold. Some desperate types were wheeling their digging equipment on barrows or handcarts and Thomas feared they might have guns in their swags.[8]

Along the skyline they saw range upon range of purple-tinged granite mountains, with deep shadows on their flanks — the incredibly beautiful MacDonnell Ranges. As they clip-clopped through the red heart of Australia, the horses followed a line of wooden poles embedded four feet deep in the earth. Thomas told the children these poles had been dug in by hand by European linesmen who had lived in camps out here for months at a time.

At last the cavalcade reached the tiny hamlet of Stuart, which would eventually be renamed Alice Springs, after the telegraph station closed its operations beside the original Alice Spring and moved to Stuart where most of the population were living.

In 1899 when the Bradshaws arrived, Stuart consisted of one hotel — the Stuart Arms — two general stores, a saddlery and three houses. One lone European woman, Mrs Charles Meyer, wife of the owner of the saddlery and harness shop, lived there. Atlanta had been looking forward to meeting her; however, they were told that Mrs Meyer's second child was expected at any time and in the absence of a midwife, desperate Mrs Meyer had made a full day's buggy drive out to Hermannsburg Mission,[9] more than 100 kilometres away on the Finke River. There she would be cared for by the missionary women, including Mrs Frieda Strehlow, rather than impose on Mrs Charles Brookes, the police constable's wife, who lived with her husband and four children in the camp at nearby Heavitree Gap.

Hermannsburg Mission had been set up by missionaries from Wurttemberg, Germany, in the 1870s. Like Thomas Bradshaw and

Ernest Gillen, missionary Carl Strehlow was a man of wide interests who learned to speak Arrernte. Strehlow was compiling an Arrernte–English dictionary, putting the Arrernte language into written form and translating the Bible into Arrernte. He was trying to turn Hermannsburg Mission into a self-supporting community with a date-palm plantation that would bring in money.

Mrs Meyer, Mrs Brookes and Frieda Strehlow at Hermannsburg were the only educated white women to live in the red centre area when Atlanta arrived.

Over the last three kilometres to the telegraph station, Atlanta gave thanks they had come through safely. None of the children had fallen from the buckboard, been bitten by a snake as they slept on the ground, or been poisoned by the decaying food. Relieved that their long arduous journey was nearly over, she could now admire the beauty of the ranges and marvel at the purity of the air — so clear it made rocks half a kilometre away look as though you could reach out and touch them from the buggy.

At the edge of the Todd River they saw a small camp of Arrernte. Naked dark-haired women and children with tousled blonde hair and dark eyes came out to look at the party and point at them with excitement. The Bradshaw children waved back as the buggy carried them on to where they caught the first glimpse of their new home — a cluster of nine stone buildings with thick walls and tiny windows that housed the staff and telegraph machinery. Some buildings still had their original palm thatch while others had roofs of corrugated iron.

Lined up beside the station office were the male telegraph operators: Mr Field, Mr Squire, Mr Middleton and Mr Jago, all wearing their best suits and waiting to greet Atlanta. As the telegraph station had to be manned all the time, these telegraph operators worked in shifts around the clock so the messages could get through. The men smiled and doffed their hats rather than shaking hands with her. Two shy Arrernte women dressed in their Sunday-best white blouses and skirts, and a traditional white *chillara* headband, which kept their hair out of their eyes, were introduced to Atlanta. Tryphena (Tryff) and Dolly had previously

PHOTO © JAKE DE VRIES, PIRGOS PRESS.

*Hermannsburg Mission where Frieda Strehlow acted as midwife to Atlanta
Bradshaw's friend Annie Meyers.*

worked for the Gillens. The women smiled and spoke in pidgin
English, calling Atlanta 'Quei' — 'senior woman' in the Arrernte
language.

Thomas led his family to the station master's house with its wide
verandas and showed them the blacksmith's workshop and stores,
the separate post and telegraph office, the stables and the buggy
shed. The station master's house was now almost thirty years old,
had ant-bed floors, and badly needed renovating, Atlanta thought.
Doors needed to be fitted to many of the rooms, she decided.

In order to both minimise fire risk and reduce heat in the main
house in summer, the station master's kitchen was a separate
building. It was joined to a dining room which had a large dining
table covered with a green baize cloth. The room was fitted with
a fireplace because in winter the nights could become very cold
indeed.

Since the station master's house lacked running water, whatever
was needed for drinking and washing had to be hauled up by hand
in buckets from the Alice Spring waterhole along the Todd
riverbed. Atlanta did not find it reassuring that the designers of the
house had fitted the exterior walls with holes at eye-level so

bullets could be fired at marauding Aborigines. But she was reassured by her husband that the Gillens had enjoyed excellent relations with the Arrernte people so shots had never been fired through these slits.

♪♪ ♪♪ ♪♪

The former superintendent, Francis Gillen, was one of a handful of people who had treated the Arrernte as rational human beings. He was disgusted by the cruelty some of the white and native police showed to the Arrernte.

The Aborigines regarded the Gillens as friends and genuine protectors. They had initially been suspicious, after their bitter experience of being hunted and killed by so many European men. However, after Gillen brought a private prosecution against a police constable for cruelty to Aborigines, he won their trust. Unfortunately, the case became a *cause célèbre* when the police paid a leading barrister to act for them and Constable Willshire got off. Nevertheless, it established Gillen as a champion of Aboriginal people.[10]

As an active Protector of Aborigines, Gillen had become very close to the Arrernte, and had been invited to secret ceremonies and

Alice Springs Telegraph Station.

COURTESY BERNARD SPILSBURY.

initiated into their ways. His 'skin name' among them was 'Oknirrabatta' or 'Great Teacher'.

Like Thomas Bradshaw, Gillen had had a passion for photography. In his eight years at the telegraph station he studied and photographed the Arrernte, who were possibly the friendliest and most artistic of all the Aboriginal peoples of the red centre.

A turning point in Gillen's life came when he met the Oxford-trained Walter Baldwin Spencer, who was a professor at Melbourne University. Professor Spencer was the official zoologist and photographer on the 1894 Horn expedition to central Australia financed by a wealthy mining magnate and investor in the fabled Broken Hill silver mines, William Horn. Horn was a keen amateur anthropologist, who also wished to investigate the land between Oodnadatta and the MacDonnell Ranges for possible mineral wealth.

Spencer realised that Gillen could supply him with invaluable information for his projected book on the Aboriginal people of central Australia. On the return journey, Spencer stayed behind at the telegraph station after the rest of the Horn expedition had departed. At nights the two men smoked their pipes and talked a great deal. Before Spencer left for Melbourne he invited Gillen to become joint author with him on a book about the Arrernte, the Papunya and Loritja of central Australia. Gillen agreed.

Spencer returned to the telegraph station the following year when Gillen 'arranged' for a corroboree to take place in his honour. The ceremony would feature in Spencer and Gillen's book *The Native Tribes of Central Australia*, a work which would make the pair of them famous. Eventually Gillen left Alice Springs in order to work on his contributions to *The Native Tribes of Central Australia*. He wrote with empathy about the Arrernte's legends and their ancestral Dreamtime, which bound them so firmly to the land.[11]

Gillen had worked hard to improve conditions for the Arrernte at a time when 'dispersing Aborigines' was a convenient euphemism among Europeans for murdering them. The Bradshaws would continue this tradition of helping the Arrernte, especially in times of drought when their game and supplies of plants and seeds ran low. Clustered around the Alice Spring waterhole, they would be fed from huge pans of boiled rice by Atlanta.

Thomas Bradshaw did not continue Gillen's anthropological research but using his glass-plate camera became a brilliant photographer of the red centre of Australia. Gillen had also taken photographs but they were not of the same quality as the glass plates of Thomas Bradshaw, whose strength lay in the composition of his subjects, the high quality of his photographs and their recording of pioneer days around Alice Springs.

Thomas also took photographs showing the family enjoying picnics at local waterholes, with magnificent reflections apparent in the water from the red rocks of local beauty spots, including Standley Chasm and Emily Gap. The unique landscape of the area inspired him and he became one of the period's great photographers.[12]

Due to its vast distance from markets the telegraph station had to be as self-supporting as possible: it had to grow its own vegetables, raise its own beef and mutton, and keep goats for milk. There were no grocery stores to go to in time of need. Dry goods like tea, sugar and rice, and all tools and fabrics came from Adelaide by camel train but only *once a year*. Atlanta had the responsibility of keeping an inventory of stores to feed and clothe the family, staff and station Aborigines, as well as supplying outback travellers who called in for purchases, and of making up the huge annual order which was telegraphed to Adelaide.

In addition to the four telegraph operators, regular station staff included blacksmith George Hablett and stockmen Bob Crann and Harry Kunoth. These men could also turn their hands to telegraph line work. Additionally there were four linesmen who went outback to keep the lines repaired, and a station cook, 'Cookie' Lloyd. An elderly man named Billy Crick acted as station gardener. Billy had planted sweet potatoes very successfully, and could grow carrots and cabbages in winter, but in the fierce summer heat had had no success with green vegetables, which withered and died, putting the Bradshaws and staff at the station at risk of scurvy — the dread of pioneer wives and mothers.

Atlanta found the summer heat overwhelming. In midsummer the temperature could reach up to 50 degrees Celsius and the only fans available had to be operated by pulling on a rope. She never came to terms with living in an unscreened house plagued in summer by flies and mosquitoes. It was impossible to escape from these insects or from the ants which infested the kitchen and pantry. Flies swarmed inside the house, settling on lips, eyes and every scrap of food they could find. After dark the flies quietened and then came the second shift, the mosquitoes, attracted by the light from candles and oil lamps.

While the telegraph office would not pay for insect screens it did pay wages for two or sometimes three local Arrernte house girls to help Atlanta clean, cook and run the house for her large family, and for the staff of boys, shepherds and water carriers — all of whom needed supervising. The house girls were liable to disappear without warning to go walkabout or take a long period of leave for 'sorry business' if a family member died. As frustrating as this was, Atlanta had to accept it. Going walkabout was like going on a pilgrimage, an essential part of Arrernte cultural life. Besides, how could girls who had lived a nomadic life be expected to know how to lay tables or do the ironing and avoid scorching delicate clothes with an iron that had to be heated over hot coals? Few of them had ever been inside four walls before, or seen a knife and fork; most did not know what cupboards or toilets were for and thought the spring water too precious to be employed for washing their bodies.

On the other hand, the Arrernte women could do many things European women could not do — like tracking people through the desert or carrying loaded pitchers of water without spilling a drop, balancing them on their heads with the aid of a *manguri,* a circle or coil of woven hair and emu feathers. Their skills had been honed over centuries to ensure survival in a harsh land where Europeans died because they could not find bush tucker for themselves, as the Arrernte could.

Atlanta found two of the women, Rungee and Amelia, much more dependable than the others and they became indispensable to her as her family increased in number. Amelia was the illegitimate daughter of an Arrernte woman and English-born Jack Pavey, who had worked for the telegraph line but did not wish to know about his daughter. The telegraph station had accepted responsibility for this delightful little girl who had become so fond of Atlanta's predecessor, Amelia Gillen, that she had renounced her tribal name and wanted to be known as Amelia.[13]

The Gillens had raised Amelia, and taught her to read and write. They had considered taking her with them when they left Alice Springs, but in the expectation of Francis Gillen being off work for a year while he finished his share of *The Native Tribes of Central Australia,* the Gillens feared it would be too much to take on additional financial responsibility for young Amelia. So Amelia remained at the telegraph station, where she became the charge of the Bradshaws.

Amelia would live happily with the Bradshaws for the nine years they spent at the telegraph station and blossom from an attractive lively child into a confident and beautiful young woman. Atlanta, who became very fond of Amelia, would form a lifelong bond with her, having come to rely on her and the much older Rungee through three difficult pregnancies and the children's illnesses.

Perhaps the Bradshaws felt that in an almost exclusively male society they had a duty to protect a young Aboriginal girl until she was old enough to decide who she wanted to marry. Much later, after the Bradshaws left, she would accept the marriage proposal of Harry Kunoth. A devout, mission-educated Lutheran, Harry never said a word about his feelings for Amelia until he considered her old enough for marriage.

Another of Atlanta's charges was another part-Aboriginal child who had been entrusted to the care of the telegraph station management during the Gillens' time there. Mumpaguila had been found abandoned as a baby, her nose and mouth stuffed with sand, making it

PHOTOGRAPHED BY JAKE DE VRIES FROM A DISPLAY AT THE OLD TELEGRAPH STATION MUSEUM.

Amelia with Edna Bradshaw.

difficult for her to breathe. One of the staff had cleaned her up and brought her to the telegraph station, where she had been fed, clothed and given a bed in the corner of the kitchen by Cookie Lloyd.

Thomas Bradshaw was not very happy about this arrangement. He wanted the youngster returned to the Aboriginal camp to be cared for by her own people. But, Doris recounted, as 'none of [the Arrernte women] were prepared to look after her my father always relented and allowed her to stay with Cookie', who fed her in his kitchen.[14]

Left to her own devices, when not in the kitchen with Cookie, wild little Mumpaguila roamed around by herself, often getting up to some mischief or other. At one time the station goats were apparently failing to give milk. Atlanta's sons Jack and Mort found that Mumpaguila had been drinking it, after catching her with a jam tin full. She flung the milk in their faces and ran away to the hills for several days before returning to the telegraph station rather than to the Arrernte camp.

Fifty years later, Doris and Consie Bradshaw visited Mumpaguila in an Adelaide hospital. By that time she was 'a very dignified, patient woman', although dying of cancer of the throat. Doris learned that Mumpaguila had been flown to Adelaide in three hours, 'over country through which we toiled for nearly three weeks'. In the intervening years Mumpaguila had settled down, married and raised a family, grateful for her life having been saved.

In learning to deal with her Aboriginal staff, Atlanta had to exercise patience. One of their most perplexing customs related to kinship rules, and Atlanta's experience of this was remarkably similar to that of Jeannie Gunn (see chapter four). Out on the veranda were wash tubs where the family washing was done with water carried from the spring by Mick the Aboriginal water boy. Since Aboriginal men were forbidden to look at or talk to particular women who were closely related to them, some of the house girls would scatter when Mick arrived. While these complex kinship rules were initially difficult for the Bradshaws to understand, they always led to lots of games and laughter among the Arrernte women, as they fled Mick and the washing suds.

It was not only the Aboriginal staff who gave Atlanta headaches. If her daughter Doris's descriptions of his meals are to be believed, Cookie Lloyd, whom Atlanta inherited from the Gillens, must have been one of the outback's worst chefs. He looked the part, at least, in his tall white cap and coat, and he could turn out tolerable bread and yeast buns in the men's kitchen. Apart from that his menus were monotonous and his cooking lacked flavour; everything the men were given was overcooked. As he was known to have a vile temper they kept quiet. Cookie's favoured dessert was a stodgy sago pudding, which he served five or six times a week, although the men hated it and sometimes threw it out of the window when Cookie was not looking.

After eating Cookie Lloyd's first meal, Atlanta decided she would do all the cooking for her family herself. She also found it hard to make the Arrernte wash their hands, another reason why she insisted on preparing and cooking the food. Many white children died in the outback from stomach infections and dysentery, so it was likely Atlanta worried about her own children.

Atlanta did her best in the hot kitchen on a temperamental stove which lacked any form of temperature control. As was so often the case in the outback, beef and mutton from the station herds were plentiful, and there was always a good supply of chops, steak and roasts. Sometimes, for a change, Atlanta would make the children an outback delicacy known as Burdekin Duck. This consisted of thick slices of cold roast or corned beef dipped in a milky batter to which finely chopped onion was added and then deep-fried in fat to produce delicious fritters. But fresh fruit was scarce or non-existent. As a special treat the family ate tinned fruit such as plums until the rations gave out.

Tea was the standard drink in those days and most pioneers automatically boiled all their drinking water fearing it might be polluted and thus cause dysentery or blackwater fever. But the water from Alice Spring was clear, unpolluted and rich in calcium, and in times of drought attracted Aboriginal groups from a wide area to camp around it.

❧ ❧ ❧

Another task Atlanta assigned herself was to set to on her hand-operated sewing machine to make clothes for the Arrernte women so they would not go about stark naked. She made five dozen skirts out of blue serge she found in the store. She could not give individual fittings but made them to a one-size-fits-all pattern with a drawstring waist.

The women liked clothes that kept them warm in winter but tended to discard them in summer and preferred brighter colours, like red and emerald green. One woman shrewdly complained that the dark blue skirts made the women look 'Allasame longa crows'.[15] Eventually many of the skirts ended up as headbands for the women's husbands. The headbands were thought to prevent headaches and were regarded as essential by the Arrernte.

The house girls wore white blouses, skirts and headbands. Atlanta insisted that the girls leave their uniforms behind before going back to their camp, a practice Amelia Gillen had initiated, knowing from bitter experience that the uniforms would be given or gambled away. During the heat of day the girls had a siesta and often slept in the red dirt surrounded by their beloved dogs, another reason for leaving their white uniforms at the station.

ℓℓ ℓℓ ℓℓ

Between her household duties and looking after both her family and the telegraph station's Aborigines and staff, Atlanta was kept busy. In her memoir of their time there, Doris Bradshaw paints a picture of her mother as dutifully tending not only her own family, but to many of the station Aborigines with food, medicine and, if that failed, attention.

The government had supplied the Bradshaws with a large medicine chest in which were old fashioned remedies like glycerine (used with honey as cough medicine), Condy's crystals (an antiseptic), castor oil (for constipation), olive oil (to soothe sores), laudanum, carbolic acid, iodine, pulverised charcoal (for bad breath), quinine (for malaria), bismuth, essence of ginger (for stomach disorders), digitalis (for heart attacks and, oddly enough, recommended for the treatment of piles) and borax (for bathing sore eyes). Doris recorded how a constant stream of people would present to Atlanta with real or imagined illnesses and all would be helped. Atlanta tended various ailments including many cases of sore eyes from sunlight suffered by the Arrernte, who arrived at the front door of the house. There were also sad cases of children who had fallen into the camp fire and had been badly burned.

As well as doctoring the Arrernte, Atlanta had to nurse her own family when they became sick. Atlanta's worst fears were realised when her son Mortimer developed a high fever and coughing fits, less than a year after they arrived at the telegraph station. His symptoms were telegraphed to Adelaide. A reply from doctors there suggested Mort had whooping cough. Over the line in Morse code the doctor prescribed doses of castor oil and belladonna, chlorate of potash, and hot fomentations to be applied to the little boy's chest.

Atlanta carried out the doctor's instructions but still Mort's condition did not improve and his temperature stayed high. Soon the poor boy had an ulcerated mouth, blurred vision, swollen glands and great difficulty in swallowing. Atlanta was beside herself with worry. Her son was far too ill to be moved. Messages sped back and forth along the wire to doctors in Adelaide and Port Darwin and soon Mort was diagnosed with diphtheria. Her son became so ill that Atlanta was in despair. She stayed in his room at night and wore herself out nursing him and worrying whether the prescriptions of doctors in distant cities, who had never examined the patient, could be effective. Mort was desperately ill with diphtheretic paralysis for three months, during which time Atlanta massaged his limbs daily while suffering all the anguish of a mother lacking medical help.

Not long afterwards Doris developed rheumatic fever with terrifying bouts of fever known as 'night sweats'. With her condition deteriorating and the doctor on the telegraph line vague on treatment, the Bradshaws sought help by getting in contact with a former hospital matron, wife of a station owner in Katherine, over a thousand kilometres away. The matron's advice was hot baths, hot fomentations, milk and salicylic acid, and total bed rest. At long last Doris started to recover.

Not all illnesses had happy outcomes. In July 1900, Thomas Bradshaw's younger brother, Ernie, arrived at the telegraph station. Ernie, a bookkeeper by profession, was suffering from tuberculosis, and had come from Melbourne to live with the Bradshaws, hoping the dry climate of Alice Springs might improve his condition and that Atlanta could nurse him back to health. But the tuberculosis slowly ravaged him and he became thinner and thinner.

At the time Atlanta was pregnant once again and in the scorching heat it became more and more difficult for her to run the household and care for Ernie. On 15 November 1900, a few months after Ernie's arrival, the Bradshaws' fifth child was born. They christened him Stuart MacDonnell Bradshaw, after the nearby township of Stuart.

There had been no time to take the long buggy journey to Hermannsburg Mission to seek Frieda Strehlow's services as a midwife. Young Annie Meyer, with no experience in midwifery except giving birth herself, helped deliver baby Stuart. Atlanta's eldest daughter, Doris later wrote in her memoirs that lack of proper obstetric and medical care resulted in her mother developing gynaecological problems.

Just as Atlanta was recovering from the birth of Stuart, Ernie's condition deteriorated sharply and he started to cough up blood and died. The Bradshaws were desolate. Due to the heat they had to bury the young man the following day. He was laid to rest in the tiny cemetery at the telegraph station, beside the late Superintendent Ernest Flint.[16]

ℓℓ ℓℓ ℓℓ

The annual arrival of the camel train at the Alice Springs Telegraph Station must have been quite a sight. Haughty-looking camels were linked to each other by ropes attached to a nose peg made of bone or ivory. The Afghan drivers made the camels lie down — grunting or squealing as they did so, folding their bony legs as they sank to the ground. Then the ropes holding the great packs and baskets, some weighing over 200 kilograms, were unfastened.

The station master was given a 'free allowance' of freight as part of his salary (which was not a large one). If he exceeded this he would have to pay for any items he shipped to or from Alice Springs — quite an expense. Thomas and Atlanta kept a running list of everything that needed replacing, from household crockery to the men's work boots, shirts and trousers. Also included were bolts of cloth from which Atlanta would sew clothes for the children and her house girls.

When the stores arrived, the children and telegraph staff rushed out to see them, and the Arrernte hurried up from the creek. Everyone would be shouting and gesticulating in excitement. They would all help carry the goods into the storeroom, which adjoined the buggy room. For the Arrernte, the arrival of rations meant less work for them hunting and gathering food.

While the Arrernte men were the hunters, it was women's work to harvest fruits like bush onions, desert raisins and shiny red *quandongs* about the size of a small plum. They would carry the fruit back to the camp in *coolamons* (oval wooden dishes). The women also went out with their digging sticks to look for witchetty grubs, which they knew nested in the roots of cassia trees, several kinds of acacia and prickly wattle. They used their long *kurupa* (digging sticks) like crowbars to break up roots and find the fat witchetty grubs, which were very rich and tasted something like scrambled egg when roasted. The Bradshaw children also loved to eat them.[17]

Gathering seeds was far more laborious. When times were good, the Arrernte women gathered and cooked the tiny seeds of woollybutt grass, native millet and seeds from a tree they called *ngalta*. The seeds were lightly singed over a fire of cassia twigs, winnowed and then ground to a fine powder on a grindstone. Once they were pulverised, the resulting fine meal was patted into little cakes, bonded together with animal fat and baked in the ashes of the fire.

The Arrernte women much preferred to use the flour Atlanta gave them, as making a paste from flour and water was far quicker than pounding seeds to a paste. Each Saturday rations of tea, flour, sugar and fresh meat were given out from the storeroom to the Arrernte, regardless of whether they worked for the telegraph station or not. The handout of rations was especially welcome in times of drought when the seeds and berries were scarce. For a special treat there were 'rice nights' when Atlanta and the house girls cooked up huge quantities of rice, just as they did in times of drought. The Arrernte loved this and came to collect the rice in old jam tins or other receptacles, sometimes with curried goat's meat as an additional treat. One elderly man, young Doris Bradshaw recalled in amusement, carried away a rice curry in his hat. Most of all they loved the special treats of treacle and small cakes. Atlanta would prepare such things on special days like Christmas and the Queen's Birthday.

Christmas Day, when Atlanta fed extensive numbers of Arrernte as well as her own children, was an exhausting day and no holiday

Atlanta Bradshaw distributing Christmas pudding mix at the telegraph station camp.
Rungee stands behind her to the left in white.
Glass-plate photo by Thomas Bradshaw.

for Atlanta at all. Each Christmas Day she and Thomas rose early and had a brief Anglican service with Christmas carols in the living room. Then Atlanta retired to the kitchen to work over huge pots on the wood-burning stove. This was the hottest time of the year and the heat in the kitchen soon became oppressive. However, the Bradshaws felt they had a responsibility to carry on the tradition of Amelia and Francis Gillen and provide at least 200 of the Arrernte with a lunchtime feast of curry, rice and Christmas pudding — which Atlanta served uncooked from a huge metal wash tub.

An undated glass-plate photograph shows Atlanta, flanked by the faithful Rungee, down at the Arrernte camp. Atlanta is wearing a hat, a white blouse and a long black skirt. Tousle-headed children in long dresses help themselves to pannikins of the uncooked Christmas pudding stiff with fruit in the wash tub. The Arrernte women, also wearing long dresses (possibly made by Atlanta), wait patiently in line to take some of the mix once the children have finished. Atlanta does, indeed, look rather tired.

In her book, Doris Bradshaw recorded that in order to give the Arrernte a happy day, the Bradshaws always postponed their own Christmas meal of bush turkey, plum pudding and Christmas cake until the evening, by which time Atlanta was usually exhausted.

ℓℓ ℓℓ ℓℓ

Washing and ironing for a large family, in which more often than not there was a new baby, was endless. The red earth around Alice Springs stained clothes very badly and it was difficult to get them white again. A great deal of Reckitt's Blue had to be used, specially imported on the annual camel train.

Soiled clothes and nappies were boiled in a copper beside the kitchen, lifted out with a stick and placed in the wash tub where they were pounded with a wooden paddle called a 'wash dolly'. Bad stains were removed by hand on the corrugated washboard. The wet clothes were rolled through a hand mangle, and the squeezed-out water used for watering the garden, since all water was precious. The washing was then pegged out by the house girls. In the heat it dried very quickly.

Atlanta had to keep an eye on everything, including the ironing which was done with heavy flat irons heated over the stove and, unlike modern electric irons, had no temperature controls.

At night, the Bradshaws made their own entertainment. Bertha Easom, and the governesses who later replaced her, would play the piano by candlelight. Bertha gave Doris music lessons and taught her to play light classical pieces and to accompany songs. With no radios or televisions for entertainment, musical ability was seen as an essential attribute of any properly educated young lady in those days. Doris also undertook a drawing course with lessons sent out to her by the Adelaide School of Art.

After the family meal, sometimes they all gathered in the sitting room round the piano for a family sing-song. But most nights, while Atlanta and the governess sewed by the light of the lamp and mended the children's clothes, Thomas retired to his book-lined study, wrote up his diary and studied the Arrernte language. He also noted down the judgements he had made in court.

As officer in charge of the telegraph station, Thomas Bradshaw also functioned as special magistrate. The Alice Springs court was held in the men's dining room at the telegraph station. At these initial hearings, Thomas had to deal with cases ranging from murder to gold miners' claims and disputes, petty pilfering and maltreatment of animals. Thomas had to send cases of arson, murder or rape on to Port Augusta, so only relatively minor offenders were sentenced at the telegraph station. Although he had no legal training whatsoever, Thomas would sit in a high-backed chair at the dining table to dispense justice as he thought fit. He was referred to as 'Your Honour' by Constable Brookes of neighbouring Heavitree Gap.

An entry in Thomas's diary refers to an Aborigine who 'broke into a store, stole 15 lb flour, 1 lb tea, butcher's knife, sugar, etc. I got the goods back, so gave him 5 lb of flour and cleared him off to Barrow Creek [further north on the telegraph line].'[18]

Doris later observed in her memoir that Thomas 'even tried to extend justice to the aborigines and temper it with mercy; at the turn of the century in Central Australia that was not at all an everyday occurrence ... any white man who demonstrated impartiality in affairs affecting the aborigines was in danger of being branded as a radical'.[19]

This was a rough, tough era and cruelty in the bush was endemic. Europeans were brutal to Aborigines, many of whom were brought to court chained by the neck. Frequently, the native constables, who were usually from different tribes, were the most brutal of all. Both the European and native police claimed the Aborigines would run away and vanish into the desert if not chained by the neck to be brought into the courtroom. Gillen and Bradshaw were outraged by this vile practice and did their best to stop it.

Thomas was also called upon to try cases of severe cruelty on the part of Aboriginal men who, on occasion, had savagely beaten their wives. Some of these cases were uncomfortably close to home. Their own servant Rungee, for example, had to suffer at the hands of her selfish husband who, according to Doris, 'regarded her as nothing more than a chattel'.[20]

Also appearing in Thomas's courtroom were Europeans and Chinese who had been brought to Australia as indentured labourers. Others on trial were drifters from the south, absconders from justice or from 'nagging wives'. In October 1905, Thomas recorded: 'White men Lennon and Gregory fined seven shillings and six pence each camel — for cruelty. Worked camels with sore backs.'[21]

ℓℓ ℓℓ ℓℓ

As the Bradshaws came to know more about their new environment, they found their interest in the local Aboriginal people deepening. Each day it seemed a new practice or belief was revealed. On one occasion, Atlanta was asked to take some special food to Tom, a horse tailer and groom, who tended the sixty horses belonging to the telegraph station. Tom was a full-blood Arrernte and had had one front tooth knocked out, a sign that he had been initiated and circumcised. He had also been a special protege of Francis Gillen, who had photographed him and taught him some English.

Atlanta and her daughter Doris went to the camp by the riverbed and found poor Tom lying on a bed of rags in a shelter by the river, looking very ill indeed. No one had been able to diagnose Tom's illness except the medicine man, who was standing over the patient, looking pleased with himself. According to Doris, in spite of his filthy appearance the medicine man had the ponderous gravity of a Harley Street specialist. He turned to Atlanta and announced that he had succeeded in solving the problem. Tom was cured.

With a theatrical gesture, the medicine man pointed to a pile of pebbles and pieces of wood and told Atlanta he had sucked them out of different parts of Tom's anatomy, where they had been poisoning him. Tom, whom Gillen had found to be a most intelligent man, seemed equally confident that the cause of his illness had been discovered and truly grateful to the medicine man. He was convinced he was cured.

But Atlanta was still very worried. In an effort to impress her, the medicine man leaned over, sucked Tom's arm and triumphantly produced a small piece of broken glass which he held out to her. When Atlanta seemed disinclined to believe that the glass had come from inside Tom's body the medicine man looked most offended.

Tom seemed both shocked and embarrassed, and assured Atlanta he was feeling much better and would soon be able to attend to the horses again. He claimed not to have any appetite for food but promised 'Quei' he would eat later. She left the food beside him and since there was nothing more they could do, she and Doris returned to the telegraph station. They knew that the medicine man did have extraordinary powers of auto-suggestion and could effect cures. He could also 'sing' a man to death by pointing the sacred bone at him. So, Doris thought, this time faith in his 'treatment' would cure Tom.

Two days later a grieving Rungee informed Atlanta that Tom was dead. According to Aboriginal custom the name of a dead person cannot be mentioned for some time so his spirit can find rest and refrain from haunting his relatives. Rungee did not actually use Tom's name, but simply implied that he was 'dead feller'.

Francis Gillen had given the Bradshaws a copy of his and Professor Spencer's *The Native Tribes of Central Australia* when it was published, and through reading this classic book Thomas and Atlanta came to know a great deal about the Arrernte's beliefs in Dreamtime spirits and totemism. They also learned much from Hermannsburg mission leader Carl Strehlow and his wife. Like the Gillens and the Bradshaws, Strehlow did not want the Arrernte to forsake their tribal life — contrary to the philosophy of most other missionaries. Strehlow was very interested in the legends and beliefs of the Arrernte who were animists. The Rainbow Serpent and the Yeperenye (the Sacred Caterpillar), their Dreamtime spirit ancestors, inspired many fine rock carvings as well as their most sacred legends and dances. Strehlow and Thomas Bradshaw recognised the Arrernte's complex system of kinship and their feeling for their land were vital to their survival.[22]

Thomas and Atlanta became good friends with Carl and Frieda Strehlow and there was frequent transit between the mission and the telegraph station. Letters held in the Strehlow Research Centre at Alice Springs addressed to Pastor Strehlow's wife, dated between 1902 and 1906, attest to the friendship between the two outback women. Attie would write to Frieda recommending a certain type of medicine for one child's cough or an ointment for skin rash for another, and Frieda would provide support and encouragement during Atlanta's uncomfortable and difficult pregnancies.

On 29 September 1902, Thomas wrote to Pastor Strehlow thanking him for the gift of some emu eggs which Thomas wanted to send to relatives in England. In his letter he also asked Frieda to call in at their house to see Attie when she next came over for the mail. Each Christmas and New Year the families exchanged greetings and small presents.

The last letter from the Bradshaws in the Strehlow Collection is dated 26 November 1906. In it Atlanta wrote to say she had sent the Strehlows a present of some home-grown tomatoes and a basket of fruit for one of their children who was sick. The fruit had been grown and packed by the Bradshaws' Chinese gardener (a new arrival at the telegraph station). Atlanta sounded very concerned for the sick boy, expressing her hopes that he would recover soon. She signed her letter, 'Your loving friend, Attie Bradshaw'.

While the Bradshaws respected the Aborigines' beliefs and rarely sought to challenge them, one thing Atlanta did insist on was gathering the house girls together with the family for religious instruction on a Sunday morning. Attending morning service was compulsory for all telegraph employees and the Bradshaw children.

Doris recorded how her mother would use illustrated Bibles to instruct the house girls. Rungee, probably trying to please the mistress she served so faithfully, became imbued with her own special blend of Christianity and animism. Knowing she was dying after she was struck with flu during the 1919 epidemic, Rungee sent a message to Atlanta who had long since left the telegraph station, via Atlanta's brother, Ernest Allchurch. 'You tell'im Quei me go alonga Jesus,' Rungee said.[23]

ℓℓ ℓℓ ℓℓ

On 27 December 1902, after a long and difficult labour, Atlanta brought another daughter into the world. The baby, once again delivered by Annie Meyer, was called Edna. She was Atlanta's sixth child.

With six children to mother, a staff of telegraph operators, station workers and camp Aborigines to nurse and cook for, and a store and home to keep in order, Atlanta was occupied day and very often night. However, she still made time for excursions with her children.

The main amusement for the Bradshaw children in these years was riding their horses and going on picnics. Like most outback children, Doris and her siblings excelled at riding and whenever possible would ride out to picnics together on their favourite horses. Thomas rarely came on these family outings, preferring to remain in his study with his beloved books, unless he wanted to take photographs of a particular place.

The birth of Edna meant there were now six little Bradshaws, plus their governess, Atlanta and Harry Kunoth the driver to cram into the buggy on outings to local beauty spots. It was fortunate then that Frank Gillen and Baldwin Spencer had called in on their return from a long and hazardous journey in central Australia (begun in 1901), researching for a sequel to their book. For such an arduous trip they had purchased a large and exceptionally sturdy buggy, a 'Rolls-Royce' of buggies in fact. It had been specially made for the former Governor of Australia, Lord Kintore, who had driven it on a journey between Darwin and Adelaide in 1891. After using the buggy to tour the centre of Australia, taking photographs and making notes, Spencer and Gillen returned to stay with the Bradshaws and Thomas agreed to purchase the large well-sprung vehicle. The Bradshaw children and Atlanta were delighted. Now they would be able to visit gorges and waterholes even further away.

Eventually there were seven Bradshaw children at the telegraph station.

That winter the children enjoyed many excursions by horse and buggy. But try as she might, Atlanta could not disguise the fact she was in considerable discomfort following Edna's birth. In September 1904, Atlanta finally decided she wanted to see a doctor.[24] She also needed some respite from blazing heat, sandstorms, flies, hard work, responsibility for nursing the sick and isolation. And of course she longed to see old friends, her parents and family, and breathe the sea air at Glenelg.

Atlanta convinced Thomas she must go back to Adelaide to consult a gynaecologist and suggested he could take leave and join her there. He agreed and they arranged to rent a house at Glenelg so the family would have a holiday at the beach. In spite of the pain she was in, Atlanta worked for weeks at the sewing machine to make the children smart new 'city clothes' so that she and their grandparents could be proud of them.

Their journey to Oodnadatta would take an estimated twelve to eighteen days by horse and buggy. The old unsprung buckboard would take the trunks, tents, blankets and food and any excess children. There were no shops en route but it would be possible to buy freshly killed meat from cattle stations and barbecue it beside their tents. Atlanta had to plan ahead for meals for a very large party.

There were her own six hungry children; three Aboriginal grooms; a former governess; Vernon South, the young son of the new owners of the Stuart Arms hotel, who was travelling to Adelaide for medical treatment; the present governess; Harry Kunoth; and another driver.

Mrs McFeat, the former governess, was near full term of her first pregnancy. Edna was almost three by now, Stuart, known as Donnell, nearly five. The older children, Consie, Jack, Mort and Doris, were now mature enough to take care of themselves most of the time.

Harry Kunoth was a superb bushman and one afternoon when a sudden storm blew up managed to locate a pitched tent that had been left behind by some surveyors and in which they could now shelter overnight. It was a miserable camp. The water seeped into the tent and the children squealed and squabbled among themselves and complained of aches and pains until Atlanta dosed them all with camphor sprinkled on a sugar lump as a prophylactic against catching chills.

One evening the buckboard, with Doris, Mort and young Vernon South on board, had problems crossing a creekbed. The tired horses refused to move on and the driver whipped them frenziedly. In frustration he threw himself down to the ground. It was then he heard the distant rumble of floodwaters on their way down the creek. Redoubling his efforts with the horses brought more disaster. The lead horse reared up and badly tore the flesh on its rump. There was nothing to do but turn it loose. Doris, Mort and Vernon realised they had to get out quickly. They struggled to the far side of the bank. The horses suddenly became compliant and moved up also.

Atlanta, unaware of the near danger, had hurried on to prepare a worker's hut she had been invited to stay in overnight. When the others didn't arrive, she sent the Aboriginal grooms back to find them. The shaken children were relieved to meet the grooms and reach the safety of their mother in the hut.

Their next hazard was the flooded Alberga Creek. First the Aboriginal grooms found the shallowest place to cross. Once the packhorses were through, Atlanta had to cross in the buggy with most of the children and the two other women. Then came the much lower buckboard with Doris and Mort. Water surged over the back and sides of the buckboard and soaked the stores. Atlanta looked on grimly, as her two eldest children stood on the seat trying to keep dry. Two of the horses began to swim but the other two remained on their feet. Finally the buckboard was through and Atlanta heaved a sigh of relief.

The horses were by then exhausted, so fresh ones were sent out from Oodnadatta. The speed of the new horses led to the kind of accident Atlanta had always feared. Holding baby Edna on her lap she leaned forward on the high front seat of the buggy to admire the new horses, just as the iron-rimmed wheel struck a hidden rock. The buggy lurched violently. Atlanta, with Edna in her arms, was thrown headfirst out of the moving vehicle. As she fell, she threw Edna to one side to prevent her being trampled.

Harry pulled the horses to a halt and jumped down from the driver's seat. Edna was examined from top to toe but there were no signs of injury. As her sobs died away it was obvious that she had only been frightened. In fact it was Atlanta who had suffered most. Her knees and calves were badly bruised and would turn black, green and blue. But at least she had saved her baby. It took several months before the livid colour of Atlanta's bruises died away. Damage to her kneecaps would plague her for the rest of her life and make walking difficult in her old age.

Finally, after two weeks' travelling on the buggy and buckboard, they arrived at Oodnadatta. After a night's rest they boarded the old steam train to Adelaide. Stopping overnight at Hergott Springs (Marree) then Quorn, the train seemed luxurious after the bumpy buggy, particularly to the bruised and injured Atlanta. Her brood of children were fascinated with the novelty of the long, powerful train. By now they were all filthy, covered in smuts from the steam engine. As they neared Adelaide, Atlanta cleaned and brushed up the children, ready to meet their relatives.

Atlanta was overjoyed to see her parents and her sister Emily. The family spent nine months beside the ocean in a rented house at Glenelg, Thomas joining them for a holiday in January 1905. By the end of February the Bradshaw family set off for the long haul back, bringing with them a new governess.

During Thomas's absence, Atlanta's brother, Ernest Allchurch, had acted as locum to run the station affairs. Ernest had previously lived in the men's barracks but moved into a small thatched cottage in the grounds when he married Elizabeth Williams, Annie Meyer's younger sister. The marriage had taken place in the tiny church at Hermannsburg Mission, the only church at that time between Lake Eyre in southern Australia and the tropical north.

The Bradshaw children were overjoyed that Uncle Ernest Allchurch had married and set up home in the grounds of the telegraph station. For them it meant new people to talk to and another household where they were welcome. The marriage of their siblings drew Atlanta and Annie Meyer even closer.

By now Doris was old enough to sympathise with her mother, watching how hard she had to work to run the household, keep six children in clean clothes and cook meals for them all. On top of this Atlanta still tended sick Aborigines and looked after travellers — all without the benefit of running water or any of the labour-saving devices that we find indispensable today.

Although Atlanta had the assistance of her Arrernte house girls, they were sometimes more of a hindrance. Not long after Edna's birth, one particular fifteen-year-old Arrernte house girl called Katie had been foisted on Atlanta by Katie's much older husband. His eagerness to get rid of Katie should have warned Atlanta something was wrong. Later it was revealed the husband had tired of Katie's irrational behaviour and her constant, foolish giggle. The poor girl, it seemed, was retarded. Katie's husband already had another wife and family (since the Arrernte were traditionally polygamous) and he wanted nothing more to do with Katie.

Atlanta was initially wary about employing Katie, who spoke very little English. But her husband pushed her inside the house and departed. As far as he was concerned, Katie was now the Bradshaws' responsibility.

Poor Katie did not mean to but she seemed to create havoc wherever she went. One evening, not long after her arrival, the family were at dinner. Baby Edna was heard crying in the bedroom. Atlanta was busy doling out the food and asked Katie to fetch the baby. There was a long wait while the baby continued to howl. Then came the sound of bumping and thumping along the veranda and finally Katie appeared tugging a large cast-iron boiler across the floor. Boiler, it seemed, was the only English word Katie understood that began with 'b'.

The next day Katie discovered that cupboards and drawers contained interesting things. In one drawer she found a pair of scissors, something she had never seen before. Unfortunately the children showed her how to use them. The following day, while Atlanta was busy cooking, Katie tried out the scissors, cutting a ragged fringe around a good tablecloth and shortening the brand-new curtains considerably. The damage was bad enough but the worst of it was that it was impossible to obtain replacements until the next camel train arrived six months later. Not long after this incident, Katie had to leave those fascinating scissors behind and return to her husband in disgrace.

A total contrast to poor Katie was the devoted, reliable and highly efficient Rungee, who stayed with the Bradshaws for the full nine years they spent at Alice Springs. Rungee was locked into an unhappy arranged marriage with a man much older than herself, infant betrothal of girls to older men being an Aboriginal tradition. Rungee lived with her husband's family, who were very unkind to her as she was childless. She poured out her love and affection on Atlanta and treated the Bradshaw children as lovingly as though they were her own. Whenever Atlanta was feeling unwell, Rungee would put a protective arm around her and say, 'You go longa bed, Quei; me shepherd'em piccaninnies.' Doris remembered she shepherded them as gently as any loving mother or auntie.[25]

Although Rungee and Atlanta had a close, warm relationship, occasionally there were misunderstandings since their two cultures had such widely differing sensitivities regarding nudity. One night, Rungee, proud of her dancing and body-painting skills and keen to demonstrate them to her adored Quei, invited Atlanta to attend a women's corroboree. Most women's corroborees were secret affairs which men were not allowed to witness, just as the men's corroborees were taboo for women on pain of death. However this corroboree, Rungee said, was different, not secret at all, so anyone could watch.

Atlanta, who had already been invited to one corroboree where the women danced stark naked, declined. 'No, Rungee . . . That other time I go you give me big-feller shame — all those girls with nothing clothes . . .'

'You come tonight, Quei, me tell'im allabout must wear shirt,' Rungee insisted.[26]

Not wanting to hurt Rungee's feelings by refusing the invitation, Atlanta agreed.

Thomas was away dispensing justice at Barrow Creek so Atlanta invited Doris, Mabel Taylor the new governess and Leslie Spicer, a telegraph operator, to witness the spectacle which Europeans rarely saw. At the corroboree place, the four of them sat and waited for the rhythmical clicking of the oval clapping sticks to start and the women to commence chanting.

Finally the women appeared in a long line, shuffling and stamping their feet in time to the beat of the clapping sticks. Their faces were painted with mask-like designs in white, yellow and red ochre, their dark eyes gleaming against the vivid colours. But, in spite of all Rungee's promises, the women were naked. As they danced, their naked breasts bobbed and bounced about, their thighs outlined by strong designs in ochres and white pipe clay which stood out vividly against their dark skins. In a crowning irony, faithful to Rungee's promise, each lady had tied her shirt around her neck by the sleeves ensuring it covered her back.

The next day when Atlanta told Rungee that she and the new governess had been embarrassed in front of the young man, Rungee was bewildered. Had she not followed Quei's instructions? Had the women not *worn* their shirts?

❦ ❦ ❦

Women's ceremonial designs for a corroboree.

Education for their children became a problem for the Bradshaws once they were back at Alice Springs. Mabel Taylor completed a term of two years but the Bradshaws found it impossible to find a new governess in Adelaide for the kind of wages Thomas could afford to pay. So sixteen-year-old Doris, who now regarded herself as a 'young lady' and rode side-saddle, taught her younger siblings in the schoolroom, something she did not always enjoy, feeling that her girlhood years had been curtailed.

Meanwhile there seemed to be an increasing number of visitors to accommodate, and, as rushes continued on the nearby Arltunga and Winnecke gold fields, more disputes over claims for Thomas to settle. Gold fever had even infected Atlanta, who in 1902 was persuaded by a couple of speculators staying at the telegraph station to invest in a mining claim. Atlanta did so — on nothing more than their recommendation — and lost her savings. Despite having shown them hospitality, Atlanta refused to blame the men, who had presumably known their vein was small and got themselves out of the investment but had not told Atlanta, much to the disgust of the old bushmen of the area.

Late in March 1906, three exhausted government geologists, all relatively young, fit men when they set out, arrived at the telegraph station suffering severe heat exhaustion, dehydration and flesh wounds from spear injuries. They had been on a mineral survey in the Petermann Ranges and had run out of water. Although they had done nothing to upset the Luritja, they had been attacked while sleeping by men of the Luritja clan who had previously been badly treated by gold prospectors and hated all Europeans.

The leader of this small geological survey party, Frederick George, had managed to find water and care for the two wounded men, one of whom had been speared through the eye and another through his leg and chest. He had removed the spear points and nursed both men until they were well enough to travel back to the telegraph station and be placed under Atlanta's care. Frederick George himself was also ill having contracted dysentery from a well that had been polluted by a dead animal.

In spite of Atlanta's devoted care and consultations with nurses and doctors over the line, Frederick George died at the telegraph station early on the morning of 4 April, aged only thirty-two. He was buried in the small cemetery beside Thomas's brother Ernest. Atlanta nursed the two other wounded geologists until they were well enough to undertake the gruelling journey back to Adelaide.

She also nursed gold miners during a typhoid outbreak at Arltunga gold fields.

In November 1907 Atlanta's seventh child was born. He was named Alan Todd Bradshaw after Charles Todd, Thomas's director of the Post and Telegraph Office. The stream of visitors continued. Only a month after Alan's birth Atlanta had to play hostess again. On a hot day in December 1907 the Bradshaw children and members of the Arrernte crowded around when the grazier Harry Dutton of Anlaby and his friend Murray Aunger

Doris Bradshaw (Blackwell) as a young woman.

arrived at the telegraph station. They turned up in a heavy open touring car, a 24-horsepower Talbot specially built and modified in England for desert conditions. The children had already seen cars before in Adelaide but for the Arrernte people and some of the telegraph operators it was as though two spacemen had arrived in a spacecraft from Mars.

The Talbot, which Dutton and Aunger had christened Angelina, had a canvas hood for protection and its heavy body was festooned with spare tyres, jerry cans, shovels, axes, rifles and water bags to undertake the journey. Dutton and Aunger's aim was to show that their motor car could penetrate places previously thought impossible for that type of vehicle. They intended to drive as far as Darwin to prove that the car could traverse vast distances of land without roads and even ford creeks — quite a journey. Young Ernest Allchurch was fascinated and hung over the engine for hours.

Dutton and Aunger were honoured guests at the telegraph station for a few days before setting off on a journey that would daunt most motorists in cars of today. Unfortunately, the weather was against them. Rain arrived early that year and they were held up at Barrow Creek Telegraph Station for four days. They set off again but before they had gone far bogged down, as the red soil turned to sticky mud and swamps. Angelina's transmission felt the strain and eventually the universal joint cracked. By now the Big Wet was upon them, which meant the end of their epic journey for that year.

Dutton and Aunger managed to obtain help through the telegraph line and a rescue party arrived, but the two men had to abandon Angelina. However, they made plans to return the following year and promised Atlanta's brother that he could make the trip with them.

Once the excitement of seeing a motor car died down, life went on with lots of riding for the children and picnics with their friends the Meyers. However, as Mortimer and Jack grew bigger and more boisterous it became harder for Doris to discipline them in the schoolroom and Atlanta became concerned.

It had also become apparent that the children needed a proper teacher who had a deeper knowledge of mathematics and science than Doris. Thomas decided they must leave the outback and return to Adelaide. Atlanta was overjoyed at the thought of seeing her parents again but sad to leave her friends the Strehlows and the Meyers, and dear old Rungee and Amelia.

A month before the Bradshaws were due to depart, the intrepid Dutton and Aunger returned in a second Talbot car with enough spare parts to rescue Angelina. They kept their promise and took young Ernest Allchurch north with them, his skills as a telegraph operator being regarded as useful on a dangerous trip of this nature. They managed to fix Angelina and restart her engine, and both Talbot cars succeeded in reaching Port Darwin after a dangerous 3200-kilometre journey lasting forty-two days. Dutton and Aunger made history as the first team of motorists to cross Australia.

Having joined the two adventurers on their trip, Ernest also attained his moment of glory. When the trip was over he went to work at the telegraph office at Hergott Springs (Marree) for a few years. Many years later he was promoted to superintendent of Alice Springs, working from 1924 to 1932.

As the Bradshaws prepared to leave Alice for good, Atlanta knew there were things she would miss. She loved the wonderful sense of space, the beauty of massed wild flowers after winter rains — the yellow *Senecio* daisies, the mauve sprays of desert myrtle and the clumps of *ptilotus*, their vivid white contrasting with the deep red soil. The great white ghost gums around the telegraph station, the dark green cycads, relics of a prehistoric age, the old house where they had been so happy and their picnics to Standley Chasm and the Wigley Waterhole had become part of her life.

The Bradshaw children were unhappy to be leaving the freedom they had enjoyed in the outback and abandoning their beloved horses to live in Adelaide. 'We've been there once; we don't want to go again; we want to stay here,' were Doris's sentiments.[27]

Amelia and Rungee, as well as the other station Aborigines, were disturbed that the Bradshaws were leaving, particularly the three children who had been born there. They were leaving their country — 'Him bin grow'up longa this place,' they pleaded.[28] Rungee could not leave since her responsibilities lay with her husband and her people but Amelia burst into tears and begged Atlanta to take her with them to Adelaide. Atlanta considered this but decided it would be foolish and risky to take Amelia to the unknown, so far away from her people and her culture.

On the day of the Bradshaws' departure there were many last-minute farewells to make. The children waved a sad goodbye to the Aborigines, to their beloved horses, and to the townsfolk at Stuart, knowing that the last link with Alice would disappear the moment they crossed the plain.

The first day they did not get very far before making camp, and this was just as well. No sooner were the tents erected when one of the Aboriginal grooms arrived on horseback bearing a message that had come in over the wire. He gave it to Thomas to read. Thomas's face changed. Without saying a word to the children, he beckoned to Atlanta and took her aside. The children heard their father talking and their mother give a long despairing wail then burst into sobs while Thomas tried to comfort her. Their father came back and told the waiting children, 'Your grandmother died yesterday, just as we left.'[29]

All her pregnancies and deliveries without the help of a doctor or midwife had seriously affected Atlanta's health. Her complexion had been coarsened by the sun and her knee joints badly damaged when she and baby Edna were thrown from the buggy. The journey to Adelaide and the shock of her mother's sudden death now took a further toll on her.

Once back in Adelaide, where Thomas returned to his old job at the telegraph office, he and Atlanta settled down in a house they bought at Glenelg. At long last Atlanta was back near the sea.

Atlanta had one more child, Sheila Pont Bradshaw, born 10 August 1909, shortly after their return to Adelaide. Her damaged knees continued to give her a great deal of pain, and no doctor seemed able to come up with a cure.

Thomas and Atlanta Bradshaw.

Once Atlanta and her children had left the Northern Territory of South Australia (as it was then known), Annie Meyer found she could not stand the loneliness. The fact her husband, Charlie, was drinking heavily did not help matters. So Annie and her children left Alice Springs as well. They were driven in a buggy to Oodnadatta and caught the Ghan to Adelaide. Eventually, Annie returned to Alice Springs and opened a boarding house, where the famous anthropologist Olive Pink would stay before moving into a converted army hut.

Both Thomas and Atlanta were shocked when they heard from Frieda Strehlow in the early days of World War I that the Strehlows, being of German origin, might be removed from the mission into which they had poured so much time and money. Most of that money had been donated by Augustine, Frieda's wealthy aunt who lived in Germany. The Bradshaws and the other inhabitants of the area wrote to the Australian Government saying that removing them was ridiculous. They described Frieda and Carl Strehlow as patriotic Australians who had done nothing wrong and should not be imprisoned. Fortunately some notice was taken at high level of Thomas Bradshaw's letter and, as a result, the Strehlows, who had done so much for the Arrernte people and for the community in general, were left in peace for the rest of the war, although many other people of German origin were interned.[30]

Atlanta Bradshaw died in Adelaide on 12 August 1929 aged sixty-three, her life shortened by her time in the outback; Thomas Bradshaw survived her by five years and died on 28 August 1934.

In Atlanta's obituary the Adelaide *Advertiser* praised the contribution she had made to life in outback Australia.

The old telegraph station, surrounded by magnificent ghost gums, operated until 1932 when, in a dark period in its history, it became a home for part-Aboriginal children who had been removed from their mothers. This period is described in a book by one of these children, *Alec, A Living History of the Alice Springs Telegraph Station*.[31] By that time the actual telegraph station and post office had been moved to the old township of Stuart. (The road north, the Stuart Highway, still commemorates the name of explorer John McDouall Stuart.)

During World War II, the telegraph station was occupied by the Australian Army. In 1963 the Arrernte were moved from the old telegraph station to Amoonguna Settlement, south-east of Alice Springs, and the area was gazetted as the Alice Springs Telegraph National Park.

Today the station master's house, the men's barracks and the old telegraph office comprise a unique museum set up just as it was during the Bradshaws' period of residence. The battery room has the instruments on the table arranged as they would have been when an operator was on duty. The interior of the station master's house, with its thick stone walls, is decorated with furniture of the period and one can imagine Atlanta, Rungee and the younger children working and playing in the house.

Although the Bradshaws took their own furniture back with them to Adelaide, Doris Bradshaw (Blackwell) would later return to the telegraph station and explain exactly how it was furnished during her childhood so the correct period furniture could be purchased. Today's visitors can see the primitive kitchen where Atlanta cooked meals for her large family. A fascinating display of Thomas Bradshaw's photographs of life at the telegraph station at the start of the twentieth century, some of which are illustrated here, recreates the scene.

The picturesque setting of the telegraph station remains as it was when the Bradshaws lived there, shaded by those gigantic white ghost gums and the lilac and purple hills of the MacDonnell ranges on the skyline. This is one of the views that the famous Arrernte artist, Albert Namatjira, who grew up at the neighbouring Hermannsburg Mission, would immortalise in his watercolours.

Clearly the contributions of Overland Telegraph Station managers and their wives who had the commitment to providing medicine and nursing to the people around them has been underestimated in the story of Australia's outback pioneers. Atlanta Bradshaw and wives like her played an important and largely unsung role in the taming and development of that beautiful and fascinating area — the red centre of Australia.

CHAPTER 4

Jeannie Gunn, OBE
1870 – 1961

THE STORY BEHIND *WE OF THE NEVER-NEVER*

Early in 1902, when Australians were anticipating the coronation of King Edward VII, Jeannie Gunn, daughter of Melbourne journalist Thomas Taylor and granddaughter of a Baptist minister, arrived as a new bride in the Northern Territory of South Australia.

There were few European women in the Territory at that time. It was seen as a wild and lawless place, scarcely suitable for a station manager to take his wife. An undeclared 'war' was being waged by some pastoral companies and graziers against Aborigines who speared their cattle. For their part, Aborigines were dismayed to lose their traditional waterholes and see their supplies of game diminishing, and considered cattle to be a communal resource. When punished by Europeans on raids, the Willeroo, Mangarrayi and Yangman of inland areas retaliated by spearing stockmen and teamsters and leaving them to die or breaking their backs by throwing rocks down on them from high cliffs.

This was a frontier war with battles just as fierce as between the wagoners and native Americans (Red Indian tribes) along the Oregon Trail. Aeneas Gunn, Jeannie's husband, had gained first-hand experience of the violence of the frontier when he joined his cousins Joseph and Frederick Bradshaw in setting up the Marigui cattle run in the Kimberleys in the 1890s, and later what was known as Bradshaw's Run, south-west of Darwin. While at Marigui Station, both Joseph Bradshaw and Aeneas were injured by spears tipped with shards of glass during an attack on the isolated homestead.[1]

Aeneas had caught malaria while at the Prince Regent River, which forced him south to recuperate in Melbourne. There he took a two-year contract as acting resident librarian at Prahran Library, re-cataloguing its collection, a job he had just completed when he first met Jeannie Taylor.

Jeannie had typical Scottish colouring, pale skin that freckled in the sun, clear brown eyes, a firm chin and a mass of reddish-gold hair, usually worn in a knot on top of her head. She was petite (only 157 centimetres tall), and an excellent story teller with a sense of humour and an ability to laugh at herself.

Aeneas and Jeannie met by chance when Jeannie was going to a concert in a buggy with a woman friend who was driving a pair of frisky horses. As her friend reined them in outside the concert hall, Jeannie tried to climb down over the wheel, intending to hold the horses' heads and steady them so her friend could dismount, but she was hampered by her long skirts. Without warning, one of the horses shied, throwing Jeannie off the wheel rim and straight into the arms of Aeneas, who had gallantly hurried forward to hold the horses' heads.

From the moment they were thrown together by circumstance, Aeneas was fascinated by Jeannie's effervescent personality, her sense of humour and by the contrast between her small frame and strong spirit. After the concert, he obtained permission to visit her at her Melbourne home.

At the Taylors' comfortable house, Aeneas met Jeannie's journalist father. The Gunns, like Jeannie's family, were fiercely proud of their Scottish Presbyterian heritage. Aeneas, who also contributed articles to local newspapers, must have impressed the Taylors. With her father's approval, Aeneas started taking Jeannie out. Theirs was a whirlwind romance, and they married at the Scots Presbyterian Church on 31 December 1901.

Jeannie had grown up in the Melbourne suburb of Hawthorn. One of five children, she was used to the give and take of family life.

Aeneas Gunn on his wedding day.

She and her sister Carrie had run a small private school from the family home which they called 'Rolyat' (Taylor spelt backwards). Their English-born mother, Anna Lush, had also been a teacher and had taught her four daughters from home, providing them with an excellent education and encouraging Jeannie and Carrie to become teachers. Jeannie had gone on to study at the University of Melbourne.[2]

Having resisted the idea of marriage for years, Jeannie was now determined to follow her charismatic husband to the tropical north, then untamed and dangerous.

Elsey Station, where the Gunns were heading, was more than 100 kilometres south of Katherine and was one of the Northern Territory's largest cattle stations, covering a million and a quarter acres (500,000 hectares) of desert and scrub. It held 40,000 cattle, Arab horses and a large number of brumbies. It was the third-oldest station in the Territory, having been established in 1880 by Abraham Wallace, who drove 2728 head of cattle out to Elsey Creek, a tributary of the Roper River. Wallace had built a thatched timber house for the manager, and other outbuildings and storage sheds, before he sold the lease to J.W. Osmand and J.A. Panton.[3]

In 1902, following the death of Osmand, Elsey Station was up for sale and a consortium, which included Aeneas's brother Bob Gunn and Bob's business partner, a Dr Bennett, was raising money to buy it. The consortium planned to give Aeneas, who lacked capital, a share if he acted as manager.

Aeneas was not planning a long-term future in the outback. He was aiming to work hard and live cheaply at Elsey Station for a few years, to increase stock numbers, sell off the brumbies to the Indian Army and then, he hoped, the syndicate would sell the lease at auction profitably. With the proceeds of his share, Aeneas planned to take Jeannie, who had never been overseas, to Europe for a few years before returning to live in Melbourne.[4]

The outback country of the north, or the Never-Never, had a fearsome reputation. Friends and relatives warned Jeannie that she would be isolated and lonely. Nevertheless, they assumed that she would live in a handsome stone or brick mansion similar to those on pastoral stations in the western districts of Victoria. They did not realise that things were very different in the Northern Territory, where cyclones frequently destroyed the timber and tin buildings. They gave Jeannie highly unsuitable wedding presents, like fine china tea services, lace antimacassars and exquisitely embroidered hand towels, which Jeannie packed to take with her on their two-week steamer voyage from Port Melbourne to Port Darwin.

Doubtless married women friends also took her aside and warned her that she would have problems if she fell pregnant — the nearest doctor would be over 400 kilometres away. But Jeannie shrugged off their grim warnings. Among the Taylor clan, Jeannie's strong will and steely determination were legendary.

Aeneas Gunn must have had some qualms about taking his bride to the Elsey, especially as Mary Jane Bradshaw, wife of his cousin Joseph Bradshaw, had stayed a mere three months at the remote

Jeannie Gunn's home in Hawthorn, a leafy Melbourne suburb.

Kimberleys cattle station Marigui, and had endured the heat as well as attacks by Aborigines on the homestead. When she found a poisonous snake coiled around the legs of the piano organ, even courageous Mary Jane gave up and returned to Melbourne by ship.[5]

The newlyweds sailed north aboard the Eastern and Asiatic lines mail steamer *Guthrie*. The route hugged the coast of eastern and northern Australia. The couple took a short holiday in Port Darwin, then a very primitive settlement surrounding a magnificent harbour.

Concerned that Jeannie would be lonely, Aeneas had advertised for a maid or paid companion to accompany Jeannie to the Elsey. No matter how high the wages he offered, not one European woman applied for the post. Darwin people knew that several station homesteads had been attacked by Aborigines.[6]

The woman who kept the hotel in which the Gunns stayed knew the outback well. She warned Jeannie that she would be lucky to reach the Elsey Station alive, as the Wet was coming on; indeed heavy rains had already started. The hotel owner invited Jeannie to stay with her until the homestead on the Elsey had been restored. Jeannie politely declined the offer. It seemed everyone but the Gunns knew the homestead had been damaged in a cyclone — a fact the executors of the Osmand estate had failed to tell Aeneas. He only received the news when a telegram arrived in Darwin from stockman Jock McLennan, who was acting as temporary manager at the Elsey.

The telegram sent by Jock — or Mac, the Sanguine Scot, as Jeannie called him in *We of the Never-Never* — was one of many the Gunns received from him advising Jeannie not to come and giving a variety of lame excuses. While both of the Gunns were prepared for the danger and isolation of the outback, Jeannie, in particular, had not been prepared for the hostility of the stockmen towards her.

The station hands did not want Jeannie at the Elsey, fearing that if the boss brought his wife there she might make them dress for dinner and stop them cursing and swearing. She might also object to the custom of station hands temporarily taking a 'station gin'. 'Black velvet' was seen as one of the perks of the life of a single man in the outback.[7]

The Never-Never was a rough, tough, male-dominated place. Those who lived there cursed the Big Wet and the clouds of red dust that replaced it. What they loved was the sense of endless space in the outback, the beauty of its lily-fringed ponds, its thermal pools and swimming holes. Most men who worked on cattle stations in the Never-Never were bachelors or escaping from failed marriages; they had their own values of mateship and codes of behaviour.

In the restrictive post-Victorian era when Jeannie Gunn went to the outback, wives were still regarded as chattels of their husbands, and lacked access to bank accounts or loans. A white woman living in the outback was considered very daring indeed. Jeannie was already considered 'modern' for her times, an 'advanced' woman who had gone to university and had run her own school. (This may explain why Jeannie married at thirty, relatively late for a time when most women were married by twenty-one.) Jeannie must only have confirmed the impression of the 'modern' woman when, in anticipation of the tough travelling conditions ahead, she shortened her skirts. Instead of being an inch from the floor as was customary at that time, her skirts now offered a tantalising glimpse of ankle (trousers being considered quite improper for a woman).

Aboard the goods train they took from Port Darwin to Pine Creek, Jeannie told her husband she could live *anywhere* as long as she was with him. She *would* make friends with those hostile Elsey stockmen and get them to accept her.

The train zigzagged through forests and open plains, stopping frequently for the driver to chase kangaroos off the line, boil a billy for a cup of tea or greet a group of Aborigines and offer them hunks of watermelon. Eventually they arrived at Pine Creek, where they made their way to the hotel. As they waited for their tea in the saloon, where ladies were allowed to sit, an angry Scottish voice was heard through the partition that separated the saloon from the public bar, which was exclusively male. The voice proclaimed to all and sundry that the outback was not a fit place for a woman.

'The telegraphing bush-whacker', Jeannie said. 'Watch me defy him!'[8]

She slid down from her seat, put her small feet firmly on the floor and marched into the next room where she confronted a brawny Scotsman. Gingerly, she held out a firm hand towards the angry man.

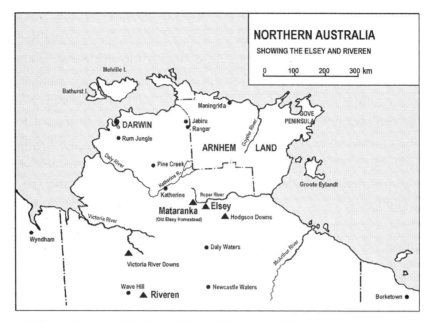

'How do you do?' she said, smiling up at him.

Mac's jaw dropped. So this petite woman was the dreaded ripsnorter! 'Quite well, thank you,' he responded, embarrassed that she had overheard him, and soon all three of them were grinning and talking away.

They had a job sorting out the luggage and picking what should be loaded onto packhorses and what had to be left behind until a team of bullock wagons could make the long journey out to the Elsey after the Wet. Jeannie said she could manage very well with just one bag of clothes for the trip, but became alarmed when Mac told her *everything* she needed had to fit in her swag. The rest could be loaded aboard the wagons when they made their annual trip bringing food and other supplies.

Jeannie could scarcely believe her ears. Wagons only went to the Never-Never *once a year*? The rest of her clothes and her household goods would only arrive at Elsey homestead in *five months time*! She stared in dismay at the one small bag she was allowed to take with her and at the pile of dresses, books and wedding gifts she was sure she could not possibly do without.

Mac said briskly, 'You'll have to cull your herd a bit, that's all.'

There was no room for books or needlework, or the pile of linen sheets, pillow cases, towels, cushion covers, lace doilies and antimacassars given by kind friends convinced that as the wife of a station owner–manager Jeannie would live in style.

'You won't need those anyway,' said Mac brutally, pointing at her pillow cases, 'for there's no pillows.' It seemed Jeannie might be condemned to use a folded jacket for a pillow, like the stockmen. 'A couple of changes of everything is stacks. There's heaps of soap and water at the station, and things dry before you can waltz around twice.'

Still anxious to please, Jeannie agreed to leave most of her clothes behind but did not realise that a couple of high-necked blouses, a cotton dress or two and a change of skirts would not be sufficient for five months' constant wash and wear. In the end, the pillow cases did go with her. By this time Mac was starting to feel sorry for Jeannie and assured her that 'all hands could be put on to pluck birds' for feather pillows as the Elsey was stiff with birds!

After a day of rain, the morning of their departure dawned bright and clear. The Elsey party decided to make a dash for the Fergusson River before the rains returned and made it impossible to reach the Elsey. Jeannie was riding side-saddle, wearing a long, cumbersome riding habit with divided skirts. The travelling was slow. In that wild country and with the Big Wet already started, they were lucky that the Cullen River, which could have been a roaring torrent, was only a stream and they forded it with ease. When they reached the Fergusson River, it was up to the top of its banks.

Mac suggested that if one of them swam a horse through the flood, the Missus could hang on to its tail. Unsurprisingly, it did not go down well with Jeannie. 'Anything but that!' she pleaded.[9]

Mac pointed to a thick wire rope stretched across the river from bank to bank. What about the flying fox? They sent mailbags and valuables on it when the river was in flood; why not send the Missus?

Jeannie felt sick at the thought of crossing swirling water holding onto a thin wire. But this was a test. She must not fail or the men would despise her. She nodded and managed a wan smile.

The crossing was put off until the morning and they made camp for the night, sleeping under nets, as the mosquitoes and sandflies were a torment. The next morning the Fergusson River was still rising.

'We'll have to bustle up and get across or the water'll be over the wire, and then we'll be done for,' Mac said.

Jeannie hurried, but getting across the river took a long time. It was an hour before Jackeroo, the part-Aboriginal stockman, managed to persuade Roper, the quietest and most reliable horse, to allow himself to be half dragged, half pushed through the flooding stream. With a good deal of urging, the rest of the horses also crossed. Then the hobbles were sent across on a pulley attached to the wire. The ever-smiling Jackeroo hobbled the horses again on the far side where he waited to take the swags and saddle bags sent over to him by Mac and Aeneas.

By the time they were across the river, it was after midday. Jeannie was still waiting, inwardly trembling but smiling so the men would not guess how scared she was. A surcingle, a long thick strap that keeps saddle bags in place on a packhorse, was buckled through the pulley. Aeneas crossed first, to test it. He was dragged through the water most of the way but called out to Jeannie that he was fine.

The surcingle came back across and Mac shortened the leather strap and reassured her, 'It's only a matter of holding on and keeping cool.' Jeannie stepped onto the strap and kept her eyes on her husband who was stationed on the other side hauling on the wire. 'Hang on like grim death,' he called out to her.

When Jeannie was halfway across, the wire began to sag and her long skirts trailed in the water, pulling her down. She feared she might be dragged under. Back on the bank Mac flung his weight on the wire making Jeannie shoot up in the air, a terrifying experience, but she was determined the men would not see her scared.

And suddenly she was on the other side in her husband's arms, relieved it was over. Jeannie looked back to the other bank, amused that Mac refused to trust the wire. He swam through the strong current.

They still had to cross the Edith River, twenty kilometres farther on. The weather had become swelteringly hot, the flies were maddening and travel was slow. By sundown they found themselves looking down at the flooded Katherine River. They had travelled a mere 100 kilometres in three days. From the far side of the deep red rocks that surrounded the area a voice hailed them. Tom Pearce (*We of the Never-Never*'s Mine Host), owner of Katherine's only hostelry, the Sportsman's Hotel, was assuring Jeannie he'd row them across in no time.

Katherine turned out to be a tiny outback settlement 'on the telegraph line' like Alice Springs. All around it, and stretching away on every side, were hundreds of thousands of hectares of what Jeannie's husband called the Never-Never, 'because in it you can Never-Never find a bally thing you want,' he said. Jeannie had her own interpretation of the term, saying that it was so named because those who go there never-never voluntarily leave it.[10]

Beside the rickety pub was Tom Pearce's house with wide verandas screened by scarlet poinciana trees. Here the Gunns would stay while the stockmen camped out in the bush. Some of Katherine's residents gave her things she would not find at the Elsey. Fresh tomatoes and a cucumber from Constable Kingston (the Wag); some eggs from Mr Little, superintendent of the telegraph line; a freshly baked cake from the policeman's wife. When Tom Pearce and his wife gave Jeannie a pile of potatoes and a flat iron she thanked them politely but was puzzled. She was too new to the outback to realise how precious potatoes were and thought taking a flat iron on such a short journey seemed odd.

'What's it for?' she asked.[11]

'To iron duds [trousers] with, of course,' replied the Wag. In Katherine its value lay in keeping the pub door open.

'But I won't *need* to iron any duds until we reach the homestead!'

'It's *for* the homestead. There will be nothing like that there,' her husband informed her.

Jeannie smiled a little uncertainly. Then Tom Pearce brought out a couple of china cups and put them with the baggage. Jeannie was delighted. She didn't know it then but the flat iron would become one of her most cherished possessions.

Jeannie was beginning to change her ideas about the kind of mansion she would be living in at Elsey. Mac decided to set her straight. The homestead on the Elsey is 'mostly verandahs and promises', he said, 'but one room is finished. *We* call it The House, but you'll probably call it a Hut, even though it has got doors and calico windows framed and on hinges.' But on the bright side, 'there's a looking-glass — goodness knows how it got there! You ought to be thankful for that and the wire mattress. You won't find many of them out bush.'

☙ ☙ ☙

With more rain expected and the flooded King River still to cross, the party was anxious to move on. When they had arrived at Katherine the Katherine River had been too swollen to take the horses across. After four days it had subsided enough for the difficult crossing to begin. Ten horses had to be dragged over the river behind a flat boat, the halter of each horse held by a man in the stern. It took a day to complete the task, but at sundown Mac nevertheless set out with the pack teams and horses. The next morning Jeannie and Aeneas climbed up onto a buckboard provided by Tom Pearce to begin the next leg.

They caught up to Mac and after a day's jolting over creek beds, successfully fording the roaring King River, and bouncing through forested country and long grass, at sundown they stopped. Aeneas and Mac bowed to Jeannie and said, 'Welcome Home!' They were at the Elsey 'front gate'. Another seventy kilometres and they would be at the front door of the homestead.

They camped the night by a wide sheet of water, Easter's Billabong. At supper, amazed to hear that Jeannie had never tasted Johnny cakes, Mac promised her some for breakfast. Producing flour, cream of tartar, soda and a mixing dish from his saddle bag, he set to work. Cutting off chunks of dough, he buried them in the ashes of the fire, cooking them until they were brown and crisp.

Rain was on the way and the mosquitoes were a torment for Jeannie's pale skin but she did not complain. They rigged their tents and Mac carried the Johnny cakes into his tent for safety, although he did not really expect the billabong to flood in the night. However, it did flood and he spent the night perched on a pyramid of pack-bags and saddles, the crisp Johnny cakes at the bottom of the pile. By breakfast time they had turned to wet, stodgy slabs, but there was no other kind of bread so they ate the crispest, crustiest bits and Jeannie fibbed that they were delicious.

That last full day, traversing the black soil flats, was the worst for Jeannie. The driving rain had turned the ground into slush. The springless buckboard bounced about like a rubber ball, Jeannie with it, as they skimmed between trees, swung through scrub, at one point avoiding a fallen tree and missing a boulder by inches. Mac pulled the buckboard up, at the right time, in exactly the right place, for their overnight camp at Bitter Springs, where Dan (Dave Suttee — the Head Stockman) and his faithful dog waited to greet them. Dan soon had a fire blazing and a billy boiling. To Jeannie's delight he also produced from a tea towel a crisp, freshly baked damper.

Dan was a shy, quiet old man, wary of women. He watched Jeannie closely as he asked her questions about the road and their journey. Jeannie knew that his shrewd hazel eyes were judging her. She wanted this kind old bushman to like her.

By the time supper was over, Dan had risked a mild joke or two and laughed loudly at the answers she gave to his questions on bushcraft. What they must do, Dan said, was to teach her some of the signs of water at hand, right off, 'in case she does get lost any time'.[12]

She was as determined as ever to win these men over. Used to finding her way about a city and sure she would soon get the hang of things in the bush, Jeannie replied confidently, 'You needn't bother about me. If I ever do get lost, I'll just catch a cow and milk it!'

This brought a roar of delight from all three men who knew how fierce the cattle could be. 'Missus! Missus! You'll need a deal of educating!' Aeneas said.

Over breakfast the next day Dan made the first joke. He was surprised, he said, really surprised, that Jeannie — the Missus — hadn't been out already to catch herself a milking cow. He had been looking forward to fresh milk for breakfast. Jeannie laughed at him, and at herself.

'She'll do for this place!' Dan declared. With all the experience of knowing eight or ten women in his forty years in the bush, he could pronounce that 'the one that could see jokes suited best'. Jeannie soon spoiled her previous good impression, however. Finding flies drowning in her mug of tea, she poured the liquid onto the ground. The waste of good tea upset Dan.

Aeneas quickly spoke up for his wife. 'She'll be fishing the flies out with the indifference of a Stoic in a week or two.'

As the jolting buckboard had no canopy, Jeannie was soon covered in a layer of reddish-brown dust. They had almost reached the Elsey when around a bend they came upon Jack McLeod (the Quiet Stockman of *We of the Never-Never*), a strong young man, who was herding out a mob of horses.

'Hallo there,' Mac shouted. 'This is the Missus, Jack!'

Another man shy of women, Jack moved uneasily in his saddle, not daring to look Jeannie in the face. Only that morning he had decided that he would not stay to meet that terrible ogre the Boss's wife. He would be gone before they arrived. Now he was embarrassed at seeing her. He couldn't stand women, always nattering about something or other and stopping a bloke doing what he wanted to.

Jeannie looked after his retreating figure, realising this man wanted to avoid her at *all* costs.

They continued their journey until Mac shouted, 'Eyes front!' and Jeannie craned her head to catch a glimpse of her new home. Mac was smiling as they bumped over the rough dirt track. He whipped up the horses and urged them through the slip-rails, past the stockyards, over the grassy homestead paddock, and they halted in front of a few down-at-heel wooden buildings.

Here at last, Jeannie thought. Descending the step, she found herself standing in the shadow of an unfinished timber building, surrounded by a mob of barking dogs. Was it a house or a hut, Mac was keen to know. 'A Betwixt and Between,' was Jeannie's opinion.

While station hands took charge of the buckboard and horses, Aeneas and Mac were greeted by Herb Bryant, the station bookkeeper-cum-drover, an educated and neatly attired man (known as The Dandy in *We of the Never-Never*). He was introduced to Jeannie and looked at her approvingly. 'I'm sure we're all real glad to see *you,*' he said.

One small victory, thought Jeannie.

Elsey Station turned out to be a group of ramshackle timber huts with dirt floors, some with thatched roofs, others with tin roofs. Jeannie was shown the cook's quarters, the kitchen, the men's quarters, a store where dry goods were kept, a meat house, a blacksmith's shop and a buggy or cart shed. In the centre was an immense wood pile. There was also a blacksmith's forge and a 'humpy' where some of the Yangman and Mangarrayi station hands lived. They were 160 kilometres from Katherine. One neighbour was 140 kilometres east, another 170 kilometres to the south and more neighbours were about 320 kilometres to the west.

Jeannie examined the manager's house and decided that Mac had been right. It *was* mostly verandas and promises. Back in 1897 a cyclone had wrecked the house. A travelling Chinese carpenter with grand ideas had arrived and started to rebuild but only one room had been completed; the second room was nothing but uprights and cross beams. The Chinese carpenter complained he had run out of wood, asked for his cheque and vanished, never to return. They would have to live in the undamaged room until the rest could be restored.

The Elsey in 1902. From left to right are the harness room, the meat house, the blacksmith's shop, the men's quarters with stockmen outside, and the Gunns' renovated homestead.

COURTESY JENNIE BLUNDELL.

The huge termite mounds of the Northern Territory impressed Jeannie Gunn as she rode among them.

The furniture in the livable room consisted of four chairs, a large dining table with one leg shorter than the others, a four-poster bed with a rusty wire mattress and a looking-glass spotted with damp. Jeannie tested a small side table made from an old packing case, the legs of which seemed solid enough, a washstand, which lacked a jug or washbasin, and an ancient, wobbly chest of drawers.

The walls were decorated with muddy footprints, as though the station dogs had pitter-pattered all over the timber as it lay in the yard.

But as she looked at her home and its furniture Jeannie tried to appear cheerful. She was glad none of her old friends who had given her all those expensive presents were here. All around the house were hillocky tussocks of coarse grass, beaten down by dogs, goats and fowls. Along the banks of the stream or billabong was a scruffy vegetable garden. Beyond it were stockyards and the house paddock and on the surrounding plains Jeannie saw reddish-brown towers of dried earth which her husband told her had been built by ants.

The primitive sanitary arrangements were one reason for men not wanting women in the bush, and consisted of a deep pit often called the 'long drop', on which the lid of an empty 44-gallon petrol drum with a hole cut in it served as a seat.

In her autobiography, *Nothing Prepared Me*, describing the Kimberleys in the 1950s, Edna Quilty is more outspoken than most about problems faced by women pioneers, one of them being the communal latrine pit shared by stockmen and boss's wife — horrific by today's standards. She describes a huge pit some distance from her main homestead, three sides of which were screened by hessian flaps, with an open doorway, no lock and hence no privacy from stockmen for the boss's wife.

Quilty, brave in other respects, was terrified of falling into the pit until finally her husband took pity on her and had a smaller latrine pit dug for her use.

Jeannie had to contend with much the same toileting arrangement, but fifty years earlier could not write about such unladylike things, so there are no mentions of such topics in *We of the Never-Never*.

After the men had shown her around Mac said, 'Well! I said it wasn't a fit place for a woman, didn't I?'[13]

Dan argued with him, 'Any place is a fit place for a woman, provided the woman is fitted for the place.'

Jeannie fully intended to fit into the place as neatly as anyone else. But some changes were needed. 'A few able-bodied men could finish the dining room in a couple of days, and make a mansion of the rest of the building in a week or so,' she said.

'Steady! Go slow, Missus!' they protested.

'We begin at the very beginning of things in the Never-Never,' said her husband. 'Timber grows in trees in these parts and has to be coaxed out with a saw.'

Jeannie looked in dismay at the distant trees against the skyline but was reassured to hear there was a carpenter 'inside' (the continent's interior) they could call on. And remember, said Mac, that they were now in the 'Land of Plenty of Time!' And so it was. 'Little Johnny', the jobbing carpenter, kept disappearing off to the pub in Katherine so progress on the new dining room was slow.

As she settled in, Jeannie began taking notes and planning a book about her experiences. But she was not the only writer in the Gunn family. Her husband was also making notes (which would later be destroyed) and writing humorous letters to the *Northern Territory Times* about life at the Elsey.[14]

He was also writing letters home in which he told of his admiration for the way Jeannie had borne the journey. In a letter to his brother, Bob, Aeneas wrote proudly of how his wife had coped with 'a roaring torrent to cross, mosquitoes and sand flies, snakes, the noxious smelling stink bugs . . . she won everyone's admiration . . . 150 miles in five days in a buckboard is a satisfactory performance for any woman'.[15]

Jeannie admired her husband, too, and soon discovered he had a talent for settling disputes harmoniously. When Jack, the Quiet Stockman, returned with some stock and told the men he was quitting, Aeneas quietly spoke to him. Whatever he said was enough to make Jack change his mind about leaving. That night at dinner the normally taciturn Jack announced, 'I'm staying on,' but gave no reasons for his change of plan.[16]

'Going to give her a chance?' Dan asked with a grin.

There were so many new things to be learned. Jeannie thought Sam, the Chinese cook, seemed cheerful but she could never tell what was going on behind his exterior. The meals he produced were often nothing like those she had asked for and could be most unusual. One breakfast consisted of pumpkin pie with raisins and mince! She didn't know how to deal with him. Nor did she know how to handle the Aboriginal women, who always said 'Yes, Missus' and 'I do it, Missus', then rarely did as she asked. Jeannie complained that she would ask the women to scrub the kitchen floor, leave them at it and then they would go walkabout in the bush, complaining the work was too tiring. Her husband suggested she should make her orders clearer. She tried hard to do so and gentle Old Nellie, one of the Aboriginal women, helped round up the girls when they showed signs of slacking off or 'knocking up', as they called it in the outback.

Mac also offered to tackle the women. In half an hour the kitchen was clean and shining and Mac was pleased with himself. 'You'll need to rule them with a rod of iron,' he told Jeannie authoritatively, but the next morning only Old Nellie appeared. Apparently the other Aboriginal women had gone for an outing to the Warloch Ponds with friends, claiming they needed a day's rest after so much hard work!

A few days later Jeannie went to their camp to see if they would give her a language lesson. The visit was reckoned a great success, with Jeannie setting off gales of laughter when she tried to say a few words in their language. The next day there were so many helpers about the place that the work was finished quickly in order to leave time for more merry-making.

All the new helpers set Jeannie a new problem: clothing them. Luckily she found a bolt of material in the station store, and it seemed that all their problems were solved — except for that of Sam the cook. Fortunately Sam decided to leave of his own accord, saying that the Missus and the 'Maluka' — 'old man', as the station Aborigines called Aeneas — were too fussy. The Maluka even insisted that the food for the men's quarters should be as good as that for himself and his wife! This would never do.

Sam announced he was going to write away for a new station cook who would arrive in about six weeks. He would see his replacement settled and then depart. Then, as if to spite them, Sam started to cook such delicious meals that they were almost sorry he was going.

ll ll ll

Station life was quite different from what she had expected, but Jeannie was beginning to enjoy it. She had plenty of free time to go riding and did not have to face the toil and financial hardship that other women in this book — Georgiana Molloy, Evelyn Maunsell, Myrtle Rose White or even Atlanta Bradshaw — had to endure. Conditions at the Elsey were primitive, but Jeannie had companionship, adventure, support and a station cook to prepare meals.

Although the Elsey was remote from civilisation, a surprising number of visitors passed through. Being within six kilometres of the Overland Telegraph Line, scarcely a week passed without one or more visitors. They were cattle drovers and stockmen, station owners, swagmen down on their luck, telegraph operators and heads of government departments. Each one brought news of the outside world and possibly extra mail. Usually they stayed a day or two and Jeannie enjoyed their company. There was only one room in the homestead but accommodation was no problem because bush travellers routinely carried a bluey (rolled blanket) and a mosquito net in their swag.

These visitors and bushmen sat among the buzzing swarms of flies and chatted about cattle camps and stampedes, dangers and extreme hardship. As she listened, Jeannie began to understand the stoic but lighthearted way these men accepted their tough life in the outback.

Not long after the Gunns had settled into the Elsey, Mac left to run a bullock team and wagons delivering goods to the inside. They could expect to see him when he returned after the Wet with Jeannie's belongings. Mac took with him Bertie, his 'boy' (as the Aboriginal men who assisted as stockmen and drovers were called) and Bertie's wife, Nellie. With Old Nellie reluctantly gone, for a while Jeannie had her hands full adjudicating between a roomful of women who rushed to take her place. Eventually two were chosen for the house with the compromise that any who wished could help outside, and Jeannie set about making these new girls some clothes.

Slowly improvements were being made to the homestead. Garden beds were built up, seeds planted and paths marked out. After a trip to Katherine, Dan returned with the welcome news that Johnny the carpenter was getting his 'tools together and would be along in no time' to finish the house.

As it turned out, Jeannie had to wait longer for her new rooms, when the demands of the outback took precedence and Johnny downed tools at the house to go out and fix a well instead. Aeneas decided to take the opportunity this provided to 'go bush' and show Jeannie the southern part of the Elsey run. The Yangman and Mangarrayi watched her depart. They could not understand why Jeannie rode side-saddle but to see the 'little Missus' mount a horse was good entertainment.

They camped overnight and the next day, on the way back to the homestead, Dan, who accompanied them, suggested that Jeannie might care to take a look at her future 'dining room'. So they turned into the tall trees on the edge of the Reach, riding on through the luxurious shade where Jeannie was delighted to see the timber for her dining room actually growing.

Jeannie made a theme of her outback education in *We of the Never-Never*. Besides teaching her to live simply, appreciate what she had, wait patiently and do it all in good humour, the men were always keen to put her instinct — or naivety — to the test. One day, when the horses were collected in the stockyard and everyone had gone to see them, Dan said, 'Let's see if she knows anything about horses. Show us your fancy in this lot, Missus'.[17]

Jeannie looked at the beautiful creatures. A magnificent brown colt, ears shot forward, nostrils quivering, watched every movement she made. She nodded at him. 'Talk of luck!' cried Dan. 'You've picked Jack's fancy.'

Jack, his voice suddenly warm and friendly, said, 'She's picked out the best in the whole mob,' before turning back to the horses again.

⁎⁎ ⁎⁎ ⁎⁎

The station received eight mails a year, with an extra delivery now and then brought by kind travellers. Everyone found a job to do at the homestead when the mailman, Henry Peckham (the Fizzer), was due to call. Peckham had once worked as a manager on neighbouring Auvergne Station, some time after the previous station manager, Tom Hardy, was speared to death by members of the 'Wild Blacks', a tribe of the Willeroo.

One day, Peckham arrived at the Elsey 'fizzing over' with news. Wagons were on their way to the 'inside'.

'Your trunks'll be along in no time now, Missus. They've got 'em all aboard,' he said.[18]

Herb Bryant — the Dandy — calculated that at ten miles (sixteen kilometres) a day on good roads and no mishaps to the bullock team, Jeannie's trunks might be there in four weeks. But, in fact, late thunderstorms and swampy ground meant they took almost twice as long. The way to make sure that at least the stores would arrive more quickly was to send a wagon to Katherine and collect them. So Bryant set off to do so.

Meanwhile, Johnny the carpenter had returned. He went on hammering the curves out of sheets of corrugated iron with which to cap the timber piles to stop white ants entering the house, all the while promising it wouldn't take long. Jeannie tried to believe him but was not convinced.

Sam had just announced dinner one evening when they looked up to see a cloud of dust along the horizon. The cloud turned into a fat, jovial Chinaman dressed in a black-and-gold robe. He dismounted, calling, 'Good day, Boss! Good day, Missus! Good day, all about.'

'You've struck Cheon,' said Johnny. 'Talk of luck! He's the jolliest old josser going.'

The 'jolliest old josser' waddled over to the assembled group, bowed low and introduced himself as the new cook. He explained that he knew all about cooking, gardening, milking, fishing and shooting wild duck, and was ready to start at once.

Next day Cheon was up at dawn, refusing any help from Sam, who, distinctly miffed, asked for his pay cheque, shook hands all around and departed, never to be seen again.

Cheon turned out to be a superb manager. Within a week he had everything under control. Everyone seemed happier and Jeannie wondered how she had ever coped without him. Cheon kept everyone, men and women, hard at work until he was satisfied. And if any of the girls had not washed hands and pail and cows' udders before sitting down to milk them, they soon toed the line.

Although Jeannie enjoyed the company of the house girls and other Aboriginal women — especially their larking about as they washed the clothes at the creek — and they seemed pleased to volunteer to work at the house, she was certain she could do the housework in less time than it took to tell her girls what to do. When she set them to work for Cheon, he only sent them back to her. The problem resolved itself when one of the Aboriginal stockmen named Larrikin returned to the property with a pleasant young wife named Rosy, who asked if she could work for the Missus. She assured Jeannie she knew how to scrub, sweep, wash and starch. Rosy was, according to Jeannie, 'so prettily jolly, clean, capable, and curly-headed' that Jeannie immediately made her head of domestic staff.[19]

'Great Scott!' Aeneas groaned. 'That makes four of them at it.' Jeannie said she was sure that Rosy would be excellent. She was right, and Rosy and Cheon worked together splendidly.

PHOTOGRAPH OWNED BY JEANNIE GUNN, COURTESY STATE LIBRARY OF VICTORIA.

Cheon at the Elsey.

Before long, Herb Bryant was back from Katherine with some of the stores — rolls of unbleached calico, mosquito netting, matting for the floors, jugs and basins to wash in and more cups and saucers. Lacking a sewing machine, Jeannie had a mountain of needlework to do by hand. The calico was intended for false ceilings in the new rooms. But Jeannie's biggest task was to make a gigantic mosquito net for the dining room, to enclose the dining table, chairs and people from flies and mosquitoes.

All the while, the house was taking better shape. Rosy and the other girls scrubbed the muddy paw-prints from the old and new walls, which were made of sliced tree trunks dropped horizontally, one above the other, between grooved posts. Inset into every third panel was a window so the new house would stay cool in the heat of summer but, of course, having no electricity there could be no ceiling fans.

Huge sheets of bark were used as insulation between the rafters and the galvanised iron roof. These were to be covered with the calico panels Jeannie had sewn to create a false ceiling.

When she announced that the tent of mosquito netting for the dining room was finished, Johnny, Dan and Herb hung it from the beams using fencing wire. As Jeannie had intended, the long net curtains reached down to the floor and ended with deep hem pockets of calico which were weighted down so the netting would not move. Jeannie hoped that snakes would not hide in the pockets in the hem. Cheon was filled with admiration, assuring the boss that the Missus was 'plenty savey', before returning to his kitchen to prepare a celebration dinner which was to be eaten inside Jeannie's mosquito-proof tent.

When Aeneas came home from visiting a far-flung corner of the property and saw how good the place looked, he was so impressed he started to build bookshelves out of old packing cases. These were intended for the much-loved books he expected to arrive any time on Mac's wagons.

However, the wagons were taking a long time, and well before they arrived Jeannie faced another pressing problem — not a thing to wear. Due to their frequent washing in the creeks, where they were beaten on stones by the house girls, her clothes were falling apart, and soon she was left with only one dress that was wearable. There was nowhere to buy new clothes, so Jeannie set about making herself a new dress from the unbleached calico she had used for the ceiling. She hadn't got far when her husband arrived from the station's own store bearing a roll of deep pink, thick, shiny cotton intended for dresses for the house girls, and some white braid. Brilliant pink was not a colour that Jeannie liked or normally wore. But she set to with her needle and soon appeared in a bright pink blouse and skirt ornamented with white rickrack braid.

Jeannie found there was so much to do in the outback she was never bored, but she missed her parents, sisters and friends a great deal. Like everyone else, she was looking forward to the next mail call by Henry Peckham, the Fizzer. It had been six weeks since his last. At sundown he arrived, covered in red dust and leading a packhorse bearing mail bags. Everyone rushed to welcome him and watched eagerly as he broke the seals of the bags and tipped out the mail. Jeannie was thrilled to receive *thirty* letters.

The next day the Fizzer was up at dawn. He ate a hearty breakfast of chops and fried eggs and climbed into the saddle, calling out, 'So long, chaps. See you again, at half-past eleven, four weeks.'[20]

The station hands knew the Fizzer would, if humanly possible, be back on time with their mail. In extremely high temperatures and with no shade, he feared that he could die of thirst out there in the bleak waterless desert and the dingoes would gnaw at his body as he lay dying. In fact, his death was quite the opposite: in later life Jeannie would learn that the Fizzer drowned while crossing a river to deliver a letter from a sick woman who lived on a remote cattle property who was asking for help.[21]

With the Fizzer been and gone, Jeannie still had the arrival of Mac's wagons to look forward to. The Gunns were up at dawn to see Mac, Bertie and Nellie rumble in with the stores — and all those lovely things Jeannie had had to leave behind at Pine Creek. For Jeannie unpacking her trunks was truly wonderful, like receiving her wedding presents all over again.

Cheon admired the silver teapot and her big brass lamp. He looked at the photographs of her friends and relatives and thought one of Jeannie's girlfriends so good-looking that she would fetch a very good bride price indeed in China! He watched in amazement as Aeneas picked up one book after another, dipping into a page here, a page there. But what pleased Cheon most was the egg-beater. He bore it away in triumph to his kitchen and used it to produce sponge cakes light as a feather.

Jeannie and her husband spent the rest of the afternoon arranging the home which they had waited four months to enjoy. By evening the dining room was transformed with ornaments on small tables and shelves, pictures on the walls, much-loved faces in silver photograph frames, a folding armchair, flowered curtains in the doorway between the rooms. Inside the shimmering white mosquito-net tent was some blue and white matting on the floor, and on the dining table a crimson cloth topped by a flower bowl which Cheon insisted was silver, although Jeannie knew it was only plate. But what made Jeannie and her husband happiest were the rows and rows of books filling the new bookshelves Aeneas had made.

Some time before Mac had left to go delivering with his wagons, Jeannie, Aeneas and Mac had gone on an overnight camping expedition to the Roper River. Noticing tracks, they followed them and found a young part-Aboriginal girl trying to cook a piece of meat over a campfire. Naked and shivering, her long hair matted with dirt and with a bone pierced through her nose, she told Jeannie her name was Dolly and that she was the daughter of Katie Wooloomool (niece of Ebimil Wooloomool — Old Goggle Eye, an elder of the Elsey Yangman) and a Scottish telegraph linesman named Lewis Cummings, a secret Jeannie did not divulge in *The Little Black Princess*, the book she published in 1905 about Dolly.[22]

Dolly told Jeannie that the Yangman had been attacked by the Willeroo, a 'wild' tribe, who came from far away searching for women. They had already speared and killed several Yangman men and captured Yangman women, who were raped and then carried off. During this attack, Dolly's relatives fled. In the confusion Dolly fell in the water and hid there, preferring to risk death from a crocodile rather than be raped or killed. The little girl survived by standing on the roots of an old tree and managed to breathe under cover of the lily leaves. Creeping out a few hours

PHOTOGRAPH OWNED BY JEANNIE GUNN, COURTESY STATE LIBRARY OF VICTORIA.

Dolly Cummings (Bett-Bett) with her spotted dog, Sue.

later, she found the camp deserted except for her little black and white dog, who was delighted to see her and licked her face.

Cold and hungry, Dolly rubbed two sticks to make fire. She huddled close and tried to cook a piece of goanna meat that had been overlooked in the raid.

Dolly was a bright little girl and said to Jeannie Gunn when they first met, in the pidgin English which most of the Yangman spoke, 'Me plenty savey Engliss, Missus!'[23]

The Gunns were worried about Dolly being so thin and cold and in a state of shock after spending a long time submerged in the river. They fed her damper and honey, which she loved. She was scared the Willeroo might return, so Jeannie invited her to sleep in the Gunns' camp and gave her a shirt to wear.

In *The Little Black Princess*, Jeannie described how the next day she invited Dolly (Bett-Bett) to come and live with her.[24] Dolly was pleased with the idea. Presumably, it was with the agreement of her relatives that Dolly continued to stay at the Elsey but Jeannie ignores this point.

Initially Dolly refused to sleep in a bed, and insisted on sleeping in a blanket roll on the bathroom floor with her dog beside her. She was free to go to the Yangman camp whenever she wanted but seemed to prefer life at the homestead and the company of Jeannie, whom she followed like a shadow.

One day when they were walking through the vegetable garden Goggle Eye passed close to Dolly and told Jeannie he was her 'little bit father' and that Dolly was 'promised' to Billy Muck, another rainmaker like himself. Under tribal kinship customs, Goggle Eye was forbidden to look at the little girl or speak to her and so was cross with Jeannie for bringing her to the garden. He worried the 'debil-debils' would get him if he caught sight of Dolly.

Jeannie was curious and asked Goggle Eye why he could speak to his sister but not to his niece. Goggle Eye replied that as his sister had been born before him he was allowed to talk to her but not to her daughters or any other nieces, including Dolly.

Jeannie grew fond of Dolly and described her as 'lovable, happy and affectionate and always constant in her affections'.[25] She made the little girl a blue dress and petticoats, which Dolly called 'shimmy shirts'. But having no concept of property Dolly gave away the blue dress to another girl and ran about naked. So Jeannie had to make her more dresses.

Dolly soon became 'bush hungry'. Jeannie realised that walkabouts were an important part of tribal life and that she had to let Dolly go, hoping she would return safely. The little girl adored Jeannie and gave her a greatly treasured possession — a sea shell — before she took off into the bush with her little dog.

Jeannie waited and worried. Three days later Dolly returned in good spirits. It is significant that she chose to return to Jeannie and the Elsey rather than to her natural mother or her aunt who 'looked out' for her.

Both Gunns wrote about Goggle Eye, an elder of the Yangman and the chief rainmaker. Jeannie described all the initiation scars on his body and called him 'a lovable old rogue'. He was forever asking her for extra 'chewbacca' or flour from the station store or a new clay pipe, and always enjoyed a joke. Aeneas referred to him in a letter to the *Northern Territory Times*:

> There is nothing substantial going on here . . . rain, though not urgently needed, would be very welcome . . . King Ebimil Wooloomool, alias 'Goggle Eye', the boss rainmaker of the Elsey, frankly confesses the inefficacy of his magic to compel the clouds to drop . . . he has been deposed by the tribe . . . Billy Muck and Big Charlie have been appointed rainmakers, and to ensure a plentiful supply, we have engaged their services. To make assurance doubly sure, we would beseech the prayers of the righteous, were there not a reasonable certainty that the natural process of the elements will in time perform their intrinsic functions . . . We have no present thoughts of building an ark.[26]

However, drought was regarded by the Yangman as a sign that the ancestral spirits were displeased. Unfortunately for Goggle Eye, as the drought continued and game became scarcer, the Yangman sought a scapegoat. According to Aeneas, this meant

Goggle Eye had to die in order to stop the ancestral spirits being angry with the Yangman, although Jeannie suggests it was because he was getting too autocratic in his old age. Goggle Eye knew he had had the bone pointed at him by someone and was resigned to the inevitable.

Aeneas became interested in the role of auto-suggestion in bone-pointing, and described how Goggle Eye was sung to death:

> so that he might waste away slowly. All possible food was
> sung so that it might not nourish him. His various organs
> were sung so that they might not perform their functions.
> The sun was sung so that it should not warm his wasted
> form. The night was sung that it might not let him sleep.
> The water that it might not quench his thirst. All other
> blackfellows were warned that if they gave him food
> or shelter or help they too, would be sung dead . . .
> Mrs Gunn disregarded her possible inclusion in the
> comprehensive curse if she gave Goggle Eye . . .
> porridge and arrowroot . . . [27]

Poor Goggle Eye, once so strong, dragged himself up to the homestead to appeal to the white folk to lift the curse from him. But Aeneas knew they were powerless against 'blackfellow magic', which had already done its work. The respected elder of the tribe who previously had been in good health and enjoyed life was now wasting away, unable to eat.

Jeannie tried to understand what was happening and described it as being 'faith dying rather than faith healing'. She went to his humpy with a bowl of porridge and treacle, which he had always loved, and some tea with sugar. The hut was dark and smelly with a dirt floor, nothing more than sheets of bark propped against a tree and she could understand why Dolly preferred a nice room all to herself at the homestead. She saw how the Yangman shunned Goggle Eye, knowing the bone had been pointed at him. He was gaunt and racked with pain, while outside the hut Jeannie heard the Yangman whispering that he would die the next morning at 'fowl sing out', as Cheon described morning.

Jeannie ordered them to be quiet, hoping this would give Goggle Eye a chance of survival but he died, as they had predicted, at dawn the following day. No one would stay in a place where a man had died, so new huts were built further upstream, and by tribal law his name (Ebimil Wooloomool) could no longer be mentioned or his spirit would haunt them. Whether Billy Muck (the man Dolly had been betrothed to since childhood without showing much interest in him), who became the new leader, was involved in the removal of Goggle Eye from his position Jeannie does not say.

ℓℓ ℓℓ ℓℓ

With her dog, Sue, at her side Dolly spent her time helping about the homestead and taking reading lessons from Jeannie. Sometimes Dolly, Jeannie, Old Nellie (after she returned), Kitty and the other women walked to the Long Reach waterhole or to the Stanley Billabong. Mindful of the crocodiles and the marauding Willeroos, who were led by a murderous man named Monkey who had already killed or raped several Yangman, Jeannie tucked a revolver into her belt whenever she went on these excursions.

With Dolly to take care of and sew for, the homestead to run, gardens and building to supervise, and a constant stream of guests, Jeannie had no time to be bored. There were also the camping trips around the property, which Jeannie loved to join. Having the reliable cook Cheon, and no children, Jeannie was free to participate in this side of station life. Her writings show how much she enjoyed the freedom and companionship of these occasions, the beauty of the scenery and a chance to be on horseback for hours at a time.

Just as the renovations to the homestead were almost ready, the Gunns left to go mustering with the stockmen. They camped at Bitter Springs, a long, looping chain of mirror-clear pools which provided a plentiful stock of freshly grilled fish for breakfast and dinner.

Many of the Aboriginal men had brought wives or partners with them, and there was also a group of Aboriginal boys Aeneas was training, so the camp was large. One small tent served as a dressing-room for Jeannie; while *gunyahs*, or shade houses, were dotted about for the Yangman. Another *gunyah* stored the supplies and a very large *gunyah*, cooler than a tent, was made for Jeannie to rest in.

Dan decided to teach Jeannie how to roast a bush turkey. Hanging from a string at the end of a sapling propped across a forked stick, the carcass twisted and turned over a glowing heap of ashes until it was roasted to perfection and still juicy inside. Accompanying it was an enormous boiled cabbage from the garden. Jeannie set about making the damper and was wrestling with the dough when a traveller rode into camp. He asked if there might be a bit of spare meat because his was fly-blown and smelled awful. Dan offered him slices of bush turkey and a plate of cabbage.

The traveller's eyes gleamed. 'Real cabbage! Gosh, ain't tasted cabbage for five years.'[28] He wolfed it down and confessed incidentally that nor had he seen a woman for five years. Jeannie commented wryly it seemed that the lack of cabbage meant more to him than the lack of a woman.

Jeannie accompanied the men on many musters and tours of the station during her year at the Elsey. In doing so she learned to respect the endurance and courage of the stockmen, and became sensitive to her surroundings. She had also 'educated' herself to the extent that 'thirty-three nights, or thereabouts, with the warm, bare ground for a bed, had made [her] indifferent to mattresses'![29]

These excursions also made her aware of the precarious nature of life in the outback. On one trip around the run, they arrived at a waterhole to find cattle — some dead, some alive — bogged deep in the mud and impossible to get out. Two poor animals stood up to their necks in mud, bellowing piteously and slowly starving to death. The only thing to do was to shoot the poor beasts and put them out of their misery.

This was not the only time Jeannie witnessed the cruelty of those outback waterholes. Taking their customary stroll while on an earlier muster, Jeannie and her husband had emerged from the bush to see a strange and terrifying sight. At their feet, protruding from the turf, was a grey head without a body — a horse's head — whinnying piteously.

The poor animal had been grazing on the turf near one of the Bitter Springs holes when the thin crust of earth it had been standing on had given way. The horse had slipped through the hole that formed and was now perched on the rocky bed of the underground river, only its head protruding. The horse was dying slowly from lack of food and water. The grass around the hole as far as its head could reach had been eaten bare, and although its feet were in water the horse's mouth could not reach any. While Aeneas went to get the 'boys', Jeannie brought handfuls of grass to the horse and used her husband's hat to bring it water.

When Aeneas returned with the men from the camp, it was hard work getting the exhausted animal out, but after an hour of digging and rope-pulling the poor horse was rescued.

❦ ❦ ❦

Following an outbreak of summer influenza among the men, Jeannie developed a sore throat and a high temperature. Aeneas was worried as the nearest doctor was 500 kilometres away in Darwin, so he stayed home to help Cheon look after her, sending the stockmen out to find enough cattle to fill an order from an Asian cattle dealer.

Cheon was delighted to have Jeannie doing as she was told and staying in bed, and he brought her in a constant supply of all invalid food possible — chicken jelly, barley water, egg-flips and junket. Her husband said she must eat and drink *all* of it. Aeneas read to Jeannie, plumped up her pillows and straightened the bed clothes every time he came in, Cheon nodding approval from the doorway.

After three days of this treatment, Jeannie thought that she would become ill from overeating! On the fourth day, with visitors in the house, she wanted to get up, but when both men begged her not to, she agreed, albeit with some reluctance. At least she could watch and talk to the visitors through the cracks in the walls.

Just as these visitors were to depart, another party arrived which forced her to leave her sick bed. This new group included two women and a brood of children and Jeannie welcomed the opportunity to lend a hand. The tired travellers were leaving the inside after fifteen years, during which three children had been born and raised, never knowing anything other than the outback. During a comfortable afternoon with tea and dinner, Jeannie later reflected, 'the women-folk spoke of their life "out-back"; and listening, I knew that neither I nor the telegraph lady [at Katherine] had guessed what roughness means.'[30]

Lack of fresh vegetables, unreliable water supplies and isolation from all medical help were constant dangers faced by inhabitants and visitors to the Never-Never.

The Gunns had only been back a few days from one of their bush trips when a traveller rode up to their veranda in search of help. 'Me mate's sick; got a touch of fever,' he said. 'I've left him camped back there at the Warlochs.'[31]

The man accepted eggs, milk and brandy which Jeannie gave him from the kitchen. But when Aeneas and Jeannie offered to ride out and bring the mate back to the homestead to be nursed, the bushman backed away, saying, 'If you please, ma'am . . . me mate's dead set against a woman doing things for him. If you wouldn't mind not coming. He'd rather have me. Me and him's been mates this seven years. The boss'll understand.'

And of course the boss did understand. These lonely, independent bushmen hated to be a trouble to anyone and were alarmed at the thought of being nursed by a woman.[32]

So Jeannie's husband rode to see the man, who had malaria, and implored him to come back to the homestead. But the sick man's mate had lugged his friend some 80 kilometres along a rough track and the sick man explained, 'He'll stick to me till I peg out — nothing's too tough for him.' The mate thanked Aeneas and said he would be grateful for some broth, fresh milk and medicines but *he* would nurse his friend.

The sick man managed to whisper, 'A good mate's harder to find than a good wife.'

For three days the sick man improved but his friend was totally exhausted by lack of sleep. Then the sick man slipped back into unconsciousness again and the Gunns knew that he might die unless he came to the homestead. The sick man still refused all help,

Roper River telegraph linesman's camp, circa 1900.

even when Jeannie sent a message that she would stay away from him unless he asked for her.

Finally, Herb Bryant — the Dandy — always good in a crisis, drove across to the camp and within an hour the sick traveller was in bed at the station, but at the first stirring of dawn he died.

Arranging the man's funeral was a problem, as even after seven years together, his mate did not know the dead man's religion or much about his next of kin. His name was William Henry Neaves, born in Wollongong in New South Wales.

'He was always a reticent chap. He never wanted anyone but me about him,' his mate insisted.

The station hands and Jeannie stood by an open grave under the pinkish-red flowers of a bauhinia tree. Aeneas read the burial service from his prayer book in his strong clear voice. Jeannie felt proud of her husband. The men shovelled earth on the grave and left him in the Elsey's little cemetery beside the graves of stockmen who had worked on the station and died there, many also from malaria, which so often followed the Big Wet.

Later, after the man's mate had packed his friend's swag for the last time, he came to the homestead and gave Aeneas two gold sovereigns, which he could ill afford, as recompense for his food and care.

'I'll have to ask for tick [credit] for meself for a while,' he said. 'He was always independent and would never take charity.'

Aeneas returned the gold coins saying gently, 'We give no charity here; only hospitality to our guests. Surely no man would refuse that.' Tactful as ever, Aeneas Gunn had said the right thing.

The man put the coins in his pocket. 'Not from your sort, Boss.'

Weak from lack of sleep and stress, the sick man's friend became their next patient. A few days of rest and sympathy, Cheon's meals and Jeannie's egg-flips brought the man's strength back. When the telegraph line superintendent sent word to say there was a job for him with the line party, the man left Elsey Station happy with the thought of work waiting for him.

House visitors arrived again in the form of Overland Telegraph linesmen with unexpected but welcome mail. Jeannie was amused to find that in two of the letters from Melbourne, her women friends demanded, 'Whatever do you do with your time? The monotony would kill me.'[33]

☙ ☙ ☙

Another trip out along the Roper River made a pleasant working holiday for Jeannie and her husband. The dark, clear water of the lagoons was filled with lilies in flower. The blue and crimson blossoms clustered on long stalks above floating leaves. On either side of the Roper River were wading birds, cranes, jabirus and graceful brolgas.

As she rode back to the homestead, Jeannie realised the Dry was almost over and the monsoon season would soon start. It was baking hot. There was no grass within sight of the homestead and dust was everywhere. The air was oppressive and there were distant rumbles of thunder, and flashes of lightning lit up the sky which had turned the colour of pewter.

The mailman was due so Aeneas wrote to his brother, Bob, and told him how they were living very cheaply at the Elsey, no rent, free game and all the beef they could eat. Jeannie had become so fond of outback life that they had decided they no longer wanted to leave the place. Bob's wedding was taking place very soon and Aeneas wrote that he hoped that Bob and his future wife, Nellie, would be as happy as he and Jeannie were.[34]

By this time Jeannie had realised that Jack McLeod (the Quiet Stockman) could not read and used this period of hiatus in activities before the Wet to teach him. She used the same text book she had in her lessons with Dolly, who was not a very attentive pupil and preferred polishing the silver or going down to the creek with Jeannie and the other women to do the washing and play in the water. Jack, however, was determined to read, tackling the letters of the alphabet in the same energetic way he tackled the colts. When he finished the reading primer, Jeannie started him on Kipling's *Just So Stories*.

Right on time the Fizzer arrived with a mail bag containing fifty letters, sixty-nine papers, dozens of books and magazines, and parcels of cuttings for the garden Jeannie was expanding. He told them Mac would soon be back, fed up with 'bullock-punching' and anxious to get back to work with horses.

But the Dry continued and each day the water from the soakage shrank. The Elsey homestead, wreathed in creepers and set amid a green garden of melons, was a pleasant oasis in the desert of dust and glare. As it became hotter and drier, Cheon, who carefully tended his vegetable garden, and Billy Muck, Goggle Eye's successor as rainmaker of the Yangman, who had against all odds successfully cultivated watermelons for Jeannie, competed fiercely for precious water which was fast running out.

The billabong dried up; the soak became so low that its water had to be kept strictly for personal needs. Everyone gasped in the stifling air and waited for the rain. Two cows died of heat exhaustion in the yards. When a few cool, gusty puffs of wind finally blew up, Jeannie and her husband ran outside to enjoy them. They didn't have long before the first shower arrived. Rain swept over the homestead and away to the south-east. Then came the deluge which filled the waterholes to overflowing.

Soon grass, inches tall, was rippling around the homestead. Jack kept at his *Just So Stories*, finished the book and asked for more.

Jeannie was pleased to see that learning to read had given him more confidence and made him more talkative.

‰ ‰ ‰

On 7 November 1902, Jeannie wrote Bob and Nellie Gunn a cheery Christmas letter telling them how happy she and her husband were together, and poignantly confided to her sister-in-law, 'I would like to grow old slowly together'.[35]

She and Cheon planned to make that Christmas a splendid one. It was decided that the homestead and the stockmen would eat Christmas dinner together on the eastern veranda, and that a vealer (an eight-month-old calf) would be provided for the meal. While they waited for the Dandy to return from Katherine with supplies, the Fizzer came and went again. He would have a merry Christmas, he said, with damper and beef served on a packsaddle!

Cheon had promised seven kinds of vegetables for Christmas dinner. But while the gardens had survived the Dry, he now witnessed them being destroyed by grasshoppers. Ever resourceful, Cheon helped himself to tins of vegetables put aside for the telegraph linesmen, donating them some fresh eggs in return.

Cheon's preparations were long and hard. On Christmas Eve he spent the night watching a huge Christmas pudding with silver threepenny bits hidden in it. Jeannie and Aeneas offered to share the watch but Cheon refused. Everyone, he insisted, must have a good sleep that night so they would be able to appreciate his beautiful dinner. Besides, he still had to make mince pies, hop beer and another big plum pudding for the Yangman camp.

On Christmas morning, when the boss and his wife went into the kitchen to be wished a merry Christmas by Cheon, they were immediately given jobs to do. The vealer was to be slaughtered and cut up; six women were needed to pluck the young hens. Anyone else available was sent by Cheon to bring in green branches and 'mistletoe' for decorating the house and kitchen.

A light breakfast of sausage without the skin was only the prelude to a superb Christmas dinner, the best they had known. Every seat on the run was retrieved, two tables were placed end to end under the decorations of greenery and covered with clean white cloths. The hop beer was set in canvas water bags to keep cool. A canvas awning was stretched from the veranda to the kitchen and more greenery was hung there, to make it a fit place for the promised procession of food.

In honour of Cheon's Christmas lunch, men who normally did not give a fig what they looked like had smartened up. They had cut each other's hair and shaved their stubbly chins. Jeannie could scarcely recognise some of them!

Aeneas, in a white shirt and white linen trousers with a red silk cummerbund and matching tie, looked even smarter than the Dandy. Jeannie wore one of her best Melbourne dresses, made of cream silk with a matching lace collar.

Then Cheon, grinning from ear to ear, rang a bullock bell to summon the guests, announcing: 'Dinner is served!' Young Nellie arrived with six chickens on a platter. Rosy carried the haunch of veal; while Bertie's Nellie brought in the ham. Dolly came last, proudly bearing the bread sauce. The higher their plates were piled and the sooner they were emptied, the happier Cheon was. And when a bottle of the hop beer he had just brewed popped its top and sent froth shooting everywhere, he beamed with joy.

Cheon went to the open-air kitchen and returned bearing a huge pudding ablaze with brandy and crowned with mistletoe. Normally Christmas Day in the Territory was hot and muggy but for some reason this was an unusually cool day, so they sat happily on the makeshift chairs and stools, telling jokes and chatting the afternoon away.

In the Yangman camp, there had also been a feast, the Aborigines deciding this Christmas dinner was the best thing the Maluka and Gadgerri (their name for Jeannie) had arranged for them. The Aborigines ate half the vealer and Cheon's plum pudding, and each of the men was given a new clay pipe as well as some plug tobacco.

At the homestead Cheon's Christmas was a triumph. Each of the 'guests' signed an autograph book for Jeannie and wrote her a special message. Only Dan was missing. He arrived two days later and pleased Cheon enormously by insisting that Christmas dinner at the Pine Creek Hotel had not been nearly as good as the one at the Elsey!

ℓℓ ℓℓ ℓℓ

Soon they reached the anniversary of the day on which the Gunns had first arrived from Darwin.

'A year today, Mac, since you sent those telegrams!' Aeneas teased Jock McLennan,[36] reminding him of his attempts to put off Jeannie's arrival. But arrived she had. And perhaps in thanks for the way she had fitted into station life and taught him to read, Jack McLeod offered Jeannie a New Year present of a beautiful chestnut filly he was breaking in. The idea of having her own horse thrilled Jeannie.

New Year 1903 brought more travellers to the Elsey but it also brought tropical rains and malarial dysentery, the scourge of the Big Wet. Some of the travellers recovered but two were very ill with high fever and, in spite of careful nursing, one died and was buried in the cemetery on the station. The other, a man of seventy, recovered and they watched him ride away again.

Jack took to the bush to train his colts. Mac and Dan went into Katherine to order supplies, while the Dandy remained at the Elsey and waited for the Wet to lift and the supply wagons to arrive.

For cheerful Jeannie, delighting in the outback and in love with her husband, life was full. She wrote to her new sister-in-law Nellie Gunn that there was a lot to discover about marriage. She joked that she had been 'led on shamelessly' for '[Aeneas] has led me to imagine I was the boss, until one day I suddenly found that I wasn't. Perhaps you have found out already there is a good deal of grim determination under a Gunn's tenderness!'[37]

As usual after the Wet, Aeneas went out mustering with the stockmen. She watched them leave the yard, the horses restive, the men enjoying it all.

A few days later, however, Aeneas was brought back to the Elsey. He was far too ill to sit on a horse, and was slumped across the front of the Dandy's saddle. Jeannie rushed out of the house and she and Herb Bryant lifted Aeneas down from the horse. They carried him into the homestead, his brow burning with fever and his lips cracked with thirst.

Herb volunteered to nurse Aeneas, as he knew all too well the terrible effects of dysentery and malaria and possibly blackwater fever caught from polluted water. Aeneas was suffering from diarrhoea, a high fever and an engorged and very painful spleen, but Jeannie would not hear of Herb nursing her husband. She took on the role of nurse, tried all the bush remedies she knew, brought cool drinks and cold compresses for his forehead, sat with him day and night and half slept beside him at night. But before the invention of antibiotics, nothing anyone could do would have lowered her husband's fever or abated the pain from his engorged spleen.

With the nearest doctor so far away, it became obvious to everyone Aeneas was getting weaker.

On 16 March 1903, Jeannie's beloved husband died with her at his side. They had been married for only fourteen months. Jeannie's grief was so intense she cried until the bones of her face ached and she lay on her bed exhausted, her head splitting with migraine.

Two days later she felt well enough to write letters to her father and sisters and to Bob Gunn telling them the terrible news. She told Bob that she had never heard strong men sob before and that knowing how fond everyone on the station had been of her husband was some comfort. The men in the Aboriginal camp had asked if they could draw the buggy carrying the coffin to the little cemetery on the hill. Aeneas had proved that treating the Aborigines like human beings had won their trust and affection, she wrote. She added that her sorrow was now too deep for tears and she must not cry any more as she needed to be composed enough to take part in the funeral ceremony.[38]

The Elsey was silent, everyone wrapped in grief. The stockmen cut down timber, made a coffin and dug a grave. The Aborigines pulled the buggy up to the small cemetery. They lowered the Maluka's coffin on ropes into the grave and piled red soil on top.

Most people present were weeping. Jeannie, however, managed somehow to control her tears and say a few words. It must have seemed incredible to Jeannie that the husband she loved was inside that wooden box. The pain of leaving the person she loved most in the world was so intense that she could write only briefly about it in her book:

> All unaware, that scourge of the Wet crept back to the homestead, and the great Shadow, closing in on us, flung wide those gates of Death, and turning, before passing through, beckoned to our Maluka to follow . . . A sobbing cry went up from the camp, as the tribe mourned for their beloved dead — their dead and ours — our Maluka, 'the best Boss ever a man struck'.[39]

The Yangman held a corroboree to mourn the loss of the Maluka and the stockmen repeated those words again and again that the Maluka had been 'the best Boss ever a man struck'.

For weeks Jeannie was in such a shocked, depressed and miserable state that she could not leave her room or eat and had difficulty sleeping. She sat there by herself, brooding on the death of Aeneas and recalling incidents from that brief but happy fourteen months of marriage. The stockmen were kind and understood her anguish and despair, which seemed as if it would never lift.

Her family were so worried about Jeannie that her sister, Carrie Taylor, sailed north to Darwin to meet her and bring her home, and so a grieving Jeannie returned with her sister to Melbourne.

Over the next few years Jeannie worked on turning the notes she had made at the Elsey and the letters she had written to friends into two books.[40] The first, published in 1905 and designed for children, was a suitably sanitised version of Dolly's story — *The Little Black Princess* — in which Dolly was called 'Bett-Bett' by Jeannie. The other, published in 1908, was designed for adults and titled *We of the Never-Never*. It was a loving depiction of the time she had enjoyed with Aeneas. The fact that Jeannie lost the husband she adored after only fourteen months gives her second book its special poignancy.

Although modern critics have sometimes charged Jeannie with racism, both her books have become Australian classics, enjoyed by people all over the world. Jeannie's style was light and amusing but showed respect for the people she met during her year in the Never-Never. She wrote with empathy and understanding about the Aboriginal house girls and the fun they had together, and did this in an era when empathy and understanding was lacking among most Europeans in the Northern Territory. She has been called patronising, but she was a woman of her times. And it is significant that all her life Dolly had nothing but praise for Mrs Gunn, and never once complained that she had found her patronising.

While never conceding her position both as a white woman and an employer, Jeannie's descriptions of the Aboriginal customs and culture she encountered — the complex kinship systems, or the bone-pointing that led to the death of Goggle Eye, for example — showed tolerance for beliefs other than her own and appreciation for the survival skills of Aborigines.

She not only donated money to various Aboriginal causes but also quite explicitly defended the Aboriginal point of view with regard to taking their land and for allowing them to spear cattle without being punished rather than go hungry:

> The white man has taken the country from the black
> fellow, and with it his right to travel where he will for
> pleasure and food, and until he [the white man] is willing
> to make recompense by granting fair liberty of travel and
> a fair percentage of cattle or their equivalent in fair
> payment — openly and fairly giving them, and seeing
> that no man is unjustly treated or hungry within his
> borders — cattle killing, and, at times even man killing by
> blacks, will not be an offence against the white folk.[41]

How much Jeannie knew about the real purpose of 'surprise parties' against Aboriginal groups, which she mentioned in her writing, and the systematic measures taken by pastoralists to destroy them, is unclear. It was certainly part of the outback she came to feel so happy in. Aeneas was presumably well aware of such practices, and had himself participated in retributive hunts of Aborigines while he was at Marigui.[42] Jock McLennan was later accused of conducting, on behalf of the Eastern African and Cold Storage Company (owners of the Elsey), systematic killing raids on 'wild' Aborigines who threatened stock.[43]

Jeannie may have been protected from this most brutal side of outback life. In a reference in *We of the Never-Never* to 'outside blacks' advancing along the river 'inside' the property while they were out preparing for a muster, Jeannie wrote that her husband considered it too dangerous for her and sent his wife back to the homestead.[44] Nevertheless, Jeannie did give hints that she knew in theory what could occur. When she wrote about the 'surprise party' she participated in herself, she explained that it 'would only involve the captured with general discomfiture', but she conceded that 'emergencies were apt to occur "down the river" and we rode out of camp with rifles unslung and revolvers at hand'.[45]

If her views on the rights of Aborigines were ahead of her time, in other ways Jeannie was still very much part of pioneer society. References to 'nigger-hunting' have been removed from some later abridged editions of *We of the Never-Never*, but so, surprisingly, have some of her most supportive statements of Aborigines. It is hard to read her books without responding to the warmth and affection she felt for the Yangman and Mangarrayi of the Elsey — and her understanding of their plight:

> A black fellow kills cattle because he is hungry and must
> be fed with food, having been trained in a school that for
> generations has acknowledged 'catch who catch can'
> among its commandments; and until the long arm of the
> law interfered, white men killed the black fellow, because
> they were hungry with a hunger that must be fed with
> gold, having been trained in school that for generations
> acknowledged 'Thou shalt not kill' among its
> commandments; and yet men speak of the 'superiority' of
> the white race, and, speaking, forget to ask who of us
> would go hungry if the situation were reversed . . .[46]

Once her royalties started to accrue, Jeannie took practical measures to help Aborigines, often anonymously. One gift that is recorded was her donation of autographed books to help raise money to build a pipeline to bring a supply of pure water to the Hermannsburg Mission in central Australia, run by Carl and Frieda Strehlow.

Jeannie's affection for the Elsey stockmen, who were so kind to her after the death of her husband, led her to protect their reputations in her books. She was careful to mask the identities of her characters by using stylised names such as 'the Dandy', 'the Sanguine Scot', 'the Quiet Stockman', as well as protecting Dolly by calling her 'Bett-Bett'.

One highly significant letter among Jeannie's papers in the National Library of Australia was written by Jock McLennan, the Sanguine Scot, dated 5 July 1906. Mac thanked Mrs Gunn for sending him a copy of *The Little Black Princess*, which he described as 'A good book written by a good woman'. He added, 'I know you could have written a slightly different tale and still have been close to the truth. I know your aim is not to give pain to anyone.'[47] Jeannie told McLennan that she aimed to present the beauty of the outback and the loyalty of bushmen, rather than showing life in the bush as 'a pandemonium of drunken orgies, black women, remorse and suicide'.[48]

The men of Elsey Station had grown very fond of Jeannie and continued to send her Christmas cards. Some, like Herb Bryant (the Dandy), the best educated of the group, wrote her letters. Jeannie also continued to correspond with Dave Suttee (Dan, the Head Stockman), who took over as joint manager with Bryant after Aeneas's death.

Jack McLeod, the Quiet Stockman, would always be grateful that Jeannie had taught him to read. He left the Elsey when it was sold, returned to Adelaide, and eventually worked for the Goldsborough Mort pastoral company, before adapting to the motor age and starting a service station at Angaston. Jack had six children, including a daughter he named Jeannie Gunn McLeod. He also included 'Gunn' in the names of another two children.

⚜ ⚜ ⚜

In its day Jeannie's book for children *The Little Black Princess* was considered the first sympathetic story about northern Aborigines in the outback, at a time when most white people feared them.

Jeannie had had to pay half the cost of publication of her first book but managed to recoup this in sales. She was urged to write a second book about the outback, this time for adults. However, getting an adult book published as a woman in a male-dominated world was hard. Several publishers rejected Jeannie's manuscript before a London publisher accepted it, but for a low 'colonial royalty', claiming that freighting the books to Australia would be expensive.

Jeannie Gunn in later life.

Ironically, in view of the fact that six publishers had rejected the manuscript of *We of the Never-Never*, fearing they might lose money, Jeannie's second book about the outback became a bestseller and one of Australia's most loved stories. It sold well in England, and was translated into German and French. In a poll conducted by the Melbourne *Herald* in 1931, Mrs Aeneas Gunn was named one of Australia's most popular authors.

Following the death of her father in 1909, Jeannie fulfilled the dream she had nurtured with her late husband to make an extended visit to Britain and Europe. After spending almost three years overseas she returned to Melbourne and planned to write a book about Aboriginal lore as retold by John Terrick, son of one of the last Victorian Aboriginal chiefs, and incorporating Aboriginal lore she had learned from the Yangman and Mangarrayi.

The writing of her first two books had been hard, as Jeannie had had to deal with powerful emotions of grief and loss, especially while writing *We of the Never-Never* in which her husband is a strong and humorous figure. She also found it difficult to write about the bush while living in the city, and periodically stayed with friends in the more tranquil atmosphere of Monbulk, a picturesque wooded area where pioneers were struggling to establish themselves on small selections and where her father had owned a block of bushland.[49] Unfortunately, as she became caught up in work for soldiers during World War I and the Returned Services League (RSL) afterwards,

Jeannie found she had come to her project with John Terrick too late, after Terrick's memory had faded, so she had to abandon the idea. Terrick died in 1921. She would nevertheless continue to regard Monbulk as a refuge for the rest of her life.

From 1914 onwards Jeannie channelled her energies into fundraising efforts for wounded Anzacs. During the war she packed gift parcels of soap, hand-knitted socks, balaclava helmets and candles, all badly needed in the freezing cold winters in the trenches of France and Gallipoli. When she was in Melbourne she saw newly enlisted men off on their tours. She wrote letters to 'her boys' in the trenches, kept open house for them and placed their photographs on her mantelpiece and walls. No soldier in uniform was ever turned away from her home without a good meal. Even if returned soldiers arrived drunk at her house, the maid had instructions to give them plenty of strong black coffee and sober them up.[50]

After the Great War many war widows and their children suffered extreme hardship. Jeannie did what she could to comfort and assist them. She also visited limbless or blind men in rehabilitation centres, and became an unpaid and unofficial liaison worker between them and the inept bureaucracy of various government departments, and when necessary fought for the entitlements of 'her boys'. In 1925 she became patron of the Tubercular Sailors' and Soldiers' Relief Fund in Monbulk.

As a former teacher Jeannie was horrified to discover that the people of Monbulk had no books they could borrow — not even an atlas. She spent ten years of her life and her own money building up a lending library in the Monbulk RSL clubhouse for returned war veterans who could not afford to go to libraries in Melbourne and borrow books. She donated the bookshelves and wrote personally to many authors to request donations of books.

In 1939 Jeannie was given an Order of the British Empire in recognition not only of her services to Australian literature but also of her work with disabled soldiers and their dependents.

Her final book — never published in her lifetime — was to have been called *The Making of Monbulk*. It told the story of the men of Monbulk who served in the Australian Imperial Force (AIF) and of the Monbulk RSL of which she would become a generous patron. It was published in 2000 as *My Boys: A Book of Remembrance*.

In 1951 Jeannie was invited to lay the foundation stone for new clubrooms for the Monbulk RSL and unveil a memorial tablet to those who had died in war. The president of the RSL described how:

> Mrs Gunn had been the friend of every serviceman from the district in two wars, sending parcel, comforts and news from home. She had been their guide and counsellor in many personal circumstances and a consolation to those who were bereaved.[51]

Jeannie died in Melbourne on 9 June 1961, aged ninety-one. Her funeral was crowded with people who had loved her books and loved her. Generous to the last, her estate was divided among the many charities and humanitarian causes she had supported.

Perhaps the last word on Jeannie Gunn should come from the eulogy at her funeral, held at the Scots Church in Melbourne's Collins Street. The Reverend A. Crichton-Barr, who had known her well, told a large group of mourners from many different walks of life who crowded the church:

> Mrs Aeneas Gunn was a modest, gentle and courageous lady. Some people will remember her for her books and others for her unremitting service to those who fought for Australia. She will be remembered by many people with gratitude and affection.

'THE LITTLE BLACK PRINCESS'

Much more might have been learned about Dolly, 'the Little Black Princess', had the correspondence and diaries of Aeneas Gunn for the year he and Jeannie spent at the Elsey not been destroyed by the new owners. However, later in her life Dolly revealed some details to H. T. Linklater and Helen Frizell and made a recording about her life, a transcript of which is in the Northern Territory Archives.[52]

In her recorded interview, Dolly revealed that her father was Lewis Cummings, the telegraph repair linesman from Glasgow, who had migrated to Adelaide and then found work in a camp on the Roper River for the Overland Telegraph Line where Dolly was born.

Dolly disclosed that she spent her first months of life in the linesmen's camp close to Elsey Station. Her mother, Katie, had wanted to call her Katherine after the town of Katherine, but her father insisted she be named Dolly, because she was so pretty, 'like a little doll'. After Katie and Lewis fought over some rice Katie had burned, Katie ran away with her daughter back to the Aboriginal camp on Elsey Creek. Cummings eventually returned to Adelaide and married a European woman.

In the camp Dolly was looked after by her Aunt Judy (it is unclear what happened to Katie)[53] until she went to live at Elsey homestead with the Gunns. Dolly was free to come and go from the homestead to the camp as she pleased. From what she said when interviewed for an article in the *Sydney Morning Herald*[54] and the letters she wrote to Jeannie, Dolly was grateful for the year she spent with Jeannie at the Elsey, bridging black and white cultures, and had few regrets at leaving the Aboriginal camp.

A month after Jeannie left the Elsey, Mr Little, Superintendent of the Telegraph Office in Katherine and Protector of Aborigines, took Dolly Cummings to Darwin, where he placed her with the family of the governor of Fanny Bay gaol, as resident nursemaid to the governor's young children. From there Dolly wrote to Jeannie telling her that she was very happy. Fortunately, through living with the children of the gaol governor — who doubtless had a governess — Dolly was taught to read and write.

Eventually Dolly's charges grew up and no longer needed a nursemaid. The governor accepted a posting elsewhere and Dolly was placed with the Ward family, whose father also worked for the telegraph line. Dolly reported that her father visited her once while she was there, bringing her a doll and promising to return the following year, but she never heard from him again, which made her very sad.

COURTESY STATE LIBRARY OF VICTORIA.

Dolly Cummings aged about twelve.

In April 1907 Mrs Ward took her children and Dolly to Melbourne, where she met Jeannie at the Spencer Street railway station. Jeannie took her back to her house at Creswick Street, Hawthorn, which she shared with her sister.

Dolly was now twelve years old.[55] Years later in Melbourne *The Age* would print a photograph that Jeannie took of Dolly when she visited Jeannie's home. Dolly was wearing a white dress and had a white bow in her long hair.

Dolly had never forgotten Jeannie and her days of fun and mischief at the Elsey homestead. She remained devoted to 'the little Missus', as she always called Jeannie. Many years later Jeannie revealed that Dolly had wanted to stay with her in Melbourne rather than return with the Ward family. It was a big decision but Jeannie decided against keeping Dolly in Melbourne with her. Jeannie later wrote that 'I was afraid of the climate and all the difficulties here [in Melbourne] for her upbringing, and her future.'[56]

Dolly returned to Darwin with the Wards, where she remained as housemaid until transferring to another home where she was unhappy.

It appears from Dolly's recorded transcript that she did not feel patronised or forced into anything by Jeannie and insisted that she would always be extremely grateful for everything Jeannie had done for her.

Through the intervention of Jeannie's friend Irene Pickersgill, Dolly became a resident ward maid at the Darwin hospital and was given a room in the staff quarters. Dolly had a loving and warm personality, was very popular with patients and fellow staff members, and got on well with Matron Pickersgill.

Two years after starting work at Darwin Hospital, and by now a very attractive and vivacious young woman, Dolly met tall English-born William Bonson on the beach at Fanny Bay, where she had gone to swim with friends from the hospital. She and William fell in love and since he had a steady job at Vestey Meatworks, he and Dolly were able to marry. He promised to build a house for them in Darwin.

The matron of Darwin hospital was Dolly's matron of honour, while a Melbourne friend of Jeannie's, at that time residing in Darwin, acted as hostess at the reception. Jeannie, who had always kept in touch with Dolly, sent a handsome wedding gift but did not attend. She and Dolly would correspond for fifty years but Jeannie never returned to the Northern Territory, possibly because it brought back sad memories.

William Bonson kept his promise to Dolly and built them a home. She and her husband had three sons and two daughters — and a share of life's ups and downs. Like many people in Darwin, Dolly's husband lost his job when the huge Vestey Meatworks closed. However, he was a hard worker and tried his hand at many different occupations, including working on the Darwin docks and owning a small banana farm at Humpty Doo, near Darwin.

During World War II, Darwin was bombed by Japanese planes and many people were killed. Dolly and her younger children were evacuated to Mildura. From there Dolly's eldest daughter travelled to see Jeannie, who was now in her seventies and living at Hawthorn. Another visitor was Dolly's eldest son who had enlisted and was for a while stationed in Melbourne. At the end of World War II, Dolly and her children moved back to Darwin.

In 1955 Jeannie publicly defended Dolly in the Melbourne *Age* against scurrilous rumours that 'little Bett–Bett' was destitute and living on the streets of Darwin, which were totally untrue.[57] Dolly was in Darwin for the arrival of Cyclone Tracy, which destroyed the city in 1974. By then eighty-two, she bravely endured a terrifying experience. The wind howled all around and there was a terrible sound of corrugated-iron sheets being dragged over the ground as whole houses were swept away. Dolly and her son Joe, a well-known footballer, sheltered under a bed while their house disintegrated around them. At length, the Bonsons were rescued and flown south to Melbourne to stay with a granddaughter who worked in a bank.

By this time Jeannie Gunn was dead, but her nephew and niece, the late Alfred and Dorothy Derham, invited Dolly to their home.

The replica of the Elsey homestead made for the movie We of the Never-Never.

They described how Dolly was taking the loss of her house with courage and dignity but, like most people who have lived through cyclones or floods, she grieved for the loss of photographs and possessions.[58] Dolly and her family were given aid by the government and eventually they had their home rebuilt and were able to return to Darwin.

Dolly died on 8 March 1988 in Darwin, at her daughter's home, having achieved a great deal. Today the Bonson family are well known and respected in Darwin, and several Bonson boys have distinguished themselves on the football field. Dolly's grandson, Matthew Bonson, a former lawyer, is now a member of the Legislative Assembly (MLA) in the Northern Territory.

In 1982 a film of *We of the Never-Never* was released, funded by the West Australian Film Corporation and Adams-Packer films, and was enjoyed on screen, video and television by a huge audience in Australia and overseas. A few years before her death, Dolly saw the movie and enjoyed it, according to her interview transcript. The movie made 'the little Missus', 'Bett-Bett' and 'the Maluka' famous to a new generation. The replica of Elsey homestead specially created for the movie is now open to the public at Mataranka Resort, 100 kilometres south of Katherine.

AFTERWORD

After the original wooden homestead near the Warloch Ponds where Aeneas and Jeannie Gunn lived was eaten by white ants, the Yangman and Mangarrayi carried galvanised iron and other building materials from Warloch Ponds to the Red Lily Lagoons in Mangarrayi country to rebuild it. But as malarial mosquitoes were a constant problem at Red Lily Lagoons, the site of the Elsey homestead was moved again and a new brick house erected at a place marked as McMinns Bar on local maps.

In 1968, following a decision of the Conciliation and Arbitration Commission, a minimum wage for all those working in the pastoral industry was instituted. In 1974 the Yangman and Mangarrayi moved to Jilkminggan, the site they occupy today.

In February 2000, Elsey Station was handed back to the traditional owners, the Mangarrayi and the Yangman, who had initially lodged their claim through the Northern Land Council in 1991, after buying the pastoral lease for the Elsey that same year.[59]

Elsey cemetery, which lies near the Stuart Highway to the south of Mataranka, contains the grave of Aeneas Gunn. A bronze plaque bears the arms of the Gunn family and an inscription 'In loving memory of the "Maluka"'. The cemetery also contains the graves of William H. Neaves, Jock McLennan, Tom Pearce, and Henry Peckham (the Fizzer), who drowned in Campbell's Creek delivering mail, and was reburied at the Elsey.

Beside the grave of Aeneas Gunn stands a smaller stone engraved 'In loving Memory of the "Little Missus", a tribute from descendants of the men whose stories Jeannie told'. Near it is a small memorial to Bett-Bett, who was buried in Darwin under her married name of Dolly Bonson.

CHAPTER 5

Evelyn Maunsell

1888 – 1977

AN ENGLISH ROSE IN THE OUTBACK

In 1912 when Evelyn Maunsell arrived at Mount Mulgrave cattle station on Queensland's Cape York, she brought with her a trunk filled with new clothes, a dinner service and two rolls of floral-printed upholstery material — a present from her bridesmaid, Paulina Fox, owner of the Imperial Hotel, Cairns. Evelyn, head over heels in love with Charlie Maunsell, the new manager on Mount Mulgrave, had been expecting to live in a gracious Queensland homestead, with wide verandas surrounded by tropical flowers and green lawns. She received a shock when she saw the tin shed that was to be their home.[1]

Mount Mulgrave Station had been owned by Paddy Callaghan, a wealthy bachelor cattle baron whose main preoccupations had been beef and beer. The 'homestead' had clearly been built by a man with no interest in homemaking. Its walls were unlined, the roof was made from sheets of galvanised iron and the floor was concrete so it could be hosed down after a drinking session. The only attempt at comfort was a wooden veranda tacked around it as an afterthought.

Evelyn peered cautiously round the back of the house and saw a big galvanised-iron water tank and a sagging clothesline. A separate shed, home to huge, hairy spiders, was fitted with a canvas-bag shower. Worst of all was the ten-metre-deep smelly latrine pit surrounded by sheets of corrugated iron. She was expected to share this with the stockmen until an outside 'dunny' could be constructed for her.

There was a dark kitchen with an ant-bed floor, a chipped sink and a wood-fired stove. The kitchen was fitted with another veranda where stockmen, fencers and visitors — all men — had their meals. Tacked onto the kitchen were two cell-like guest rooms. One was occupied by elderly Rudolph Morisset, a former gold miner who had been a drinking mate of Pat Callaghan. Callaghan had let Morisset live there for free in return for milking the cows.

Beside the creek was a gone-to-seed vegetable garden. There were no fruit trees and no green lawns, only gigantic gum trees. Evelyn's new abode was scarcely the tropical paradise she had dreamed of as her matrimonial home.

Evelyn had grown up in a large, well-furnished home at Ilford near London, with comforts such as carpets, paintings, a music room, central heating, running hot water and well-trained servants. Her father, Frank Evans, owned his own import-export business in the City of London. He was an alderman and also a Freeman of the City of London.

The Evans children took after their father — they were hard-working and adventurous in spirit. Two of Evelyn's brothers were army officers, hoping for postings to Australia. The eldest, Rupert, did go to Australia as a civilian, eventually working on a station in northern New South Wales.

Sweet-faced, elegant Evelyn, known as Evie in the family, had always longed to travel, and when she turned twenty-one the opportunity arose to go out to Australia also. Her round-the-world ticket had come about through a friend of her aunt, a Mrs Dean, recently widowed, who was about to take a world cruise to visit her married daughters, in Australia, New Zealand and South America. Mrs Dean wanted a paid companion, it being considered quite improper for ladies to travel alone. Evelyn jumped at the chance to see her brother and persuaded her parents to let her accompany Mrs Dean. It was a daunting journey, at a time when there were no aeroplanes and most British people travelled no further than Europe.

In Australia, Rupert Evans had made friends with the family of Thomas Hall, chief accountant of New South Wales Railways. As Rupert would not be in Sydney when she arrived, Evelyn wrote to young Harry Hall asking him to meet her when the ship came in.

Evelyn had had many admirers but hoped she might meet the man of her dreams on board ship. If she did not, she could always come home and marry nice, kind Reggie Grimwood, a friend of one of her brothers, who had loved Evie since they were children.

So, three years before the start of World War I, Evelyn and Mrs Dean were booked aboard an ocean liner from Marseilles to Sydney and allocated pleasant first-class cabins. Mrs Dean planned to spend four days sightseeing in Paris en route so she could shop for clothes in the fashion houses. She found Evie sweet and helpful and with a good sense of humour, and treated her like a long-lost daughter. In Paris she bought her a beautiful silk dress as a present. The two women went by train from the Gare de Lyon to Marseilles, where they boarded the SS *Osterley* for the six-week voyage to Sydney. But there was no shipboard romance. The male passengers were either married or elderly — and Evelyn resisted the romantic attentions of the ship's officers.

They arrived in Sydney on the Thursday before the Easter weekend. At Circular Quay, Mrs Dean was met by her daughter and Evie was met by Harry Hall and his wife, Maude. Harry, Maude and Evie drove in a horse-drawn buggy to Thornleigh, where Harry and his brother Arthur had homes on their father's property. Staying with Arthur Hall and his wife, Frances, were Frances's widowed mother, Jane Maunsell, and her sister, Phoebe.

Evie stayed on and off with the Halls for the remainder of the year, during which time she was reunited with her brother Aubrey (later to be renamed the less formal 'Tim' by Evelyn's future husband). Tim had quickly followed Evie out to Australia and was given a job by Thomas Hall in his orchards. In due course Rupert

Evans also arrived back in Sydney from his stint in the bush. Love blossomed at Thornleigh and Evelyn was pleased when Rupert and Phoebe Maunsell announced their engagement.

Evelyn frequently met up with Phoebe Maunsell and Frances Hall, who spoke with pride about their elder brother, Charlie. Charlie had just been appointed manager of Mount Mulgrave Station on Cape York Peninsula and was coming south by train to spend a week with them. Both Maunsell sisters were very attractive, tall and blonde, and Evie hoped their brother was as good looking too.

Her first impression of Charlie, however, was a disappointment. She saw him when he arrived from the railway station — a dusty-looking travel-stained figure, his face shaded by a battered hat. Oh dear, was this Charlie Maunsell, she thought.

That evening they met at Arthur Hall's home and Evelyn found herself confronted by a tall, handsome young man. Surprise, surprise, it was Charlie Maunsell. After a refreshing bath he had brushed his blond hair until it gleamed and then changed into a well-cut suit. When Evelyn started a conversation with him, she found that he had a sense of humour very similar to her own. He made life in the outbck sound like an adventure, but he was still very much a gentleman.

The more Charlie talked, the more Evelyn realised why his mother and sisters were so proud of him. He was the sort of man she had dreamed of meeting on board ship, and just as good looking as his sisters.

Charlie had only a week's holiday before taking up his new position. During that time he and Evelyn were scarcely apart. She felt very at ease with him; it was as though they had known each other for years. And not only was Charlie the most attractive man she had ever met, but he treated her like a princess. Having found him and being so much in love, how could she bear to go back to England and staid old Reggie Grimwood?

As his week's holiday drew to a close, Charlie realised that he, too, had found the girl he wanted to marry. As cattle mustering was scheduled on Mount Mulgrave, it was impossible for him to extend his visit. He knew he must act quickly and propose before Evie left Australia. If he did not do so now, she would leave with Mrs Dean for South America and he would never see her again. It was now or never.

Fired by love and admiration, and encouraged by his sisters, after dinner one night Charlie took Evie into the rose garden. He told her that he loved her and wanted to marry her. He also confessed that they would have to wait. Charlie was very honest with Evelyn and told her that although he knew a great deal about cattle and horses he had nothing in the bank. All he had inherited from his father was a crumbling old house in distant County Limerick, an estate that made no money and was unsaleable.

The Maunsells were Anglo-Irish landowners, with a pedigree going back to the Normans. Charlie's grandfather had been a kind and compassionate landlord to his tenants during the Irish famine of the 1840s when the potato crop had been attacked by blight, foregoing rents from the estate's tenants. Unlike many other landlords who evicted their tenants, Charlie's grandparents had funded soup kitchens. Being left deep in debt, they emigrated to Australia and settled in the Manning River district.

Charlie's father had grown up in Australia but was proud of his Anglo-Irish heritage. When he died, Charlie had been only sixteen, but had had to assume financial responsibility for his mother and sisters. He took a well-paid but boring job in a bank, paid his sisters' school fees and did his best to replace his father as the breadwinner. When Frances married wealthy young Arthur Hall, his mother and other sister were able to take up residence as long-term visitors with the Halls, and Charlie had been able to return to the land. For more than ten years now he had worked on properties in Queensland, including Paddy Callaghan's Mount Mulgrave Station. Following Callaghan's sudden death in a shooting accident, the executors offered Charlie the job of getting the property into shape and listing all the stock in order to sell it for a good price.

What if she were to rough it with him, Evelyn proposed. Could they manage on his salary? Charlie was delighted.

When Evie told Tim and Rupert that Charlie had asked her to marry him, she expected them to advise her to return home and think it over. But no — her brothers liked and admired Charlie and thought he was the right man for her. Rupert pointed out that a young man who was such a devoted son and brother would make an excellent husband.

Mrs Maunsell and her daughters were also very keen that Charlie should marry Evelyn. They felt she had the necessary strength of character and sense of adventure to face the hardships of pioneering.

Charlie wrote to Evelyn's father asking for his consent. Evelyn also wrote a letter, filled with praise of the Maunsell family and about New South Wales, which was all she had yet seen of Australia. She described Charlie's widowed mother as 'very ladylike' but with 'the saddest face [she] had ever seen'.[2] Jane Maunsell had lost her parents in the Indian Mutiny, then buried two children of her own who had died of dysentery, and finally lost her husband.

Once the week was over, Charlie headed north to his new job on Mount Mulgrave. Evelyn longed to go with him but cared enough about her family in England to wait for their response. In the meantime her brother Rupert had secured a job in Mitchell, Queensland, and left to find a home there for Phoebe and himself, as well as Mrs Maunsell, who would now live with them.

While waiting for a reply from her parents, Evelyn decided to take up an invitation from Rupert to stay with him and help prepare the house.

While Evelyn had written to her mother explaining she was in love and wanted to go and live with Charlie on a Queensland cattle station, she had said nothing of Charlie's finances. Nor had she mentioned the fact that Queensland was known as a place of tropical disease, where Charlie's two brothers had died of malaria and where the wet season lasted for months.

There were other dangers too. Far north Queensland in 1911 was the scene of some of the bloodiest fighting in Australia between Europeans and Aborigines. It was hardly the place for a delicately reared girl to live. But Evelyn was certain that she wanted to marry Charlie. Once she received her parents' approval, she began the long journey north to begin her life with him.

From Mitchell, Evelyn travelled to Brisbane then took a steamer to tropical Cairns, at that time a small, rather ramshackle port largely surrounded by rainforest. A crowd of men waited at the quay. Just as tall and handsome as she remembered him, Charlie was there among them. With a lump in her throat and fighting back tears of joy and excitement at seeing him again, Evie walked down the gangplank and fell into her fiance's arms. Two days later, on 21 July 1912, they were married.

For years afterwards Charlie would tease Evelyn about having to pay half a week's wages to obtain a special licence so they could get married immediately in St John's Anglican Church, thus avoiding the delay of calling the bans in church. Evie was totally unused to the tropical heat and high humidity. Although she looked elegant, she felt hot and uncomfortable during the noisy wedding reception. There were no relatives present but Charlie's racing friends and Queensland cattle barons, as well as most of the hotel residents, attended. It seemed to her that almost everyone in Cairns knew Charlie and wanted to wish him luck.

She heard some guests at the wedding reception talking about Mount Mulgrave Station as though Evie was off to Mars, which she found rather alarming. Some of them seemed convinced that Charlie Maunsell was crazy to take her to the wilds. 'That English girl will never stick it out,' said one of Charlie's friends to Dick McManus, who had worked as a station hand on Mount Mulgrave before becoming its purchasing agent in Cairns. Dick knew how tough it was out at the station, and how dangerous, but said nothing about that to Evie.

The wedding guests had underestimated Evelyn Evans — she was much tougher than she looked. Despite the primitive conditions and isolation Evelyn faced on her arrival at Mount Mulgrave Station, she was determined to stay there and make a success of the property — and her marriage.

❦ ❦ ❦

They arrived at Mount Mulgrave after a 400-kilometre journey by train, buckboard and buggy. Evelyn was exhausted but Charlie went

The buckboard which carried Evelyn on her honeymoon.

straight to the stockmen's quarters to find out what was going on and left it to old Maggie to show Evelyn around. Evelyn found it unnerving watching Maggie, a Palmer River Aborigine, smoke a pipe. Maggie showed her to the main bedroom, which had galvanised-iron walls and roof, a concrete floor, no ceiling and exposed rafters. The room lacked a wardrobe or a chest of drawers. All Evie found there was a small, cracked toilet mirror, a few wooden pegs on which to hang clothes and an iron bedstead with a lumpy horsehair mattress.

On isolated Mount Mulgrave Station, whose cattle runs and outstations made it one of the largest properties in Queensland, Evelyn was amazed to realise how frugally Paddy Callaghan had lived. In England, possession or management of broad acres automatically included a handsome home with all amenities and perhaps an art collection and a library of leather-bound books. Mount Mulgrave Station was stark and uncomfortable, the ceilings unlined so that without the protection of a mosquito net, spiders, bats, carpet snakes and even the odd small goanna fell from the ceiling onto the bed below. Floor-length windows in both the bedroom and sitting room led to the veranda; they were fitted with heavy wooden shutters with holes bored in them at eye-level so Callaghan could shoot at 'those damn myalls' (wild Aborigines) who might attack the station.

As Maggie showed Evelyn around, she told her about Mr Bowman, of the neighbouring Rutland Plains cattle station, who had recently been speared and left for dead by the 'myalls' — wild Palmer River people. Evelyn now realised that her new surroundings were not just primitive but also highly dangerous. Charlie had not told her anything about Mr Bowman's murder, although she had noticed the conversation had gone very quiet at the wedding reception whenever the Bowmans' names were mentioned.

That night after dinner, when Charlie and his new wife went to their bedroom, Evelyn was horrified to find it full of fruit bats squeaking away in the rafters. Eventually the noise quietened as the bats flew out to their nocturnal feeding places, but it was soon replaced by the distant drone of a corroboree from the Aboriginal camp celebrating the arrival of 'new Missus belonga Boss'.[3]

It puzzled Evelyn that as soon as she had arrived, Mrs Lakeland, the station cook, had prepared to depart. Mrs Lakeland, whose

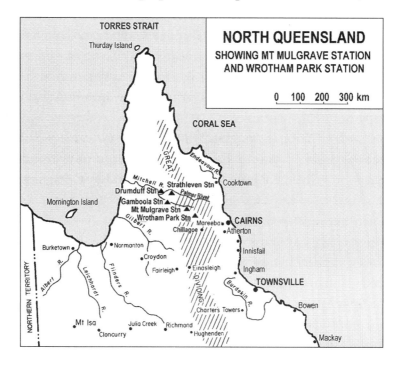

husband was a gold prospector, could shoot a gun as well as any man. As she was saddling up her horse Evie begged her to stay. Having come from London she knew nothing about outback cooking. But Mrs Lakeland refused, replying that it was nothing personal, but she just could not work with another woman in her kitchen. Her swag was packed and nothing Evie could say would change her mind.

Tom Graham, the odd job man, took pity on Evelyn, who was now faced with running the domestic side of things. Tom taught Evie how to make damper and bread, staples of the station diet. Bread was made in an old wooden tub, covered with a blanket and placed close to the fire all night. The next morning the dough was kneaded, made into loaves and replaced in the tub until midday when, having risen, they were baked in a hot oven.

Evie channelled all her energies into trying to improve conditions on Mount Mulgrave: running the store, cooking, creating a garden and making the property a success.

She encountered none of the antagonism that had met Jeannie Gunn arriving at the Elsey. The stockmen on Mount Mulgrave were very polite and respectful. But apart from Tom Graham and old Rudolph Morisset, who both became good friends, she did not see a great deal of the other men, who ate in their own quarters.

One of the many jobs that Evelyn took on was overseeing the washing of not only her own and Charlie's clothes but the unmarried stockmen's as well. This was not a simple job. She had first to make cakes of soap rather than getting expensive loads brought in from Cairns. Making soap entailed dissolving caustic soda in water, then pouring in melted fat that had been strained through muslin. The mix was then boiled gently before being poured into trays. Once hard, it was cut into cakes.

One of the Aboriginal hands, Albert, turned out to be Evie's most loyal helper. Usually dressed in a white jacket and trousers, he was far better at doing the washing and ironing than the house girls Evie had to help her. Albert also did most of the heavy work around the house. Albert came from the Wide Bay district near Brisbane and had been trained as a doorman and driver by a local doctor who had later taken him to Cooktown. Albert's Wide Bay people were enemies of the Mitchell River people around Mount Mulgrave — he was so scared of them and their fearsome reputation that he refused to venture far from the manager's house.

Albert and Maggie told Evie that Aborigines from the Mitchell, Palmer and Coleman rivers hated Aborigines from other tribes entering their territory nearly as much as they hated the Europeans who had taken their land. Some years later, a Coleman River Aboriginal girl Evie named Mary came to work at Mount Mulgrave Station. Evie promised Albert he could marry Mary if he taught her to speak English. There were no kinship laws that prevented them from marrying, even though the Coleman River people were reputedly unfriendly with Albert's tribe. When they eventually did marry Charlie built them a separate house on the property and the couple would stay with the Maunsells for years.[4]

Evelyn's recollections in the book *S'pose I Die* reveal the warmth of her long-term relations with, among others, Maggie, Mary, Albert, and Finlay Callaghan, who was believed to be Paddy's illegitimate son. These people served the Maunsells devotedly at Mount Mulgrave and later followed them to the Atherton Tableland. Charlie Maunsell had grown up on a cattle property where he had played with Aboriginal children as a boy, and he spoke several Aboriginal languages fluently. Although he had worked with both Paddy Callaghan and 'Terrible Jimmy Collins' of Koolburra Station,[5] both of whom had reputedly treated the Aboriginal people appallingly, Charlie did his best to treat indigenous people fairly. He followed the custom of the time of employing them as stockmen in return for the right to rations for themselves and their dependents and distant relatives. He saw that each Sunday Aborigines who lived on the property received rations of tea, sugar, meat and tobacco from the station store and, when necessary, new clothes and work boots. The men also received a small wage, which was supposed to be kept in trust for them by the Queensland Government.[6]

✤ ✤ ✤

While many of the stockmen at Mount Mulgrave Station were rough gold miners, Evie found to her surprise that Rudolph Morisset, who lived in a shack built onto the outside kitchen, was a highly educated man who had been to Sandhurst. He was the son of Lieutenant-Colonel J.T. Morisset, one-time commandant of the Norfolk Island convict settlement.

Morisset had once been a dashing officer in the Queensland Native Police Force. Despite living roughly for most of his life, he maintained gentlemanly habits and was a fount of local knowledge. Like many men who came to Cape York as gold miners and were now living in or around the property in ramshackle slab huts, Morisset had gambled his money away. He still owned an impressive library of leather-bound books, kept up to date with gifts from his sister. One of Morisset's books was a copy of Jeannie Gunn's *We of the Never-Never*, published a few years earlier and then very popular. Morisset lent it to Evelyn but made her promise not to read the final chapter, in which Mrs Gunn's husband dies of malarial dysentery (the same disease which had killed Charlie's brothers).

Over dinner Rudolph and Charlie would reflect on life at the station during its previous owner's reign. At meals old Paddy Callaghan, a giant of a man, had sat like an Irish chieftain at the head of a long trestle table, surrounded by his stockmen, including his part-Aboriginal son, Finlay.

Paddy, the rough, tough cattle baron who had started Mount Mulgrave, had arrived in Australia from the peat bogs of Ireland with the proverbial shilling in his pocket. He was a hard man who had worked in far north Queensland as a bullocky, carting telegraph poles for the telegraph line. Later he had gone into business for himself in partnership with a butcher to supply gold prospectors with meat. He had made more money doing that than the miners. When Paddy and his mates Jack Edwards, Tom Leslie the butcher, and Jack Duff had arrived at the river, they had encountered trouble from Aborigines, who rolled rocks down on them as they drove cattle up to the Palmer River. This was virtually unmapped country, and a war was going on between Aborigines and the white men who pushed north with their cattle. From then on Paddy and Jack Duff had carried guns everywhere and made a point of shooting as many Aborigines as possible.[7] Ruthlessness and cruelty made these men a great deal of money.

Paddy had bought leases on a number of properties to hold his stock, including Mount Mulgrave. Although he was a millionaire by the time he came to live on the station, he lived frugally. While some pastoral owners let the Aborigines take a few bullocks now and again, Paddy had been a man who felt outraged every time a beast was speared. He also had a reputation for kidnapping Aboriginal women and raping them.

The horrific stories Evelyn must have heard were hinted at in articles written by Jessie Litchfield, editor of the *Northern Territory Times* and one of the first women journalists in the north of Australia to write about the legacy of hatred the evil dealings of some white men had engendered. In her *Far-North Memories* Litchfield described how:

> fully nine out of every ten murders in the North have
> been due, directly or in part, to unauthorized interference
> with gins [a usual term for Aboriginal women at this
> time]. Not all the true facts ever get into print, of course,
> but those who have been privileged to peep behind the
> scenes know more than the general public can ever know,
> or ever want to know.[8]

Evelyn could understand why the Aborigines hated Callaghan and men like him and looked for opportunity to take revenge.

Paddy Callaghan lived and died by the gun. Fearing an attack by the Mitchell River people, he slept with a loaded revolver by his side. One morning as he was rolling up his swag the revolver accidentally discharged and killed him.

❦ ❦ ❦

Besides Maggie, Albert, Mary and Finlay, Finlay's Aboriginal sister, aged about nine, also helped in the house. The European staff included Johnny Seibel, the head stockman, whose father had been a butcher on the Palmer River during the gold rush, and Tom Graham, who looked after fences, brought in the firewood and sometimes went out on the musters as cook.

Following Mrs Lakeland's departure, a new cook, Sin Sin Yu, arrived from Cairns, but proved very disappointing. He could not bake bread and had no idea what to do with dried and smoked salt beef — both standard fare in the outback. Fortunately, once again Tom Graham came to Evie's rescue. He taught her how to soak the beef overnight, change the water a few times to get rid of most of the salt and soften it up before making a beef stew.

Evelyn learned a great deal from her Aboriginal staff. Before the Aborigines at Mount Mulgrave became accustomed to European food or 'tucker', they supplemented the station diet of salt beef with other meat including roast crocodile. They also regularly caught fish in the river. The Aboriginal boys often caught young pigs and brought them in for fattening. Lizards, goannas and rock pythons, which looked like chicken when cooked, were wrapped in green leaves and covered with hot ashes in the camp fire.

The Aboriginal women on the station would sometimes take Evie with them when they went out hunting or to have a *bogey* (swim). Evie was fascinated to see they ate all kinds of food that were virtually unknown to white people, lily roots from the lagoons being one delicacy that they would dive for. They were excellent swimmers and never seemed to tire of frolicking among the blue lilies. The Mitchell River women collected seeds and fruit and wove intricate long fish-trap baskets from reeds. They also made a kind of bread from the nuts of the pandanus palm.

The women taught Evelyn how to make fire by spinning between her palms a firestick, which was inserted into a small hole cut in another stick and held firmly on the ground with one foot. As sparks appeared, grass was pushed down with the other foot. The spinning was kept up until there was enough smouldering grass to create a flame.

Despite their company, Evie was often lonely when Charlie was away on musters or other station work. She would eat her evening

A woman of the Mitchell River (Yir Yoront) people, painted and feathered for a corroboree.

meals alone, with time to reflect on the society she had once enjoyed in a life that now seemed so far away. She missed her large family dreadfully.

When Charlie returned she would be so glad to see him that she chattered away nineteen to the dozen about petty incidents and domestic concerns. Charlie rarely talked in the saddle except to issue orders and was not comfortable with such a flow of words. Without speaking, he would get up from the table and walk outside, preferring the silence of the outdoors.

This must have hurt Evie but she forgave him. Charlie was a good man and for Evie what mattered was her husband and her marriage. She was determined to stick it out and make things work. She knew how much Charlie wanted to make a success of this job and that he would hate to have to go to London with her and seek employment in an office.

Charlie was a thorough bushman, and like so many bushmen who had worked hard and endured tragedy, he was loath to show his emotions. He had never known his two elder brothers, who had died before he was born. Later, when his father died he had had to make the coffin and bury him.

To occupy herself while Charlie was away, Evie kept a journal. She was also kept busy with the store and garden, and tending to any crisis that developed.

As she was neat and methodical, Evie found she enjoyed the job of storekeeper. All dry goods and tools came out from Cairns by bullock wagon at six-monthly intervals. Evie ordered dry goods and clothing through Charlie's old friend Dick McManus, the man who had given her away at her wedding.

The six-monthly order to the station agent was always similar and included goods for her and Charlie, for the stockmen's kitchen and to sell in the store when travellers called in.[9] Evie also did the book-keeping and sewed dresses for the Aboriginal women, who would otherwise have gone around half naked or in rags, as they had in Callaghan's day. She cared for the station Aborigines when they fell sick or injured themselves, relying on her limited medical knowledge and using her own small supply of medicines and bandages.

Nothing was ever wasted in the outback. Evelyn made pillowcases or tea towels from used calico flour bags, while smaller calico bags were used to hang salt beef. Evie used the jute bags from the coarse salt to line the walls of the tin house in an attempt to make it more 'homely'.

When she arrived at Mount Mulgrave Station, the only vegetable available was pigweed, which had spread over the damp ground where the kitchen waste was thrown away. People ate pigweed to avoid scurvy at a time when the bush diet consisted almost exclusively of salt beef and damper.

Evie was very keen to supplement the pigweed with crops from a vegetable garden. She had listened to Charlie's advice about what to plant in the fertile river flats after her first Big Wet. The Cape York Peninsula was known as a place where 'nine months [were] summer and three months Hell'.[10] The wettest months were January and February after which the rains eased off. April to October was largely dry, with November seeing a build-up in humidity and the beginning of the Wet.

It became obvious during Evelyn's first Wet that while Pat Callaghan's corrugated iron house could resist white ants, he had built it too close to the river. As the rain fell the house became invaded by red-back spiders, scorpions and centipedes. Snakes also became a pest. There were snakes in the store, snakes in the saddle room, snakes in the blacksmith's shop, snakes in the kitchen, in the bedroom and behind the chintz curtain that covered Evelyn's dresses. On one occasion Evelyn was bitten by a scorpion and on another by a red-back spider; both bites were extremely painful. Charlie sterilised his penknife in the flame of a match, cut the bites, sucked out the poison and sterilised the wounds by pouring methylated spirits over them.[11]

Floodwater from the Little Mitchell, a tributary of the main river, joined the Mitchell River a quarter of a mile downstream from the house. Often it threatened to bank up the main stream and flood the house. If that happened, large canvas bags were hurriedly made in which to hang food. Old timber was carried to the base of the highest tree in case a platform had to be built in the branches as a last-ditch retreat should the river continue to rise.

During the first wet season Evelyn experienced, the water rose until it lapped the edge of the veranda, then the rain stopped, and slowly the water level receded. At least for that Wet the worst was over.

After April, once the waters had subsided and the ground was dry enough, Evie was keen to begin the garden. She spent many days down on the river flats supervising the ploughing and planting — maize, sweet potato, silverbeet, turnips, carrots, potatoes and more.

The subsiding waters had left stagnant pools — breeding grounds for *anopheles* mosquitoes, which plagued Evie. Unfortunately, the *anopheles* mosquito spreads malaria, but Evie was ignorant of this.

On the western end of the homestead veranda, Charlie also built a fernery for Evelyn. Evelyn loved the fernery and hosed it down each evening before dinner. She also ordered ornamental plants from catalogues and received cuttings from various neighbours. Before long the homestead was surrounded by a beautiful tropical garden.

Mango seedlings, a present from their neighbours at the much larger Wrotham Park Station, flourished as did the banana trees, pawpaws, custard apples, oranges and lemons which Charlie and Evelyn planted together with the help of Albert.

By the following November, Evie was pregnant. With heavy storms signalling the start of the next Wet, Charlie and the men set out to make their last trip around the property before Christmas.

Charlie had only been gone a few days when Evie was hit by malaria. Feverish and drenched in perspiration, she collapsed into her bed. The weather was extremely hot and humid, and without a generator there was neither refrigeration nor overhead fans. In an attempt to lower Evie's temperature, faithful Albert placed her on a wicker stretcher on the back veranda.

Malaria causes a painful enlargement of the spleen and total loss of appetite. Unable to eat and perspiring heavily Evelyn became delirious. At times she called out 'Charlie, Charlie' even though she knew that he was far away and could not hear her.

Before World War I and for many years after, the standard treatment for malaria was a teaspoon of quinine, made from *chinchona* bark (eventually replaced by far more effective anti-malarial drugs). Evie had already suffered mild bouts of malaria which she had treated herself. Quinine was extremely bitter to taste and was taken dissolved in hot water or alcohol (to make it act faster) and recommended to be taken twice daily. There was no doctor around to warn Evelyn that quinine was a toxic substance that all pregnant women should avoid.

Between bouts of fever, she dosed herself twice daily with quinine in water. The third dose of quinine brought on a show of blood, followed by a searing pain in her lower abdomen. Then the foetus came away from the womb.

Too weak to help herself, all Evelyn could do was to lie there bleeding, convinced she would die. The once white sheets and nightdress were dark with her blood, her long hair matted with perspiration. The bleeding would not stop, she had no anti-coagulants and no possibility of blood transfusions.

Her brow damp, Evelyn tried to collect her thoughts to speak to Albert. As she became weaker and drifted in and out of consciousness she was afraid that Charlie would return and be confronted by the terrible sight of her putrefying corpse, since Albert and Maggie would be too scared to bury her without Charlie's permission.

Charlie had been haunted by the memory of burying his father and Evelyn wished to spare him another harrowing experience. She wanted Albert to bury her as soon as she died. Charlie could read the funeral service over her grave later. Albert scarcely left her side but could do little to help, apart from trying to fan away the flies which gathered on her lips and around her eyes. The nearest doctor was five hours away on horseback. Rain had turned the surrounding country into a bog. Even had Albert been able to contact neighbours they would have been unable to come to Evelyn's rescue.

'Albert,' she whispered through cracked lips. 'S'pose I die, you dig a hole and put me in it, and cover me up, and tell Boss I bin lose em piccaninny.'

Albert looked horrified and pleaded, 'You no more die, Missus. You no more die.'[12]

The next day Albert asked her permission to borrow Charlie's gun. Although Charlie had told her never to let any of the Aborigines take a gun, Evelyn was too sick to care. She told Albert he could take the one which she kept loaded by the bed whenever Charlie was away.

Albert was gone for so long that Evelyn thought he must have tripped over and shot himself like Paddy Callaghan. Finally he returned driving a cow and her calf before him and holding a brolga's egg and two dead wild ducks. He told her he would make her something nice to eat. He milked the cow and baked a custard with the brolga's egg and brought them to her. Evelyn had not eaten for more than two weeks and felt nauseated by the custard but she allowed herself to be spoon-fed because she did not want to hurt Albert's feelings. He had steamed the duck and she managed to eat a little of the flesh and drink some duck broth, which gave her strength.

Evelyn knew the Mitchell River men would have speared or clubbed Albert to death had they caught him away from the homestead and on foreign ground. She was grateful he had risked his own life to save hers.

Finally Evelyn heard the clatter of hoofs that signalled Charlie and the stockmen were home. She tried to rise from her bed but was still so weak she fell over. The sight of his wife lying on the concrete floor, her long hair matted, her clothes stained with dried blood, gave Charlie a dreadful shock. He picked Evelyn up, her emaciated body light as a feather, and laid her on the bed inside. He stripped off the soiled sheets from the stretcher she had been lying on, dumped them in the tub in the laundry and told Albert to take the stretcher away.

Charlie returned to the bedroom with a bucket of warm water from the kitchen. Gently and tenderly he gave Evelyn the first wash she had had for three weeks. He combed her tangled hair, fetched clean sheets and a nightgown, propped her up with four clean pillows and gave her a shot of rum. The wash and the clean sheets made Evie feel better than she had done for weeks.

Once Evie was settled, Charlie went out on horseback and rounded up another cow. He came back, took Evelyn's temperature, which was still high, and gave her another dose of quinine in hot milk. He removed his spurs and revolver, had a shower outside and then sat beside her on the bed.

When Evelyn awoke Charlie was lying on his back, eyes wide open staring at the ceiling. 'What's the matter?' Evie inquired.

'I haven't been to sleep all night. I never thought you'd see it through,' Charlie admitted stroking her hair tenderly.[13]

The next morning Charlie killed one of the cattle. He went into the kitchen and made beef broth by boiling down a fresh shin-bone.[14] Evelyn reckoned Charlie looked after her far better than any paid nurse would have done. The contrast between the tender side of his character and his rugged masculinity never ceased to amaze her. Underneath his tough bushman's exterior, Charlie was the most gentle and considerate man she had ever known. It was clear he loved her deeply and would do anything in the world for her.

After four days of his loving care she felt strong enough to walk to the shower unassisted. Charlie found excuses to do small repair jobs around the house instead of going out on his horse, which was totally unlike him. Normally he was never happier than riding about with his men mustering cattle and Evie realised what a sacrifice he was making for her. From her window she could see that the wet season was approaching. She knew that her husband should have been supervising the moving of cattle away from woodland areas where the gums and cedars were huge and dead branches could fall on the cattle and kill them.

Whenever the weather was not too hot, Charlie would take a mattress out, put it under a shady tree and carry Evelyn to it so he could keep an eye on her while he worked. She was still skeletally thin, her once manicured hands were freckled claws. He would now joke that he had paid 'two pounds five shillings for just skin and bone', referring to the money he had spent on their special marriage licence in Cairns, half a week's wages at that time.[15]

In spite of Charlie's care, it became apparent that Evie was not recovering and needed treatment by a doctor. Christmas had come and gone. The Wet was at its height, and the ground so soggy that the sturdy buckboard would never get through. If they could get to the railhead at Mungana, Charlie said, she would be fine. Was it possible she could sit on a horse? The trip to the railhead 100 kilometres away — two days' journey in the buckboard — could easily take five days on horseback, especially if Evelyn had to rest for long intervals.

Evelyn had been telling her husband that she was not as sick as she really was in order not to worry him. But the idea of spending days in the saddle feeling as ill as she did horrified her. She was not a brilliant horsewoman. She liked riding quiet, gentle Biddy but the last thing she wanted was a long ride on horseback in her present condition. But there was no alternative. She would have to ride to the railhead or stay at Mount Mulgrave.

As if Charlie did not have enough to worry about, a letter arrived from Evie's brother Rupert saying that Charlie's mother, Jane Maunsell, had had a severe stroke and was unlikely to live longer than a few days. Since Charlie's mother could no longer recognise anyone, Rupert said that it was pointless for him to make the long journey to see her. Poor, poor Charlie, Evelyn thought, so much responsibility and I who want to help him have become an additional burden. Once again she felt she just had to get well soon for Charlie's sake. Eventually Evelyn gave in to Charlie's wish to travel to the railhead on horseback, as long as she could ride Biddy.

The heat and humidity were stifling and Evelyn was often barely conscious. When she felt as if she was going to faint she had to cling to the pommel of the saddle to stop herself falling while Charlie supported her. Evelyn was so weak that Charlie rode beside her, putting his arm round her and urging her to 'try and do another mile or two'.[16]

Even so, Evelyn had to dismount every so often to rest under a shady tree. Charlie would give her a nip of brandy from his flask and by the end of each day Evie felt light-headed.

After six days they reached Mungana. Charlie had to leave Evie and go straight back to work at Mount Mulgrave. He put her in a first-class compartment on the train for Cairns in the charge of the guard, phoned his old friend Dick McManus and asked him to meet the train.

Dick was distressed at the sight of the once elegant and beautiful Evie. He drove her to the Imperial Hotel where she was looked after by Paulina, who had been maid of honour at Evelyn's wedding and was now married to Dick. Dick had to admit people had been totally wrong in their estimation of Evelyn. 'The English girl' had grit and pluck; Charlie was very lucky indeed to have a wife like her.

At the hotel Dr Kerwin examined Evelyn. He sent her to hospital immediately, saying that she must have had a constitution of iron to have survived. After two weeks' bed rest and treatment, Dr Kerwin allowed her back to the care of her friend at the Imperial Hotel. By then Evelyn was feeling much better and desperate to return to Charlie. Without telling Dr Kerwin what she intended to do, she asked Dick to book her a seat on the train and wire Charlie that she was returning.

Charlie met her at Mungana railhead with a hired buckboard and a driver who took them as far as the Walsh River crossing. They crossed the river by boat and found Finlay waiting for them on the other side with the Mount Mulgrave buckboard and the billy on.

For the rest of that year Evelyn suffered recurring bouts of hot and cold sweats due to intermittent malarial fever. Gradually they decreased but her malaria would reappear at unexpected times for years.

ᐤᐤᐤ

Charlie had been entrusted with the responsibility of getting the cattle station in order and making it pay so that Paddy Callaghan's relations could eventually sell it. Evelyn had never seen anyone work as hard as Charlie and his stockmen. Day after day and week after week they went out mustering while she was left alone on Mount Mulgrave with only Maggie, Albert and Mary, and some of the other locals for company. When Charlie was away Evie prayed that the Mitchell River warriors would not come to steal supplies or take revenge on her for atrocities other white people had committed against them.

Despite her prayers, one day a group of men from the Mitchell River tribe appeared at the station. Alert to their arrival Maggie walked out to meet the approaching men, who were brandishing spears tipped with broken glass. Inside, a terrified Albert and Evie listened quietly. As an Aborigine outside his territory Albert was in greater danger than Evie.

Aware that the boss and his stockmen were away mustering cattle, the tribesmen asked Maggie where the Missus and Albert were.

Even though the men were her distant kinsmen Maggie knew that they would spear her if she refused to answer. She told the men that the 'white Missus' was planting vegetables down by the river with Albert. To get to the vegetable garden the men had to pass the station store and Maggie knew that if they went down there, it was likely they would break in, take the sugar and treacle they loved and return to their camp with as much as they could

Evelyn at Mount Mulgrave with two young Aboriginal children.

carry. As long as they went to the store she would have time to warn Evie to hide.

Some of the Mitchell River men set off in single file towards the vegetable garden, but two of the most ferocious-looking padded up to the veranda intending to go into the house. It was impossible to scream a warning or they would all be speared.

While Maggie was talking to the men, Evelyn and Albert slipped into Evie's bedroom, Albert clutching a gun he had picked up. Although she could not understand what they were saying outside, it was clear from the men's threatening stance and the way they brandished their spears that they were looking for trouble. How she wished Charlie was there.

Evelyn's heart beat wildly as she heard the two Aborigines make their way into the house, spears in hand. She knew she had only seconds to find a hiding place or she could be dead.

Without a word Albert disappeared under the bed like a frightened dog in a thunderstorm and the long quilt hid him from sight. Evelyn thought quickly, then knelt down also and slid out of view as well.

Hardly daring to breathe, she heard the men in the living room. She watched terrified from under the bed as the barbed point of one of the men's spears pushed aside the curtain separating the bedroom from the living room and its owner peered around the room.

After what seemed like an eternity the two men retreated and the curtain fell back. Evelyn wanted to scream but held it in, remaining stiff as a corpse, far too scared to move. She stayed like this, praying she would not sneeze. The room was silent, suggesting the men had gone, but Evelyn did not come out until she heard Maggie say, 'All right now, Missus, him gone now.'[17]

Still shaking with fear, Evelyn crawled out from her hiding place followed by Albert, who with trembling hands attempted to brush the dust off his trousers. Evelyn clung to Maggie, shedding tears of relief.

ll ll ll

In 1914 World War I broke out. Rupert and Tim Evans, Evelyn's brothers, enlisted as did three of her brothers in England. Not to be outdone, Charlie went to the Cairns recruiting station and volunteered but was turned down on medical grounds. He had continuing problems with his hip and lower back dating back to a fall from a horse while he was working on his first station job in 1904. He was also told that producing food was vital for the war effort, which was a great relief to Evelyn.

During what was known as the Great War, station life went on much as it always had, except that Evelyn and the others did whatever they could to help the war effort. Evelyn taught the Aboriginal women how to knit scarves and socks, and they made huge quantities of beef extract to send to military hospitals overseas. In the second year of the war Evelyn sent dozens of jars of this nutritious 'beef tea' to Australian Army hospitals at Rouen and on the Somme. According to letters she received, it was much appreciated by wounded Anzacs who could not eat solid food.

She also made fruitcakes, using plenty of butter, eggs and dried fruit, which the Red Cross sent out to soldiers at the front. The Aboriginal kitchen hands thought cake making was great fun and never tired of beating the eggs. Evelyn added plenty of treacle to keep the fruitcakes moist. The Red Cross wrote to Evelyn and asked her to add glycerine and plenty of rum, so they would arrive in one piece.

Letters from England were depressing. Evelyn's home town of Ilford had been bombed by the Germans in an attempt to destroy the big Kodak factory that had been built there. Fortunately, Evelyn's parents were safe, but her mother's letters were full of news about young men Evelyn had known and who had been killed at the front in France or at Gallipoli.

Evelyn's brother Tim was one of the Anzacs who landed at Gallipoli in 1915. Evelyn was in Sydney with Charlie, who was trying to enlist there, when she heard that Tim would be arriving home on the hospital ship *Ballarat*.

Tim had apparently lain unconscious on the battlefield where he fell after a shell had burst over his trench. Five days later when a truce was called to bury the dead, Tim was found still alive.

Shell-shocked and a long time recovering his memory, Tim was sent from Sydney by train to a hospital in Brisbane. Eventually, Evelyn and Charlie arranged for him to be nursed back to health with them at Mount Mulgrave.

℘ ℘ ℘

The Big Wet of January and February 1917 was a very bad one, hot and humid, with a lot of Gulf fever (malaria). Evelyn came down with another bad attack and once again it caused her to lose a much-wanted baby. Although depressed, Evelyn had a strong and stable character and the motivation to get better. For Charlie's sake she picked up the pieces and started again in the hope that one day she would be able to bear a child.

But things were starting to look up for Charlie and Evelyn. By living modestly and working very hard they had saved enough money to fulfil their dream of buying their own land for the time when they would leave Mount Mulgrave. They decided that dairy farming would be the coming thing and they purchased fifty hectares of partly cleared land at Malanda on the Atherton Tableland and then bought another lot filled with gigantic trees, some of which had to be felled to make room for cows.

Mount Mulgrave was finally to be put to auction, and the O'Briens, Pat Callaghan's relatives, were grateful for everything Charlie had done to improve the station. They gave him some racehorses which he had bred and raced successfully, as well as twenty heifers from the station herd to start the Maunsells off with stock for their own new farm.

Leaving Charlie to finish business at Mount Mulgrave, once again Evelyn became a pioneer. She set off to the Atherton Tableland with their cattle and Charlie's beloved racehorses, accompanied by faithful Albert and his wife, Mary. They had insisted on leaving Mount Mulgrave and coming with Evelyn to help her to get the place into some sort of order. From the railway at Malanda they all rode in an open cart out to the property, sitting on top of their suitcases and small items of furniture. It proved to be a bumpy, uncomfortable journey.

On either side of the track Evie could see a tangled forest of huge cedars, silky oaks, rosewood and pine trees. She was relieved to find that, even when the days were hot, the nights were fairly cool. Often clouds hung so low over the mountains that one could walk through them, like mist on Scottish or English moors.

The southern part of the tableland was year-round far wetter than the open forest country around Mount Mulgrave. It seemed to be raining all the time in those pioneering days at Malanda and finding dry firewood was a problem. Evelyn made them all raincoats out of unbleached calico, waterproofed with lampblack and raw linseed oil. In spite of the constant rain, she appreciated the tableland because the climate was mild and more like that of England. She did most of the cooking in the open over a cast-iron camp oven, which she had never used before. She soon got used to it, and even managed to make bread, though some of it was hard as any stone.

There being no lovely homestead, once again Evelyn lived in a corrugated iron shed, this time much smaller than the one at Mount Mulgrave. The shed would remain 'home' until Alby Halfpapp, a pioneer settler and carpenter on the Atherton Tableland, at last built them a cottage and outhouses from black-bean timber. Then they could settle down to enjoy life on the edge of a wonderful rainforest.

With no shops nearby, Evelyn still had to plan ahead for all her purchases. Rations were brought in by bullock wagon and, as usual, some of the flour had weevils in it. But the sugar was no longer in one damp, sticky mass as it often had been out at Mount Mulgrave.

One morning, before Charlie had yet joined them at Malanda, Evelyn awoke to find all the heifers gone. If they could not be located, it would mean a huge financial loss, just as they were starting out on their own. There were no fences to keep the cattle in and the tracks through the scrub led in all directions. Even though the rain poured down, it was crucial to start searching for the herd immediately.

Evelyn knew she could not ask Albert and Mary to go separately to search for the heifers. Being from Wide Bay and the Coleman River they were afraid of what the Atherton Tableland Aborigines might do to them. So Albert and Mary set off searching for the cattle together while Evelyn went alone to adjoining farms asking if anyone had seen the missing herd.

Eventually Evelyn found the heifers and brought them home, but she resolved they *must* erect fences. She had a crosscut saw, maul and wedges, but the trees were new to her and she had no way of knowing what the best timber to use was. When she saw a fencing contractor fixing a bridge she asked for his advice. Armed with some local knowledge she located logs which Albert and Mary sawed into lengths and they all split into posts. They worked with extreme caution because venomous red-bellied black snakes were everywhere. It was back-breaking work but eventually they got the fences up.

Not long afterwards, Charlie and Finlay joined them, bringing more horses from Mount Mulgrave.

Finlay and some of the other Aboriginal hands from Mount Mulgrave decided to stay on at Malanda rather than return to Mount Mulgrave. They found the noisier and densely populated area diverting — and rich in game.

Before going into town on Saturday nights Finlay would often ask Evelyn, 'Missus, you want fowl for dinner tomorrow?'

Innocently Evelyn thought that Finlay was being given the chicken by kind friends in Malanda. So she thanked him and they had several nice Sunday lunches of roast chicken before she realised that Finlay was raiding the neighbour's hen house.

'Finlay, where are you getting these hens?' Evelyn demanded.

He looked genuinely surprised.

'Doesn't matter, does it Missus?' he asked.[18]

After that Evelyn refused all Finlay's kind offers of chicken for dinner.

♧ ♧ ♧

They were just about settled into their new wooden cottage at Malanda when Charlie received a letter offering him the position of general manager of the huge cattle runs of Wrotham Park and its three outstations, Gamboola, Highbury and Drumduff. Cattle and horses were in Charlie's blood far more than dairy farming and Evelyn recognised this. The Maunsells put a manager onto the Atherton property and went back to the hot, steamy Cape York Peninsula.

Wrotham Park, one of Queensland's largest cattle stations, now owned by the Australian Agricultural Company, lies 300 kilometres west of Cairns. Its 596,000 hectares of rich red soil in a good season today carry up to 35,000 head of cattle.[19] When the Maunsells arrived to manage it, Wrotham Park was a property of cleared land bisected by a broad winding river, which meant it was rarely affected by drought, and running 55,000 head of cattle.

At long last Evelyn was the mistress of a large station homestead complete with all amenities, the sort of home she had dreamed of having when she first came north to live in a tin shack on Mount Mulgrave Station.

Tranquil Wrotham, in the county of Kent, had been where Wrotham Park's founder, A.C. Grant, had been born. He had started his Queensland property as a holding station for beef cattle to be sold at top prices to the European and Chinese miners panning for gold along the Palmer River.

While Mount Mulgrave had remained in the hands of Paddy Callaghan, who had started it in 1874 at the height of the gold rush,

Wrotham Park had had many owner-investors. There had always been friendly relations between the two adjoining properties and joint musters were often held.

At the time Charlie Maunsell was invited to take it over, Wrotham Park and its outstations were owned by Tom Purcell, one of those cattle barons who, like Paddy Callaghan, could scarcely read and write but had a knack of predicting cattle prices, assessing risks and forecasting weather conditions.

Purcell was a good boss to work for. Under Charlie's skilful management, Wrotham Park set records and turned off about 3000 bullocks a year. Evelyn went back to her former job of running the station store and under her capable management they never ran short of food or work clothes. Charlie worked hard with the stock while Purcell remained in Brisbane and organised the sale of the beef cattle, eventually becoming immensely wealthy.

Evelyn was paid the piffling sum of two pounds a week to run the store, which carried enough supplies to service the entire district. Every quarter, Evelyn ordered dozens of shirts, trousers, and elastic-sided boots in different sizes, as well as plenty of blankets and everything else that men in the bush needed. Once more she ordered brooms, flour, jams, raisins, tomato ketchup, tobacco and clay pipes by the dozen for Wrotham Park and the outlying districts.

Wrotham Park Station was only about six miles from the Walsh Telegraph Office and the homestead was connected to it by telephone. The Maunsells had their own private line strung from tree to tree out through Gamboola and Highbury to Drumduff, nearly 160 kilometres away. With a large (by today's standards) 'mobile phone' Charlie could connect to the line anywhere he pleased so the head stations and the outstations were always in contact.

Before long, old Aboriginal friends and staff from Mount Mulgrave Station arrived looking for work at Wrotham Park. The first to arrive were Billy God-help-us, his wife, Kitty, and their children, who had walked forty kilometres across country to announce they would only work for Charlie.

Evelyn and Charlie Maunsell (on the right) with a group outside Wrotham Park homestead.

'Other feller boss no good,' said Billy, whose son was now old enough to go out mustering cattle.[20] So father *and* son signed on at Wrotham Park in order to work with Charlie.

Next to arrive were Maggie, her husband and their young son Robin. Evelyn was especially pleased to see Maggie whom she would never forget had saved her life by sending the threatening Aborigines down to the river when they had come to kill her. Evie and Maggie hugged each other joyfully.

Wrotham Park already had its own workers — Topsy, Dinah and Jessie — helping in the kitchen and in the vegetable garden. Work had to be rearranged to keep them all occupied or, as Evelyn knew, grievances could surface and they might fight among themselves. Evelyn kept Mary and Albert, who had also come with the Maunsells, on household duties, put Maggie in charge of the garden and told Kitty to help with the washing. They soon had a good vegetable garden, watered by hand from buckets carried from a creek by Maggie and other Aboriginal staff.

While relations between the Maunsells and their staff were good, the coming years would prove to be unhappy for many station Aborigines as government policies were implemented to round up Aborigines and send them to Palm Island Reserve. In 1919, the flu epidemic which swept the world hit the Cape York Aboriginal population particularly hard. Evelyn and Charlie were extremely concerned about the fifty or so Aborigines reliant on Wrotham Park, and wrote to the Minister for Health asking for medical supplies for them. In reply they received a large box of medicines, equipment and instructions, which they set about following immediately.

Slowly but surely the flu began taking its toll. As the Aboriginal stockmen and their relatives became ill they were brought to the homestead to be nursed. At one point Evie had more than thirty patients in the house. Using a combination of medicine, feeding and judicious periods in the sun (which Evie thought the best treatment), none of their patients died, unlike on neighbouring properties which had death rates amongst their Aborigines of more than fifty per cent. When they were well enough Evie sent her patients on walkabout so they could use their own bush remedies and build up their strength.

Towards the end of 1920 Charlie wrote to Tom Purcell to say he would be resigning early in 1921 because he wanted to take Evie home to visit her family and he wanted to see his own family property in Ireland.

Purcell refused to accept the resignation and suggested Charlie take twelve months' holiday on full pay and find a suitable person to take over as manager while he was away. The Maunsells persuaded Jack Hamill, head stockman and an extremely responsible man, to act as manager.

Charlie and Evelyn were due to sail for Europe in March 1921. Jack Hamill and the rest of the staff organised a 'surprise leaving party', any trip overseas in those days being a once-in-a-lifetime event to be celebrated in style.

On the night of the party, Evelyn and Charlie were out taking a walk. As they returned, the homestead seemed to be unusually brightly lit. They went inside and found that all the lights and lanterns had been put into service. The staff and stockmen had gathered in the dining room, which was decorated with coloured streamers. The table was groaning under the weight of plates of savouries and cakes and a selection of bottles of wine and spirits which, Evelyn noted, the mailman must have been smuggling in for weeks.

Jack Hamill read a testimonial signed by twenty-two of the staff of the four stations. 'We, the undersigned . . . wish you both a safe journey to the homeland and a safe return back to us all at Wrotham Park, and hand you this presentation.'[21] The gift was £75, a large sum for those days. As some of the station hands received only about £2 a week wages it represented a very generous gift indeed.

At the right moment Jimmy Ah Say, the Chinese cook, gave the Aborigines who remained on the station a signal to leave their own supper and to come inside the homestead. They gathered in the fernery and sang a song of farewell before inviting the Maunsells to their camp to attend a special moonlight corroboree. The men had painted their bodies and wore white feathers in their hair; the women beat time on their thighs with their hands, their eyes gleaming in the light of the fire. The rhythm of their chants and the tapping of the music sticks filled the air. Evelyn was touched to be witnessing the unique, mysterious ceremony, a sign of affection and loyalty from her Aboriginal friends. She was determined to bring back special gifts for them all — musical instruments she felt would be ideal.

Evelyn and Charlie spent two days in Sydney visiting Charlie's family, as well as the Halls at Thornleigh, and five Maunsell aunts, who were delighted to learn of the planned visit home and to County Limerick to see Ballybrood, the Maunsell family home. Each aunt took Evie aside and whispered how nice it would be if Charlie and she were to have a son to continue the family line and suggested that perhaps Ireland might work its magic on her.

The sea voyage to England was long and far from pleasant. Charlie and Evie both needed the ship's doctor in the Indian Ocean when ten days' rough weather brought on a flare-up of the malarial fever from which they both suffered intermittently.

In the Red Sea their ship passed through a sandstorm so thick the land became invisible and the deckhands were forced to sweep sand from the decks. The banks of the Suez Canal were lined with British soldiers in uniform who called longingly out to the ship bound for England, 'Tell [King] George we want to go home.'[22]

Evelyn and Charlie left the ship at Toulon in the south of France and took a train across the country. When they crossed the English Channel, Evelyn recalled how she had made that crossing as a young girl, a paid companion to an elderly widow, and could hardly believe how much her life had changed since that fateful voyage.

After landing at Dover, they took the boat train to Victoria Station, marvelling at how green the countryside looked. From Victoria Station they drove down the Mall, past Buckingham Palace to Liverpool Street Station, and took the train to rural Ilford.

They were disappointed to find no one on the station to greet them. Then old Jock, the ticket collector, recognised Evie and told her that her father had met every single train from London from morning to night and had only just returned home. There were no cabs to be had so they decided to walk and paid the only porter to help Charlie wheel their luggage on a trolley.

When they reached Evelyn's childhood home, the porter tipped all the luggage on the front drive, leaving Charlie to guard it. Evie rang the front door bell and hammered with her fists on the door, so excited was she at the thought of seeing her family again after so many years. Evie's mother opened the door and burst into tears and then her sister arrived. They cried, laughed and hugged each other and were so excited that they forgot all about poor Charlie sitting on the suitcases.

Evie's letters had described Charlie as a typical Australian bushman, tall, sunburned and at home in the saddle, but ill at ease in cities. So her family had expected him to be awkward, a little uncouth and unsociable. Discovering their Irish-Australian son-in-law was a handsome, quietly spoken gentleman with perfect manners was a pleasant surprise for Alderman and Mrs Evans.

Evie felt good to be living in a solid, handsome brick house again. The house had not changed; it was just as she had remembered it with bow windows on the ground floor, the wide curved staircase, and bedrooms and bathrooms upstairs. That tin-roofed shed on Mount Mulgrave, with its concrete floor and holes in the shutters to shoot threatening Aborigines, seemed a long, long way away.

After a happy time at Ilford they stayed with one of Evelyn's brothers in Wiltshire. He drove them around Bath and Bristol and to the beautiful villages of the Cotswolds area, with their mellow stone houses and walled gardens full of hollyhocks and herbaceous borders.

Their next step was to take the boat from Liverpool to Dublin. In 1921 there was still a great deal of unrest in Dublin, following the Troubles and the War of Independence. Roads and railways had been damaged in fighting between the Irish Republican Army and British troops. At the port of Dublin their luggage was searched on arrival by customs officers looking for guns.

Charlie hired a taxi-cab and they paid the driver's hotel expenses to drive them to Limerick. One night on the main road to Killarney they saw the door of a cottage fly open and an old man and his wife come running out, scattering pigs and fowl in all directions. 'Stop, stop!' they shouted. 'The bridge was blown up.'[23]

Had the couple not warned the Maunsells, they would have fallen ten metres into the river. Their driver managed to find an alternative route to the charming town of Limerick. They stayed at the Royal George Hotel, which had bags piled round the windows and doorways in case of shooting or bombs thrown by the patriots. The Sinn Fein, Eamon de Valera and his followers wanted an independent Ireland with its own parliament. They felt Michael Collins had sold them short signing the treaty with the British Government which meant that Eire had to acknowledge the British king. This act would cost Collins his life.

Their driver took them to Ballybrood, where the Maunsells had lived for 400 years, now standing deserted except for a farm manager occupying the servants' quarters. Ballybrood was built in Georgian style from imported stone. It had a long drive, a handsome front door, and a large stable yard behind the house with quarters for the servants. Ivy had run wild and covered most of the walls, clogging the gutters.

Evelyn was fascinated to see the house, especially the drawing room which contained beautiful old furniture covered with striped silk. It wasn't hard to imagine the house in the days when the Maunsells had entertained the cream of Anglo-Irish society.

The estate of Ballybrood still had nearly 200 hectares of arable land, which was rented out to tenant farmers. Ireland was desperately poor and their meagre rents were just enough to pay the rates and the farm manager's salary. Charlie, heir to the mortgaged property, had never had a penny from the place and nor had his father.

The bailiff-caretaker, whose name was Breen, showed Charlie the estate's books, and invited them to a very modest meal. Clearly, with the Troubles raging in Ireland and the Sinn Fein burning down country houses, selling Ballybrood was out of the question.[24]

The trip to Ireland was like a second honeymoon for the Maunsells, as Charlie had no cares or work to occupy him. And Evelyn would never forget the green of the fields of southern Ireland and the romantic appeal of Ballybrood. After they returned to stay with her parents at Ilford, Evelyn discovered to her delight that what Charlie's aunts had whispered *had* come true. The magic of Ballybrood had made her pregnant.

In October it was time for them to leave. They decided to take a ship that went via Canada and the United States. Their voyage from Liverpool to Quebec in the SS *Minnedosa* was a rough one. Evelyn, pregnant and worried about the baby, stayed in their cabin resting most of the time. Charlie, who enjoyed the rough seas, often ventured onto the deck. By the time the St Lawrence River was in sight, the weather was calm and Evelyn was able to join Charlie to gaze at the approaching Quebec shores lined with beautiful maple trees in autumnal shades.

They visited Montreal and New York as well as Niagara Falls, then travelled by train across the prairies and over the Rockies, eventually arriving at Vancouver. There they boarded a ship bound for Sydney. Though the Pacific crossing was smooth, Evelyn consulted the ship's doctor, anxious that nothing should go wrong after her previous miscarriages.

On their way north from Sydney, they stopped off at Brisbane to see Tom Purcell, by now in his seventies and very wealthy indeed. Purcell had bad news: he was planning to sell his interest in Wrotham Park. Charlie was taken by surprise at Purcell's announcement and wondered about his and Evelyn's future.

They arrived in Cairns in the first months of 1922 and Evelyn went straight into St Anthony's nursing home. Charlie returned to Wrotham Park to relieve Jack Hamill as manager. The staff were puzzled that Evelyn was not with him but Charlie, probably scared of yet another miscarriage, said not one word about the pregnancy, promising she would return soon. The staff were consumed with curiosity, but did not like to ask too many questions.

He handed out the presents he and Evelyn had brought back in their shipping trunks. They had purchased accordions and mouth-organs for the Aboriginal men, a gramophone and records for the staff, a new white suit for Albert, and fishing lines for Maggie and the other Aboriginal women.

On 8 May 1922 Ron Maunsell was born in the nursing home in Cairns — a perfectly healthy and sturdy baby. One of the first things Evelyn did was wire the good news to Charlie's aunts. Charlie came to Cairns to see his infant son and take Evelyn back to Wrotham Park.

Everyone was surprised to see Evelyn arrive holding a newborn baby wrapped in a shawl. Charlie had still not told anyone about her pregnancy. The staff were delighted and made a great fuss. Evelyn had never been so happy.

෴ ෴ ෴

As he had warned, Tom Purcell eventually sold Wrotham Park for a very good profit. By 1925 Charlie had had enough of working for the new owners and resigned. He and Evie now had their young son's future to safeguard and their dairy farm at Malanda to build up.

Leaving Wrotham Park was hard. They had become fond of their many staff, who were now like family. Charlie and Evie felt they could not leave behind faithful old Albert and Mary — or Kitty's

Charlie, Evelyn and Ron Maunsell on the Atherton Tableland.

daughter Josie — so the three staff came with them. It was a sad day for Evelyn when she left Dick and Maggie and the other faithful friends she had known since Mount Mulgrave days.

Jack Hamill, who had done a fine job as surrogate manager, also asked for his final cheque the day they departed and rode away from the homestead with them.

The Maunsells subsequently spent nearly twenty years on the Atherton Tableland carving out their home and farm from the scrub and watching young Ron grow up tall and strong like his father. Evelyn loved the crisp air and cool nights, the green grass and clear running creeks on the tableland. She worked hard but no harder than all the other women dairy-farming in the area. Cows always had to be milked, the separating done, the cream cans made ready for collecting early in the morning, and the butter churned and sent away by rail.

Dr Jarvis Nye from Atherton believed that these pioneering women worked far too hard and often kept them in hospital longer than necessary because he knew that as soon as they were home with a new baby or recovered from an illness or injury the women would go straight back to work milking cows — as Evelyn did.[25]

Albert and Mary, in spite of their attachment to Evelyn, could not take the cold and wet of the tableland and asked Charlie to arrange for their return to Cooktown, where Albert wanted to spend his old age. Josie also left to return to her Mitchell River people.

Once their son Ron went to boarding school, Charlie arranged for a teenaged boy from an orphanage to come to the farm to help. Evelyn mothered the abandoned Tony, who had been left on the steps of a Townsville orphanage, and helped him manage his wage as well as earn some additional money.

By October 1939 young Australians were enlisting in another world war. Ron signed up to the Royal Australian Air Force (RAAF) as soon as he was old enough. On his last day on the farm he helped his father with the afternoon milking as usual and in the evening they went into Malanda for his send-off party. It was pouring rain the night they farewelled Ron and the following morning he departed. Evelyn felt as if 'the bottom had fallen out of the world'.[26]

As soon as he was of age, Tony, too, left to enlist. Evelyn and Charlie were now working the farm on their own. Ron had told his parents that when the war was over he did not want to continue dairy farming and preferred beef cattle. When the opportunity arose, Evelyn and Charlie sold the property and retired for a while to a much smaller farm on the outskirts of Brisbane. By now Charlie was sixty and Evelyn was fifty-six, and the long hours of milking had become too much.

After his discharge Ron worked at sinking dams for a while and then went into a partnership with his parents. They bought Rio sheep station, close to Longreach in central Queensland.

Once again they experienced the pitfalls of the pioneering life. The house was basic and the laundry block was only four posts with a few sheets of galvanised iron over the top, a bench with two round tubs and a copper boiler set on an open wood fire. Winters can be freezing in Longreach, and Evelyn did the washing in two thick overcoats.

Charlie and Evelyn spent a year living there with Ron. During that time Rio Station was hit by a plague of black rats which gnawed away busily through the bottom of doors to get to food. It was horrendous, with rats everywhere. There was little the Maunsells could do but wait until the thousands of rats moved on, heading north for the Gulf of Carpentaria.

Evelyn had been longing for grandchildren and she and Charlie were happy when on 17 April 1954, Ron married Joan Meekin. Now with Rio in good hands, the Maunsells retired to Brisbane for the second time, where Evelyn worked very hard for the Country Women's Association (CWA). She was very fond of her daughter-in-law and thrilled by the arrival of three lovely granddaughters: Joanne, Margaret and Barbara.

Evie was very proud, too, when in 1968 Ron, who was extremely popular locally, was elected as a Federal senator. He remained in that position until 1981. Ron Maunsell would eventually sell his outback property of Rio to a neighbouring station owner, retire to Buderim and then move north to Cairns to live with one of his daughters.

Charlie Maunsell died in May 1970 aged eighty-seven; Evelyn died seven years later. One of the last things Charlie said to Evelyn was that he had never realised until he visited her home what a sacrifice she had made leaving a life of comfort behind to go with him to Mount Mulgrave.

Evelyn was able to reassure Charlie that it had not been a sacrifice for her. She had enjoyed pioneering the outback and sharing his life, tough as it had been. He had been the only man for her; and their long and happy marriage, and their handsome, successful son had rewarded them for a life of struggle.

CHAPTER

6

Catherine 'Katie' Langloh Parker

1856 – 1940

COURTESY NATIONAL LIBRARY OF AUSTRALIA.

Myrtle Rose White

1888 – 1961

ON THE DESERT FRINGE

'The outback is a cruel place,' wrote Jeannie Gunn to Jock McLennan, a former Elsey stockman, on hearing of the death of 'the Fizzer', the intrepid postman who had drowned crossing a river in the Never-Never.[1] Catherine Parker and Myrtle White would also experience the cruelty and pain of the bush, including flood, drought and red dust. Both of these determined, resourceful women had a gift for writing and both followed their husbands into some of the harshest regions on the planet.

Born during a sandstorm near Broken Hill, Myrtle Rose Kennewell nearly died when her tiny nostrils became blocked by flying sand. Her mother had been seven months pregnant and travelling by covered wagon in the Broken Hill area when she went into labour prematurely, miles from a doctor. Frantic with worry, Myrtle's father pitched their tent, placed his wife inside and drove hell for leather to try and find someone to deliver the child. Alone in the tent the labour continued until Myrtle was born. Swirling sand coated the baby and almost suffocated her before Myrtle's father returned with a woman who unblocked Myrtle's air passages and cut the umbilical cord.[2]

Katie Field was born over three decades before Myrtle. Her birth was supervised by her maternal grandmother at the Newland family home at Encounter Bay, South Australia. Martha Newland and Katie's grandfather, the Reverend W. R. Newland, would take a special interest in the education of their grandchildren, as they had their own children. They saw that Katie was a clever little girl and intended for her to learn Latin, Greek and French.

The Reverend and Mrs Newland were cultured people, well-travelled classicists in love with ancient Greece. They were determined that their granddaughters would not suffer by living in the outback when the family moved there around 1859, after Katie's father became interested in land opening up around the Murray and Darling Rivers. At Marra Station, the five young Fields — two boys and three girls — and their later siblings were tutored by their well-schooled mother and their classically educated father who exposed them to Greek myths and legends.

Katie's father, Henry Field, had come out from England as a young man in 1837 and run a pastoral property with his brother at Yankalilla, supplying meat to whalers at Encounter Bay. He and Sophy Newland, Katie's mother, were married in 1849. After his brother's death in 1860, Henry farmed around Encounter Bay until the move to Marra Station.

Once at Marra the children maintained contact with their grandparents, accompanying their mother on several visits back, including the one she made for the birth of Rosa Emily (Rosina) in 1860.

At Marra Station the girls, Jane, Katie and Henrietta, were cared for by an Aboriginal nursemaid named Miola. At bedtime she introduced the girls to the myths and legends of the Yuwaalaraay (Euahlayi) people, one of the largest Aboriginal linguistic groups in northern New South Wales. Miola related the ancient Aboriginal legends of Byamee, the sacred being or 'All Father' of her ancestors, as well as tales of Yuwaalaraay ancestral spirits like Yubbah the Carpet Snake, Ooboon the Blue-tongued Lizard, and Mouyi the White Cockatoo.

On hot summer afternoons at Marra Station while baby Rosina rested with her mother, Miola would take twelve-year-old Jane, six-year-old Katie and four-year-old Henrietta for a paddle in the Darling River. One fateful afternoon Miola and Jane swam to the middle of the river leaving the two younger girls in the shallows. A current seized Katie and Henrietta and swept them out of their depth. Both little girls screamed for help and thrashed about in terror. Miola and Jane swam over to save them. Miola dragged Katie to the bank thereby saving her life. Jane tried to save little Henrietta but Henrietta clung to her in terror and dragged Jane down.

Alone on the beach with Katie and unable to see either Jane or Henrietta, Miola ran to find Henry Field who was working close by. They returned to see Henrietta's corpse floating by the river bank but no sign of Jane. All hands were mustered to drag the river and finally it gave up Jane's body.[3] Clever, pretty little Jane had been the apple of her father's eye and he never forgot her. Katie, the second daughter, suddenly became the eldest but always felt that her sisters' deaths were her fault; had Miola not saved her she could have saved them instead.

In 1871 Sophy Field learned she was pregnant with her eighth child. As she was now in her mid-forties, doctors feared the birth could have complications. At this time Katie's two elder brothers were at school in Adelaide and perhaps the family decided it was time to rest from running a property. Henry Field left Marra Station in the hands of his brother-in-law and took a six-year lease on a house called The Lodge in Adelaide.

In the 1870s birthing practices were hazardous and maternal mortality rates very high. Katie took over the running of the house while her mother was in labour. After giving birth to a son named Edward on 11 April 1872, Sophy became weaker with puerperal (childbed) fever. As her temperature soared it became apparent the doctors could not save her and she died an agonising death.

Katie turned sixteen three days later. She was then in her final year at Miss Senner's School for Young Ladies in Palm Place (later part of St Peter's College, Adelaide, which her brothers had attended). She engaged a housekeeper to run the house and a nanny for Edward and, after they came out of a period of mourning, acted as hostess for her father.

Following Sophy Field's death, Katie's father decided to leave The Lodge and move to Glenelg. Although she wrote nothing down about their introduction, perhaps it was at one of her father's functions that she met tall, broad-shouldered Langloh Parker, a dashing grazier just as successful as her adored father. Langloh Parker was much older than herself, with the confidence and charisma of a successful man who has travelled the world. In fact, he was in many respects very similar to Henry Field. Both were tall, athletic, distinguished-looking men, and their careers had followed the same path in the wool boom. Both had gambled by borrowing large sums from the banks to buy stock — gambles which, due to seasons of good rainfall, had paid off handsomely with large wool cheques and stations sold for profits.

Katie, by now a very attractive young woman, seemed far more mature than her sixteen years. She knew her father was thinking of remarrying — to Mary Servante, a woman in her early forties, whom they both felt would make an excellent mother for baby Edward. Henry Field did not object when Langloh Parker, twice Katie's age, started sending flowers and paying his respects to Katie.

The highly eligible Langloh Parker was reckoned to be an extremely 'good catch'. A brilliant horseman, winner of many amateur steeplechases, he was charming, considerate and believed to be very rich. Langloh seemed fascinated by Katie. They went out riding together, suitably chaperoned, as Katie loved horses and riding as much as Langloh did. Katie was flattered by Langloh's attentions, enjoyed his company, and was the envy of her former classmates when she accepted a proposal of marriage from this charismatic, handsome, urbane man who had resisted marriage for so long. In her journal written later in life, Katie claimed Langloh had virtually 'plucked her from the schoolroom'. Today psychologists might deduce that Katie was marrying a father substitute.

Katie Field and Langloh Parker were married on 12 January 1875 at St Peter's Anglican Church, Glenelg, then a small fishing village. The bride was eighteen and the groom was thirty-five. She was taken everywhere by her proud husband, keen to show off his attractive, amusing young wife to friends and relations at balls and parties. They made a handsome couple. Langloh's investments were doing well and Katie was deeply in love. Since she was a superb rider, happiest on horseback, Katie was pleased to accompany her husband on brief trips to the outback, but the couple spent most of their time in the city — in Adelaide, Melbourne and Sydney.

In 1879 Langloh was planning to take his wife on her first trip to Britain and Europe when his business partner, Colonel Ward, announced he wanted to sell out. He asked Langloh to buy him out of the properties they owned.

The banks were loath to lend Langloh any more money, so reluctantly he had to borrow at eight per cent interest from the tight-fisted cattle baron Jim Tyson, to take control of all his isolated grazing properties. The largest of Langloh's properties was Bangate Station situated north-west of Walgett on the New South Wales–Queensland border.

In those days few educated women were prepared to endure the isolation, hardships and deprivation of bush life, especially if they had young children. Langloh told Katie he would live on Bangate Station, 800 kilometres from Sydney, and run the other properties from there, and gave her the choice of staying in Sydney or braving the outback with him.

Katie could not bear the thought of staying in Sydney without her husband, and insisted she would accompany him. Langloh was delighted but warned her she would be surrounded by rough boundary riders, stockmen and drovers; it was an almost exclusively male world. Knowing of Sophy Field's death in childbirth, Langloh insisted that, since there was no doctor close to Bangate, if Katie became pregnant she must spend the period of her confinement in Sydney. He did not mince his words when he told Katie:

> The bushman, out and out, will be terrified of you, and
> will think I'm a blamed ass to take you out there . . .
> However he may object to your being there, he'll do his
> level best for you when you are there![4]

Langloh also warned Katie that, without the diversions of Sydney, she might be bored in the outback. Furthermore, she would be

surrounded by hundreds of Aborigines. His words amazed Katie, who replied that she wasn't in the least afraid of Aborigines. She had played with Aboriginal children at Marra Station and been saved by an Aboriginal girl.

Katie told Langloh that while he was away she would spend her time riding and keeping a journal 'to remind me of things in my old age'.[5] In that journal Katie described lavish farewell parties and festivities to mark their departure. At one dinner given by Langloh's male friends she was presented with a pair of silver entree dishes — a token of their admiration that she had *chosen* to accompany her husband to the outback.

The vast Bangate sheep station was situated on the Narran River (Narran being a Yuwaalaraay word for 'winding'), a tributary of the upper Darling. The region had been explored by Sir Thomas Mitchell in 1846, who spotted its potential as sheep country. The Parkers' journey there was arduous and took almost a week by train, coach and buggy.

The journey started in Sydney. The Parkers went by narrow-gauge railway across Emu Plains and up the steep slopes of the Blue

Mountains, with the Nepean River lying far below them 'like a silvery carpet snake'.[6] Then came a bumpy, rattling journey by coach to Bourke, followed by several hundred more kilometres in the jolting station buggy drawn by four horses.

They stayed in bush inns whose patrons were 'in various stages of intoxication'.[7] Those not already dead drunk leered at her, and Langloh would hurry Katie away from them and into the private parlour which, more often than not, had a cracked mirror and armchairs draped in crocheted antimacassars stained with hair oil. Such bush inns, Katie dryly noted, nearly always boasted grand names like The Imperial or The Royal Hotel, whatever the socialist allegiances of the publican.

They ate dinners of greasy mutton and boiled potatoes followed by suet pudding, or jam roly-poly, or fried eggs and bacon from wild pigs. After one particularly vile meal, Langloh joked that when travelling through the outback you had to 'be prepared to eat a dead horse, and you generally are, so invigorating is the bush air'.[8]

Soon they were passing through black soil plains, which turned into sandy soil with grey-green saltbush and spinifex. Katie found the plains had a strange beauty of their own — with drooping, silvery-grey myall and coolibah trees bearing pink flowers hidden among their grey leaves under intensely blue skies. At first Catherine loved these skies. But the long years of drought which ate up their money meant that in time she would grow to hate them.

Beyond Lightning Ridge they passed through groves of casuarinas whose branches sang in the wind. It reminded Katie of the surging of the sea at beloved Glenelg, where her father had bought his house. Katie would later write that the Aborigines claimed the noise was the wailing of boys who had died before they could take part in initiation ceremonies designed to turn them into men.[9]

Bangate Station comprised 90,000 hectares of grazing land, some freehold and some leasehold, with a frontage of forty-seven kilometres along the winding Narran River, a tributary of the Darling, the river of Katie's bush childhood. The Narran flooded after rains and in drought seasons became a series of muddy waterholes. The sheep station itself resembled a small village with wooden huts and outbuildings, a station store, a saddlery and a blacksmith's shop.

The climate was a harsh one, varying from blazing heat in summer to freezing cold in winter. Katie's journal ignores the lack of sanitation and running water, nor does it mention the isolation. To Katie none of this mattered. When she arrived in 1879, she found Bangate delightful and spent her time riding with Langloh or on her own.

She soon discovered that the Aborigines who lived on Bangate and its surrounding lands were called the Noongahburrah, a branch of the Yuwaalaraay-speaking tribes whose hunting territories had stretched as far as Marra Station. Katie wrote of employing three part-Aboriginal girls as maids. One of them was an orphan whom Katie wanted to take under her wing, but she did not think it right for her to grow up alone at Bangate and was delighted when another Noongahburrah mother agreed to let Katie train her daughter to become a maid.

Katie Parker started what she called her 'bush book' long before Jeannie Gunn had published *We of the Never-Never*. In a strange co-incidence Katie wrote of Langloh by his Aboriginal name 'the Matah' ('senior man' in the Yuwaalaraay language) in the same way Jeannie called Aeneas Gunn, 'the Maluka', the term used by Yangman Aborigines. The Noongahburrah called Katherine 'the Innerah' (mistress), a term of respect.

Katie's writings show her determined to see the best side of outback life, and she wrote whole chapters about the beauty of the trees, wild flowers and birds. *Australian Legendary Tales* was published in 1896 by Mrs K. Langloh Parker, using her husband's name, just as Jeannie Gunn published as Mrs Aeneas Gunn. *My Bush Book* ends in 1901, the year Jeannie Gunn married and arrived at Elsey Station, and over a decade before the younger Myrtle White went to isolated Noonameena Station.

ℓℓ ℓℓ ℓℓ

Katie was not long at Bangate before she returned to town briefly and there had an accident. She did not tell much about this in her journal except to say that the fall broke one wrist and cracked a few ribs. She also suffered unspecified pelvic damage which would make it impossible for her to have children.

After her accident, horse riding, formerly Katie's passion, was beyond her and she was frequently in pain from bones that had been broken and not set very well. But as always, she was dogged and determined. When she returned to Bangate she set about developing new interests, in particular 'domestic skills'. Learning to cook became increasingly important, as a series of drunk, incompetent or worn-out cooks and 'married couples' came and went from the station.

Another blossoming skill was gardening. Fearing that she would be miserable and alone on the property, a city friend sent her a gardening encyclopaedia. With the aid of a series of either opinionated or incapable gardeners, Katie managed to produce fruit and vegetables deemed exotic at a time when most people in colonial Australia lived on cabbage and beans and scurvy was endemic in the outback.

She grew Jerusalem and globe artichokes, squash of various types, kohlrabi, salsify, okra, endive, eggplants, chillies, capsicums and sweet potatoes. In summer, there were watermelons and rockmelons, passionfruit, mulberries, grapes, figs and oranges; and mandarins in winter. She also grew pomegranates on learning that the rind was excellent for summer dysentery, or Barcoo fever, as it was known. Apple trees, however, resolutely refused to fruit in spite of all her efforts.

Katie's gardens had to withstand not only the vagaries of uncertain weather, but of human nature as well. The employment of one pigtailed Chinese gardener with psychiatric problems was terminated when he ran amok with a knife and nearly killed one of the Aboriginal house girls. Another gardener tore out all Katie's precious carnations and replaced them with cabbages while she was busy nursing a sick stockman. This made her so furious she refused to speak to him again and he soon also departed. In time, floods would mean the ruin of the precious flower gardens and vegetable beds Katie had worked so hard to establish.

Bangate Station.

Katie's accident meant that she could no longer participate in the musters that she had enjoyed when she first came to Bangate. But there were other sides of pastoral life that she voluntarily avoided. 'I get no amusement out of sheep,' she wrote in her journal. 'Shearing can be cruel, and smelly it certainly is.'[10]

The outback life still brought her pleasure. She took an interest in the native plants around her, troubling to learn the botanical names of many, and she was a keen observer of the bird life at Bangate. In the summer, she was careful to leave out dishes of water and birdseed on the verandas for the birds. She had a horror of birds kept in cages and wanted to see them free and happy. She fed oatmeal to the ring-necked doves and the butcher birds, and the top-knot pigeons, with their neat little heads, pink toes and pink flush on each side of their plump breasts. She watched entranced as birds came to splash in the water dishes — cheeky yellow-headed mynahs and raucous kookaburras. She even had a pet black swan she named Diogenes, which swam in a tub and which she thought something of a philosopher. Diogenes had been brought to her by a Noongahburrah man when it was wounded and became so tame it ate from her hand.

ll ll ll

With a good complement of staff and no children to occupy her, Katie was able to spend time listening and learning from the Noongahburrah. She described the Noongahburrah as:

> a very fine tribe both as to physique and intelligence . . .
> plenty of fish in their creek, plenty of game — kangaroo,
> bustards, emu, duck . . . and in good seasons, quantities
> of grain from luxuriant grasses on their creek banks . . .
> abundant eggs of swans, emu, duck, water hens . . . and
> native fruits.[11]

Like her contemporary Daisy Bates, who also observed Aborigines at first hand and wrote about them, Katie Parker started off by learning some of the Yuwaalaraay language in order to compile vocabularies of the commonly used words of the Noongahburrah.

She found the Noongahburrah women fascinating. She respected their complex law system and their tribal government by elders, and was always very polite to them. In return they respected her. As she gained their trust, the women and the elders of the tribe went on walks with her to show her places and objects that were sacred to them — things they would not have revealed to any other European, male or female.

At various times the women and the elders gave her painted digging sticks, *nulla nullas* or war clubs, throwing boomerangs and incised shields painted with ochres and pipeclay. She used these as decoration on the wooden walls of the long verandas.

On one occasion she was presented with a *nulla nulla* by one Aboriginal woman for the express purpose of murdering 'the mortgagor' (presumably James Tyson). The woman had heard how if the mortgagor foreclosed, the Parkers would be forced to leave. When Tyson visited the property, the woman called Katie away from a conversation with him and pushed the *nulla nulla* onto her to 'gib him one crack longa head'. The woman reassured Katie it had 'bin kill plenty black peller'. Katie was further touched that the woman was prepared to do the deed herself if Katie was too squeamish, and to face the magistrate, to whom she would explain that the man was taking things that 'belongin' my Missus'.[12]

In addition to speaking their language, Katie took great interest in Aboriginal myths and legends, at a time when few Australians were interested and most thought the Aborigines would soon die out.

Using various Aboriginal friends as interpreters to help her with Yuwaalaraay words she did not know, Katie wrote down their stories in her notebooks, translating as literally as possible to retain the Noongahburrah view. She would often invert an object and verb, just as is done in Yuwaalaraay, giving her sentences a curious flow, but otherwise she wrote in clear English which made the books she would publish popular with readers.[13]

She described how:

> During the eleven years which I practically devoted to
> the study of their folklore . . . [they revealed] how all
> their natural world is divided into totemic families . . .
> I shall never forget my rambles through the Bush with a
> retinue of natives. I learnt that every distinctive bit of
> nature — say, a heap of white stones, the red mistletoe,
> the gnarled dark excrescences on the trees . . . each had its
> legend.[14]

Katie also tried to help the Aboriginal children with the eye afflictions they so often suffered. On her arrival at Bangate, she had been distressed to find:

> . . . every second person seemed to have sore eyes . . .
> I seemed to be always issuing eye lotion according to a
> prescription given me by an old squatter doctor in
> Melbourne . . . [Some] had swelling blight — 'bungey
> eye', colloquially called — from a fly sting which the
> blacks used to cure by pressing on hot budtha twigs and
> the whites with the blue-bag.[15]

She taught the Noongahburrah children to bathe the affected eye with salt water and made her staff do the same whenever their eyes became infected. She was also careful to wash her own eyes frequently and in this way avoided getting ophthalmia.

Now that she was living in the outback, Katie bitterly regretted she had no nursing experience. She wrote how among her 'amateur ministrations' were:

> attending to the fleshy part of a hand nearly blown off by
> a bursting gun. The flesh had to be cleaned, disinfected
> and patched up. Then a broken arm had to be set . . . a
> baby to be helped into the world prematurely owing to a
> buggy accident . . . a man practically drowned swimming
> in the river in floodtime, to be resuscitated.[16]

To their many visitors who called socially, or the bush folk who came looking for assistance, Katie and Langloh Parker appeared wealthy and successful. They had a vast property, a handsome homestead, Aboriginal maids in uniform, and the services of cooks, gardeners and married couples to help them.

Like many bush people of the era, whenever the Parkers entertained they did so lavishly. Guests arrived from all over and were housed in the huge homestead. There were dancing and amateur theatricals with programs designed by Katie. These were the golden days of Bangate and photograph albums recorded the fun — musical evenings with Katie and other guests playing the piano, sing-songs, and amateur theatricals on the veranda. To amuse the guests on one occasion she organised a competition to see which man could make the tastiest damper and the ladies acted as judges.

But the drought was taking its toll. Lack of rain was turning the land into a fissured mass of red dust. Normally an excellent source of water, the river was drying up until it consisted of a chain of muddy waterholes in which scrawny half-starved sheep and cattle bogged down and had to be dug out before they died of thirst or starvation.

By 1887 after a number of bad seasons the Parkers were struggling financially. Although the district had seen improvements, such as the new bridge across the Narran River, some of the infrastructure had cost landowners dearly. The rabbit-proof fence Langloh had been forced to erect cost 'enough to buy a snug freehold in more civilised parts', mused Katie.[17] As the expenses mounted, Langloh, already in debt to James Tyson for the original purchase, sought to take out a second mortgage from Dalgety and Company. Dalgety's sent an inspector to write a report on the situation at Bangate. He found Langloh Parker was running it well but needed still more water tanks. Langloh had already built five large tanks, but this was considered inadequate for a station carrying 96,000 sheep and 4600 head of cattle. And by the next year the number of sheep had risen to 138,000.[18]

Despite their financial difficulties, the Parkers continued to help their less well-off neighbours. Katie described one dreadful day in the relentless heat when she was putting up a neighbour and her two children. One of the children developed a raging fever, which no amount of bathing or fanning could cool. Used to the deaths of so many children in the bush, Katie and the mother agonised over whether to incur great expense and have the possibly drunk doctor called for or take the feverish child into town. Katie observed that they were almost as poor as their neighbours, but she nevertheless consulted Langloh.

'Poor little devil. Doctor of course,' declared Langloh. 'What's a few more pounds to an overdraft?' So he rode off in the morning and brought the doctor back late in the afternoon. Thankfully the child recovered but that wasn't always the case. Just a few weeks before, a woman had appeared at the homestead looking for a place to bury her treasured daughter who had suddenly died. Reluctant to bury her 'among the deadbeats' in the cemetery alongside the pub, she had noticed the well cared-for graveyard at Bangate, where her little Janie might be given 'a thought now and agen', as the woman and her husband made their way about the outback looking for work. The Parkers let them bury their child at Bangate.[19]

The drought continued over seven long years, and it proved impossible for the Parkers to meet the mortgage repayments. In 1890, in spite of Langloh Parker's hard work and Katie's stringent economies, most of their sheep and cattle had died and Tyson foreclosed on his mortgage. Dalgety's repossessed the property, keeping Langloh on as manager. It was dispiriting and a great financial loss, but the Parkers still had a small nearby property, Grawin South, to call their own.

Off to the Sandhills

In many respects Myrtle Kennewell had a happier childhood than Katie Parker, although she had no loving nursemaid and no loving grandmother to encourage her studies.

Myrtle was raised amid the rough and tumble of a large family of ten siblings in the Barossa Valley. This meant money was always short in the Kennewell household, although there was always plenty of love and laughter. As the eldest, Myrtle had to become the practical daughter who cared for younger siblings.

By the time Myrtle was sixteen, the family had moved to Williamstown, near Adelaide. Myrtle left school and was sent away to help her Aunt Elizabeth, who owned the Packsaddle Hotel, north-west of the Darling River. Here she would meet the man she would marry and follow to the outback.

Cornelius White was a muscular, good-looking but shy young man of whom her aunt spoke highly.

Con White had left his parents' home near the Murray River at age eleven to go and live with a guardian at the local

Mechanics Institute. At fourteen he felt the call to adventure too strong to ignore, and he left the security of town and the labour of school books for a life in the open air. He headed towards Queensland and soon found work droving cattle. He loved outback life and was offered a job as a stockman and then some years later promoted to manager of a large cattle station, something very unusual for a young man still in his early twenties.[20]

Myrtle Rose White as a young girl.

Used to spending most of his time in the company of men, Con was shy and awkward with women, had no gift for small talk and few social skills. However, he found warm-hearted Myrtle, with her relaxed sense of humour, easy to talk to. Con was no drinker but started haunting the Packsaddle Hotel hoping he might get a chance to talk to the owner's pretty niece. Myrtle found him attractive and the two of them took long walks together in the afternoons when she was free.

The friendship blossomed. Soon Con confided to Myrtle that his ambition was to own a cattle property, but obtaining the necessary capital was a problem. Myrtle reminded him how Sir Sidney Kidman had started out with only a few shillings and had become Australia's wealthiest pastoralist.

The year was 1906, only five years after Federation, Australia was still a pioneering society and cattlemen were the aristocracy of the bush. But those who worked the land hardly lived like lords. There were few of the tinned food products that enliven meals in the outback today, and none of the frozen products available today. Before refrigeration the diet was limited; fruit and vegetables withered in the heat. Most bushmen lived off corned beef, damper with treacle and black tea, their only vegetable being 'fat hen' or wild pigweed.

When Myrtle left Packsaddle to return to her family, Con returned to droving, writing to her when he could. When Myrtle did not receive her weekly letter, she worried that Con might have had a riding accident and so wrote to her aunt at Packsaddle asking for news. She was distressed to learn that Con had collapsed with pain to his heart and been sent to hospital. Doctors had warned him that he must eat a more balanced diet or he would die of heart disease.

Myrtle decided to take a job as a domestic servant at a nearby property, and and went about seeing (as far as she could) that Con ate a healthy diet and recovered. Since there was no dole or sickness benefit, Con had to return to work as soon as possible. He had always loved horses and managed to find a job driving a horse-drawn cab. He worked hard, saved up, bought his own horse and carriage and was granted a cab driver's licence.

Con wanted to have money in the bank before he asked Myrtle to marry him. Although he owned very little apart from his horse and carriage, he promised Myrtle that as soon as he was well enough he would go back on the land as a cattle station manager and earn a good salary. They could live in the manager's house, save hard and fulfil his dream of buying a property.

For Myrtle money did not matter. They could get married and she would continue to work as a cook. She urged Con to take things slowly, aware that his health would take some time to recover fully before they could return to the outback.

On 19 October 1910 Miss Myrtle Kennewell and Mr Cornelius White were married quietly at St Peter's Church, Broken Hill. Con continued to work as a cabbie. A year after they married Myrtle gave birth to a little girl whom they named Doris.

Con applied for several station manager's jobs without success, and in 1914, when Australia went to war, volunteered for army service. When he was examined by an army doctor he was rejected on health grounds, which upset him badly.

Con's knowledge of beef cattle was profound and he had a reputation as a very hard worker. In time he received an offer of a station manager's job. His prospective employer was a man Con had worked with years ago and whom Myrtle referred to in her memoirs as JDD.

Con and Myrtle talked things over. Noonameena (Lake Elder Station) in South Australia[21] was in a very remote area but the job was a highly responsible one. Having been offered the inducement of free bores by the Government of South Australia, JDD had taken out pastoral leases on seven vast cattle runs in the north-east of the state, near the Broken Hill region where Myrtle had nearly died at birth. Con accepted JDD's offer, sold his horse-drawn cab and in 1915 he, Myrtle and little Doris prepared for the move to sandhill country. The whole area was a virtual desert of sandy plains and dunes. In summer, temperatures hovered around 50 to 60 degrees Celsius. One of Australia's driest and harshest places, the annual rainfall was less than 100 millimetres per year. Few Europeans had ever lived there. In fact, it was so dry Myrtle noted that Aborigines rarely roamed in the area. Previously it had been impossible to raise any cattle or crops at all. Only the deep, government-funded bores made the area viable for farming.

In effect, Con, now the manager of seven remote cattle runs, had become part of an ill-fated experimental project to raise beef cattle in sandhill country. In wartime, fired by patriotism, Con saw this as an important job with the added benefit of a free house for the manager. Besides, getting the job was a boost to his ego. He regarded it as an exciting challenge.

By now Australian troops were fighting at Gallipoli and in northern France. To feed the army vast quantities of corned beef were needed. The Whites planned to work hard, live frugally, save money and reckoned that their savings would mean that once the war was over they could buy and stock a cattle run of their own. Although Myrtle was reluctant to leave the city with all its diversions, for Con's sake she was prepared to 'give it a go'.

Con left for Noonameena before Myrtle to inspect all the cattle properties, meet his jackaroos and stockmen and make the living quarters as comfortable as possible. They had made plans for Myrtle and Doris to travel to an old homestead at the outstation called Mirrabooka until a proper homestead could be built. 'I'll be in fairly often, and JDD tells me there is a very capable couple at Mirrabooka,' Con promised.[22]

Broken Hill would be their nearest town. A bitumen road from Broken Hill to Mirrabooka, where goods were stored, petered out before Mirrabooka and was replaced by sand.

Myrtle learned that Noonameena was regularly reached by camel track through eighty kilometres of sandhills. All goods and foodstuffs arrived at the homestead by camel train. Indeed, camels would become Myrtle's lifeline. Although it was 1915, there was no telephone and Myrtle would spend years without access to a phone or radio.

Six weeks after Con departed, Myrtle and four-year-old Doris bundled into JDD's big open-topped touring car for a day-long journey to Mirrabooka. What she saw as they drove along were acres of reddish sand blown into furrowed patterns by the wind, contrasting with the deep blue of the sky. Towards the end of the day, the car became stuck in sand, still a few kilometres short of Mirrabooka. Seemingly undaunted JDD jumped out of the car to begin the march on foot to the station. Tired and disappointed, there was nothing Myrtle or Doris could do but follow. Stumbling through sand they reached a lake which had formed after rains: another delay as they detoured around it. With shins bruised and skin torn the trio finally reached the four-roomed cottage in the dark.

They were met by Mrs Smithers, a surly, elderly housekeeper who clearly disliked having another woman around. The 'Boss' was out on the property and not expected back for a week. The grumpy housekeeper provided them with something to eat and Myrtle retired to a sleepless night.

The next morning as JDD was leaving, he informed Myrtle that the housekeeper and her husband had handed in their notice and would be off in a fortnight. Myrtle would be alone in the house with only a young child for company, surrounded by 12,000 square kilometres of sand and silvery-grey mulga. There was no inside toilet, only a large latrine pit to the rear of the homestead surrounded by a few flapping bits of hessian. The bathroom, which Myrtle conceded was a modern affair, was blocked off with a door only about a metre tall. There was no refrigerator or cool cellar. All butter, milk and meat had to be kept cool in a hessian-lined Koolgardie safe. Mail was collected by camel once a fortnight. There was no telephone and as far as Myrtle knew no other woman living within miles.

However, to Myrtle's surprise, a man arrived that morning looking for the housekeeper to attend his wife who had gone into labour two months early. Declaring she could not possibly go, Mrs Smithers ordered Myrtle to attend. Myrtle remembered back to Doris's difficult birth. The doctors had given Doris one chance in a thousand of surviving. What chance would this woman have with only inexperienced Myrtle attending the birth?

It was a tense journey back to the man's home as he wondered how his wife was faring and regretted the fact that he had missed JDD and his car by only two hours. When they finally arrived they

The Noonameena homestead under construction.

were met by the man's three terrified children. Myrtle felt justifiably nervous. She entered the house and found her patient. When she met the woman's relieved eyes, all fear disappeared and she set to with commonsense. It was a long night, and in the end the baby died. But the mother survived. From the moment she had known another woman would be there to help, the mother had seemed to rally.

Myrtle and Doris stayed with the woman for two weeks after the birth and came to appreciate all the personal touches the woman had made to her humble earthen-floored shack in the outback. Whatever was to hand had been converted into something charming and useful — packing cases into gaily covered furniture, goat-skins tanned by the woman herself into floor covers, and everywhere flowers brought in by the children. Myrtle felt ashamed that she had had any reservations about her own more comfortable home.

She returned to Mirrabooka to take up her duties running the house somewhat buoyed by the experience. Once Mrs Smithers and her husband left, she decided to take on the job of cooking for fourteen men herself. With Con often away and the men quartered in their own area, it was a lonely life, but Myrtle thought of the determination and fortitude of the 'Little Mother' she had stayed with and cheered herself up.

Con and the men spent much of their time working the cattle at the main run at Noonameena and building a new homestead there. On one occasion Myrtle accompanied JDD on a trip with cattle-buyers out to Noonameena. The sand was so soft that JDD's custom-built touring car sometimes sank up to its axles in sand but having been fitted with special large tyres it managed the trip. Myrtle faced almost perpendicular descents down the sandhills with her heart in her throat.

She was horrified by her first sight of Noonameena. Its vastness and the inaccessibility of its 'treeless waste' disturbed her.[23] But the work on her new home was well under way, and a few months later the house was ready enough to move into.

Myrtle, who loathed sand, was now surrounded by acres and acres of the stuff. Sandstorms were frequent. For days on end red sand, fine as dust, hung in the air, making them all cough and splutter. Day after day the wind blew clouds of sand over everything — food, furniture, curtains, bed linen, books. On waking in the morning the only clean place in the whole house would be where they had lain their heads on the pillows. Myrtle hated it but was determined to stick it out, for Con's sake.

She described the red soil as 'stretching away and away and away'. The view was always the same — red sandhills with patches of greenish-grey mulga and occasional splashes of a more vivid shade of green from bullock bushes which provided fodder for the cattle, the leopard trees with their mottled grey trunks, and the greenish-grey saltbush.[24] The area had its own wild beauty but, used to the lush green of the Barossa Valley where she had grown up, Myrtle found the aridity depressing.

Their bore water tasted disgusting, so finding unsalted drinking water, as well as fresh and nutritious food, was a constant problem. Housekeeping was exhausting in the torrid heat. Hot water had to be run off each morning from the taps so that the water supply would be cool enough to drink later. Myrtle had 'an endless job' filling earthenware coolers with water and, on the rare occasions when they had some, with milk.

Myrtle craved fresh vegetables but whenever she ordered a case from the station agent, they were withered or rotten by the time they arrived.

Replacing household items was also a problem. Even a lost pair of scissors could be a disaster with no possibility of buying another unless an Afghan pedlar arrived with a camel train.

Once it was finished, Noonameena homestead was more comfortable than Mirrabooka. It had cement floors, a dining room, office, pantry, guest-rooms, bathroom and separate men's quarters and kitchen. A flour store was built up on piles to allow circulation and other stores were kept in a large underground cellar. Myrtle ordered carpets, wallpaper and curtains. Once the materials arrived by camel train and the wicker baskets and bales were unloaded, she got busy, sewed curtains and papered over large cracks in the plastering. To create an illusion of coolness, she ordered a moss green carpet for the bedroom. She had chosen curtains patterned with roses, the sort of tea roses her mother had grown at home in the Barossa, determined their bedroom would be a refuge from the sandhills and mulga that surrounded them.

As unpaid store manager, her job was to place bulk orders for everything needed to feed and clothe the men. She did the orders twice a year. Supplies came out from the agent at Broken Hill by bullock dray or by camel and took over a week to arrive.

The station relied on its own supply of meat. They killed a beast or two each month and lived on fresh beef for two days and salt beef

A camel team would bring supplies to Noonameena from Broken Hill.

for the next twenty-nine. In the fierce heat, with no refrigeration or ice house, keeping things fresh was a nightmare. As Myrtle wrote, 'Butter was a hope of the future and a thing of the past.'[25] It was too hot even for jellies to set.

Still craving fresh green salads and juicy tomatoes, fresh apples or peaches, Myrtle tried growing them. But, no matter how hard they tried, vegetables and fruit proved impossible to grow, watered only by the salty bore water. To prevent scurvy Myrtle dosed them all with cod liver oil and lime juice if she could get it.

When the Whites arrived at Noonameena they were true European pioneers, farming country that had never been fenced or farmed before. JDD had been attracted to take the land up by the sinking of bores but also the nutritious grasses that grew after the rains. But the rains had stopped just as he took possession and, by the time the Whites settled in, there were only a few drops falling each month.

In a good season, Noonameena and its outstations could carry about 5000 head of beef cattle. But over the seven years the Whites stayed, the land degraded considerably. The hoofs of so many thousands of cattle caused the sand to 'dreft' around the waterholes, cutting the natural 'skin' of the land's surface. When finally the drought ended and it rained, mobs of cattle would bog down in quicksands that developed around the waterholes.[26]

Little Doris thrived in the harsh surroundings. She was thrilled with the beloved pony she acquired, as well as a cattle dog pup she named Bluey and from whom she was inseparable. A tomboy, Doris loved the freedom of outback life. Mounted on her pony she seemed fearless and the station hands taught the little girl to crack a stock whip and round up cattle. By the time she turned eight, Doris was out mustering cattle with the station hands.

Riding around on her pony one day Doris found a human skeleton, which Myrtle presumed was that of an Aborigine. Myrtle rarely encountered tribal Aborigines in the area; presumably even they considered food too hard to find in this arid wilderness.

A year later Doris found more skeletons. She rode out with Con to see them and he reckoned they were of two stockmen who had died of thirst in the sandhills. They had, it seemed, been taking a short cut across country and had lost their way. With only one water bag between them, it appeared they had died a slow and miserable death.

Doris was a healthy active child, and did not seem to mind that she had no playmates of her own age. With the help of textbooks sent out by camel train from a library at Broken Hill, Myrtle did her best to educate Doris. She read the books with her daughter, who proved to be a quick learner.

✿ ✿ ✿

Even though Myrtle and Doris had now settled into the Noonameena homestead, Myrtle saw little of Con. His duties ranged from as far afield as the Lake Frome basin to Milparinka in the north-west of New South Wales. As well as the stock, Con had to manage a large number of men. Some of the stockmen were reliable, others drunkards and troublemakers. Con had to deal with fist fights and accidents in which stockmen were gored or fell off their horses and broke arms and legs.

Whenever she could, Doris tagged along with the men so Myrtle sought refuge in the mundane routine of housekeeping — Monday washing day; Tuesday ironing with flat irons heated on the stove which had to be stoked with firewood; Wednesday sewing and mending; Thursday baking; and Friday 'turning out' rooms, moving the furniture, sweeping and polishing.

Not only was the heat stifling in summer but the mosquitoes were voracious. There were no flyscreens, only citronella to keep the pesky creatures at bay. When

In the days before refrigeration, butter and milk were cooled in a Koolgardie safe. Water dripped down hessian or cloth into a tray.

the family tried sleeping out in the front garden believing it would be cooler, they were kept awake by not only the droning mosquitoes but the howling of dingoes.

But the wind and sand were Myrtle's firm enemies. She described the silence that heralded the coming of a cyclonic storm. The wind would drop and then the fierce storm would sweep through the depressions between the sandhills, the house taking the full brunt of the clouds of stinging, whirling sand:

> Timber creaks and strains, roof-iron begins to lift and flap, and window-sashes rattle and shake . . . Meanwhile, the dust thickens and deepens . . . until one stifles and feels that all hope is lost . . . If you can take it with a Christian spirit, thankfully, uncomplainingly, you are the salt of the earth. Personally I never could.[27]

As at Katie Parker's Bangate, domestic staff came and went. Some of the married couples were unsatisfactory; some individuals drank to excess; one employee deliberately scorched Doris's best dress out of spite. In fact, most of the domestic staff Myrtle employed to help her cook for the station hands proved more trouble than they were

COURTESY REDLANDS SHIRE MUSEUM, QUEENSLAND.
PHOTO © JAKE DE VRIES, PIRGOS PRESS.

A wood-burning stove (with no temperature controls) of a type popular just before World War I.

worth, and Myrtle would frequently take on cooking for the men herself, as she had done at Mirrabooka.

During her first year at Noonameena, Myrtle became pregnant again. Having no telephone and no doctor to call anyway, it was necessary to go to the city to give birth. On the appointed day the skies opened with rain so the journey had to be delayed. For two more days they waited until the skies cleared. Con, Myrtle, Doris and a maid set out in the station buggy. They made good progress to begin with and eventually changed horses, sending the old team that had pulled the buggy back with a stockman. But not much further on the first of a series of problems arose. The reins of the leading horse became unbuckled and slipped from Con's hands. Without his guidance, the lead horse began to turn in ever decreasing circles, until it seemed certain the pole yoked between horse and buggy would break. Myrtle was ever grateful that it held, as Con jumped down and placated the leader. It would have been a forlorn place to have been stranded.

Back on track, they soon reached what had previously been a dry lake they would have crossed comfortably. Now it was a stretch of oozing mud. They had no alternative but to go round it.

To help ease the load for the poor horses struggling along the heavy ground at the lake's edge, Myrtle, Doris and the maid climbed down and walked. Eventually the horses were too tired to move. They rested a bit and set off again. The next hitch was a thunderstorm which wet them through and turned their route into another lake. They continued on painfully slowly, and just before darkness met up with the change of horses Con had arranged to come from a depot.

But luck was against them again. The horses were changed, and as they proceeded the new leader seemed to go forward erratically. Con realised the horse had a form of sandy blight or blindness. The poor old previous leader had to be harnessed up again.

Late that night, six kilometres short of their destination, they finally stopped when the horses sank deep into some soggy ground and the pole that had held out so splendidly before broke. There was nothing for it but to make camp. A boy accompanying them was sent off to get a tent and blankets from the depot.

And so pregnant Myrtle cooked a meal on the camp fire, boiled the billy and settled down for a night on branches cut from buck bushes. A new buggy arrived the next day with fresh horses and they reached the place where a car was expected to take Myrtle on to Adelaide for the birth of her second child.

Hardly were they out of the buggy than a cyclone hit the town and they had to wait three days for it to blow over. In the meantime the car still had not arrived, so the party set out again in the buggy. Finally, after another two days on the road, they met the car.

In comparison with the awful journey, the birth was uneventful. Proud Myrtle returned to Noonameena with a five-week-old baby boy whom they named Alan. He was chubby and good-natured with cornflower-blue eyes and Myrtle adored him. She also took back with her a young girl of seventeen to help with Doris and Alan and decided to have the stock and station agent look for another married couple. The prospect of caring for her family, as well as cooking for the men without the labour-saving devices we now take for granted, was daunting.

The couple located by the agents arrived. They claimed they had been in service with Dame Nellie Melba at her home in Victoria, luxurious Coombe Cottage, not really a cottage but a mansion, surrounded by green lawns and a swimming pool. The wife took one look at the red sand around Noonameena and in the house and decided she'd been totally misled. She told Myrtle that when she had been employed by Madame Melba, all she had had to do was to cook vegetables and wash up — light cleaning duties only!

The couple also had a child, who unfortunately arrived with a raging temperature. Whatever the illness was, everyone at the station came down with it except baby Alan and Myrtle. Their start was not a good one. Instead of getting help, Myrtle now had three extra people to cook for. They had come so far there was nothing for it but to give the couple a try. Myrtle may have wished she sent them packing in view of what happened next. Hoping to cash in on the bounty for dingo hides, inexperienced Cecil the husband laid baits around the wood heap without tying the dogs up. Poor Bluey, Doris's beloved dog, was killed along with all the other station dogs.

Next Myrtle employed two single girls, in the vain hope they would be company for each other. Unfortunately the two girls loathed each other. Bertha, the elder, was a hard worker but had a sharp tongue. Ruth was an unstable girl who was teased unmercifully by Bertha over her fondness for a good-looking station hand.

One morning Bertha taunted her colleague, saying that one of the station hands had boasted to his co-workers that he had had sex with Ruth. Ruth turned white and then red with rage. As luck would have it, when Ruth was in the boning room cutting up the meat for the next meal, in walked that particular station hand for his breakfast. Enraged to think that he had been discussing her like that, Ruth picked up the boning knife and slashed the handsome stockman across the face. The knife was razor sharp, and almost removed the man's nose and carved a deep gash in his chin.

The injured man was brought to Myrtle, bleeding copiously. She did her best for him but had no anaesthetic or morphine to ease the pain. Ruth departed on the next mail run from the station, along with Bertha.

Although she provided first aid to injured stockmen, Myrtle found it hard when her children had accidents. She could not bring herself to insert a needle and stitch up her beloved daughter when she fell and gashed her shoulder on the metal roof of the homestead's cellar. She took a deep breath and disinfected Doris's wound. She held both sides of the wound together by applying sticking plaster, and prayed it would heal without becoming infected. Eventually Doris's wound did heal but forever after her shoulder had a long red scar.

The addition of 'Miss Seventeen' (as Myrtle called her), the girl who returned to Noonameena with Myrtle after Alan's birth, livened things up for the stockmen. Miss Seventeen played the young men off against each other but seemed to prefer one station hand above the rest. Tim was a tall, bronzed, broad-shouldered young man with deep blue eyes, and the two of them spent their evenings on long walks amid the sandhills. It seemed wedding bells were in the air. Then suddenly Miss Seventeen seemed to lose interest in him.

Fortunately for Tim a new housemaid arrived. Myrtle called her 'Miss Dimple' because she was all smiles, sweeping lashes and long blonde hair. Before long, Tim and Miss Dimple were spending a lot of time together. Both of them asked to take leave at the same time and when they returned Tim started to fix up a tent which he pitched behind the homestead. Miss Dimple demurely sewed cushion covers and bedspreads. Eventually their secret leaked out. They had been married by special licence and would only be staying at Noonameena for another six months, as they were saving hard to buy a place of their own. To Myrtle it seemed that the only permanent residents of Noonameena were the White family.

While Doris had been a relatively easy baby, Alan seemed to have a constant problem with his tonsils or stomach. On one occasion he went into convulsions, his tiny body alternately rigid or gyrating in spasms. For days Myrtle kept sponging and fanning him in an effort to bring his temperature down. It was too hot to take a feverish baby on the many days' journey to a doctor.

To make it worse she had influenza herself and was shivering and shaking with fever. She was also pregnant again. Alan's convulsions grew worse and worse and Myrtle feared her baby son would die. Little Miss Seventeen was so terrified that she fainted — which was not much help to Myrtle. For days Alan suffered in a feverish state. Finally a cooler change came through and Myrtle decided to embark on the long trip by car over sandhills and risk a rise to searing heat to reach the nearest doctor.

Con and Myrtle had spent some of their savings on a Ford car they named Henrietta, which Myrtle described as 'a 1914 buckboard, hoodless and comfortless.'[28] Once they had a car, what they most needed was a road through to the depot. Helped by the station hands Con had bravely attempted to pack down a graded track through the dips in the sandhills. Despite the hard work the

*Sandbogged cars in the sandhill country of north-eastern South Australia
often had to be hauled out like this.*

road was not very successful. Now, in desperation, Alan, Con and
the very pregnant Myrtle set out in the car on the half-made road,
accompanied by some station hands on horses for the first forty
kilometres.

Then the worst happened: the Ford bogged down in soft sand.
Four men tried to push and two horses tried to pull Henrietta out
of the sand. They placed baulks of timber under the wheels. But the
car was heavy, loaded up with a tuckerbox full of food and two days'
supply of drinking water in metal canteens. It remained stuck fast.

The midday heat was terrible and little Alan suffered as the
temperature soared. Myrtle was beside herself, as she tried to cool
her baby boy. She sat under a mulga, desperate for shade from the
blazing sun, fanning Alan's burning body with wet cloths. She
watched as the men and horses slowly progressed, until they reached
the last and biggest sandhill which blocked their path to the better
stretches of road.

As Con revved the engine two of the horses panicked and fell. For
a dreadful moment it looked as if their flailing hoofs might kill one
of the stockmen. But the men kept calm and soothed the horses.
Finally they were over the sandhill and safely on the other side.

All the while, Alan's temperature was so high Myrtle feared he
would be dead by the time they reached a doctor. Still driving by
evening, the party was held up again by a sandstorm. Finally they
reached the depot where they spent the night. Next day after
covering twenty kilometres, Henrietta became stuck in a creekbed.
Pushing and pulling, they could not move the car. Myrtle knew that

the only passing traffic on this road was the fortnightly mail lorry or an occasional private car.

'My son will die,' she thought as Alan's fever mounted. She cradled him on her lap in the shade of a big gum tree, the only shade around, and offered up a silent prayer for a lorry or car to pass by.

Her prayer was answered. The mail truck with sixteen passengers came into view. It stopped and took Myrtle and Alan in the cab. Poor Con had to walk back to the depot in terrible heat.

The trip still took Myrtle another fourteen hours and Alan was barely alive when they reached Broken Hill.[29] Declaring it a miracle that Alan had survived, the doctor warned Myrtle that he would most likely suffer convulsions again. He prescribed a long period of convalescence in a cooler climate. How on earth could she manage that? The doctor sat Myrtle down and suggested she rent a room in a private house by the sea until her third child was born.

Myrtle took his advice in part. After her baby was delivered, she set up a home in Broken Hill, where a doctor was on hand, as were other amenities of civilisation. Myrtle would always be convinced that her period of worry over Alan caused her third baby, Garry, to be a nervous and highly strung little boy. Suffering reflux, Garry was unable to keep food down, and a stressful and anxious time ensued for Myrtle. She stayed on in the city for nine months after Garry was born, but ironically began to think about safety in the sandhills again as the children came down with measles, whooping cough and chickenpox. Con was eager for Myrtle to return, and after hiring two new girls to help her back at Noonameena the family rejoined him.

❧ ❧ ❧

It was apparent to Myrtle that Con was wearing himself out, working seven days a week at the expense of his health and his family. By this time JDD had sold Noonameena (Lake Elder Station) to Sidney Kidman. Myrtle felt that Kidman's company was taking advantage of her husband's good nature and resented the fact that they underpaid and overworked him.

Operating a station on the desert fringes was tough. Even when the seasons were passable and the market good, Con was at the mercy of sometimes inexperienced stockmen to get the herds to market. As well as plagues of dingoes, there were rabbits.

The constant battle with sand continued. In 1920 a severe drought began to take its toll. When the main bore which watered the cattle silted up, pressure was placed on swamp waters. Diversions from the bore were not enough. Myrtle watched weakened cattle struggle to find water, pausing at the foot of sandhills with heads hanging waiting to gather strength, the crows hovering overhead then swooping down on sick and dying animals and pecking out their eyes. Soon hundreds of cattle were dead. The drought dragged on for a year, with heartbreaking promises of rain as clouds formed only to fade away.

When rain finally did come it surprised everyone. It rained in torrents, flooding the homestead at Noonameena to a depth of seven centimetres. With the flooding came scorpions, spiders, snakes and disease. The steamy heat and the flies gave the children Barcoo fever, making them vomit.

But the rain also brought life back to the sandhills. Around the bore, the flowers burst into colour — bluebells and wild geraniums blossomed and a convolvulus put out pink flowers. As the swamps refilled, the birdlife returned. The station seemed in as good a state as ever.

After seven years at Noonameena, Con decided it was the right time to leave. As if in answer to a prayer, the newly installed telephone tinkled with the offer of management of Mordern and Wonnaminta stations in far western New South Wales. But the Whites had to make their decision quickly — they would need to be there in three days' time.

After three frantic days packing, the family left Noonameena, driving Henrietta the Ford along behind a neighbour's borrowed Dodge tourer, hoping to reach Mordern, some 240 kilometres east as the crow flies, that day. Shortly before dusk the lights of the Ford fused, leaving them in darkness. They continued to drive on in the wake of the Dodge, guided only by the light fanning out beyond the car's black bulk.

Suddenly there was a crash and a jolt, as the Ford driven by Con slewed and rolled into a ditch. The others in the Dodge piled out to see what had happened. They were thankful Con was safe but dismayed to see the Ford damaged. By now the younger children were tired, hungry, cold and fretful.

The men decided to take the family on in the Dodge to a bush pub on the Tibooburra mail road, only a few kilometres away. Con would spend the night by the wreck and be on the job at daylight and save precious time.

Arriving at the pub, they settled in but not for long, as the jolting and extreme fatigue had brought on one of Alan's gastric attacks. The castor oil bottle, Myrtle's 'trusty friend', which usually helped settle Alan's stomach, was in the stranded Ford. The night was a terrible one. No one slept.

By mid-afternoon they were off again and finally reached Wonnaminta. In bygone days Wonnaminta had employed between eighty and ninety men and three maids. Myrtle thought the collection of old buildings she confronted was more like a small village than a farm. The big old house now had a ghostly haunted feel, its rooms bare of furniture and the wallpaper peeling away in festoons.

However, it was to Mordern, another twenty kilometres away, they were heading so they pressed on. They reached Mordern homestead in darkness, tired and hungry. The house was chilly and damp, and Myrtle was appalled to find one main bedroom with only one bed to hold all five of the family. The manager Con was replacing lived at Mordern, helped by a married couple, but the housekeeper had not even lit a fire in welcome, let alone made the beds. Indeed, she proved so unwelcoming that a housemaid Myrtle had brought with her and come to rely on left within the first fortnight.

There was one improvement in Myrtle's new home and that was the presence of trees, but just as at Noonameena she saw Con only rarely, when he called in from some far corner of the properties. The married couple soon departed, having first raided the vegetable garden, and Myrtle took to cooking, cleaning and establishing a new garden. She grimly observed:

> Domestic help remained a never-ending problem —
> either because we didn't have it or because we did. One
> short week in the bush was sufficient for the first cook
> and housemaid we acquired. They came out on one mail
> and departed homeward on the next, and I took up the
> daily round again . . . I dreamed of a few days in bed as
> one might dream of Paradise.[30]

Soon she became overtired and ill. The doctor at Wilcannia was consulted by phone and prescribed two weeks in bed. Capable little Doris had to take over as head cook, housekeeper and bottle washer for twelve hungry people, as indeed she did the next time Myrtle was sick and was forced to go to hospital.[31]

But there was little rest for Myrtle. She had been in hospital for more than two weeks when she was finally able to hobble from her bed to make a telephone call to Mordern. There, she discovered, everyone but Doris had been confined to bed with flu. Immediately she organised someone to take her home the next day.

ll ll ll

After three years at Mordern, the Whites were beginning to feel unhappy. Promised rises in salary had not been honoured and the dream of owning their own land was fading. Con decided to make the break with Kidman's company, and announced it just as Kidman was touring his properties in the area. Kidman was not about to let such a hard worker go, and made more promises of money. Much to Myrtle's regret Con changed his mind.

Kidman also suggested Myrtle might go 'south' to Adelaide for a break. There was sense in this suggestion as the boys had continued to be plagued with sicknesses such as tonsilitis that required expensive long trips to hospital there. So the family travelled to Adelaide where they bought a house for Myrtle and the children to live in.

It was a lonely existence for Myrtle in Adelaide, and despite Kidman's assurances to Con, the money he had offered never materialised. Con and Myrtle revived the plan to buy their own

The manager's homestead at Wonnaminta Station, New South Wales, circa 1930.

land, but with the Depression just beginning, the Adelaide house was now worth only a fraction of what they had paid for it.

In something of a reverse, doctors were also now advising Myrtle to take Garry to a warmer climate, and when Con suggested she come back to the outback Myrtle agreed. She let the 'White Elephant', as she called the Adelaide home, and returned this time to Wonnaminta, where Con and the other men had moved the manager's residence.

Reviving the gardens and putting the buildings back into order were Myrtle's first priorities. The children took up their correspondence courses and Con returned to mustering, shearing and the daily grind of station life. Myrtle rued the fact that the Depression and what turned out to be cuts to Con's salary meant the boys could not go to boarding school and participate in the education and sporting activities available there. But they made the most of what they had to hand, with cricket matches between station teams and others in the district, or golf games on improvised station courses.

Out of all the worry and anxiety came one thing — Myrtle's book titled *No Roads Go By*, based on her journal. The book found a publisher and received wide acclaim when it appeared in 1932.

It drew attention to the difficulties of women with sick children in the outback. Through a chance meeting with the Reverend John Flynn, who was on a bush tour, and a talk about her difficulties to some businessmen, she was able to help Flynn raise money for his Australian Inland Mission Aerial Medical Service based at Cloncurry.

Flynn would travel around Australia with a copy of *No Roads Go By* in his suitcase. He found it helped fundraising for his Flying Doctor Service to read from the chapter about Myrtle's terrible journey with Alan over the sandhills to hospital.

John Flynn's work would continue and the Flying Doctor Service would grow to employ, through the assistance of public donations and government grants, radio transmitters, aeroplanes, pilots and doctors to bring what John Flynn called 'a mantle of safety' to outback families.

Myrtle was delighted she had been able to help raise funds to relieve the lot of outback women like herself. But the Whites' financial situation was not improving.

In 1937 the Depression began to ease. Myrtle described that year as one of:

> . . . much portent . . . Prosperity was steadily returning — but not for us. At the beginning of the depression one hundred and fifty pounds a year had been cut from the Boss's [Con's] salary, a further one hundred pounds followed a little later. We expected to share in the lean years, but, having done so, also expected to share in the fat — which we didn't. The cuts in the Boss's salary — much more than fifty per cent — were never restored . . .[32]

Another property had been added to Con's management with no addition to his salary. Sidney Kidman, who, despite letting Con down on occasions, had valued his management, died in 1935. Con finally understood Kidman's promises would never be fulfilled. The 'White Elephant' in Adelaide was still worth less than the money they had paid for it many years earlier, and too often their tenants were late in rental payments. Con was now fifty-five, Myrtle forty-nine. The dream of owning their own land was at an end.

During the year Con was struck down with flu which turned into bronchial pneumonia, but he continued to work hard. He had not taken more than six weeks' sick leave in twenty-two years. To his surprise he received a letter from the board of directors asking for his resignation. Despite having eventually received a substantial bonus, Myrtle was disgusted by Con's treatment. She wrote bitterly:

> 'Owing to ill health and advancing years' the Boss was deemed incapable of doing his job; yet on his departure the Powers that Be found it necessary to allot that same job, or jobs, to not one man, but three . . . in addition, the car that had played such a sinister part in our lives was replaced by a *new* one without loss of time . . . [33]

A Bitter-sweet End

Similar feelings of frustration and depression experienced by the Whites were felt by Katie and Langloh Parker when Langloh was bankrupted. Langloh had stayed on as manager at Bangate working for Dalgety's for a short time, but there were differences of opinion. Eventually the Parkers held a final auction sale and moved to the neighbouring and much smaller run called Grawin South, which they had purchased some time before. Here they lived in a humble bush dwelling with a bark roof and ant-bed floor. It cannot have been easy for Katie but she bore it far better than Langloh. He was now sixty, felt his life had been a failure and became immensely depressed.

Katie, however, had her writing to fall back on. She worked to collate and refine the Aboriginal stories she had collected, and sent a manuscript copy to the publisher David Nutt in London. The manuscript was accepted and Katie's first book appeared in 1896 with an introduction by the noted anthropologist Andrew Lang. Sales of *Australian Legendary Tales* were strong enough to warrant a second edition in 1897, and a second collection of stories, *More Australian Legendary Tales*, in 1898.

While Katie continued to write about the bush and her Aboriginal friends in contributions to journals and newspapers, Langloh could not shake off his depression. Hoping a change of environment might cheer him, the Parkers went to stay with Katie's brother George Field on his station in western Queensland. But the drought continued there and Langloh found little relief.

Katie and Langloh moved into rented rooms in Sydney. Early in 1903, Langloh suffered pain in his stomach and could not eat. He was eventually diagnosed with cancer of the stomach. Katie, now forty-seven, nursed him through six months of terrible suffering before he died.

Katie still had a small income from Grawin South where the seasons were now better and in 1904, two years after Langloh's death, she decided to take a trip to England. It was a chance to see where her ancestors had come from, a place she had always wanted to visit.

On board ship, published authoress Mrs Langloh Parker, by now quite a celebrity, met a tall, quiet bachelor lawyer who was fond of books. His name was Randolph Percy Stow and they saw London together. Perhaps Percy fell in love with Katie's warmth, energy and quick wit. Katie knew he could never replace Langloh, who had been the love of her life, but she was older now. She craved different things from when she was eighteen, and she and Randolph had so many interests in common. Neither of them had children to worry about, so when Stow proposed they get married in London and surprise their relatives with a *fait accompli* Katie accepted.

They married quietly amid the splendour of St Margaret's, Westminster, and returned to South Australia to live at Glenelg, where Katie and her family had lived before her marriage to Langloh.

Their lives were agreeable. Both she and Percy loved books and art and led an interesting life, entertaining writers and artists and travelling overseas every year. The Stows were close friends of Hans Heysen and his wife and owned a marvellous collection of Heysen's paintings.

In 1905 Katie revised and enlarged some chapters from her children's book on Aboriginal legends and republished them as an adult book in London under the title *The Euahlayi Tribe: A Study of Aboriginal Life in Australia*. This book also included twelve chapters that were originally part of the *My Bush Book* manuscript, as well as a long and detailed introduction by Andrew Lang.

Katie corresponded with ethnologists all around the world and in 1930 wrote another book *Woggheeguy: Australian Aboriginal Legends*, published by Preece of Adelaide. It was beautifully illustrated by her friend Nora Heysen, daughter of Hans and the first woman ever to win an Archibald Prize. (This book has now become a valuable collector's item.)

Katie died at her home, No. 5, Kent Street, Glenelg, in March 1940, and was buried in St Jude's Anglican cemetery. *Australian Legendary Tales* continued to be read overseas and was republished after her death in both American and Russian editions. *The Euahlayi Tribe* was recently placed on the internet as part of the Gutenberg Project for disseminating important books internationally.

Escape from the Sand

After selling the 'White Elephant' the Whites had just enough money to buy an old rambling guesthouse at Aldgate in the Adelaide Hills. Doris had already set herself up in an employment agency catering for the needs of people on the land. She left her business to help Myrtle run the guesthouse. Then she met Jim Chambers, a man who loved horses and the outback as much as she did. They became engaged and after marrying, Jim and Doris returned to the outback — eventually in 1948 to manage Wonnaminta.

With the guesthouse to run, Myrtle was kept busy cooking, cleaning and trying to make time to write between domestic chores. When World War II broke out in 1939, both White boys were old enough to enlist, which meant another heartache for Myrtle. But she was nevertheless proud of them.

In the second year of the war tragedy struck. Con died of a massive heart attack. She soldiered on alone at the guesthouse but there was another bitter blow in store: Garry's plane was declared missing on a flight over Malaya. Devastated by the news, Myrtle refused to admit Garry could be dead. She attended spiritualist meetings and had her belief that Garry would eventually return bolstered by mediums.

'There is no death,' she wrote at the end of her second book, published in 1955, thinking, as always, of Garry lost somewhere over Malaya.[34] Sadly the dead were dead and would never return.

Author Myrtle Rose White, as pictured on the jacket of No Roads Go By.

At the end of the war, Alan was demobilised and returned to his favourite way of life — like his father he was happiest on the land.

Gradually Australians recovered from the effects of World War II. Publishing and paper supplies became easier to obtain. Myrtle's best-selling book *No Roads Go By* was republished in 1952 and became popular with a younger crop of readers.

In 1954 a special edition of *No Roads Go By*, illustrated by Elizabeth Durack, was published in Britain where it also proved very popular. The book showed British people what the outback was really like. It brought Myrtle a swag of letters from English wives and mothers who admired her courage in raising children under great difficulties. She donated some of her royalties to the Flying Doctor Service in memory of her old friend John Flynn, who had died three years previously, his ashes interred under a cairn of stones in the shadow of Mount Gillen, near Alice Springs.

In those days Myrtle wrote her books by typing them slowly using two fingers on an old Corona portable.[35] She typed and retyped her manuscripts, making carbon copies and undertaking all the corrections slowly and laboriously.

The wonder is that she managed to complete *No Roads Go By*. She had written it while running a large homestead, ordering all the supplies, caring for three children and a husband, supervising meals for station hands and battling sand in a home which lacked any of the labour-saving conveniences that women take for granted today.

The title *No Roads Go By* was a quotation from a poem by Banjo Paterson. The book's grim humour and its account of the gritty realities of outback life, so different from *We of the Never-Never*, touched a chord in the heart of the public. It was praised by the *Times Literary Supplement* and the *Times Literary Review.* Myrtle was asked to write another book and produced a novel the following year titled *For Those That Love.*

In the Adelaide Hills, while answering letters from readers, Myrtle continued to run her guesthouse efficiently. She would tap away at her latest book in what little spare time was left. Her style was humorous and unpretentious.

As a thank you for years of patient work for her family, Myrtle was taken to India on holiday by Doris and Jim Chambers. Myrtle insisted on visiting an orphanage near Bombay to which she donated some of her royalties from *No Roads Go By*.

In her later years Myrtle enjoyed attending meetings of the Fellowship of Australian Writers, met fellow authors, such as Kylie Tennant, and visited art exhibitions with Miles Franklin and her artist friend Pixie O'Harris.[36] Myrtle's final book was *From That Day to This.*

In July 1961, when Myrtle was seventy-two and visiting Alan who was running the vast Lalla Rookh Station in the outback near Port Hedland, she complained of feeling tired and retired to bed early. That night she died in her sleep. After cremation, half her ashes were interred in her husband's grave, the other half taken to Wonnaminta.

PART 2

SUSANNA DE VRIES

HEROIC AUSTRALIAN
WOMEN
in War

Astonishing tales of bravery from Gallipoli to Kokoda

Heroic Australian Women in War *is dedicated to my friend*
Alexander Freeleagus, AM, Greek Consul for Queensland,
who has done so much to promote the life and work of Joice Loch,
Australia's forgotten heroine, whose life and work
emphasise the strong bonds that bind Greece and Australia.

There is no poetry here... only pain, misery and death.

SISTER ALICE KITCHEN, 1915

INTRODUCTION

✤ ✤ ✤

Research by historian Caroline Viera Jones reveals that women's heroic role was played down by Australia's official historian of World War I. Acting on instructions from publisher George Robertson to up the mateship and increase the larrikinism, author C.E.W. Bean contrived to make the Great War seem a blokey, all-male affair.

In 1900 a group of Australian nurses, including the redoubtable Sister Nellie Gould, accompanied the 2nd New South Wales Army Medical Contigent to the Boer War.[1] On her return Sister Gould founded the Army Nursing Reserve, which supplied the first nurses to military hospitals in Egypt in 1914.

By the second year of the Great War, Australian nurses, doctors and volunteer ambulance drivers were helping wounded Serb soldiers in Greece. Why were they there?

The answer lay in the racial melting pot known as Sarajevo. The assassination of Austrian Archduke Franz Ferdinand on 28 June 1914 in the predominantly Serb town of Sarajevo would escalate a small local war of retribution into a world war that killed millions.

The pretext for waging war was the fact that Archduke Franz Ferdinand, heir to the Austrian empire, was murdered by Gavrilo Princep, a young Serb, and member of a terrorist gang called the Black Hand. Princep and his fellow terrorists wanted to use the assassination of the archduke to highlight the religious and racial grievances of thousands of Orthodox Serbians and Bosnians living under the rule of the Catholic Austro-Hungarian Empire.

Unfortunately, their plan misfired, bringing years of misery and conquest to the very people they aimed to help. As Princep was a Serb, Austria believed the Serb government must be involved (which it was not). The Austrians were outraged. As a result Austrian soldiers attempted to capture Belgrade, capital of Serbia. Initially they were repulsed, but they returned with German guns and planes and overran most of Serbia.

In the midst of winter the Serb Army, accompanied by a group of brave Australian nurses who had enlisted as volunteers, retreated through thick snow to Albania and then to the port city of Salonika (Thessaloniki), held by Greece. The retreat was forever after known as the 'March of Death', because so many died while crossing the snow-covered mountains.

It was against this background that Germany's Kaiser Wilhelm falsely claimed that France was planning to invade Germany. He seized the opportunity to strike first, sending German soldiers to march through neutral Belgium en route to capture Paris and northern France. While there they committed atrocities against women and children which feisty Australian-born war correspondent Louise Mack would document for London's *Daily Mail*.

Britain defended Belgian neutrality and declared war on Germany. Australia, as part of the British Empire, supported Britain and, lacking a permanent army, raised what became known as the Australian Imperial Force (AIF) to fight in Europe. It was this force — a combination of men from every state in Australia — which helped forge Australians together as a nation.

On the way to Europe there was a change of plan. Australian troops were sent by British High Command to the Gallipoli peninsula to fight against the Turks, who supported Germany and had been supplied with German armaments.

On Anzac Day we remember the brave men who fought at Gallipoli and in northern France, but few people remember the 'forgotten Balkan campaign' in which Australian nurses, doctors, ambulance drivers and engineers took part, some giving their lives.

World War I was supposed to be an all-male affair. Experienced surgeons such as Dr Elsie Inglis, Dr Agnes Bennett and Dr Lilian Cooper, who volunteered to serve in the Army, were turned down by contemptuous recruiting officers and told to stay home and knit.

However, these determined professional women refused to take no for an answer. Led by Dr Inglis, who had spent some early years in Tasmania, they ran their own all-women hospitals. After being turned down by the British and Australian Armies a dozen or so Australian women doctors paid their own sea passages to Britain and enlisted with the privately funded Scottish Women's Hospitals for Foreign Service — or SWH — which ran field hospitals in France, northern Greece and Serbia. These were countries unable to staff their own hospitals and deeply grateful for the women's help. The SWH employed women as doctors, nurses, cooks and ambulance drivers. Later the determined Dr Inglis commissioned a time-and-motion study, which revealed that in the Scottish Women's Hospitals, five unpaid female VADs (Voluntary Aid Detachment workers) got through the same amount of work as eight paid male orderlies.

An enterprising young Australian, Olive King, offered to serve as an ambulance driver in the British Army and even to donate an ambulance. Her offer was brusquely rejected and she was told that women were not tough or smart enough to do such a demanding and stressful job.

Exhibition poster dated 1918.

Baffled and annoyed by her rejection, Olive decided to join the SWH and took her ambulance to France and later to Salonika in Greece, where she won five medals for her valour and service.

In 1916 the writer Virginia Woolf, angered by the pointless slaughter of her male contemporaries, called newspaper articles that glorified war 'preposterous masculine fiction'. Woolf, a supporter of women's economic freedom, pleaded for 'another Joan of Arc to arise and lead the Allies to victory'.[2] However, Australian and British generals made sure that a second Joan of Arc would not interfere with their all-male war.

Before World War I few Australian women attended university or had careers or meaningful employment. Most girls stayed home and helped their mothers until they married. But after the men had gone to war the door of the 'Doll's House' finally opened. All across Australia strong-minded young women left the kitchen sink or the drawing room and volunteered to serve in Europe as ambulance drivers, nurses, nursing aides, cooks or Red Cross workers. They also took on jobs within Australia that were previously reserved for men. 'Cowgirls' or land girls worked on the land, dipping sheep and helping on farms in a thousand other ways; women played an important role, moved into offices, became telephonists and secretaries (once male occupations), journalists, even porters.

With so many men away at the front some women even managed to slip into places in schools of law and medicine as enrolments were low. Joan Rosanove, for example, who later became a QC, was allowed to study law at Melbourne University. In the world of journalism, Joice NanKivell Loch got a job on the *Melbourne Herald*, as did Katharine Susannah Prichard, and Sydney's Louise Mack was employed as Europe's first female war correspondent by London's *Daily Mail*.[3]

Australian nurses served with distinction in France, Belgium, England, India, Burma, the Persian Gulf, Palestine, Egypt, Italy and Greece. They could enlist in the Australian Army Nursing Service (AANS) in Australia's state capitals or pay their own fares to London and enrol with Queen Alexandra's Imperial Army Nursing Service (QAIANS) or the Scottish Women's Hospitals (SWH).

Australian nurses found themselves in demand to work in at least a dozen private hospitals in France or on ambulance trains, funded by British aristocrats, by royalty (for example, the Queen of Denmark) or by French charitable organisations. In 1914, the British-run QAIANS employed 463 trained nurses, including a percentage of Australians. By 1916, that number had increased to 6864 nurses and 3580 nursing aides.

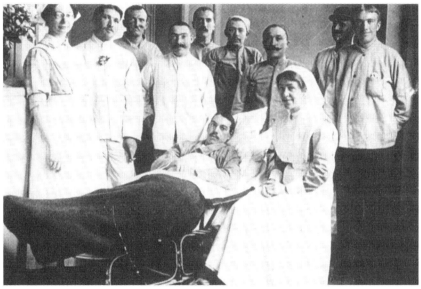

Sister Claire Trestrail with colleagues and a patient.

Nearly 3000 Australian nurses served in World War I.[4] Twenty-one of them paid for their dedication with their lives. Sister Claire Trestrail, for example, went to London in 1913 to improve her qualifications. She was there when war was declared, enrolled with the SWH in Brussels and narrowly escaped being captured by the Germans. In October 1915, Claire joined the QAIANS on a one-year short-term contract. Having enjoyed freedom and responsibility in her previous nursing positions, she found one particularly bossy matron unbearable. When her contract expired Claire did not renew it. She then worked for a variety of private organisations and in a private hospital in the Marne district around Paris where she nursed wounded French and Belgian soldiers.[5]

Friendships forged amid the horrors of war helped nurses and volunteers face danger and deprivation. 'It's hard to face danger alone, but having a pal besides you makes you feel stronger,' as Patsy Adam-Smith once wrote.

Alice Kitchen was one of twenty-five senior Australian nurses recruited to join the newly established Australian Imperial Force. Alice and three other nurses left Melbourne on 19 October 1914. On the long sea voyage Alice developed a supportive friendship with Sister Hilda Samsing and they both volunteered to nurse on dangerous and exhausting rescue missions to Gallipoli aboard the hospital ship *Gascon*. Nursing on hospital ships was certainly not for the faint-hearted.

Alice Kitchen's war journal is memorable because she was so frank about the terrible conditions endured in the evacuation of the wounded from Anzac Cove. 'This isn't war, it's mass murder,' recorded Alice, describing wounded Anzacs left like 'run-over dogs' on the beach at Anzac Cove.

Alice Kitchen's diaries have a special resonance for Australians. She wrote about the moral questions posed by war and the conduct of the war itself — moral questions that concern all Australians today.

ℓℓ ℓℓ ℓℓ

By the second year of the war, casualties from Gallipoli and France were pouring into military and private hospitals, and hospital ships and trains, all of which needed more and more well-trained nurses.

John Galsworthy, later to become author of the bestselling *Forsyte Saga*, personally funded a hospital ship which rescued wounded men from Gallipoli. Serving aboard as orderlies were several young authors and the future poet laureate John Masefield. Masefield echoed the anger of Sister Kitchen in his book *Gallipoli*, describing how many men died of septic wounds because they had to wait for days on the beach amid flies and burning sun.[6]

Nurses who served overseas were governed by strict conventions. The 'top brass' of the Australian Imperial Force were convinced soldiers were sexual predators and young nurses feeble creatures who could not resist their advances. They feared that unwanted pregnancies and venereal diseases would result if young men and women were allowed to socialise. To prevent this, the AIF did its best to keep nurses and soldiers apart in their free time. Contraceptive advice for women did not exist in this prudish era.

The feminist Scottish Women's Hospitals were fiercely puritanical. 'No lipstick, no rouge, no high heels, no jewellery and no dancing in uniform,' the selection committee warned all applicants. Spirited young women like Olive King, who risked their lives in war, resented such constraints on their new-found independence and the SWH's demands for chaperonage at all times. Since the average life of a soldier at the front was brief, some girls wondered how they could possibly refuse the pleadings of a young man who might soon be dead.

Nevertheless, serving in World War I *did* bring women increased freedom. Skirts became shorter as women complained they needed to clamber in and out of trains and lorries. The war changed women in many ways. While they became more masculine in their desire for freedom, in other ways they became more feminine. Pretty factory-made clothes were now within the reach of many more women and faces became more attractive thanks to the products of Elizabeth Arden and Helena Rubinstein. For the very first time 'respectable girls' could use lipstick, face powder and eye shadow, formerly the province of actresses and prostitutes. Virginia Woolf's novel *Mrs Dalloway*, refers to young women 'taking out rouge or a powder-puff and making up in public', previously unacceptable.[7]

War also provided many Australian women with the opportunity to leave home, travel and live in foreign countries. For some, like Sydney's Louise Mack, the first woman to report on the horrors of modern war in Belgium as a reporter for London's *Daily Mail* during the German invasion of Brussels, it meant freedom from restrictions and instant fame.

At the start of World War I several married women aimed to join the AANS but were discouraged from doing so, although the daughter-in-law of Prime Minister Joseph Cook *did* manage to enlist. Another woman, Sister Mary Kennedy, an AANS nurse serving on Lemnos Island, secretly married an Australian doctor but had to pretend she scarcely knew him. Had the Army discovered their secret, Sister Kennedy could have been sent back to Australia, while her husband, who had broken no Army ruling, would not have been penalised.[8]

Despite the sacrifices made by women in wartime, once the men came home, most wives and daughters returned to the subservient role of 'the Angel of the House'. The concept of separate spheres for men and women continued to bind most women to the home. World War I had been responsible for the deaths of over eight million men, wiping out a substantial part of what became known as the 'Lost Generation'.

At the outbreak of World War I Australia had a population of less than five million people but sustained a shockingly high casualty rate. Of the more than 400,000 men who enlisted in the AIF alone, 61,720 died in the conflict, a calamity for so young and small a nation.[9] As a result of such a high death toll, a large percentage of women would never have the chance to marry.

'They walked like princes, they looked like kings,' wrote John Masefield about the Anzacs at Gallipoli before the bloodthirsty massacres at Lone Pine and the Nek turned healthy young Anzacs into crippled wrecks. No one who went to war escaped damage, either physical or emotional.

Those Anzacs who survived and came home would later face the worst economic depression Australia has ever known. After the Great War women lived with husbands and sons scarred in mind and body, who turned to alcohol and were often violent. Many men could not find a job at all, an image author George Johnston showed in his novel *My Brother Jack*, which depicts very movingly the problems of a sensitive boy trying to adjust to having his mother bring home disabled soldiers to nurse.

FROM CORSETS TO CAMOUFLAGE AND CONCENTRATION CAMPS

When the Great War ended with the German request for an armistice, France (supported by America and Britain) imposed stiff penalties on Germany in the Treaty of Versailles. These in turn led to severe recession and unemployment in Germany and the rise of Hitler's

National Socialist Party. Within two decades the Third Reich defied the terms of the Treaty of Versailles and started to re-arm. Unfortunately, the League of Nations was a toothless tiger, lacking the power to send weapons inspectors to the Ruhr, where German factories like Krupp and Thyssen were manufacturing large quantities of armaments in contravention of the Treaty of Versailles.

In 1939, Germany invaded Poland. When in response Britain declared war on Germany, the Australian government announced it was also at war. The Japanese attacked Pearl Harbor in December 1941, thus entering the war. Japan had already seized Manchuria, a region of north-east China, in 1931 and invaded China proper in 1937 but felt obstructed by US policies towards its expansion in the Far East. It now looked towards the Philippines, Malaya and Indonesia as desirable sources of oil and rubber.

Following the fall of Singapore in February 1942, it became clear that the British Empire could not and would not defend Australia against Japan. Accordingly the Curtin government sought help from America. In response, General MacArthur arrived in Brisbane to run the Pacific campaign.

Women played a far more public role in World War II than in the previous war. Women were now employed in the Australian Army as decoders, cracking complex coded messages from Japanese ships and planes; they also worked in General MacArthur's planning rooms, moving models of troops and ships around large wall maps by means of billiard cues. Stella Bowen and Nora Heysen served as official war artists overseas, producing powerful images of war, Bowen with her scenes of Australian airmen, Heysen with her transport drivers and nurses at the blood bank.

With the Women's Auxiliary Air Force (WAAF), the Australian Women's Army Service (AWAS) and the Women's Royal Australian Navy Service (WRANS), women became an essential part of the war effort. They also worked as drivers, telegraph operators, clerical assistants, telephonists, draughtswomen, seamstresses, tailors and in munitions factories.

Once more, Red Cross volunteers were vital. Dr Lucy Bryce set up the Red Cross Blood Transfusion Service, which was responsible for saving many thousands of lives. During World War II gift parcels packed and sent by Red Cross volunteers provided huge moral support and helped keep many prisoners of war alive.

With so many men enlisted, the Curtin government made a landmark decision to support the employment of women, as land girls, railway porters, bus conductors and even as station masters. As a result, child care facilities had to be established to help these women cope with paid work *and* family responsibility. The Australian government nervously assured male voters that the employment of women was only a wartime measure and that everything would go back to normal when war ended.

The president of the Women's Employment Board, established to adjust women's rates of pay, expressed surprise that women were actually *capable* of handling complex machinery. Having inspected women working in factories, Judge Alfred Foster wonderingly observed:

> It was an amazing revelation to see women who were yesterday working in beauty salons or who had never worked outside the home, actually operating machines with a skill and a mastery that was little short of marvellous.[10]

Reluctantly, the men on the board raised female rates of pay to between 60 and 90 per cent of the male wage. However it was made clear that the concept of equal pay for equal work was an unnatural one and that, once the war was over, pay scales would revert to the old inequalities. It would take almost fifty years for women to claw back the economic gains that had been so hard-won in wartime.

In World War II, 3477 AANS nurses were posted as far afield as Britain, Egypt, Libya, Greece, Crete, Palestine, Syria, Eritrea, Ceylon, Malaya, New Britain, the Solomon Islands, Borneo, the Philippines and Morotai, off the coast of the Northern Territory.[11] By the second year of the war, Army nurses were given the rank of captain or major and expected to salute superior officers. This regimentation did not suit most AANS nurses, who responded by smiling instead of saluting and asked to be addressed as 'Sister', 'Miss' or 'Matron' rather than by military titles. This gained them the respect and co-operation of the roughest and toughest Aussie diggers.

ee ee ee

Nancy Wake was the only woman to be awarded a George Medal by Britain and a Croix de Guerre and the Legion d'Honneur by France. Nancy and her close friend Violette Szabo, one of only four women awarded a George Cross, trained with the British Special Operation Executive (SOE) and risked their lives when parachuted into France to help the French Resistance with money and arms. Nancy Wake survived, but Violette, who steadfastly refused to reveal the names of her comrades, was tortured to death. Violette Szabo had attended the same school as me, and her courage was commemorated on a stained glass window in our school chapel.[12] Violette's life shows all too clearly the difference between heroism and our modern and warped cult of celebrity.

Not all women who behaved heroically in the war are quite so well known. Queensland-born Joice NanKivell Loch, who died in Greece in 1983, received eleven medals for humanitarian work and for risking her life to save 1000 Polish and Jewish women and children from the Nazis.

Other well-known war heroines are the 'Paradise Road' nurses. Just before Singapore fell to the Japanese, sixty-five Australian Army nurses escaped aboard the yacht SS *Vyner Brooke*. The yacht was bombed and strafed by Japanese planes and sunk off Bangka Island. Amongst the survivors were AANS Sisters Vivian Bullwinkel, Sylvia Muir, Joyce Tweddell and Betty Jeffrey, who spent the remainder of World War II as Japanese prisoners of war.

Despite all their hardships, these heroic women never gave up. Vivian Bullwinkel's miraculous survival has been the inspiration for several books, films and documentaries, and Betty Jeffrey's account became the basis of the film *Paradise Road*. Here their story is supplemented by the stories of Sisters Sylvia Muir and Joyce Tweddell who have never spoken about their ordeal before. Likewise, the stories of Mavis Parkinson and Sister May Hayman who faced the Japanese in New Guinea deserve to be widely known.

HEROINES VERSUS CELEBRITIES

The Ancient Greeks gave us the word 'hero', a word they applied to people they believed were supermen, even braver than the gods because, unlike the gods, they were mortal and risked death. A hero meant someone outstandingly brave, one who would give their life to save others.

In those days no female equivalent of the hero existed. Women were regarded as physically and intellectually inferior to men, because they had smaller brains and because of the strange medical misconception of internally 'wandering wombs' causing hysterical behaviour. Hence, it was concluded, women were incapable of truly heroic acts.

The word 'heroine' is a relatively modern concept. The term did not come into general use until the early eighteenth century when it was used to describe the female protagonist in a novel. By the middle of the reign of Queen Victoria, the meaning had morphed into 'a woman of exalted spirit' or 'a brave woman'. Over a century later, feminist principles held that 'heroine' was politically incorrect and should be replaced by 'hero', defined in several dictionaries by the more gender-neutral phrase 'those who are admired'. The *Oxford English Dictionary* defines hero as 'someone brave, selfless and compassionate, who shows true greatness of spirit'.

Today, television programs, teenage magazines and PR specialists create 'heroic' female figures for young girls to emulate. These are often plastic Botoxed celebrities from the world of fashion and entertainment, shallow characters preoccupied with money and publicity, who do little for others and appear to lack any moral compass. The sporting media must also take some blame for having devalued the word 'hero' for their own ends. These days, anyone who wins a race or kicks a ball can be referred to as a hero, a term that should be reserved for *real* heroes — men and women like these who save the lives of others.

Of the brave and compassionate women described in this book, it is evident that none of *them* saw themselves as heroes or celebrities. In fact, apart from Vivian Bullwinkel, who was embarrassed by her fame, all are virtually unknown. These heroic women were compassionate and altruistic rather than narcissistic and inflated by silicone. Their lives say a great deal about the nature of female heroism and the fact that heroism is not gender specific.

Their names deserve to be known and remembered along with those of our Anzac heroes.

Out of the night that covers me,
Black as the Pit from pole to pole,
I thank whatever gods may be,
For my unconquerable soul.

W.E. HENLEY, 1849–1903, FROM 'INVICTUS'

CHAPTER 7

Olive May Kelso King

1885 – 1958

Serbian Order of St Sava
Serbian Good Samaritan Cross
Royal Serbian Memorial Medal
Serbian Silver Bravery Medal
Serbian Gold Zealous Conduct Medal
George V Silver Jubilee Medal
George VI Coronation Medal

In Greece you acquire wisdom and meet your destiny.

TRANSLATED FROM AN OLD GREEK PROVERB

When Miss Olive King died in 1958, her half-sister, Hazel, had to go through Olive's possessions to see what should be kept and what thrown away. It was not something Hazel enjoyed doing. Half-sisters are often jealous of each other, but she had greatly loved Olive, who, because of the twenty-five year difference between them, had been more like a loving aunt than a sister.

Hazel unlocked a red morocco-leather jewel box, aware that her elder sister, although reasonably wealthy, had never worn much jewellery. Inside was a pearl necklace with a sapphire clasp, a small brooch inscribed on the reverse 'To Olive from Mrs Harley, 1915', two commemorative medallions bearing the portrait heads of Kings George V and VI, and some other medals with foreign inscriptions.

Gently, Hazel lifted the tray that divided the box in two. Underneath lay what she knew had been Olive's most cherished possession: a large blue and white enamelled cross hanging from a gold crown. It was the Order of St Sava, Serbia's highest award for humanitarian service, which had been presented to Olive by King Alexander of Yugoslavia for serving in the Serb Army in World War I, a period in Olive's life she had rarely spoken about.

Beside the medal lay two matching miniature gold crowns, badges of rank worn by officers. And then Hazel found something that Olive must have cherished all these years. It was a faded photograph of a handsome young officer with blond hair, wearing a uniform jacket with similar crowns on his epaulettes. Written in ink on the right-hand corner of the photograph were the words 'With fond love, Yovi'. Obviously there were wartime secrets her sibling had not shared with her family.[1]

ℓℓ ℓℓ ℓℓ

Olive May Kelso King was the younger and more unconventional of the two attractive daughters of wealthy Sydney philanthropist Sir George Kelso King, director of Colonial Mutual Insurance, the Bank of New South Wales and the hugely successful Mount

Kelso King, to whom most of Olive's letters were addressed.

Morgan gold mine. Kelso King, as he preferred to be called, was the seventh son of a Protestant clergyman from Ulster, known for his devotion to the Anglican Church and his generosity to Anglican charities. His wife, Irene Isabella (née Rand), also a staunch Anglican, whose grandmother was French, had died of cancer when Olive was only fifteen. Her lingering and painful death affected her daughters in different ways. Sunny, the elder daughter, reacted by wanting to meet the man of her dreams and start a family of her own. At the age of twenty, Sunny married Harold Waring, an Englishman she met at a debutante ball at Government House, and moved to England with her husband. She had two boys, and the sisters, always close, kept in weekly contact by letter and phone.

At fifteen, Olive was old enough to realise how much her mother had suffered. The experience traumatised her, making her into a 'difficult' teenager. Once a brilliant student, Olive lost interest in studying and left Sydney Church of England Girls' Grammar School without taking any public exams.

What was she to do with her life? Olive was born in the same decade as Virginia Woolf, a period when intelligence and independence were not valued in young women. Instead, marriage and motherhood were seen as their destiny. But Olive did not want to settle down and get married, although she wrote love poems claiming that she wanted 'a great love in her life'. She was fascinated by the idea she had a French great-grandmother and loved the idea of going to Europe. She showed a flair for European languages so her father sent her first to a German and then to a Swiss finishing school. Olive loved her life in the Swiss Alps, learned to speak fluent French as well as German and became an excellent skier and mountain climber. With her teachers she visited Paris, Venice, Rome and Florence, and learned to appreciate art and architecture.[2]

When Olive returned to Sydney she missed Europe and her freedom. She wanted to be financially independent but her father forbade her to get a paid job, telling her that young ladies did not work for money. As Olive and her father were very similar in character they quarrelled a great deal. Strong-willed Sir George Kelso King was proud of his spirited younger daughter, although at times he despaired of her tomboyish ways and her passions for surfing, tennis and ice-skating. Olive had to do as he wished. So she acted as her father's hostess. Being a good bridge player, she partnered her father in the game, as well as being his unpaid chauffeuse, driving him around to board meetings in his Rolls-Royce and involving herself with his fundraising activities for the various charities to which he acted as financial adviser.

Olive's father was an unusual man. Unlike many businessmen of the period, whose main goal was to make vast profits, he devoted much of his free time to raising money for charities, including those for cancer research, the disease which had killed his wife.[3]

As well as being a dutiful daughter, Olive managed to enjoy her own pursuits. Out of the trust fund her mother had left her, she was allowed to buy a large open touring car and took up rally driving, at which she won numerous cups and prizes. Encouraged by her aunt, Georgina King, a renowned amateur anthropologist and ethnographer, she also took up mountain climbing as a sport. Georgina was a well-travelled, adventurous woman, way in advance of her time. She had written scientific papers, which were published in the journal of the Royal Anthropological Society of Australia, and she also funded the indomitable Daisy Bates. Aunt Georgina encouraged Olive to delay marriage and children as long as possible.

Despite expending her energies on the sports she loved, Olive still missed her mother greatly and she was not very pleased when her father told her he had fallen in love with young Alicia Kirk, ward of his late wife's good friend, the well-known philanthropist Eliza Hall.[4] Alicia Kirk, known by her pet name of 'Belicia', shared King's interests in charity work. Kelso King rather naively hoped that Belicia and his younger daughter would become good friends. Naturally Olive was outraged at the idea of his marriage to a woman who was not much older than herself. Doubtless she felt, like most young girls presented with a stepmother, that no one could possibly take her mother's place, and may have feared that Belicia was only after her father's money. Had Olive felt that, she would have been wrong. Alicia Kirk was an admirable young woman and worked as tirelessly for charities as had Olive's own mother. It was through her charitable work that she had contact with Olive's father.

After their quiet wedding in November 1907, Belicia joined Olive and her father in his large apartment at The Astor, in Macquarie Street, Sydney. From its long windows the apartment had a magnificent view over Circular Quay, Sydney Harbour and the grounds of Government House.

Initially, Olive resented her stepmother and the situation between them became more strained when Olive learned her stepmother was pregnant. To add to the tension, Kelso King disapproved strongly of Olive's latest boyfriend, a racing driver, whom her father referred to as a 'lounge lizard' and a 'fortune hunter'. Her father feared the handsome young man was after the money Olive had inherited from her mother. However, the money was invested in a trust fund, of which her father was sole trustee. His daughter had to ask his permission before spending any of it. Her father hoped it would be spent on educating his grandchildren.

In 1908 when Olive was twenty-five, her stepmother gave birth to a pretty little girl, whom they named Hazel. Olive was initially jealous, but soon she grew extremely fond of her baby sister, who was more like a favourite niece than a stepsister.

Olive eventually realised that Belicia was a generous and sweet-natured young woman who genuinely wanted Olive to like her. Her stepmother soon became pregnant again and both Kings were delighted when she gave birth to a healthy boy they named Nicholas.

To remove her from the racing driver boyfriend, Kelso King sent Olive to Mexico in 1910, accompanied by Isabelle Hay, a close friend of her mother. Olive terrified Isabelle when she decided to join three young English climbers in a brave attempt to be the first woman to climb the volcano of Popocatepetl, the second highest peak in Mexico. Olive succeeded and entered the annals of mountaineering history. What is remarkable is the fact that Olive accomplished this daring feat wearing a long skirt, as in that era 'young ladies' were not allowed to wear trousers.

Olive's passion for adventure remained unquenched. In 1914 she won another prize for rally driving and stayed out late celebrating her win with a crowd of friends, incurring her father's wrath. Olive thought of moving out and getting her own apartment but in 1914 unmarried daughters of 'good' families did not live alone. Then she received a welcome letter from her sister Sunny, telling her that a third baby was on the way. Sunny asked if Olive could come to England, run the house and oversee the domestic staff while she was in hospital having the baby.

Urged on by her father, who was still keen to separate Olive from the 'fortune hunter', Olive sailed to Europe and took over the running of Sunny and Harold's comfortable home and the care of her two young nephews.

On 28 June 1914, Olive tuned the radio to the BBC news and heard that Archduke Franz Ferdinand of Austria had been shot by a Serb student in the city of Sarajevo. Olive had no idea this act would trigger a chain of events that would lead to World War I or that this news item would so profoundly affect her life.

The assassination of the Archduke, heir to the Emperor of Austria, served as a pretext for Austria to invade Serbia. Austrian troops burned down homes and farmhouses and killed thousands of Serbs. They assaulted the Serb Army with superior forces and German-made arms and planes, killed large numbers of Serb soldiers and forced the remainder to flee over the mountains into northern Greece.

The German Kaiser, in turn, declared war on Germany's traditional enemy, France. German troops marched through Belgium and attacked France from the north, an act that violated Belgian neutrality. When Belgium appealed to Britain for support, Britain declared war on Germany.

On the other side of the world, shortly before he became prime minister, Andrew Fisher promised that Australia would send a large force to help Britain, 'down to our last man and our last shilling'. At the time Australia had only a tiny regular army and a volunteer part-time militia. Among the young men who enlisted in the newly formed Australian Imperial Force was Olive's cousin, Selwyn King, whom Olive more or less regarded as an elder brother. From Australia, cousin Selwyn wrote to Olive in London predicting that the war would be won by Christmas.

Olive became excited by the idea of going to war herself. She decided to volunteer as an ambulance driver. When Olive informed Selwyn of her decision he infuriated her by insisting that war was men's business. Women, in his opinion, should keep the home fires burning.

In those days, relatively few women drove cars. Driving was complex, as vehicles lacked synchromesh gearboxes and drivers had to master the skill of double declutching. But Olive had gained plenty of experience in car rallies, and the idea of helping to save lives had huge appeal for her. Not only that, it also offered a chance of adventure and escape from domesticity and possible marriage.

In England, many girls from affluent families who had never done paid work in their lives were now volunteering to drive ambulances or serve as volunteer nurses with volunteer aid detachments (VADs), which sprouted like mushrooms in northern France.

From Sunny's comfortable home Olive wrote to her father and

asked him to allow her and her sister to use some of their capital to buy an ambulance, which Olive could take to France. Reluctantly, Kelso King gave his consent. Olive was overjoyed. However, she soon found that the Army had bought up all ambulances not already in service. Undaunted, she bought a lumbering second-hand lorry and sent it to a professional firm of coach builders who converted the vehicle into a well-equipped ambulance. The large and heavy vehicle, which Olive christened *Ella the Elephant*, was capable of seating sixteen patients or taking four stretcher cases in bunk beds. A cupboard had been installed for emergency medical supplies and a primus stove provided for making hot drinks.

Olive with her ambulance *Ella*.

To prepare for her role, Olive attended a crash course in First Aid with the St John's Ambulance Brigade and took lessons in motor repairs at Sunny's local garage, a very unusual practice for a woman in an era when so few women drove cars.

Olive submitted her credentials to the Allies Field Ambulance Corps (AFAC), a privately funded organisation, and passed her commercial driving test easily. The AFAC was short of funds so could only supply its drivers with caps and badges. Apart from these, drivers were free to wear their own clothes. Olive bought herself several pairs of jodhpurs and warm sweaters. These would be far easier for climbing in and out of the ambulance than a long skirt. She generously helped the AFAC by paying her own passage and that of *Ella the Elephant* to cross the English Channel and for the fuel to get them to the Franco-Belgian border close to the front line.

ELLA AND OLIVE GO TO WAR

Joining the AFAC proved to be a baptism of fire for Olive. She was billeted in a deserted château near Rouen, along with the rest of the drivers, and given the job of driving wounded soldiers to a British military hospital.

As no morphine had been provided, the wounded men cursed and raved with pain. On her first day Olive transported a man in agony, his right arm hanging by a thread of muscle. Another of her patients had lain untended on the floor of a deserted farmhouse for days and had a gaping gangrenous hole in his thigh. Knowing he would die, the young man laughed bitterly as Olive, overcome by the stench of putrefying flesh, had to put down her end of the stretcher, turn away and vomit. 'You women, you'll *never* make proper ambulance drivers,' he jeered, his face twisted in pain.

At other times Olive had to transport soldiers so shell-shocked they could not speak and stared straight ahead, their limbs moving in spasms. The trauma of shell shock presented itself with a wide variety of symptoms, but had never been properly acknowledged before. Consequently, Olive was ignorant as to how to treat such patients and was left to cope as best she could.

For warm-hearted Olive, hardest of all to cope with were young boys, terrified of dying alone in a strange land, begging her with pain-filled eyes to sit beside them and hold their hands. Olive and her orderly worked up to seventeen hours at a stretch, frequently with only four or five hours' sleep a night.

Strangely enough, in spite of all the hardships Olive faced, she felt happy and fulfilled. Supervision was minimal in the AFAC and a great deal of decision-making was left up to their drivers, which suited Olive very well, as she detested rules and regulations. She also appreciated the easy camaraderie among the women drivers, the informality and the absence of ceremony. Each night they had a kind of rough-and-ready picnic meal around the dining table of the château with a few bottles of good French wine from a well-filled wine cellar. Olive was having the time of her life. She knew that she looked her best in trousers, enjoyed flirting with the young British officers stationed nearby and ignored the possibility of being hit by enemy gunfire — in fact, she revelled in danger all that summer.

Winter arrived with biting winds, sleet and snow. On New Year's Eve, 1914, Olive and the other drivers celebrated with a crate of French champagne discovered in an abandoned farmhouse. They drank the champagne out of tooth mugs. To keep warm, they burned worm-eaten kitchen chairs and ancient garden furniture, told jokes and sang songs in French and English.

The lives of Olive and the other drivers were placed in jeopardy when the AFAC headquarters, sited close to the French front line with Belgium, was captured by the Germans. Those who were able to escape looked after their own skins and took off for Calais, terrified they could be shot as spies. Those in charge at AFAC omitted to warn the ambulance drivers that they were in grave danger, and consequently Olive and two Canadian women drove back to the headquarters and into enemy hands. They were arrested by the Germans, locked in a damp basement and denied food. The officer in charge threatened that if they did not reveal all they knew they would be executed.

Later that night the women were interrogated one by one, as a Prussian officer shone a light into their eyes to confuse them. Olive kept calm and replied to the questions in German, which she spoke fluently after her time at finishing school. She explained that she was from Sydney and the other two drivers came from Toronto in Canada. And how did she, from the land of kangaroos, know how to speak German so well, one officer demanded. He was convinced that her knowledge of German proved she must be a spy. Olive gave the name of her finishing school and the names of several girls from prominent German families who had attended it with her. Luckily for Olive, they believed her. The officers decided Olive and the Canadian girls were harmless, a bunch of misguided idealists from the colonies caught up in a war they did not understand.[5]

Finally they released the women. Impressed that Olive had actually bought *Ella* out of her own money, a young officer, who had been friendly to Olive, returned the ambulance to her. However, the Germans impounded the other ambulances for the use of the German Army.

The girls climbed into *Ella* and roared off, singing at the tops of their voices in relief that they were alive and free. Olive drove at top speed in case the Germans changed their minds. They reached Boulogne and boarded the Channel ferry. On arrival in London they discovered that the AFAC had collapsed.

Hearing what had happened to Olive in a letter from his elder daughter, Kelso King was so worried about badly organised private relief organisations in France, he urged Olive to sell *Ella* and return home. Olive replied that, rather than returning home, she would apply to join the British Army as a driver, which would be far safer.

She did so but found the British Army refused to take women as ambulance drivers even when they had their own ambulances. One can imagine the recruiting officer scornfully declaring women far too hysterical to be ambulance drivers and unable to read maps. They could join the Red Cross and knit socks for soldiers instead. Olive probably gave him a withering glare, stood up and walked out.

Defying her father's wishes, Olive applied to another voluntary organisation, the independent Scottish Women's Hospitals for Foreign Service (SWH), run by Dr Elsie Inglis. The service's field hospitals and ambulances were entirely staffed by female volunteers from Britain and other parts of the British Empire.

The SWH received funding from American women and from the all-women's Cambridge colleges, Girton and Newnham. Their British supporters, mainly suffragettes, hoped that by showing courage and competence in war, British women would eventually obtain the right to vote, something Australian women had received in 1902 as a spin-off from Federation.

The SWH conducted several admission tests. Olive took an advanced driving test with *Ella* and a French language test and passed both with no difficulty. She was asked to leave for France as soon as she bought her uniform from the Army and Navy stores. This turned out to be so hideous that Olive believed it must have been designed by someone with a grudge against women. It consisted of a grey felt hat like an upturned pudding basin, a badly cut grey flannel shirt, a thick grey woollen jacket with large pockets and matching ankle-length skirt. A long grey woollen overcoat which reached to her ankles, a tartan headscarf and a narrow black tie completed the attire.[6] Olive attacked the pudding-basin hat with a hairbrush but nothing would make it more flattering. The uniform was nothing like the elegant outfit of cream jodhpurs, sweaters and well-polished riding boots, which showed off her legs to such advantage, she had been allowed to wear when working for AFAC. It was also far less practical. As Olive viewed herself in the mirror she winced.

For dinner in the mess, SWH staff were expected to wear a white silk blouse with their regulation long grey skirts. For 'special occasions' they could wear a plain black silk dress, which must have a high neck, but could be of any style they liked. Olive bought a black dress that showed off her slim figure and her long legs. However, in the SWH, high heels were taboo, as were lipstick, eye make-up and jewellery; even the gold charm bracelet she had worn since childhood and the little gold cross her father had given her on her confirmation into the Anglican Church were banned.

As men vastly outnumbered women at the front, Olive was warned that the conduct of SWH personnel with members of the opposite sex must be 'above reproach'. If invited to lunch or dinner by a man a woman could accept, but only if she was chaperoned by another woman. Olive, being typically Australian, loathed petty rules, regulations and rigid hierarchies. However, she crossed her fingers and agreed to these galling conditions, as she was desperate to get back on active service.

In the spring of 1915 Olive and *Ella the Elephant* crossed the English Channel once again. Last time Olive had been a free agent driving the ambulance with a minimum of supervision. Now she found herself taking orders from the elderly Mrs Harley, sister of autocratic General Sir John French. This stubborn general has entered history books by refusing to use tanks in World War I, claiming that they 'will never work and are no substitute for well-bred horses!'

Old Ma Harley, as the girls called her, was stone deaf. In a vain attempt to counteract this she wielded a huge ear trumpet. Due to her advanced age and the fact that the ear trumpet was useless, Mrs Harley proved difficult to work for.

However, Mrs Harley liked Olive very much and was kind to her. On her monthly conduct report she wrote that she found Olive conscientious and an excellent driver, and asked the SWH top brass to allow Olive to act as her personal chauffeuse.

Initially Olive was pleased by such rapid promotion. However, she soon discovered that her new boss had the time sense of an ant! She would tell 'dear Olive' she would be popping in to see some Army general who was a chum of her brother and would be back in five minutes. Olive, who would wait for her outside, kept the engine running. But invariably Mrs Harley would not emerge from her visit or meeting for hours. Sometimes she would go shopping and forget 'dear Olive' altogether. On other occasions, Mrs Harley would tell Olive she would be in a meeting for two or three hours and suggest Olive find herself a cup of coffee and read a book. When Olive finally returned, she would find her boss standing beside the ambulance tapping her feet in annoyance at being kept waiting. She liked Mrs Harley but found it impossible to carry on working for her.

Eventually Olive requested a transfer, just as all Mrs Harley's previous chauffeurs had done. But Olive had a kind heart and still regarded Mrs Harley as 'a nice old thing'. They parted on good terms, Mrs Harley believing Olive had been requested for field hospital duty. She kissed Olive on both cheeks and presented her with a brooch as a farewell gift. This had the effect of making Olive blush to think what she had said about Mrs Harley and her ear trumpet when requesting a transfer, and she continued to keep in touch with Mrs Harley and her daughter by letter.

Olive was posted to Troyes field hospital, which lay south-east of Paris and to the south of the cathedral city of Rheims. Rows of wounded French and British soldiers lay in canvas tents connected by duckboards across the surrounding mud in the grounds of the sixteenth-century Château de Chanteloup, with its pepper-pot

Olive King with fellow ambulance drivers including Kirstie Guthrie, aunt of the author, in France in 1914.

towers, elegant salon and mirrored ballroom, where Olive and her fellow drivers were billeted. The château had been abandoned by its owners at the start of the war, its ornamental *parterre* and vegetable gardens now overgrown with weeds.

Mice capered around the interior and over a few remaining Louis XV gilt chairs and Aubusson carpets. Most of the curtains and mirrors had been stolen during the first months of the war. As a result, Olive and her colleagues slept on camp beds in near empty chilly rooms, where fabulously expensive hand-blocked *toile de Jouey* paper peeled in long festoons from damp walls. They hung their clothes on nails knocked into the walls and set to work with buckets of water and scrubbing brushes to make their rooms habitable. In a letter to her sister dated 14 May 1915 written from the château, Olive described sleeping on a broken stretcher for a bed, and how they 'worked like lions and ate like wolves'. She also joked that the drivers had renamed their new home 'Château des Chauffeurs'.

Many of Olive's fellow ambulance drivers came from aristocratic or middle-class families. They were delighted to escape from parental control and worked hard and played hard. Olive found the company of these amiable young women stimulating; they were young, fancy free and high spirited. Together they planned a dance in the château's ballroom, to which they would invite the young British officers billeted nearby and play gramophone records, wear fancy dress and dance the night away.

However, the fancy dress party never eventuated as the next day a British officer arrived and warned them to expect an intake of two hundred wounded men. They were to be housed in the château's grounds and the girls were given ancient tents, poles and mallets and told to erect more tents. Some of the girls were completely flummoxed but as Olive had been a keen Girl Guide at school, she took charge and they got the tents up in good time.[7]

The Getting of Wisdom

In Greece you acquire wisdom and meet your destiny.

TRANSLATED FROM AN OLD GREEK PROVERB

After some months in France, Olive was told she could transfer to the recently opened Balkan front, where, on Greek soil, what remained of the Serb Army was fighting the Austrians. A new SWH field ambulance unit officially attached to the Greek Army, would be leaving for the northern Greek port of Salonika very soon.

Olive realised that she knew absolutely nothing about Salonika. So each morning she studied *The Times*. From it she learned that the city, with its large and strategically important harbour on the Gulf of Salonika, had been captured by the Greeks only a few years previously from the Ottoman Turks who had occupied it for centuries. To the north of the city lay beautiful but rugged country, filled with canyons, gorges and steep mountain peaks. Here on the Greek side of the border, the Serb Army was fighting a combined force of Austrians and Bulgarians. The Bulgarians, who were staunch Muslims and loathed Orthodox Serbs, were fighting with the Austrian Army because the German Kaiser and Emperor Franz Joseph of Austria had promised the King of Bulgaria part of conquered Macedonia, then part of Serbia, if the Bulgarians would join the war on the German side. Bulgarian bandits now filled the hills, harrying and murdering local peasants, as well as Allied soldiers and ambulance drivers who were bringing back the wounded from the front line.

To help the Serbs, an advance party of British and French troops who had been fighting at Gallipoli had landed at Salonika in October, under the command of General Sarrail. In Salonika, as well as Russian and Italian troops, a few British, Canadian and Australian engineers from the Gallipoli peninsula were helping to dig fortifications and earthworks to defend the city's northern frontier.

Olive prepared to leave for Greece. The SWH advised her that Salonika was extremely hot in summer but in winter could be snowed in. So Olive packed her fur coat, extra sweaters, her jodhpurs, her swimming costume and tennis racquet, just in case. She travelled by train to Marseilles where she and her group met up with another SWH unit. This unit was commanded by forty-three-year-old Dr Agnes Bennett, also from Sydney. *Ella the Elephant* and the other ambulances arrived at the same time on open goods wagons attached to the rear of the train.

From here, their journey continued on a troop ship, an ancient freighter called the SS *Mossoul*. Aboard were Olive's Girton and Newnham unit and Dr Bennett's SWH field hospital, whose ambulances (unlike *Ella*) had failed to catch the boat. On the voyage the ship had to keep changing course to avoid German submarines. Everyone on board was aware the *Mossoul's* sister ship, the equally ancient *Marquette,* had been torpedoed by the Germans and sunk, and that all the passengers and crew had drowned.

On board the *Mossoul* was a group of SWH doctors, thirty-eight female drivers, the same number of nurses, and crates of medical equipment. After three days' sailing, the *Mossoul* steamed safely through the high stone walls of the Corinth Canal and headed for Piraeus, the port of Athens.

After leaving Piraeus, the *Mossoul* chugged northwards, hugging the Greek coastline and heading for the port of Salonika. Olive, who loved mountains, was excited to see handsome Olympus, the mountain of the Greek gods, with its peak clad in snow and hillsides covered in rows of sugar-cube houses. The *Mossoul* docked at Salonika on 3 November 1915, just as the weather was turning bitterly cold. The passengers were greeted by a small group of Australian engineers. Delighted to see a fellow countrywoman, some of them immediately volunteered to help Olive unload *Ella*. The ambulance was swung across the deck by crane and lowered onto the shore.

While they watched *Ella* being hoisted up by crane, an elderly Australian colonel, who had served as an engineer at Gallipoli, explained to Olive that he and his men were digging ditches and fortifications around the landward side of the city.

Olive was told how a number of Serb soldiers had fled from the advancing Bulgarian and Austrian Armies by retreating across the snow-covered mountains of Serbia and Albania, where many had died of frostbite on what was now called 'the March of Death'. The remnants of the Serb Army were fighting the Austrians in northern Greece but had their headquarters in Salonika. They planned to recapture Monastir (today's Bitola) on the Macedonian border from the Austrians, the first step in a joint French and Serb campaign to recapture the Serb capital of Belgrade, now occupied by the Austrians.

Olive also learned that the British hoped the Greeks would break their neutrality and join the Allies. But King Constantine of Greece was descended from the German royal house and his wife was related to Kaiser Wilhelm. The result was conflict between King Constantine and the Greek Prime Minister, Eleutherios Venizelos, who was keen to join the war on the British side. Venizelos hoped that by doing this Greece would defeat Turkey, Greece's old enemy, and obtain a larger share of Macedonian territory.

Ella had now been landed on the quayside where she was surrounded by crates of bully beef, tea and marmalade imported by the SWH. The soldiers unhooked the clamps and chain from her wheels and, after a cursory customs inspection, Olive was free to drive her north to a French-run dressing station close to the front line at Guevgueli.

Olive and her three fellow drivers had to make their way carefully over the winding, potholed mountain roads with their hairpin bends, to Guevgueli. Sometimes *Ella's* radiator boiled and emitted clouds of steam, and Olive had to stop at intervals and top up the water in the radiator with melted snow.

Deep snow surrounded Guevgueli. In a letter to her father dated 12 November 1915, Olive mentions that the nights were freezing. *Ella* had no heating, so Olive wore her fur coat over her uniform. On the other hand, she was pleased that there were fewer fleas here than at Château de Chanteloup and wrote that the snow-covered mountains were glorious and reminded her of Arizona.

Guevgueli dressing station was overloaded with patients and there were fears that the Bulgarians might attack staff and patients. A decision was made to scale down the dressing station. However, the nurses had heard tales about the rape and murder of female prisoners by the Bulgarian Army and were terrified. They pleaded to be allowed to return to Salonika with their patients.

Sixteen talkative and flirtatious French ambulance drivers, half a dozen French soldiers and a young lieutenant arrived to help dismantle the dressing station. They were to load the wounded French soldiers into waiting French ambulances and take them by road to Salonika before the Bulgarians arrived.

Olive and the French drivers tried hard to dismantle the tents. It was not easy as the ground was frozen solid and a biting wind tore at the canvas. Olive struggled on one tent with the help of two jolly French drivers, who told her their names were Jean-Luc and Henri. They were pleasant young men who said they had become ambulance drivers because they preferred saving lives to killing people.

Striking camp took most of the night but the gale-force wind abated just before dawn and they managed to load the least seriously wounded men into the ambulances.

The SWH nurses sedated those seriously wounded patients due to undertake the uncomfortable journey back to Salonika. Meanwhile, the drivers, who had had little sleep, took the chance to have a quick rest in their ambulances before the return journey.

However, they didn't have long. Within half an hour Olive and her orderly were woken by one of the young volunteer nurses. The French lieutenant had received a morse code message warning that a detachment of the Bulgarian Army was advancing on Guevgueli. Unfortunately, no more French troops could be spared from the front line to help them. They were on their own.

As Olive spoke French fluently she was chosen to act as interpreter with the French ambulance drivers, who were arguing over the best route to take. As the senior SWH driver, Olive was fully aware of the gravity of the situation. She emphasised that *none* of them stood much chance of escaping from the Bulgarians if they took the mountain route. Even on the flatter road around the Doiran Lakes the ambulances were so overloaded they could still be overtaken by the Bulgarians on the terrible potholed roads.

She reckoned their only chance of escape was to drive to Guevgueli station, load the ambulances onto the next goods train for Salonika, and pray it arrived before the Bulgarians.

Olive knew they were taking a huge risk in relying on the train but she knew that the lorries transporting the Bulgarian troops had more powerful engines than the British or French ambulances. Catching the train was their only hope, although there was the risk that the train might have been cancelled.

Henri and Jean-Luc agreed with Olive but the other French drivers shouted them down and insisted they could easily drive faster than the Bulgarians. Male bonding and group solidarity won. Henri and Jean-Luc agreed to take the road to the Doiran Lakes along with their colleagues. Olive shrugged and wished the Frenchmen good luck before they revved up their engines and started off.

From where they were camped Olive and the other drivers could hear the sound of gunfire. Mesmerised, they watched the flickering headlights of the Bulgarian Army advancing on the opposite hillside. Olive knew they were gambling with their lives *and* those of their patients, but what else could they do?

Olive told her colleagues they must make their own choice. They could follow the French drivers or they could drive to Guevgueli station, as she had suggested, with her and load their ambulances and passengers onto the next goods train for Salonika. After some discussion the others agreed to her plan. Olive had butterflies in her tummy as she crank-started *Ella* into life and warmed up her engine. Slowly and carefully so as not to hurt the wounded men, Olive set off down the steeply sloping road to Guevgueli station. The other drivers followed, bouncing and jolting their way over potholes that threatened to break the suspension of their vehicles.

Once they reached the station it was nerve-racking for the women to see the lights of the Bulgarian lorries drawing closer. Luckily, the train was already standing in the station and the station master assured them that it would leave any moment now. The drivers bought tickets for themselves and their patients and drove the ambulances up the loading ramp.

Closer and closer came the lights of the Bulgarian lorries but the train did not move. Olive took her pistol from its holster, determined to kill the first Bulgarian who attempted to rape her or any of the other women. Still the train did not move. Then a whistle blew and with a flurry of steam they were off, only minutes before the Bulgarian convoy arrived.

As they drew out of the station they saw Bulgarian soldiers shaking their fists and making crude gestures at them. But it was too late — the Bulgarians could never catch them now. The train was gathering speed and was faster than any lorry. Soon they would be safe in Salonika. The women hugged each other with relief and several of the young VAD nurses burst into tears. After they had been travelling for ten minutes they heard a distant *crump crump crump* and saw flashes of light in the sky. German planes were bombing Guevgueli.

When they reached Salonika they heard over the radio that Guevgueli and its railway station had been reduced to rubble and the friendly station master had been killed by flying shrapnel.

Bulgarians armed with German machine guns had shot any Greek and Serb men of fighting age. As Olive had feared, Jean-Luc and Henri and the other ambulances *were* overtaken by the Bulgarians and forced to stop. Although the French ambulances had red crosses painted on them, Bulgarian soldiers did not respect the conventions of war. The massacre and genital mutilation of the French ambulance drivers and their wounded passengers horrified everyone in the French and SWH ambulance services.[8]

When the harrowing news was told to Olive, the blood drained from her face and she had to sit down. Poor poor Henri and Jean-Luc. She recalled how they all agreed to have dinner together in Salonika. She remembered how they had wanted to take the train — tears filled her eyes at the sheer horror of it all.

Olive knew she had survived by a fluke. Her main worry was that her father would find out what had happened and demand that she return to Sydney. Hoping reports of the Doiran Lakes massacre had not been picked up by the Australian press, Olive wrote a light-hearted letter to Kelso King saying nothing about Bulgarian atrocities. Instead, Salonika filled most of her letter. She told her father it was 'a fascinating spot, a real eastern town with bazaars, lovely Turkish coffee and quaint narrow streets aligned with old wooden houses with balconies'.

Her letter to Sunny gave a very watered down version of the truth and she warned her sister to say nothing to their father. Fortunately for Olive 'the forgotten Balkan campaign' did not attract the attention of the British or Australian press and her father never learned about the massacre on the Doiran road or Olive's narrow escape from Guevgueli.

However, Olive's bravery at Guevgueli had made her famous among the Serb garrison in Salonika. She was praised in the local press and awarded the Royal Serbian Memorial Medal.

MEETING ONE'S DESTINY

On return to Salonika, Olive's unit was camped uncomfortably on a windy beach outside the city. The next supply ship from

Britain had been wrecked, so the SWH staff were living off tins of corned beef, rock-hard army biscuits, tinned marmalade and a soup made of boiled weeds. To supplement this strange diet Olive bought treats for her fellow drivers, such as fresh fruit from market traders in Salonika.

Serbia had been totally overrun by Austrians and Bulgarians and thousands of Serb civilians had been killed. The nurses and ambulance drivers worked long hours trying to cope with a massive influx of wounded Serb, Montenegrin and Rumanian soldiers.

The Serb Army was still busy regrouping and reorganising its shattered forces in various camps around Salonika and trying to get hold of new equipment and ambulances to bring down the wounded from the front line.

Olive had worked for weeks without a break and was due some time off. She used her free days to drive into the centre of Salonika, park *Ella* and walk around the city. She was fascinated by what she saw. To Olive, brought up in a relatively young society, Salonika seemed incredibly ancient. It had been founded by a Macedonian leader named Cassander and ruled by Philip of Macedon, father of Alexander the Great. Centuries ago it had been invaded by successive waves of Romans, Normans and Saracens. As part of the great Byzantine Empire it had been second only in importance to Constantinople (now Istanbul) when Athens was nothing but a village. Now Salonika was becoming strategically important once again; its port thronged with ships and soldiers from many different countries. The city was connected by rail to Belgrade, Paris and Athens, a vital cog in what was known as the Balkan Campaign against the Austrians and their German and Bulgarian allies.[9]

In the narrow streets Olive learned to recognise Macedonians and Albanians by their black baggy trousers and brightly embroidered waistcoats of many different colours, and their white linen shirts. The women wore long black skirts with white linen blouses and white headscarves.

Wealthy Greek women, on the other hand, wore Western dress, silk stockings and high-heeled shoes. Olive also learned to distinguish Orthodox Greek or Serb priests from rabbis by their flowerpot hats. Both groups seemed to have bushy beards, flowing black robes and long hair, but the rabbis also had ringlets that hung down beside their cheeks.

Each day more British soldiers and a few Anzacs arrived from Gallipoli, shivering in their thin summer uniforms. As well, there were kilted Highlanders, Indians in turbans and Africans from the French colonies in blue jackets and white breeches with red fezzes on their heads.

Olive enjoyed her visits to the picturesque Turkish quarter of Salonika so much that she asked permission to move out of her tent in the SWH camp at Mikra Bay to rent accommodation there. Prices were amazingly cheap. She did not tell her father until she had moved into the city, delighted to have a home of her own at last, albeit temporary. The apartment already had some furniture and beds and Olive added dark wooden chests, ceramic plates and sheepskin rugs, which she bought cheaply from a shop owned by a Turk. He told her that his ancestors had lived in Salonika for centuries and that he and his family intended to remain here even though the city was now part of Greece.

Olive's new apartment overlooked the bay. It was surrounded by ancient Turkish-style timber houses, their balconies braced by timber supports to withstand earthquakes. The balconies were sheltered by and decorated with lattice, which gave privacy and made an additional room for summer living. As the houses of the workers were highly flammable few of them had stoves, so peasant women in black carried their casseroles of food to the local bakeries to have it cooked for them.

Olive was kept busy ferrying cases from the camp at Mikra Bay to the British tented hospital at Mount Hortiack,[10] almost 20 kilometres away. She also ferried supplies up the Vardar Valley to the Serb battle lines on the slopes of Mount Kaimaktsalan, or the 'Peak of the Buttercups'. To get there she drove over 'perfectly poisonous, simply indescribable roads which were a mass of shell-holes'. On the return journey she brought back wounded Serbs to the new army hospital out at Kalamaria run by Canadian and British doctors, and to the SWH hospital at Charilaos run by SWH volunteers.

Olive serviced *Ella* herself, not wanting to entrust her to Greek mechanics who had never seen an Alda engine, let alone serviced one. One day after changing tyres and doing some work on the engine, Olive lunched at the SWH mess at Mikra Bay. Afterwards she was called into the office of a senior staff member and told that there had been complaints that she had arrived at lunch with grubby fingernails. Olive, angry and annoyed by the reproach, said they could hardly expect her to service her vehicle *and* look as if she had just come from the beauty parlour.

Two weeks later, Olive received a letter telling her that women drivers were no longer expected to service their vehicles. An agreement had just been confirmed between SWH administrators and the Serb Army under which Serb mechanics would service all SWH ambulances, including those that were privately owned.

The following week, as Olive was driving casualties to the hospital at Mount Hortiack, one of *Ella*'s front wheels ran into a large pothole, causing a spring to break, 'going with a click like a broken back', as she put it. Driving very slowly, Olive managed to get the ambulance to the Serb military garage where she asked to talk to the most experienced mechanic. He turned out to be a tall, shy young man named Artsa, with crisp black curly hair, startlingly white teeth and a friendly smile.

Artsa was extremely polite and respectful. He called Driver King 'Gospojitsa' or 'Most Honoured Lady' in the old fashioned Serbian way and explained that, due to the bad state of the roads, he had thirty vehicles with broken springs awaiting repairs, so her ambulance would be off the road for some time. He suggested Olive talk to Captain Milan Yovitchitch, the liaison officer, to arrange replacement transport. Olive waited to see him but the officer never arrived. Nothing more happened for two weeks and Olive was becoming increasingly angry with that wretched liaison officer. She planned to tell him just what she thought of him when finally he *did* arrive.

Aware *Ella* would be off the road for some time, Olive bought herself a Serb–English dictionary and a phrase book, hoping to learn the Cyrillic alphabet and some Serb phrases so she could try to converse with the wounded men. She also walked everywhere around the inner city, climbing cobbled streets and walking through ancient archways in the thick walls. Once she found herself high on the ramparts overlooking the bay, enchanted by the magnificent views. She enjoyed herself sitting at pavement cafés watching the world go by and developed a fondness for eating almond-filled *baklavas* dripping with honey and drinking sweet, gritty Greek coffee, thick as mud and just as dark.

Finally, she received a message that Captain Yovitchitch would meet her. His English was rather halting so they communicated in French, which he and Olive both spoke fluently. Olive had intended to be furious with the captain. However, since he apologised so nicely and told her he was overwhelmed with work and meeting relations who had come to bury their sons or visit the wounded in hospital, she forgave him. The fact that he was tall, broad-shouldered and extremely handsome helped her to forget how annoyed she had been.

For his part, Captain Yovitchitch had been told by Artsa the mechanic that Olive was one of the most heroic ambulance drivers, and that she had saved many wounded Serbs at Guevgueli. The captain wrote out a docket which would give Olive a substitute vehicle until *Ella* was repaired. Their official business over, the captain asked Olive how she was getting on in Salonika. When he learned that Olive had been spending her free time trying to learn Serbian, a most difficult language, he was impressed. He bought her another cup of coffee and told her how to pronounce some useful phrases. She would have no trouble communicating with educated Serbs, he told her, as French was their second language. The captain told Olive he had perfected his French in Paris where, before the war, he had been a junior attaché at the Serb Embassy.

Initially, the captain had thought Olive a rather plain young woman in her drab grey uniform. However, when she smiled her whole face lit up and her cropped blonde hair gave her a boyish charm. The fact that Driver King was risking her life to save wounded Serbs made him feel protective towards her. He promised her that she would receive a replacement ambulance very soon.

Olive thanked him but secretly wondered if he could be trusted. In her experience, handsome men rarely *were* trustworthy. However, within two days her liaison officer was back with a replacement ambulance. They made a short drive to get her accustomed to driving the new vehicle. When he said goodbye the captain kissed her hand in the French way.

THE PURSUIT OF LOVE

On Olive's next free day the captain drove her around the Byzantine landmarks of Salonika. He pointed out beehive-domed churches, some of which had had minarets added to them by the invading Turks, and the famous White Tower, a Salonika landmark. Then he parked his staff car and invited Olive for a cup of coffee. Sitting at a marble-topped table in a café she talked about her life in Sydney, mentioning that she had partnered her father at bridge and had played it for many years. The captain invited her to take part in a bridge tournament to be held the following week at the Serb Officers' Club.

The night of the tournament, Olive spent a long time dressing and washed her hair till it shone. Ignoring the regulations, she wore her gold charm bracelet, pale pink lipstick, eye-shadow and French perfume. That little black silk dress bought in London and a pair of high-heeled shoes showed off her slim figure and long legs.

The evening was a huge success. The captain was impressed by Mademoiselle King's skilful and rational bidding and the cool way she played her cards. Rationality was not something he had previously associated with women. He invited her to play bridge again and this time suggested they dine beforehand at the Serb Officers' Club. This did not break SWH rules — there would be plenty of other women around to act as chaperones — so Olive accepted with a clear conscience.

One can picture how the meeting might have gone: Olive arriving at the Serb Officers' Club, the captain once again kissing her hand and saying, 'Mademoiselle King, please call me Yovi. I know my family name is difficult for English people to pronounce.'

'Call me Olive,' she might have responded. 'Australians don't go much for ceremony.'

'Oleev,' he possibly repeated uncertainly, finding it strange that her parents had named their daughter after a fruit instead of a saint. 'I prefer, if I may, to call you a Slav name. How does *Olinka* sound to you?'

Olinka, what a beautiful, exotic name.

That night at dinner Yovi and his fellow officers spoke in French for Olive's benefit. They told her that their family estates had suffered from the Austrian invasion, crops and barns had been burned and tenants' cottages razed to the ground. Yovi's father had died of a heart attack, probably from the horror of it all. Olive was filled with sympathy. How these young men had suffered on the March of Death from Serbia to Greece and how brave they were, how determined to win back their homeland from the Austrians.

Yovi escorted Olive back to her apartment, said goodnight formally and kissed her hand.

Olive must have felt that this time her father had no need to be alarmed — even *he* could not accuse Yovi of being a fortune hunter.

Olive King in her Serb Army uniform.

Captain Milan Yovitchitch. The print was inscribed, 'To my dear little pal with fond love, Milan (Yovi)'.

Yovi enjoyed Olive's company more and more. He admired the fact that she could dismantle an engine, change a tyre, and play bridge and tennis well.

They went to restaurants together, heard *bouzouki* music with Yovi's fellow officers, danced to gypsy music, intoxicated by the rhythm. One night, after a few bottles of Samian wine, Yovi confessed to Olive that he had allowed himself to follow tradition and become betrothed to a seventeen-year-old girl whose parents were friends of his mother. He hardly knew the girl. According to his family it would be a good match. She was a descendant of Black George the Liberator, the famous Karageorge, ancestor of the present royal family. Yovi told Olive he wanted to wait until after the war before marrying his fiancée.

Olive was upset but not surprised by Yovi's confession. Although she knew the sensible thing would be not to get emotionally involved with him, it was too late — Olive was head over heels in love with Yovi and convinced that he loved her.

Soon they were dining and dancing several nights at week at the White Tower restaurant. Yovi admired how well she danced. He laughed at her jokes, enjoyed her company, did everything he could to please her, no doubt squaring his conscience about his fiancée by telling himself that this was wartime and he and Olinka were ships passing in the night.

On a mission up to the front line to confer with Crown Prince Alexander, Yovi narrowly avoided death when the car he was in was fired on by a Bulgarian patrol. The bullet grazed his forehead. On his return to Salonika, Olive sat him down on one of the bunks in the rear compartment of her ambulance, unwound the bandage a Serb orderly had placed around his head, disinfected the spot where the bullet had drawn blood, then rebandaged the wound. She hoped the bullet graze would heal without leaving a scar on that handsome face. Leaning over him and looking into his eyes as she tended his wound was her undoing. The tension between them was electric. He drew her down beside him and it was impossible to resist his kisses.

Olive may have rationalised her surrender to Yovi the same way he did: by saying that things were different in wartime. He could be killed by the Bulgarians any day — she could have been killed at Guevgueli or die next week. What were they waiting for?

They tried to keep their affair discreet but they were so obviously in love that people started to talk. The more prudish members of the SWH staff heard the gossip and demanded that Driver King be dismissed. With pursed lips they pointed out that she had broken the rules by dining unchaperoned with a member of the opposite sex. And it seemed the matter had gone further, much further. They had danced cheek to cheek in public and Driver King had been wearing eye-shadow and lipstick.

Olive was interviewed by the SWH director who reprimanded her. SWH rules were spelled out to Olive. Furthermore, the committee members (who were all over fifty) pointed out that Dr Inglis and other feminists had set up the SWH to prove women were as good as men in order to win British women the vote. Driver King was letting the side down.

The elderly woman who headed the SWH told Olive her relationship with Captain Yovitchitch had become a scandal and would be considered at next week's committee meeting. Her resignation might be demanded.

'OLINKA' JOINS THE SERB ARMY

To forestall Olive being sacked by the SWH, Yovi suggested she resign and join the Serb Army.

He added teasingly that *his* army had no rules forbidding female staff from wearing lipstick or high heels. Yovi suggested that Olinka apply to be his personal chauffeuse and promised he would keep better time than Mrs Harley! It seemed like a heaven-sent opportunity to be together.

In July 1916, Olive shocked her critics by resigning from the Scottish Women's Hospitals, taking her ambulance with her.

In a letter to her father dated 20 July 1916, Olive told him that she was about to join the Serb Army as an ambulance driver. She did not mention that she had upset the SWH but added revealingly, 'I've had *enough* of women's discipline.' Worried that her father might learn about her and Yovi, Olive mentioned that her liaison officer thought it was an excellent idea, as the Serbs were so short of drivers. But Olive gave no hint of her feelings for Yovi.

Olive's father had continued the King family tradition of upholding the Protestant faith, was a lay canon of St Andrew's Cathedral and churchwarden of All Saints' Anglican Church, was on the Board of Governors of King's and Sydney Grammar School, and involved in various Anglican charities. The idea of his younger daughter abandoning the Protestant faith and marrying into the Eastern Orthodox Church, which denied the authority of the Bible, Olive knew would be anathema to Kelso King, no matter how well-connected her bridegroom might be.

In her letters home to her staunchly Anglican father, Olive was careful not to mention any emotional involvement with Yovi. She made their relationship sound professional, referring to him as a 'good pal' who was only helping her as her liaison officer.

Mrs Harley, Olive's former boss in France, arrived in Salonika, heading another SWH unit. She was delighted to see Olive but puzzled as to why she had joined the Serbs. Olive did not enlighten her.

As a corporal in the Serb Army, Olive was issued with a uniform consisting of a khaki tunic with brass buttons, cream-coloured breeches, long boots of supple leather and a thick khaki pullover. She found these clothes far more practical for work than the cumbersome long skirts provided by the SWH.

Olive's ambulance was one of three attached to the Serb medical headquarters. The other two needed constant repairs, which meant that, as the only person insured to drive *Ella*, she had to let someone else drive Yovi around. She was promoted to the rank of corporal and was sent to the front line on the slopes of Mount Kaimaktsalan near Monastir to collect wounded Serb soldiers to be transported to the British Military Hospital at Mount Hortiack, about 30 kilometres north of the city.

As the roads were potholed and precipitous, *Ella's* tyres were frequently punctured. Olive had to get out and change them and was often on the road for sixteen hours at a stretch.

When she wasn't carrying out rescue trips in *Ella*, Olive acted as staff driver to Yovi and his immediate superior, Colonel Derok. She worked long hours and spent as much of her free time as possible with Yovi. She was deeply in love with him and, it seems, so was he with her.

On one trip, Olive was ordered to take *Ella* to fetch Serb soldiers wounded in a skirmish high in the hills. The rescue trip meant crossing the rickety Gumendjie Bridge, a narrow structure only just wider than the ambulance, whose parapets had collapsed. A steely nerve was needed to drive *Ella* over the dilapidated bridge, which had a drop of 30 metres on either side. One false move on Olive's part meant that she and the wounded men would plunge to their deaths. Fortunately, Olive kept a cool head and a steady hand on the wheel. Although the stretcher cases were terrified, she got them back across the Gumendjie Bridge without mishap. 'Excellent work,' said Colonel Derok when he heard about Corporal King's success. 'Women keep their nerve when men lose their heads.'

On another dangerous mission, driving with her orderly on a rescue mission along the steep and potholed road that led north to Vodena (today's Edessa), *Ella*'s gearbox broke down completely and it was beyond Olive's capabilities to repair it. Clearly the engine, gearbox and suspension also needed time as well as money spent on them. However, Artsa and the other mechanics were already working around the clock and lacked the time to do a complete overhaul on *Ella*.

Olive wrote to Sunny describing *Ella*'s deterioration. She explained how desperately the Serbs needed another ambulance. Three weeks later she received a reply. Her father had agreed that each of his daughters could pay half the cost of a new ambulance from their joint trust fund as a contribution to the war effort. They should buy a smaller more economical and manoeuvrable ambulance and Olive should use *Ella* only for emergencies. But where could Olive buy a brand new ambulance? They would have to buy a new lorry in England and get it converted into an ambulance there.

Olive thought of Mrs Harley. She made frequent trips home to see her brother and intended to buy the SWH another ambulance out of her own pocket. Surely she could look for two ambulances? So Olive wrote to Mrs Harley outlining the problems with *Ella*. Mrs Harley wrote back offering to find a suitable lorry and get it converted by a coachbuilder when she was in England the following month. She would see the suspension was reinforced as she knew what the potholed roads out here did to lorries. Olive must have felt a warm glow when she read Mrs Harley's letter.

On her next visit to London Mrs Harley was as good as her word. She bought a Ford lorry, organised its conversion and arranged for the new vehicle to be shipped to Salonika. Olive named the second ambulance *Bridget* after a hardworking Irish girl who had cared for her and Sunny as children. *Bridget* could not accommodate as many wounded men as *Ella* but had far more responsive steering and so she handled better over the terrible roads.[11]

Olive was thrilled with *Bridget*, and Yovi invited Mrs Harley to a special luncheon held in her honour at the Serb Officers' Club to thank her for what she had done for the Serb Army.

※ ※ ※

Olive, who up to now had had plenty of admirers but never lost her heart, must have been suffering the torments and jealousies as well as the delights of love as she reflected about the seventeen-year-old girl to whom Yovi was betrothed. Her diary for 1917 revealed that whenever she was with Yovi she felt blissfully happy but she found his behaviour perplexing. He treated her like a younger sister, teased her affectionately, rumpled her hair and was annoyed when she beat him at tennis.[12]

His fiancée, a Karageorge, was apparently distantly related to Crown Prince Alexander, Yovi's great friend since childhood. And in Serbia, Karageorge was a name to reckon with. The wedding would take place in the Eastern Orthodox Church which did not acknowledge divorce. If he married, that was final. Yovi, like most men, avoided matters that embarrassed him and refused to discuss his fiancée. Olive thought he regarded this betrothal as an obligation. In the midst of a war his family obligations seemed unreal. What was real was the here and now.

There was also the problem of Olive's age. Being over thirty, Olive was not regarded as being in her prime child-bearing years. She could easily bear him a mentally defective or a deformed child. And a healthy male heir was needed to secure Yovi's estates in troubled times.

Ironically enough, at this time Crown Prince Alexander himself was under pressure to marry and produce an heir. The prince was being urged to marry a Russian princess, whose church was also of the Eastern Orthodox faith. Tsar Nicholas, who had sent a detachment of Russian troops to help the Serbs, had several beautiful daughters all younger than Alexander Karageorge. It was believed that when the war was over Prince Alexander would announce his engagement to one or other of the Tsar's daughters.

While the romantic in Olive might have been disappointed that Prince Alexander would not marry his French girlfriend, Yovi explained that as regent to an ailing and elderly king, the Crown Prince could not make a morganatic marriage to the girl he loved. He must make a dynastic alliance to an Orthodox princess, and one from a wealthy country that could support Serbia.

Like most people who are desperately in love, Olive could not prevent herself mentioning Yovi's name in letters home. On several occasions she told her father how lucky she was to be working with Captain Yovitchitch, a close friend of the Serbian royal family who saw that whenever she drove to the front line she had an armed guard with her. She told her father how much she admired the Serbs' unconquerable spirit and their determination to repossess their country from Austrian and Bulgarian invaders. She explained that there were now about 80,000 Serbian troops garrisoned in northern Greece and Greek Macedonia, once part of the great Macedonian Empire.

Olive also explained to her father how war had changed her. Now she would gladly 'work day and night for the Serbians without pay'. She begged her father to use his financial skills to set up a fund to buy ambulances and medicines for the Serbian Army. While there was wide publicity for the suffering of the Belgians and the French, the suffering of the Serbs remained largely unreported. Unless her father did something, no one else would take up the Serbian cause in Australia.[13]

On receiving his daughter's cry for help, Kelso King responded by setting up an appeal for funds to buy ambulances for the Serbs. Australians were generous, and money was raised and more ambulances and medicines were purchased. Colonel Derok, Olive's commanding officer, was extremely grateful to her and her father. Best of all in Olive's eyes was the fact that Yovi was delighted. Yovi was convinced that under the leadership of Crown Prince Alexander the Serbs would recapture their country from the enemy. After the war, the prince would build 'Greater Serbia' — a huge federation of Slav countries. This was the 'Grand Plan' Crown Prince Alexander and Yovi believed in and which, as a diplomat after the war was over, Yovi would help implement.

The spring of 1917 was hot and very dry. Olive and Yovi got up early and after working-hours played tennis and often went to the beach for a swim. Most nights they ate dinner together and sometimes attended concerts, as Olive shared Yovi's love of classical music.

In March 1917 Olive was directed to drive Yovi north over the hazardous mountain road to the SWH base hospital attached to the Serb Army, which Dr Agnes Bennett was running near the village of Ostrovo. Yovi was to represent the Crown Prince and award three women — Dr Bennett, Dr Lilian Cooper[14] and the head of the Ostrovo ambulance service, Miss Josephine Bedford — with the Order of St Sava, the highest award for humanitarian service in Serbia. After three hours of skilful driving over precipitous roads they reached Dr Bennett's hospital, situated under some elm trees, and visited Mrs Harley's daughter who was suffering from malaria. The camp had a magnificent view across the waters of Lake Ostrovo and the surrounding snow-capped mountain peaks. Unfortunately, mosquitoes bred there in droves and were more dangerous than Bulgarian bandits — some of Dr Bennett's staff had already died from malaria.

In a simple ceremony as 'stand in' for Crown Prince Alexander, Yovi presented Dr Bennett, Dr Cooper and Miss Bedford with the

Order of St Sava, a blue and white enamelled Maltese cross hanging from a large golden crown. The medals came in individual velvet-lined cases and had been made by a leading Bond Street jeweller. The medal had been named after Prince Sava, who renounced the world to become a monk, and was awarded to outstanding Serbs and foreigners but rarely to women.

Yovi read out the commendation personally authored by Crown Prince Alexander, pinned the medals on each woman and made a short speech commending their dedication and bravery. Then he spoke a few words to each of them. Yovi found Dr Agnes Bennett and Miss Josephine Bedford pleasant but Dr Lilian Cooper hard to talk to. She was brusque and ill at ease. Little Miss Bedford was overcome by the honour and had tears in her eyes as Dr Cooper received her medal. Yovi did his best to make the ceremony informal and to put Dr Cooper at her ease but she was coughing badly and in need of a good rest as, like all the SWH women, she had been working under primitive conditions for months.

After the ceremony, they all drank a *vin d'honneur* from tooth mugs.

Aware of the gossip about Olive's abrupt resignation from the SWH and her relationship with him, Yovi politely declined Dr Bennett's offer of a spartan lunch. Then Yovi said polite farewells and climbed into the vehicle. Olive crank-started the engine for the return journey. Yovi placed his pistol on the dashboard as protection against the Bulgarians in the high mountain passes. Then they drove away from Ostrovo and its mosquitoes.

They stopped at a high vantage point where they could look out over miles and miles of surrounding territory and were relieved to see no troops were in sight. All around them were masses of blue, yellow and white wild flowers amid the grass. They sat down and Olive unpacked some food and a bottle of wine for a romantic picnic.

Hours later they reached Salonika and congratulated themselves that the day had gone so well. Olive had never felt happier.

Despite Olive's care to sleep under a mosquito net at all times, she still caught malaria. One morning she found her temperature had soared. By the evening she shivered and shook and was covered in perspiration. Yovi called the doctor and was so worried by Olinka's condition that he visited her twice a day, sat beside her bed for hours and had special broth and minced-chicken dishes cooked for her in the Officers' Club. He brought the food to her apartment himself or had it sent over by one of the mess staff, but nothing seemed to bring down Olive's temperature.

In the second week of her illness Olive lost consciousness and Yovi feared she might die. He would not leave her bedside and once, as Olive regained consciousness, she found him wiping her forehead with tears in his eyes, whispering, 'Olinka, my love, don't die. Olinka, stay alive for me.' But Olive's blackouts and fever continued. The doctor asked Yovi to bring an Anglican clergyman to Olive's bedside just in case . . .

Yovi climbed into his car and scoured the city until he found an Anglican clergyman. He dragged the poor man out of bed and made him come to Olive's apartment. By the time Yovi was back at Olive's bedside with the clergyman the fever had abated and she was fully conscious. Yovi was convinced that the Mother of God had heard his prayers and intervened.

Olive's health gradually improved but she was aware that she had had a close shave with death. When Yovi felt that Olive was strong enough to bear the shock, he told her that poor Mrs Harley was dead and buried, and a memorial to her aid work was being erected in Salonika. An enemy shell had landed on her house in Monastir.[15] Olive remembered the little brooch Mrs Harley had given her and how she had bought *Bridget* for her in England. It highlighted the fact that in wartime they all were at risk. She and Yovi could die any time. Marrying or not marrying did not seem so important now. What mattered was staying alive.

The doctor now allowed Olive to get up for a couple of hours each day. Yovi still brought her special meals and told her that what mattered most to him was that she got well. It was a touching demonstration of his love. Olive had now lost so much weight that her clothes were far too big for her. In response to Olive's urgent SOS, Sunny sent out an elegant silk dress and a couple of pairs of well-cut black trousers — very daring for a woman to wear at that time. They showed off Olinka's long legs to best advantage.

Sometimes Olive ate with Yovi and several of his fellow officers in their favourite *taverna,* run by an Athenian who, in spite of the food shortage, managed to produce assorted *mezedes* of grilled vegetables and plates of grilled fish. Greek women of that era rarely ventured outside the home, so that *kafenions* and *tavernas* were almost exclusively male. With her cropped blonde hair, her tight black trousers, her scarlet cummerbund and knee high boots and in one of Yovi's crisp white evening shirts, Olive often passed as a boy. It amused Yovi when she dressed like that.

The previous summer Olive's father had written saying that he was worried about Olive living alone in a garrison city where there would be many drunken soldiers. Olive jokingly told him that she was 'more horribly independent' than ever. However, alleviating his worries she told him two English girls, Barbara M. Allen and D.K. (Mimi) Percival, who were also working as drivers for the Serbs, were sharing her apartment with her. But she never told her father that Yovi spent nights with her when he was not on duty.[16]

Both Miss Allen and Miss Percival had fallen foul of the SWH for dining unchaperoned with Serb officers and had followed the example of Olive in enlisting in the Serb Army. Olive called her new flatmates 'Barb' and 'Mim' and they called her 'Ollie'. They were nice girls with a good sense of humour and they and their Serb boyfriends often joined Olive and Yovi for dinner.

Olive was well satisfied, with a modest home of her own, friends and a purpose in life. In her letters home, she carefully continued to make it appear that she, Yovi and Corporals Percival and Allen were just 'good pals'. She told her father that Captain Yovi was kind enough to escort them to restaurants or concerts in Salonika as part of his official duties.

The Serb drivers admired Olive for her bravery at Guevgueli and for her generosity and kindness to them. The drivers were fiercely protective of their *Gospojitsa.* They gave her a little medallion of the Holy Mother of God to hang from her driving mirror. Artsa swore he would fight to the last to ensure she would not fall into the hands of those terrible Bulgarians. Artsa, the head mechanic with his broad smile and dark curly hair, was a typical Slav: tall, broad-shouldered and ruggedly good looking. He did everything possible to help Olive keep her ambulances on the road.

The Serb drivers' garage doubled as a combined mess and recreation area. At lunch the drivers, the mechanics, Olive and Corporals Percival and Allen ate at a rickety wooden table in a corner of the garage. In an effort to improve things Olive hung a flowered curtain around the dining table to block out the pieces of dismantled car engine and the oily floor. She bought tablecloths and napkins and a set of comfortable dining chairs with padded seats for which her fellow drivers were grateful. Their lunches were a thin spartan soup with barley, gristly stewed meat and dried beans with boiled rice. Olive, generous as ever, bought *baklavas* or other delicious Greek cakes and pastries and fresh fruit to supplement them.

With Yovi's help Olive had become reasonably fluent in Serbian, which was not an easy language to master. She learned from Yovi that the Serbs had paid a heavy price for recapturing the bleak slopes of Kaimaktsalan and Monastir: almost 125,000 deaths and an even greater number of wounded or maimed men.

Olive vowed that since her life had been spared at Guevgueli and she had recovered from malaria she would donate any money she earned from the Serb Army to help her fellow drivers and their families. There was no point in saving it. She might never live to see the end of the war. 'Shrouds have no pockets' was a proverb she had heard from several wounded Serbs.

Dining with Yovi at the Serb Officers' Club was like eating in a good restaurant in pre-war Paris. In marked contrast, the food and living conditions of the Serb drivers was woeful. Unlike their British and French counterparts, they did not even have subsidised canteens selling hot drinks, lollies, chocolate and warm clothes. Serb soldiers were paid a pittance by their exiled government and could not afford to buy chocolate or warm clothing at the inflated prices charged by Salonika's black marketeers.

Olive, who received a good income from the interest on her mother's money in the trust fund, did indeed spend her Serb Army wages on buying her fellow drivers some additional comforts. Another thing she felt she could do was to set up a canteen for Slav soldiers. Practical as ever, Olive noted the top-selling items in YMCA and Red Cross canteens. These were tins of barley sugar, nourishing hot drinks like Ovaltine and Horlicks, cough sweets, packets of chocolate biscuits, woollen sweaters, vests and socks. So Olive wrote to her father asking him to raise money to set up a couple of mobile canteens for Serb soldiers.

He wrote back saying that at present Australians were concentrating on raising money to buy additional comforts for Australian soldiers. However, her father did send a handsome personal donation to what they decided to call the Serb Comforts Fund. So Olive was able to set up the first of her canteens, employing a Serb-speaking Greek woman to serve hot drinks and snacks to the Serb soldiers.

ℓℓ ℓℓ ℓℓ

As part of the Eastern Orthodox Church's celebrations for Easter (1917), the highlight of the religious year, Olive was told she and Corporals Allen and Percival had been promoted to sergeant. Yovi was delighted that Olinka's dedication to the Serb cause and her generosity had been recognised.

Celebrating the Orthodox Easter meant a great deal to Yovi, just as celebrating Christmas with her family meant a great deal to Olive. Olive was invited to a special Easter dinner at the Serb Officers' Club where everyone was in ceremonial uniform and she wore uniform as well. Afterwards, she and Yovi attended the midnight service at the Church of St Demetrios.[17]

After dinner they left the Officers' Club and walked slowly through streets crowded with worshippers, carrying lighted candles. In the open square in front of the church, Yovi bought long white candles from a street vendor. Then, like everyone else, they carried their lighted candles inside the historic church, where mosaics sparkled under the light of hundreds of candles. In the dimly lit interior, candles cast a golden glow on gold brocade robes of the priests and on gold-ground icons studded with jewels.

Around them the voices of the choir soared and then fell to a whisper as the ancient liturgy revealed the promise of Christ's resurrection, man's redemption and life after death. Yovi repeated the words of the Orthodox liturgy, his eyes fixed on the officiating patriarch, or bishop, in his richly embroidered cope. A huge silver-covered book was brought out and presented to the bishop, who resembled an Old Testament prophet with a long white beard. But instead of opening the book and reading from it the bishop kissed the book reverently and then closed it. As the chanting soared to a crescendo the big book was solemnly borne away while younger priests and acolytes waved silver incense burners that gave out clouds of perfumed smoke.

Olive gazed around the huge church, one of the oldest and largest in Greece, recognising a mosaic of St Demetrios, the Roman centurion who had embraced Christianity and been martyred for his faith on this very spot. She was amazed by the amount of gold and silver ornaments all around her, in a church situated in one of Europe's poorest nations.

Most of the ceremony was a mystery which pulled Olive and Yovi apart rather than drawing them together as she had hoped. She could not understand the litany that Yovi was intoning so fervently or why bells kept ringing at intervals. She examined the icons with golden backgrounds, depicting black-robed sad-eyed Madonnas cradling Christ children, realising how much these icons meant to Yovi.

Inside the vault of the dome over the altar was a huge mosaic featuring a stern-faced olive-skinned Christ Pantocrator with one hand upraised, a gesture which Olive found more menacing than reassuring. She imagined her father's shocked face if she wrote to him saying she would be marrying Yovi in an Eastern Orthodox church complete with bells, smells and icons.

Finally the Easter Mass was over. They emerged from the church into the bustling traffic and walked up the street that led to the oldest part of the city, under the archway in the city wall near the Trigonian Tower. From the terrace of their favourite *taverna* they watched firecrackers exploding in the narrow streets below.

Over a bottle of Samian wine, Yovi announced he had an Easter present for her. She felt her heart miss a beat. Was he going to give her a ring?

Afterwards, they walked hand in hand to Olive's apartment. They stood at the window, looked down at the city lights and out over the wide bay of Salonika far below them. Then Yovi took the gold stars from the epaulettes of his uniform jacket and clipped them onto Olive's khaki jacket.

'To celebrate your promotion, Olinka,' he said.

It was not quite what she had hoped for.

HEROINE OF THE GREAT FIRE OF SALONIKA

With Monastir recaptured and over 1200 Serb soldiers dead or wounded, and a push north to take back Belgrade now being planned, Yovi was often working late or sometimes in conference with Prince Alexander. Olive was glad of the company of her flatmates, Barb and Mim. But on 4 August 1917 the two English girls, who were only on short-term contracts, returned to London. On the night before they left, they celebrated with a farewell dinner in the apartment. The girls presented 'Ollie' with a beautiful antique silver belt and Yovi with a bottle of very expensive French brandy bought on the black market.

Olive's apartment seemed lonely without the chatter and laughter of her English friends. Due to Yovi's heavy work commitments she now saw much less of him, increasing her loneliness. She moved out and rented a room in the home of a large and noisy Greek family in the Kastra district, closer to the city centre. Having mastered Serb and its alphabet, the next step was to learn Greek so she could find her way around the city better, as all street names in Salonika were written in Greek. She had her meals with the family, so she could practise speaking the language.

On the afternoon of 17 August 1917, after four hot and dry months, a huge fire swept through the wooden houses of Salonika.[18] It was rumoured that the fire had been started by Bulgarian saboteurs.

Fanned by the hot wind from the north, flames leaped from house to house until much of the Turkish quarter was a blazing inferno. Then the flames leaped across the Via Egnatia and into the modern part of the city.

Seeing the flames, Olive climbed into *Bridget* and drove into the city centre. There she saw men with grappling hooks pulling down the old wooden houses to try and stop the flames from spreading. But in spite of their frantic efforts to control the fire, it leaped over the debris and ignited still more buildings. All around Olive's ambulance pedestrians screamed, as sparks and flying embers filled the air and landed on them. Without a thought for her own safety, Olive climbed out of her vehicle, braving falling masonry and beams to help as many burns victims into the ambulance as possible. Then she drove out to the British military hospital at Mount Hortiack.

When Olive returned, dusk was falling but the sky over the city was as bright as day.

Olive drove past the Church of St Demetrios. The roof had fallen in and an end wall had collapsed. She could have wept to see its marble panels and columns stained by fire and smoke and its centuries-old mosaics cracked and peeling due to the fierce heat. Then she drove back to the Via Egnatia where buildings were crumbling and crashing in clouds of dust. She filled up the ambulance once again and returned to Mount Hortiack.

Olive worked until midnight without a break. The fire stretched in an arc that measured over 2 kilometres in width. On the skyline she could see minarets blazing away like tall candles. Time and time again Olive drove back into the burning city, rescuing terrified Greek women and children as well as Serb officers and soldiers and their families.

With flying sparks and embers all around her, Olive realised that many lives depended on her keeping calm and staying awake. Via Egnatia was now a solid wall of fire, its elegant shops in ruins and their plate glass windows shattered by searing heat. Everywhere Olive drove, she saw panic-stricken people carrying away their belongings on their backs, on handcarts or bullock wagons. The streets were filled with terrified people desperate to save their lives and their possessions.

Olive had another load of badly burned victims on board when the front wheels of her ambulance started to wobble. She climbed down and saw that, due to a flat tyre, the wheel had been riding on its metal rim. It was too dangerous to continue driving until *Bridget* could be fixed. By now her ambulance was blocking the road behind a mob of screaming people and, in addition, two Greek women in the rear of the ambulance were panicking. Olive had no choice — she had to fix the flat tyre immediately. She dismounted, lifted up the rear door of the ambulance, got out the jack and changed the wheel. Roaring flames came closer, while terrified bystanders implored her to get out of the way.

An elegant Greek woman in the crowd was in hysterics, sobbing and shrieking after her silk dress caught fire from a flying ember. The woman moaned over and over again, 'O*yos mou, oyos mou*' ('My son, my son'). She explained that her boy was trapped inside their burning house, and then she collapsed at Olive's feet.

Olive hauled the Greek woman into the ambulance but when she regained consciousness she could not remember her address. With the aid of some friendly Greeks Olive finally coaxed the location out of the distressed woman.

Arriving at the house Olive wrapped a damp scarf over the lower part of her face and rushed into the blaze. She felt her way around the walls and managed to rescue the woman's terrified little son and get him outside, moments before the house collapsed. Overcome with gratitude, the woman kissed Olive's hand. No time for thanks. Olive set off once more with a full load of patients for Mount Hortiack.

On another desperate dash to the home of a Serb friend, *Bridget* ran out of fuel. Olive hunted desperately around the darkened streets for petrol but found none. In despair she hailed an Army lorry. Luckily, the driver happened to have a spare can of petrol, enough to get her to a French Army ambulance station a kilometre away. There, she found to her relief that the French tanks still had some petrol in them.

With *Bridget's* tank replenished, Olive returned to the city centre crowded with bewildered people running in all directions. She rescued Greeks, Serbs and Albanians from blazing buildings. But a hot wind was blowing in the direction of the medical supplies stored in the Serb Army's depot.

Arriving at the Serb Army's depot, Olive found the place in uproar. She and Artsa and five other drivers worked through the night, dowsing canvas tents and ground sheets with water and laying them over their precious medical supplies in a desperate effort to protect them from the fire.

Adrenalin lent Olive strength and stopped her feeling sleepy. The phones were down so it was impossible to get a message through to Yovi. She imagined he would be out fighting the fire, just as she was.

During the night Olive drove more fire victims along the rubble-strewn quay and kept looking for more casualties she could take to the British Military Hospital. Around the harbour law and order had broken down — looting from shops, warehouses and abandoned homes was taking place. The gutters were running with wine as the intense heat had burst wine barrels in the stores. Soldiers lying full length in the gutters drank and drank 'or lay there sleeping it off', wrote Olive to her father after the fire.

Tram wires were hanging in festoons across the road and in places the overhead power lines were down, so she had to give them a wide berth. Around one of Scottish Women's Hospitals buildings, now reduced to a smoking ruin, were people with terrible burns, some unable to move. Olive helped them into the ambulance and took off again. Later, assisting burns victims into the crowded casualty department at Mount Hortiack, Olive suddenly realised that she had been working without pausing to eat or drink for fourteen hours.

Fortunately, Matron Jessie McHardy White, a fellow Australian, realised she must be exhausted.[19] The matron grabbed Olive by the shoulder and insisted she sit down and have a sandwich and a cup of tea. Olive wanted to go back to the city right away but Matron White made her lie down in the casualty tent for an hour.

Rested a little, her face grimed black with smoke, Olive finally returned to her lodgings at six in the morning. She found the house filled with homeless Greeks — friends and relatives of the owners, and who were now refugees in their own city where the fire was still raging. Olive washed herself and lay down, quite spent. She slept for a few hours and then awoke with a start, remembering she had arranged to have dinner with Yovi and Captain Shapovitch in the Officers' Club the previous night. What had happened to Yovi? Had he been injured? To her relief she found Yovi at the Officers' Club. She hugged him, relieved and delighted that he was unharmed.

He kissed her on both cheeks, overjoyed to see her. Yovi told everyone how proud he was of her. He too had been at the fire with soldiers from his unit. He had received reports of her rescue work from those who had seen her in action and had heard about her saving the Greek child in the blazing building.

All that night the fire raged on, fanned by the wind that blew down from the Vardar River valley. Olive reflected on the day in a letter to her father: 'I carted refugees from 7 am till 10 pm and the following day started at 5 am.'

The city of Salonika was now in ruins, historic monuments, offices and warehouses destroyed, and thousands of people left homeless sleeping in the streets or on the hillsides above the city. Over the next few days Olive would learn that more than 4200 homes and business premises, all the hotels in Salonika and most of the banks, including her own, had been destroyed by fire. The

PHOTO BY COM. J.G. ADAMSON, RN, OBE, AUTHOR'S FATHER. AUTHOR'S COLLECTION

Church of St Demetrios after the Great Fire, 1917.

Turkish quarter was largely destroyed. Only Kastra, high on the ramparts with its wooden houses where Olive had lived, was left intact. Many of the Byzantine beehive-domed churches were smoking ruins, their roofs collapsed, leaving marble-lined interiors open to the sky, and their art treasures stolen or damaged.

Olive worked long hours in her ambulance and not until 29 August did she find time to write a long description of the city's destruction. She wrote to her father telling him that she was unharmed. She described how the churches, cinemas, the best hotels, the Nursing Sisters' Club, the shops, bars, banks and restaurants had been destroyed. She told how thousands had died in the flames, suffocated or burned to death. Thousands more were left homeless and many hundreds of children were now orphans.

To her father and Sunny, Olive modestly played down her own part in the rescue but did eventually admit she was to receive recognition by the Serb and Greek governments. The Serbs had awarded her their Silver Bravery Medal immediately and she would soon receive a Gold Medal for Zealous Conduct and an official commendation from the Greeks in Salonika. Yovi was promoted to major for his rescue work. Now there were three pips on his shoulder instead of two.

The horror of those burning buildings and the charred corpses of those who perished in the fire gave her nightmares for months. She implored her father to raise money for fire victims and for the housands of homeless refugees. He promised to do so and set up a special Save Salonika appeal. Within a few weeks funds started to roll in. Olive involved members of the Orthodox Church, friends of Yovi, to distribute funds to those most in need. She also decided to fund an orphanage since there were so many children sleeping in the streets.

One day, without warning, Yovi came to see Olive. He knocked on the door, and when she opened it said, 'Put on your best dress. Crown Prince Alexander of Serbia is here. He wants to congratulate you personally for your rescue work during the fire.'[20]

So Olive put on the silk dress Sunny had sent her and a pair of high-heeled shoes and they drove to the only cinema in Salonika still standing. Inside, the Crown Prince was standing under the giant screen. Olive was spotted by one of the equerries and beckoned forward. She walked up a small flight of steps and stood in front of Crown Prince Alexander, who raised Olive's hand to his lips and thanked her for everything she had done for his people. Then he pinned the Order of St Sava onto the shoulder of her dress.

After the ceremony Olive and Yovi came out of the cinema to find a huge storm had caused flooding in the street. Olive was wearing flimsy shoes so Yovi picked her up and carried her across the flooded street to his car and they drove to her home.

A Corfu Idyll

That night Yovi told her that, at the request of the prince, he had been ordered to leave Salonika and travel to French-occupied Corfu where the Serbs still had a military base. Yovi had been entrusted with a delicate diplomatic mission. He was to liaise with the French authorities and find common ground for peace negotiations once the war was over, since the Allies would be re-aligning borders. He explained that it was vital that France support Crown Prince Alexander's aims of a pan-Serb federation under Serb rule to include Dalmatia, Croatia, Bosnia, Hertzegovina and Montenegro. Yovi swore her to secrecy. He promised he would use his influence with the Crown Prince to obtain a driving job that would take her to Corfu so they could enjoy a holiday together once his conference with the French generals was over.

The next day he was gone and no one seemed to know where, not even his Army batman. At the end of that month, Olive had still heard nothing from Yovi and was starting to worry about him. Then, true to his word, she received a personal request from an equerry to drive friends of the prince, a Mr and Mrs Beshitch and their baby, from Salonika across the Ipeiros mountains to the port of Santa Quaranta (now Sarande in Albania) and on to Corfu.

Colonel Derok gave her permission and asked her to take three convalescent soldiers with her to Corfu so they could recover in the milder climate of this most beautiful of Greek islands.

Her orders were to drive to Santa Quaranta, leave the ambulance there, buy tickets and accompany her passengers on the ferry to Corfu. Obviously she would have to use *Bridget*, as *Ella* was not reliable enough, although a more comfortable and spacious vehicle.

What she was not prepared for was the nightmare journey which would take three days over potholed roads and through violent storms. Olive was forced to drive very slowly and edge her way around a succession of precipices. Despite the failure of *Bridget*'s foot brake and Olive's worries that the heavy vehicle might skid over the edge of the precipice, Olive managed to bring her passengers safely to Santa Quaranta on the Adriatic coast, opposite the northern tip of Corfu.

The bad roads had damaged *Bridget*'s suspension, and Olive had to leave *Bridget* in the town to be repaired by a local garage. She bought ferry tickets for everyone and accompanied her passengers on an ancient caique to Kerkyra on Corfu, where she was to meet Yovi.

As they approached the jetty, Olive saw pink and blue sugar-cube houses climbing up the hill with, here and there, some gnarled and ancient olive trees and other vegetation. Yovi stood on the quayside in his splendid ceremonial uniform, a short-cropped jacket with the gold braid on its high collar accentuating the breadth of his shoulders. His blond hair gleamed against the dark blue uniform. He explained that he had had to leave a conference at French Army headquarters before it had finished in order to meet the ferry.

As they were surrounded by uniformed Serb soldiers she could only salute him. He helped her load the convalescents and Mr and Mrs Beshitch into a horse-drawn cab and then hailed another *fiacre* for the two of them.

As the *fiacre* took them up the steep streets of the old town, Yovi explained that talks with the French Foreign Minister and General Sarrail had gone well. The Serb Foreign Minister had been pleased with Yovi's presentation of the Crown Prince's ideas. The upshot was that Yovi was to replace the present military attaché at the Serb embassy in London, an ideal way of returning to the world of diplomacy.

The fact that Yovi was leaving Salonika for London was a bitter blow to Olive but she felt she should not show it. She reckoned that if she truly was Yovi's best pal, she should be *glad* of such a promotion. But deep down she knew that his transfer to London was probably part of his mother's plan to take him away from Salonika and from her. She put on a brave face and told him she was delighted by his promotion.

He had booked her a room with a balcony in the luxurious hotel where he and the other diplomats were staying.

When he had free time, they hired a horse-drawn *fiacre* and a driver and drove to unspoiled fishing villages with curved sandy beaches. They swam in crystal-clear turquoise-blue water, lay in the sun for hours talking, and lunched on grilled fish cooked over charcoal braziers by fishermen.

Olive was enchanted by Corfu, its mild climate, the amount of greenery everywhere, the magnificent olive trees and abundance of wild flowers. It was the first leave she had had for two years. As always, Yovi was kindness itself. However it became apparent that ambition would take him into a wider world of European diplomacy, the world he had been in before the war started. The parting of the ways had come sooner than expected: he was to leave Corfu for London without returning to Salonika. His mother would be waiting for him there.

Their time together was perfect but far too brief.

On their last day an orderly arrived from the Serb barracks with orders for Olive to drive three convalescent soldiers back to Salonika. Then came the dreadful moment when Olive had to say goodbye to Yovi.

She wanted to kiss him. But as they were both in uniform any display of emotion was impossible. Holding back her tears, all Olive could do was shake hands formally and say goodbye as a sergeant would do when farewelling a superior officer.

She and the three Serb soldiers she was transporting mounted the gangplank and settled themselves on the ferry. Yovi stood waving as the caique pulled away. Gradually the waving figure on the jetty got smaller and smaller and eventually faded into the distance. That evening she wrote in her diary: 'I couldn't help a couple of tears falling on my cheek but with the soldiers there couldn't howl my eyes out as I longed to.'[21]

Olive feared separation would change everything for them. Theirs had been a wartime romance — two people of different backgrounds, religions and cultures thrown together in a foreign city. Now it was over.

'The return journey was no joyride' was how Olive described it in a letter home. The weather turned cold and to make matters worse when she stopped at an inn to get some hot soup for the convalescent soldiers and tried to restart the engine the starter failed to fire. Cranking it herself Olive injured her wrist. Then climbing a steep mountain pass on a potholed road, one of *Bridget*'s springs and part of her chassis broke. Olive had to rope the chassis together to complete the journey.

On the long trip she had plenty of time to think about Yovi. For years her father had insisted men would try to marry her for her money and had tried to protect her against fortune hunters; now her money was powerless to get her the man she really wanted. How could she *ever* explain the truth to her father, tell him that Yovi was her lover, that he was *not* a fortune hunter and was breaking her heart.

One thing was certain. Her father and Belicia must never know the *real* story. But Olive could not help herself mentioning Yovi's name. Her next letter to her father dated 15 November 1917 contained the revealing statement: 'Yovi was my most constant pal and Salonika is desolate without him.' She also added that Colonel Derok was very pleased with her work. As her fellow drivers referred to her as '*Gospojitsa*' (Honoured Lady) she felt she had to live up to their high opinion of her. Olive added wistfully: 'although at times I feel bewildered and hopeless and at a loss.'

Salonika without Yovi

Olive was now used to living rough, eating and sleeping at odd hours, wearing a uniform and yarning with men round camp fires. But she yearned to return home when the war was over.

By now her family had left the Macquarie Street apartment and were living at *Quambi*, a large house in Woollahra, with sufficient room for her. But she was worried she might not be able to take up her old life in Sydney. Could she go back to attending tennis parties, swimming and surfing, driving her father around in the Rolls and playing bridge with him as though the independence she knew in the war had never occurred? She described in a letter home how she could only marry someone who had shared the strange masculine life to which she had become accustomed.

At Christmas she organised a party and was delighted when her fellow drivers, for whom she had bought presents of food and warm clothes, gave her a beautiful evening bag which hung from a chain of solid silver. When she chided them affectionately for spending so much on her, the drivers insisted: 'It's *not* extravagant — *Gospojitsa,* you have done so much for us so we wanted to give you something that you will remember us by when the war is over.'

With tears in her eyes she thanked them for their gift. In an undated letter she wrote to her father describing the gift, saying, 'I wish they hadn't given me something so extravagant, none of them can afford it. But I will value their gift all my life as a remembrance of the dear fellows.'

To repay their kindness, on 6 January 1918 (the day when the Orthodox Church celebrates Christmas and Anglicans celebrate Epiphany), Olive entertained her fellow drivers. With her Greek landlady's help she served what she described in a letter home as a 'feast of ham and eggs' bought on the black market, and which she knew the Serb drivers could not afford.

The feast turned into a party. The drivers brought records of Serb folk music, which they played on Olive's wind-up gramophone and tried to teach her Serb folk dances. She found to her surprise that Artsa was light on his feet. Olive loved dancing and Artsa whirled and twirled her around in a Serb folk dance until they both collapsed on a low divan, out of breath and laughing. He was really very nice, she thought.

Olive missed Yovi and wrote chatty affectionate letters to him each week. He replied with brief notes at irregular intervals, revealing very little about life in London. His letters were friendly but he might as well have been writing to a male comrade. Worrying about Yovi, she did not eat the stodgy food served by the Serb Army, lost weight and looked better for it.

By 1918, the Austro-Hungarian Empire, which had begun the war by invading Serbia, was collapsing. Franz Joseph, Emperor of Austria and Hungary, King of Dalmatia, Slovenia and Croatia was dead. The Dalmatians, Slavs and Croats were demanding freedom.

But while the Austrians still had food, the Serbs, whose farms and barns had been burned by the retreating Austrian Army, had nothing. Much of the populace, already weakened by war, had died of starvation and from the flu epidemic that now swept through Europe like a plague.

At last the Americans awoke to the suffering of the Serbs. President Wilson ordered the Serb flag to be flown over the White House to honour the bravery of the Serbs and their wartime losses. The American Red Cross sent the Serb Army a gift of twenty-nine brand new ambulances. Artsa, Olive, Dushan and Lukar, as the most reliable of the drivers, made numerous journeys over dangerous mountain roads delivering the new ambulances to the battle lines.

On these journeys Olive became aware that Artsa was head over heels in love with her. She was flattered as he was a very handsome young man but felt she could never love anyone but Yovi.

Just at this difficult time in her life, Olive was told by her Greek landlady that she needed Olive's room for some relatives who had been left homeless by the fire. Olive had only two weeks to find somewhere else to rent in a city where accommodation was scarce and so many other people were homeless after the Great Fire.

Artsa and the other drivers were appalled at the thought of their *Gospojitsa* without anywhere to live. In their free time they built a little house from a huge wooden crate in which an Australian light plane had been shipped out to a unit of the Australian Flying Corps in Salonika.

Artsa's father was a carpenter by trade. Artsa was able to turn the crate into a little chalet and build partitions inside, so she had a separate living room and bedroom; he also built cupboards. Olive's new home had a pitched roof, eaves decorated with scalloped barge boards, small windows with shutters, and its own front door. The diminutive home was installed in the garden of a Greek woman friend by the name of Mrs Papadopoulos,[22] whose toilet and bathroom Olive could use. Olive lived there without paying rent for the rest of her time in Salonika.

To thank her workmates for their time and effort, Olive spent the money she would have paid in rent buying them little luxuries on the black market — chocolate, warm clothes and medicines.

In Salonika, homeless men, women and children slept in the streets, on park benches, around the harbour and on the hillsides outside the city. Their suffering made Olive feel that her own

The Balkans and Greece during World War I.

unhappiness was trivial by comparison. Artsa told her that the Serbs in Belgrade were also homeless and starving, and were slaughtering their horses for meat. 'Hard work is the way to get through troubles,' her father had always claimed. Olive decided she would drown her sorrows by doing everything she could to help the homeless.

Her father was still raising money in New South Wales for the Save Salonika appeal and sent it to Olive. She used the money to buy and equip mobile canteens in caravans. They were fitted with small stoves and ice boxes to provide simple meals and hot and cold drinks to the homeless. She also donated money to an orphanage run by Katharine MacPhail, a Scottish doctor who had left the Scottish Women's Hospitals and was doing marvellous work with the Quaker War Victims Fund, helping orphans and destitute families.

Eventually some of the homeless people *were* rehoused, but Olive could see Salonika would take many years to rebuild. A French architect named Hébrard was appointed to design blocks of apartments and wide boulevards to replace many of the old and narrow streets.

In February 1918 Yovi wrote to tell Olive that he was following his family's wishes and formally announcing his engagement to the Crown Prince's cousin. He gave no details, aware that saying any more about his bride or his impending wedding would only hurt Olive more.

Desolate, she sought comfort from an overjoyed Artsa, who told her he had always loved her. She was the woman he wanted to marry and cherish. It was a clear case of love on the rebound, but the fact that this handsome young man loved her so devotedly was balm to Olive's self-esteem, which had taken a severe beating after Yovi's rejection.

Olive wrote to her father telling him she was thinking of marrying Artsa a 'comrade in arms'.[23]

She was distressed to receive a disapproving cable from her father on 24 April 1918. She replied immediately saying,

> I am afraid you think Artsa is a fortune hunter, your views
> are quite natural because you can't know anything about

him — I respect them and fully understand them, but oh
Daddy darling, how I wish you could see the other side
and try to understand.

Olive's father was so concerned he wrote to Colonel Derok and
learned to his further dismay that Artsa was a peasant from a huge
family who lived in a hovel in a Serbian village.

Kelso King wrote back to Olive: how could his darling possibly
wed someone of a different race and a different religion, who had
left school at twelve? Artsa might be good with cars but could he
read and write? Ironically enough, her father actually suggested that
she should write and discuss the matter of her marriage with 'her
good friend Major Yovi', who would explain the impossibility of
such an alliance.

In her next letter Olive attempted to explain that this was not a
spur-of-the-moment decision. She and Artsa had been friends for
years and she valued his loyalty and devotion. She did not admit to
her father that her brave 'companion in arms', was in fact illiterate,
but insisted she would not give him up.

Artsa continued to profess his affections. When they were on a
trip to the Vardar River, Artsa swore on his mother's life he would
die rather than let Olive fall into the hands of the Bulgarians, who
might rape her. If necessary, he would defend her to the death.

Nevertheless, paternalistic forces strengthened against Olive.
Colonel Derok called Olive into his office for a fatherly chat. He
explained that Artsa and the other poor mechanics and drivers had
lost touch with their wives, sweethearts, sisters and mothers —
everyone they held dear. He made it clear that Artsa was only one
of the *many* Serbian soldiers who were in love with Olive. 'You are
their *Gospojitsa*, all of them would kill anyone who would harm a
hair on your head.' The colonel stressed that he liked Artsa very
much and considered him an excellent soldier and mechanic. But
he was definitely *not* a husband for *Gospojitsa*. 'You are an educated
woman, you must not think of marrying *any* of our soldiers — their
ambitions, their way of life and their family circumstances are too
different for such an unequal marriage to succeed.'

Colonel Derok was too tactful to refer to the fact that Yovi would marry the girl his family had chosen.

Without warning, Yovi returned from London to confer with Crown Prince Alexander, who was now back in Salonika from the front line. Yovi was worried and annoyed to find that 'his Olinka' could consider marrying an illiterate peasant. He declared he was in total agreement with Colonel Derok and with Olive's father. 'You *cannot* marry Artsa,' he told Olive. 'I forbid it.'

Justifiably annoyed, Olive replied that she could not understand how Yovi could abandon her for someone else and *still* believe he could run her life. He had chosen to marry someone else, so she was free to make *her* decision and she chose Artsa.

Cousin Selwyn King, whom she had known since childhood and who was more like an elder brother, had been promoted and was now Major King in the 3rd Division of the Australian Imperial Force. Urged on by Olive's father, Selwyn arrived in Salonika to meet Artsa. Through a Serbian–English interpreter Selwyn told Artsa that Olive's father would never consent to their marriage.

Having thoroughly upset poor Artsa and left him distraught, Selwyn proceeded to lecture Olive on the impossibility of marrying Artsa. He also added that her father was very worried and wanted her to come home.

Olive, by now in her mid-thirties, was furious at being told what to do by Yovi and by Selwyn. 'I've had quite enough of men lecturing me and I'm quite capable of running my own life, thank you very much,' she said cuttingly.[24] Yet she yearned to talk to her father, whom she had not seen for five years, and to Sunny, the only person in the world to whom she could confide the truth about the emotional turmoil she was in.

Olive wanted to obtain leave from the Serbs, and go to Sydney to see her father and discuss her future with him, possibly even tell him the truth.

The war in the Balkans was now reaching a crucial point. The Serbian and French Armies were fighting their way back through Serbia to Belgrade where they were horrified to find people starving, crops and houses burned and many Serbs reduced to begging.

Colonel Derok implored her to stay in Serbia, saying 'You are the only member of my staff I simply cannot spare for any length of time.'[25] The only way of getting from Salonika to Australia was by cargo boat and that trip home would take months. He said he would give her a few days off to go to Athens, Vodena or Corfu if she needed a break to think things over, but marrying Artsa was not fair to him or her. After all, there was a war on, and she *had* enlisted in the Army and was under Army discipline unless she resigned. They needed drivers and ambulances — the driving team could hardly spare her.

Olive was shocked that this was how the colonel saw it. But she wrote to her father telling him she had changed her mind. She had applied for leave to go to England to buy stock for her canteens. She would *not* marry Artsa after all. As soon as the Serbs had control of their country once again, they would work together on an aid project to run canteens and shops in war-torn Serbia, similar to the canteens she had set up in Salonika to feed the homeless after the fire. She knew Artsa would be excellent at running the transport side of this venture and she knew she could trust him implicitly with money.

In May 1918 Olive wrote letters to her father and the editors of the *Bulletin*, the *Sydney Morning Herald* and the *Telegraph* appealing for funds to help the Serbs through her canteens. Her father's reply was to send money but insist she stop seeing Artsa completely, or she would only hurt him even more. Involving Artsa in her new project was simply not fair on him and only asking for trouble.

By August 1918 Artsa had been advised by Selwyn, Colonel Derok and by his own parents that such an unequal marriage would cause grave problems. He was resigned to the fact *Gospojitsa* would never marry him. It was left to Colonel Derok to solve the matter by posting Artsa away from Salonika to Monastir. Olive had by now realised that such a marriage was impossible. It was time to leave Salonika. Put her memories behind her and move on.

THE SAVE THE SERBS FUND

Sergeant Olive King was demobilised from the Serb Army in April 1919, five months after World War I ended and which revealed the desperate straits the Serbs were left in. Olive had already written to Australian companies Arnotts Biscuits, the Queensland Meat Preservative Company and various sugar companies begging for supplies to be donated to help the Serbs. She received crates of goods for her canteens.

What Olive needed now was ready cash to buy more food for starving Serbs. She hardened her heart and sold *Ella* to a motor dealer. She made a short trip to London to see Sunny and buy more supplies, returning promptly to Salonika.

Then, leaving her Salonika canteens in charge of two Quaker aid workers, Olive packed up her possessions inside *Bridget* and drove north, up the steep winding road to Vodena (Edessa) until she crossed the frontier.

Serbia turned out to be an attractive country of mountain ranges and wooded valleys, bisected by the wide basin of the Danube and its tributaries, the Sava, the Marova and the Tisza. She drove along the valley of the River Sava, through plundered towns and villages, where barns and crops had been burned to the ground by the retreating Austrians and their German allies. Everywhere Olive went she found homeless families sleeping in drainage ditches or in damp pine forests. Some had crawled into underground trenches, others had dug holes in the ground and made shelters of boughs, and were surviving on berries and roots. Hunger, typhoid and cholera were everywhere. The graveyards were full.

So many people were left homeless and begging. She gave out the tins of food she had brought with her and then had so little more to give them she could have wept.

She arrived at the capital, Belgrade, on 11 November 1919, and wrote to her father about street upon street of burned-out buildings, just like Salonika after the fire. Everywhere she went was the same: piles of rubble, people trying to find shelter in bombed-out cellars, and long lines of the homeless waiting at soup kitchens or making fires on street corners to keep warm.

The retreating Catholic Austrians had slaughtered Serb cattle, ripped out their vines and burned fields of maize, barley and wheat before it could be harvested. Serb farmhouses and cottages, barns and onion-domed churches were in ruins. She thought how strange that these horrors had been inflicted by men on innocent women and children in the name of religion.

The Serb economy was in ruins: there was no money in the exchequer to import food. Summer was past. What would happen when the snows came?

The tinned food she had brought had all been distributed. Olive lived on black tea that she brewed in a billy. Now she had only a couple of packets of biscuits left and one jar of marmalade. Her throat felt constricted and she could scarcely eat. Everywhere she went hungry children clamoured for food.

Starving children haunted Olive's dreams. She wrote to her father again explaining to him how guilty she felt that before the war she had led an idle, selfish life. Now at last she had a chance to show that one person could make a difference. She would make that difference to the best of her ability.

In his reply her father claimed that he understood how she felt but implored her to come home. He feared that after three years of hard work, after several bouts of malaria and now surrounded by victims of cholera and typhoid her health would suffer. Surely she had done enough by setting up canteens for the homeless in Salonika?

Olive wrote back. She said she had to do something for those in need and this was her way of showing Christian charity. Far better to do something here than sit in St Andrew's Cathedral just *talking* about doing good for the underprivileged and the starving. Surely her father and Belicia must recognise that this was what mattered to her. Kelso King the clergyman's son took the point.

Accustomed to raising large sums of money for various charities, Olive's father formed an Australian branch of the International Save the Serbs Fund. Belicia also organised fundraising functions among her friends.

Olive's letters to her father in 1919 reveals how much she was helped by the war veteran Colonel Derok and his network of contacts. After *Bridget* was involved in an accident (while being driven by another driver) and smashed beyond repair, Olive travelled around by train, persuading local mayors to give her space for her canteens. She was allowed to park the canteens in Belgrade, the former Bosnian city Sarajevo, and in other ruined cities such as Skopje, Nish, Brod, and the walled city of Ragusa (now called Dubrovnik).

Practical as ever when it came to fundraising, her father sent more money to London to buy food and warm clothing at bulk prices. The Save the Serbs appeal took off, and there was a generous response from every state in Australia to advertisements and newspaper articles about famine in Serbia. Sufficient funds were raised to replenish the original canteens and to stock ten more canteen/shops in the villages.

To buy more food, Olive took the night sleeper from Belgrade to Paris, although the rail lines were badly damaged, changed trains and caught the Calais–Dover ferry, and from there travelled to stay with Sunny near London. She was planning to buy two large and reliable lorries and fill them with crates of tinned food and warm clothing, then ship them to Salonika, which was still the closest port to Belgrade.

Buying a lorry was relatively easy. However, in postwar England food was either rationed or in short supply.

But strong-minded Olive was determined to bring aid to the starving before it was too late. She contacted Sir Charles Wade, a former attorney-general of New South Wales, who was now the state's agent-general in London and an old friend of her father. Sir Charles had also become chairman and honorary treasurer of the London Committee of the Save the Serbs Fund.[26]

Sir Charles made the necessary contacts with British government departments so that Olive could obtain permits enabling her to buy bulk supplies of tinned corned beef, tinned sardines, canned fruit and vegetables, packets of biscuits, powdered milk, coffee, chocolate, tea, blankets, woollen socks and scarves. She even bought a consignment of primus stoves at wholesale prices.

Olive paid the accounts, checked the items and arranged for the food and medical supplies to be shipped to Salonika. She asked for and was given a cabin on a cargo ship, the only woman on board. When the shipping company protested that a woman could not travel alone and unchaperoned on a cargo ship, Olive produced her Serb Army identity papers showing she had been a sergeant in the Serb Army, and as such was allowed to board.

Arriving safely at Salonika, Olive found thousands more Slav and Albanian refugees had flooded there, joining those who had been left homeless after the fire. Hundreds of people were living in the streets, using sheets as impromptu tents or sleeping rough in the hills around Salonika. There were homeless families everywhere, in every square and open space, their possessions in wicker baskets or pillow cases.

To help alleviate the desperate situation Olive set up two more canteen shops in Salonika and donated money out of her trust fund to the International Red Cross and the Quaker War Victims Appeal. These were staffed by English and American volunteers, who were also running free medical clinics. Apart from the old Turkish quarter high on the hill, most of Salonika (now reverting to its former name of Thessaloniki) was still in ruins. The French military architect who had been appointed to redesign the city was still working on his plans and progress was slow.

After establishing four more canteens in Salonika and hiring staff to run them, Olive employed a Serb to drive one of her lorries while she drove the other to Belgrade.

Olive kept her pistol handy on the dashboard in case there were attempts to rob the lorry. At night she placed her army sleeping bag on top of the crates and slept there, the gun beside her.

Living frugally and using some of her own money, Olive employed two English girls she met in Belgrade, former VADs with the SWH who spoke a little Serbian, to operate the new canteens. She also found additional part-time female staff from among the Serb community to help run her network of canteens.

Everywhere Olive went in Serb cities she saw desperation. Trees had been stripped of leaves which people boiled up to eat, and even the bark of birch trees was consumed. Cats and dogs were slaughtered for food, dead horses were cut up and turned into sausages, even leather harnesses were boiled up in water and the resulting liquid drunk for its nourishment.

Olive saw long queues materialise after the merest rumour that a shop had something to sell. Ration cards had been issued, giving each inhabitant the right to a small quantity of bread, potatoes and sugar, but the shops quickly ran out of supplies.

It was the same with Olive's canteens. The starving queued for hours to get food. Eventually the lines were so long, staff had to limit how many tins or packets of food each family could buy.

Yet Olive was absorbed by her work. One day she realised that her father had been right. Hard work and thinking of others had lifted her depression. Another letter to her father described how she made a trip to Salonika by boat to check the canteens there, and how beautiful she found Salonika after being away from it. On the return trip the captain gave up his cabin to her but then became a pest wanting to share the cabin with her. Olive wrote with humour about the incident, describing him as that 'wretched old skipper'.

Olive's Save the Serbs chain of non-profit making canteens serving hot soups and stews free of charge to starving people saved thousands of war victims and rescued Serb soldiers from malnutrition and starvation. The warm clothes the canteens sold at cost price saved many families from frostbite in winter. Eventually she had her big van and two smaller vans she called 'Tin Lizzies' to service the canteens.

Olive continued to open more canteens until eventually there were seventeen outlets. She seemed fearless as she drove or travelled by train around the ruined countryside, seeking food from as far away as Fiume and Constantinople. She and two of her staff were travelling on a Serb goods train when their carriage was derailed; many passengers were killed but miraculously all three of them escaped unscathed. When her father heard about the train accident he implored her to return to Australia, but she refused saying she had to stay until the famine was over.

By 1920, starvation no longer stalked the land. The last of Olive's canteens finally closed in June 1920. It was time to think about the future. It was six years since she had seen her father. She told him how much she missed him. 'If only Australia were not so far away,' she wrote in a long letter to her father. 'I would buy a house on the Adriatic and grow vines there.'[27]

When Olive received disquieting news from Belicia about her father's health, she decided to go back to Australia immediately. Much as she loved living in Europe, going home to see her father had priority.

In recognition of her work Olive was decorated by the Serbs with the Good Samaritan Cross for setting up canteens for starving refugees in Salonika. She received a card from Yovi congratulating her.

Before leaving Serbia, Olive sold her lorries and all the cooking equipment, foodstuffs and clothing in the canteen/stores. She donated some of the money from the canteens to a child health unit being established in the University of Belgrade. The rest she gave to a Serb children's hospital and orphanage in the city, set up by her friend Dr Katharine MacPhail.[28]

RETURN TO SYDNEY

At the time Olive arrived back in Sydney by ship, her father and Belicia and young Hazel and Nicholas were living in a large house in the harbourside suburb of Point Piper. Back in Sydney, Olive's reunion with her father was an emotional one. He had aged greatly and every moment she spent with him was precious. Her father steadfastly refused to let her take a paid job or buy a pastoral property and run it herself. So, out of love for her father, she compromised by taking an interesting but unpaid position as state secretary of the New South Wales Girl Guides Association, an organisation with which Belicia (now Lady Alicia King) was involved.

Olive's Serb friends kept her up to date with news from Serbia. The Crown Prince's father had died in 1921 and he was now King Alexander. The King had set up new factories with foreign capital and given people jobs but there were growing tensions between Serbs and Croats in his new amalgamated kingdom of Serbs, Croats and Slovenes. He was now looking to marry but his choice for a spouse was very limited. There was scarcely an Orthodox princess of the right age left, because the Great War had seen the fall of so many kingdoms and empires. The best option seemed the daughter of King Ferdinand of wealthy Rumania, who was Orthodox and of the right age. In the end matters were settled. Rumania had not only common borders with the kingdom of Serbs, Croats and Slovenes but also valuable oil wells. So diplomats were sent to arrange a marriage to young Princess Marie of Rumania.

When Olive read about King Alexander's engagement she wondered what part Yovi had played in it. His Christmas cards gave details about his postings and various addresses but never contained any news about his wife or whether they had children. Olive was too proud to ask.

Olive returned to Serbia only once. Early in 1922, she received a gold-edged card inviting Miss Olive King and Sir George Kelso and Lady Alicia King to attend the wedding of King Alexander of Yugoslavia and Princess Marie of Rumania.

Belicia and Olive's father were thrilled. Kelso King's heart condition had stabilised and they longed to visit Serbia, the Dalmatian coast and Greece. For Olive the trip would mean meeting Yovi again. Yet how could she refuse?

Olive, her father and stepmother and little Hazel and Nicholas spent the summer of 1922 in England with Sunny and her husband, but her father's angina prevented him from travelling to attend the wedding. In the end Olive did return to Belgrade for the King's wedding, chaperoned by Belicia. Bells pealed from the churches, there was folk dancing in the squares, and the streets were garlanded with ropes of wild flowers. Olive met up with old friends like Dr Katharine MacPhail.

In a colourful ceremony in the cathedral the bride and groom were crowned with diadems. After the ceremony hundreds of guests streamed out of the cathedral and were taken in fleets of chauffeur-driven cars and wedding carriages decorated with flowers to the reception in the royal palace.[29]

Determined that she would not look a frump in front of Yovi and his wife, Olive had bought a beautifully cut silk gown. She only hoped that she could keep her feelings under control and that nothing would betray to her stepmother just how much Yovi had meant to her.

To her surprise Yovi arrived at the reception with his sisters but not his wife. He wore a blue sash with the medal of the Order of St Sava and other decorations over white tie and tails in which he looked even more handsome than she remembered. Yovi behaved impeccably, every inch the 'old comrade in arms'!

Belicia was charmed by Yovi. Newspaper accounts of the wedding describe how, after a sumptuous dinner, the King and Queen led the dancing. Alexander wore his ceremonial uniform and rows of medals. The royal couple waltzed together surrounded by floor-length mirrors that reflected their every movement. Olive described to her father how 'the King was charming but the new Queen looked bored to the point of insolence'.

Yovi requested a courtesy dance with Belicia. Duty done, he invited Olive onto the dance floor, and waltzing with Yovi was as magical as it had been at the White Tower Restaurant years ago. They chatted about the old days in Salonika and mutual friends. Olive summoned up courage to ask after Yovi's wife. Apparently she was recovering from the birth of their second son. Olive was surprised that she did not attend the wedding, and Yovi observed that some women preferred their children to their husbands.

Colonel Derok stood back, looked Olive up and down, admiring the dress of shimmering floating silk, her Order of St Sava pinned to one shoulder, her bare tanned shoulders, shining blonde hair and polished fingernails. Olive reported that Colonel Derok said she looked 'so beautiful that he would never have known me'. She talked about the old days in Salonika, and wrote to her father: 'I met heaps of friends and had a most delightful evening.'

Olive and Yovi never met again, although they exchanged Christmas cards each year. One of these cards revealed that Yovi had been transferred from his position in Vienna to Athens, where he did well. Later he served a few years in Geneva as the Yugoslavian representative to the League of Nations, followed by a posting he had always wanted: ambassador in Paris, his favourite city.

In the Australian spring (European autumn) of 1934, Olive opened *The Times* and read how, on 9 October, King Alexander of Yugoslavia had been assassinated while on a state visit to France.

The King had been shot while driving through Marseilles in an open Rolls-Royce. There were grave fears the assassination could be used as a pretext for war in the same way the assassination of Archduke Franz Ferdinand had been a pretext.

In another paper Olive saw a photograph of the King in the open Rolls-Royce in which he had been assassinated. Could that be Yovi sitting with him in the car? As Serb ambassador to France he could easily have been present. She found a magnifying glass and peered through it. The third man in the car, sitting beside French Foreign Minister Louis Barthou, *was* Yovi. King Alexander and Foreign Minister Barthou had died instantly, while the Serb ambassador to France had died later in hospital.[30] Yovi dead — she could hardly believe it.

le le le

In 1939, World War II broke out. Olive was now fifty-five but she was determined to join the Australian Army as a driver. When they told her she was too old she was annoyed. Undaunted, she put her mechanical knowledge to good use, studied aircraft manufacture and engine inspection techniques and became an examiner of engines at the De Havilland aircraft factory at Mascot. It was a most unusual role for a woman at that time.

Sir George Kelso and Lady King and his daughter continued to be involved with many charities and volunteer organisations until his death in 1943. Olive suffered a double blow when she learned that Sunny had developed heart disease and needed her help. Without a thought for her own safety, Olive managed to get on a boat to London to be with her sister.

Olive spent the final years of the war caring for Sunny. Later, she lived with Sunny and her husband, who had bought a villa at Kyrenia on the island of Cyprus. Gradually the island of Cyprus became turbulent and dangerous as Cypriot Turks and Cypriot Greeks became locked in a bitter conflict.

After Harold's death, Olive continued to nurse her sister until Sunny died too. Olive thought about buying a house in Cyprus. However, the conflict on Cyprus was growing worse and several

English expatriates were killed by terrorists. Olive, who had already lived through one bitter racial and religious war, decided to return home. Olive returned to Australia and lived with Belicia at Point Piper, caring for her widowed stepmother until Belicia also passed away.

After Olive's death in 1958 at the age of seventy-three, Dr Hazel King, her half-sister, now an academic at Sydney University, published a small edition of Olive's letters to her father. These gave readers an insight into the remarkable courage and determination of her extraordinary sister.

War's purpose was destruction, which appeared to be the opposite of our function as artists or as women.

Stella Bowen, Official War Artist, from
Drawn from Life, London, 1941

CHAPTER 8

Dr Lilian Violet Cooper

1861 – 1947

Serbian Order of St Sava
Imperial Russian Order of St Anne

Dr Agnes Elizabeth Lloyd Bennett

1872 – 1960

Serbian Order of St Sava
Cross of Honour of the Serbian
   Red Cross
Officer of the Order of the
   British Empire

At the beginning of the twentieth century, in line with the prevailing male opinion of the time, it was generally thought that women were too illogical and hysterical to serve as army medical officers or surgeons. These ideas were not new. The German philosopher, George Hegel,[1] for example, wrote at the beginning of the nineteenth century:

> Women's limited mental capacity equips them only for housework and child rearing. Women cannot succeed in science or allied fields and are incapable of intellectual achievements . . . '

William Balls-Headley, Professor of Obstetrics at Melbourne University,[2] thought them incapable of becoming doctors:

> If young women were allowed to undertake tertiary education the energy needed by the uterus would be diverted to the brain, rendering them infertile.

However, dedicated young women like Agnes Bennett and Lilian Cooper proved these professors wrong. Despite encountering prejudice and opposition from male students and professors, both young women studied medicine and passed their final examinations with flying colours. And fortunately, too, many women doctors managed to enlist in voluntary medical organisations during World War I and save thousands of lives although risking their own.

Their heroism went largely unnoticed by the governments of Britain and Australia — though the French, Serb and Russians, with whom they worked, awarded them medals.

AGNES BENNETT — THE EARLY YEARS

Agnes Bennett was born in the Sydney suburb of Neutral Bay, sixth of seven children of William Christopher Bennett, a quiet and cultured professional man, and his wife Agnes Amelia.[3] The family comprised four boys and two girls. In 1878, when Agnes was six, her strong-minded English-born mother, who believed in the superiority of an English education, took Agnes and her two elder brothers overseas to place them in English schools. Agnes was sent to the famous Cheltenham Ladies' College.

Tragically in June 1881, while still in England, Mrs Bennett fell victim to smallpox and died a horrific and painful death. Agnes was with her mother in her last hours and her sufferings made a deep impression on the sensitive, highly intelligent little girl. Agnes's father, alerted to his wife's illness, took a boat from Sydney but arrived in England too late to see his wife alive and had to escort his children back to Sydney.

W.C. Bennett was a busy man so he employed a resident housekeeper named Sarah Darling to care for his large and motherless family. Relations between the Bennett children and Sarah were not pleasant but several years after his wife's death Mr Bennett married her. She bore him two more children. Agnes in later life would claim her stepmother only cared about her own children's welfare and was cruel to her stepchildren.

Agnes and her siblings and half-siblings moved from Neutral Bay to a larger house at St Leonards. Agnes was doing well at Abbotsleigh, a private school, where she was a member of the tennis team.[4] Then Agnes's father, who was very fond of his eldest daughter, died of a heart attack when she was only fifteen. At this crucial time when Agnes needed security and continuity, she was removed from Abbotsleigh and the comfort of close friends and familiar teachers.

392 | THE COMPLETE BOOK OF HEROIC AUSTRALIAN WOMEN

Agnes's stepmother sent her to a school where the fees were cheaper, Sydney Girls High School, in the Francis Greenway-designed building now occupied by David Jones on Elizabeth Street. Although it must have been difficult for Agnes at first, Sydney Girls' High encouraged its brightest girls, and Agnes's classmates included the future writers Ethel Turner and Louise Mack. Many pupils went on to tertiary education but Agnes was told by her stepmother that there was no money for university fees for *her* — her father's money would be better spent on her brothers' education.

Agnes's stepmother was sole trustee of her father's will so she held the purse strings. In her opinion, Agnes would do well to get married as soon as possible and stop costing the family money. Fortunately, Agnes received a small legacy from an aunt on her father's side, which enabled her to pay what were then relatively expensive tuition fees to study arts at Sydney University. This was the only faculty that admitted women at that time.

In 1890, after a year of studying arts, Agnes applied for a scholarship and was thrilled to receive one. As a great privilege she was allowed to switch from arts to science, so she grasped the opportunity to study geology and biology. She was a good all-round student, intelligent as well as strong and athletic. She loved tennis and played for Sydney University.

While playing in a tournament near her home she met a young naval officer with whom she fell deeply in love. They announced their engagement and Agnes was ecstatically happy planning a future with the man she loved. Then came terrible news. Agnes's fiancé had drowned in a boating accident on Sydney Harbour. For Agnes, already grief-stricken by her father's death, this was the final blow. No one would ever take her fiancé's place. His loss marked a turning point in her career — from now onwards Agnes channelled all her energies into studying for a career, determined to be financially independent. In 1894, she became the first woman at Sydney University to gain a science degree and passed with first class honours.

But Agnes Bennett's dream of a career in science was soon shattered. Her responses to job advertisements received no acknowledgement — male employers did not want a woman. Her stepmother refused to continue supporting her: Agnes had to earn a living or starve. She did one of the few things open to educated young woman who lacked money in that era. She responded to an advertisement for a governess and went to teach children on a remote sheep property in outback New South Wales. It wasn't what she had spent so many years studying for but she tried to make the best of it.

AGNES BECOMES A DOCTOR

One day by chance Agnes opened the newspaper and read an article about the remarkable Dr Elsie Inglis (pronounced *Ing-alls*). Elsie had been born in India in 1864 where her father was a colonial administrator. When Elsie was five he had been given a job in Tasmania but the family returned to Scotland in 1878 and Elsie went on to do her medical training in Edinburgh and Glasgow.

What impressed Agnes was that Elsie Inglis had managed to qualify as a doctor at a university where *female* students were banned from using the dissecting room. She had fought against this restriction and opened her own medical college so that the female students could acquire the practical knowledge that would help them get through their medical exams.

Agnes was fired with enthusiasm by the story and decided she too would study at Edinburgh University Medical College to become a doctor. Elsie Inglis would be her role model. But once again her stepmother disappointed her by refusing to loan her any money or pay her fees to undertake a second degree. Undaunted, Agnes applied to her late father's bank manager and told him that she felt that medicine was her vocation in life just as engineering had been that of her father. The bank manager agreed to provide her with a low-interest loan so she could enrol at Edinburgh but warned her that she had only a few years to pay back the loan plus interest.

When she arrived in Edinburgh, Agnes was forced to live very frugally. She rented cheap but damp lodgings in a basement apartment. After the warmth of Sydney she found Edinburgh the 'coldest, grimmest place I've ever seen'.

By now Dr Inglis had managed to obtain a teaching post at Edinburgh University Medical College, the first woman to do so. Agnes was one of her students.

However, due to the cold winter Agnes went down with bronchitis and had to miss several of her tutorials. She had been a keen student and the fact that she did not appear at tutorials for some weeks worried Dr Inglis. She looked up Agnes's address and came to visit her. When examining Agnes, Dr Inglis realised she had bronchial pneumonia. She provided medical care free of charge until her student had fully recovered.

Elsie Inglis had a soft spot for her young Australian student. Mindful of her own poverty-stricken days as a student and her own problems as a woman pioneer, she befriended Agnes. She invited her home to tea on many occasions and became her mentor and friend. Agnes was well aware she must pass each and every exam and qualify as a doctor as soon as she could. Today, when female students walk our medical schools in large numbers, it is hard to imagine how badly they were once treated. University lecturers ridiculed their intellectual capacity and often tried to embarrass them by telling salacious stories in class while the male students tittered if their female counterparts showed the least sign of discomfort.

Agnes ignored such jibes. She worked hard and passed her medical exams. Subsequently, she took examinations in surgery and was elected a member of the illustrious Royal College of Surgeons of Edinburgh. But because she was a woman, the male-dominated Appointments Committee turned down Agnes's application for the position of surgical registrar at the Royal Infirmary, Edinburgh's main teaching hospital, in favour of a male graduate whose examination results had not been nearly as good as hers.

Other jobs she applied for were denied her, often for ridiculous excuses, such as the fact there were no staff lavatories for women doctors and she could not use the nurses' lavatory.

At long last she found a position at the lunatic asylum at Larbert, a grim and grossly under-funded mental hospital near the town of Stirling in Scotland. For fifteen harrowing months Agnes worked in this asylum, where conditions were primitive and Dickensian. Mental health was a Cinderella specialty in those days. In the absence of tranquillisers and anti-depressants, violently disturbed patients were held in straitjackets or 'restraining chairs', and kept on locked wards. Sexual abuse of female patients by male staff was commonplace. Dr Bennett struggled to improve conditions for her patients but found male hospital trustees rarely wanted to listen to a woman.

Eventually Agnes decided to return to Australia and look for a position in Sydney. However, in spite of her excellent qualifications she was no more successful than she had been in Scotland. Agnes soon realised that the specialty of surgery was the biggest boy's club of all.

By this time she was short of money and still had to repay much of her loan to the bank. So in 1904 she accepted the post of medical officer at Callan Park Hospital for the Insane, which, she soon found, had the same abuses as the horrific lunatic asylum at Larbert.

When a friend wrote to Agnes from New Zealand offering her a partnership in a leading private practice in Wellington, Agnes took up the offer. She went on to become chief maternity officer at Wellington's St Helen's Hospital. However, she had not given up her dream of practising surgery, and in 1911, returned to Edinburgh to complete her degree in surgery. She went back to New Zealand with this additional postgraduate qualification and fought against male authorities who opposed tertiary education for women on the grounds that the health of the nation's future mothers would suffer due to the stress of too much study.

Dr Lilian Violet Cooper — No Shrinking Violet

On the other side of the world another determined and highly intelligent young woman had also dreamed of becoming a surgeon but suffered from prejudice against women in medicine.[5] Lilian Cooper came from an affluent middle-class family but had to struggle just as hard as Agnes to be allowed to study medicine in an era when boys had careers and girls married and had children. Lilian's parents were very kind to her but they gave priority to educating their sons.

Although Lilian's middle name was Violet, she was no shrinking violet. She had strong opinions and a strong will. She yearned for financial independence and wanted a career, a very unusual concept in the late 1870s when she was an adolescent.

Lilian was very tall with beautiful brown eyes, a large nose and large hands and feet. Extreme shyness about her appearance made her appear brusque, especially in the presence of young men. She was interested in books and science and totally uninterested in acquiring the 'ladylike' accomplishments which were so prized by her mother and aunts.

On the contrary, she loved science and anatomy and read books on these topics. Eighteen-year-old Lilian secretly used her dress allowance to pay fees to attend a cramming establishment to obtain tuition in the scientific subjects which fascinated her. Seven years later, in 1886, Lilian Cooper found a loophole in the regulations that banned women from studying at the London School of Medicine: her qualifications in science and maths from the London Society of Apothecaries, which blithely used the word 'person' rather than 'man' on admission forms for their qualifying exams.

Once Lilian gained admission to the London School of Medicine she was determined that nothing would stop her qualifying. She studied very hard and passed her medical exams. At this critical and stressful time in her life, she formed a deep and abiding friendship with a young art student, Josephine Bedford, a friendship which aroused hostility among her colleagues.

In 1890, the only professional job newly qualified Dr Lilian Cooper could obtain was as assistant to a general practitioner in the small Essex town of Halsted. Whether the GP in question was difficult to work with or whether he suspected Lilian Cooper of a lesbian relationship with Josephine Bedford is unclear but after a few months he dismissed Dr Cooper without a reference.[6]

DR COOPER PRACTISES IN BRISBANE

Dr Cooper must have placed advertisements in foreign medical magazines for her next job because she received a letter offering her the post of 'assistant with a view to partnership' in a general practice in Brisbane, at that time a primitive frontier town with few amenities and a very humid and exhausting climate in summer.

In June 1891, Lilian and Josephine sailed 16,000 kilometres from Britain to the subtropical city of Brisbane, and Lilian became the first female practitioner to be registered in the State of Queensland.[7] She soon discovered that her employer was a temperamental alcoholic and Lilian feared his alcohol problem was endangering his patients. Once again Dr Cooper stood up to a bullying employer, consulted a lawyer and finally secured the cancellation of her contract.

For standing up for herself she was unjustly pilloried and boycotted by male colleagues in Brisbane, who refused to give anaesthetics whenever she was asked to operate on patients. Alternative employment was denied her. In fact, there was a concerted effort among male specialists and GPs to freeze Dr Cooper out of medicine altogether so that she would be forced to return to Britain.[8]

Strong-minded Lilian was determined not to be beaten. She was lucky that Josephine had a private income so that they had the means to live in Brisbane until Lilian once again found paid work. Dr Cooper was determined the medical establishment of Queensland would acknowledge her skills, even if she had to work without pay. She knew she was a good doctor in a city that badly needed well-trained physicians and surgeons.

Lilian Cooper was eventually allowed to join the Medical Society of Queensland and appointed as an unpaid 'honorary' at the Lady Lamington Hospital for Women. Lilian also worked at the Brisbane Hospital for Sick Children, which had been established by another woman, the pioneer settler Mary McConnel.[9] To see her own patients, she conducted her daily rounds in a two-wheeled horse-drawn carriage driven by a groom, who looked after the horse while Dr Cooper was inside tending to patients.

On one occasion she narrowly escaped death. She was in the carriage when the groom took the blinkers off the horse, which took fright and bolted, smashing the carriage against a lamppost, throwing Dr Cooper headfirst onto the road and damaging her lower back.[10] Lilian never minced her words and her language when she reproved the groom would have done credit to a bullock driver.

After that experience, Dr Cooper bought a bicycle and became known as the 'Lady on the Bicycle', as she pedalled around the streets of Brisbane in cumbersome long skirts or in the very modern 'bloomers' invented for women cyclists.

Her patients loved her and found her a warm and caring doctor. She was especially kind to the children of large, impoverished families and would buy toys for them out of her own money when they were in hospital.

By 1905 Dr Cooper was a senior doctor and appointed an honorary staff member of the Catholic Mater Misericordiae Hospital, newly established across the river in south Brisbane, and would later be employed in a salaried capacity there. She was devoted to the work of the Mater, which was run by well-trained and very dedicated Irish nuns, and would be connected with this hospital and its staff for the rest of her life.

In 1907 Lilian Cooper moved away from The Mansions on George Street and she and Josephine Bedford set up in handsome Auckland House on the corner of George and Mary Streets.

To update her surgical skills, in June 1911 she and Miss Bedford travelled to the United States and visited Minnesota's famous Mayo Clinic, and the Johns Hopkins Hospital in Maryland. A year later Dr Cooper gained further postgraduate qualifications in surgery at the University of Durham. Back in Brisbane, she now received warm congratulations (feigned or genuine) from male colleagues who at one time had done their best to prevent her practising medicine there by fair means or foul.

WORLD WAR I: EVERYTHING AND NOTHING CHANGES FOR WOMEN

At the outbreak of the war, Agnes Bennett was forty-two and a paediatrician with a long operating list. Dr Cooper was fifty-three and had a thriving practice acquired through twenty-five years of hard work.

Financially secure and successful though they were, both women would feel driven to offer their skills to help those injured in war, even if it cost them money to do so.

Three of Agnes's brothers had enlisted in the Australian Imperial Force (AIF), and every day the papers brought news of young men dying in the trenches of northern France and Belgium. Keen to help in the war effort, Agnes returned from New Zealand to her home city of Sydney and offered her services to the AIF. The interviewing officer, who was far less well qualified than Dr Bennett, rudely told her that, if she wanted to help the war effort, she should 'stay home and knit'. Agnes left the room seething with rage. She wrote to her old friend and tutor Dr Elsie Inglis, asking if she could help her. Dr Inglis was setting up a chain of hospitals called the Scottish Women's Hospitals for Foreign Service in countries like Belgium, France and Serbia, which were unable to fund military hospitals and ambulances. In her reply to Agnes, Dr Inglis told her that there would certainly be work for her and promised a surgeon's position in an all-women hospital in France.

Several months later Dr Inglis received an application from Dr Lilian Cooper, who had similarly been rejected by the British Army. Dr Cooper also recommended Miss Josephine Bedford for the post of orderly/ambulance driver and added that Miss Bedford was an excellent driver (a skill possessed by few women at that time).

In the middle of 1915, Dr Agnes Bennett sailed from Australia to join the Scottish Women's Hospitals, hoping to work with Dr Helen Sexton, an Australian surgeon in charge of a tented hospital at Auteuil in France. The SWH now had five tented hospitals in the north of the country assisting Belgian soldiers whose country had been overrun by Germany. When the ship made a stop at Alexandria, Egypt's main port, Agnes looked over the rail and saw wounded soldiers being carried down the gangplanks of hospital ships flying the British flag. They were then dumped unceremoniously on the dockside in the burning sun to wait for horse-drawn ambulances to take them to Army hospitals. She descended the gangplank and discovered the wounded men were Anzacs. These were soldiers from the fighting at Gallipoli, on their way to various military hospitals in Alexandria and Cairo. Due to the influx of so many patients, she learned, these hospitals were short of surgeons. Terrified one of her brothers might be among the wounded, she walked through indescribable chaos, overworked orderlies and Australian Army nurses trying to attend to men with terrible injuries. Many of the men had gangrenous wounds and needed limbs amputated immediately or they would die.

Agnes told the medical officer in charge she was a trained surgeon on her way to England to enlist. His face brightened and he asked if she could give them a hand as they were so short-staffed. Agnes made a quick decision. She had her surgical instruments with her and she would be useful here. She could continue on to Britain once the crisis was over. Agnes called for a steward to bring her trunk up from her cabin and left the ship. The commander of the medical services in Alexandria was delighted with his new recruit. Agnes was asked to escort wounded men to Cairo where she was received with open arms.[11] There, she signed the necessary papers and became the first woman surgeon commissioned into the British Army, albeit on a temporary basis. Captain Bennett was attached to the Royal Army Medical Corps (RAMC) accredited to the staff of the British Army Hospital in Cairo. At last she was doing what she loved most — working as a surgeon. Agnes had that rare combination of qualities that made her an excellent physician, a brilliant surgeon and a good administrator.

In Cairo she found overcrowded wards and long operating lists. Wounded soldiers from the Dardanelles poured into the Army hospital. Typhoid and dysentery were common. Beds were scarce until Agnes and some other doctors commandeered a car, drove to the river and ripped out bunks from laid-up tourist steamers on the Nile.

After nearly six months spent in an operating theatre and in the wards with little free time, Dr Bennett received news that Bob, her favourite brother, was in Alexandria. She took the train there from Cairo and they spent the day together before he left for London.

With the evacuation of Gallipoli the hospital ships ceased bringing loads of wounded men to Egypt. It was time for Agnes to move on. She caught the train to Alexandria and boarded a ship for London, arriving there early in 1916.

The crying need now was for doctors and nurses to go to what had once been Macedonia, where the Serbs and the French — Britain's allies — were fighting Austrian soldiers, who were armed with German guns and German planes. As regent for his ailing father, Crown Prince Alexander of Serbia had applied to Dr Inglis, asking her to set up field hospitals on the border between Greek-owned Macedonia and Serb-owned but Austrian-occupied Macedonia, both of which had been ceded to Greece and Serbia after the recent Balkan Wars. Soldiers from the Irish Fusiliers and the famous Scottish regiment, the Black Watch, who had served at Gallipoli, were now being sent to help the Serbs fight the Austrians in an attempt to regain their captured country. A large British field hospital had been established for British troops in Salonika. But the Serb Army, now exiled from its own land, had no hospitals and very few ambulances.

Dr Bennett contacted Dr Inglis, who offered her the command of a field hospital in Greek Macedonia.

The new field hospital was to be set up near the front line, out of range of the guns. Wounded men would be sent down from the front line in lorry ambulances, driven by a team of women who would be under her command. Excited about the idea of running her own unit, Agnes signed on with the Scottish Women's Hospitals as a senior surgeon for a salary of £200 a year, plus expenses. This was far less than she received in civilian life, but war was not a time to argue over money.

From London, Dr Bennett took control of ordering tents, medical equipment, emergency rations, ambulances, spare parts and bedding to be shipped to Salonika. She also interviewed large numbers of volunteers. From the British and Canadians who had applied she selected two experienced surgeons — Dr Sybil Lewis and Dr Josephine Muncaster — and an Australian general practitioner with surgical experience named Dr Jessie Scott. Agnes was told that Dr Lilian Cooper from Brisbane would be joining the unit shortly.

For her field ambulances Dr Bennett was allocated several Australian nurses including Agnes Kerr, who had served with Agnes in the military hospital in Cairo, Caroline Reid from Melbourne, Florence Grylls from Cue in Western Australia, and Robina Ross and Mary Stirling of Adelaide. Much later the author Miles Franklin would join the unit as a volunteer, working initially as a cook and then as a nursing aide. She became a great admirer of Dr Bennett.

The nurses and doctors were paid substantially less than their counterparts in civilian hospitals. Their fares to Greece and back were paid but many, including Dr Bennett and SWH nurses, would be out of pocket when the war ended. All staff had to pay for their own SWH uniforms, which consisted of a grey woollen coat with lapels faced with tartan, a grey skirt, three thick grey flannel shirts, a grey cotton suit for summer, a Gordon tartan scarf and a felt hat for the nursing staff and a peaked cap for the doctors.[12] Agnes, who hated military pomp and ceremony, made up her mind that in *her* hospital all the women would be on first name terms. There would be none of the saluting she had disliked in Cairo. As for the uniform, she would have to put up with it, but she was determined to wear her own Akubra hat.

At last all was ready and the new unit and its equipment caught the train to Marseilles and then boarded a rusty old tramp steamer to Greece. There was insufficient room for all the crates of equipment and vehicles, so much of it had to follow on another cargo ship.

The ship called at Piraeus, the port of Athens, and then sailed north along the coastline, arriving off Salonika in mid August 1916. Agnes noted the turquoise-blue sea bordering the rocky coastline and a harbour crowded with troop ships from Britain, France and Italy.

While they waited for their ambulances and equipment to arrive, Dr Bennett marshalled her nursing staff, surgeons and twenty ambulance drivers and they pitched their tents at Mikra Bay on the outskirts of the city. Dr Bennett met several generals of the Serb Army with whom she would be working at the staff headquarters in Salonika. Then she set off with the chief of Serb Medical Services to select a suitable site for the new field hospital near the Greek–Serb border. Their Chief Medical Officer advised her to select a sheltered spot under spreading elm trees, a kilometre or so north of the railway station at Ostrovo (once part of Serbia; the town is today known as Arnissa and is part of northern Greece; Lake Ostrovo is known as Lake Vegoritis).

Eventually all was ready and the convoy, consisting of forty supply lorries and several dozen ambulances and cars, rumbled over the dusty Vardar plain and then drove north over winding, potholed roads and hairpin bends bordered by precipices. The area was wild but hauntingly beautiful. One lorry lost a wheel and had to be abandoned. German aircraft flew overhead and a big attack was expected any moment. Dr Bennett knew the area had been the site of fierce battles between Serb and French troops against a combined force of Austrians, Croats and Bulgarians. They drove with loaded revolvers beside them, fearful of Bulgarian bandits who were known to hijack lorries and kill their passengers. One of Dr Inglis' field hospitals, including its doctors and nurses, had already been captured by the Austrians.[13] A French field hospital had been attacked by Bulgarian troops and the staff had had their throats cut. It was scarcely encouraging news to the women in Dr Bennett's unit.

WOMEN ON THE BATTLE LINE

The site selected for their hospital was located in a small hollow on the slopes of a mountain 5 kilometres from the small town of Ostrovo. It had a superb view across a valley to snow-covered peaks. Below them were deep gorges, canyons and steep roads.

The field hospital consisted of a row of tents — each tent taking at least ten patients — and had an overall capacity of two hundred beds. There were smaller tents for orderlies and even smaller individual tents for doctors and nurses. The main operating theatre was in a long low barn, divided into two compartments, and beyond a hastily erected partition was a small X-ray room. A second operating theatre was housed in a large tent. More tents were added at a later date. The nurses and female doctors were issued with revolvers and ammunition, so they could defend themselves in case the Bulgarians, who had a reputation for rape, attacked.

On the slopes of neighbouring Mount Kaimaktsalan ('The Peak of the Buttercups') and around the ancient Macedonian town of Monastir, the Serbs were fighting a combined force of Austrian and Bulgarian troops.

Agnes wrote:

> Our first evening in camp star shells were being sent up over the enemy lines and preparations made for a big advance. Heavy guns wakened the unit and by 6.30 am, our breakfast hour, the great Serb and French advance which ended in the fall of Monastir had begun.[14]

Ostrovo Base Hospital was soon overflowing with casualties, far too many for the tents available. Not all patients had been wounded. Some had typhoid or dysentery, the common diseases of trench warfare.

Badly wounded Serbs arrived in lorry-ambulances driven by courageous women. Due to the terrible conditions of the roads, many patients were in agony and sometimes died in transit. In the midst of so much horror and pain, Agnes was amazed to find herself working in a place of outstanding natural beauty. The view of snow-covered mountains resembled postcards of the Swiss Alps. The nearest peaks were 40 kilometres away but in the clear sparkling air they seemed much closer. Now, in high summer, the fields around them were filled with daisies and scarlet poppies.

Their Serb orderlies, seconded from the front line, had dug the latrines far away from the lake, fearing the malarial mosquitoes that lurked in its rushy swamps. However, the stream beside the camp soon ran dry as that summer it had not rained for months. This meant all water for drinking, washing and cooking had to be carried several kilometres in buckets. The mosquitoes seemed undeterred by the distance. Agnes had been assured by the Serb Chief Medical Officer that malarial mosquitoes would not venture from the marshes surrounding Lake Ostrovo but, it turned out, he was wrong. Malaria became a serious problem for the staff who were ordered to cover their heads and shoulders with veils, which soon proved too cumbersome and were abandoned.

Shortage of drinking water also became such a problem that the camp had to be moved closer to the lake where the mosquitoes were even worse. Each staff member was issued with mosquito nets and gaiters or knee-high canvas boots and told to wear the boots after dark. Although they were given massive injections of quinine, large numbers of the staff had at least one attack of malaria.

In August, the weather was very hot and dry. Food was cooked and eaten outside, which meant they were subject to another plague — wasps. Most people were stung and a few were unlucky enough to swallow a wasp, which meant their throats swelled and they required emergency tracheotomies. Snakes frequently invaded the camp and in autumn, as the weather turned colder, a mouse plague infested the tents. The pesky little rodents ate holes in uniforms and nested inside mattresses and between spare blankets.

Early in October came the rain. Later it started to snow. The rain and snow were a huge problem for soldiers ankle-deep in water in the trenches. The poor men were soon suffering from soggy feet, which led to trench foot, in which soldiers' feet swelled and their toes blackened with gangrene. Those affected had to be brought down by ambulance so their toes could be amputated.

The battle for Monastir, and the Serbs' eventual recapture of their country, marked a turning point in the war and a psychological blow for the enemy. But the death toll was huge. Serb casualties numbered many thousands — of these, over four hundred men died in ambulances while being driven over rough mountain roads to Ostrovo Base Hospital. After the final battle of Mount Kaimaktsalan ended on 28 September 1916, Serb officers drove Dr Bennett up the mountain to the battle site. There she saw rows and rows of dead Serbs and Bulgarians, far too many to bury. The long wet winter was over. Their corpses were already mummifying in the dry atmosphere of summer.[15]

On 18 September 1916, Dr Lilian Cooper and her friend, Miss Josephine Bedford, arrived at Ostrovo Base Hospital. From Brisbane they had taken a steamer to Port Said and a P&O liner to Salonika. They had signed a contract to serve at Dr Bennett's hospital at Ostrovo, attached to Unit 3 of the Serb Army, Dr Cooper as a surgeon and Miss Bedford as an unpaid orderly or ambulance driver.[16] They arrived just in time for the final stages of the battle for Monastir and the ongoing battle on the slopes of Mount Kaimaktsalan.

Dr Bennett was delighted to have an experienced surgeon and mature ambulance driver join her unit, as some of the younger drivers were feeling immense strain or had had accidents. She and her junior doctors were operating long hours, carrying out amputations and removing bullets and shrapnel from wounds. The operating theatre was in constant use and sterilising of surgical instruments had to be done at night to keep up the supply. The women ambulance drivers were working round the clock, making the 45-kilometre round trip to the battle front and back.

Summer was well and truly over and now the weather had turned cold and wet. The track down to Ostrovo was not only potholed, but slippery as well. One ambulance went over the edge and the driver was killed. On 25 September Agnes wrote in her diary: 'The chauffeurs are still a trouble but I have given them entirely to Miss Bedford, who has arrived with Dr Cooper. Both are simply splendid and going to be an enormous help to me, being older women.'[17]

By mid October the rain had changed to snow and sleet. The shivering ambulance drivers would arrive at the base hospital with icicles hanging from their eyebrows. The staff were very uncomfortable in tents with no heating. At night, snow drifted in under the tent flaps and they piled every single piece of clothing they owned on top of themselves. Dr Bennett wore a battered sheepskin coat bought from a Vlach shepherd over her uniform jacket.

By November, with snow piled up around their tents, food became scarce. A ship from Britain, loaded with tinned peaches and jars of marmalade, was hit by a German mine and sunk without trace in the Gulf of Salonika.[18] The retreating Austrian and Bulgarian soldiers had plundered the villagers' barns and fruit trees and killed their cattle so there was little food to be had in the villages and many of their inhabitants were starving.

Due to the shortage of local supplies including butter and milk, all food for the hospital had to come by road from Salonika. By now they had eaten the stores they had brought out from Edinburgh. Their rations consisted of tinned sardines, packets of biscuits, corned beef and marmalade, eternal marmalade. Bread was scarce and even the flinty, bitter greyish Greek 'famine' bread to which acorns had been added to make it go further, was welcome.

The cooks looked at the diet of the Greek and Macedonian villagers and copied their resourcefulness, picking weeds and boiling them into a traditional Greek dish known as *horta*. Eventually, the camp was reduced to eating a soup made from weeds and stewed rats with boiled rice. If asked, the staff said it was chicken.

It was now so cold the doctors operated wearing woollen mittens rather than rubber gloves. Dr Bennet still wore her sheepskin coat over her uniform and her bushman's hat.

Day and night they heard the distant booming of the guns from the front line. The Aussie women became known for their coolness under fire, their laconic sense of humour and their uncomplaining acceptance of horrific working conditions.

Agnes worried over the agonising deaths of wounded Serbs as they were being transported. Since Mount Kaimaktsalan had been captured, the Serbs were pressing further north towards their homeland. She decided to set up an advanced dressing station nearer the battle line to reduce the number of deaths, and chose a bleak mountain hamlet called Dobraveni as its site. The dressing station consisted of enough beds for thirty-nine patients, a lean-to shed used as a makeshift operating theatre and some ambulances in which emergency operations could be performed and wounds dressed.

Working close to the battle line was dangerous but at least the wounded could be transported in panniers by mules along grassy tracks. This was far less painful for badly wounded men than travelling over potholed roads in bone-shaking ambulances.

Agnes Bennett decided that Dr Cooper was the ideal person to run the dressing station. She had worked well with Lilian and trusted her skill and competence completely.

Arriving at Dobraveni Dr Cooper asked her staff to make a dining room or mess house of timber framing with tin cladding using a tarpaulin for the roof. The resourceful Josephine Bedford made a chimney out of kerosene tins so they could light a fire to keep warm. There were three ward tents, each of thirteen beds, and the patients and staff slept on lumpy straw mattresses. By now temperatures were down to below freezing and air raids were frequent. In sub-zero temperatures and howling winds, from mid January to early March, the ambulances under the direction of Josephine Bedford carried 1840 patients from Dobraveni to Ostrovo. Miss Bedford's talent for organisation kept the service going. Whenever spare parts were needed for the vehicles, Miss Bedford had to drive down to Salonika and beg, borrow or steal them. Indeed, she soon became known as 'Miss Spare Parts' at the SWH headquarters.

Naturally, tempers flared under such pressure. One can only imagine the oaths used by Dr Cooper when things were specially trying. She must have sent crisp notes to Dr Bennett, furious about the working conditions, the diet and the lack of so many essentials to run a dressing station. Not that the lack of equipment or food was Dr Bennett's fault. Everyone was suffering in the Balkan or 'forgotten' campaign. Agnes obviously valued Dr Cooper, but she did write home to a relative in Australia saying, 'It has not been easy getting on with Mesdames Bedford and Cooper . . . but their work is so good, one can forgive them a great deal.'[19]

Then a typhoid epidemic broke out among a detachment of Russian soldiers who had been sent to help the Serbs win back their country. Dr Cooper and Miss Bedford shifted their advance dressing station to the far side of the Czerna River, so they were nearer the Tsarist Russian camp.[20] The Russian commanding officer was so impressed by Dr Cooper's skills in operating under primitive conditions that he recommended her to be awarded the Order of St Anne (an Imperial Russian decoration given to foreigners).

But the cold winds, the snow and bleak living conditions were taking their toll on Dr Cooper and she went down with bronchitis. Eventually she became so ill she was driven by Miss Bedford to Salonika to rest and recuperate in a convalescent home. Dr Mary De Garis, an Australian surgeon who had just arrived, took over until Dr Cooper was well enough.[21] Dr Cooper returned in March 1917 and continued helping the Russian and Serb soldiers.

By now the Serb Army had advanced closer to the Serb border. This time, to be close to the wounded, the advance dressing station had to be moved further north to Skocivir, which was only 8 kilometres behind the battle lines. Then they had to move further north again, this time to Yellac, another desolate spot amid the mountains. On several occasions storms blew the tents over and rain flooded through the shed Dr Cooper used as a field kitchen, carrying their precious pots and pans down into the stream below it.

Eventually the terrible winter of 1916–17 was over. Spring arrived and the mountain slopes became covered with wildflowers. But with the warmth, plagues of flies also arrived, and it was impossible to keep them away from the wounded men over whose wounds and lips they swarmed.

In March 1917 Crown Prince Alexander Karageorge awarded the Order of St Sava, the Serbs' highest award for humanitarian service, to Dr Bennett, Dr Cooper and Miss Bedford.[22] He sent his *aide de camp,* Captain Milan Yovitchitch, to present the medals to them in a special ceremony. Dr Cooper and Miss Bedford both drove down to Ostrovo for the occasion.

By May, Dr Cooper's advance dressing station had been in operation for eight months. Nearly 300 badly wounded men had been admitted as patients and 144 operations had been performed under the most primitive conditions imaginable. In such a harsh environment, it was a tribute to the nursing and medical skills of her team that only sixteen deaths were recorded.

By the time Dr Cooper's one-year contract was over, she needed to recuperate in Britain before taking the long return journey by ship through the tropics to Queensland.

Meanwhile, malaria was taking a toll at Ostrovo. Miles Franklin, one of the camp cooks, went down with the disease as did another Australian, Sister Agnes Kerr, who died from it.[23] Eventually, after two nursing sisters and several patients died, it was decided that malaria was now such a severe risk for staff and patients that the field hospital must be moved down to Salonika. Dr Bennett had been feeling feverish for some time but refused to admit it and carried on working.

The day before the hospital was due to move, Agnes received the shocking news that her favourite brother, Bob, had been killed fighting in France at the Battle of Passchendaele. There was no time to mourn him.

As commander of a field hospital attached to the Serb and French forces she had to attend a formal farewell dinner with Crown Prince Alexander and the Serb and French commanders who were leaving to go north, aiming to recapture the Serb capital, Belgrade, from the Austrians.

Following the dinner Agnes arrived back at her field hospital to find the tents had had been shelled by the Austrians and many orderlies and patients wounded. The operating theatre in the old barn was ablaze and had to be hosed down. She was exhausted but took command, helping to fight the fires. Once the danger was over, Agnes went to her tent and, out of sight of everyone, she collapsed.

The next morning she staggered to her feet, shaking with malaria, to say her goodbyes. The Serb orderlies, with whom Dr Bennett had such an excellent rapport, lined up to kiss her hand. Her Serb driver wept unashamedly as, pale and wan, she climbed into one of the ambulances determined, in spite of her fever, not to depart on a stretcher.

In spite of her brave stance, on the way to Salonika, Agnes collapsed once again. At Salonika she tried to get back on her feet but failed. She was too weak to protest when the orderlies carried her off on a stretcher to the British hospital at Mount Hortiack where she spent a few days recovering.

She had left Ostrovo just in time. After her departure, the skeleton staff that remained to care for patients too ill to be moved to Salonika were bombed and strafed by German aircraft. The surviving patients, doctors and nurses were massacred by the Bulgarians, another sad chapter in the history of the gallant SWH.

※ ※ ※

Agnes made a good recovery on her journey home to Sydney on a troop carrier. However, bouts of malaria occasionally returned as she recuperated at the home of one of her brothers. When she felt stronger she gave lectures about her time at the military hospital in Cairo, nursing the Anzacs from Gallipoli, and the exploits of Australians working for the SWH in the Balkans.

The fact that Bob Bennett had been killed at Passchendaele made Agnes all the more determined not to give up. As soon as she was well enough, she volunteered for war service once again and in view of her excellent war record was accepted. This time, Agnes sailed to Britain on a troop ship as medical officer to a returning Anzac regiment. They had a narrow escape when the convoy was torpedoed and several ships were sunk.

With her regiment off to France, Agnes was discharged from the Army and went to work in a civilian hospital, the overworked Royal Infirmary in Glasgow. Normally the infirmary had a staff of fifteen to twenty residents. Now she and one other doctor were assisted only by a couple of third-year medical students. Her clerical workload as well as her operating list was enormous. Casualties of war included workers from the local munitions factories, with arms and legs blown off in accidents.

'I had to do major operations without the assistance of another doctor,' Agnes wrote. 'There was no option and medical students gave the anaesthetics.' However, for a woman who had performed complex operations under primitive conditions at Ostrovo, surgery in a hospital theatre was child's play.

Later she worked at a British military hospital at Netley, in Southampton Water, until the war ended.

RETURN TO THE ANTIPODES

Once the war was won Agnes Bennett returned to Australia, but in spite of her many commendations, testimonials and medals, men dominated the world of medicine and she *still* could not find a surgical post in Sydney. Serving in the war had cost her a great deal of money and she needed to work so she returned to her old job in New Zealand.

Just before the outbreak of World War II the death of another sibling brought Agnes back to Sydney.

This time, in her seventies, still active and alert, she went north and worked for the Royal Flying Doctor Service in Burketown in north Queensland, something that suited her sense of adventure. Between 1940 and 1942, Agnes returned to England to work as a medical officer in hospitals. For her wartime service and for her dedicated work in the remote Chatham Islands, Agnes Bennett was made an Officer of the Order of the British Empire.

Five years before her death, in memory of her beloved father, W.C. Bennett, Dr Bennett donated the sum of £10,000 (then a very considerable amount indeed) to her alma mater, the University of Sydney, to further pioneering research into aviation. The university inherited the residue of her estate after her death in 1960.

Back in Brisbane after the war Lilian Cooper resumed her work at the Mater and other Brisbane hospitals. She bought herself a car and initially employed a male chauffeur, but eventually learned to drive it herself. With Miss Bedford's help she did her own motor repairs. Dr Cooper was famous in Brisbane for uttering fearsome curses whenever the car failed to start, which must have been fairly often, considering the unreliability of cars in the pioneering days of motoring.

Both Josephine Bedford and Lilian Cooper were devoted to children. Lilian enjoyed voluntary work with children in kindergartens which Miss Bedford had founded. Embarrassed by displays of emotion, Dr Cooper would visit her young patients in hospital and gruffly say a few words of comfort before placing a toy into their hands. She often refused to accept fees from poorer patients and was very popular with those who realised that underneath her stern exterior Dr Cooper was a sincere, caring woman and a dedicated doctor.

In 1926, Lilian's health started to deteriorate, either as a result of her war service or from the high humidity in Brisbane's subtropical summers in the days before air-conditioning. She went into semi-retirement, moving from Auckland House in the centre of Brisbane to Kangaroo Point, where she was cared for by Miss Bedford. Two years later, Lilian Cooper was honoured by being invited to become a foundation fellow of the Royal Australian College of Surgeons and its first female fellow.

She died in 1947 and was buried in Brisbane's Toowong Cemetery. St Mary's Anglican Church at Kangaroo Point has a memorial window to Dr Lilian Cooper and its altar cloth is embroidered with a reproduction of the blue, white and gold medal of St Sava, to serve as a reminder of her service in the Great War.

In her will, Miss Bedford donated the large tract of land she and Dr Cooper owned jointly at Kangaroo Point to the Sisters of Charity to build what is now Mount Olivet Hospital and Hospice. Miss Bedford was very unselfish and made no claims for her own name to be preserved but insisted one building be named in memory of a remarkable female pioneer of medicine.

Today, the Lilian Cooper Aged Care Centre is regarded as one of Queensland's best centres for aged care. In commemoration of Dr Cooper's difficulties in gaining the right to study medicine, as well as in due recognition of her achievements, the Queensland Medical Women's Society and the Queensland Branch of the Australian Medical Association maintain an annual Lilian Cooper prize. It is awarded to the female medical student with the highest grade point average during the course of their medical studies.

To leave injured soldiers in the blazing sun for days without dressing their wounds or giving them water is mass murder. Our poor boys, if only the world knew how badly they are treated.

SISTER ALICE KITCHEN, ABOARD THE HOSPITAL SHIP *GASCON*
AT GALLIPOLI, 12 AUGUST 1915

CHAPTER

Sister Alice Elizabeth Kitchen

1873 – 1950

British Campaign and Service Medals
Victory Medal

At 2 pm on the afternoon of 19 October 1914, Her Majesty's Australian troopship *Benalla* drew away from the dock at Port Melbourne, taking some of the newly formed Australian Imperial Force to fight overseas. Four Army nursing sisters in brand new uniforms, filled with excitement about their overseas trip, leaned over the *Benalla*'s rail. They were surrounded by soldiers of the 8th Battalion, yelling and waving at friends and relatives on the quayside below.

As the distance between ship and shore widened, the paper streamer linking dark-haired Sister Alice Kitchen with an elderly woman in a wheelchair grew taut and snapped. With a thrill forty-one-year-old Alice realised that she was free.[1]

Alice Kitchen had been born at Amherst near Ballarat. After her father, William Barratt Kitchen, died, Alice had moved to inner-city Carlton with her invalid mother, Mary Collway Kitchen, a former nurse, and looked after her devotedly. While Alice was away, Sister Mary Perpetua and the other nuns would take care of her mother in a Catholic nursing home. It wouldn't be for long, as the general opinion was that the war against Germany would be over by Christmas.

Alice's three fellow nurses were her cabin companion bespectacled, shy Hilda Samsing from Adelaide; Janey Lempriere, daughter of a wealthy Melbourne merchant; and statuesque Jessie McHardy White, who was a widow and, like Alice, in her early forties.[2] Both Jessie and Alice had grown up in country Victoria.

Each nurse had been given ten guineas as a uniform allowance. The uniforms consisted of a floor-length grey serge dress, black ankle boots and an antiquated black bonnet like that of a Salvation Army sister, with chestnut coloured silk ribbons tied under the chin. Over their dresses they wore ankle-length grey woollen cloaks with scarlet facings, which fastened with genuine silver buttons.

Rules and regulations governing the conduct of nursing sisters were as outdated as their Boer War uniforms. They were forbidden to smoke, drink or wear lipstick or other make-up while in uniform. Matron Grace Oram, Lady Superintendent of Nurses who would be heading the Australian Army Nursing Service (AANS) in Cairo, warned the nurses they would be court-martialled if found disobeying orders.

On the first night of the voyage, the nurses were invited to a formal dinner in the Officers' Mess. Alice and Hilda were at a table of senior battalion staff. Alice found herself seated between grey-haired, moustached Colonel 'Jock' Gartside and Colonel William 'Bill' Bolton, a family friend. On either side of Hilda were Captain John Fowler, a handsome young medical officer from the Light Horse Field Ambulance, and beside him Frank Mathieson, Medical Officer to the 8th Battalion. Also at their table were Colonel McPhee, Captains Graham Coulter and Frank Dale, and Dale's dashing cousin, Lieutenant Rupert Barratt. During the long voyage these three men would become part of Alice and Hilda's 'family'.

The 8th Battalion had been raised in country Victoria. All the men were crack shots and had already trained as volunteers in the militia. Shared values and backgrounds strengthened shipboard friendships.

Colonel Bill Bolton's eldest and youngest sons, Lieutenant Jack Bolton and young Private Hunter Bolton, were also aboard the ship. Alice's friendship with the Bolton family gave her an *entrée* into the inner circle of the 8th Battalion.

The convoy assembled off Albany in Western Australia. It comprised thirty-six ships, carrying 29,185 Australian and New Zealand officers and men, eight dozen doctors and nurses, over 11,000 horses and quantities of guns, ammunition, tents, medical and surgical supplies and three cruisers. According to Alice's journal the *Benalla* left Albany on 3 November 1914.

The sea was rough and the nurses were confined to their cabins with sea sickness. Alice was the only one to keep her sea legs. She took Mothersill tablets in water with a dash of Worcestershire sauce, a remedy used by the nurses who sailed to the Boer War, her mother had told her.

Alarming reports had come in that the *Emden* was in their vicinity. This huge enemy cruiser with its powerful long range guns was greatly feared, as it had sunk twenty-three British ships.[3] After receiving information that the *Emden* had been sighted near the Cocos Islands, the cruiser *Sydney* left the convoy to pursue it.

Concerned about the possibility of having to abandon ship, Alice went on deck with Hilda to inspect the lifeboats. Practical Alice also decided to sleep with a candle and matches beside her so she could see when going down to the sick bay, after the night patrols had switched off the lights for security reasons.

Later that week the captain announced that HMAS *Sydney* had torpedoed the *Emden*. They were all relieved but the captain warned them they must still be vigilant as a second German cruiser, *Koningsberg,* was still in the vicinity.

Convinced they would eventually be serving in France, since the Germans had invaded Belgium and were threatening the north of France, Janey Lempriere gave the three other nurses conversational French lessons. On 11 November 1914 the crew and passengers were told by the captain that Turkey had entered the war on the side of Germany. At the time nobody had any inkling that this event would change their lives.

As the convoy approached the equator the temperature soared. The nurses in their heavy uniforms, designed for a British winter, were drenched with perspiration. 'Today was so hot I felt that my bones were burning,' Alice complained in her journal.

The nurses started a program of inoculating the troops for typhoid and paratyphoid. Some soldiers did not wish to be inoculated, but Colonel Bolton announced that anyone who refused presented a health risk to the others so would be court-martialled and sent home.[4] This had the desired result. Long lines of apprehensive men formed outside the medical centre.

On 28 November, everyone was told that they would be stopping at Cairo rather than continuing on to Britain. Salisbury Plain, where it had been planned they undergo combat training, was overcrowded with troops and bitterly cold. It was thought better that the AIF train in Egypt, where it was warmer.

At that stage the troops were *not* told that Lord Kitchener, the British Minister for War, had decided that the joint Australian and New Zealander forces (later known as the Anzacs) would take part in the forthcoming expedition to the straits of the Dardanelles.

ARRIVAL IN EGYPT

On their last evening on the *Benalla*, the nurses and officers enjoyed a formal dinner followed by coffee on deck. Against a crimson sky that faded to yellow they watched Alexandria's minarets and domes gleam in the last rays of the setting sun, and Alice felt sure she would find Egypt fascinating.

The following day the happy voyage was over but firm friendships had been forged. The 8th Battalion disembarked and marched to the main station of Alexandria, where they boarded troop trains to Cairo.

The nurses boarded a separate passenger train. The journey to Cairo took five hours in a hot, close compartment.

Alice and Hilda were to live and work at Mena House, built in 1869 at Giza as a hunting lodge for the Egyptian royal family, and later a luxury hotel before becoming an Army hospital. Alice had feared they might have to live in tents and was delighted with her accommodation, which turned out to be large and luxurious, its ballroom filled with rows of beds with screens around them. From her bedroom Alice had a superb view of the Great Pyramids, which were within easy walking distance.

Colonel Neville Howse, who had a reputation as an excellent doctor and administrator, would be in command of the new Army hospital. The nurses had to work eight-hour shifts but could be called out at any time during the night should there be an emergency. They had three or four hours off for a siesta during the heat of the day.

AUSTRALIAN WAR MEMORIAL NEG. A05410.

One entertainment off duty was visiting the Sphinx, where the nurses could enjoy a camel ride.

In addition to the 8th Battalion, two other brigades of infantry and some light horsemen were camping near Mena House. While the officers had huts and a house to serve as their mess, the enlisted men had nothing. They had to sleep on the sand, which blew everywhere, causing severe respiratory problems like pneumonia, bronchitis and throat infections.

Food poisoning also caused many hospital admissions. In Egypt, vegetables were often fertilised with human excrement so dysentery became rife. Talks on hygiene and the dangers of infection were regularly given by medical officers and nurses, but their warnings were often ignored.

Another problem was syphilis. During World War I there was no effective cure for this disease. Treatment was ineffective and consisted of applications of mercury and an ointment laced with arsenic called Salvarsan, which often caused the sufferer's hair to fall out and had other serious side effects.

Mena camp's inadequate washing and toilet facilities horrified Colonel Howse, so he granted permission for the men to swim every day in the large marble-lined pool. The nurses watched admiringly as the bronzed, fit young Australians waited in line for their turn. 'Our lads were the finest groups of men I ever saw,' wrote Alice in her journal the week she arrived, blissfully unaware that within a few months, many of them would be crippled, mutilated or dead.

As yet no clear rules had been laid down for authority over Australian doctors and nurses and this led to bitter in-fighting between Australian medical and nursing staff and British military administrators. The Australian-run hospital inherited almost two hundred British soldiers suffering from respiratory infections, food poisoning and syphilis. Having to care for these patients rather than for men wounded in war annoyed some of the nurses; they complained to the matron in charge that caring for syphilitics was not why they had enlisted.

Soon ten per cent of all Anzacs were suffering from syphilis and three times that number from gonorrhoea.[5] Gonorrhoea, although infectious, was curable and detected by a penile discharge, and the nurses were told that it could also be spotted when the men's ankles swelled after route marches. 'Getting a dose of the clap' was regarded as a sign of sophistication and a symbol of manhood by many soldiers, who ranged from young farmhands and stockmen to clerks and farmers' sons with no previous experience of war.

The Army regarded nurses as officers but did not extend to them the same rights and privileges or appropriate pay as male officers. The nurses did not have batmen and had to look after themselves, as well as mend soldiers' clothes and prepare special meals for those too ill to eat standard hospital food.

The nurses received nine shillings and sixpence a day, only sixpence more than an Army corporal. However, corporals were provided with free meals whereas the nurses had to pay for their own food and were charged the same high mess fees as the better-paid officers and doctors. Consequently, the AANS nurses had a struggle paying for basic necessities as well as laundry and food. Colonel Neville Howse, who was married to a former nurse, was sympathetic to the nurses' plight and did his best to sort out various anomalies, but he was often obstructed by Matron Nellie Gould.

Matron Nellie Gould was a martinet and in charge of nurses' dress codes and behaviour. She insisted that all nurses wear their hot, uncomfortable winter uniforms — ankle-length long-sleeved dress with stiffly starched collar and cuffs, a white webbing belt and a long, stiffly starched white apron. Thick grey stockings and black lace-up walking shoes completed an outfit totally unsuited to the tropics. Matron Gould ruled with a rod of iron. All nurses had to be back in the nurses' home by 10 pm each evening and were not allowed to drink even one glass of an alcoholic beverage. She even attempted to ban the nurses from dancing in public, without much success.[6]

Alice dared to defy Matron Gould and created a lifelong enemy when she headed a movement among the nurses for new summer uniforms. To silence all comment Nellie Gould placed a notice on the bulletin board stating that 'The Imperial Government requires *all* nurses to wear the regulation uniform of grey serge or grey cotton dresses. A stiff white collar will be worn at the neck of the uniform dresses, topped by a black bonnet when going outdoors.' Eventually the nurses won the right to wear white solar topees, but only if they paid for them out of their own pocket.

Alice kept her journal under lock and key fearing Matron Gould might exact revenge by confiscating it and handing it to the Censor's Office with dreadful consequences for Alice.

'CRY HAVOC AND LET SLIP THE DOGS OF WAR'

For years Alice had cared for her invalid mother without much in the way of a social life. Now at Mena House she enjoyed her new-found popularity and freedom. She and Hilda felt the need for new off-duty clothes. They had elegant white linen dresses made by a local dressmaker, who had learned her craft in Paris. Cotton, linen and silk were good value in Egypt and the dressmakers charged the nurses very reasonable rates. Alice and Hilda bought red silk poppies imported from Paris to trim their wide-brimmed straw hats and matching red silk ribbons to make coloured belts to wear with their new outfits.

Elegant in her new white linen dress and a belt, Alice attended a garden party in the grounds of Mena House, in honour of General Bridges. The moustached, silver-haired general stood on a raised podium with the newly promoted Colonel Neville Howse beside him. In his speech General Bridges emphasised that the AIF, being the first force to fight as an all-Australian unit, was creating history.

As meals at Mena House were unappetising, the nurses were often asked out by affluent Red Cross lady volunteers from Sydney and Melbourne. These ladies would drive the nurses to Groppi's Tea Rooms, a favourite spot for unaccompanied European ladies, and treat them to a truly delicious tea. Groppi's became a kind of home-from-home for the nurses, who enjoyed choosing French patisseries, brought to their tables by waiters, along with Indian or China tea, real French-style coffee or hot chocolate in silver pots.

The nurses were permitted to receive officers or male

COURTESY JENNY BLUNDELL.

Mena House as it was in 1999.

relatives to visit in their sitting room, providing they had a chaperone. Old friends from the *Benalla* were frequent guests, dropping in unannounced for a warm cup of tea and a chat and bringing their 'sisters in arms' Australian magazines and newspapers. Colonel Gartside even made a presentation to Alice and Hilda of brass shoulder badges in the form of an '8' to wear on their uniform jackets. They treasured these and wore them with pride on their lapels when they were invited to meals at the 8th Battalion Officers' Mess.

On Christmas Eve 1914 the nurses decorated the wards with greenery and bought each other presents. Alice and Hilda also bought presents for their friends in the 8th Batallion. Alice wrote in her journal: 'We allowed ourselves a little latitude . . . stayed up till 11 pm entertaining old friends from the *Benalla* and from 1 AGH [Australian General Hospital in Cairo] in our private sitting room, and talking nostalgically about old times in Australia.'

On Christmas morning the 8th Battalion's brass band arrived to serenade the nurses and patients, playing for them old favourites like 'Home Sweet Home' and 'Waltzing Matilda'. Colonel Bill Bolton came round the wards to wish the boys a happy Christmas. The nurses distributed Red Cross parcels, each containing a home-made cake, a hand-stitched pillow case, a cake of soap, a note pad and pencil, and sometimes a hand-knitted pair of socks.

By the new year Surgeon-General William Birrell had arrived in Cairo to run the medical corps of the AIF. Birrell clashed bitterly with Neville Howse over the allocation of money for medical care. Howse wished to spend more money on hospital ships but this plan was vetoed by Birrell. However, Neville Howse was responsible for the Australian Army acquiring the hospital ship *Gascon*, which would save thousands of lives.

It was whispered in the 8th Battalion Mess that the AIF would soon be off to foreign parts. There was talk of Lord Kitchener as Admiral of the Navy involving the Australian Imperial Force in a 'big stunt'. The British War Council had adopted Winston Churchill's ambitious plan for ships of the British Navy to force a way through the heavily mined Dardanelles.

Winston Churchill's daring but impractical plan involved British warships steaming through the Dardanelles channel and landing Allied troops, who would capture the forts and guns that protected the narrow straits. Churchill expected little opposition. He envisaged that Constantinople would fall immediately, ensuring the collapse of Germany's ally, the Ottoman Empire. The Allies could then attack Germany from the east, aided by Russia. To Churchill, the idea of capturing the Hellespont had a ring of Homeric glory, making the somewhat impractical Dardanelles plan irresistible. (Of course, had the plan succeeded Churchill would have been a hero.)

Secretary for War Field Marshall Herbert Kitchener was just as single-minded as Churchill. Kitchener suffered from the delusion that 'if a British submarine surfaced opposite the almost uninhabited Gallipoli peninsula and waved the Union Jack the Turkish garrison would turn tail and run'.[7] Kitchener and Churchill agreed that the newly raised Australian and New Zealand Imperial Forces had to play a vital role attacking the Dardanelles, in company with British, French, Indian and West Indian troops.

To lead the military side of the expedition, Kitchener chose Sir Ian Hamilton, a retired general with a passion for books and ancient history. Unfortunately, General Hamilton's practical knowledge of the area was non-existent. Hamilton and Birrell's plans for the evacuation of wounded soldiers from the Gallipoli peninsula were based on a brief report and a map made nine years previously.[8]

It was unclear to whom the Australian Army Nursing Service would report. Were they officially under the Royal Medical Corps or under the command of the colonel of the regiment to which they were attached?

TRANSFER TO HELIOPOLIS

In February 1915, Sister Alice Kitchen was transferred to 1 Australian General Hospital (AGH), which operated in the former Palace Hotel, Heliopolis, an affluent suburb on the other side of the city from Giza.

The Palace Hotel was so big it occupied two city blocks and it lacked the charm of Mena House. Alice missed her friends and the homelike atmosphere of the nurses' sitting room at Mena House.

On the wards, vital equipment was lacking. There was no steriliser so the nurses were forced to sterilise surgical instruments in a saucepan full of water, which they boiled on a primus stove. The Art Nouveau-style lift, imported from France at the time the Suez Canal was built, was so old it frequently broke down. As a result, after a hard day's work the nurses often had to walk up four flights of marble stairs to their rooms. 'Marble is very very hard on the feet at the end of the day,' Alice observed wryly in her journal towards the end of February.

Matron Jane Bell, the administrator, found her orders blocked by the hospital's commanding officer Colonel Ramsay Smith, a stickler for etiquette and female propriety. Matron Jane Bell was a competent and fiery Florence Nightingale in steel-rimmed glasses. Alice knew the matron well and admired her from the days when they had worked together at the Melbourne Hospital. It was inevitable that Matron Bell would arouse the enmity of the autocratic colonel. Because Alice supported Matron Bell she also incurred Colonel Ramsay Smith's anger. The fact that Ramsay Smith was in alliance with Alice's old adversary Matron Nellie Gould, now in charge of nurses' welfare at Heliopolis, aggravated things. Constant disputes between the CO and Matron Bell only made life harder for the already overworked nurses.

Colonel Ramsay Smith issued a vengeful order restricting the nurses' right to entertain male friends and relatives in their sitting room. Nurses had to obtain written permission from Colonel Ramsay Smith twenty-four hours in advance of receiving male visitors. Alice was one of the chief protesters against the newly imposed rule, pointing out that the nurses and their visitors often did not know when they would be off duty beforehand, making it impossible to predict their visiting hours.

Censorship of letters and personal diaries became even more stringent than before. Like all military and medical staff Alice had signed the *British Official Secrets Act* of 1911. This Act had severe penalties for revealing 'information of potential benefit to the enemy' and included dismissal from the service, court-martial or imprisonment if information was written down in any diaries, letters or documents, which could be handed to the enemy.

Understandably, Alice felt uneasy about the CO or Matron Gould learning she was keeping a journal detailing her experiences as an *aide memoire* to writing a book. In her journal Alice made guarded reference to 'hospital management problems' and 'discord between nurses and administrators', but did not elaborate.

Meals provided by a caterer were unappetising, grease-laden and expensive. Matron Jane Bell put in a complaint, but the CO refused to take any action and meals continued to get worse.

The caterer employed by Ramsay Smith was, in Alice's words, a 'canny money grubbing person', who charged each nurse a flat fee for 'breakage and replacement costs' even when nothing had been broken. In desperation the nurses bought their own cutlery and crockery, carrying it down the long marble corridors from the wards to the dining room and then back again.

Alice became so angry with the CO that she jeopardised her chances of promotion by heading a deputation to complain about the poor treatment of nurses. In return Colonel Ramsay Smith and Matron Nellie Gould gave Alice bad work reports, which, in accordance with custom, she was shown each month and had to sign. Alice stopped being cautious and vented her outrage in her journal when she wrote on 18 February, 'Everyone here *loathes* the C.O. [Ramsay Smith] and J.W.B. [Colonel J.W. Barrett] like poison. No one would grieve if anything happened to them.'

Colonel Ramsay Smith countered protests by making the nurses account for every meal or snack sent to the wards. Each patient's meals had to be ordered on special sheets which were then sent down to the hospital kitchens. All this paperwork was time-consuming for the already overworked nursing sisters. On 1 March 1915 Alice's journal records that 'this evening I was so tired I was nearly reduced to tears while trying to make the diet sheets tally and fill in prescription forms'.

Alice could accept working long hours for low pay but constant friction with Colonel Ramsay Smith and endless red tape wore her down.

Colonel J.W. Barrett (later Sir James Barrett), who had previously lectured the troops on the dangers of syphilis, was a good doctor. But like Ramsay Smith he was a stickler for discipline. Both men blamed the nurses for patients leaving the ward at night to slip into the bars and brothels of 'The Wozzer'. The nurses were aware of the dangers of syphilis but were not happy to take on the role of jailer.

One evening the CO called for Sister Kitchen and told her sternly the military police had reported that *three* of her patients had been seen in the streets in their blue hospital pyjamas. Alice assured him that none of her patients was missing, but the colonel insisted on inspecting every bed on her ward. He stormed about, pulled covers off the beds and thumped pillows to see whether the beds were occupied. To Alice's relief every one of her charges was in bed. In her journal she wondered if the soldiers had deliberately hoaxed the colonel by making the call themselves, pretending to be from the military police.

A few weeks later Alice and Hilda (who was now working at the Citadel Hospital) had lunch at Shepheard's Hotel with their friends Captains Dale and Coulter and Lieutenant Barratt. On leaving Shepheard's Alice and Hilda were confronted by an uproar in the street outside. Alice recorded the scene in her journal:

> Motor cars, horse-drawn fire carts and military police everywhere. We heard shots fired. Was told afterwards that Australian soldiers had burned down undesirable places, defied the 'red caps' [as the British Military Police were known] and fired at them, killing one man and injuring several others and that police had cleared the street using fixed bayonets.

Alice later learned that the spread of venereal disease amongst the soldiers had triggered the riot. In retaliation drunken Anzacs had evicted prostitutes and pimps from the brothels and gaming houses, and set bedding and furniture alight. When a fire cart arrived they had cut its water hoses so that several of the bars and brothels burned down.[9]

꙰ ꙰ ꙰

General Sir Ian Hamilton arrived in Egypt on 29 March. Five days later the 8th Battalion was ordered to pack up camp.

Every bootblack on the streets of Cairo and Alexandria seemed to know that the troops were off to the Dardanelles, but ironically the Anzacs themselves were kept in the dark.

On 4 April 1915, the 8th Battalion boarded the *Clan McGillivray* for a two days' voyage to Lemnos Island. 'May God have mercy on them and protect them,' Alice wrote in her diary that night.

Australian military hospitals in Cairo and Alexandria were told they should prepare a few hundred beds for the arrival of wounded soldiers. All leave for Army doctors and nurses was cancelled.

Colonel Neville Howse had warned that casualties could be extremely high on the Gallipoli peninsula, but his requests for more hospital ships and more medical supplies and equipment continued to be ignored.

On the evening of 24 April 1915, the 8th and other battalions steamed out of Mudros Harbour at Lemnos, past the island of Imbros, 24 kilometres away from the Gallipoli peninsula. The men lay on deck wrapped in their greatcoats and gazed up at the stars, reminiscing in low voices about 'home' and speculating about the 'Big Stunt' to come.

According to historians Les Carlyon and C.E.W. Bean, the following morning at dawn between 15,000 and 16,000 men prepared to land on the Gallipoli peninsula. Due to an unexpectedly strong current and a faulty marker buoy the landing crafts were dragged towards a narrow strip of beach more than a kilometre north of their original target. This meant the Anzacs were facing almost impossible terrain with steep cliffs rising only some 20 metres from the waterfront.

A handful of Turkish sentries patrolling the coast from the cliff tops spotted the approaching boats and quickly summoned reinforcements. As soon as the British were within range, Turkish soldiers opened fire — not with the ancient muskets the Anzacs had been told to expect, but with brand new German rifles, machine guns and howitzers.[10]

Some of the Anzacs were killed by shrapnel even before the boats ran aground, others clambered out into waist-deep water and drowned under the weight of their heavy packs. Within minutes the shallow waters of Anzac Cove were stained red with the blood of the dying.

Those surviving the first wave waded ashore and found themselves at the foot of steep scrub-covered cliffs. Anzac Cove resembled an amphitheatre with the Turks in the gallery and the Anzacs on stage. On the beach, the Anzacs rushed towards the cliffs to shelter from a rain of Turkish bullets. Then orders were given to ascend the slopes. Hundreds of Anzacs were killed and wounded in the attack. The wounded lay in the blazing sun until the stretcher bearers could reach them. Many died a lonely, painful death.

Evacuation of the wounded to the hospital ships was a huge problem. Over 1700 wounded men were placed on mine sweepers and taken out to two hospital ships, the *Gascon*, and *Guildford Castle,* and the transport ship *Osmanieh,* which had no nurses and only one doctor on board. No one had allowed for so many casualties, and with the impossibility of setting up a hospital on the Gallipoli peninsula many more hospital ships staffed by trained personnel were needed.

Such was the carnage that commander of the Australian and New Zealand forces, General Sir William Birdwood, sent a message to General Sir Ian Hamilton, seeking permission to withdraw and return to the waiting ships. General Hamilton, who had just received a radio message that an Australian submarine had slipped through the Dardanelles into the Sea of Marmara, refused Birdwood's request. Instead of allowing the Anzacs to retire and saving thousands of lives, Hamilton sent back a message: 'Your news is indeed serious. There is nothing for it but to dig yourselves right in and stick it out. It would take at least two days to re-embark you.'[11] And so those valiant men began to dig.

Alice's former CO at Mena, Colonel Neville Howse, had kept his head amid the chaos which he had predicted. Heroic Dr Howse set up a small casualty clearing station (CCS) at one end of the beach and disinfected and stitched wounds and splinted limbs, ignoring his own safety.[12] As Howse had foreseen, there were not nearly enough stretchers or supplies of drinking water, morphine and surgical dressings. As a result men were left in the blazing sun injured and their wounds became infected by sand, dirt and flies.[13]

THE RETURN OF WOUNDED ANZACS

Alice recorded in her journal that the first load of wounded Anzacs arrived at Alexandria on 29 April 1915. Those who arrived on hospital ships were in better condition than the unfortunate men assigned to transport ships. Most had not been washed for days, were badly dehydrated and had wounds swollen with pus or black with gangrene.

Half the wounded were hospitalised in Alexandria while the rest were sent another 320 kilometres to Cairo. On 30 April, Alice, disobeying censorship restrictions, recorded that 2849 wounded men had been shipped from Gallipoli to Alexandria. Lieutenant Rupert Barratt had been killed and Colonel Bolton wounded.

Alice's ward at No 1 AGH at Heliopolis was swamped by wounded men, many of them on the point of death. Camp beds and rubber mattresses overflowed into the hallways, corridors and wherever nurses and orderlies could find space for them. Some of the men were too tall for the hospital's flimsy camp beds, which had to be extended with chairs.

Some of the wounded men had been left lying in pools of their own blood for so long they were stuck fast to their canvas stretchers. The nurses and orderlies had great difficulty prising them off the canvas, and often caused the men excruciating pain. By now Alice was in despair about the appalling treatment of wounded men at Gallipoli. Angry and frustrated, she wrote in her diary: 'If wounded animals had been treated as these soldiers were, the RSPCA would have raised a storm.'

The nurses were overwhelmed with the flood of distressing cases: men who vomited blood or haemorrhaged, tetanus victims with their jaws locked rigid and men whose faces or genitals had been shot away. Young soldiers terrified at the thought of having a limb amputated clung to Alice's hand for comfort. The suffering was terrible and no effective pain killers as yet existed apart from morphine, and supplies of this were limited.

Each morning the nurses had to drain pus out of infected wounds. Fortunately, Red Cross volunteers helped the nurses to feed those patients who could not feed themselves. These ladies also provided small luxuries, such as bars of chocolate, tobacco, books, magazines and shaving gear. Alice was amazed that, in spite of their suffering, the patients rarely complained. They could see the nurses were overworked and were grateful that at long last they had *someone* to attend to them.

More casualties arrived each night by train. Alice worked ten- or twelve-hour shifts. When she finally did get to bed she had terrible nightmares in which wounded men with shattered faces and bleeding stumps instead of arms and legs haunted her. On the morning of 30 April she awoke, feeling as though she had not slept a wink. The horrors of Gallipoli and the bungling that cost the lives of thousands had shattered her illusions about the poetry of war. She had enjoyed reading the poems of Rupert Brooke. Now she wrote her own memorable words: 'There is no poetry here . . . only pain, misery and death.' Her journal entry for 2 May 1915 reads:

> This is not war but mass murder. Poor boys, if only the world knew how badly they are treated. There are not nearly enough hospital ships to cope. Another strenuous day. Over fifty officers admitted in my section. We are all worked to breaking point with so many dressings to do, meals to provide and so much marble underfoot.

Heliopolis had two hundred medical orderlies, but Alice described some as 'pretty hopeless'. There were only thirty-five overworked doctors. Each nursing sister was responsible for forty wounded officers and between one hundred and fifty and two hundred enlisted men. The nurses worked on average twelve hours a day, six days a week. However, in cases of an emergency they had to work on without a break. They could also be woken to assist the night staff if necessary. On 5 May Alice wrote in her journal:

> Everyone is working long hours. Scarcely time to think of snatching a meal. So many patients have arm and hand injuries. One poor young lad had his leg amputated due to gangrene. Work gets heavier each day. Some say [Gallipoli] casualties reached 6,000: others say 8,000 is nearer the mark.

On 7 May Alice was overwhelmed with the arrival of another thousand casualties. She wrote in despair:

> By this time perhaps all the men we looked on as friends have been blotted out of existence. All our leave has been stopped until further notice. Another turmoil of a day. I have charge of forty-two officers, some of them good friends. The work is harrowing. If we had been nursing strange troops we may have felt it less, but among our own people the horrors of war are brought home. Almost everyone on the nursing or medical staff has a relation or friend at the front so you dread the latest news, in case it is someone you know.

On the open wards, shell-shocked men raved and screamed. Some crawled under the beds, terrified of gunfire, while others tore off their bandages. Being a danger to themselves and other patients they were moved to a special lockable ward. Over half the men in the wards, debilitated from a poor diet, were suffering from dysentery or enteric fever (typhoid). These men wanted water and more water, which had been in short supply during transport from Gallipoli.

The mental and physical strain on the nurses was immense. Alice and her colleagues were haggard from overwork, lack of sleep and worry about friends and loved ones. Eventually the situation grew so desperate that more Australian nurses were enlisted, but it would be a long time before they arrived.

Catering at Heliopolis was still tendered out and the food became worse by the day. Some patients could not keep down any of the hospital food and relied on the nurses to buy them fresh eggs and milk. Frequently, Alice paid for these out of her own money, because the enlisted men would not get paid until after leaving the hospital, and so many were penniless.[14]

Once again the nurses complained about the food. This time Colonel Ramsay Smith took action. The following day the caterer departed in a huff, taking everything in the hospital's larder with him. The nurses survived on tea and biscuits until a new caterer arrived with fresh supplies. The food improved, but only marginally.

On 11 May 1915, Alice started a week on night duty. In a contemplative mood she wrote:

> The morning star rises outside our ward windows. It and
> the white desert sand are lovely at dawn and compensate
> for the fatigue that accompanies a spell on night duty.
> I have grown to love Egypt and shall be sorry to leave it.
> The jacaranda trees are in bloom everywhere: have never
> seen such fine blossoms.

On 19 May, Colonel Cunningham from the 8th Battalion told Alice that General Bill Bridges was wounded and Captain Mathieson, another good friend and a medical officer to the 8th, had been killed at Anzac Cove. Alice wrote with sadness, 'Captain Mathieson was such a nice kind man.'

A group of younger nurses arrived on the SS *Kyarra* a week later and brought new energy to Heliopolis. Among them were Sister Olive Haynes, a clergyman's daughter, and her flirtatious, exuberant friend Sister 'Pete' Peters, both from Adelaide.

As well as their medical duties, Alice and the other nurses mended the men's uniforms, listened to their troubles and wrote letters home for amputees or those with arms in slings.

Following the example laid down by Florence Nightingale during the Crimean War, Alice did her best to write letters of condolence to families whose sons had died. Her letters were filled with praise for the dead men's courage in their last moments, even when this was not entirely true.

By now Alice was aware that young soldiers did not die happily. They called for their mothers, some cursing the day they had enlisted. However, the older men showed extraordinary courage and most confronted death with stoicism. 'I would like you to know your son died bravely,' she would write. 'He was happy to know he had given his life for his country and the Empire.' Sometimes at a loss for words and wanting to provide comfort she would quote a few lines from Rupert Brooke. What she could not tell grieving mothers was that if only their sons had received prompt treatment at Anzac Cove or on the filthy transport ships, their wounds might not have become infected with gangrene and their sons might still be alive. After witnessing the deaths of many young men whose lives had been needlessly sacrificed due to bungled evacuation processes Alice was finding it harder and harder to write these letters.

Over the next few months Alice received replies from the boys' mothers thanking her for caring for their sons in their last hours. Some of the letters were so sad they made Alice bite back her tears.

♧ ♧ ♧

The hottest time of year was fast approaching and the nurses joked that Heliopolis should have been named 'Hell–iopolis'. Their heavy uniforms were hotter than ever. Matron Jane Bell had already lobbied the administration in London who, after months of deliberation, grudgingly conceded that nurses in Egypt could be issued with lighter weight dresses and summer capes of red cotton rather than wool. Measurements were taken for new uniforms, but nothing arrived.

Alice accepted an invitation to a luncheon at Shepheard's Hotel for Colonel Bill Bolton, who had been invalided out of the Army and was to return home. He had been mentioned in despatches for bravery at Gallipoli, in particular for the capture of an important Turkish stronghold on top of a ridge, which had been named Bolton's Ridge in his honour.

At the dinner Colonel Bolton, who had his arm in a sling, related how the men of the 8th Battalion had charged up the beach and climbed those terrible cliffs while being strafed by Turkish bullets. Then he told the sad story of Lieutenant Rupert Barratt's death, killed as he stepped ashore. There was a gasp from the audience, many of whom had known Rupert well. Alice remembered that first night at dinner on the *Benalla,* when Rupert and his cousin Frank Dale made them all laugh with their funny stories. Now this young man, heir to a vast grazing property, lay in a grave at Anzac Cove.

With a grave face Bill Bolton went on to tell them that, during the battalion's first month of battle, 251 of its members had been wounded, 58 killed and 79 reported missing and believed dead. At this, he turned towards Sister Kitchen and Matron Bell and as representatives of the AANS in Cairo thanked both nurses for everything they were doing for the wounded men.[15] There was a burst of clapping among the officers. Glasses were raised to Sister Alice Kitchen and Matron Jane Bell before Bill Bolton sat down amid a chorus of cheers.

In the Aegean and at Gallipoli

In the first week of May 1915, Matron Jane Bell called Sisters Kitchen and Samsing into her office. She congratulated them for running their wards so efficiently. As a reward for all their hard work she was recommending them for a more pleasant job — taking convalescent patients back to Australia.

Alice and Hilda discussed Matron Bell's kind offer. It would be nice to return to Australia and see their families but they decided that as they had enjoyed working on the *Benalla* they would now like to do a spell as nurses on a hospital ship. Hopefully, they would be sent to Gallipoli and could look after wounded men from the 8th Battalion, which they regarded as their 'special' regiment. Matron Bell promised to support their application. However, she warned them that work on hospital ships was very hard and carried no extra pay or overtime allowance.

For weeks and weeks they heard nothing from the War Office. The temperature in Cairo was soaring and they were still wearing the winter uniforms in which they had left Melbourne. Finally, after months of waiting London sent out their new lightweight summer uniforms. Matron Nellie Gould posted a notice stating that even though the new summer uniforms came with soft muslin cuffs instead of starched ones, all nurses had to continue to wear 3-inch (75 mm) high starched collars.

On 7 June 1915, almost a month after their interview with Matron Bell, Hilda burst into Alice's room with exciting news. The War Office had granted their wish. They were to join the hospital ship *Gascon* in Alexandria as replacements for two nurses unexpectedly returning to Australia. One poor nurse had collapsed when she learned her younger brother had been killed at Anzac Cove. The other nurse had refused to go back on board saying she could no longer endure such terrible sights.[16]

At Alexandria, Alice's former colleague and friend from Melbourne days, Grace Oram, now Lady Superintendent of Nurses, was there to meet them. She filled them in on the hospital ship *Gascon's* situation.

It seemed that the War Office in Whitehall

Hospital ship Gascon.

AUSTRALIAN WAR MEMORIAL NEG. P01287.006.

was to blame for the hospital ship *Gascon*'s chaotic last voyage from Gallipoli. Instead of sending out bandages and bottles of morphine, those wretched clerks in London had sent babies' feeding bottles and nappies. The nurses had had to tear their petticoats into strips to bandage the wounded. Without enough morphine to last the voyage the cries of pain from badly wounded men had been heartrending. These poor men had lain out in the blazing sun for days before the stretcher bearers could reach them, so their wounds were badly infected. This had caused grave problems for the medical team. Matron Oram warned Alice and Hilda that this was not a job for the squeamish. She shook Alice and Hilda by the hand. 'Goodbye and good luck. You'll need it,' she said ominously.

The *Gascon* had once been a passenger liner operated by the Union Line on the route between London and South Africa. Its lower cabins had been converted into hospital wards, its elegant furniture stripped out and the white hull painted with huge red crosses to show the enemy it was a hospital ship. But the Germans did not always observe these rules: to date, two hospital ships had been torpedoed and sunk.

On board the *Gascon*, they were presented to a tall Englishman in a gold braided uniform. In a plummy voice he told them that he was the captain and seemed less than delighted at the idea of two *more* women on what he obviously thought should be an all-male ship. He informed them stiffly that the nurses did not eat with 'his' naval officers but at a special sitting of their own in the mess. Women were only admitted as long as they did not break any of the rules of the British Navy, whose officers staffed this ship.

They were shown around the ship by the chief engineer, a friendly Geordie. He showed them the big box-cradle in which two stretcher cases at a time could be hoisted aboard and told them the procedures to follow when the wounded arrived. First, the men's wrist labels were checked and names and ranks written on a record card. Urgent cases were 'red carded', a sign they should be given priority. Five wards were assigned to seriously wounded patients, and these could accommodate a total of 450 patients. The *Gascon* could transport another 200 to 300 men known as 'sitting' cases — those who could sit up but needed food brought to them — and 'walkers', who could get their own food from the Patients' Mess. Walkers slept on mattresses on top deck or wherever they could find space in the companionways.

Alice and Hilda were shown to a small cramped cabin which they were to share. It was on the lowest deck near the engines and was very, very hot. On the wards they met up with a former colleague from Heliopolis, Sister 'Pete' Peters, who told them that on the *Gascon*'s previous voyage from Gallipoli to Alexandria, fifty-two soldiers had died from badly infected wounds.

They were bound for the small rocky island of Lemnos, approximately 40 kilometres off the Turkish coastline, which the Greeks had allowed the British to use as a supply depot and to set up tented hospitals. These were run by British, Australian and Canadian nurses, who were functioning under difficult circumstances. The island was only two hours by sea from the Gallipoli peninsula but, like Gallipoli, was short of drinking water, which had to be shipped in by a tanker from Alexandria.

On 11 June 1915, the *Gascon* steamed into Mudros Harbour, the main harbour on this parched island. The ship lay at anchor amid rows of British and French warships, transport ships bringing food and water to provision the tented hospitals, and converted trawlers used to sweep the area for German mines. The captain warned them all through the loudspeaker that they were under an hour's notice to sail to Anzac Cove where the *Gascon* would replace the *Sicilia* as duty hospital ship. There they would wait until nightfall, load the wounded and take off for Alexandria again.

On Sunday morning they were still awaiting orders to leave for Gallipoli. While Hilda wrote letters home Alice wrote to her mother and updated her journal. After a traditional roast Sunday lunch with a joint of beef, two naval officers on an adjacent supply ship offered to take them sailing in a dinghy. As it was highly unlikely they would sail that day, Colonel Hugo, as the senior medical officer on board, gave them permission to leave the ship, something that did not please the captain. It seemed there was an uneasy truce between those two, each believing the Army nurses were under their command.

Alice, Hilda, Ella Tucker and Major Ilias (a surgeon with the AIF whose Greek-born parents had migrated to Melbourne from Athens) were taken by the two friendly young British naval officers for a sail round the harbour. Alice, who had grown up in inland Victoria and never learned to swim, initially was nervous but discovered she enjoyed small boat sailing. They landed on a beach near the Australian tented hospital and found soldiers of many different nationalities camping along the waterfront. There were French and French-colonial troops from Africa, brown-faced Ghurkhas from the Himalayas, turbanned Sikhs, and West Indians with broad smiles and gold teeth.

They walked through a camp of French soldiers whose officers wore elegant pale blue-grey uniforms and were extremely polite. But Alice, suspicious of their flowery compliments and hand kissing, called them 'chocolate soldiers' and thought the French looked as if they belonged in a comic opera. She and Hilda politely refused invitations to join the French officers for a glass of wine while marvelling at the comfort with which the French surrounded themselves. The mess tents used by the French contained barrels of wine shipped over from France. The men had also set up a long row of camp ovens which baked long crusty loaves of bread fresh each morning.

From this French enclave they walked to the Australian camp whose dining room rarely served fresh bread but provided hard biscuits and a never-ending supply of tins of salted bully beef or stewed lamb. The Australian camp, with its rows of white tents, was surrounded by borders of white pebbles and had pathways with evocative names like Collins Street and Macquarie Street.

They were greeted by Colonel Bryant, the Australian CO, who showed them over the tented field hospital. Alice looked at the lines of stretchers lying on the ground in the blazing sun. They had no mosquito nets over them. Blowflies buzzed round the mouths of men too ill to brush them aside — surely it *must* be possible to do better than this for men who had risked their lives for their country.

AT ANZAC COVE

Just before midnight on 14 June, Alice was woken by the rattle of the *Gascon's* anchor chain. With relief she realised the continual throbbing and droning of the ship's engines had ceased. They had arrived at Anzac Cove safely. Alice turned over and went back to sleep.

When she woke, Alice looked through the porthole and saw the hospital ship they were to replace lying about 50 metres away. She glimpsed a narrow strip of sand above which reared cliffs sharp as fish bones, with slopes scarred by steep ravines. In the distance Alice could see trenches that traversed the buff-coloured or reddish cliffs like a fine network of veins.

On the beach were two small tents with a white canvas awning slung between them which she realised must be the tiny casualty clearing stations. Beside them was a much larger tent with a red cross on its roof. It was a hospital tent where serious cases could lie in the shade until nightfall. However, it was not large enough to accommodate all the wounded and many of the men had to lie on the beach, in the hot sun plagued by blowflies.

Most of the beach was covered with packing cases, and mules were dragging stores to the gullies. Men in khaki shorts surrounded two water carts. With a shock Alice realised they were lining up for their daily water ration. Others braved the shells which pock-marked the water and went for a swim. The water looked exquisite — turquoise-blue and clear as glass. Alice looked down and saw dolphins gambolling around the *Gascon's* hull, giving the impression she was on a luxury yacht anchored in a millionaires' playground rather than a hospital ship hopefully anchored out of range of the enemy guns.

Alice watched a small boat rowed by a young midshipman coming towards them. He tied his dinghy to the *Gascon's* rope ladder and climbed up on deck, removed his braided cap, saluted the chief engineer and told him that the *Sicilia* would be leaving for Alexandria at midnight.

His message delivered, the midshipman saluted, turned on his heel and made for the rope ladder. He climbed down into his dinghy, untied it and started to row back to the *Sicilia*. As he reached a point half way between the two hospital ships Alice heard a shrill whine overhead then a hissing as an object hit the water. The enemy shell created a surge which rocked the *Gascon* and nearly swamped the tiny dinghy.

Alice watched in horror, fearing the dinghy would be sucked down by the rapidly spreading whirlpool.

Rowing like a man possessed, the young midshipman managed to reach the *Sicilia*. Alice felt uneasy, knowing another German shell could be aimed at the *Gascon*. Engines throbbed and propellers churned. Slowly the *Gascon* moved out of range of the gigantic German-made gun known as Asiatic Annie.

Alice went below. The ward reeked of carbolic soap. That meant the orderlies had been hard at work cleaning up. She checked each bedside locker to see it contained a china urinal and that each water carafe was full. In order that they would not spill when the sea was rough the carafes were slung from metal gimbals beside each cot. Just to make certain, she rechecked her dressings cupboard and was relieved to see the large stock of neatly wound bandages, gauze dressing pads, bottles of iodine and Eusol disinfectant.[17]

Reassured that the ward was shining clean and ready to receive the next load of wounded, Alice returned on deck. Here, the chief engineer was chatting animatedly with Sister Peters. Their conversation was interrupted by a droning sound high above them. The three of them looked up. Alice saw a small plane circling overhead, its wings glinting silver against the vivid blue of the sky.

'Theirs or ours?' Alice asked.

'Theirs,' said the chief engineer laconically, 'Looks like a Taube.'

There was a burst of gunfire from Anzac Cove. Seconds later a tiny piece of cotton wool appeared in the sky close to the German plane. In response, the Turkish fire increased in volume until the noise was deafening. Like a lazy wasp the German plane droned away over the lion-coloured hills of the Gallipoli peninsula, one of the most lonely and desolate places on God's earth Alice thought.

She wrote up the scene in her journal:

> . . . heavy booms from Turkish guns echo round the hills
> and over the sea, dealing out destruction and death. From

the hills opposite we constantly hear the sound of snipers' rifles cracking. There is dust everywhere. Destroyers patrol around like watchdogs in case of German submarines.

Having experienced the searing heat, Alice felt sympathy for the Anzacs trapped in the hot and dusty trenches, deafened by gunfire. She could understand why soldiers would risk their lives for a swim in the sea, the only diversion in such a bleak place.

After dinner the doctors and nurses watched the sunset, one of those crimson and golden skies slowly turning to a mixture of grey and lilac. The hills behind Anzac Cove resembled a recumbent elephant, whose wrinkled trunk pointed inland to the hills that ran down the spine of the Gallipoli peninsula. At midnight, when the guns had fallen quiet, their sister ship, the *Sicilia*, slipped away for Alexandria, her hold full of wounded soldiers.

Shortly afterwards, a small fleet of pinnaces, tugs and barges ventured out from the shore and surrounded the *Gascon*. Wounded men lay pressed tight together; others sat bolt upright, due to lack of space, their faces gaunt with pain.

Alice, watching the scene from the ship's rail, thought the rolling of these small boats must be agonising for men with stomach wounds or broken limbs. She saw how the first patients, their faces ghastly white in the light of flares, were swung aboard. Those with less serious wounds were able to climb the *Gascon*'s rope ladder unassisted. Those men who had sustained serious injuries, 'cot cases' in Army medical jargon (after the metal cots they were given on the wards), had to be swung aboard the *Gascon* on its box hoist. Patients who had been

PHOTO BY COM. J.G. ADAMSON, R.N., OBE, AUTHOR'S FATHER.

Wounded soldier being lifted onto the Gascon *in a box hoist.*

Stretcher cases on a barge await loading onto the Gascon. To the rear of the barge are the walking cases; on the left orderlies carry wounded men over their shoulders up the gangway.

AUSTRALIAN WAR MEMORIAL NEG. A020740.

given morphine by the doctors at Anzac Cove arrived with a large 'M' written in indelible ink on their foreheads or on the red wrist labels to indicate they needed urgent attention.

Fearful of showing too much light, which could attract German planes, the crew worked by flickering flares. Again and again the large wooden cradle soared high into the air and hovered over the deck. Slowly and carefully, over two hundred stretcher cases were lowered onto the deck. The stretchers were then carried by the orderlies into the lifts that disgorged them directly onto the wards.

The medical orderlies were Hindus or Sikhs seconded from the Indian Army. Alice called her orderly 'Billy' because she couldn't pronounce his name. Hilda's medical orderly was named Selim. Neither Billy nor Selim could read but they were kind to the patients and very hard workers. Alice and Billy worked their way along the right side of the ward while Hilda and Selim took the left side. The stretchers and their occupants reeked of stale blood and excrement. Alice helped Billy to cut soiled and torn uniforms off the wounded, swab them down, using the minimum of water which was in short supply, and dress and disinfect their wounds so the doctors could operate if necessary. Changing field dressings often took a long time as dried blood encrusted the area. Sometimes an anaesthetic was needed before the dressings could be removed. The nurses had learned to administer these as the surgeons were too busy carrying out amputations and other urgent operations. Some of the Anzacs had hacked off the legs of their uniform trousers with pocket knives in an effort to keep cool. Sadly, for some of them, this problem of short trouser lengths would soon be resolved by amputation.

Men who had been lying out in the blazing sun in 'No Man's Land' (where it was very dangerous for the stretcher bearers to rescue them without being killed themselves) often had third-degree sunburn, and swollen and blackened tongues that protruded from their mouths. The nurses and orderlies had to restrain them from gulping down water too greedily.

Washing the wounded, Alice noticed how many of them were infested with fleas as well as lice. Since most men were crawling with lice, whose eggs nestled in the seams of their uniforms, all clothes were sent to be deloused and disinfected in a machine the staff jokingly referred to as the Detonator. The name was given to it because if any unused cartridges were left in pockets, they would explode in the heat of the machine. Many soldiers had festering sores around their mouths and on their arms and legs, due to months of living on an inadequate diet without fruit or vegetables. Others had the distinctive red rash that Alice knew denoted scabies.

After the orderlies had washed their patients they eased them into clean pyjamas. One young lad with shrapnel wounds that had ripped through his body and lodged in his genitals was left mute from shock. So was a young officer who could not stop shaking and shivering. Alice was told by other soldiers that the officer had been forced to spend days trapped by enemy fire beside the decomposing body of his younger brother and was now in shock.

The concept of shell shock was very new. It had not existed as a diagnosis in the Boer War, which had consisted of cavalry charges and infantry manoeuvres by men armed with sabres or bayonets attached to their rifles, and no machine guns or trench warfare. But at Gallipoli the Anzacs had spent weeks in tiny dug-outs or trenches, waiting for Turkish shells to land beside them, aware they were unable to escape. The sheer horror of seeing men blown apart and having to pick up the body parts afterwards had badly affected them.

From her experiences with shell-shocked men at Heliopolis, Alice was convinced that some of them, given rest and quiet, could be cured. However, in an open ward on the *Gascon*, surrounded by throbbing engines and other hallucinating patients, these shell-shocked men raved, screamed and disturbed soldiers who were very sick or dying.

What amazed Alice was how brave many of the wounded men were — most did not complain despite being in terrible pain. And if they *did* complain it was in soft moans rather than loud curses. A sergeant with a broken leg asked her how long it would take for him to get 'fixed up' so he could get back to Anzac Cove 'and have another go at the Turks'.

Abdominal wounds were the hardest of all to deal with. One unfortunate case had entrails protruding from his stomach like a string of sausages. Alice had to steel herself to push the guts back inside the body and bandage them in place until he reached the operating table. Now at last she understood why one of the young nurses on the previous voyage had refused to go back on the ward.

'Abdominals' were often in grave danger of haemorrhaging to death. They had to be made ready for the operating table immediately (since at that time there were no blood transfusions, no blood bank, no intravenous drips). Alice knew that no matter what they did most of these men would die, but nevertheless tried desperately to keep them alive.

On 10 June the second group to be made ready for the operating theatre were amputees. A soldier with an arm missing and a pair of bleeding stumps where his legs should have been told Alice: 'That shell knocked me arse over tit, sister. An' when I saw what the buggers 'ad done to me, I wished to Gawd the Turks 'ad finished me orf.' Alice's heart went out to the poor man but she could do little except give him morphine to ease the pain.

Another high-priority group were those with broken limbs. Most needed splinting, a skill Alice soon mastered. She never forgot one patient, a senior officer from Brigade HQ Battalion, who in her journal she called Colonel X. She had last seen him in Cairo, tall and handsome, mounted on a chestnut horse, riding beside the other colonels — Gartside, McPhee and Bolton — leading the 8th Battalion as they rode from Mena camp to Cairo station. And now here he was, a cripple, on board the *Gascon*. A shell had shattered the bone in his right leg, ripping the muscle to shreds.

On 18 June, Alice was told an old friend from 8th Battalion had come aboard and would like to see her, if she could spare a moment.

Directly she had finished changing the dressing on a patient's wound, Alice patted her hair into place and went up on deck. There she found Colonel McPhee, now looking years older than when she had last seen him. He handed her a parcel wrapped in old newspaper. Inside was a small but very beautiful watercolour of Allied warships in Mudros Harbour with the grey granite hills of Lemnos silhouetted against a vividly blue sky.

She thanked the colonel profusely for his gift, touched that he had thought of her.

Another soldier from the 8th Battalion that Alice remembered from the *Benalla* was Ross, a cheerful boy who had once delivered bread to her parents' home in Ballarat. He had been hit while having a swim in Anzac Cove and arrived on her ward, his guts full of shrapnel. Poor Ross held Alice's hand and made her promise she would write to his mother and tell her that he died bravely. In the event, he died screaming with pain in spite of the morphine injections, but Alice honoured his last wish.

> . . . poor Ross died shortly after admission as did two more 'abdominals' . . . hit while swimming. The work gets heavier daily, the flies are a continual pest and the atmosphere oppressive down below on the ward. Several large shells were fired at a store ship close by and rocked our poor wounded boys on the *Gascon* causing them to cry out in pain.

Whenever she had a spare moment, Alice tried to help the 'sitters' up on deck, including those suffering from typhoid or severe bouts of dysentery. Over a hundred men lay sprawled on the deck under a big white awning because the wards were too full to accommodate them. Some had the luxury of mattresses, others did not.

These poor men had been waiting to board the hospital ship for five days. Most were badly dehydrated, weak as kittens and unable to get up and fetch a cup of tea or a bowl of soup from the Patients' Mess down below. Alice did her best to help those who were dehydrated but, before the discovery of penicillin, there were no really powerful drugs for enteric fevers.

When the supply of clean pyjamas ran out, the 'enterics' had to be left in their soiled khaki trousers until they reached Alexandria. These poor men were pathetically grateful for the smallest attention by the 'walking' patients, by overworked nurses or the orderlies. Few of them complained of how the Army had treated them, although Alice felt they had every right to do so. Some died of dysentery or typhoid aboard the hospital ship; others had their health permanently damaged.

After a scare when a German submarine attempted to torpedo the *Gascon*, each night, at 9 pm, the crew now closed the portholes. Alice described in her journal for 17 June how:

> . . . each night after dark, the mine-sweepers bring over
> patients. The watertight doors can be closed quickly so it
> would take us longer to sink. We continually hear guns
> and shells being fired from the beach and from torpedo
> boats but now we scarcely give them a thought.

Alice got very little sleep but knew she could cope provided she kept focused on the task in hand. Throughout her shifts, Billy kept her supplied with cups of strong sweet tea and she cat-napped in an armchair on the ward whenever she could, only leaving the ward at dawn to change out of her bloodstained uniform. She would put on a clean white apron, a clean grey cotton dress and a freshly laundered set of muslin cuffs. By now she did not give a fig *what* Matron Gould wanted — she was *not* going to wear one of those dreadful starched collars: they were far too hot and uncomfortable.

Fleas were a problem. They were brought on board from the trenches and hopped from the patients to the nurses. Alice's midriff became raw from flea bites. Her nails were often rimmed black with dried blood after a patient haemorrhaged and she had had to use a tourniquet on arms and legs to staunch the bleeding. Bleeding could be fatal as there were no blood transfusions and nurses had to cope unaided with patients bleeding to death.

Major Ilias, Colonel Hugo and the other two Army surgeons also worked flat out almost round the clock. Tin buckets containing severed legs, hands and arms mounted up outside the operating theatre. Finally, the orderlies took the buckets up on deck and heaved their contents over the side, which caused a flurry of activity among the sharks.

Alice's ward lay below the waterline. It was hot, humid and poorly ventilated. Try as she would to keep the area fresh and clean, it often reeked of stale sweat and tobacco. Although the patients were not meant to smoke, what nurse could forbid such heroic men anything that might ease their suffering?

The death of Ross had been hard to bear. Alice was experienced enough to understand why nurses were not meant to get involved with their patients. She vowed this would not happen again but of course it did, because underneath her efficient exterior Alice had a warm and loving heart. Another *Benalla* boy by the name of Gooch, riddled with shrapnel was red-carded for her special attention. She was with him when he went to theatre and offered up a silent prayer that this time the surgeons could save him.

After Gooch returned from the operating theatre, Alice stayed by his bedside holding his hand and talking to him as slowly he regained consciousness. It seemed as though he would recover, but then his condition deteriorated. White as death, he haemorrhaged from a wound the size of a dinner plate. It proved impossible to staunch the flow of blood and soon Alice was drenched in it, blood staining her white apron and the hem of her dress. The poor boy gave a sigh and held tight to Alice's hand. She remembered Gooch confiding to her that he had raised his age to enlist — he had just had his seventeenth birthday.

Not wanting to let the patients see her cry she went below and wrote a letter to Gooch's mother. In her journal on 21 June she wrote:

I wonder when this awful destruction of life will cease.
There seems no safe spot for the men anywhere at this
rough spot, except in their dugouts. They seem to take their
lives in their hands whenever they move about, whether in
search of water, food, fresh air or any form of recreation.

When all the 550 cots were full, Alice and Hilda gave up their
cabins to two badly wounded men and slept on deck chairs for the
return journey. A dozen patients died en route and were buried at sea.

At Alexandria there was no time for an overnight break which
regulations recommended. They were under orders to go straight
back to Gallipoli. They saw their patients off onto the quayside and
immediately took on more crates of bandages, morphine, food and
other supplies. At least they could rest on the outward journey.

After they had anchored off Anzac Cove, the procedure of
loading patients at night was repeated again.

There was no intensive care ward but a system of 'special' nursing
for the worst cases. One of Alice's colleagues, Sister Rachael Pratt, was
ordered to relieve Alice of general duties so Alice could 'special' or
monitor closely four young soldiers in need of intensive care. The first
died just before midday, holding tight to her hand. The second did not
regain consciousness. The third — another boy from the 8th Battalion,
not yet twenty — remained conscious right up to the last moment.
He complained of terrible headaches and Alice tried to soothe him by
massaging his temples. In his last moments he confused Alice with his
mother and asked her to give him a hug. Then, as darkness finally
descended on him and he drifted into unconsciousness he cried out,
'Mum, I wish I'd never volunteered.' The wretchedness of it all made
Alice want to cry. Her fourth patient was a young man from Singleton
in the Hunter Valley, 'a fine young fellow, far too young to have his life
blotted out so quickly', wrote Alice on 25 June.

Alice hated laying out the dead. They represented failure to her as
a nurse. Fortunately, Billy did the lion's share of the work and with
the help of other orderlies carried the corpses out of the wards. In
the ship's mortuary they were sewn into canvas shrouds and placed
in rows on the top deck, each one draped in the Union Jack.

After a burial service was over, the shrouded bodies were placed on the *Gascon's* hoist and winched down onto the deck of a mine sweeper. Naval ratings removed the flags so they could be used again and slid the shrouded corpses, now weighted with lead, down a wooden chute and into the sea.

In addition to wounded men, Alice was trying to cope with almost fifty patients with dysentery. They were running high temperatures and demanded water constantly, which was a problem on a ship where drinking water was precious. Dysentery seemed worse than on her first trip. And still the admissions poured in.

During daylight hours the whine of 100-pound shells was sometimes so loud Alice found it hard to hear what her patients were trying to tell her. On deck when she was bending over a typhoid sufferer, a shell landed beside her and Alice felt stinging pain as shrapnel grazed her leg, drawing blood. A nursing sister working on deck and a patient were killed by shrapnel from the shell.

In all, thirteen AANS nurses died during World War I, ten of them Alice's fellow Victorians.

Alice wondered how *could* they hope to conquer the Gallipoli peninsula when it seemed the Turks were able to obtain reinforcements, supplies and drinking water more easily than they were?

As soon as the *Gascon* was relieved by the next hospital ship on duty it began the journey back to Alexandria. The weather was fine and the sea not too rough, and this time the voyage took only three days. Nevertheless, thirty-eight more men died en route and were committed to the deep.

At Alexandria, the orderlies, assisted by stokers and crew, hoisted the stretcher cases ashore in the cradle. Alice and the other nurses soon had the walkers and sitters dressed in their newly fumigated and laundered uniforms. With their nurses' help the wounded men managed to walk off the boat with their heads held high.

After tidying their wards, the nurses went ashore. They hoped to get a decent night's sleep in a hotel, collect their pay and pick up letters from home. In the meantime, the *Gascon* was fumigated, restocked with provisions, medical supplies and coal, and her tanks filled with drinking water before returning to Lemnos for another rescue mission.

'Lemnos, Imbros and Chaos' (A popular saying among the Anzacs at Gallipoli)

The *Gascon* returned to the island of Lemnos on 27 June. The ship entered Mudros Harbour as the sun came up, flooding the sky with pale light. Alice recognised the softly rolling hills with their brown, fawn and lilac shadows, the lower slopes masked by the olive trees that turned silver as the wind stirred their leaves, just like the watercolour Colonel McPhee had given her. She hoped the colonel and all her other friends in the trenches were still alive.

Overcrowded, waterless Lemnos, only two hours away by sea from Gallipoli, was now designated as the place to send dysentery cases. Surgeon-General Birrell believed once the dysentery cases were removed from Gallipoli and its plague of flies they would get better rapidly and be able to return to the fray. What he failed to realise was that the flies were just as bad on Lemnos as they were on

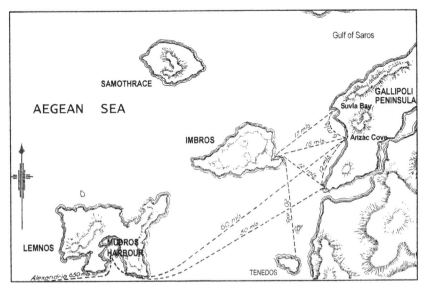

Gallipoli and surrounding islands (60 miles = 96 kilometres);
Gallipoli to Alexandria = 1000 kilometres.

Gallipoli, and Lemnos was also short of drinking water. As a result, many men got worse or died in agony.

There were now three tented hospitals at Lemnos, all overflowing with patients, so it was impossible to keep the dysentery patients in tents. The only option was to leave them out in the open air where they were tormented by malarial mosquitoes and plagues of blowflies.

By now the death rate from dysentery was so bad that Whitehall decided dysentery patients should be moved to Alexandria, where there was an adequate supply of drinking water.

The *Gascon* was ordered to take on as many of the dysentery sufferers as possible plus a hundred badly wounded men. Alice prayed they would survive the journey.

The nearer they came to Alexandria, the hotter and more humid it became in the belly of the ship. On Ward 2 forty men had already died. Alice found some consolation in Padre MacAuliffe's words: 'You are helping to ease the end of the dying,' but she knew that if the men had been treated better in the first place far fewer would have died.

After unloading at Alexandria Alice bade her patients goodbye with a cheery smile but a heavy heart, knowing some were so badly wounded it was unlikely they would see Australia again.

By now two of the original nurses from the *Gascon* had had enough. They had requested a transfer to work in military hospitals in Egypt. After attending a farewell lunch for their colleagues, Alice and Hilda threw a few overnight things into their kit bags. They were rowed ashore in the *Gascon's* tender and would have twenty-four hours' shore leave before returning to Gallipoli.

The Australian Army Nursing Service had booked the nursing sisters into a relatively modest hotel with poor facilities. The medical officers were provided with far more luxurious accommodation in the magnificent Hotel Beau Rivage.

On the quayside, Alice and Hilda hailed a horse-drawn *gharri* to take them to their hotel, eagerly looking forward to their first night off in eleven days. In the lobby the concierge apologised profusely that their rooms were not ready. Alice and Hilda were too tired to argue. They left their kit bags with the concierge and went shopping.

On leave they often found release in shopping in bazaars, sometimes bargaining fiercely for things they didn't even want. However, the shopping expedition was not a success for Hilda. Already stressed and tired she was upset at being hassled by touts and had difficulty making up her mind *what* to buy. In the end she was so annoyed by them she bought nothing at all.

Hot and thirsty after lengthy negotiations with the shopkeeper, Alice and Hilda adjourned to the Alexandria branch of Groppi's Tea Rooms, which acted as a home-away-from-home for Australian Army nurses. There they found a group of AANS sisters sitting at a round table reading the latest newspapers from London which were now several weeks old.

As usual the despatches from the Dardanelles reported the Allies' successes against the Turks who were expected to surrender very soon. It was obvious to Alice that the censor's blue pencil had removed all references to the large numbers of wounded, the soaring rate of deaths from dysentery, the awful diet, biscuits as hard as rocks, salt beef that made them thirsty, and the shortage of drinking water. With all this talk of surrender, victories and happy soldiers, Alice seemed to be reading about a totally different war from the one she was living through.

&& && &&

On 2 July 1915, the *Gascon* once again left Alexandria for Gallipoli to take over from the *Neuralia* as receiving hospital ship. The old system, under which hospital ships anchored off Anzac Cove and took on as many wounded each night until their wards were full had now been replaced by fixed timetables and regular sailings, with the aim of reducing the long hours medical staff had to work.

On the *Gascon*'s arrival Alice was glad to hear that the 4th Australian Field Ambulance had set up two more first-aid posts, including one in Hotchkiss Gully, so now there was a good chance the wounded could be treated more promptly and kept out of the burning sun.

Despite the new system, Alice found she was working just as hard:

> . . . another poor 'abdominal' begged me not to leave him
> as he was dying. The nursing staff is not adequate for the
> heavy demands on it, especially at night when the
> wounded come in two or three batches. Shells whistled
> and shrieked over or beside us and made huge splashes as
> they fell alongside.

The following day, 11 July 1915, after a number of narrow misses from the enemy guns, the *Gascon* sailed back to Alexandria with a full load of patients.

Without time for an overnight break they were ordered to load more medical supplies and water and return immediately to Anzac Cove where they would receive another cargo of wounded men. So much for regular timetables and shore leave, grumbled the nurses.

This time there were fewer men wounded but the number and severity of dysentery and typhoid cases had soared. Clearly this was an epidemic, probably due to the open latrine pits, Major Ilias reckoned. Most of the poor 'enterics' were so weak they arrived on stretchers and had to be hoisted aboard the *Gascon* on the cradle.

At Anzac Cove Hilda and Alice worked from eight in the morning to one o'clock at night. Thirty more stretcher cases arrived needing their details recorded, dressings changed and some amputations. Since the cots were full, even badly wounded men and dysentery cases had to lie on deck. Alice had three deaths that day, and a fourth critically ill patient on her ward. All day she flew up and down steps between these poor men, but in spite of all her dedication could not prevent their deaths. She felt powerless, never having imagined conditions on board a hospital ship could be so terrible. She also had responsibility for another two dozen wounded men. The stress and rushing about all over the ship were wearing her out. How long before she too had to resign or become ill herself?

By now all the hospitals in Alexandria were full and the War Office was desperate. On the return trip from Lemnos, the captain of the *Gascon* received orders that the ship should proceed to Malta, another British colony.

And so on 18 July, the *Gascon* anchored in Valletta's grand harbour. Then it was back to Gallipoli for another load. A major attack on the Turks was about to begin.

THE HERO OF LONE PINE

The August attacks on Lone Pine and the Nek by the Anzacs were intended to divert the attentions of the Turks while the main attack took place several kilometres north of Anzac Cove at Suvla Bay. To achieve this, fresh troops were to be landed at Suvla Bay and the attack would involve British, Irish and Gurkha soldiers.

The Anzacs held the Turkish trenches for three days, surrounded by the reeking corpses and severed limbs of their comrades. Handsome Captain Frederick Tubb of the 7th Battalion killed twenty Turks who advanced into the trench he and his men had captured. Fighting the Turks off with his bayonet, Captain Tubb saved the lives of two of his comrades, but a third friend died in front of his eyes.

'Tub', as he was affectionately known in his battalion, survived Lone Pine but spent twenty-four hours half-dead from his wounds and thirst out in the sun. Finally, the stretcher bearers found him and carried him down to the tiny casualty clearing station. There was insufficient space inside so Tubb spent more agonising hours on the beach, tormented by blowflies, waiting to be loaded onto a barge and taken out to the *Gascon*.

Alice had been cooped up in the heat of the ward and emerged on deck to see the first of the wounded swung aboard. An orderly indicated she should look at an officer who had been 'red-carded' for priority treatment with a label noting 'Recommended for Victoria Cross. Provide special care.'

AUSTRALIAN WAR MEMORIAL NEG. H06786.

Captain F.H. Tubb., V.C.

The wards were nearly full with wounded men. Alice made sure that Captain Tubb was taken down below *immediately*. From his records Alice saw he was a fellow Victorian from the town of Euroa, in his late thirties. As she had done with Gooch, Alice became attached to Frederick Tubb. She was determined he would not die like Gooch but survive to receive his Victoria Cross. She felt honoured to have the responsibility of looking after such a brave man.

Other wounded men who could still hobble around came to see the hero of the hour. They whispered to Alice what a good fellow he was and how he deserved recognition. The Victoria Cross was the highest award for bravery presented in battle — Captain Tubb, who was promoted to major for his heroism, would be the first recipient of the award Alice had nursed.

On 7 August, a day of unbearable heat, the 11th Battalion had landed at Suvla Bay under heavy fire. The *Gascon* was ordered to steam north, and load more casualties there, even though space was at a premium and men were jammed like sardines on the decks and in the companionways.

Alice thought Suvla Bay resembled Anzac Cove, with the same background of steep-sided hills and ravines but with a huge salt pan behind them.

The *Gascon* anchored beside a fleet of destroyers, mine sweepers, hospital ships, and transport ships which had brought horses and mules and heavy equipment there.

Alice's journal for 11 August shows that the *Gascon* received fifty to sixty Ghurkhas and Irish troops, many suffering from third-degree burns. She was told that some of the wounded men had crawled for safety under gorse bushes to find shade from the burning sun. But when the tinder-dry scrub had been set on fire by Turkish shells, many of the wounded men had been badly burned.

The Ghurkhas had been ordered to cross Suvla's salt lake, a huge sparkling white salt pan against which their khaki uniforms and pith helmets stood out clearly. The Turks had been able to pick them off one by one from the top of a hill. Some survivors had lain out in the open for twenty-four hours dying of thirst or their burns. Others had managed to crawl back to Suvla on hands and knees or had been brought back by stretcher bearers who braved enemy fire. The wounded Ghurkhas were stoic but in spite of all Alice's care several died from burns and were buried at sea.[18]

On 11 August she worked from 7 am to 11 pm. 'Truly this is a dreadful war . . . more like wholesale murder,' she wrote at the end of that terrible day.

Alice had planned to let Sister Pratt take over the running of the ward and spend as much time as possible with Major Tubb, who still needed special nursing. But the arrival of so many bad burns cases from Suvla Bay prevented her spending as much time with the hero of Lone Pine as she had hoped. 'We heard the authorities were preparing for 22,000 casualties so are not surprised there are thousands already. So many septic wounds,' Alice wrote sadly when she reached her cabin after midnight.

After another nightmare five-day voyage to Malta, the *Gascon* delivered Major Tubb and Alice's other patients to Valletta's crumbling and ancient military hospital.

Major Tubb recovered and was later shipped to Britain to convalesce at Lennel House near Coldstream. Alice never forgot him, her first patient honoured by the Empire's highest award for valour.

By October and early November 1915, military hospitals in Egypt were so overcrowded that the *Gascon* was ordered to make the long trip via Gibraltar to England. However, Alice was no longer in London on 16 December, when Major Tubb went to Buckingham Palace to receive the Victoria Cross. One by one the seven heroes of Lone Pine went forward to receive their awards. Afterwards, standing in front of the iron railings in front of Buckingham Palace, Major Frederick Tubb, Lieutenant William Symons, Captain Hugo Throssell and Private John Hamilton posed together for a historic photograph of four Australian holders of the Victoria Cross.

After only a brief stay in London the *Gascon* returned to the Mediterranean and through the Aegean to Anzac Cove. By now winter was almost upon them and Gallipoli had turned freezing cold. Many Anzacs were suffering from severe frostbite — lack of warm clothing meant that the poor men were still obliged to wear light-weight summer clothes, although it was snowing.

On 4 December 1915 the *Gascon* took on board dozens of Anzacs with badly frostbitten toes who had been lying in the snow for days. Another contingent of frostbitten patients arrived the next morning. Their feet were turning gangrenous and some toes needed amputating. Six soldiers had frozen to death — one had been buried under snow over a metre deep.

WITHDRAWAL FROM GALLIPOLI

Towards the end of 1915, with the Gallipoli Campaign conceded a failure, Churchill resigned and finally it was agreed to pull out. Ironically, it turned out that the evacuation was one of the few successful operations of the whole Gallipoli campaign.

To mislead the Turks, automatic firing devices kept the Anzacs' rifles firing spasmodically. Covered by darkness the men quietly slipped away with their equipment, their boots muffled by sacking. They managed to pull out without the loss of a single life. 'Every inch of the Gallipoli peninsula was dyed red with Anzac blood,' Alice wrote when she heard that the Anzacs had left the peninsula.

By 22 December Alice was once more nursing at Heliopolis. On Christmas Day 1915, Alice and Hilda were invited by Graham Coulter, the new colonel of the 8th Battalion, to eat a special Christmas meal with some of the 'original' Anzac officers. Alice described in her journal entry for that day how they were greeted warmly with presents and glasses of champagne. They sat down to eat and raised their glasses in a 'Loyal Toast' to the King and a 'Silent Toast' to those who had died at Anzac Cove. They drank a third toast to success in France where the 8th Battalion would soon be going.

By February 1916 most of the patients had returned to Australia, so the long line of beds in the ballroom at Heliopolis stood empty. Free of responsibilities at last, Alice decided to realise one of her dreams. She booked herself onto a cruise steamer which took her up the Nile to Luxor and Memphis.

On her return to Heliopolis Army Hospital Alice heard rumours that the nurses and administrators of her unit were off to Rouen in northern France under the command of Colonel de Crespigny. She tidied up her ward for her replacement, supervised the packing of the medical equipment into shipping crates and packed her suitcase and kitbag. She bought a French phrasebook she intended to study on the ship bound for France, a country she had always wanted to visit but under different circumstances.

ALICE IN FRANCE

In April 1916, Alice, Hilda and the other Australian nurses disembarked from their rusty transport ship at the southern French port of Marseilles. Their journey north was scheduled to take sixteen hours: instead, it took four days and nights. The carriages were so crowded the AANS nurses had to sleep sitting upright. There was no restaurant car, lavatory or washing facilities. They sprinkled themselves with eau de cologne, the only way to keep fresh. It was a hellish journey, broken at stations where they could use the toilet and buy French bread and cheese and beakers of ersatz coffee to warm themselves.

From the train windows Alice admired the soft green fields, so different from Australia. As the train advanced northwards most villages they passed through seemed to be in ruins. British soldiers, mules, gun carriages and horses lined the roads. It rained unceasingly and ambulances, lorries and guns were bogged in mud that reached up to their axles.

Hilda and Alice had been selected to work in a British military hospital, nursing troops from Britain and Commonwealth countries, in the port of Boulogne, from where the ferries left for Britain. Tired and stiff from their journey they arrived at 7 pm, 'Our *sixteenth* day of travelling since we left Egypt,' wrote Alice in her journal.

The European spring was very late in arriving. Though it was now mid April it was still very cold. Being wartime, heating fuel was in short supply. Alice wrote that she and Hilda were glad of those thick grey winter uniforms they had hated so much in tropical Egypt.

Although the nurses slept in unheated rooms, Alice was grateful that at least the wards were heated. In her journal she wrote:

> The wind [is] so wild it tore the doors out of your grasp
> and the breath from your body and the air is icy. Each
> ward has a nice coal stove.

The Australian Imperial Force (or what was left of it) was now renamed No 1 Anzac Corps. German trenches stretched across France to Switzerland, and for many months there had been a virtual deadlock across the entire Western front. Lord Kitchener was determined to break the stalemate, no matter how many men died in the attempt.

On 8 June 1916, Alice realised that a year ago she had boarded the *Gascon* full of hope that the war would soon be over. And now after a year of deadlock in France the slaughter of young men on a grand scale was happening again. Thinking about her time aboard the *Gascon* Alice wrote in her diary:

> Sad memories mingle with happy ones of superb sunsets and
> sunrises at Anzac Cove and Lemnos, over the Grecian Isles
> and the lovely Mediterranean . . . One can almost forget the
> days full of heat, hard work and misery . . . after Gallipoli
> was evacuated it seems the heartbreak was for nothing.

In June the nurses were shocked to hear that Lord Kitchener had been lost at sea on the ship HMS *Hampshire*. Meanwhile Scottish-born General Sir Douglas Haig had been appointed commander in chief of the British Expeditionary Force. He would be responsible for more deaths than Lord Kitchener.

On 2 July 1916, Alice and Hilda received orders to take the train to Rouen Australian Auxiliary Hospital. The hospital, which had been set up on the site of a former racecourse, was overcrowded with wounded men and badly needed more nurses.

Alice and Hilda had less than an hour to pack their bags, say their goodbyes and board the train for Rouen. The journey was exhausting. There were no seats so they sat on their suitcases in the corridor amid stale tobacco fumes. Tired and grimy, they arrived at Rouen station at three in the morning of 3 July to be met by an ambulance driven by a young woman in the uniform of a volunteer driver. Alice recorded the converstaion in her journal the following day.

'Welcome to Ruin,' the VAD said crisply.

'Ruin?' Alice queried.

'That's what the lads call it, due to its awful death rate!' the VAD replied cheerfully.

At the newly established field hospital with its tents and tin roofed Nissen huts they were pleased to meet up with former colleagues from Cairo. Less pleasant were their immediate sleeping quarters, which consisted of a dank storage shed with a concrete floor. During the night there were ominous rustlings and skitterings and in the cold light of dawn they discovered a dead rat in one corner. The other rats had fled, doubtless to return the following night.

The tents had been rented for a high price from the British and leaked like sieves, and the Australians had to make do with substandard supplies. On 10 July, Alice made her feelings clear in her diary:

> . . . that rubbishy medical equipment should have been burned long before it left Egypt. One feels ashamed to be part of such a muddle . . . No water laid on, either hot or cold, so all drinking and washing water has to be carried some distance.

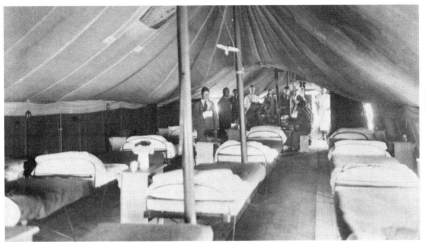

Interior of a tented ward.

The eight nurses and ten inexperienced VADs looked pale and pasty-faced from poor food, overwork and exhaustion. By now Alice was too tired to write a separate entry for each day, as they were working under immense pressure on long shifts, six days a week. In her usual forthright style in the second week of July, in the heat of the European summer, she described their situation:

> Meals are disgusting and good food is spoilt. Potatoes are
> served out of a billy, likewise pudding. There are no
> hospital trays for the sick and no way of keeping food hot
> in the meantime. The nurses resent that the medical officers
> have a total of twenty-two batmen between them while
> the sisters have to do everything but stretcher bearing.

On Alice's ward one severely shell-shocked patient was hallucinating that a German officer was standing over him with a gun. He begged over and over again not to be shot. Other severe shell-shock cases moaned and hid under their beds, as they heard in their imaginations the crash of falling shells and saw their comrades blown apart.

The summer of 1916 was the wettest for decades. By now the roads around Rouen were ankle-deep in dark sticky mud and the nurses' skirts and shoes were covered with it. The ground outside the tents was a morass of mud; the wounded arrived with mud on their uniforms and on their bandages. No matter how hard the nurses worked, it was impossible to keep anything clean for long and drying clothes and bed linen was a problem. Early in July Alice wrote:

> How long can we last in this unhealthy spot? We are
> worn out. The nurses have to drag heavy men off their
> stretchers, undress them, live and sleep in damp
> surroundings without even the comfort of a warm bath
> after the working day is over.

Several nurses were killed by German bombs. In another undated entry in July Alice instructed Hilda that should she be killed, Hilda was to give her diary to a Melbourne newspaper to be published, in the vain hope that if they printed her descriptions of life at Rouen, the working conditions might improve for nurses and VADs.

Bombing on this British hospital resulted in the deaths of nurses and patients.

As usual, the British Army administrators at Whitehall had not cooperated with Australian administrators. As a result the Rouen hospital was constantly running low on medical supplies, food and even on cutlery and crockery, and nothing was done to make life more comfortable for the nurses. For the first few months, the nurses had to drink their morning tea out of jam jars and eat with their fingers as they had no knives and forks. They were issued with tin hats and knee-length rubber boots. They were given cumbersome gas masks, fitted with glass eye pieces, which came in boxes with shoulder straps. The nurses put these on whenever they heard the air raid warning. Alice was terrified of bombs but was determined the patients would not know she was afraid. She found the best way of dealing with fright was to ignore it and concentrate on soothing the patients' fears.

On 15 July 1916 Alice heard the whine of a shell followed by a *crump* and a scream. She grabbed a tin hat and went outside. In the light of her torch she saw that an Indian orderly had been blown off the duckboards and lay dead face-down in the mud, one of his legs lodged in the fork of a tree. Alice felt sick but forced herself to continue working on the ward for the rest of the night. The following morning a fatigue party arrived and removed the corpse and its lonely leg.

The next staff fatality was Sister Jacobsen, who had been suffering from tuberculosis. Alice attended her funeral. On 20 July she wrote in her journal:

> In a few months' time there will be few of the original staff left. Sister Jacobsen has been ill since we came but no notice was taken of her cough until now. Convoys in and out with a stream of sick and wounded men. The great offensive seems to be failing and another winter of cold and misery seems to be before us.

Each night after dinner they listened to the distant boom of guns and were told this was part of another 'Big Push'. The generals would proclaim there was no chance any Germans could survive this particular barrage but somehow they always did. General Haig promised that the war would soon be over.

When Alice had arrived in Rouen the fields and hawthorn hedges around the old racecourse had been green and leafy with the white flowers of hawthorn everywhere. When autumn arrived there was hardly a leaf left due to shelling and bombing. Birds no longer sang, the days were shorter and patches of frost whitened the grass each morning. Summer was almost over.

On 26 September 1916, the next big battle involving Australian troops took place at Polygon Wood, near Ypres. One casualty was Major Tubb, who had returned from Australia at his own request. Hit in the chest he was carried on a stretcher to the ambulance train. In one of the tragedies of war, Major Tubb, VC, was hit by 'friendly fire' while the stretcher bearers were crossing open ground and died without recovering consciousness.

A week later Alice wrote in her journal: 'The only man I could have loved and married has died.'[19] It made her wonder what sort of a country Australia would become if the bravest men died in battle, while cowards and shirkers stayed home in safety. She also wrote about the morality of persuading so many immature boys that it was glorious to enlist and die for king and country before having experienced much of life.

Northern France where Alice Kitchen nursed.

By November most of the nurses were coughing and sneezing and had chilblained hands and red noses. Casualties were pouring in, including soldiers with severe cases of rheumatism contracted in the damp trenches. 'Some of us sisters are working five or six days on twelve hour shifts without a break,' she commented on All Saints' Day, the first day of November, as the weather turned even colder and the wind howled around them. She continued:

> . . . paddling about in rain and wind with a mackintosh and an umbrella is most uncomfortable and scarcely satisfactory. Leaky tents make the work harder than it need be. Motor ambulances have bogged down, some of the wounded are half drowned in mud in flooded shell holes and trenches.

In her unheated hut Alice slept badly. She had nightmares in which she saw young soldiers with terrible wounds crying out to her for help, and wounded boys begged her to hold their hands.

The bitterest winter of the war had arrived. On 13 November, Alice wrote, 'The whole place is covered in a mantle of snow, dry as sugar and bitterly cold.' Snow etched the bare branches of those trees that were still standing and lay thick on the ground. By now the British, Australian and Canadian tented hospitals were filled to bursting with casualties. Finally they had some kerosene heaters, but their effect inside the draughty tents was minimal. The nurses slept in wooden huts without heaters but by now had a few cane chairs and a table. They wore woollen gaiters, mittens, muffs and knitted jackets to try to beat the cold. Nevertheless, several of them suffered frostbite and had to be admitted to the sick bay. Many of their patients were also suffering from frostbite.

Alice piled all her clothes onto her bed in a desperate effort to keep warm. The icy conditions and long hours had weakened her health and brought on rheumatism and a persistent cough. The wan pale face that looked back at Alice from the mirror was nothing like the tanned healthy woman she used to be.

One night the mess hut was hit by a bomb, which destroyed every stick of furniture including the piano. Fortunately no nurses were in the hut at the time.

So-called 'trench fever' killed many patients; other fevers such as typhoid were carried by lice. Patients with trench foot gave the nurses a great deal of work. This condition was caused by standing ankle-deep in water for days on end, while damp puttees, which the men were ordered to wrap round their trouser legs, restricted the blood supply. As a result, the soldiers' feet turned soft and puffy, causing them to hobble around painfully. After several days the feet turned black and blistered and oozed with pus. Socks became stuck fast to the wound and the smell was fearsome. Nurses and orderlies alike dreaded the job of removing the boots from these patients. The only treatment was to rub the blackened and gangrenous feet morning and night with whale oil, keep them warm in heavy socks, and try to get the bedridden men to rotate their ankles and feet as much as possible and bring back the circulation.

During the first big attack in the Somme surgeons were so overworked that the nurses had to amputate blackened, gangrenous toes themselves with or without anaesthetic. The nurses received a brief course in administering anaesthetics as the hospital was short of anaesthetists, although they were not paid extra for this. Alice observed wryly that Australian Army nurses were seen as 'general dogs-bodies, called upon to do just about everything except stretcher bearing'.

Dozens of shell-shocked men continued to be admitted to the hospital. To add to the nurses' workload a severe outbreak of meningitis occurred. Known in Army medical circles during World War I as 'cerebro-spinal fever', this lethal disease, which seemed to thrive in Army camps, transport ships and ambulance trains, caused a swelling of the brain followed by a rapid death.

In December 1916, Alice's persistent cough grew much worse. She recorded that she 'coughed like a sick cow before falling asleep'. She gargled with salt water and prayed her sore throat would clear up of its own accord. A week later, however, she was still coughing badly and feared it might be due to anaemia or bronchitis. She confided her fears to the matron on duty but received only a barbed comment that she was no longer young so must expect to tire easily. Alice had already noted bitterly that 'Nursing sisters may give gentleness and attention to wounded men but should not expect too much attention if they fall sick themselves'.

Despite her ill health, Sister Kitchen carried on until she collapsed while accompanying a doctor on a ward round. She was then admitted to a special ward for nurses.

> They can't say I'm faking being ill or 'swinging the lead' as they put me off duty themselves and I [have] no voice but only a cough and a squeak. Snow drifting softly down. Matron R (British) expected to do an inspection so I kept my bed tidy, being told she did not like Australians. Matron R's dislike is based on our independent spirit and the fact that Australians are supposed to take no notice of rules! . . . My voice not much better and I shudder at the thought of pneumonia or lung disease [by which she probably meant cancer].

During the first week of December, Alice's inflamed throat grew worse and she was diagnosed with what she described as 'purulent bronchitis'. However, her sense of humour did not desert her and on 17 December she wrote:

> The loss of a voice is a worry especially to a woman used to
> airing her opinions. Marked for evacuation to Blighty. Feel
> as if I were deserting Sister Samsing in all her worries but
> have no choice in the matter. Sister Rogers and Sister Curtis
> came in today as patients, both with broncho-pneumonia.

Once Alice made it to 'the sick list' she was given every care
and attention. After enduring weeks of misery, kindness and
consideration were as good as a tonic. Alice's throat was examined
by a consultant physician, who insisted she be sent to London by
the next available vessel, which was the *Aberdonian,* a black-hulled
transport ship. Feeling sad and guilty that she was 'letting her fellow
nurses down', Alice said tearful goodbyes to her colleagues.

Unlike hospital ships, Alice knew that transport ships were not
allowed to fly the Red Cross flag, so they were vulnerable to enemy
torpedoes. By now she was feeling too ill to care if she lived or died.
She nevertheless arrived safely in England, and was taken to
Southwell Gardens in South Kensington, a special clinic for Army
nurses. Having cared for others for so long Alice was very appreciative
of the care shown to her.

> I have a room to myself with a radiator, nice furnishings,
> good food and much kindness. I shall always be grateful
> to these people for their kindness. Don't know what the
> next move is — perhaps more laryngoscopes and mirrors
> etc though am constantly assured it is not chronic.

A week later, Hilda, who had also become seriously ill, joined
Alice at Southwell Gardens. Alice spent Christmas 1916 in the
clinic and was told she should not return to the cold and damp of
France. Instead, she was posted to more comfortable surroundings
at Harefield Park in the heart of rural Hertfordshire.

A FAREWELL TO ARMS

Alice spent the next two years nursing crippled and paraplegic
soldiers at Harefield Park Hospital, a square neo-Georgian

mansion which had been loaned to the Australian government for the duration of the war by the Billyard-Leake family of Western Australia. The general hospital was housed in a Nissen hut; three operating theatres and an X-ray department were also in prefabricated buildings.[20] The grounds included a lake, tennis courts, croquet lawn and bluebell woods, where Alice used to pick armfuls of flowers for the wards.

Alice was assigned a ward of thirty-two men who had only fourteen legs between them. The men had left Australia young and fit and were terrified of going home to be objects of pity. Caring for them was hard work and demanded great tact.

Whenever the weather was warm enough Alice would wheel her patients outside onto the terrace in front of ivy-covered Harefield House. Here the blind and the crippled and maimed sat in rows in the pale English sun, one of the saddest sights Alice had ever seen. What would be their future? Who would care for these unfortunate war victims? Some would go home to their wife or mother, others would be forced to live in institutions.

Alice often described writing letters for men who had no arms. She always dreaded being asked to read the replies to these letters as sometimes they revealed that the patient's wife or girlfriend had found someone else.

On 25 April 1917, which had just been gazetted as Anzac Day by the Australian government, they observed two minutes' silence on the wards at Harefield to remember the dead.

Even at rural Harefield Park Alice was not safe from air-raids. In June a bomb landed on the roof and flames roared through the upper storey of the mansion. Nurses and orderlies risked their lives to get the patients to safety. As Alice checked the rows of patients massed on the front drive, she realised that two of them were missing. She and Sister Pearl Corkhill tied wet handkerchiefs around their faces and climbed the servants' staircase through clouds of smoke. They located the missing men in a burning ward and dragged them down the stairs before the upper storey caved in.[21]

Publicity about the fire brought King George and Queen Mary to Harefield to inspect the damage for themselves. Sir Francis

Newdegate, a former governor of Tasmania, also visited Harefield. He was so upset by the sight of the crippled and paraplegic soldiers that he purchased a large burial plot beside Harefield Parish Church in which Australians who died at Harefield could be buried with no cost to their families.

By now Hilda had been posted to an Army hospital for limbless soldiers at Southall. They managed to meet up occasionally on their free days.

Alice and Hilda took leave together in February 1918 and visited Dublin and the west coast of Ireland, which Alice greatly enjoyed, in spite of the cold weather. During her three-week stay in Ireland, she wrote in her journal:

> The Irish don't like the Huns but hate the British even
> more although they seem to like Australians. Our landlady
> told me that the Irish and Australians had been colonised
> by the English so we had much in common. So many
> people here would like to come to Australia.

By then over a million and a half soldiers had been killed. The AIF had lost over 59,000[22] men, a relatively large number for a nation with a population of only four million. The average life expectancy of a young officer in the trenches of northern France was a matter of weeks. More men were constantly needed as replacements. In Britain even the elderly and arthritic maintenance men and gardeners at Harefield Park were being called up.

On 28 May, just as the spring flowers were coming out in the gardens at Harefield, Alice received her first patient suffering from Spanish flu, a highly contagious disease. The nurses were issued with surgical masks but were not immune. Wearing a black armband over her uniform, Alice attended various funerals including those of two nurses. This lethal disease reached epidemic proportions and would eventually kill more people worldwide than were killed during the entire war.

Alice continued working long hours, now nursing flu victims, eventually catching the disease herself. She was nursed at Harefield Park and was lucky enough to recover quickly, although other nurses died. She was now in her mid-forties and whenever she looked in the mirror she saw that her dark hair was streaked with grey and her handsome face had become lined. Age had caught up with her.

There were rumours that the enemy was short of food. Civil unrest in Germany meant Kaiser Wilhelm was planning to abdicate, so possibly the war might end soon.

Alice started to worry about her future. Due to the low rates of pay for nurses she had been unable to save any money. New regulations stated that Army nurses returning to Australia would be laid off if they were over the age of forty. Alice wrote in her journal, 'It seems a polite way of asking us nurses to go home and be scrapped.'

In October Alice was saddened to learn that Hilda would be sent back to Australia as escort for twenty soldiers who had been blinded by gas. They said goodbye at a final meeting and realised that in Australia the long distance between Adelaide and Melbourne would separate them. Alice would miss her outings and holidays with Hilda, her closest friend, but intended to continue working in England as long as possible. Several of her crippled patients were 'sweet' on her but she knew that eventually she would have to go back to Melbourne to care for her mother. She did not say so but it would appear from the tone of her journal entries that she had no intention of caring for a crippled mother *and* a crippled spouse.

At 11 am on 11 November 1918, the Germans' request for an armistice was granted and the fighting ended. Sirens blew, bands played, but Alice kept on working. That night she wrote:

> I don't trust the Germans . . . they are probably preparing
> for *another* Great War. We are still too near the sorrows
> and heartbreaks to feel like rejoicing. One sees as many
> sad faces as merry ones. The general feeling is relief rather
> than joy that it is finally over.

Senior nurses were told that the Army would pay them to do a course of their choice, which might help them find jobs in Australia. Alice took a course at the Institute of Public Health.

On Saturday 28 June 1919, six months after the armistice began, a victory parade took place in London. Huge gaps in the marching men revealed just how many had been killed. Some battalions had only a few dozen survivors. Back at Harefield, most of the crippled and wounded men had been sent home and Harefield Park estate was about to be handed back to its owners.

Before returning to Melbourne Alice decided to visit Australian war graves in France and Belgium. Her plan was to photograph the graves of the men she had nursed and send photos to their mothers. At various cemeteries Alice was horrified to see piles of bones and skulls lying around awaiting identification. In marked contrast to the well-tended French graves with their marble angels and crucifixes, most Australian graves were still raw mounds of earth with here and there a wooden cross, some unmarked, others with a name scrawled on in pencil.

She visited the cemetery at Lijessenthoek in Belgium where Major Tubb was buried. Scarlet poppies resembled clots of blood among waist-high corn. Fertilised by human blood and bone, the poppies grew large and in abundance — the harvest of war. She was shocked to find that many of the dead did not have their names painted on the wooden cross that marked their graves — instead the names were scrawled on pieces of paper pinned to the end of each row.

The Australian War Graves Commission had as yet not identified all the graves.

Between the pages of her journal Alice pressed a newspaper clipping containing a poem dated 1918 by John McCrae, who had fought in Belgium.

> *In Flanders fields the poppies blow*
> *Between the crosses, row on row*
> *. . . We are the dead. Short days ago*
> *We lived, felt dawn, saw sunset glow*
> *Loved, and were loved, and now we lie*
> *In Flanders fields.*

It was the best epitaph she could find for Major Frederick Tubb, VC, for Rupert Barratt, golden boy of 8th Battalion, and for poor Gooch and Ross, the soldier boys.

On her trip to Australia Alice served as an escort to twenty crippled war veterans aboard the troopship *Kanowna*. The homeward voyage was a sad one and very different from the outward voyage on the *Benalla*. 'So many legs and arms gone, so much optimism and boisterousness evaporated,' Alice wrote late in July 1919.

æ æ æ

There were as yet no Australian medals. Alice Kitchen was awarded British Campaign and Service Medals and a Victory Medal.[23] She was formally discharged from the AANS on 28 August 1919 with severance pay and a small annual pension.

Alice, heroine of the hospital ship *Gascon*, faded into obscurity. According to information provided by a reader, Alice Kitchen's last years were spent running a boarding house on the Victorian coast. She died aged seventy-seven in the Melbourne suburb of Carlton.[24]

I realized that only one thing counted . . . and that is kindness.

JOICE LOCH, FROM *A FRINGE OF BLUE,* LONDON, 1968

CHAPTER 10

Joice NanKivell Loch

1887 – 1982

Polish Gold Cross of Merit
Serb Order of St Sava
Greek Order of the Phoenix
Greek Order of the Redeemer (2)
Greek Gold Medal, National
    Academy of the Arts
Rumanian Order of Elizabeth
Member of the Order of the
    British Empire
Polish Gold Cross of Virtue
Greek Order of Beneficence (2)

Joice Loch's courage took her close to death in several theatres of war and her life was one of astonishing heroism. In this chapter, which relies on extracts from my biography of Joice, *Blue Ribbons, Bitter Bread*, I am concentrating on her exploits during World War II.[1]

Joice NanKivell Loch was born in the middle of a cyclone — a suitable entry into the world for a third-generation Australian who would face danger and be involved in rescuing the victims of war and ethnic cleansing in World War II.

In the booming 1880s, Joice's paternal grandfather, Thomas NanKivell, was one of Australia's richest men. His company, Fanning & NanKivell, owned a fleet of ships and leased four huge cane plantations near Ingham in North Queensland. One of them was managed by Joice's father, George NanKivell. Joice's first years were spent on a large plantation surrounded by Pacific Islanders as house servants and a Kanaka nanny. This pleasant life came to an end once the Queensland Government acted to prohibit the importation of Kanakas. Since it was impossible to cut the cane without imported labour, the plantation faltered and Joice, her brother and her parents were forced to leave their home with almost nothing but a few clothes and some books.

The swift descent from riches to rags led to the NanKivells moving to a dirt-floored hut without running water on a run-down property in the wilds of Victoria's Gippsland. With no money to send Joice away to school, she was taught by her mother. Joice loved books and writing and longed to become doctor. But there was no money for a girl to attend university. Instead Joice worked as an unpaid labourer, cook and general rouseabout on her father's struggling farm.

When war was declared in 1914, Joice's beloved younger brother, Geoff, enlisted. Serving with distinction at Gallipoli, he was later killed in the trenches of Northern France, and to deal with her grief Joice wrote a book about their childhood, *The Solitary Pedestrian*, published in 1918.

In the later years of the war, Joice moved to Melbourne, became a book reviewer and journalist, and worked as a secretary for a professor of classics. She also developed a longing to visit Greece.

After reviewing a book about Gallipoli[2] Joice met and eventually married its author, Sydney Loch, a young Gallipoli veteran, but even when married Joice continued to write under her own name of NanKivell. Once the war ended, the Lochs went to London. They were commissioned by the prestigious publishers, John Murray, to write a book on the Irish war of independence (the Troubles).

The Lochs' book, *Ireland in Travail*, published in 1922, displeased the IRA and the Lochs were warned by a member of the British Secret Service to get as far away from London as possible.[3]

Hearing of Quaker-run refugee camps in war-torn eastern Poland, the Lochs volunteered to work there. Eastern Poland had been left devastated after World War I, with villages burned, farmland destroyed, and people slaughtered or transported to Russia. The population began to return but malnutrition and disease were rife.

The Lochs remained in Poland until 1923, when they heard from Quaker headquarters about the 1.5 million Greek Orthodox refugees fleeing persecution in Turkey and other areas in Asia Minor, and who were now pouring into Thessaloniki where a large refugee camp had sprung up on the grounds of the American Farm School. Joice worked in the camp tending the sick. She was later joined by Sydney, who taught refugee children at the American Farm School. Gradually the refugees were resettled in villages, including Pirgos (now Ouranoupolis) to which the Lochs eventually moved. There they established a home and became involved in helping the villagers both medically and economically.

Before fleeing Turkey the refugee inhabitants of the village had been rug weavers. From her royalties as a writer (the Lochs were still writing for British papers and John Murray), Joice paid the village carpenter to build looms and started a women's rug-weaving cooperative.

The rug-weaving cooperative was successful and by September 1939 Pirgos was thriving. The Lochs were celebrating at a Greek wedding when the BBC Foreign Service announced that Hitler had invaded Poland.

The Lochs contacted Quaker headquarters at Friends House in London and, since they still spoke some Polish and had no idea Hitler would later invade Greece, volunteered their services to help Polish refugees.

The Quaker War Relief Service appointed Sydney head of an aid centre for Polish refugees who had fled to Bucharest, the capital of neutral Rumania. The Lochs took the overnight train to Bucharest, a city of huge contradictions — lush restaurants and cafés, elegant boutiques and fashionable women alongside starving refugees and gypsies begging in the streets.

Joice was by now in her early fifties. She found herself with the huge responsibility of feeding and clothing hundreds of refugees. Most were Polish women and children, but there were also some Jewish orphans. Male Polish refugees were being interned by Rumania's King Carol II, who was juggling allegiances to his British and German royal relatives.

Joice was overworked and badly needed an assistant — preferably someone middle-aged and sensible. Father Ambrosius, priest to the internment camp where the Polish men were held, recommended Countess Lushya, sole survivor of one of Poland's aristocratic families. The countess was young and beautiful. She had lost her home, her family and her money. Nevertheless she was, it seemed, good at figures and book-keeping. To Joice, who hated having to keep the accounts of the Polish Refugee Mission, this was a definite point in Lushya's favour.[4]

After interviewing the young countess it was apparent she was not just a pretty face. Lushya (pronounced Loo-shah) showed Joice a list she had compiled of wealthy Rumanians prepared to allow Polish families to 'house-sit' their holiday villas on the Black Sea free of charge until the next summer.

The winter of 1940 was a particularly cold one and a disastrous year for Rumania. The Rumanian capital of Bucharest lay under a deep blanket of snow that muffled the clip-clop of horses pulling the *trasuras* (hansom cabs) along the streets. The children of the rich kept warm in fur coats and snow boots, while beggars and refugees shivered.

A sub-zero wind from the Carpathian Mountains whistled through the thin walls of the Quaker Refugee Mission. Joice would sit at her desk wearing a fur hat, woollen mittens, her old fur coat over her Quaker uniform, and a huge pair of fur-lined pilot's boots over two pairs of Sydney's thickest socks. Sydney worked in a Harris tweed coat and a grey knitted balaclava helmet of the type the Mission had given out to the thousands of interned Polish men.

Lushya had turned out to be a brilliant fundraiser. She set up a Save the Polish Refugees Committee made up of Rumanian princesses and countesses, and which encouraged the wives of bankers, industrialists and oil tycoons to join and raise money for the Polish women refugees and their children.

The committee met once a month at the Café Mavrodaphne. All the proceeds of their fundraising luncheons were used to support their Polish charges. Joice also paid for the school fees of Jewish orphans under her care.

As funds accumulated, so the Lochs were able to move many of the Polish women to better accommodation and organise classes in typing, hairdressing and other skills to help them obtain jobs to feed their children.

The Lochs' resourcefulness in organising these courses was drawn to the attention of King Carol. Although he had interned the Polish men for political reasons, and after several assassinations of ministers by the Iron Guard ruled as a virtual dictator, the King was a reasonable man in an unenviable position. As well as having divided loyalties between Britain and Germany, he was also romantically linked with a Jew, Magda Lupescu. Wanting to help refugees but nevertheless afraid of what would happen should Hitler invade his country, he awarded medals to volunteer workers helping displaced Polish refugees. Joice was to receive the Order of Elizabeth while

Sydney was awarded the Order of the Star. Their investiture was to take place at King Carol's palace in mid April 1940.

On the day of the investiture, the Lochs crossed the huge square in front of their hotel. From far away the brand new royal palace seemed most impressive. Through the vast reception hall the Lochs were ushered into the throne room, where they sat side by side on gilt chairs. King Carol, a very tall man, wore a white uniform with gold epaulettes and stood on a raised dais to award the medals.

The Lochs rose from their chairs when their names were called. They came forward down a long strip of red carpet, and the King pinned on their medals and had a few words with each of them.

Joice found the King knowledgeable about their work with refugees and easy to talk to, but clearly his political situation was distressing.

That evening the expatriates and foreign journalists who gathered at the English Bar at the Athenée Palace Hotel toasted the Lochs.[5] Yet a gloomy note pervaded the occasion: what if France should fall and Russia and Germany raced to seize Rumania's oilfields? How long would the Rumanians remain pro-British once they realised the British could not protect them? For Joice there was the further question: what would be the fate of her Polish refugees? More urgently, how could they get 2500 Poles out of Rumania if the Germans or Russians were coming to invade it?

The first thing was to get money. The Save the Polish Refugees Committee organised a fundraising dinner at Capsa's restaurant. The champagne was French, the caviar from the Black Sea, and tickets enormously expensive. Rumania's super rich chewed their way through mountains of food. The function was a great success. The Polish refugees' escape fund was building up.

One day Lushya relayed an unusual request. Friends in one of the internment camps needed a printing press to produce a Polish newspaper. Could they be given one from the Save the Polish Refugees Fund? When pressed, Lushya admitted another reason. One of the inmates of the camp had been an art forger. He could use a press to print exit visas so good that no one would be able to tell they were forgeries. If provided with skis and funds to bribe

Joice and Sydney in a rare period of relaxation.

their way out of camp, hundreds of Poles would be able to cross the mountains and the frontier to Turkey and from there to reach Cyprus and Palestine. Among them were young men thirsting to fight for Poland if they could reach England, and serve as pilots for the Polish Air Force.[6]

'I don't want the Quakers to know about the printing press,' Joice told Lushya. 'We'll donate it to the camp and ask no questions. What the eye doesn't see and so on.' Lushya smiled and hugged Joice, and many hundreds of Poles subsequently escaped using forged visas.

By Easter 1940 the two huge barbed-wire encampments that had housed Polish soldiers and officers were nearly empty of men of fighting age. Those who could had escaped to fight with the Free Polish or the British forces. Only the middle-aged and elderly, politicians and senior government officials, and a sprinkling of Polish professors remained.

❧ ❧ ❧

As the thaw set in and the snow turned to slush, King Carol found himself under increasing pressure from Hitler, as the main buyer of

Rumania's oil, to lift his ban on the activities of Rumania's Fascist Party. Carol announced an amnesty for acts of violence committed by the pro-Nazi Iron Guard who were terrorising Jews and pro-British citizens.[7]

Spring 1940 arrived late. By the time the chestnut trees that lined the boulevards were decked in pink blossom King Carol had attempted to salvage his situation by offering to sell Rumanian oil to the British government, which unaccountably turned down his offer and bought oil from Mexico instead. Rejected by Britain, the King next received a demand from Hitler to increase Rumania's food and oil exports to Germany. He had little choice but to accede. If Rumania stopped trading with Germany its entire economy would crash.[8]

The mild spring weather transformed Bucharest into a city of gardens and pavement cafés. The pretty streets, however, contrasted with deteriorating social conditions. As exports to Germany lifted, domestic prices rose. The Lochs' landlady, Doamna Popescu, complained bitterly, telling Joice that butter and milk had almost doubled in cost and she would be forced to raise the prices of her breakfasts.

With increasing freedom, jackbooted Iron Guard members could be seen marching along streets, or hanging around street corners looking bored and sullen.

In neighbouring countries, including Austria and Slovakia, new police restrictions based on those in Germany were issued on Jews working or going to public places. Slowly Hitler was tightening a noose around the Jews. Amid this atmosphere, Jews in Bucharest began applying for visas to America and Palestine. Suddenly everything they owned was for sale or being auctioned off, homes, cars, silver, rare books, paintings, jewels, as they attempted to raise enough money to bribe their way out of Rumania.

Joice asked their friend and co-worker 'Brownie', who acted as liaison officer between the US and Rumanian YMCA, why the United States would not accept more Jews.

'We're doing what we can,' Brownie told her sadly, 'but it's a difficult time for any government to accept large numbers of immigrants. Americans still remember the Depression and mass unemployment.'

At this critical juncture, Francesca Wilson, Head of Friends War Relief in Budapest, Hungary, visited Bucharest. She explained that the Quaker Relief Mission in Hungary was experiencing problems. Fear of the Germans had made moderate Hungarians turn against Polish refugees; Admiral Horty's pro-Nazi party was now popular and Hungary would soon be under German rule. Francesca had closed her mission down and was advising Polish refugees in Hungary to escape to Rumania.[9]

Joice explained that there was room in an old and dilapidated jail at Czernowicz, capital of the Rumanian territory of Bessarabia, which would at least be roof over the refugees' heads.

The Germans had rented offices for their Propaganda Bureau in Bucharest; its full-length window featured a huge map of Europe on which German conquests were charted. As Hitler's troops invaded Scandinavia, Holland and France, the citizens of Bucharest saw black arrows advancing across the map. The Lochs and British Legation officials walking past the Bureau looked at the map with foreboding.

In June 1940, Rumanians were devastated by the news that France, their erstwhile protector and the source of everything they considered civilised, had surrendered to Hitler's troops. The French government left Paris and fled south to Vichy where it followed a program of collaboration with the Nazi regime. The British Army presence in northern France had to be evacuated from the port of Dunkirk by a fleet of small ships, while German planes bombed them ferociously.

Under threat of invasion, the Rumanians were no longer so generous to Polish refugees. The evacuation of the British Army from Dunkirk was regarded by the Rumanians as a crushing defeat, though the British journalists the Lochs met in the English Bar viewed it as a victory. The British talked of 'the Dunkirk spirit' in the same way that Australians talked about the spirit of Gallipoli. How strange that we both celebrate defeat, Joice thought. It must be something in the Anglo-Saxon character.

The map of Rumania, too, was shrinking rapidly. In June the Soviet Union demanded that Rumanians cede within twenty-four hours the Rumanian territory of Bessarabia and its 'Russian' oilfields, as well as northern Bukovina.[10] German diplomats advised

King Carol to cooperate with Germany's Soviet ally, on the understanding that these territories would be returned once Germany had won the war — which could only be soon.

With a Soviet takeover of Bessarabia imminent, Joice and Sydney drove to the capital, Czernowicz, loaded the Polish refugees who had sought refuge there onto a fleet of lorries and brought them back to Bucharest. The following day, 24 June, the Russians invaded Czernowicz.[11]

Rumania relied for her defence on the 'King Carol Line of Fire', a series of huge trenches into which jets of oil could be pumped. In the event of an invasion, these were to be set alight by Rumanian soldiers. Unfortunately, King Carol's plan failed. Instead of pumping oil into the trenches and lighting it, the soldiers fled before the advancing Russian Army, which scarcely had to fire a shot, so terrified were the Rumanians of its brutality. With the King Carol Line of Fire out of action and without a shot being fired, the Russian troops advanced a few kilometres each day.

Cars bearing Rumanian and Jewish refugees from Bessarabia were pouring into Bucharest full of horror stories of the looting and pillaging of Bessarabia and the killing of Jews. Joice later wrote in her memoirs:

> Many Rumanians we talked to or lunched with in
> Bessarabia were hung from the lamp-posts by the Russians
> within a few days. Everything movable on hoof or in store
> was sent back to Russia. Bessarabia was picked bare.[12]

Stalin had given orders to be brutal with the Rumanians as a warning to the rest of the country not to resist. Russian troops, fuelled with alcohol, were encouraged to rape and destroy. In contrast with the Russians, the Germans began to seem positively civilised. Despite earlier assurance, it was obvious that no help would be coming from Britain.

As the Rumanian members of the Save the Polish Refugees Committee resigned, Joice realised there would be no more charity concerts in Rumanian mansions. The Poles were now a living reproach to the Rumanians.

Rumania continued to be threatened from all sides. In August, under German pressure, King Carol was forced to return the territory of Transylvania to Hungary. In September part of the Dobruja district was lopped off by the Bulgarians.[13] Bucharest was seething with rumours of the imminent invasion of Britain by the Nazis. Dr Goebbels' propaganda machine broadcast a barrage of misinformation.

In Bucharest's Athenée Palace Hotel, the English Bar was filled with officers in grey uniforms. The German Military Mission occupied every chair and bar stool, toasting each other and behaving so arrogantly that it was clear they believed the war as good as won. Showing great restraint, the British expats retreated to the chilly inner courtyard, ordering their pink gins and glasses of *tzuica* to be sent there, forced to sit outside on hard wooden chairs at metal tables covered in dead leaves while the Germans lived it up in the main hotel. To Joice it seemed like a foretaste of the future.

With the Hungarian Quaker Mission now defunct Joice undertook to collect the funds from the Budapest Mission and use them to help Polish refugees in Rumania. Just before she set out, she was summoned to the British Legation: Old Etonian, the 'Honourable Nigel Fraffly-Fraffly', as Joice and Sydney nicknamed him, was nominally a third secretary but also working for British Intelligence.[14] Somehow he had discovered she was about to leave for Budapest. Had he got the Mission's telephones tapped, Joice wondered.

Nigel had a difficult request to ask: would Joice take a spot of government money to one of his Hungarian contacts — or pay his contact out of Quaker funds and be reimbursed later?

It seemed that what Nigel referred to as 'the Powers that be' had decided this was an undercover assignment that would arouse less suspicion if carried out by a woman. Joice and the Legation's press secretary, Olivia Manning, were two of the few women left in Bucharest with a British passport and a high-security clearance. Possibly the Legation felt they could not spare the much younger Olivia Manning, or that Joice as a more mature woman would be more suitable. Joice was amazed to learn that the British Legation had security-vetted both her and Sydney.

For his part, Nigel tried hard to make his mission sound about as dangerous as a shopping trip to Harrods, but eventually he admitted that a Polish-Jewish scientist desperately needed by the Allies for the war effort, was being 'slipped from jail'. He was asking her to take a bribe intended for the scientist's jailer. Joice realised that the operation was important, but she also knew that it was dangerous. If things went wrong it could jeopardise her role in getting funds from the Hungarian Mission to the Polish refugees.

'Not scared are you?' sneered Nigel.

Joice hesitated before replying, but she could never resist a challenge. 'Perhaps not. But who else have you got?' she countered.

Nigel explained that the rail lines between Bucharest and Budapest had been damaged the previous night by Rumanian partisans, protesting against the handing back of Transylvania to Hungary. With the railway out of action, Joice would have to fly, but all commercial flights to Hungary were fully booked. Her only option was by a privately owned light aircraft which was taking charter passengers at double the normal price. The Legation's travel agent duly booked her seat.

The next day, wearing her old grey serge uniform with the red Quaker star on the sleeve, Joice was driven to the airport in a Legation car. She was slightly late and was the last to climb the gangway. Inside the cramped plane she found her seat as the door closed and the engines began to roar. Looking around at her twelve fellow passengers, she realised with horror that all the seats were filled by jackbooted men in long military overcoats with swastikas on their lapels. She looked across at the opposite seat and met the eyes of Herr von M,[15] Minister of Kultur in the German Mission to Bucharest, the only civilian aboard the plane apart from herself.

The rest of the plane had been chartered by the German Mission to transport high-ranking officers to Budapest. As an Australian (before Australia issued its own passports) Joice was travelling on a British passport — and Germany was officially at war with Britain and Australia! Under her uniform jacket was the money belt containing cash to bribe a Hungarian jailer to release a Jewish prisoner. If the Germans caught her she could be shot or sent to a concentration camp. This had happened only the previous month when a charter plane carrying a young Englishman working for British Intelligence had been diverted to German-occupied Vienna. He was arrested by the Gestapo when the plane landed and was presumed dead.

Joice's palms were damp. Her stomach churned. She prayed for good weather so there was no risk the plane would be diverted to Vienna.

She had already met Herr von M at a reception held by the Rumanian princesses. He had seemed impressed when she was introduced to him as the author of several books and had been very charming to her. During their flight, the German minister smiled at Joice and pointed out the beauty of the land they were flying over — the mists swirling around mountain peaks, the huge pine forests.

Politely Joice agreed with him, hoping he would not notice how nervous she was.

Joice's flight was becoming nightmarish. As visibility was poor, there was a real possibility the plane might bypass Budapest and land in Vienna. Joice wondered if the German minister who was being so nice to her suspected anything. Had there been a leak at the Legation? Were they being diverted to German-occupied territory so that she could be caught and arrested by the Gestapo? She prayed for the visibility to clear . . . within half an hour it did.

The passengers left the plane and filed past Hungarian customs and passport control. Joice handed in her blue British passport, which stood out among so many green German ones. The German minister stayed close beside her and together they were driven to the city in his car.

Leaving the minister's car and peering over her shoulder to check she was not being followed, she took a horse-drawn *fiacre* to Nigel's prearranged rendezvous, a café on tranquil Margaret Island in the middle of the Danube. She chose an outside table under a striped awning.[16]

Nigel had arranged for Joice to meet his 'contact' at one o'clock. He was to carry a copy of Langenscheidt's German–English dictionary and wear a red rose in his buttonhole. Joice thought the whole device corny, as though Nigel had been reading too many bad spy novels. But at least having her Hungarian contact carry a dictionary was a better idea than a rolled-up copy of *The Times*.

She ordered a pot of coffee, then waited — and waited.

At a quarter to two, just as she thought something had gone wrong with Nigel's arrangements, a man arrived with a rose in his buttonhole, carrying a bulky dictionary. He was built like a prizefighter. He sat down opposite her, smiled and she caught a flash of gold-capped teeth.

A trio in black waistcoats and tight trousers played gypsy music on their violins. No one appeared to be observing them.

Gold Teeth ignored Joice, clicked his fingers to summon the waiter and demanded a glass of the most expensive tokay on the wine list. He swallowed it as though it was lemonade and ordered another. As the gypsy trio launched into another of its glissando-filled *czardas* Joice's heart pounded. This was the moment.

She got up, went to the ladies' room, unbuckled the money belt, placed Nigel's banknotes in an envelope she had brought with her, put it in her handbag and returned to their table.

She sat down and said a few words to Gold Teeth in English. He looked puzzled. She picked up the dictionary and opened it, pretending to be searching for the right word. Then she unfastened her leather shoulder bag and nonchalantly slipped the envelope containing the money between the pages of the dictionary, thanked Gold Teeth for lending the book to her and passed it back across the table.

Gold Teeth picked up the dictionary and placed it under his chair. In fractured English he quoted the date and time his Jewish prisoner would be 'allowed to escape': on no account should Joice write down the time and place. He drew a finger across his throat which said more than words. She shuddered inwardly — obviously Gold Teeth feared she might be captured and killed by the Nazis.

Gold Teeth drained the last drops of golden tokay, reached under his chair, picked up the dictionary and tucked it under his arm. Without a word, he stood up and strode away, leaving Joice to pay for his expensive glasses of wine.

She strolled through the beautiful gardens of Margaret Island, took a bus back to the city centre and found the Quaker Mission headquarters. There she talked to the elderly Hungarian who was the last Mission volunteer left, signed for the money remaining in their safe, and received a list of exiled Poles who had fled to Rumania.

She recalled her conversation with Herr von M about the beautiful view over Pest from the heights of Buda. Her watch said half-past four — there was still time to watch the sun set over Pest. She took a *fiacre* up the steep hill to the castle ramparts of Buda. The Herrengasse that Herr von M had called Buda's oldest street, as though he felt Budapest was already part of Germany, was as fascinating as he had claimed. Its Hungarian name was the Uri Utca, and it was lined with tall houses painted in pastel shades of pink, green, turmeric and terracotta. The houses had arched oak doors with their former owners' coats of arms embossed in gold leaf, and steeply tiled roofs with distinctive 'eyebrow' windows to light their attic rooms. A few had been turned into hostelries, their inn signs showing double-headed eagles, golden stags and roses.

From the ramparts of Ober Buda, Joice looked out over a magnificent panorama. Steeply terraced slopes, green with trees, were crisscrossed by flights of steps, some arched and roofed like small cloisters, which descended abruptly to the wide streets that bordered the silvery loops of the Danube. Six huge bridges linked Buda with Pest. Far below her she picked out the spires of what must be Hungary's House of Parliament, its Gothic pinnacles topped by a huge dome. It looked like a cross between Brunelleschi's Duomo in Florence and London's Houses of Parliament. Far below sprawled the nineteenth-century business and shopping centre of Pest, its wide boulevards slicing through dense rows of shops, offices and apartment blocks.

As the last rays of the sun disappeared and the lights came on, Joice thought Herr von M had been right — this *was* the most breathtaking view she had ever seen.

The next morning Joice rang the railway station, determined not to return to Bucharest on a charter plane. To her relief, the stretch of railway line damaged by the Rumanian partisans had now been repaired. What luck! She took a *fiacre* to the station, where she telephoned Sydney, careful to say as little as possible in case the Nazis had tapped the line. She gave her expected time of arrival at Bucharest station. Sydney said he would be waiting for her under the railway clock.

When the train drew in at Bucharest, Joice felt almost light-headed with relief that her spy mission was accomplished. That afternoon she rang Nigel and gave him the message from Gold Teeth.

ESCAPE FROM THE IRON GUARD

German domination of Rumania was becoming increasingly heavy handed. Germany had been instrumental in the loss of all the Rumanian territories, as it traded off Soviet ambitions in return for the oilfields of the Ploesti area, close to Bucharest where it would establish Nazi headquarters.

The loss of Bukovina and the failure of the British to save them had now turned the populace against the King. He was jeered as his chauffeur drove him through Bucharest in his bullet-proof Rolls-Royce. Carol had already alienated the peasants and the working class, who resented the fact that he spoke English and French better than Rumanian and had spent huge sums on his new palace and his Jewish mistress. Posters appeared in the streets calling for the King to resign in favour of his son by his estranged wife, Princess Helen — Crown Prince Michael, now a boy of nineteen.

Carol, who had already spent a period in exile with his mistress Magda Lupescu before being invited to return to Rumania after his father's death, had no intention of spending another exile in penury. Realising that his days were numbered he had been hoarding gold ingots from the Treasury to take with him to Estoril in Portugal.

Meanwhile the Iron Guard, sinister in their dark green uniforms and jackboots, no longer stood around on street corners but goose-stepped proudly down the Calea Viktorei, Bucharest's main street. Joice felt shivers run down her spine. Clearly they must get the remaining Poles out of the country as soon as possible.

The Lochs continued to bombard Friends House and the British

War Office with information about the plight of Polish and Jewish refugees trapped in Rumania and to plead for more funds to get them out. Finally a very senior British civil servant granted permission for a group of 2000 civilian refugees from Poland to be accommodated in an Army camp in British-run Cyprus. But no more than 10 per cent of the escape party could be Jewish. They were to cross the Black Sea from Constantza to Istanbul and sail via the Turkish port of Mersin to Cyprus. Should Cyprus be invaded, the Polish refugees would have to escape to Palestine, although the Arabs, Britain's oil-rich allies, had made it plain they did not want too many refugee Jews in their country.

On receiving the go-ahead to what Whitehall called Operation Swordfish, Sydney spent days drawing up escape routes out of Rumania. The Lochs' plan was for Sydney and five hundred Polish men to leave Bucharest by river steamer to the Black Sea resort of Constantza. Joice, Lushya and Father Ambrosius, in Operation Pied Piper, would follow with four hundred and fifty Polish women and children and fifty Jewish children. They would leave by train for Constantza as soon as they had the funds. They would be joined at Constantza by as many as possible of the four hundred Polish women and children who had been living in the holiday villas of wealthy Rumanians.

Many Polish women and their children were also scattered through outlying Rumanian villages. Some of the women had found paying jobs which, understandably, they were reluctant to leave. Having been in an economic limbo they were now trying hard to build new lives for themselves and their children.

Using Quaker funds Joice purchased a roneotype machine. With Lushya's help, she sent out circulars advising the women of the danger they faced. The circulars explained that the Free Polish government in exile was urging them to flee from Rumania if they could. The women were told about the escape plans, and warned not to take suitcases. All they could take was a beach bag, so that the Iron Guard would think they were off to the coast for a day trip rather than fleeing the country. Joice had instructed the women to sew any jewels they had not pawned into the hems of their dresses.

On 6 September 1940, with demonstrators screaming for his blood outside the royal palace, King Carol issued a statement. He would abdicate in favour of his son, who would reign under the name of King Michael of Rumania.

Carol had also appointed Pro-Nazi General Ion Antonescu premier, with the result that, the Iron Guard could exercise its force freely. In the violence that followed Carol's abdication, shop windows were smashed, there was shooting in the streets and many dead. Corpses piled up and no one dared bury them for fear of becoming a target.

Guns were firing as the Lochs crossed the square in front of the royal palace to reach their hotel. In the hallway their landlady, Doamna Popescu, threw herself into Sydney's arms weeping and laughing wildly. As the group came upstairs Sydney insisted that they lie face-down on the floor. A stray bullet winged through the long windows and embedded itself in the wardrobe. Doamna Popescu's hysterics returned.

Eventually Doamna Popescu revealed the reason for her hysterics. Although she had not told a soul, her bedridden eighty-year-old mother was Jewish. Neither her father nor her late husband had Jewish blood, but under Rumanian law, having a Jewish mother meant that she and her children and grandchildren were Jewish, even though they followed the Catholic faith.

'Come with me to Cyprus. One or two more will make no difference,' Joice advised her.

Doamna Popescu thanked Joice but said she could not leave her mother, who was far too ill to travel. She told Joice, 'Doamna Loch, I am more Rumanian than Jewish. I was educated in a convent. They will not touch us.'

Their landlady sounded so convincing that Joice almost believed her. Sporadic firing continued. Joice described how:

> Each boarding house . . . was seized and behind each door stood an armed man. At midday a man bearing a white flag emerged from the royal palace and declared a truce. Shooting stopped; everyone went out to lunch and stacked their guns under their tables. For an hour all was calm. Then we poor foreigners slunk out and bought

sufficient supplies for another twenty-three hours of rage and ruin . . . Rumanians take their stomachs much more seriously than their revolutions.[17]

The following morning the police informed the British Legation that the body of a young man had been brought into the morgue. The body had been thrown from a bridge onto the cobblestones below, the spine broken on impact, the face so battered it was almost unrecognisable. A British Legation official was asked to go to the morgue and had no difficulty identifying Nigel, whose striped Old Etonian tie was still knotted around his neck.[18]

It was time for the Lochs to put their plans into action. With regular Danube ferries already crowded with refugees, Sydney managed to charter a huge pleasure steamer for his escape party. When he received a message from the captain that his river steamer was ready, Operation Swordfish was under way.

Joice kissed Sydney goodbye, trying to sound unconcerned about what lay ahead but inwardly scared. It was agreed they would meet up at the small Turkish port of Mersin — or, should something prevent this, on the British-held island of Cyprus. Joice would somehow get the Polish women and children to the Black Sea port of Constantza, and from there by ferry to Istanbul and on to Mersin. If she had problems she was to contact the British Embassy in Ankara or the British High Commissioner in Famagusta, Cyprus, who would pass messages to Whitehall, but for safety's sake she must not give her name; just use her code name: Pied Piper.

By now most of their Bucharest funds as well as the money Joice had brought back from the Budapest Mission had been used up. Joice cabled Friends House in London, pleading for money to help the women and children escape. But no money arrived. The banks kept erratic hours during what was a state of emergency. Whenever they did open long queues of people formed, desperate to leave Bucharest before the invaders arrived. Day by day the Russian troops drew nearer. They would be caught between the Nazis and the Reds and it would be cattle trucks and labour camps for the Poles, Joice knew, if she did not act soon.

The day before Operation Pied Piper was due to depart, the promised Friends War Relief Fund money had still not arrived. Joice had almost enough to buy tickets to Istanbul for those who could not pay but nothing to spare should anyone fall sick or to get them to Cyprus. They would have to go and trust to providence, she thought.

Mr Brown, the Lochs' American friend and colleague, had kindly agreed to look after those Polish women and children who had opted to stay behind. Brownie was extremely upset that the US government (which was still not involved in the war) had not done more for Poles and Jews, and insisted on taking Joice, of whom he was very fond, to a farewell lunch at Nestor's restaurant. 'Got to see you have a square meal before you leave,' he said.

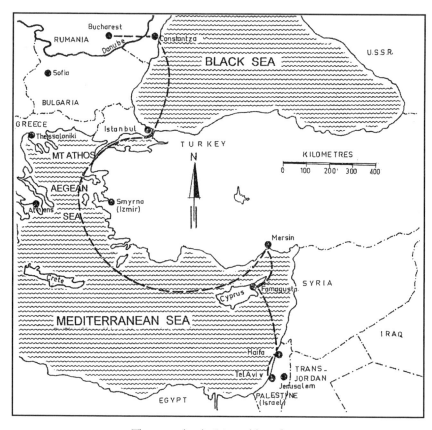

The route taken by Joice and her refugees.

At the door of the restaurant, Brownie greeted a pair of German-speaking Rumanians, who said they had been listening to the radio and that Churchill was on the point of surrendering to Hitler.

Joice and Brownie both laughed. 'Don't believe a word of Dr Goebbels' propaganda,' Joice responded.

Inside the restaurant they were shown to a table where a well-dressed couple were already seated. Brownie introduced them as Mr and Mrs Gluckstein, of Solomon and Gluckstein's Bank.

'This is Mrs Loch, a woman on whom you may depend,' he told the Glucksteins. They shook hands.

Mrs Gluckstein was from a Jewish banking family, owners of the famous Dresdner Bank. Her brother-in-law, who ran a branch in Bessarabia, had been killed by the invading Russians; her sister had been raped and killed by Russian soldiers.

'We sent our chauffeur to bring my nieces to Bucharest. He hid them on the floor of the car under a rug,' Mrs Gluckstein told Joice, biting back her sobs.

Brownie had told the Glucksteins about Joice's flight and asked them if they could donate enough money to help the escape of the Jewish orphans on Operation Pied Piper. The Glucksteins agreed on the condition that Joice would include their recently orphaned nieces and their only daughter in her escape party. Mrs Gluckstein had another sister living at Haifa who had agreed to look after the three girls until the Glucksteins could wind up the bank's affairs and leave the country for British-run Palestine.

'Of course, we'll make it worth your while to take our girls to Haifa,' Mrs Gluckstein told Joice, pulling a large envelope out of her handbag. 'Here are ten thousand *lei,*' she whispered. Joice realised with gratitude that this money would cover emergencies during the long and dangerous journey that lay before them.

'Mrs Gluckstein, please understand that I am not in this for the money,' Joice said. 'But it would come in handy with so many mouths to feed. I can't sleep worrying about what happens if we encounter delays.'

'Take it, take it, my dear. Get my daughter and my nieces to Haifa, where there is a large Rumanian-Jewish community, and we will join them there, or the Nazis will kill them. Mr Brown tells me very good things about you. So give me your word that you will take my beloved girls to Haifa.'

'I will, as long as their passports are in order and they don't say they are Jewish.' Joice knew that prominent families such as the Glucksteins were high on the Iron Guard's wanted list.

Mrs Gluckstein reached into her handbag again. She produced three blue British passports bearing the royal coat of arms, in the names of Sally, Susan and Janet Brown. Joice examined them. They looked just like her own passport. Surely no one could tell.

'Doamna Loch,' Mrs Gluckstein said nervously, 'I swear on my sister's life, no one but God himself would know these girls are Jewish. They had an English nanny so they have a good English accent and their hair is so blonde they don't look *Jewish*!'

Joice agreed to take the three girls to Haifa. They arranged to meet next morning at eight under the clock at Bucharest's main railway station.

That night, as Joice made her final preparations, she thought about Sydney. By now his party must have reached Constantza, taken the ferry to Istanbul and, God willing, be at Mersin.

By six o'clock next morning Joice was ready. She bade a sad farewell to her landlady, who gave her a thermos of coffee and a bag of rolls filled with smoked ham for the journey.

'*La revedere* is Hungarian for *au revoir*,' Doamna Popescu said as she kissed Joice on both cheeks.

I only hope we do meet again, Joice thought to herself.

OPERATION PIED PIPER

Although he abdicated on 6 September, the former King Carol did not depart from Rumania until 16 September.

Operation Pied Piper[19] also began its journey from the main station of Bucharest on 16 September 1940. By good luck and because it was still in the school holidays, Joice had selected the very day the royal train departed with King Carol and his Jewish mistress, Magda Lupescu, taking them and their possessions first to Belgrade and then to exile in Portugal. Aware of rumours of crates of gold bullion from the Treasury and Old Masters' paintings leaving with the former king, the Iron Guard had stationed marksmen by the approaches to a railway tunnel where it estimated the royal train must slow down. From there the Guard could shoot King Carol and his mistress through the train window and take the gold. The plot only failed because King Carol had his *own* team of marksmen, who shot the assassins first, and his train arrived in Belgrade riddled with bullets.[20]

An inner-city rally of the Iron Guard was also scheduled that day, which further distracted their attention from the ordinary travellers at the railway station. The next day Horia Sima, the Iron Guard commander, and his thugs would go on a killing spree: hanging their victims from meat hooks in abattoirs was to become their trademark. Over 6000 Rumanian Jews perished in one week.

Meanwhile Joice and her hundreds of refugees were getting ready to board the train heading for the Black Sea. As it was the school holidays, the train was crowded with Rumanian parents and children bound for the twin resorts of Constantza and Mamounia.

To play the role of holiday maker, Joice had exchanged her grey Quaker uniform for a blue cotton frock, sandals and a straw hat with blue ribbons.

Just as Joice and Lushya had insisted, the Polish children wore sundresses or shirts and shorts and carried spades, and their mothers had their night things in beach bags rather than in leather suitcases.

The three bewildered little Gluckstein girls arrived at the previously arranged meeting place under the station clock, delivered by the very Jewish-looking Mrs Gluckstein. They bobbed little curtsies to Joice and Lushya and announced in beautifully enunciated English that their names were Zara, Magda and Dina.

Joice put her arms around the little girls and promised to see that they reached their aunt and uncle in Haifa safely. The three girls kissed Mrs Gluckstein goodbye. She burst into tears and soon all of them were crying. Then, shepherding the weeping children, Joice and Lushya boarded the train.

For the moment it seemed as if they were safe. However, Joice worried that the Iron Guard might decide to board the train further down the track, make an inspection of passports and discover that some of the children were Jewish, with terrible consequences for her and her charges.

A ticket inspector informed Lushya that the train was being diverted in order to load a big export consignment of Black Sea caviar from the processing factory at Tulcea. Lushya said it would mean an hour's delay before they reached Constantza. Joice prayed they would arrive in time to catch the afternoon ferry to Istanbul. She wanted to get out of Rumania as quickly as possible.

Their train clattered alongside ripening fields of wheat and maize and orchards loaded with fruit. The day was warm and the journey had such a holiday feel to it that the excited, chattering children were oblivious of the danger they were in. After passing the town of Giurgeni, the steam train ran beside the banks of the Danube whose brown muddy waters were spliced by the mint-green waters of streams from the Carpathian Mountains.

Gradually the Danube grew wider. Finally they arrived at a siding beside the huge canning factory of Tulcea. The train waited while crates of tinned caviar were loaded into the goods wagon. Then the whistle blew and they set off again through the flat lands of the Danube delta where Joice kept the little girls busy counting pelicans and flocks of creamy-white storks.

They finally reached Constantza, a thriving Black Sea holiday resort with concrete Art Deco-style hotels bordering a wide sandy beach. As arranged, they were joined at the ferry terminal by four hundred more Polish widows, wives and children who had been 'house-sitting' holiday villas for wealthy Rumanians. Accompanying them were some Polish teachers and priests, who helped Joice and Lushya buy ferry tickets from the expedition's slender funds. Fortunately luck remained with them: Joice was relieved to see that the Istanbul ferry was in port and waiting for them.

They filed through customs apprehensively. However, the Rumanian officials were not very interested in schoolchildren on an outing. Still no members of the Iron Guard were in evidence.

Joice, playing the role of an English-speaking governess taking her charges on holiday to Istanbul, steered the three little Gluckstein girls through passport control, while Lushya took the rest of the Jewish orphans with their forged passports. The ferry set out.

Just as Joice and Lushya were congratulating themselves that everything was going to plan, announcements in Rumanian and German boomed over the ship's loudspeakers. Lushya frowned and translated for Joice's benefit: 'We are returning to Constantza on the orders of the Iron Guard.'

At this change in plan, beads of perspiration trickled down Joice's back. The Iron Guard would be there waiting to herd them into cattle trucks.

Back at the dockside an armed detachment of Iron Guard was drawn up in a dark green line, waiting for them. Joice feared the worst. They watched from the deck as the gangplank was lowered. Jackbooted guards swarmed aboard. Joice thought the moment of reckoning had come. It was all up now, those poor children would soon be in a labour camp or worse.

Ignoring the apprehensive Polish women who gathered their children protectively to them, the Iron Guard clambered up the steep companionway that led to the top deck.

The passengers watched a detachment of men swarm around eight huge shipping crates roped to metal rings inset into the deck. Was the Iron Guard fussing over that export order of tinned caviar that had been loaded onto the train? Surely not.

As the Iron Guard untied the ropes that held the shipping crates, the ship's captain argued with them, waving his arms and gesticulating. Obviously he did not want the crates moved. The officer in charge barked an order and members of the Iron Guard drew their pistols from their holsters. The captain dropped his arms to his sides and stood very still indeed.

The boom of a crane swung overhead, a huge net dangling from a hook. The wooden crates were loaded into the net, swung over the side of the ship and deposited carefully on the dock.

At the sight of them, more Iron Guard waiting below uttered cheers of delight and started to prise open the crates using heavy crowbars. From the deck Joice caught a glimpse of something inside the crates that glinted like gold.

'That's not caviar! It's the gold bullion King Carol was shipping out of the country,' Lushya said, laughing so much that tears of relief poured down her cheeks. So gold was what the Iron Guard was after, not their refugees.

With their gold back, the Iron Guard wasn't interested in inspecting the passengers.

Very slowly the ferry pulled away from the dock and they steamed past the lighthouse for the second time that day.

This time the crossing of the Black Sea passed without event. As they approached Istanbul, on each side of the placid waters of the Bosphorus they saw picturesque timber houses painted pink and blue, with latticed balconies lining the shore. Thank God, Turkey at last.

They were met by a group of Polish refugees who had escaped from Bucharest a few months before. Listening to the BBC Foreign Service they had heard that the German Army had marched into Bucharest a few hours earlier. It had been the signal for the Iron Guard to commence a reign of terror, throwing Jewish people out of high windows to their deaths or hanging them from meat hooks in the city's abattoirs. Joice felt sick, thinking what might have happened to poor Doamna Popescu and her mother. Why, oh, why had their landlady not come with them when Joice had begged her to?

Joice and her huge party of refugees walked through street markets where men in baggy trousers and pointed slippers sold exotic-smelling spices, pastries filled with nuts and honey, and glasses of drinking water from huge copper urns carried on their backs.

The group had been booked for the night into several large inexpensive *pensiones* near the Topkapi Palace, in the old part of town known as the Sultanahmet.

They were to catch the overnight ferry for Mersin the following night, which left Joice and some others enough time the next day to visit the ancient Topkapi Palace. There they were shown an immense faceted diamond, larger than a duck's egg, jewelled daggers encrusted with rubies and emeralds, and coffee cups glittering with diamonds, worth enough money to feed and house their refugees for years, Joice thought. Their guide took them through the 'gilded cage', where the sons of various Sultans, born to their many wives, used to be confined to prevent them being strangled or poisoned and where some had gone mad as a result.

The time came to board the ferry from Istanbul to the south-eastern port of Mersin, near the Turkish-Syrian border. For the next two nights everyone had to sleep on deck. On the second morning Joice woke stiff but tremendously exhilarated to think they had managed to escape from the Iron Guard and the Nazis.

The quayside and town of Mersin were filled with Polish refugees from Rumania and Hungary, all using this tiny port to reach Cyprus and Palestine. The number of refugees was so large that the British and the Germans had opened consulates to process their passport applications.

Joice visited the British Consulate and learned that the Consul was ill with typhoid. She was given a letter addressed in Sydney's firm handwriting. Opening it, she read that he had got a very good price on three large fishing boats to take his party to Cyprus. Joice must wait at Mersin and one of the boats would return to take them to Cyprus. She should contact the Turkish harbour master: he would arrange everything in return for a good tip.

Faced with the prospect of spending some time in Mersin, Joice realised she would have to organise accommodation, food and clothing. After some hard bargaining with a Turkish hotel owner, Joice managed to install most of the refugees in his clean but totally empty hotel for a nominal charge, provided they slept on the floor. The hotel was in process of being sold and all the beds, bedding, linen and cutlery had already been auctioned off. This meant that out of her diminishing funds, Joice also had to buy mattresses and cooking utensils. Once they were in Cyprus, Joice assumed the British government would contribute to the Polish refugees' living expenses, as the Poles were Britain's allies.

Joice, Lushya and a few of the older Polish women stayed at the nearby Hotel Gazelli, which fortunately had a telephone. From there Joice sent a telegram to Friends House in London, explaining that food was expensive in Mersin and they needed more money to buy fresh milk and eggs for the children.

The German Consul ate his meals in the rooftop restaurant of the Hotel Gazelli, where, it seemed, anyone who was anyone in Mersin's diplomatic world stayed — apparently all spying on one another. The dapper Italian Consul pleaded dyspepsia. He flatly refused to share a table with his German counterpart, even though by now Mussolini had entered the war as Hitler's ally. The French Consul looked supremely unhappy, refused to eat with either of the other consuls, but grudgingly consented to eat with Joice and Lushya. There was no sign of the British Consul.

Over dinner the Frenchman told Joice that doctors believed the British Consul might die — apparently typhoid was a constant health risk in Mersin because the underground sewers were so close to the water pipes, and the sanitation was poor. Here was another thing for Joice to worry about: the children might catch cholera, dysentery or typhoid. She would need to rent a ship with a purified water supply to take them to Cyprus. In the meantime she had to persuade the Turks to sell them fruit, vegetables, bread and fresh milk at prices she could afford. Meat was far too expensive for their budget but they did manage to get some fish. The women took it in turns to cook meals in the hotel's huge kitchen, using equipment and crockery Joice had bought at the market.

After a week of waiting, the largest of the three boats that Sydney had hired returned. The captain contacted the harbour master, knowing he was in touch with Joice.

A Turkish sea captain brought Joice a second letter from Sydney. She read it. The letter was something of a shock. Sydney explained that the voyage had not been nearly as easy as he had hoped. In fact his party had had a hellish four-day voyage under sail. The wind had dropped, leaving all three sailing ships becalmed for two days. Each one had run out of drinking water which had turned out not to be purified after all. The 'modern flush toilets' promised them by the captain and the harbour master had proved to be nothing but a few buckets filled with sand. Many of the refugees went down with food poisoning; the stench had been vile.

Sydney warned Joice that she must, on no account, hire the boat of the captain who brought her this letter. She must not trust the harbour master. He was a complete rogue and was only helping them because he received a good commission from the captain. Indeed the two of them were rogues, in league to get as much money out of refugees as possible.

Joice could not run the risk of her party getting dysentery, especially with children on board; polluted water and 'sanitary buckets' were out of the question. She would have to stay in Mersin until she could find a modern ship. Sydney had suggested that the British Consul would help, but Joice realised that she could get little assistance from him.

There were many picturesque but unseaworthy sailing boats for hire in Mersin harbour but none of them was suitable. The sea passage between Turkey and Cyprus was not long but if the wind blew up it could be dangerous — vessels had been shipwrecked in the past. This was a terrifying prospect. Many of the Polish children could not swim and there were no lifeboats or life rafts on board any of these old *caiques*.

By now Joice had been advised that the German Consul was spying on her party, trying to learn their destination. Was he plotting to pass on the information to the German Navy so that their ship could be attacked and torpedoed?

Even with unlimited money, finding a trustworthy captain prepared to take a party that included many young children to Cyprus would have presented problems. Meanwhile, the Turkish harbour master, fearing the loss of his introductory commission from the captain, was insisting Madame Loch and her band of refugees should charter the captain's boat and two other ancient sailing vessels and leave Turkish waters immediately.

In desperation Joice sent Lushya with flowers to the Consul's home but was told he was critically ill. Joice managed to get two Polish doctors to attend him till he recovered, but it seemed she had only one option for her refugees left. She telephoned the British Embassy in Constantinople, giving the telephonist her code name, Pied Piper. She was terrified her phone might be tapped by the German Consul but she had to take that risk.

She was put through to an embassy official and asked him to be kind enough to radio British Naval Command to see if they could provide a ship capable of taking a party of some eight hundred refugees to Cyprus. The official was flabbergasted by her request. 'The British diplomatic service, was governed by strict protocols,' he said and he had not been instructed by the Foreign Office to help.

Joice held her ground. She insisted that on humanitarian grounds he *had* to help. The Poles were their allies, weren't they? Some were fighting in the British Army and Air Force. Sensing his quandary, Joice gave the name of an old friend, an admiral in charge of the Mediterranean Fleet, and suggested the official contact him. There was a long pause. The official had obviously gone to consult someone higher up the ladder. Finally he came back to the phone and suggested Joice phone back tomorrow.

Although Joice belonged to no church or religious denomination, their situation seemed so precarious that on the way back to their hotel, she entered the cool, dark interior of what had once been a Greek Orthodox church. She prayed that God or Divine Providence would, by some miracle, protect the women and children in her care and send them a ship.

The following day she rang the British Embassy in Constantinople, not confident of receiving help. But there was good news. British Naval Command *had* found her a suitable vessel. The ship was called the *Warszawa,* affectionately known by the British Navy as the *Warsower.* It had flush toilets, water tanks and was manned by a volunteer crew whose aim was to rescue refugees from the Nazis. Joice was amazed. It was as though her prayers had been answered.

Joice was informed that the *Warszawa* was due to arrive in Mersin harbour within twenty-four hours to pick up Polish soldiers who had escaped from Hungary and were on their way to join the British Army in Palestine. Since the *Warszawa* was already bound for Cyprus the fare for each refugee on Operation Pied Piper would be a nominal one. However, there was one problem. The ship's cook had his work cut out to provide food for the Polish soldiers and the crew. Joice must buy all the provisions for her group and they must arrange to cook their own meals. This was easy to arrange and Joice and Lushya hugged each other at the thought that they could get out of Mersin before anyone got sick.

The following day when the *Warszawa* steamed into Mersin harbour, it was easy to see why the British Navy had nicknamed her the old '*Warsower*'. She was a battered hulk with a strong list to port, resurrected from a breaker's yard at the beginning of the war by a volunteer crew, some of whom were Polish, others British. No one had given her a coat of paint for decades and her hull was red with rust. She did have piped water but the pump-action toilets only worked intermittently and the smell was fearsome.

But this battered steamer and her volunteer crew had saved British soldiers from the beaches of Dunkirk, as well as carrying boatloads of Jews to safety. To Joice and the Polish refugees, she seemed like the *Queen Mary*. They were overjoyed to board her and leave disease-ridden Mersin.

The *Warszawa*'s captain, who as luck would have it was Polish, handed over his cabin to Joice. 'Madame Loch, as the commander of Operation Pied Piper, you must have my cabin,' he insisted gallantly.

The Turkish harbour master, baulked of his commission from Joice's party, was furious. He tried to delay their departure by demanding changes in their paperwork. Joice wondered if he was radioing the German Navy to tell them in what direction they were heading.

Also observing them was the German Consul, who had been tipped off, probably by the harbour master, that the *Warszawa* should be watched. He hired a dinghy and sailed around her hull. Yet unknown to the German Consul or the harbour master, just before they left under cover of darkness the old tramp steamer stealthily loaded its large group of Polish soldiers on board. Had the German Consul spotted any of the Polish soldiers in their khaki jackets and breeches boarding the ship on the landward side, he could have pressured Turkey to intern them. If they were caught on board, the captain of the *Warszawa* would have been deemed to have broken international shipping rules by not declaring he had Polish soldiers aboard.

But everything went without a hitch. The *Warszawa* slipped out of Mersin harbour the same night she arrived, so quietly that not even the harbour master suspected her departure.

After an anxious night, Joice was relieved to see the island of Cyprus appear on the skyline. The sea had been calm and there had been no mines to impede them. They docked at the down-at-heel harbour of Famagusta, where Joice was relieved to see the Union Jack was flying.

British Army doctors came on board to do a health inspection. Because the women and children had spent time in Mersin, they insisted on inspecting them for symptoms of typhoid but found no signs. After the refugees disembarked the old *Warsower* and her crew sailed on, taking the Polish soldiers to Palestine.

Joice and her party were escorted to a tented quarantine camp, by now overflowing with Polish and Jewish refugees. She was delighted to find Sydney there. He had been anxiously awaiting their arrival.

Sydney's own group had been housed in an Army camp; since so many of them were members of the Polish Parliament they were considered official guests of the British government until transport planes could be organised to fly them to Britain. However, no authority wanted to take any responsibility for the Polish women and children, financially or otherwise. The British military authorities were also anxious about having so many women and children to care for, and warned the Lochs they might have to evacuate again if the German Army invaded the neighbouring island of Crete.

In wartime there were many empty luxury hotels beside the beaches and beauty spots of Cyprus, but their owners refused to rent rooms to refugees who might damage expensive fixtures and fittings.

After some haggling by the Lochs and the British Consul — who pointed out that these Polish refugees were educated people who would not allow their children to wreck the premises — a bulk rate was negotiated with two smaller hotels. Joice felt that she and Sydney had secured a real victory when, after much discussion, it was agreed that the British government would pay accommodation costs for the women and children on Operation Pied Piper. They managed to obtain a small weekly allowance for each refugee, plus a grant of five pounds per adult and three pounds per child for new clothes and shoes.

⊱ ⊱ ⊱

By the spring of 1941, Joice was still negotiating for places on a troopship to take the Gluckstein girls and the rest of the Jewish orphans to Haifa, where she hoped the large Rumanian-Jewish community would take care of them.

She had written several times to the Glucksteins' address in Bucharest but had heard nothing and was worried. Perhaps the Glucksteins had planned their escape before the Nazis arrived and were already in Haifa waiting?

And then came terrible news. Unexpectedly, the German Army invaded Greece. Cyprus seemed likely to be the next island to be invaded after Crete. Cypriots heard on the radio that Germans on the Greek mainland and several of the islands had slaughtered British and Australian soldiers, as well as Greeks suspected of being friendly to the British. In the days that followed there was a rush by pro-British Greeks to escape Greece, some of whom headed to Cyprus.

With the Nazi threat so near, the Polish government in exile (some of whom had been part of Sydney Loch's escape party) requested the British government to evacuate all the Polish refugees in Cyprus to British-run Palestine. It now seemed likely that the whole Operation Pied Piper group would be going to Palestine, not just Joice and the Gluckstein girls.

In June 1941, after an anxious period for Joice, Sydney and their refugees, the British government sent a naval cruiser to evacuate as many of them as possible from Cyprus to Palestine. Australian troops who had arrived on Cyprus after the battle for Crete helped load the refugees aboard the vessel. Hearing Aussie voices again made Joice feel quite homesick.

The Lochs were so busy with last-minute arrangements, buying food and medicines for the women and children and settling outstanding hotel bills, they had no time to buy food for themselves. As the Polish refugees formed a long line and edged slowly up the gangplank, Joice and Sydney managed to have a cup of tea and a biscuit in an English teashop beside the harbour. When the Cockney proprietor of the teashop learned they were in sole charge of many hundreds of refugees, she insisted on packing up four cheese sandwiches and a thermos flask of tea for them. 'Good luck dearie,' she said to Joice. 'You'll need it.' Her gift was very welcome and would be the only food Joice and Sydney had for the next two days.

As they left Famagusta harbour the sea was as flat as glass under a scorching sun. The British cruiser made slow progress, twisting and turning to avoid floating mines. Father Ambrosius and the other priests on board gave lessons to the Polish children under striped canvas awnings, while the Jewish girls and boys played under another awning and Lushya looked after any children suffering from sea sickness.

Joice and Sydney ate their sandwiches in the gun room, far too anxious about floating mines or German bombers to relax. At dusk they went on deck to find the sky overcast. A cigarette butt flickered for a moment and the captain yelled down from the bridge, 'Stop those Poles smoking!'[21] The last thing they needed was a signal to German planes that they were there.

After some reconnoitring on board, Joice and Sydney were disturbed to discover that the ship did not have enough lifebelts or lifeboats for all the passengers. If the ship were bombed or blown up by mines it would be a disaster. Some hours afterwards the drone of German planes could be heard overhead. Huge waves surged around them as the dropped bombs made a wall of water on either side of the ship. At times the ship seemed as if it would be swamped. The raid seemed to last for an eternity, then, as dawn came, denied their quarry, the German planes flew away.

During the morning the captain was advised by port control at Haifa that mines had been placed at the approaches to the harbour. The Germans had succeeded in blowing up a British ship the previous night and had bombed two more so fiercely they had sunk and everyone aboard had perished. Tenser than ever, he invited the Lochs up to the bridge. Just then over the horizon steamed a battered tramp ship. As it came nearer they realised it was the old *Warsower*. At the sight of her and the hundreds of soldiers in Polish uniform waving from her rails, an answering cheer came up from the Lochs' Polish refugees.

'The old *Warsower*. Now we're all right ... That ship has a charmed life and nothing will hit us as long as she is here,' the captain breathed.[22]

The captain was still very gloomy about their chances of getting the Jewish orphans into Palestine. He knew that several British ships had been refused permission to land because they carried Jewish refugees. He told Joice how one captain had been so desperate he had risked a court-martial and beached his ship so he could offload his Jewish passengers in Palestine rather than sail on from port to port. (In 1941, before the world was aware of the Nazi death camps, it was hard for ships to arrive anywhere with Jewish refugees aboard, as few countries would accept them.)

To the dismay of Joice and Sydney, the captain told them that Palestine had demanded a reduction in the numbers of Jews entering, down from the maximum 10 per cent originally agreed. Palestine was part of the Arab bloc, and Britain desperately needed Arab oil (as well as Mexican) to win the war.

Joice believed firmly in the Quaker principle that *all* refugees regardless of religion or race *must* be accepted. She had promised the Glucksteins she would deliver their daughter and orphaned nieces to Haifa. *Nothing* would stop her getting those children to their aunt, even if she had to take a lifeboat and row them ashore herself.

The captain radioed his vessel's whereabouts to the officer in charge of port control. A reply crackled back: 'Cut engines, drop anchor and wait for clearance.' They followed orders, hove to and waited anxiously for over an hour.

To distract the children, Joice and Lushya got the teachers to play games with them. They plaited the hair of the Gluckstein girls and made them change into clean dresses and ankle socks so they would look their best. The three little girls, overjoyed at the thought of seeing their aunt and uncle, chattered away nineteen to the dozen. Joice marvelled at the resilience of children. She wondered how Doamna Popescu and Mr and Mrs Gluckstein had fared in Bucharest during the full rampage of the Iron Guard, and only hoped they might find the Glucksteins waiting for them.

Finally a British mine-sweeper appeared and removed the mines which the Germans had laid the previous night. They were advised by radio that it was safe for them to dock. British medical and port officials came on board. To Joice's relief there were no difficulties about the Jewish children and no awkward questions asked about their passports.

Once they had ushered the refugees through customs, Sydney and Joice telephoned the British High Commissioner, who had already been advised of their imminent arrival by Whitehall. The High Commissioner promised that a special train would be sent to the port to deliver the refugees to two camps outside Haifa. He also invited Sydney and Joice to dine at the High Commission that night.

Then Joice dialled the number Mrs Gluckstein had given her weeks ago in Bucharest. The phone rang for some time before anyone answered.

'Mrs Gutman, this is Joice Loch. Your nieces are safe and longing to see you. How soon can you collect them?'

A sharp intake of breath at the other end of the phone was followed by sobbing. Mrs Gutman replied haltingly, 'Mrs Loch, forgive me. My sister and her husband were murdered by the Iron Guard two days after you left Bucharest.'

She added, 'How can we thank you for saving our girls?'

'I am so sorry. Please, I don't want any thanks,' said Joice, shocked and horrified at the news. Then she thought about the orphans with no relatives or homes to go to and added, 'If you really want to thank us, please find foster homes for the other Jewish children in our party.'

'Anything, Mrs Loch, anything. We have a large Rumanian community in Haifa. We will do all we can. You have my word.'

THE CAMP OF A THOUSAND ORPHANS

As the British High Commissioner had promised, a special train was sent to the rail siding beside the ship to take the refugees to a transit camp in Haifa. Mrs Gutman kept her word, and the Jewish children found their relatives or foster homes among Haifa's large Rumanian Jewish community.

From Haifa the Polish refugees who had come with the Lochs from Bucharest were transferred to a much larger camp outside Tel-Aviv. Sydney was given a liaison post with the British Army, and Joice spent the rest of World War II running what became known as the Camp of a Thousand Orphans.

When Hitler broke his pact with Stalin and invaded Russia in June

1941, Stalin joined the British in the war against Hitler. His huge slave labour force of transported Poles then became an embarrassment. Stalin gave orders to release all Polish prisoners from Siberian labour camps, and the Lochs' Polish refugees from Operation Pied Piper were eventually joined by a cohort of starving Polish orphans who had been held in labour camps in Siberia and used as slaves in salt mines. The International Red Cross had helped many of them to reach Iran where the Shah then helped by chartering ships to bring them to British-run Palestine. Many of these refugees included the wives and children of the more than 20,000 Polish reserve officers who, on Stalin's orders, had been shot in the head by Russian firing squads and buried in the Katyn forest and other locations.[23]

It was from this group that Joice's camp received a large intake of emaciated Polish orphans, many of whom were so weak from lack of vitamins and minerals they could hardly walk. Joice used all her skills as a writer to compose an emotive plea to the Quakers for funds. In a letter to the Quakers, she described the orphans as:

> khaki-clad midgets . . . with thin necks like wobbly stalks,
> making their heads seem larger. Their eyes burning with
> fever and starvation stand out against their white faces.
> Most are suffering from scurvy or pellagra due to vitamin
> deficiency.[24]

Joice and Sydney fought the British authorities for food and suitable clothing for the orphans, who had been issued with Army uniforms too big for them and boots too heavy for them. Practical as ever, Joice obtained supplies of rope and canvas and organised the inmates of the camp to make rope-soled canvas *espadrilles* for them. The Lochs bargained with the Palestinian owner of an orange grove for fruit to feed the malnourished children. Slowly the orphans lost their pallor and listlessness and started to gain weight and strength.

Meanwhile the British Army, which was in charge of all refugee camps, was insisting it had no funds to feed so many Poles: the Quakers or the Lochs must pay for food for 'their' refugees. By now the Lochs' relief fund was almost exhausted. If 'their' Polish women and children were not to starve, the Lochs would have to confront the director of the Ottoman Bank at his headquarters in Jerusalem. So taken was he by the story of their escape, he agreed to allow them enough credit to feed and clothe 'their' refugees for the duration of the war.

As they had done in the camps and villages around Bucharest, the Lochs arranged for instructors to give courses in engine maintenance, electrical repairs, bricklaying, lorry driving, sign writing and other practical trades that would help the Polish men to find work once they had emigrated from the refugee camps. Joice set up courses to benefit Polish women who would also need jobs in their new countries. They managed to place their Polish refugees in Rhodesia (now Zimbabwe), New Zealand, Britain, Australia (which only took a small number) and America.

Joice encouraged Polish refugees to stitch dolls in national costume as a means of earning a living.

For the beautiful and talented Lushya, the story was not to end happily. Lushya fell in love with an English Army officer and was given permission to travel on board a naval vessel from Haifa to join her fiancé in England. The ship hit a German mine and sank with no survivors. Joice grieved deeply when she heard the news.

At the end of the war, Sydney and Joice returned to work at the American Farm School near Salonika (Thessalonika), Greece, where Sydney was made head in the absence of his close friend Charlie House, who had been imprisoned by the Germans. Joice taught girls in the Farm School and they both also worked in the refugee camp in the grounds of the Farm School.

But peace had still not come to Greece, as Joice described:

> The joy of getting back was shadowed by the horror of
> the new situation. Murder was afoot — and such murder.
> For civil war had broken out in Greece . . . a war of
> extermination on the part of the poor against the deadly
> poor.[25]

Finally after eighteen months of bitter fighting and attacking the villages, the communist guerillas, or *Andartes*, were defeated and the Lochs were able to return to Pirgos, now renamed Ouranoupolis. There they helped the villagers rebuild lives shattered by the years of world war and civil war. Again Joice organised the village women into the rug-weaving cooperative, which had saved the village in the 1920s. She sold the rugs to British and American friends and brought some to Australia. She also restarted her free medical service for the villagers, and ploughed whatever income she received from writing articles and books back into the village to help fund such amenities as the services of a doctor and a road to connect them to the outside world, which were both eventually achieved.

In the winter of 1954, Sydney Loch, his health weakened by his service at Gallipoli and in Polish and Greek refugee camps, suffered a massive heart attack and died.

Joice, by now in her mid sixties, stayed on in the village of Ouranoupolis in northern Greece. Until the villagers had a supply of unpolluted water, a road and a resident doctor, she believed her work was not complete. She became 'Kyria Loch', the saviour of the village, loved, and greatly honoured by the entire community to which she selflessly devoted her energies and what little money she had.

During her long and productive life Joice Loch was awarded eleven medals and several international awards, more than any other Australian woman.

In 1924, Poland's President Pilsudski awarded Joice the Polish Gold Cross of Merit for helping homeless refugees in eastern Poland. Two years later, while working in a refugee camp in the grounds of the American Farm School near Salonika, she was awarded the Order of St Sava for work on mosquito eradication programs to prevent malaria. In 1926 Joice became the first woman to be honoured with the Greek Order of the Phoenix, a medal for 'outstanding Greeks and foreigners', for her work with refugees.

On two separate occasions, Greek authorities honoured her with various grades of the Order of the Redeemer. The first was for running free medical clinics in 'her' refugee village of Ouranoupolis. The second and higher grade of the Order was awarded for establishing a women's rug-weaving cooperative which rescued refugee villagers from penury; for this achievement she also won the Gold Medal of the National Academy for the Arts. At a time when Australia did not award its own medals, Joice was also made a Member of an Order of the British Empire for medical rescue work following an earthquake which decimated the village of Ierissos, near Ouranoupolis.

In 1940 she received the Order of Elizabeth from King Carol of Rumania for her work with Polish refugees. At an award-ceremony held in Jerusalem in 1945, just before returning to her Greek home, Joice received from the exiled Free Polish government, the Polish Gold Cross of Virtue for her organisation of Operation Pied Piper.

In 1950 she received her first Order of Beneficence from the King of Greece for reviving the Pirgos rug-making cooperative. A second and higher grade of the Order was awarded over a decade later for funding a supply of unpolluted water for the villagers of Ouranoupolis.

Joice also received several awards from the International Red Cross.

Joice died in 'her' village, at the ripe old age of 95, loved and honoured by everyone. By now Ouranoupolis had become a thriving port bringing travellers to the monasteries of Mount Athos. The village closed down completely over three days for her funeral: people wept openly in the streets. In his funeral oration, Orthodox Bishop Kallistos Ware proclaimed Joice Loch 'among the most outstanding women of the twentieth century'.

The tower of Prosforion, Joice's home in Ouranoupolis, has been restored by the Byzantine Museums Authority, and plans are afoot to open a Joice Loch museum inside the tower to commemorate her life and work.

Ingham in North Queensland, birthplace of Joice Loch, has honoured her with a brass plaque in the Botanic Gardens. At the dedication ceremony, Alexander Freeleagus, Queensland Consul for Greece, placed the Greek flag beside the plaque.

Once totally unknown in Australia, slowly the fame of this remarkable Australian is increasing. Her story is being used by the author to raise funds for the work of Austcare, which has offices in every state capital. This work continues today. Donations for refugee programs will be gratefully received by Austcare in memory of Joice Loch.

The full story of Joice NanKivell Loch is told by the author in *Blue Ribbons, Bitter Bread* (Pirgos Press). The book is distributed by Scribo Group, French's Forest, Sydney, and can be ordered from leading bookshops. It is now an e-book obtainable from www.smashwords of amazon.com or sony and titled *Joice Loch, the woman who rescued 1,000 Poles and Jews from the Nazis and saved a Greek village from starvation* by Susanna de Vries.

Her heroism, courage and humanitarian achievements are unique.

CHAPTER 11

COURTESY SYLVIA (MUIR) McGREGOR.

Sister Sylvia Muir

1915 – 1999

Member of the Order of the
British Empire
British Campaign and Service
Medals

COURTESY SYLVIA (MUIR) McGREGOR.

Sister Vivian Bullwinkel

1915 – 2000

Member of the Order of the British
Empire
British Campaign and Service
Medals
Officer of the Order of Australia
Royal Red Cross Medal
Florence Nightingale Medal

COURTESY J. GRIFFITHS.

Sister Joyce Tweddell

1916 – 1995

British Campaign and Service
Medals

Sister Betty Jeffrey

1908 – 2000

Officer of the Order of Australia
British Campaign and Service
Medals

And Other 'Paradise Road' Nurses

In 1996, when I came to write their stories,[1] Joyce Tweddell was dead but Sylvia (Muir) McGregor, Betty Jeffrey and Vivian (Bullwinkel) Statham were still alive.

Sylvia, who had always refused to talk to journalists, agreed to tell me about her years as a prisoner of the Japanese. She knew that her breast cancer was advanced, and each week an ambulance took her for treatment at Brisbane's Wesley Hospital, which is very close to my home.

We agreed to meet in the hospital's café following each treatment session but after six weeks Sylvia was too ill to continue with our interviews. Aware she had only a short time to live she spoke frankly to me about her war experiences, the sexual harassment of nurses by Japanese guards, those women captives who had agreed to become 'comfort women', and her feelings about the Japanese captors who had refused to provide the medicines that would have prevented her closest friend from dying.

As Sylvia spoke to me, it became increasingly obvious how the nurses' deep loyalty to each other had enabled them to endure horrors, hardships and privations that might have caused psychiatric breakdown among women who were less stable, disciplined and courageous.

In spite of Sylvia's Christian faith, with its precepts to forgive, and her wish to put the past behind her, it became clear that she had not come to terms with her emotions. Neither did she seem to realise the underlying reasons why Colonel Yamasaki had encouraged the camp guards to treat the women in such brutal fashion. Under the ancient Japanese code known as *bushido*, warriors (*samurai*) were taught to despise anyone who did not fight to the death. The only other alternative for any honourable *samurai* was to commit suicide (*hari-kiri*).

The Australian Army Nursing Service (AANS) nurses were wearing uniforms when they surrendered to the Japanese soldiers. They had mistakenly believed they would be treated according to the terms of the Geneva Convention. Unfortunately, the fact that they were wearing uniform and accompanied by wounded soldiers meant the Japanese to whom they had surrendered regarded them as cowards and hence without honour.

To those who embraced these old ideas, the nurses were degraded beings who could be starved and used as beasts of burden till they dropped dead.

Once the war ended and the nurses returned home they made a point of going to visit the parents of dead colleagues. When doing so Sylvia Muir, Vivian Bullwinkel and others appear to have experienced survivor guilt similar to that experienced today by people who have been involved in terrorist attacks or hijacking attempts.

GROWING UP

Sylvia Muir was born on a property near Longreach in the Queensland outback in 1915, the second year of World War I. She spent her early years on 'Aviemore', a vast and isolated cattle station where her father was employed as station manager.

Childhood memories included fierce droughts, when most of the cattle sickened and died through lack of food and water, swirling dust storms, bushfires that nearly engulfed the homestead, and Christmases when the temperature soared — all the joys and heartbreaks of the pioneering life.

Sylvia loved horses and became a fearless rider. As there was no doctor or vet for hundreds of kilometres, she learned to care for wounded animals and to treat simple ailments from reading a battered home encyclopedia of bush nursing she found on the shelf in her father's office.

Dark-haired and elfin, the little girl was taught to read and write by her mother. At the age of eight, Sylvia was sent to Rockhampton where she boarded with relatives so she could attend Rockhampton's Central Girls' School where, fortunately for her, she was taught to swim. Sylvia conquered homesickness and did well at school but always loved returning home for the holidays.

Sylvia was one of a large family so there was never much money, but her mother valued education and books and insisted the little girl read a great deal. At that time, nursing and teaching were two of the few occupations considered suitable for bright girls who needed to earn a living.

'I'm going to nurse overseas if there's another war. Then I'll come back and marry a grazier and have four sons,' Sylvia told her mother, who hated war, as several male relatives had been killed in the trenches in World War I.

Armed with her leaving certificate, Sylvia enrolled as a trainee nurse at the Brisbane General Hospital. She was an attractive, extroverted girl who made friends easily. Sylvia's best friend was Pearl Mittelheuser, known as 'Mitz'. Her other close friends were Joyce Tweddell, ('Tweedie') and Florence Trotter ('Flo').[2]

As enthusiastic young nurses they enjoyed their training at the Brisbane General Hospital (now the Royal Brisbane Hospital), shared rooms in the spacious Lady Lamington Nurses' Home, attended parties and dances, but worked very hard.

Sylvia gained her midwifery certificate and worked as a nurse in Townsville and in the sugar town of Ingham, where, for a year, she was both district nurse and local midwife.

After finishing her training at the Brisbane General Hospital, Joyce did additional training as a radiographer but decided she would continue as a nurse.

In 1940, Sylvia, Joyce and their group, enlisted in the AANS. Although Sylvia was the minimum twenty-five years of age, Joyce at twenty-four was so determined to join the Army that she raised her age to gain admittance.

Sylvia, Joyce, Mitz, Flo and another nurse, 'Mickey' Syer, were posted to Redbank Military Hospital for further training. Like all AANS nurses they received a small uniform allowance, which was not enough to pay for their mess kit and outfits, which cost them almost a month's pay. Soldiers and officers were instructed to address them as 'Sister'. They were given the honorary rank of lieutenant and permission to use the Officers' Mess but ordered not to fraternise while off-duty with 'other ranks'. (They were never formally gazetted as officers, however, which did not help them when they were captured by the Japanese, who showed them no respect whatsoever.)

lC lC lC

Vivian Bullwinkel (or 'Bulli' to close friends) was born in Kapunda in South Australia. At the age of twelve, she went to live in Broken Hill, where her father worked in the accounts department of South Mine. After leaving Broken Hill High School she tried without success to get jobs in several banks but was persuaded by her widowed mother to become a nurse instead.

Vivian began her nursing training at Broken Hill Hospital, aged eighteen. Initially Vivian had no great commitment to nursing. While she enjoyed the challenge of learning new things she saw it more as a way of earning a living and gaining independence. However, she soon found she had a natural aptitude for it and went on to nurse at Hamilton in the Western District of Victoria and later at Melbourne's Jessie McPherson Hospital. At the Jessie McPherson Hospital, Vivian greatly admired the matron, Irene Drummond, for the way she ran such a happy hospital so efficiently, and she became very fond of the older woman.

Vivian may have been shy and reserved but she had a warm, generous personality. While a trainee nurse she received several proposals of marriage but had no intention of settling down before she had seen something of the world.

In May 1941, Vivian enlisted in the AANS, as nurses were urgently needed in wartime. She was sent to the Army base at Puckapunyal, 100 kilometres north of Melbourne, from where she hoped to be posted overseas.

ℓℓ ℓℓ ℓℓ

Betty Jeffrey, always known by her friends as 'Bet' or 'Jeff', was a tall, athletic young woman born into a family of six children. Her father was a manager with the postal service and the family moved around a great deal for his work. Betty attended schools in Tasmania, Queensland and Victoria.

From childhood onwards Betty kept a diary. She was a good writer with a lively sense of humour and extremely intelligent. However in the 1930s few young women received tertiary education, which was seen as the prerogative of men.

After leaving school Betty took a shorthand and typing course and became a secretary but soon tired of the monotony of office work. She felt restless, dreamed of travelling overseas but lacked the money to do so. In 1935 Betty applied to become a trainee nurse at Melbourne's Alfred Hospital, hoping that eventually she might get a nursing job on an ocean-going passenger liner.

As a late entrant to nursing, Betty had turned thirty by the time she finished her training, somewhat older than most of her fellow trainees. Like Vivian, she did her midwifery certificate in Melbourne.

In 1940, aware that the Australian Army was short of nurses, Betty joined the AANS. She was assigned to 2/10th Australian General Hospital (AGH) and left Melbourne for Malacca aboard the *Zealandia* in May 1941.

READY FOR ACTION

On 25 August 1941, Sylvia, Mitz and Joyce, nine other nursing sisters, two radiographers and two doctors (also assigned to the 2/10th AGH) left Brisbane on the SS *Wanganella,* bound for Melbourne, where they picked up the main troopships and an escort of destroyers.

Boarding the *Wanganella* in Melbourne was a group of nurses with the newly raised 2/13th AGH, to which Sylvia was also assigned. They included Vivian Bullwinkel — as Betty Jeffrey would later describe her, 'a tall, slim girl with very fair straight hair, cut short, and blue eyes'[3] — and Vivian's close friend Wilma Oram. The 2/13th would later be commanded by Matron Irene Drummond.

The Brisbane contingent had been led to believe they were going to the Middle East. However, one morning they were amazed to find all the other ships in the convoy had vanished. The *Wanganella* was steaming towards the Far East instead.

The hospital where they were to work was not ready to receive them, so Mitz, Sylvia, Joyce, Vivian and some of the others were briefly seconded to the 19th AGH on the Malay Peninsula in the picturesque colonial town of Malacca, where Betty had been posted.

There the Australian nurses had the time of their lives. Living in a military garrison, the younger prettier nurses were in great demand and constantly invited to dances and tennis parties by the single officers.

The girls worked hard and played hard, glad to escape from the conventions whereby young women saved for their glory boxes and married early. Yet these high spirited young women were protected by the extremely strict conventions that surrounded nurses on duty and off.

All the younger nurses, including Sylvia, enjoyed male attention: flowers and phone calls from young officers inviting them to dances and dinners, swimming parties and fancy dress parties. As far as they were concerned, marriage could wait. Wartime was a crazy time. No one made long-term plans.

One patient on Sylvia's ward was a tall, broad-shouldered soldier from Queensland named Colin McGregor, who was suffering from a severe case of prickly heat. The boys in the beds around Colin were all competing for the attentions of the prettiest nurses, but he warned them to lay off ogling Sister Muir. He was in love with her and once the war was over he would ask her to marry him.

Part of Colin's treatment was to lie face-down on his bed while Sylvia rubbed his back and shoulders to reduce the severe inflammation caused by prickly heat. If the rash was too bad she would paint it with iodine. Once Mitz had to do this for him and as a joke she painted 'I love Sylvia Muir' on his back, amid roars of laughter on the ward.

Betty Jeffrey and a colleague in 1941.

One day Colin followed Sylvia out to the sluices and right there among the bedpans told her he was in love with her. Sylvia was most surprised. She had hardly paid any attention to him — in fact, she knew his lean muscular back far better than his face.

She told Private McGregor that she liked him but at this stage in her life she was not looking for a serious relationship.

Colin smiled down at Sylvia. She never forgot how he replied calmly and confidently, 'Once the war's over, I'll find you, no matter *where* you are. Then I'll propose properly in much nicer surroundings than this.'

Sylvia was touched by his faith that they would both get through the war but was fairly certain their paths would never cross again.

The following day Colin's back was better. The medical officer discharged him as cured and he returned to his regiment which was by now 'up country'. Sylvia put the good-looking soldier from Queensland out of her mind.

On 8 December 1941, Japanese assault troops landed in northern Malaya near Kota Baharu. Betty Jeffrey described in her journal how 'when [war] did come . . . our group were right in the thick of it. Early in the New Year our [Malacca Army] Hospital was forced to evacuate to Singapore.'[4]

Back in Singapore, by 10 January 1942, the returned nurses under the charge of Matron Olive Paschke found themselves also working alongside Vivian's old colleague, Matron Irene Drummond, and her staff, turning the buildings of Oldham Hall School and St Patrick's School into hospitals.

As more and more wounded soldiers arrived, the hospital expanded and took over adjacent private houses. All leave was cancelled and the nurses found themselves working increasingly longer hours to cope with the influx.

Yet morale was high. They were part of a close-knit and disciplined team. Life for the Australian nursing sisters on the tropical island of Singapore was far more comfortable than for those serving in war-torn Europe. Similarly for the men. Those single officers lucky enough to have been posted to Singapore seemed to Sylvia to be obsessed by the seemingly endless round of cricket matches, golf, cocktail parties, fancy dress balls and amateur theatricals. They continued to believe the myth that Singapore was safe because the Japanese were too short-sighted to shoot straight.

No defences had been constructed on the vulnerable north-west of Singapore island. Everyone thought the Japanese would attack by sea from the south and could easily be beaten off.

However, throughout January the retreat of British forces down the Malay Peninsula continued. The seemingly unstoppable force of Japanese soldiers could apparently live on a handful of rice a day and carried no unnecessary equipment to impede their progress southwards. Some even travelled by bicycle.

On 31 January, the causeway between Singapore and the Malay mainland was blown up. With their guns trained on the sea rather than the land, this came as a huge shock to the garrison.

The nurses were working hard when the sirens sounded a warning.[5] Japanese planes flew overhead and bombed the docks: chaos and confusion reigned. The RAF could not muster nearly as many planes as the Japanese. By now the Japanese artillery had arrived on the far side of the Strait of Johor from where they were shelling selected targets on the island of Singapore.

ESCAPE FROM SINGAPORE

In early February 1942 the British began the process of evacuation. Betty Jeffrey recalled how 'on 10 February, six of the sisters left early on a Chinese hospital ship taking wounded patients with them'.[6] The following day a second group left to board the SS *Empire Star*, which would manage to take them to Australia, although the Japanese bombed it on two occasions.

Betty and Sylvia both pointed out that in spite of the danger there was no panic among those nurses who remained. They wished to stay with their patients rather than leave.

The next day, the remaining nurses were told they were all to be evacuated. They must be ready to leave at a moment's notice. Yet, however great the danger, the Australian nurses did not *want* to be evacuated. They did not want to walk out on wards full of badly wounded soldiers and said as much to Matron Paschke, who pleaded on behalf of all the nurses to be allowed to stay with their patients.

The military authorities, being aware that the Japanese would soon be surrounding the hospital, refused to listen. Plans for evacuation had been made: the nurses had to leave by whatever boats were available.

Some wounded men, fearing the Japanese would gang-rape the nurses as they had done in Hong Kong, urged them to go. Others, especially those who were badly injured, were distressed to see them leave.

'Whatever the risk, I just hated having to leave my patients,' Sylvia said, still emotional as she remembered it. 'Especially since in hindsight we realised we would all have been far better off had we only stayed in Singapore.'

Matron Paschke gathered her nurses together and gave out white armbands with red crosses printed on them, to wear in case they were caught by the Japanese. Sylvia and the other nurses grabbed a few personal belongings and stuffed them into their handbags. Flo Trotter snatched up a pair of scissors (precious objects during their imprisonment). Sylvia took a few pencils and a notebook.

The nurses were given backpacks containing iron rations, field dressings, morphine and other medical supplies before they scrambled into the waiting ambulances and set off for the port area. Meanwhile, Japanese planes zoomed overhead. As they drove through the Chinese quarters buildings were burning all around them and thick black smoke was pouring from the oil terminal.

At the docks bombs were falling on the warehouses or 'godowns', and finding suitable ships on which to evacuate the remaining nurses was not easy. The port and the dockyard were in chaos. Civilians panicked as they hunted for a ship — any ship at all — on which they could leave what they now saw as a doomed island. Enemy planes screamed overhead: wives bade sad goodbyes to husbands and frightened children howled as they farewelled their fathers.

Amid the chaos, the Australian nurses and Matrons Paschke and Drummond were ferried out to a relatively small yacht flying the Red Ensign. The date of their departure — 12 February 1942 — would be one Sylvia, Vivian, and other survivors would remember.

The nurses, outwardly calm in their uniforms and white headdresses, helped the women civilians and their children climb on board. In the crisis all available yachts had been pressed into service, including the SS *Vyner Brooke*, a small vessel designed and built for Sir Charles Vyner Brooke, the former 'rajah' (white ruler) of Sarawak, to take guests on pleasure cruises round the islands. Into this yacht were jammed over two hundred people — British Army wives and children, wounded soldiers and the Australian nursing sisters.

The *Vyner Brooke* had no food aboard and a relatively small water tank. It had only two lavatories or 'heads' and one washbasin. Sylvia and Joyce, who had spent a lot of time on boats in Queensland realised there were not nearly enough lifeboats should they be bombed by the Japanese.

Sylvia described the scene:

> In our group there were sixty-five nurses. Only twenty-
> four would survive but of course no one knew that at the
> time. We each carried a haversack with tinned food in it
> and we were wearing our working uniforms, grey with
> short sleeves. When we got on board, we pooled our food
> because the ship had no provisions. There were about two

hundred civilian women and some children, some elderly men, and some selected service personnel. The crew consisted of Malays and some survivors from the *Prince of Wales*, which had been sunk.

Well, we were briefed and told that in case of bombing we were to go below decks and obey instructions from the ship's officers. The mood was calm because we were all sort of stunned. The overall enormity of the experience was just too much to take in at the time. We'd been working hard and I suppose we were all desperately tired. Fortunately, the good old Australian trait of humour emerged and this helped break the tension. I remember we had lifeboat drill and the chief officer said that the nurses were expected to get everyone safely overboard before we left ourselves.[7]

Once again Matrons Paschke and Drummond took charge, outlining the procedures should they have to abandon ship. Matron Paschke had drawn a plan allocating places in the two lifeboats to the children and those mothers who could not swim. She warned the adults that, in an emergency, they should remain calm in order to save their children. Matron Drummond insisted that the captain fly a flag with a red cross on it to demonstrate there were nurses on board.

Space was severely limited. At night there was not even enough room to lie flat on deck, which meant everyone was short of sleep.

The yacht moved slowly ahead. Sylvia thought they were heading for Colombo, the capital of Ceylon (now Sri Lanka). Some optimists even believed the tiny overloaded yacht would attempt to reach Australia. They zigzagged a slow course, the captain worried about the dangers of mines.

Two days after leaving Singapore, Japanese aircraft spotted them. They were by now in the Bangka Strait, off the Indonesian island of Sumatra. The planes strafed the *Vyner Brooke* with gunfire, deliberately aiming for the yacht's lifeboats, which were damaged but still useable.

Sylvia and several civilian women received shrapnel wounds but Betty and Vivian survived unscathed. The medical supplies and bandages were stored below and unreachable so Sylvia tore up her petticoat and hastily bandaged her wounded arm and the wounds of several civilians. The yacht was in chaos, women and children screaming and yelling, many of them injured. As the yacht started to list alarmingly, canvas life jackets were given out by the crew.

The planes circled and returned. A bomb exploded in the water near where Sylvia and Mitz were standing. The force almost knocked them off their feet. As it exploded, a wall of water rocked the yacht. Mitz grabbed Sylvia's good arm with one hand and the rail with the other. A second plane whined above them and they ducked for cover. The yacht rocked again as a bomb exploded. A third bomb landed on the funnel and exploded in the engine room below, killing several of the crew and setting the vessel on fire.

Amid the mayhem, the nurses remained calm. They helped the aged and women and children into the lifeboats, which the crew managed to lower from davits into the sea below. Rafts, duckboards, loaded kitbags — absolutely anything that would float — were thrown overboard to act as emergency life rafts.

By now the *Vyner Brooke* was listing badly to starboard and smoke and fumes were everywhere. There was no time to lose. Sylvia put on her life jacket with difficulty, kicked off her shoes and jumped into the sea, blood pouring from her wounded arm as she hit the water. She was a good swimmer and had won many swimming prizes at school, so the prospect of a long swim with only one good arm did not concern her unduly. What really worried her was that sharks could be attracted by the scent of blood.

Betty and several other nurses slid down ropes into the water and received severe rope burns which tore all the skin away from their fingers and palms. Others dived or, like Joyce, held their noses and jumped into the sea. Soon Betty's hands became badly swollen, causing her great pain, but she managed to clamber onto a floating raft.

In spite of the pain from her arm, Sylvia tried to swim against the strong current that was taking them further out to sea. She stayed afloat for several hours, exhausted by the effort. She could not have lasted much longer, but fortunately she was saved by being hauled into one of the lifeboats by Mitz.

On board Sylvia's badly damaged lifeboat, a soldier took the tiller and told the passengers that since the engine had been damaged a makeshift sail was necessary if they were ever to reach land. He was shirtless like the rest of the men aboard. Would two of the nurses sacrifice their uniforms which could be buttoned together for a sail?

It was no time for false modesty. Sylvia and another nurse undressed then buttoned their pale grey dresses together and watched them flap in the breeze as the lifeboat picked up some speed. The two girls sat there in their underwear trying to look unconcerned and hoping they would not get too sunburned.

The sail worked well for some time and they made good progress before the lifeboat was becalmed in a gigantic oil slick. By now the boat was dangerously low in the water. Some of the nurses attempted to plug the jagged shell holes with their pants but without much success. Sylvia, having no outer garments, kept her pants on and attempted to bail out the lifeboat with an old tin but the water kept rising. The boat was soon so low in the water it was time to take to the sea again.

> We saw a raft with men and women in uniform aboard, and made for it. It was overcrowded and so, for the next sixteen hours, I used my good arm to hang onto a trailing rope at the side of the raft. The worst thing was being thirsty and surrounded by sea water but knowing I could not drink it or I would hallucinate and die.

For some time this raft stayed afloat but eventually it too started to tilt dangerously. One nurse sighted ships in the far distance. The rest of them raised a faint cheer, thinking it must be the British Navy come to their rescue. However, as the ships approached Sylvia realised these were *Japanese* warships. The Japanese ignored the perilously tilted raft and the waving people, presumably believing that if they did not help them, the occupants would drown or die of thirst.

But they did not drown. Instead, they drifted on through the night. Those who had been burned or wounded by shrapnel were in a bad way. Some were hallucinating. As night fell, they heard the groans of the dying on other rafts floating around them or in the water. It was like a scene from Dante's *Inferno*.

Sylvia recounted seeing a raft holding Matron Paschke and five nurses with babies and toddlers on their laps. It seemed dangerously low in the water. A strong current swept them past Sylvia whose attention was distracted by a crying child. When she looked up again the raft with Matron Paschke and the other sisters had disappeared. None of the nurses or the children were ever seen again.[8]

Watching them disappear also were Betty Jeffrey and Iole Harper, a nurse from another unit whom Betty had never met before. Betty and Iole had left the raft Matron Paschke was on to swim alongside and therefore lighten the load. The current that swept Matron Paschke's boat away somehow missed Betty and Iole. The girls swam together for hours until they were eventually carried into the mud and mangroves of Bangka Island.

There was little respite for them here, however, as they swam up tidal streams to search for fresh water. They injured themselves on the mangrove roots and spikes. As night fell they floundered amongst the mudflats and mangroves, trying to keep ahead of the rising tide until daylight. The next day they swam again. That night they found a river to swim up and eventually saw signs of a native village ahead. When finally they were rescued by Malay fishermen, they had spent three exhausting days in the water.

ℓℓ ℓℓ ℓℓ

The day after she had watched Matron Paschke disappear, the raft Sylvia was on and its cargo of thirsty, exhausted nurses and wounded soldiers floated ashore at Muntok. Although they did not know it at the time, they had landed on Bangka Island, on the far side of the Bangka Straits offshore from Sumatra. Near them was a pier full of Japanese soldiers who had disembarked from the very same ships that had ignored the nurses' cries for help the previous night.

Sylvia was horrified that she would have to face the soldiers while she was wearing only bra and pants. The nurses had been told terrible stories about Japanese soldiers pack-raping British nurses on the mainland. Would this be their fate?

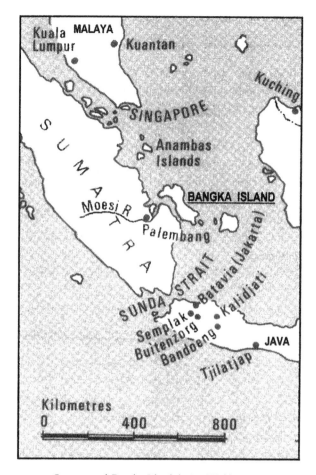

Sumatra and Bangka Island during World War II.

'We'd been warned in Singapore to keep our uniforms and Red Cross armbands on if we were captured,' Sylvia explained. 'But in my case that was impossible.'

On the wharf they were surrounded by leering, jeering Japanese soldiers pointing at them gleefully. Sylvia, expecting to be raped or shot, had already made her peace with God. They were not assaulted, however, but lined up and marched off to a hot and airless cinema. For another six hours they were held without any food, while the Japanese discussed what to do with them. At least they had cold water from a hand basin in the cinema's cloakroom.

By now other rafts were arriving with nurses, including Joyce, as well as English soldiers and civilians and their children. They too were brought under guard to join them in the cinema while their fate was discussed. There was no chance of escape as they were guarded by two armed soldiers. Having followed orders to remove their shoes before they jumped from the *Vyner Brooke* they were also barefoot. Those girls who had been on the rafts had bad cases of sunburn and some were feverish.

The nurses were starving and very thirsty as by now their water supply had been cut off by the Japanese. Towards nightfall they were brought a bucket of water, to which a little rum and sugar had been added. A second bucket containing boiled rice arrived, plus the news that Singapore was now in Japanese hands. All British and Australian soldiers there had been taken prisoner, they were informed by a Japanese guard who spoke a little English.

Bangka Island was rich in tin deposits. Before the Japanese occupied it, Dutch colonists had prospered from mining the metal. Rickety wooden barracks had housed the coolies imported from China to work the mines. These were now empty and the Dutch in captivity. It was to these dirty unsanitary buildings with their open sewers that Sylvia and her fellow nurses were eventually transferred.

VIVIAN AND THE BANGKA ISLAND MASSACRE

Unlike Sylvia and Joyce, who were strong swimmers, Vivian could not swim well. Later, she told me her story of the shipwreck.

> I was wearing a life jacket in which I had no faith
> whatsoever. However, after jumping ship I was astounded
> to find myself coming to the surface again. I'd read
> somewhere that the first thing you did was get away from
> a sinking ship as quickly as possible. It was a sunny
> tropical day, waving palms in the distance and very much
> like a travel poster — if it hadn't been for the gunfire and
> the sinking ship and people floundering for their lives.
> I saw an upturned boat in the distance with people
> clinging to it, so I dog-paddled over there. We all looked
> back and saw the ship roll over on top of some lifeboats

— though we saw one get away — and then the poor old
Vyner Brooke had gone and I realised Sister [Mona] Wilton
who could not swim had not jumped and must have gone
down with the yacht.

It was all over in fifteen minutes. We began to paddle
and push and jolly the upturned boat towards an island
which, before the attack, we'd guessed was about 16
kilometres away. The chief engineer took control. Finally,
we got ashore at about ten o'clock that night. When we
were on the beach, someone pointed out that the water
had probably been infested with sharks but, as someone
else said, all the bombing and so on had probably driven
them away.[9]

The boat carrying Vivian, Matron Irene Drummond and others
had floated ashore at what they would later learn was Radji Beach
on Bangka Island.

Among the twenty-three AANS sisters on Radji Beach were
some who were badly wounded. Also on the beach were the
surviving crew members from the *Vyner Brooke*. While Vivian and
other nurses tended the wounded, others gathered driftwood and lit
a bonfire, hoping any other survivors would see it and join them.
They also found a spring of fresh water at which to slake their thirst.
Soon they were joined by a second raft containing twenty-five
British soldiers and a group of British wives and children and more
shipwrecked nurses who had been saved by clinging to floating
spars or duckboards.

Vivian described the scene:

The older civilians were beginning to show signs of strain
and the children were getting a bit tearful because they
hadn't had a meal for about twenty-four hours. It was
decided that a party would go inland, find a village and
try to get help. The chief officer and five of the *Prince of
Wales* crew and five women, of whom I was one, went
inland and found a village. The local people said no, they

couldn't help because the Japanese had arrived and it was worth more than their lives to be seen helping us. So we went back to the beach.

On the Monday morning, the chief officer called everyone together and said, 'These are the facts: we can't get away from the island, we haven't any food, but we've got plenty of fresh water from a spring. We can either give ourselves up to the Japanese or we can stay put.'

A vote was taken, and it was unanimous that we couldn't do any good staying there. The only alternative was to give ourselves up, and although we service personnel knew that the Japanese hadn't been taking prisoners in Malaya, we realised that there were so many civilian lives to think of as well as the wounded men. Then the chief officer and two of the *Prince of Wales* crew volunteered to go and contact the Japs and tell them there was a party of us on the beach. The nurses all put on their Red Cross armbands to protect them. I felt chilled as I remembered the words of an officer in Singapore: 'You can't put any faith in your Red Cross armbands because you're fighting an enemy that doesn't play cricket!'[10]

The chief officer and two of the crew and most of the women and children went off to find some Japanese to whom they could surrender.

Some of the nurses stayed on the beach, trying to construct rough stretchers on which to carry the injured men. On Matron Drummond's instructions they fashioned a crude cross from driftwood to highlight the fact they were non-combatants under the terms of the 1906 Geneva Convention to which they hoped the Japanese would adhere.

After an hour one of the crew returned accompanied by a Japanese officer and fifteen armed soldiers. He told the group on the beach that the Japanese had taken the women and children prisoner. The senior officer from the second raft obeyed the rules of war and informed his soldiers they should give the Japanese officer their ranks and serial numbers. He then formally asked that they be taken prisoner according to the Geneva Convention. The officer spoke little English and ignored the request. He held a brief conference with his men. Then, without warning, the Japanese soldiers rounded up those soldiers who could walk and marched them away over a bluff, leaving the wounded men on their stretchers behind. They disappeared from the view of the nurses, who sat on the sand in a state of shock, waiting to see what would happen to them and their patients.

From around the bluff came the sound of distant gunfire. No one said a word. There seemed nothing they could say or do. Five minutes later, the soldiers returned grimly wiping their bayonets and cleaning their rifles. The soldiers now made signs to the nurses that they were to walk into the sea. Vivian described Matron Drummond calling out, 'Girls, I love you all and I'm proud of you. Walk into the water with your chins up. Don't be afraid.' For the rest of her life those words would haunt Vivian.

The group obeyed.

> No-one panicked. We marched ahead with our chins up
> until we were waist-deep in water. Matron Drummond,
> Sister Casson and Sister Wight, injured when the ship
> went down, were killed by the water's edge.[11]

Vivian did not cry out but thought how sad it was that her mother would never know what had happened to her.

The other nurses were equally stoic. No one whimpered, cried or screamed. Some girls prayed aloud as they stood in shallow water and waited for the Japanese to shoot them in the back.

Vivian was near the end of the line on the far left between her friends Alma Beard and Jenny Kerr. She thought how strange it was that such a terrible thing could happen in such a beautiful place. She heard the *rat-tat-tat* of machine gun fire. And then the full force of the bullet slammed into her like a giant fist, knocking her off her feet into the water. She lay there face-down, swallowing a tremendous amount of sea water until she was violently ill, expecting to die any moment.

From the stabbing pain in her side Vivian knew she must have been shot in the region of her left loin. How was it that she was still alive? Had the bullet gone through her, missing her stomach and intestines by some miracle because they had shrunk from lack of food? She dared not look at her wound, knowing she must pretend to be dead or the Japanese would finish her off with another bullet. So she stayed motionless, rocked by the waves, floating limp as a corpse, turning her head surreptitiously in order to breathe.

After what seemed like an eternity she raised her head and turned round. The waves had carried her closer to the shore in shallow water. The Japanese had disappeared. Neither Alma, Jenny nor any of her fellow nurses or Matron Drummond were to be seen. No corpses floated beside her. She was alone, sole witness to a nightmare in which the sea was awash with blood.

Vivian stood up, shivering with shock. She examined her left hip with its trail of blood and saw that her dress had two holes, one where the bullet had entered and another where it had emerged. She managed to crawl up the beach and into the surrounding jungle, where she hid among the thick tropical vegetation, a little away from the track that led to the village.

The pain from her wound was intense and, feeling light-headed, she slid in and out of consciousness. When she awoke it was dark. She dozed off again and it was light when next she awoke. She thought about going down to the spring for a drink of water but felt too exhausted. Vivian drifted off again but awoke as soldiers passed very close to her hiding place, returning in single file to the beach, doubtless hunting for survivors. With a shock she realised that had she gone to the stream for that drink they would have killed her.

The question going round in Vivian's mind was why had *she* been spared. Why her and not Matron Drummond, who would have known exactly what to do and was far more worthy of being saved?

Vivian waited for another hour to make certain the Japanese had gone. Then she made her way slowly back to the spring and had a drink of fresh water. Suddenly a male voice with a strong Yorkshire accent asked, 'Where've *you* been, Nurse?'

The voice turned out to belong to Private Pat Kingsley, who had been one of their stretcher cases and been bayoneted on the beach. He had managed to crawl to a fisherman's hut and take shelter. One of his arms had been badly wounded and he had lost a great deal of blood. He had also received a bayonet wound to his side but by some miracle he too was still alive.

Vivian had nothing to dress Private Kingsley's wounds but bathed them in salt water. Then he wanted to return to the fisherman's hut but Vivian convinced him that it was safer to stay in the jungle. Somehow they managed to walk back up the beach and into the surrounding jungle. She pulled bark off a tree and wrapped it round his wounds as best she could. She did nothing to her own wound, believing that the long immersion in salt water would act as a disinfectant.

They lived in the jungle for twelve days, eating berries they thought would not be poisonous and some grass. Vivian brought Pat Kingsley fresh water from the spring. On her trips to the beach she saw bloated corpses of the nurses washed up by the sea. But as Vivian and Private Kingsley lacked the necessary strength to bury them, they lay there undisturbed, rotting away in the tropical heat.

Finally, they were so hungry they managed to walk as far as the village. A woman took pity on them and gave them a handful of boiled rice and a few small fried fish. However, the men, doubtless terrified the Japanese would kill them if they knew they had helped their enemies, drove them away with menaces.

By now they were very weak with hunger. Eventually they decided it was better to be shot by the Japanese than die slowly from starvation.

As it was Private Kingsley's thirtieth birthday they waited for another day before surrendering. They spent the time telling each other stories about their lives. The next morning they set off very slowly along the track to give themselves up.

They were found by a naval officer and taken to Muntok by car for questioning. Vivian and Private Kingsley had already agreed that neither of them should mention the massacre on the beach, only too aware that in order to cover the evidence of their crimes the Japanese would shoot them as well.

Fortunately, Vivian had found an old water bottle with a leather strap on the beach. She slung the bottle over her shoulders so it covered the bullet hole in her bloodstained uniform and answered the questions the Japanese put to her as to how many troops were in Singapore by saying that as a nurse she knew nothing at all about troop movements.

Private Kingsley and Vivian were taken to the Muntok jail, where Sylvia and the other thirty nurses were now being held, and where Private Kingsley died a few days later. Up till now Vivian had believed she might be the only one still alive out of the nurses who had left on the *Vyner Brooke*. It was a relief to see so many other survivors.

Then, out of the crowd, she heard a voice: 'It's Vivian.' Her friends were overjoyed to see her alive. They showered her with questions about what had happened to her and the other nurses. At first, fearing the guard would overhear her story and kill them all, she refused to tell them anything. Then, as they continued with their questions, her iron self-control snapped and she broke down in tears and fell into the arms of Nesta James. Between sobs, Vivian recounted the story of the massacre.

Also in the group were two Australian Intelligence officers. They warned the whole group they must *never* mention the massacre at any time or they could all be shot. So during the three long years of their captivity, the massacre on Radji Beach was never spoken of again.

'We had to keep Vivian's secret. We had to adapt to circumstances or die,' Sylvia told me.

AT THE COOLIE LINES

For the next three years Sylvia, Vivian and the other nurses learned the art of survival on very little food in a series of overcrowded, unsanitary prison camps. At the jail in Muntok, they were reunited with Betty and Iole.

Betty and Iole had received food and some medical attention from the Malays who rescued them, but knowing the island was in Japanese hands the women resolved to give themselves up. The Japanese soldiers to whom they surrendered brought them to Muntok and gave them some more food and water. The Japanese showed the two nurses some of their own wounded soldiers. But hands of the nurses, now wrapped in bandages, were so damaged Betty and Iole could do nothing to help.

Some time later the two nurses were led from what appeared to be the Japanese headquarters to the jail, where Betty was surprised to be hailed by a strange woman dressed in a sarong. With relief to find that others had survived the wreck of the *Vyner Brooke*, Betty recognised two of her colleagues and was soon among the rest.

The nurses and civilians women were moved and then moved again from Bangka Island to Sumatra. At times they shared accommodation with the wives and children of wealthy Dutch-Indonesian planters and colonial officials. These women tended to be rather snobbish because they had been allowed to take money, jewel cases and other luxuries into the camps with them.

Many of the Dutch women managed for years to live quite well off the proceeds of selling these various items, or off stored money hidden in pillows or bedding. They were able to buy eggs and fruit or the occasional chicken from the locals and survive, although by the second or third year of imprisonment most of their money was gone. It meant that there were two distinct castes in the camp: the haves and the have-nots. Those who had been shipwrecked had absolutely nothing other than the clothes they stood in. 'Long-distance breast stroke isn't much good for carrying luggage,' Sylvia observed wryly.

The nurses kept themselves occupied. They drew up rosters of who should cook, clean and tend to the sick. They did everything possible to earn money to buy extra food for themselves and their patients from the locals who were allowed into several of the camps to trade.

They nursed the British wives and children who had been with them on the *Vyner Brooke* and shared any food they had with them. The nurses also cared for sick Dutch-Indonesian civilians. In this vital humanitarian work they were assisted by Dutch Charitas nuns. At first the nurses cared for the sick who lay on narrow wooden platforms or *bali bali* in the huts. Eventually, the Australian nurses were allowed a building to use as a hospital, which they shared with

Dutch nursing sisters. As medicines were unobtainable, all they could dispense was care and keep the patients clean.

Many of the British were elderly and the first to fall sick and die. Although most of the British officers' wives were strong-minded women, others lacked the discipline and group loyalty that kept the Australian nurses going.

Sylvia, who had no clothes, apart from her bra and pants, and no shoes, found a trunk belonging to a planter who had returned to Holland. When she lifted the lid she found a few old books, a blank diary, several pencils, work boots and wooden clogs, and a very large thick blue woollen suit, totally unsuitable for life in the tropics. A Dutch nun took pity on her and gave her a needle and thread and Flo Trotter lent her that precious pair of nail scissors. Sylvia cut the legs off the suit and altered the waist to make herself a pair of shorts. She unpicked the lining of the jacket to turn it into a halter top and created a pair of sandals out of two strips of bark. She kept the book to record life in captivity and made little pencil drawings to illustrate her accounts.

With little money to buy additional food from the natives who came to the barbed wire fence with baskets of fruit and vegetables for sale, the nurses had to survive on meagre rations including a handful of soya beans each day. Sylvia expanded on this:

> We'd be given our rice ration in cigarette tins — enough
> for ten days at a time. The rice often contained weevils
> or rat droppings. Hunger pains were a daily occurrence.
> Food became an obsession.

All through their three years of capativity, the Australian nurses proved themselves extremely resourceful and adaptable. They were able to earn a little money by acting as nannies to the planters and mining officials' children in the camp. At times they cared for the sick children of the locals and bartered their services and their knowledge for scraps of food. Iole and Betty ran a cookery business making cakes of fried rice and selling them to the Dutch, and a kind of fish paste, made from the remnants of the meals of the Dutch women. Betty roasted fish heads and bones, pounded them to a paste and added salt and lime juice.

Any money the nurses managed to earn from child minding, cooking or sieving the weevils out of the rice rations for the Dutch–Indonesian women was spent on little luxuries, such as eggs or an ancient scrawny chicken. The nurses shared all food, and the luxuries always went to those who were the weakest.

'If you managed to find a banana you'd sell it to the Dutch women so you could buy something else you desperately needed. Then you would ask them if they would give you the skin to eat,' Sylvia told me, explaining how she and her friends would fry and eat banana skins and banana flowers — *anything* that increased their meagre diet of boiled rice and soya beans.

Always hungry, the nurses dreamed about food, talked about food, swapped recipes and pined for the roast dinners their mother had made. Most of the Australians loathed the taste of soya beans. However, hunger being a great spur to ingenuity, Sylvia and Vivian and some of the others learned how to soak the beans for days and then pound them down to make soya milk. They either drank the milk or sold it to the Dutch-Indonesian women, who gave it to their children, or made a paste from it which Betty and Iole used in the little cakes they sold.

Several nurses earned money by making straw hats from dried local grasses, while Flo, who still had her pair of nail scissors and a comb with a few teeth in it, became the camp's hairdresser. Both Flo and Betty earned money by cutting the hair of the Dutch women. Sylvia made toy kangaroos from scraps of material and sold them to the Dutch women for their children.

On a virtual starvation diet even the tallest of the nurses dropped to 6 stone (38 kg) while some weighed only 5 stone (32 kg) and now lacked resistance to disease. Red Cross parcels that had been sent from Australia by relatives convinced the nurses were still alive were either lost or stolen by their guards, with the connivance of Colonel Yamasaki, the officer in command of the camp. He was responsible for its policy of starving the prisoners and denying them medicines.

In most of their camps the living conditions were horrific. At one time the nurses were made to sleep on a sloping concrete floor beside stinking latrines used by the Japanese soldiers, who would delight in splashing them with urine. They were forced to shower under buckets of cold water in cubicles without doors while the soldiers enjoyed making lewd comments about their bodies.

The brutality of some guards was beyond belief, treating their captives worse than animals. At *tenko,* or roll call, some women had initially worn make-up until one guard (later named Lipstick Larry by the prisoners) smashed the teeth of women wearing it as a punishment. Another guard they named Rasputin would hit them with his stick at *tenko.* The guards despised their prisoners; their ancient culture of *bushido* honoured only those who fought to the death or committed suicide rather than surrending. Sylvia saw it this way:

> They treated us with disdain or indifference: many of
> them blamed us for the fact they had to guard us. They
> hoped we would die as soon as possible so they could go
> home to their families in Japan . . . They practised refined
> tortures, hoping that they would break our spirit . . . This
> was why they withheld the medicines that could have
> saved so many of us.

One of the 'refined tortures' that the guards enjoyed most was withholding food.

> If they did give us some meat or fresh vegetables, they'd
> put it down on the road outside the barbed wire around
> the camp. They knew that we knew that if we ventured
> outside the wire to get it, we'd be shot. The food that was
> ruined by the sun could have saved many nurses from
> dying of beriberi [caused by vitamin deficiencies].
>
> So instead of us eating it, that precious food would sit
> there for hours, rotting away in the boiling sun. By the time
> the guards let you go and get the vegetables, more than half
> would be ruined and stinking. Or they'd bring us a bag of
> dried soya beans and empty them on the ground or in the
> latrines, hoping to see us grovel in the dirt at their feet.

Sylvia counted those friends who died of beriberi off on her fingers: Irene Singleton, Pauline Hempsted, Shirley Gardam, Win Davis, Dot Freeman and eventually Pearl Mittelheuser (Mitz).

Colonel Yamasaki (behind his back we called him 'Saki the Sadist'), the military commander, was the man we all loathed. Saki insisted we make a low bow to any guard who spoke to us at roll call. If your bow was not low enough, you got a slap in the face. They were very good at slapping faces.

If you did anything wrong, they would stand you out in the sun for hours. One of our girls, Ray Raymont, had heart trouble. They trussed her and Val Smith up with ropes so they couldn't stand but only kneel and left them there in the blazing sun for not bowing low enough at *tenko*.

Poor Ray fainted and she lay out there in the sun for hours. We were terrified she would die. It was agonising, knowing we could do nothing or the guards would have been happy to shoot us. Eventually we got her in and both she and Val had severe sunstroke, which undoubtedly shortened their lives.

Most of those guards enjoyed being cruel. They were sadists and really took pleasure in finding ways to humiliate us . . . We stuck together and presented a stubborn, united face, insisting we were officers and they should obey the rules of war. They could jeer at us but sticking together was our only weapon against them. We vowed they would not kill us or break our spirit.[12]

As a result of being tortured, 'Ray' Raymont was never able to do heavy work again. She died in camp only a few weeks before the end of the war.

WHITE COOLIES AND 'COMFORT WOMEN'

On 2 March 1942, the nurses and their fellow captives were moved to a camp at Palembang in Sumatra, built by male internees who were soon sent elsewhere. The men at Palembang included Australian prisoners who would eventually alert the outside world to the plight of the captives. Sylvia described conditions there:

Over five hundred women and children, including Dutch, German and English women and our large group of twenty-five Australian nurses, were jammed into a barracks intended for one hundred men with only two bathrooms and lavatories among the whole group. We slept on concrete floors during the wet season. We were often ankle-deep in mud as the camp had been built on a swamp and there was no drainage. The mozzies were terrible. Most of us, including myself, got malaria and the Japanese refused to give us quinine.

Eventually we were so thin we were like X-rays, only skin and bone. They despised us, used us as white coolies, made us clean out their filthy latrines as well as our own. We were tired of cleaning shit for them and being used as slave labour for a bunch of illiterate Japanese sadists.

We had to till their vegetable garden with heavy wooden hoes but were not allowed to eat the vegetables.

We were white coolies. We had to cut wood for them, cart water for them and do all this on the most meagre of diets imaginable . . . Somehow many of us managed to survive on less than 90 calories a day. We grew sweet potatoes to eat whenever the Japs let us do so. We did better than many of the civilian women, because we had group discipline and group loyalty.

The Japs punished us for any infringement of discipline by cutting our rice rations even further. No wonder so many of us died. Can you imagine what it is like to sit beside a close friend you have known for years, holding their hands and watching them die? When Mitz died I swore I'd never forgive the Japs. Now I'm not so sure.

Each time a colleague died of malnutrition or disease the nurses would get out their stained grey uniforms, dig a grave and hold a funeral. As they grew weaker it took more and more of them to carry the coffin. The little money they had been able to earn from the Dutch planters' wives was drying up as the Dutch women themselves were running out of money.

Sylvia said:

> Somehow, we survived by helping each other. We kept up
> our morale. Our shared friendships got us through thick
> and thin. It was no good thinking about escape. What
> was the point of escaping into dense jungle miles from
> anywhere where the mosquitoes were even more lethal
> than the Japs? All that escape meant was dying even
> sooner.

Then a new ordeal arose. The nurses were ordered to 'entertain' the guards in the house the Japanese had nominated their 'social club'. Four of the youngest and most attractive women, including Joyce Tweddell and Pat Gunther, were ordered to attend the club. To protect them, a large group of nurses accompanied the selected group.

They prepared themselves for the ordeal by continuing to wear their AANS uniforms (or what was left of them) and the armbands with red crosses that Matron Paschke had given them when they left for the *Vyner Brooke*. Viv and her friend Wilma Oram rubbed dirt on their faces, Wilma and Sylvia wore men's work boots, others went barefoot or wore old sandshoes sold to them by a local trader. Some of the girls cut each other's hair close to the scalp, and a few of them even sprinkled their hair with their own urine.[13]

Sylvia recounted what happened that evening:

> Each of us made ourselves look as ugly and dirty as
> possible. Inside the club house we sat on chairs and ate all
> the peanuts and biscuits we could find, refusing to accept
> any of the alcoholic drinks they plied us with. We made
> lots of visits to the cloakroom, stole toilet paper and
> stuffed it into our knickers, as we didn't have any paper in
> our latrines. We tried to behave as though we were
> lesbians to discourage the guards.

We had agreed beforehand we wouldn't have any
alcohol to drink. When one of the Japs asked in
amazement 'What do Australian girls drink when they go
out?' Blanche Hempsted, one of the Queensland
contingent, lied 'We never drink anything but milk!',
which made several of us want to burst out laughing, in
spite of the danger we were in. Unfortunately they didn't
give us any milk.

Conversation was limited as the guards were
uneducated fishermen who only had a few phrases of
English. However, one of them could write a little
English. When it became apparent after an hour or so that
any advances were repelled and that sex was not on the
agenda he wrote: NO SEX MEANS WE'LL STARVE YOU TO
DEATH. One of the nurses wrote back laconically under
his message. OK, SO WE DIE SOONER RATHER THAN
LATER. WHAT'S THE DIFFERENCE?

Sylvia continued with amusement:

Stalemate. After a few hours of getting nowhere the Japs
in the social club seemed to abandon the idea of having
sex with us that night.

The group walked out, their heads held high. However,
outside the 'club' four Japanese officers were waiting for
them. There was a nasty struggle as they tried to take four
of the younger nurses back to their quarters. One of them
was Val Smith, who had been made to stand out in the
sun as punishment with Ray Raymont. Val was a heavy
smoker and had observed the behaviour of many patients
with TB. Val and two others now put on a hacking cough
as though she had TB, a disease the Japanese were terrified
of catching. As Val rolled around doubled up with
coughing, the officers took fright and ran away.[14]

Next morning, an angry Colonel Yamasaki sent an
interpreter to tell the nurses that the inauguration of the
club had not been a success. He insisted that next time

the nurses must take more care with their appearance and the social evenings would continue.

The nurses were horrified. Not only were they being slowly starved to death, some of them were also to be used as prostitutes or 'comfort women'. Their rank as lieutenants and their uniforms would not protect them. Sister Win Davis was chosen to go to the Officers Club and put the sisters' views that they were fellow officers, prisoners of war and should not be subjected to such indignities.[15] Win was ordered to sign a paper agreeing to the Japanese terms and one officer hissed at her, 'You no sign, you die.'

Another nurse, Sister Blanch ('Blanchie'), was called in and also refused to sign the document. Finally the officer stopped the interview, realising that these pressure techniques were getting them nowhere.

Sylvia related that for days the Japanese put enormous pressure on the group to hand over the four young nurses selected to be comfort women. They withheld their rice ration as a punishment, hoping this would make the nurses cooperate in their plan. The same tactics were applied to Dutch, Eurasian and English women captives who had no money to buy food.

> Their demands placed even more stress on the rest of us
> and now some of the guards became quite open in their
> demands that nurses would masturbate them to orgasm.
> From then onwards we slept badly, fearing the guards
> would enter our huts at night and rape us.

The supplies of sour rice and withered vegetables dried up. By now the nurses had lost half their body weight. Joyce Tweddell was the skinniest of all, and Betty and Sylvia feared Joyce's amoebic dysentery was so severe she could not live much longer. The pain of watching another close friend die was almost more than Sylvia could bear. Joyce and Mitz had become like sisters to her.

Last-minute relief occurred when a Dutchman in another camp near Palembang, who still had hidden money with which to buy food, heard of their plight and managed to smuggle a small quantity of flour into the camp. The nurses lived off that and a soup of grass and berries for several days rather than give in.

Although not all accounts of the 'comfort women' stories agree, Sylvia claimed that at a secret meeting held in the Japanese Officers' Club, four older nurses agreed to replace the younger ones and become comfort women to spare the rest of the group from being starved to death. The other nurses swore on the Bible that the names of 'the four' would never be revealed, to spare pain to them and to their relatives, and no one ever broke this promise. (At the time of writing only one of the captive nurses is still alive.)

The four women were thereafter kept in a separate house with some Dutch and British women who had also agreed to cooperate. They were given good supplies of food and nice clothes but, regarded as prostitutes by their jailers, they were repeatedly raped.

Sylvia told me this very quietly so that no one in the hospital café could overhear what she was saying. 'Those girls were truly heroic — I couldn't have done it. Mitz and I would have rather kissed a leper than a Jap, let alone have *sex* with one of them!'

After the war the survivors put out a story that Japanese demands for sexual services ceased after Dutch prisoners reported the incident to a Dutch Red Cross official who protested on their behalf. This was clearly not true because throughout the war the Japanese paid no attention to the Red Cross.[16]

THE PALEMBANG CAMP CHORAL SOCIETY

To keep their spirits up, a group of British wives and Australian nurses, including Sylvia, formed a choir which rehearsed at night. Betty joined slightly later. They used their voices to hum classical music specially adapted for them by two talented English women, Nora Chambers and Margaret Dryburgh. Dryburgh was an accomplished pianist and choir director, and Chambers was a professional violinist, with a huge knowledge of music. The choir was highly professional and their concerts did wonders for the prisoners' morale. For light relief Sylvia, who passed an audition to get into the choir, decided that for their third Christmas concert, she would change the mood, and organised a 'mock ballet' during the interval.

> A few of us who had done ballet at school put on a
> sort of comic ballet after one particular camp concert.
> I remember that I wore a short skirt of banana leaves and
> a pair of men's boots. Three of us did a comic rendering
> of the 'Dance of the Little Swans' from *Swan Lake*. We
> knew we must keep our sense of humour and laugh
> whenever possible or we were finished.

The Palembang choir continued to give concerts until the women were too weak to sing and the organisers were dead of malnutrition.

Just like the Jewish choirs that performed under leading Jewish conductors at Theresienstadt concentration camp before the organisers were sent away to Auschwitz, the Palembang choir performed inspiring music and reached a high standard of performance. Their repertoire included Ravel's *Bolero*, Dvorak's *New World Symphony*, adaptations of requiem masses by Mozart and Fauré, and the slow movement from Beethoven's *Moonlight Sonata*. Later, they added Mendelssohn's *Song Without Words*, extracts from Bach's *St Matthew Passion* and *Jesu, Joy of Man's Desiring*, music that helped to comfort them.

Hearing the choir perform meant for many of the captives that the camp, with its dilapidated shacks, seemed to fade into the background. The music took over and their spirits soared on wings of sound. Betty and Sylvia felt that singing in the choir set them free. They realised that although the Japanese might starve them to death, they could never conquer their spirit. As Sylvia related, 'Singing in the choir did wonders for us. The Jap guards couldn't understand how we could still sing after everything that had happened to us.'

'I'm Not Going to Die a Prisoner' – Sylvia Muir

The nurses were allowed to write home 'just to keep us quiet', Sylvia said bitterly. Letters had to be brief, not more than twenty-five words. Plump, well-fed Colonel Yamasaki, who ate the food in the Red Cross parcels intended for the prisoners, forbade them to mention where they were held or the terrible conditions under which they lived.

Vivian wrote a brave letter to her mother pretending they were all well and enjoying themselves, not wanting to upset her. Sylvia did the same for her parents. (After the nurses were freed they found most of their letters unposted, stored in a box in the guard room.)

A move from Palembang on Sumatra back to Muntok on Bangka Island, where their captivity had begun, took place in October 1944 and after that many more prisoners died from malaria.

Up to then the nurses had been housed in a variety of government buildings, primitive log huts or deserted coolie barracks without any protection from mosquitoes. A few people had managed to scrounge strips of mosquito netting, which they used to place over their faces at night as some protection. When anyone died they bequeathed these pieces of netting to a friend along with their ragged clothes and treasured possessions, like a comb or a sewing needle.

By now their complexions were yellowed, their faces lined and wrinkled, and many of them had lost several teeth, which made them look grotesque. When they were moved back to Bangka Island most of the group suffered from 'Bangka Island fever', a virulent form of malaria which gave them a high fever and affected coordination of their limbs. The slow painful deaths from amoebic dysentry and beriberi continued among the civilians and nurses.

The sanitation in all their camps was extremely primitive but in this particular camp on Bangka Island the latrines were dangerous, the narrow deep pits often overflowing. Using them was precarious. By now all the women captives were so thin that several of them slipped between the poles that ran across the narrow slit trench as they squatted over them. If someone fell into the pit their screams alerted the next hut. Although the unfortunate person was hauled out and buckets of water thrown over them by the nurses, each woman died from swallowing excrement.

One of Betty's most haunting descriptions in *White Coolies* records how, in January 1945, the last year of the war, Iole Harper, Vivian, Wilma Oram and Jean Ashton worked as night soil cleaners. For performing the revolting chore of cleaning out the latrine pits, these 'white coolies' were paid eight cents a day each. The nurses pooled the money they earned in order to feed the rest of their group.

Those nurses who had volunteered to be part of what they called the 'carrying squad' rose each morning at the crack of dawn to start work. Already weak and emaciated, the nurses knew the money was vital to ensure the survival of the rest of the group, who were stricken with beriberi, recurring bouts of amoebic dysentery and malaria. As nurses, they also knew the camp must be kept free of typhoid and dysentery which spread like wildfire once the latrines were allowed to overflow.

The tools of their foul-smelling trade were kerosine tins and two half coconuts shells nailed on sticks to use as scoops. Each pair of nurses was given a long bamboo pole to carry the loaded kerosine tin nearly a kilometre away from the main camp and they were ordered to bury the reeking contents in the jungle. Each nurse had to make six trips before breakfast. By the sixth trip each of them was faint with exhaustion. On one occasion the pole slipped and cracked two of Iole's ribs.

By now Betty was down to skin and bone, suffering from amoebic dysentery, which meant she absorbed very little of what she did manage to eat. She was also suffering from beriberi. Game as ever Betty wrote in her journal: 'Wish I could help them [the girls on the 'carrying squad'] but am back in bed again and down to six stone.'[17]

On 8 February Betty wrote sadly of the death from a severe bout of malaria of Ray (Wilhelmina) Raymont, who had been tortured by being left out in the burning sun for hours without water. Since friendship was so precious to all of them Betty wrote sadly 'Val Smith has lost her best friend.'[18]

In the final three months of their captivity — now at Loebok Linggau — many of the remaining twenty-six nurses were so sick and depressed they no longer cared if they lived or died.

Mitz Mittelheuser, who had saved Sylvia's life by hauling her into the lifeboat, was even thinner than the rest. She was suffering a severe case of beriberi, which covers the sufferer with painful sores and causes their limbs to swell up. Mitz lay on her bunk, resembling a

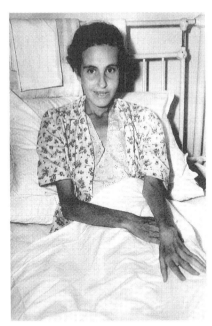

*Joyce Tweddell before incarceration on Bangka Island
and recovering in hospital in Malaya after the nurses' release at the end of the war.*

skeleton, her ribs protruding, her cheeks sunken, eye sockets hollow, covered by an old rice sack. Sylvia sat beside her in despair, trying to soothe her. Lacking medicine, all Sylvia could do was wipe the sweat from Mitz's face and limbs with a damp cloth and give her sips of water from an old milk tin to stop her dehydrating even further.

Mitz died on 18 August 1945, a date Sylvia told me she would never forget. By that time Sylvia was too weak to cry. Drained emotionally and physically, the tears would not come.

Ironically enough, three days before Mitz died, unknown to any of them, the war in the Pacific had ended. The only sign the nurses had that something was happening was reports of air raids, which they took as a sign that the Allies were advancing.

Now it seemed that it must be Joyce's turn to die. Weak as a kitten, she could hardly move her stick-thin limbs. A tall, big-boned girl, she had weighed over 10 stone (63.5 kg) at the start of their captivity. She now weighed only 4 stone (25 kg). Suffering from an advanced case of beriberi, she lay on the raised bamboo sleeping platform where Sylvia sat beside her, sponging her face and body covered with peeling skin and open sores with the same rag she had used for Mitz. Would help arrive in time to save Joyce?

Like the rest of them, Vivian was weak and emaciated and half her hair had fallen out. She was far too frail to do manual chores such as sweeping the compound or hauling water or cleaning out the sewers, all tasks which drained the prisoners of energy on their meagre diet. Vivian had saved the life of a little English girl named Betty Kennieson by nursing her through a high fever. As a result, little Betty adored Vivian and through a trader, Betty Kennieson had sold her only surviving possession, a gold bangle, which she had kept covered in tar and hidden from the Japanese. The money enabled Vivian to buy fresh limes and other foods from the natives and the pair of them to stay alive.

'THE WAR IS OVER, SISTERS'

Fearful of reprisals, the Japanese authorities kept quiet about their female prisoners on Bangka Island. Of the sixty-five sisters who had left Singapore, by late August 1945 only twenty-four were now still alive and more were admitted to hospital later that month. By now all the nurses were so wasted and weak from malaria and malnutrition they could not survive much longer.

Had there been a very senior matron to negotiate with Colonel Yamasaki they might have achieved better living conditions but Matron Drummond had died in the massacre on Radji Beach and Matron Paschke was swept out to sea. As it was, all the nurses were relatively young when they were imprisoned and therefore lacked authority in the eyes of the enemy.

In their final camp, a disused rubber plantation 13 kilometres from Loebok Linggau, they lived in leaking dirt-floored huts provided for the rubber workers. The camp was surrounded by a barbed wire fence and plagued by mosquitoes.

Fortunately for the nurses, help was at hand.

Since the Japanese now realised they were losing the war, their attitude changed. Colonel Yamasaki was aware that eventually his prisoners would be found and as the senior officer he would be held responsible for their deaths. After years without proper food and medicines, he issued orders that the nurses were to receive the parcels denied them for so long. The degrading *tenko* roll calls were abandoned.

On 24 August 1945, Sylvia's thirtieth birthday, she received what she described as 'an unexpected present'. Colonel Yamasaki summoned the prisoners and, standing up in front of them, said, 'The war is over, sisters'. With an impassive face he announced, as though past events had never happened, 'Now we can all be friends.'

Sylvia thought, 'I'm a Christian but I *can't* be friends with you. I can't forget what you did to Mitz and Ray and the others who have died. If you had given them the medicines we asked for they would still be alive.'

And then an amazing thing happened. Nesta James, as the senior nursing sister, received a telephone call. An unknown male voice told Nesta that an Australian rescue plane was searching for them and would get them out as soon as they were located. This gave the remaining nurses the strength to hang on until they were found.

To keep herself going, Vivian ticked off on her fingers the things that she wanted most when she was back home: a comb, a cup of tea and a piece of toast and butter, toothpaste, talcum powder and soap. She vowed if she ever had those items again she would never take them for granted, neither would she ever again waste food.

The day after Colonel Yamasaki's announcement, the Japanese released European male prisoners from the neighbouring camp. They arrived in the women's camp: battered men in rags and on crutches — Dutchmen, Englishmen and Scotsmen, who had once held important positions as school principals, administrators, mining engineers and rubber planters. The men were as gaunt and as thin as the women.

There were cries of joy as husbands and wives were reunited and tears as they heard of loved ones who had died. Amid the throng of those weeping with joy and sorrow the Australian nurses found themselves on the fringes of the crowd. They were acutely aware that it would be a long time before they would see their homes and their loved ones again.

THE END OF THE ORDEAL

When they were finally found by the Australian Army, the emaciated nurses resembled scarecrows in their tattered rags and homemade straw hats. Their faces were gaunt, yellowed skin stretching tight over bones, their hollow eye sockets and sunken cheeks bearing witness to malnutrition and starvation. Black holes marked the gaps where teeth had fallen out through lack of vitamins. Some of the girls had lost much of their hair and bald patches showed through lank locks.

The Army rescue team had been provided with photographs but could not recognise these walking skeletons as the carefree, jaunty girls in smart uniforms who had landed in Singapore at the outbreak of World War II.

Vivian described the scene:

> I don't know what they thought of us. We'd lost teeth. We looked awful. We heard about the atomic bombs. Later, some of us talked together and thought perhaps we'd better stay where we were. We felt frightened of the changed world we would have to cope with.[19]

The prisoners, wearing their tattered uniforms, were driven to the nearest station to Lahat airport. Such were their pride and dignity that Sylvia, Vivian and the other nurses still capable of shuffling insisted they did not need help to board the train.

Joyce Tweddell was the worst affected of the group. Before the war she had been a most attractive young woman with her magnolia complexion, dark expressive eyes and regular features. From June 1943 she was badly weakened by severe amoebic dysentery. Malnutrition had given her pellagra (caused by lack of Vitamin B), and beriberi had coarsened her complexion, darkened her hair, and given her sores all over her body and legs. By now her body was so shrivelled that her hands resembled freckled claws and her eyes looked huge in her gaunt wasted face. It seemed as if her bones might crack if she moved. She was carried to the train on a stretcher and it was feared she would die on the journey.

From Lahat airport the nurses were flown to Singapore. At Singapore airport, journalists and well-wishers pushed and jostled to take photographs of the women. 'As though we were something in a freak show,' Sylvia observed wryly.

They were taken to St Patrick's Hospital, the very place they had worked as Japanese bombs rained down on them back in 1942. There, bunches of flowers and goodwill messages awaited them.

At the sight of these starved and skeletal survivors, the nurses of St Pat's burst into tears, wondering how these poor women could have endured so much and still be alive.

One of the first things the survivors noticed was that the St Pat's nurses were wearing safari jackets and trousers. 'Women wearing trousers!' they exclaimed. 'Whatever next!'

There were also gasps of horror from the male patients — Australian survivors from Changi — when they saw twenty-four human skeletons hanging onto the banister rail in a valiant attempt to haul themselves up the stairs. The diggers asked one of the hospital nurses what had happened and when she told them, with one accord the men cried out in rage, '*We'll* get the bastards who did this to them!'

Those warm-hearted soldiers collected their dinners and took them straight up to the ward, wanting to give their own plates of steak and chips to the starving women. But a matron told them that the women would have to be on a special diet. To the survivors' indignation the precious food they had been dreaming about for years was taken away from them.

The women protested they were being starved by their own people but the medical authorities were right. What the nurses needed now was a gradual change of diet: rich food would have had a terrible effect. Initially, they could only take broth, so shrunken were their stomachs. Later, they were given a strictly controlled diet of eggs and milk, with other richer foods being introduced gradually.

As a young student nurse, Joyce had worried she was overweight. Now she was the thinnest and most scrawny, and she took the longest to recover. She weighed only 4 stone (25 kg), a stone lighter than the rest, and resembled a stick insect lying back on the pillow. Only her eyes, still beautiful, huge and luminous, reminded anyone who had known her what an attractive girl she had been. Even when she was well enough to get out of bed Joyce shuffled around like an old crone. The rest of the group were not much better.

Their bodies had an unpleasant acetone-like smell, a result of living on stale rice. It took almost a week for the smell to disappear and many months before their menstrual cycles resumed.

Provided with cotton nightdresses and dressing gowns, for the first time in many years they slept between sheets and with pillowcases, the greatest luxury they could imagine after spending years sleeping on wooden floors or narrow bamboo platforms. Another treat was a bath or a shower, complete with soap and talcum powder, things none of them had seen for years. Hairdressers and beauticians were sent for. Shampoos and manicures made them feel better and took their minds off their ailments.

Only when their shrunken stomachs could accept a normal diet could they sail home.

The nurses returned to Australia on the hospital ship *Manunda* and were overjoyed to see their families again. Meeting the press, however, was an ordeal for all of them. Everyone wanted to interview Vivian as the survivor of the massacre at Radji Beach. Although the nurses had not spoken of the event, word had nevertheless spread, as apart from Pat Kingsley, two other soldiers from the group marched over to the bluff and shot had survived.

The press popped flash bulbs into her face until Vivian told them in no uncertain terms to leave her alone: she had not seen her mother for years and was going home to catch up.

All the nurses steadfastly refused to discuss what had happened to them in the camp. Nevertheless, stories still appeared in the press about their captivity and how they had been used as slave labour by their Japanese guards.

CRIME AND PUNISHMENT IN JAPAN

After her return, Vivian initially did her best to lead a normal life, enjoying the company of friends and her mother but found it hard to disappear from the public eye.

War crimes tribunals were taking place in Germany and in Japan. Survivors of prison camps were being assembled to give evidence against their captors.

As the sole survivor of the Bangka Island Massacre, the Australian government sent Vivian to Tokyo to give evidence against the Japanese officer who had ordered the atrocity and against camp comander Colonel Yamasaki.[20] Vivian went with some trepidation, as she still felt nervous about speaking in public and was far from the accomplished performer she would become in later years.

In Japan, Vivian took the opportunity to visit the grey wasteland that had once been Hiroshima. She could not cry for the dead there either, remembering only too well the three and a half years of misery she and her friends had endured. But the sight of the devastation of what had been a large city removed all desire for revenge from her mind. She wanted justice for her friends but to rebuild the world, to make it a better place, and to make sure the young did not repeat the mistakes of their elders.

In Tokyo, in spite of her fears, Vivian turned out to be a brilliant witness at the tribunal. Cool and collected, she had written out her speech, point by point, on cards and rehearsed it carefully.

Trim and composed in her grey uniform, Vivian's voice was low but firm as she spoke into the microphone. It never faltered as she told the tribunal about the conditions under which they had been forced to live. She gave approximate dates and details of violence, such as when the nurses had their front teeth knocked out when they did not bow low enough to Colonel Yamasaki at *tenko*; of women being forced to stand out all day in the sun without water; of being made to do heavy manual labour when they could scarcely lift a hoe; of how they had been moved from camp to camp, forced to carry the heavy luggage of the Dutch prisoners, so they would weaken and die and of how the group had sustained each other.

She told the assembly of the nurses who had died of beriberi and other fevers and how the food and medicine that had been sent by the Red Cross could have saved them. She described how Colonel Yamasaki had refused to release the medicines to them; how he and his guards would jeer at their prisoners when they pleaded for the medicines and say: 'No matter — plenty room to bury them in the ground.'

During her evidence there were no tears, no histrionics. She put the facts clearly. When Vivian ended her speech she was trembling with the effort of holding her emotions in check.

Taken together with written testimonials from other nurses read out in front of the Tribunal, it was a spine-chilling portrait of Japanese scorn and hatred of their prisoners.

A far thinner Colonel Yamasaki appeared in front of the Tribunal. He was no longer the arrogant commandant but a beaten and resentful man.

He was sentenced to fifteen years' imprisonment for the ill-treatment of prisoners, mainly on the evidence provided by Vivian. Absent was Captain Orita, who had given the order to shoot the soldiers and nurses. He had been found in Russia, sent back to Tokyo to be tried but true to the cult of *bushido* committed suicide in his cell before the start of the tribunal.

LIVING AGAIN

Sylvia also received a hero's welcome and, albeit briefly, became a celebrity, something she found disconcerting. She soon discovered she had a real talent for organisation but disliked speaking in public. At a victory parade in Brisbane, Sylvia and several other nurses were driven slowly down Queen Street in an open car past cheering crowds standing six deep, which embarrassed Sylvia.

Suddenly a tall, dark, muscular man leaned over the side of the car and said, 'Sister Muir, it's me, Colin McGregor, the soldier who said he'd propose to you when the war was over. Can I see you later?' Sylvia agreed, amazed by his persistence.

Colin, she discovered, had also been a prisoner of the Japanese and they had a great number of experiences and attitudes in common. A year later Colin and Sylvia were married.

The McGregors moved from Brisbane to Bega, where Colin became a dairy farmer. Sylvia gave up full-time nursing to become a farmer's wife and rear their three sons, Iain, Neil and Ross.

Once her children had grown up Sylvia dedicated herself to voluntary work in the community. She remained close to the other nurses and eventually was elected president of their Prisoner of War Association.

'Unfortunately, I outlived Colin by many years. But I can't complain. I'd say I've had a very happy life. After all, I did tell my mother I wanted to be an Army nurse, then marry and have four sons, though I only managed three.'

My last memory of Sylvia was when our interview session ended. She told me she needed to pick up some tablets from the pharmacy before the ambulance arrived to take her home. I immediately jumped up to do this for her.

'No, thanks, Susanna,' she said firmly. 'I'm not dead yet. *I'll* get them.'

And off she went down the long passage clinging onto her walking frame. Sylvia was just as determined to refuse help as she had been when, weighing 5 stone (32 kg), she turned down any assistance to board the train that took her away from their last camp.

♥ ♥ ♥

Joyce was a very private person who never once spoke to the press about her harrowing years of captivity. Her ordeal at the hands of the Japanese became a catalyst for an outstanding career in radiography and a truly heroic life dedicated to the welfare of others.

It took years for Joyce to recover after her release. Joyce's niece remembers her mother helping Joyce peel away the top layer of skin from her hands, which was flaking away due to beriberi.

Back in Australia, with loving care from her family, Joyce slowly recovered her strength and was finally well enough to consider what she would do with the rest of her life. She had no wish to exist on an invalid pension. She wanted to do something to help others. When she asked her doctor for his opinion, he told her that returning to nursing was out of the question, as she lacked the physical strength to lift patients. Why not go back to radiography? All she needed to do was to update her qualifications.

Through guts and determination this quiet woman had the strength of character to transform herself from a physical wreck into a leading figure in the world of cancer treatment. In time, she acquired an international reputation for her pioneering work in the field of therapeutic radiography.

In May 1950 Joyce Tweddell was admitted to membership of the Australian Institute of Radiography. At that time Royal Brisbane Hospital had a vast treatment area stretching from the north of Queensland, the Torres Strait Islands and Papua New Guinea. In 1959 Joyce was sent by the Queensland Radium Institute to set up a radiotherapy department in Papua New Guinea.

'Tweedie' became a senior, much-loved figure in the Royal Brisbane Hospital. Tall, silver-haired and imposing, she was generous with her time and helped many younger women achieve careers in radiography. She was extremely kind, loyal and supportive to her staff and she had a wonderful sense of humour. Later she became deeply involved in the planning of new buildings and the upgrading of radiation facilities at this hospital, and watched it become the most important centre for radiography in the southern hemisphere.

In 1972 Joyce was appointed chief radiographer and radiation therapist at the Royal Brisbane. She travelled the world, attending conferences and speaking on her treatment methods for cancer. She finally retired from professional life in 1979.[21] She went to live in Caloundra, where she cared for her ageing mother, played golf and coped bravely with several bouts of illness. She died in 1995.

In the 1970s when my late husband, Dr Larry Evans, worked at the Royal Brisbane, Joyce was a legendary figure, loved by her staff and famous as one of the Bangka Island nurses ill-treated by the Japanese.

A handsome state-of-the art oncology building at the Royal Brisbane has been named the Joyce Tweddell Building after her, a fitting memorial for a woman who bravely endured so much and still managed to turn her life around to help others less fortunate than herself.

ee ee ee

Vivian confided how hard it had been to adapt to civilian life. After living so tightly packed together in the camp, she and the other nurses found it most disconcerting to be on their own. Like the others, Vivian and Sylvia 'wanted to be with one of the group all the time'.

Vivian admitted that it had been worse for her when she returned to Australia because, though naturally quiet and shy, she suddenly found herself in the public eye, followed about by journalists and photographers. Her wish was to let the world know how heroically the *whole* group had behaved in the camp rather than concentrate on the Bangka Island Massacre. To do this, she had to overcome her natural reticence, and embark on a busy program of public appearances.

> I'd never been involved with public speaking before but Betty and I went around Victoria raising money for a memorial to the nurses who had died. I was still emotionally involved with the girls we had lost. The way they behaved on the sinking *Vyner Brooke* was heroic. I could never forget the heroism of Matron Drummond. She was so calm organising us all, helping civilians and children into the lifeboats, and sacrificing her own life to save others. All the nurses were brave. We only left after everyone else was safe.
>
> What none of us will ever forget was how Mitz and other girls who died thanked us for caring for them and apologised for dying so slowly. It was so terrible just remembering these things. At first I had a lump in my throat and could scarcely talk about them in public and I had to overcome that.
>
> Those journalists pestered me and wanted to take my photograph and wanted me to answer stupid questions. I didn't want to talk about the Japanese and the details of the massacre. I wanted to talk about my friends and their bravery. But most of the press didn't want to hear about that, they wanted to know about the violence and the sordid aspects of it all.
>
> I spoke at RSL branches, school graduation nights; I opened things, unveiled things. I was propelled into

becoming a different person, a new and totally different person, Sister Bullwinkel, the survivor of the massacre. Sometimes the whole thing seemed unreal as though it was happening to someone else, not me. Often, if I had problems to deal with, I thought, 'How would Matron Drummond have dealt with them?', and tried to act accordingly. But there was always the guilt that I had been saved rather than her. I know she would have been far better at negotiating with Colonel Yamasaki than any of us.

Guilty thoughts kept returning. I would say to myself, 'Why were *you* the only one to be saved? Why weren't you killed when girls who were far better than you were killed?' For three days, I wouldn't allow myself to pray. Then finally, I did pray, and found a measure of peace but I couldn't cry for the others. I never shed a tear for them but I never forgot them. Never for one single day.[22]

Returning to Melbourne, Vivian left the Army and nursed wounded soldiers at the Repatriation General Hospital, Heidelberg. Later, she took a diploma in civilian nursing administration. She was appointed assistant matron of the Heidelberg 'Repat' serving from 1956 to 1960.

Vivian became matron and then director of nursing of the Fairfield Infectious Diseases Hospital in Melbourne, and in 1974 president of the College of Nursing. She received a host of honours in the field of nursing administration. She also became a lieutenant-colonel in a Royal Australian Nursing Corps training unit and the first woman trustee of the Australian National War Memorial in Canberra. She was also instrumental in the establishment of nursing scholarships to enable Malaysian nurses to undertake training in Australia.

Vivian attended many ex-servicemen's functions, and became known for her willingness to help ex-servicemen and women, especially those down on their luck.

As well as working hard, Vivian took care of her ageing mother and led an active social life. She received various proposals of marriage, but none of them seemed right. In spite of those years of extreme hunger and deprivation, she remained a strikingly attractive woman who always managed to look elegant for her speaking engagements.

Vivian had planned one day to go to London with her best friend, Wilma Oram,[23] but Wilma was now married to a former prisoner of war, nursing him and living on a farm. In the end Vivian went to London with Betty Jeffrey and other members of the group. In 1973 Vivian returned to London to receive a Member of the Order of the British Empire award. Later she received nursing's highest award, the Florence Nightingale Medal.

After the nurses' release, two films and a TV series described their capativity and ill treatment by the Japanese. Vivian found to her dismay that the media had turned her into something of a legend. She tried to guard her privacy fiercely, as did Sylvia and Joyce, but it was Vivian's name everyone remembered, while Sylvia and Joyce were able to slip into relative obscurity.

ᴸ ᴸ ᴸ

On her return to Australia, Betty was down to skin and bone and weighed less than 5 stone (32 kg). She spent the next two years in hospital. For a long time afterwards, her great-niece Emily Malone remembers, she needed to be treated with injections of cortisone. Her limbs bruised easily and it took a long time for her to recover her former strength.

But as soon as Betty felt well enough, she came out of hospital and, energy reviving, moved into a block of units in East Malvern, Victoria. She became involved in plans with Vivian to raise money for a 'living' memorial to their dead colleagues. This was to take the form of a Nurses' Memorial Centre, which would include a lecture theatre and accomodation for visiting nurses. Betty and Vivian borrowed a car and toured hospitals throughout rural Victoria, giving fundraising talks together. By a great deal of various hard work and public speaking, these two indomitable women collected the sum of £78,000, a considerable amount in those days.[24]

The money they raised was used to build and furnish the Nurses' Memorial Centre in St Kilda. Betty became the centre's administrator and ran the facility very well. In 1950 she went to London with Vivian and they were presented to King George VI, Queen Mary, the Duchess of Gloucester and the young Princess Elizabeth. Eventually, continuing ill health forced Betty to retire on a pension from the Federal government.

In her retirement Betty continued to keep herself busy and active. She was always very involved with her close-knit family and her sister's two daughters, who were her special favourites. Betty's great-niece Emily Malone records her aunt as being very generous and loving. Betty also took on voluntary work for ex-prisoners of war, attended reunions of the group and played a great deal of golf at Huntingdale Golf Club.

At the same time Betty was hard at work preparing an edited version of her 'war' diary for publication by Angus & Robertson under the title *White Coolies*.

The published book was Betty's personal view of those bleak years of captivity, a dark story enlivened by flashes of the author's characteristic wit and good humour. It also revealed to Australians the heroic side of the story, describing how the nurses grew weak but carried on trying to save the lives of those around them.

Betty Jeffrey at the launch of White Coolies. *Vivian Bullwinkel is on the left.*

As a senior nurse, Betty who by the third year of captivity was feeling very ill indeed, described with grim foresight, how even if they survived, few of the nurses would emerge from captivity unscathed by the terrible diet and shortage of vitamins, and the fevers. She wrote:

Thirty-one of our thirty-two sisters now have malaria quite badly . . . We are . . . praying for our freedom. If this doesn't happen soon we shall be a mess for the rest of our lives.[25]

White Coolies caused an overnight sensation when it was published. Over the course of the next two years it was reprinted eight times and copies were sold in England, at that time something rare for an Australian book.

A popular drama series on commercial radio based on Betty's book was later produced by Gwen Friend, sister of the well-known artist Donald Friend. June Salter starred in it as Betty. June and Gwen became great friends with Betty and enjoyed her keen sense of humour.

In 1954 after her edited journal was published, Betty donated her battered war diary to the Australian War Memorial, along with her nursing uniform and a watch from which the Japanese had removed the hands so she could not tell the time. Later she gave the War Memorial drawings of the camp, produced, like her diary, at great danger to herself. Had the diary, which she had kept hidden in her pillow, been found she could have been shot, as could Sylvia for her diary. The Japanese guards were keen to destroy anything that might incriminate them should the Allies win the war. Typical of Betty's spirit and sense of humour was a 'soldier' doll with Japanese features that she made out of a shirt-tail stolen from one of the guards.[26]

In 1987 Betty was made an Officer of the Order of Australia, an honour bestowed on Vivian in 1993.

In 1996 Betty was invited to act as script adviser to the film *Paradise Road* in which Betty's character was played by Ruth Cracknell. Betty attended the premiere of the film but told her great-niece, Emily Malone, who accompanied her, that she felt that after the shipwreck of the *Vyner Brooke* the film deviated too far from the truth.[27]

However *Paradise Road*, directed by Bruce Beresford, received great critical acclaim for its sensitive portrayal of the heroism of women in wartime. It differed from Betty's diary substantially because it was intended for an international audience and omitted the Bangka Island Massacre, possibly because it was just too gruesome for general viewing.

The film was superbly well acted. It also depicted the British civilian wives in the camp and featured the little Eurasian girl named Nellie who acted as a go-between and traded with the local people and sold the gold bracelet that saved Vivian and Betty Kennieson's lives.

Betty Jeffrey's journal was concerned with life as she experienced it rather than as an overall picture of concentration camp life. Betty and Sylvia both wrote about the struggles of the Australian nurses to stay alive and the overwhelming kindness of the Dutch Charitas nuns to the Army nurses and civilians. Both Betty's diary and Sylvia's briefer account, as well as the film, pay tribute to the work of British missionary Miss Margaret Dryburgh in sustaining morale by conducting her 'humming' choir, of which Betty and Sylvia were keen members. Like the diary of Anne Frank and the diary of Vera Britain in World War I, Betty Jeffrey's poignant journal and *White Coolies* are among the great anti-war testaments written by women.

Betty Jeffrey died of a heart attack in a Melbourne nursing home on 13 September 2000, managing to survive to the ripe age of 92.

At Betty's funeral at St Peter's Church, Eastern Hill, Melbourne, Wilma Oram (Young), the youngest of the nurses' group, praised 'Bet' for her strength and her courage and ended her speech by saying 'We have all lost a gifted and sincere friend.'[28]

THE FINAL YEARS AND A MEMORIAL ON BANGKA ISLAND

The surviving 'Paradise Road' nurses remained close, had frequent reunions and sent birthday and Christmas cards to each other. Vivian and Sylvia corresponded regularly, particularly since Sylvia had taken over the arrangements for their annual reunions.

In 1975 Vivian was part of a rescue mission to bring a group of Vietnamese orphans to Australia for adoption by Australian parents. Quietly and unobtrusively Vivian did everything possible to help those less fortunate than herself.

In 1977 Vivian appeared on *This is Your Life*. In the television studio she was surprised to find assembled Betty Jeffrey, Mickey Syer, Flo

Trotter, Sylvia, Nesta James and her closest friend, Wilma Oram. Each of the nurses spoke with love and respect about the things Vivian had accomplished and what her friendship represented to them.

Finally it was Vivian's turn. She spoke about some of her war experiences but glossed over others that were still too painful to mention. Vivian won the hearts and minds of the audience, who repeatedly applauded her. The television program was seen all over Australia and letters of admiration for Vivian poured in. As a result, she was deluged with speaking offers and had she been so minded could have gone on the speaker's circuit around Australia and overseas. But money and fame were not what she wanted. She still dreamed of a memortial on Bangka Island.

In the year she was due to retire as matron of the Melbourne's Fairfield Hospital, Vivian surprised everyone by announcing she was about to get married. Her husband-to-be was a much decorated army colonel she had known for a long time. Frank Statham had been one of the war heroes known as the 'Rats of Tobruk'. He was a widower whose wife had died of tuberculosis after a long illness. Vivian and Frank had met at the Naval, Military and Airforces Club in Melbourne. Vivian wished her marriage to be a low-key affair, away from the media spotlight. She had her farewell party at the hospital and then packed up her house and took herself and her elderly mother to Perth where Frank lived, and quietly got married.

Vivian and Frank settled into a happy retirement. With shared interests, a great deal of community service and a few overseas trips to Penang and Singapore, the next twenty-three years of happy married life flew by. One sadness was the death of Vivian's mother.

In March 1993, Vivian finally succeeded in getting a memorial to the victims of the massacre erected at Bangka Island. Sylvia McGregor was one of the group of seven nurses who flew to Indonesia for the dedication of the memorial. She, Jessie Simons, Wilma Oram and the others watched as Vivian, wearing her Order of Australia and other medals, laid a large wreath at the foot of an engraved block of granite. The monument was as close as possible to the spot where the survivors of the *Vyner Brooke* came ashore. On the brass plaque was the following inscription:

8th Australian Division
2nd Australian Imperial Force

This memorial honours the heroism and sacrifice of members of the Australian Army Nursing Service who served in the Bangka area during the years 1942–1945.

Lost at sea off Bangka Island after the bombing of the SS *Vyner Brooke* on 14 February 1942:
Matron *O.D. Paschke*
Sisters:

L.M.J. Bates	C.M. Ennis	M. Schuman
E. Calnan	K. Kinsella	A.M. Trenerry
M.D. Clarke	G.M. McDonald	M.M. Wilton
M.H.M. Dorsch	L.J. Russell	

Killed on Radji Beach, Bangka Island, by Japanese soldiers, 16 February 1942:
Matron *I.M. Drummond*
Sisters:

E.L Balfour-Ogilvy	P.E. Farmaner	K.M. Neuss
A.M. Beard	C.I. Halligan	F.A. Salmon
A.J. Bridge	N. Harris	E.S.J. Stewart
F.R. Casson	M.I. Hodgson	M.M. A. Tait
M.E. Cuthbertson	E.L. Keats	R.J. Wight
D.G.H. Elmes	J. Kerr	B. Wilmott
L.F. Fairweather	M.E. McGlade	

AANS sisters who died in Japanese Prisoner-of-War Camps:

W.M. Davis	P.B. Hempsted	W.R. Raymont
R.D. Freeman	G.L. Hughes	I.A. Singleton
D.S. Gardam	P. Mittelheuser	

AANS sisters who survived and returned to Australia:

J.C. Ashton	J. Greer	C.S.M. Oxley
K.C.Blake	E.M. Hannah	E.M. Short
J.J. Blanch	I. Harper	J.E. Simons
V. Bullwinkel	N. James	V.E. Smith
V.R. Clancy	A.B. Jeffrey	A.C. Syer
C.E.M. Delforce	V.I. McElnea	F.E.O. Trotter
J.G. Doyle	S.J. Muir	J. Tweddell
J.P. Gunther	W.E.F. Oram	B. Woodbridge

This monument was dedicated on 2 March 1993 in the presence of seven of the above including Matron Vivian Statham AO MBE ARRC (the former Sister V. Bullwinkel), sole survivor of the massacre at Radji Beach.

Speeches were made by government officials from Australia and Sumatra. Vivian, her emotions tightly in check, held a small circlet of flowers. As the Australian flag was unfurled Vivian threw her little wreath as far as she could into the sea. She watched as it bobbed about in the waves where the lives of her companions had ended.

She had fulfilled her promise to honour her dead comrades. Now at last she was able to weep, to release the tangle of emotions she had held at bay all those years. Tears rolled down Vivian's cheeks as she sent up a silent prayer for all the dead nurses and for Matron Irene Drummond who had helped them all to leave the sinking ship and made an inspiring last speech just before they were killed.

In her final years Vivian suffered a series of strokes but fought back bravely and learned to overcome most of the after-effects. She was able to be present at the dedication of the Nurses' Memorial in Canberra, close to other military memorials, in October 1999, the centenary year of Australian military nursing.

Then, in December, Vivian had occasion to weep again after her husband died of a heart attack. In March 2000, her biography, written by fellow West Australian Norman Manners, was launched. To guests at the launch it was evident that Vivian had been deeply affected by Frank's death — much of the spark had gone out of her life.

Vivian died of a heart attack on 3 July 2000, in Perth's Hollywood Private Hospital. At her funeral, Australia mourned a woman who had never sought publicity for herself but only for humanitarian causes.

A state memorial service for Vivian Bullwinkel was held in Perth's St George's Cathedral to honour the heroic woman who had done so much for others. The funeral cortège, accompanied by nurses in uniform, passed slowly along St George's Terrace, where flags were flying at half mast. A month later, a memorial service was held in Melbourne, a city which also claimed Vivian as its own.

Major-General 'Digger' James summed up the life and work of this determined yet extremely modest woman. Vivian Bullwinkel, he said, had been a, 'superb role model for all who care for the sick in war and in peace. Her life and her work made our world a better place.'

If I do die, I've had an . . . adventure . . . I wouldn't have missed for anything.

MAVIS PARKINSON, PAPUA, 1942

CHAPTER 12

Sister Frances May Hayman
1906 – 1942

Mavis Parkinson
1915 – 1942

One of the shortest and saddest stories of Australian women in war is that of Mavis Parkinson and May Hayman. These two young women loved the Papuan children they cared for but their refusal to return to Australia until Japanese soldiers landed on the beach beside the Anglican mission where they worked would cost them their lives.[1]

Mavis Parkinson attended Ipswich Girls' Grammar School near Brisbane. She was a vivacious girl who enjoyed sport and work, and became a school prefect. On Sundays she worshipped at St Paul's Anglican Church in Ipswich with her parents. She was also a keen Girl Guide, enjoying outdoor activities, including bushwalking, with fellow members of her church.

Mavis was a petite girl with brown hair and brown eyes — and a lively mind and a good sense of humour. She once devised what seemed to be a good method for avoiding an exam. She and a classmate ate large boxes of chocolates in the hope they would become too ill to sit for the test. Although the girls did become sick they were made to sit for the exam along with the rest of the class. It says a great deal for Mavis's intelligence that she passed the exam easily.

After leaving school Mavis found herself a clerical job locally with Cribbe & Foot in Ipswich but her ambition was to become a teacher. She was fortunate in being accepted at Sydney University, where she studied languages and anthropology before gaining her degree in theology.

Mavis was accepted to teach at Gona Anglican Mission in Papua, which had been established in 1929. Formerly governed by the British, Papua was then under Australian administration. The Australian government spent very little on education in Papua and it was left up to various missions to provide most of the educational services. Only primary education was given to most Papuan children.

At the time of Mavis's arrival at Gona Mission, Sister Frances May (Merry) Hayman had been working there for some years and provided the only medical services in the area. Small and delicate, with light hair and bright blue eyes, May Hayman was nine years older than Mavis. Born in Adelaide, she had grown up in Canberra and trained as a district nurse in Melbourne.

Gona Anglican Mission had extensive grounds which sloped down to the Pacific Ocean. Its timber houses with wide verandas sat on the large, well-tended grounds less than 90 metres from the beach. Massive tulip trees with scarlet flowers lined paths that ran parallel to the sandy beach. Flowerbeds were bright with canna lilies and red and yellow crotons, brightly coloured hibiscus and variegated 'Busy Lizzies' with white, pink and scarlet flowers. The school was a happy place which gave children, who would otherwise have had no chance of an education, a variety of skills. There was a kindergarten, a primary school and the All Souls' Senior School. Mavis and her associate Simon Peter Awoda were assisted by several pupil teachers. Mavis was an inspiring teacher. She and her team tended the gardens with pleasure and the plants provided a teaching resource for Mavis's botany lessons.

The head of Gona Anglican Mission was the Rev. James Benson who, like the rest of his staff, was dedicated to improving the lives of Papuan villagers.

Behind the mission was a coconut plantation leading to the village of Bepore. Beyond the village were hectacres of jungle with mangrove swamps and tangled undergrowth. In the low-lying swampy ground, millions of mosquitoes bred, including the dreaded anopheles, carrier of malaria.

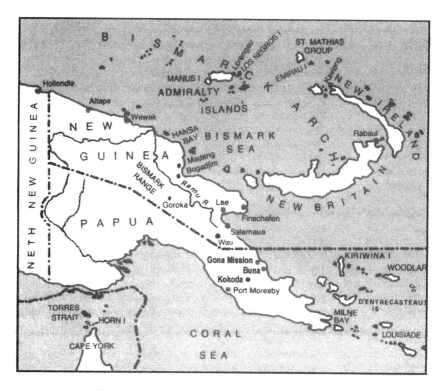

New Guinea showing Gona Mission during World War II.

In 1937, after training May for two years to act as his replacement, the mission's resident doctor returned to Australia, leaving May in sole charge of the medical centre. She dispensed medicines, delivered babies, stitched wounds, splinted broken limbs and coped with the thousand and one ailments of the Papuan population in the surrounding villages. The medical centre and the small hospital provided care for the mission staff and the surrounding villages, and many Papuans would have died or had far less productive lives had it not been for May's nursing skills.

May and Mavis shared a bungalow and soon became close friends. Life at the mission lacked many material things we take for granted today but the environment was a happy one. Both these capable young women felt a sense of achievement at what they were accomplishing.

Mavis acted as housekeeper for the mission and ordered all the stores. She organised breakfast for the staff, then walked each morning across a small bridge to open up her school. Mavis had a knack of creating order, happiness and harmony around her, and a capacity for hard work.

During the day May worked in the dispensary and the isolation hospital, and undertook what she called her 'walkabouts'. These were conducted on foot or by lorry to the outlying villages for which May, in

Vivian Redlich.

her role of district nurse and 'barefoot doctor', provided medical care.

Both women had attractive and outgoing personalities and were deservedly popular among the expatriate community, as well as with the Papuan villagers. May was also attracted to a shy, bespectacled English priest named Vivian Redlich, described by Anglican Bishop Philip Strong as 'happy, youthful, gifted', who had been working for the Bush Brotherhood in Queensland and was now posted to Papua.

THE JAPANESE INVASION

In December 1941, Japanese forces attacked the American fleet at Pearl Harbor. In the same month the Japanese invaded Malaya and struck the first blows in their well-planned onslaught on the South Pacific region. They seized Guam, the Wake Islands and Sarawak in British Borneo, and ousted a small Australian force in Rabaul, the main port on New Britain island. There they captured a group of Australian nurses and sent them to a prison camp in Japan.

On 19 February 1942, Japanese soldiers landed on the island of Timor in the Malay archipelago and invaded the island of Sumatra, part of Dutch-Indonesia, and neighbouring Bangka Island. British and Australian forces in Singapore capitulated to the Japanese in February 1942.

Despite the danger of an invasion, in January 1942 the Anglican Bishop of New Guinea, Philip Strong, had made a radio broadcast urging all committed Christians to set an example and stick to their posts, come what may. He said 'We must endeavour to carry on our work. God expects this of us . . . the people whom we serve expect it of us.' Much later, when tragedy ensued, Bishop Strong insisted he had also stated that it was up to each individual's conscience what *they* chose to do. In his radio message he had added a thinly veiled warning to women — that 'terrible things could happen, worse than death', by which he meant rape and torture by the Japanese. In the bishop's defence very few believed it possible the Japanese would land at remote coastal areas like Gona or at Buna with the aim of using the heavily forested Kokoda Track and attacking Port Moresby by land.[2]

How May and Mavis interpreted the bishop's warning is unclear but undoubtedly in the light of later events, his stirring and emotional words did influence them to make a major and fatal decision not to leave the mission.

Lae and Salamaua, in the Mandated Territory of New Guinea, were occupied by the Japanese on 8 March. Port Moresby was also bombed by the Japanese although planes continued to arrive from and depart for Australia from its tiny airport.

In April, General Douglas MacArthur arrived in Brisbane from the Philippines to command the now desperate battle against the Japanese in the Pacific. By now Mavis's parents were anxious for her to return home but the staff at Gona were convinced that the war would pass them by and life would continue as normal. So the two young women stayed to teach and run the medical centre.

The Japanese advanced relentlessly along the coast of Papua. Although Gona was isolated, some news reached the mission via an ancient radio, which had an unfortunate habit of fading out at critical moments.

News also reached them through Europeans fleeing from the Japanese, who were arriving at Gona on foot and by sea, exhausted, hungry and tired. Many of them had made their way across the border between Papua and New Guinea, desperate to escape from the Japanese, and reach Kokoda and Port Moresby and its airport. Thirty American and British refugees travelled south by canoe from Salamaua. The staff at Gona took them in, fed them and sent them on their way refreshed.

Mavis gave all the refugees a warm welcome, fed them home-cooked meals and gave them clean clothes. She and the rest of the mission staff believed that giving food and hospitality to refugees was part of their Christian duty, and that by showing kindness and love to those in need she was following the precepts laid down by Christ.

Allied servicemen whose planes had been shot down and who were cut off from their fighting units were also given hospitality by Mavis.

Meanwhile, American planes were harassing Japanese shipping off Midway Island. When an American plane crashed in the jungle near Gona, survivors brought with them disturbing reports of events that followed the fall of Singapore. The gruesome tales of rape in particular increased Father Benson's belief that May and Mavis must leave as soon as possible. He was convinced that no matter how difficult it was to make their way on foot, the two women should try to reach Port Moresby, which lay south of Gona on the opposite coast over the mountains. There they could board a plane to Australia and safety.

The only way out of Gona was by sea or along the narrow walking track to Kokoda. The Kokoda Track twisted its way through 240 kilometres of dense jungle and traversed the heights of Papua's Owen Stanley Range.[3] It took about five days of hard walking to reach Port Moresby.

The Australian government administrative centre at Buna was a few hours away from Gona and was staffed by Magistrate J. Atkinson and his assistant, Alan Champion. These two men had previously attempted to persuade May and Mavis to trek inland with them where the people were predominantly Christian and would hide them from the Japanese. However, May had refused to leave, claiming her medical work was vital.

For her part, Mavis truly loved the children entrusted to her care, especially the orphans, and did not wish to leave them. She was also committed to the vital task of providing shelter, food and clothing for the refugees. Finally May and Mavis insisted they would only leave if directly ordered to do so by Bishop Strong.

Rightly or wrongly, they were not ordered to leave. So, based on humanitarian motives and Christian principles, these two Australian women and several English and Eurasian women at other missions made the altruistic decision to stay on and care for others rather than saving their own lives.

As the head of Gona Mission, Father Benson was still convinced the two women were in danger and should leave. He warned May and Mavis they must keep a bag packed with essentials, just in case they had to escape in a hurry. In her bag Mavis packed arrowroot biscuits and two slabs of chocolate for emergencies.

Local radio messages also advised residents to be ready to leave at a moment's notice. The warnings were couched in curiously stilted English, which aroused suspicion among some expatriates that the warnings were broadcast by the Japanese to lower their morale.

One broadcast in heavily accented English announced, 'For you people on the north-east coast, I have no definite instructions. But if you don't want to leave your bones on the beaches, I think you had better clear out too.'[4]

These dire warnings had the effect of terrifying the villagers on the north-east coast of Papua. Father Benson was unsuccessful in contacting the bishop of New Guinea for more advice. He learned that the bishop was on his motor launch, the *Maclaren King*, visiting other mission stations by sea and could not be contacted by radio.

In the midst of Father Benson's dilemma, a messenger arrived from Magistrate Atkinson, saying that he accepted the wireless announcement from Salamaua as genuine. He would be leaving the following morning for Kokoda with his staff. Did any of the staff at Gona Mission want to accompany his party?

Father Benson, who was a widower and had no surviving family, intended to stay on at Gona and care for the mission but he encouraged May and Mavis to be ready to join Mr Atkinson's party. It was somewhat reassuring that Mr Atkinson was taking a radio transmitter along.

Late in the afternoon a motor launch arrived at Gona from Eroro Mission, some 110 kilometres down the coast, bringing Father Newman who wanted to know what the Gona staff intended to do. Father Newman said he did not regard the radio message from Salamaua as official and, like Father Benson, he would stay at his post until advised to leave by Bishop Strong.

However, both men agreed that due to the danger of rape the women should leave. In spite of the fact that the trail to Port Moresby was long and difficult, Father Newman was so worried by the thought of what Japanese soldiers might do that he was entrusting his wife to Mr Atkinson's party. Father Benson persuaded May and Mavis they too should go with this group.

The following morning, Mavis and May left Gona surrounded by tearful children wishing them goodbye and good luck. They were accompanied for the first kilometre or so by twelve of the senior pupils who competed fiercely for the honour of carrying the women's overnight bags.

'They could have had a couple of hundred devoted helpers had they wished,' wrote Father Benson years later, remembering how the children had wept as May and Mavis departed.[5]

Father Benson and Father Newman accompanied the group for the first few kilometres, and with considerable relief watched them heading off in the direction of the Owen Stanley Range. May and Mavis were young and fit. The prospect of a long walk through the damp and steamy jungle didn't worry them.

Each night they listened to the news and heard it had now been confirmed that the radio announcement about not 'leaving their bones on the beach' had definitely been put out by the enemy. The teacher and dedicated nurse felt annoyed they had been deceived by it into leaving.

RETURN TO GONA

From now on it weighed heavily on Mavis and May that they were deserting their charges. Another fact that influenced their wish to return to Gona was a meeting at Sangara with two strong-minded women like themselves, Sister Margery Brenchley originally from Kent in England, and a young Eurasian teaching assistant, Lilla Lashmar. These two women had decided to defy the broadcasts and stay on at Sangara Mission.

After talking it over, Mavis and May likewise decided to return to Gona. Mavis asked Mr Atkinson to radio her father in Ipswich asking his permission to stay.[6] Her father agreed, although both her parents were unhappy about it and they later sent a letter demanding she return home. Having contacted her parents and explained to Mr Atkinson and the rest of the group how they felt, Mavis turned around and headed back along the track to Gona with May, hearts light and filled with the optimism that nothing unpleasant could happen to *them*.

Five days later, Father Benson was surprised to see Mavis back at the Mission surrounded by a flock of laughing, happy children delighted to see her return. Father Benson was amazed that Mavis was as fresh and neat 'as if she had been down town shopping'.[7] May had not returned directly with Mavis but gone to Eroro to spend a few days with Father Newman's wife (who had also returned), possibly hoping to see Vivian Redlich, who was due to visit. When May returned from her stay at Eroro, thanks to the hard work of the women, Gona school, the little bush hospital and the medical centre opened again. The shy, dark-eyed children with their wide smiles streamed back into the classroom. Life was back to normal. Or was it?

Mavis and May thought they were safe. They had no way of knowing that Lilla and Margery would later be beheaded by Japanese soldiers, as would Vivian Redlich, who ran Sangara Mission. Their devoted assistant and fellow teacher, Papuan-born Lucian Tapiedi, who stayed behind to protect them when the rest of his countrymen fled, would also be beheaded by a fellow Papuan, a man called Hivajapa.

On 7 and 8 May 1942, the Battle of the Coral Sea was fought off New Guinea's eastern tip. It involved planes from Japanese aircraft carriers and Australian and US aircraft based in north Queensland. The Japanese lost two aircraft carriers and their convoy turned back to Rabaul.

A month later, between 3 and 6 June, American planes engaged with the Japanese fleet off Midway Island, some hundreds of nautical miles to the north-east of Gona. In the ensuing battle the Japanese lost four troop carriers and some 250 planes. As a result, the Japanese changed their strategy and decided to attack Papua by land. They selected isolated Gona as the place they would land. From there, following the inland track, their commanders planned to send a large detachment of Japanese troops to cross the wild and rugged Owen Stanley Range to Port Moresby, hoping to capture its airport.

Meanwhile, at remote Gona Mission, the staff were blissfully ignorant of the Japanese plans, believing that large ships could not pass through the reef and enter Gona Bay and that they were therefore safe from attack.

That same month May announced her engagement to Vivian Redlich. The newly engaged couple received the good wishes of both the locals and expatriates, who felt that May's extroverted nature and sweetness of character and Vivian Redlich's more intellectual approach to religion would combine very well. When married, they would be an ideal couple to run a mission station.

But war was coming closer. One morning, when the children were playing in the gardens, a US fighter plane flew low over the station, its engine on fire and losing height rapidly. The mission staff heard a loud crash and saw a plume of smoke rising from the jungle.

Mavis took some of the older boys with her and set off to investigate. They found the pilot, who had bailed out and broken his neck on landing, and carried his body back to the Mission. The two women had to lay out the body. They held a funeral service for the pilot in Gona church and buried him there.

ℓℓ ℓℓ ℓℓ

Late in the afternoon of Tuesday 21 July, Father Benson was in the Mission's repair workshop when one of the pupil teachers, Lancelot, rushed to the door, shouting, 'Father! Come quick. Great big ships are here.'

Father Benson followed Lancelot to the beach. To his horror he saw steaming towards the shore a huge ship bearing the emblem of the rising sun, escorted by four smaller destroyers.

Amazed that the Japanese were able to enter the bay through the reef, Father Benson ran back to his house, where he had a bag packed with essentials. He added his vestments and Office Book, a watch, tobacco, pencils, a notebook and some notepaper (which Mavis would later use to write a letter to her parents) and a few other necessities.

The remaining villagers, simple people who had never seen a ship larger than the bishop's motor launch, took fright at the sight of the destroyers. They gathered up their sleeping mats, cooking pots, babies and piglets, and fled along the bush track into the depths of the encircling jungle.

Father Benson, May, Mavis and the senior teacher, Simon Peter Awoda (who had already sent his wife and family away), watched more Japanese transport ships and destroyers anchor offshore. When four planes arrived soon after, Mavis declared: 'They are Japs, and they are shelling Buna.'[8] However, eventually their Allied markings were revealed and the planes flew over and strafed the ships. The battle was bitter but eventually the Allied planes flew away, their ammunition exhausted.

Now that the danger from the air was over, rowing boats and barges were lowered from the Japanese ships as hundreds of armed soldiers prepared to come ashore.

Shells were now landing in the compound and a barrage of fire swept the beach. It was getting dark and time to go. Adding some mosquito nets, tinned food and the precious compass to their bags, Father Benson, May, Mavis and Peter set off on the little track at the back of the mission into the jungle with three boys who volunteered to act as their guides. They were just in time. Hundreds of armed Japanese soldiers were now coming ashore.

Escape from the Japanese

Their stressful experiences over the next nineteen days were described by Mavis in a brave and lively letter to her parents. In the memoirs of Father Benson, Mavis comes across as an entertaining woman with a vivid turn of phrase, not easily afraid of anything. Father Benson records Mavis saying:

> Golly, think of it. In the past twenty-four hours I've seen
> a naval battle, been driven out of hearth and home,
> crossed the enemy lines, been lost in an impenetrable
> forest, on the edge of a first-rate aerial bombardment, and

now I'm one of the babes in the wood. Me! Who feared I was going to die without any adventure. Scrummy! Scrummy! If I do die tonight I've had a day's adventure anyhow. I wouldn't have missed it for anything.[9]

Her letter to her parents was written in pencil on a piece of crumpled notepaper from Father Benson's bag. Months later, as though by a miracle, the letter was discovered in the jungle.[10]

It reveals nothing of her own fears for her safety but demonstrates her strength, her courage, her altruism and concern for the peace of mind of her parents.

> Dearest Mummy, darling,
>
> I know how terribly worried you all must be, but if thoughts can comfort, I know you must be comforted . . . Father Benson, May and I are in a little hide-out in the bush and, indeed, are doing what probably few white men have done before, living deep in the heart of the Papuan jungle . . .
>
> On Sunday, July 19, Sergeant Hewitt and Signals Officer Palmer arrived at Gona on their way through from Buna and as they had a few days to spare decided to salvage the American plane which had crashed on our station . . .
>
> As we had visitors at night, May and I dressed for dinner in our long frocks. Afterwards, as it was rather warm, we took the light and gramophone out under the palm-trees on the lawn where we talked and ate chocolate the boys had received in Comforts Funds Parcels.
>
> Tuesday passed as usual (I was examining the schools) and early in the afternoon I pressed my pretty blue georgette evening frock to wear that night.
>
> About 4.45 pm I heard yells from Lancelot, one of my pupil teachers: 'Sister, Sister, are you there? Oh Sister [a courtesy title commonly used for medical and teaching staff], come quickly!' as he ran up the path from the beach.

I simply could not believe my eyes. There were four big ships not far out to sea, and another two on the skyline. Then the boats farther out opened fire on those nearer the beach, burst after burst of shellfire until the ground shook with the explosions. Then ensued a most thrilling naval battle. The warships, both ours and Japan's seeming to move around like tiny boats, they were so quick. Then the transports put down dinghies, and men got into them, so we decided we'd better move to a healthier spot.

We rushed up to the house, grabbed a box, and flung as much as we could into it, our nicest dresses, some undies, comb, toothbrushes, soap, shoes, etc. The soldiers had meanwhile gone up the beach. Our mission-boys were so frightened, but so brave, and carried our things for us along the only road we could take — the mission road to Kokoda. It was by then 6.30, and as it was fairly dark we stopped at the first garden house along the track, a mile from Gona. There we said Evensong with the boys, put up our mosquito nets and prepared to settle down.

About a quarter of an hour later we heard footsteps on the road, and voices. We thought they were village people going into hiding, and I called out to them first in English, 'Boys, come here, we want you,' then the same in Motu (the local dialect), but only silence answered.

Soon another lot came, and again we called out, and Father whistled, but again silence. Then we saw a torch flash, heard a clank of a bayonet, and knew we had been calling out to patrols of Japanese soldiers passing by up the mission road. Our way to the villages of Isivita and to Sangara was cut off, and we could hear the Japanese all around us on the various Kokoda roads. May and I thought we'd like a run for our money so suggested that we should wait our chance of getting across the main Kokoda road and into the bush on the other side. We grabbed our mosquito nets, ground sheets, a blanket each, a tin of biscuits, and some chocolate, a billy can for water and Father Benson took his walkabout haversack.

We left everything else, and crept down the path to the track where the Japs were, and as soon as the way was clear, between patrols, we went for our lives across that road and into the thick wet grass on the other side. We pushed through the undergrowth to a log, a damp rotten one, where we spent the rest of the night.

We were glad to see dawn, and after eating a biscuit each pushed on through the bush. By a great mercy Father had a compass in his bag, one given us by Lieutenant Dickenson, an American pilot who had crashed nearby and stayed at Gona for some weeks.

We'd not gone far when the first raid . . . occurred. We crouched under a big tree, hoping to get some protection. The air seemed thick with bombs and shells, the planes roared over our heads, and the air seemed full of dog-fights.

Things quietened down after eight or ten minutes, and we said Matins, then continued our journey through the bush. Less than every half-hour throughout that day there was a raid. We had lunch (two milk coffee biscuits and a piece of chocolate each), and again pushed on, but about 3.30 pm we came to a big tree with a brush turkey's nest at its foot, and decided to make our camp for the night. There had already been nineteen raids on Gona that day (surely a record) and as soon as the moon rose we started again.

Next day, to our dismay, we got into a sago swamp, and only if you'd been in this country could you know what that means — prickly, almost impenetrable undergrowth, slushy mud underfoot, into which it is possible to sink up to one's waist or even one's neck. And there is always the chance of crocodiles. However, we decided to go east, retracing our footsteps, and try to get around that way.

Soon we came to a clean running stream, and while Father went farther up the river, May and I stripped and got into the water. Oh, it was heavenly to feel the cool water on our bodies, and to bathe our poor legs, torn by the prickles and thorns of the bush. Then we went on for some distance until, to our great joy, we came to some [Papuan] natives. They made a great fuss of us and prepared food for us. My word, we were pretty hungry too, and just ate taro and sweet potato out of the cooking pot — no salt or anything! They told us of Japs on the tracks nearby . . . and also told us we were on the right track to Siai, our outstation [on the Kumusi River].

We walked hard the next morning, and about lunchtime met three boys from Bakumbari [a village about 16 kilometres from Gona] on the track. We were quite overwhelmed by their affectionate greetings. They carried our swags and on we went and arrived at Sageri about mid afternoon. From there we sent a letter on to Siai, telling Father John Yariri, our assistant native priest, who happened to be at Siai, to meet us the next day.

Next morning off we went again, the Sageri people carrying our swags, and just beyond Orosusu met Father John, Nathaniel [the Siai teacher] and a crowd of Siai people.

As long as I live I shall never forget the welcome they gave us. They hugged us and patted us for ages, and actually cried over us. They took us on to Siai station and there we had another demonstration of affection, this time by the women who brought us food and hot water for a bath. May and I took off our filthy dresses and washed them and while they dried, May wore a cassock of Father John's and I wore an alb [a church vestment].

The people decided the best thing to do would be to build us a cottage in the bush where we should be hidden until things cleared up. We could still hear the bombs falling on Gona. So we came to this house just a fortnight today. Mr Chester sent May and me some clothes belonging to a woman who had evacuated in January —

dresses and scanties, and a few towels and two
nightdresses, so we are beautifully fitted out.

We've simply no idea what is happening, though we do
know that the bombing of Gona has stopped. Of course
we hear all sorts of rumours. We heard of fighting at
Kokoda at Olive Hill, and on the Port Moresby road. We
also heard that the Japs' cartridges are finished and the
fighting is now hand to hand.

Their situation was extremely worrying. They had heard
disturbing tales about Japanese atrocities against prisoners and harsh
reprisals against any Papuans who sheltered Europeans and knew
they must leave their hut at Siai. By staying there, they were putting
the villagers' lives at risk.

Father Benson's worries increased when he learned that the
sorcerer or 'medicine man' at the neighbouring village of Oitanandi
had told the elders they should kill all Europeans in the area or the
Japanese would punish them.

There were strong anti-European feelings in many villages in the
interior because in the past gold miners had exploited the Papuans
and treated their women appallingly. This hostility increased after
missionaries of various denominations had endeavoured to end the
'old ways' of head hunting and cannibalistic practices and, in doing
so, break the power of the sorcerers. There was a deep rift between
the Christianised pro-mission villages and those that remained true
to traditional ways.

On 9 August, Father Benson decided they must head towards the
more isolated but mainly Christian Mamba district.

Later that afternoon, two Australian soldiers arrived, part of a
group which included five wounded American airmen and soldiers
from the Papuan Infantry under the command of a brave young
Australian subaltern named Lieutenant Arthur Smith. The group
was heading for a track across the Owen Stanley Range (not the
Kokoda Track) to walk to Port Moresby. They asked Father Benson
and the two women if they would like to join them. The Gona
Mission group, who had met Lieutenant Smith when his coast-

watch unit was stationed at Buna, was in two minds.[11] May and Mavis approved of Lieutenant Smith's daring plan. Father Benson did not. He reckoned such a difficult journey would take between six and eight weeks and they would be crossing harsh country which few Europeans had succeeded in traversing. By then the soles of the women's shoes had been worn away and they were finding it painful to walk on the rough jungle track.

Later Father Benson wrote: 'I think I was unwise in not insisting on following my own plan that we should all go to the Mamba area and live out the war in peace there.'[12]

However, Father Benson allowed himself to be persuaded by May and Mavis that they could manage the long trek and would prefer to join Lieutenant Smith's group and walk to Port Moresby, although to date only one woman had ever accomplished this difficult journey over the Owen Stanley Range.

Father Benson thought the presence of Papuan soldiers would provide some protection but in reality it did the opposite, providing a pretext for the Japanese Army to regard the entire group, including May and Mavis, as military personnel.

On that last morning, just before dawn, Father Benson woke May and Mavis and they prayed together and took Holy Communion. Then, as dawn was breaking, they set off. They walked through the jungle for the next four days, plagued by mosquitoes and in danger from poisonous snakes. Fearing capture by sentries, the group retraced their steps in order to be further away from Popondetta, which they realised was the site of Japanese Army headquarters.

By morning on the fifth day, they felt safe from pursuit and rested until noon. That afternoon, they set out for the Gona road and were soon within a few hundred metres of it. Before they could cross the road, a Papuan soldier guarding the rear of their group ran up and yelled that Japanese soldiers were approaching them from the rear.

They stayed in the bush until another of the Papuan soldiers reported that the way was clear. By now it was almost dark. Accordingly they ran across the road and into the jungle. They kept running for ten more minutes before stopping to catch their breath.

Father Benson recalled shaking Lieutenant Smith by the hand in relief and saying to him, 'That's our biggest hurdle crossed.'[13] He remembered the women smiling before a blast of gunfire caused them to swing around in terror.

To his horror, Father Benson saw that between eighteen and twenty armed Japanese soldiers were less than fifty metres away. He heard the crack of their rifles and dived for cover amid the bushes. Then came a burst of rifle fire on his right. In the dark he could see nothing at all. He heard low moans and feared one of the girls must have been hit by a bullet. Father Benson called out but received no reply.

In his headlong dive into the jungle Father Benson had dropped his blue bag containing the food and the compass and was now completely lost. For the next five days he wandered around in circles. He managed to survive by drinking the morning dew. Ravenous with hunger, by the sixth day he decided that his only chance of staying alive was to surrender. He found a patrol and gave himself up.

Father Benson was put in an all-male prison camp and spent the next three years in captivity. Whenever he asked his Japanese guards about the women from Gona he was told they were being held in another camp.

Only when the war was over did he learn the sad and awful truth.[14]

REVELATION OF THE TRUTH

Neither of the women had been hit by a Japanese bullet as Father Benson believed. What he had heard was a wounded Papuan soldier groaning. May and Mavis were unharmed and had retreated through the bush with some of the Papuan soldiers, several of whom were slightly injured. Other Papuan soldiers had turned tail and fled.[15]

That night May, Mavis, Lieutenant Smith and a few soldiers slept in the jungle, plagued by mosquitoes but otherwise unharmed.

The next morning they walked briskly to the village of Upper Dobodura, the women keeping up well with the rest of the party in spite of the fact that their worn shoes gave little protection from thorns underfoot. Two soldiers from the Papuan Infantry offered to go into the village and see how the land lay. They returned with the news that the villagers appeared friendly.

Reassured, the rest of the party entered the village and found the inhabitants playing football. Lieutenant Smith asked if some men could be spared to act as stretcher bearers and guides, as two of the soldiers in the party were limping badly and in great pain. The villagers promised to supply stretcher bearers the following morning.

That night the group camped outside the village. Next morning, no one from the village arrived to help.

When Lieutenant Smith and an interpreter inquired at the village, they received flimsy excuses for the delay and overheard hostile mutters among a few of the men.

As the sun mounted overhead, Lieutenant Smith became worried. He decided it was better to continue walking towards Port Moresby and so the group set off again without any help. The men carried improvised stretchers and the two women took turns to help, but their progress through the dense undergrowth was slow.

What the group did not know was that after some discussion the elders of Upper Dobodura, fearing Japanese vengeance if they helped Europeans, had instructed a boy to go to Popondetta and inform the Japanese that two Australian women and some soldiers were nearby. In consequence, when Lieutenant's Smith's group was still only a few kilometres away from Popondetta, a Japanese patrol caught up with them and opened fire.

Amid a hail of machine gun bullets Lieutenant Smith, May and Mavis took cover in the jungle. Their remaining soldiers fired back but were either killed or badly wounded. One Papuan soldier survived by feigning death and he went on to give evidence of what happened at the Webb War Crimes Commission after the war ended.

May and Mavis wandered around in circles all night, totally lost and separated from Lieutenant Smith. By morning, they were exhausted and once more near the hostile village of Upper Dobodura. However, by chance they met a friendly villager named Tionda who was out hunting. He warned the women against entering his village.

Seeing how thirsty and hungry they were, Tionda took pity on them. He went to his hut and returned with pieces of paw-paw, for which the women were very grateful. With Tionda were two young boys whom he introduced as his nephew and a friend. Tionda instructed both boys to guide the women to the neighbouring village of Jegarata, advising them that Embogi, an elder and sorcerer who lived there and spoke a little English, would act as their guide and lead them to a predominantly Christian village.

Accordingly, May and Mavis accompanied the boys to Jegarata, where they found Embogi digging in his garden. That night they slept in the village longhouse beside the women and children.

In the morning, Embogi told them he would take them to an even remoter Christian village where they would be safe. This seemed to be their only option and it looked promising. However, Embogi had a hidden agenda.

He was resentful towards the missionaries whom he felt had undermined his power, and extended his anger to all Europeans.[16] He decided to seek revenge by betraying the women to the Japanese at Popondetta. Embogi had already had one meeting with the Japanese and been offered a bribe to act as their spy. He believed he would acquire some financial or personal advantage from the betrayal.

May and Mavis, who had never received anything but kindness from Papuans, naturally trusted Embogi and were unaware of any danger. They followed him into the jungle. However, instead of leading the women to safety he took a round-about route back to Popondetta.

Tiondo's nephew and his young friend did not trust Embogi so they followed him from a safe distance. They soon realised the elder was taking the women in the wrong direction. They ran back to Upper Dobodura and reported to Tionda that it seemed Embogi was taking the women to the Japanese at Popondetta.

Another uncle of the boys, Aitere, had received much kindness from Anglican missionaries. He was horrified at Embogi's treachery and hurried along the track after the women, hoping to warn them while there was still time. However, by now the group was so far ahead of him that Aitere could not overtake them.

By the time Aitere reached Popondetta,[17] Embogi had handed the women over to the Japanese. Their captors had taken them to Ururu plantation, where they locked them inside a large cage made from wire-mesh and used for storing coffee beans.

As dusk fell, Aitere crept close to the cage. Fearing he would be caught and imprisoned, the women waved him away. So Aitere hid behind some bushes and stayed there, keeping watch throughout the night.

By now, Mavis and May were desperately thirsty in the tropical heat. Through the mesh of the cage Japanese soldiers amused themselves by offering the captives water and then snatching it away before they could reach it. They repeated the same cat and mouse game with a plate of rice. After an hour or so the women refused to react and sat on the floor of the cage and wept, doubtless aware of their probable fate.

At eight o'clock, the following morning, Aitere saw four Japanese soldiers appear, two carrying rifles and two carrying shovels. They unlocked the cage and at rifle point escorted May and Mavis into the heart of the plantation.

Aitere followed at a safe distance so the soldiers could not see him. The Japanese halted at the site of a freshly dug grave. They handed the women the shovels and made signs to them to make the grave deeper. They stood over the two women menacingly as they struggled to do this.

Then one of the soldiers approached close to Mavis and tried to embrace her and paw her chest. She struggled fiercely. Angered by the rejection, the soldier stepped back and plunged his bayonet into her side. Mavis fell to the ground in agony, her life blood ebbing away.

The sight of her friend's sufferings was so unbearable that May covered her eyes with her handkerchief. A second soldier then plunged his bayonet into May's throat. The sharp edge of the weapon severed her jugular and May died almost instantly.

According to Aitere, the four soldiers lifted up the women's lifeless bodies and threw them into the grave without the least sign of remorse. They covered the bodies with a thin layer of earth and then departed.

After the war the murders of Sister May Hayman, Mavis Parkinson, May's fiancé, Vivian Redlich, Sister Margery Brenchley, Lilla Lashmar and Lucian Tapiedi were considered as war crimes against civilians. Under the terms of the Geneva Convention the women were unarmed non-combatants who had only entered a war zone for humanitarian reasons.

Embogi was tried for treachery and hung.[18]

Years later, the bodies of May Hayman and Mavis Parkinson were exhumed and reburied at Sangara Mission alongside those of Margery Brenchley, Lilla Lashmar and Lucian Tapiedi, whose statue stands in Westminster Abbey along with a plaque to the mission women who died in Papua.

Each year on Martyrs' Day in September, Anglican churches around Australia remember all those Australians and Papuans slain by the Japanese in Papua and New Guinea.

The original buildings of Gona Mission were destroyed by bombs during fighting between Australians and Japanese troops. Subsequently, a new and more modern mission complex was built. A white-painted wooden cross remains from the old mission, and a stone altar near Popondetta commemorates the lives and deaths of May Hayman and Mavis Parkinson.

COURTESY ANGLICAN BOARD OF MISSION — AUSTRALIA LTD.

The altar at Popondetta commemorating Frances May Hayman and Mavis Parkinson.

In total thirty-three Europeans were killed by the Japanese when they invaded Papua. Hivajapa, Lucian Tapiedi's killer, was overcome with guilt and converted to Christianity, taking the name of his victim and building a church dedicated to Lucian's memory.

Although unknown to the wider population of Australia, May and Mavis are remembered in the Anglican Church in Australia and elsewhere. May Hayman had been a parishioner of Canberra's St John's Church in the suburb of Reid. The church erected a stained glass window in her memory. She is also represented in a beautiful stained glass window at St Mark's, in Camberwell, Melbourne. Well-known Brisbane artist William Bustard commemorated May's life in a memorial in St John's Cathedral, and there is another icon commemorating various martyrs including May Hayman in St Nicholas's Church, Guildford, in Britain.

In Mavis's home town of Ipswich, a small, simple bamboo cross commemorating her is displayed near the altar in the Martyrs' Chapel in St Paul's Church where Mavis worshipped. Another bamboo cross commemorates May Hayman in Adelaide. Mavis's niece and namesake, Mavis Mathieson-Frame, told me that similar bamboo crosses were donated to Anglican churches in places where other murdered mission staff had worshipped.

The one bright note in this tragic story is that those bamboo crosses were donated in a spirit of reconciliation by Japanese bishops.

ACKNOWLEDGEMENTS

Thanks are due to Judith Stove, the granddaughter of Emma Withnell; Rosalie Kunoth-Monks, granddaughter of Amelia Kunoth, star of the movie *Jedda* and a worker for Aboriginal rights; the descendants of Dolly Bonson in Darwin; Ron Maunsell, son of Evelyn Maunsell; and to the Archives Service of the Northern Territory and the AITSIS (Australian Institute of Aboriginal and Torres Strait Islander Studies) Library for its help with the names of various Aboriginal groups.

I would also like to thank Stuart Traynor, Senior Interpretive Officer with the Northern Territory Department of Primary Industry, Planning and Environment, for information on Atlanta Bradshaw; Rob McDonald, Librarian at the Arid Zone Research Institute, Alice Springs; Graeme Shaughnessy of the Strehlow Research Centre, Alice Springs; Graeme Powell and Valerie Helson of the Manuscripts Department of the National Library of Australia; Gisela Triesch, German translator; my publishers Helen Littleton and Amruta Slee, and all the staff at HarperCollins who have worked on this book.

Special thanks are due to my husband, Jake de Vries, who read through the manuscript and suggested amendments, scanned old photographs and drew the maps which are such a help in a book of this nature. And, of course, not forgetting my loyal literary agent, Selwa Anthony, whose encouragement and support throughout the publication of this series of five books has been phenomenal. Special thanks go to Terry Underwood, a great contemporary woman of the outback.

Susanna de Vries

Permission to quote from Hector Holthouse's *S'pose I Die*, courtesy Sybil Holthouse. Every effort has been made to contact copyright holders of quoted extracts. The author apologises for those cases where it has been impossible to obtain permission, and invites copyright holders to contact her care of HarperCollins.

I would like to thank Irene Papadopoulos, who provided stories her mother related about Olive King's stay with her in Salonika (Thessaloniki); my good friend, Michael Wilson, former high commissioner to Papua, for his background information on Papua and for material on Serbia from his time as Australian ambassador to that country; Dr David Ritchie for medical information; Reit Dekker for information about Dutch women imprisoned by the Japanese; Mrs J. Griffiths and Mervyn McNee for information about Joyce Tweddell; Mavis Mathieson-Frame, Graeme Barron and Jenny MacLennan, OAM, for information on Mavis Parkinson, Sister May Hayman and Lieutenant Arthur Smith; and Joyce Welsh for information on Joice Loch. Thank you also to Barbara Angell, author of the biography of Wilma Oram, for putting me in touch with Gwen Friend, Betty Jeffrey's radio producer, and to Gwen Friend who kindly shared her memories of Betty with me; also to Emily Malone, great-niece of Betty Jeffrey.

I am also indebted to Mavis Parkinson's niece, Mavis Mathieson-Frame for permission to print a large part of her aunt's last letter; to

Glenda Murrell, Diocesan Archivist of the Anglican Archives Centre, Church House, Anne Street, Brisbane, for help with research; the Anglican Board of Mission — Australia Ltd for permission to use photographs and text from *The Road to Gona*; and to the Rev. John Cuffe for drawing the story of Mavis Parkinson and May Hayman to my attention. Excerpts from Alice Kitchen's diary have been reprinted with permission from the State Library of Victoria.

Every effort has been made to contact copyright holders and the author and publishers apologise in any case where this has not been possible.

I would also like to thank my literary agent, Selwa Anthony; my assistant, Marusia McCormick; my husband, Jake de Vries, for map design and photographs; and the team at HarperCollins, a publisher that supports writing the hitherto ignored histories of some great Australian women.

This book has taken a long time to research and compile, covering as it does so many women and so many different fields of battle. It has been fascinating to write but at times disturbing for me, who as a child lost my home during the bombing of London in World War II and detests war and its effects.

Biographies are more than just paper and string, they are ideas about and investigation of past lives and past eras. I am grateful to all those who have helped by furnishing information, loaning books and allowing me to reproduce photographs and correspondence.

Susanna de Vries
Brisbane, 2004

ENDNOTES

PART 1: GREAT PIONEER WOMEN OF THE OUTBACK

CHAPTER 1: FARMING FRESH FIELDS

1 Two accounts of the life of Georgiana Molloy and the Bussell family can be found in Hasluck, Alexandria, *Georgiana Molloy: Portrait with Background*, Oxford University Press, Melbourne, 1955; and Lines, William J., *All Consuming Passion: Origins, Modernity and the Australian Life of Georgiana Molloy*, Allen & Unwin, Sydney, 1994. The more recent Lines book frequently adopts a different view from Hasluck's, especially regarding Aboriginal and colonial relations.

2 *The Australian Dictionary of Biography*, Vol. 2, 1788–1850, Melbourne University Press, Melbourne, 1967, relates that Captain John Molloy was named after his foster father, Captain A.J.P. Molloy, a penniless sea captain dismissed from the British Navy for cowardice in 1795. The registration of John Molloy's death in October 1867 at Busselton Court House gives his birthdate as 5 September 1780. In an article entitled 'Links with the Past', published by Horace Stirling in the Perth *Sunday Times* of 22 May 1921, the author records that John Molloy's fees at Harrow and Oxford were paid by an unknown benefactor. Stirling records, too, that on reaching his majority Jack Molloy was handed a sum of money by lawyers acting for the Duke of York to buy himself a commission as an officer in the army or navy.

 Captain Molloy's regiment was widely known as the 'Green Jackets' because, instead of wearing red jackets, like the rest of the British Army, they camouflaged themselves in dark green.

3 For details about the Swan River Association, see Battye, J.S., *Western Australia,* Clarendon Press, Oxford, 1924; Uren, Malcolm, *Land Looking West: The Story of Governor Stirling in Western Australia,* Oxford University Press, London, 1948; the James Stirling papers, Battye Library, State Library of Western Australia, Perth; and Cameron, J., 'Information Distortion in Colonial Promotion: The Case of the Swan River Colony', *Australian Geographical Studies,* Vol. 12, No. 1, 1974. See also *ADB*, Vol. 2, *op. cit.* entries on Thomas Peel and on Solomon Levey.

4 Ogle, Nathaniel, *The Colony of Western Australia. A Manual for Emigrants,* James Fraser Publishers, London, 1839, the unfortunate Ogle being another of the Swan River settlers.

5   Bussell Family Papers, Battye Library, State Library of Western Australia, Perth.

6   Letter from Georgiana Molloy to Helen Story, 25 January 1830, Battye Library, Perth.

7   Friend, Mary Anne, Journal, 1834, cited in de Vries-Evans, Susanna, *Pioneer Women, Pioneer Land*, Angus & Robertson, Sydney, 1987, pp. 243–51. Captain and Mrs Matthew Friend, who had been interested in receiving a land grant, took their ship to Tasmania and were given a land grant there instead. Mary Anne's story was related in *Another Two Years at Sea* by Jane Roberts & M.A. Friend, London, n.d.; see also *ADB*, Vol. 1, *op. cit.*, pp. 417–18.

8   Georgiana Molloy to Helen Story, 1 October 1833, Battye Library, Perth.

9   The duties of a Government resident magistrate were listed in a decree from Lieutenant Governor Stirling dated 21 March 1831, cited in Hasluck, *op. cit.* appendix D.

10   Captain Molloy named various points on his land at Augusta, WA, after a different title of Frederick, Duke of York, such as Point Frederick, York Street, Duke's Head and Osnaburg, the duke being also Duke of Osnaburg.

11   Georgiana Molloy to Maggie Dunlop, 12 January 1833, Battye Library, Perth.

12   Fanny Bussell to Mrs Frances Bussell, 21 April 1833, Bussell Family Papers, *op. cit.*

13   *Ibid.*

14   Bessie Bussell to Fanny Bussell, 5 November 1833, Bussell Family Papers, *op. cit.*

15   In fact Georgiana was wrong. The Bibbulmun used broken glass for *tipping* their spears to make them far more deadly, as glass splinters had terrible effects on wounds.

16   Georgiana Molloy to Helen Story, 8 December 1834, Battye Library, Perth.

17   Georgiana Molloy to Mrs Kennedy, 29 May 1833, Cumbria Record Office, Carlisle, and Georgiana Molloy to Elizabeth Besley, 13 November 1833, Battye Library, Perth.

18   Georgiana Molloy to Helen Story, 8 December 1834, Battye Library, Perth.

19   Bussell, Bessie, Journal, Bussell Family Papers, *op. cit.*

20   Bussell, Bessie, to Capel Carter, 13 September 1835, Bussell Family Papers, *op. cit.*

21   Bussell, Bessie, Journal, Bussell Family Papers, *op. cit.*

22   *Ibid.*

23   *Ibid.* See Hasluck, *op. cit.*, pp. 164–5. Lines, *op. cit.*, who is far more sympathetic to the Bussells, does not mention the noisy corroborees at Windelup. On p. 299 he details the story of the Vasse settlers and the gradual extinction of the Wardandi whom Lines refers to simply as 'Nyungar'. AITSIS Library states that 'Nyungar' is a generic word and the clan around Augusta and the Vasse were Wardandi-Bibbulmun.

24   Georgiana Molloy to Helen Story, 8 December 1834, Battye Library, Perth.

25   Georgiana Molloy to Captain Mangles, 25 January 1838, Battye Library, Perth.

26   The fine was so small that in spite of the efforts of the Exeter Hall reformist movement, who wanted native people treated as British subjects with the full rights of any subject of the British Crown, settlers continued to murder members of the Wardandi-Bibbulmun. The end result was that by 1907 the largest group of Aborigines in Western Australia had died out, either murdered by settlers or dead from imported diseases such as measles, mumps and syphilis, or from alcohol addiction. The death of the last member of the Bibbulmun was recorded by Daisy Bates, who had made an anthropological study of various Bibbulmun groups and their language. In 1907 Daisy described burying Joobaitch, the last of the Bibbulmun. She recorded in her memoirs that when Captain Stirling arrived at Swan River in 1829, he estimated over 1500 Bibbulmun roamed the country from Perth to the Vasse.

27   Georgiana Molloy to Captain James Mangles, 31 January 1840, Battye Library, Perth.

28   In the 1830s, decades before the great Hungarian scientist Ignaz Semmelweiss made his important discovery that puerperal or childbed fever could be prevented using antiseptic methods, infection was frequently passed to the mother from the unwashed

hands and blood-stained clothing of the doctor or midwife. These discoveries came too late to help Georgiana and many women like her.

29   Georgiana Molloy to Captain Mangles, June 1840, Battye Library, Perth.

30   The account of John Ramsden Wollaston's stay with the Molloys is contained in Wollaston's *Picton Journal*, Paterson Brokenshaw, Perth, 1948.

31   Wollaston, *Picton Journal*, *op. cit.*, pp. 34–6 and 161.

32   Georgiana Molloy to Captain Mangles, n.d., Battye Library, Perth.

33   Cited by Hasluck, *op. cit.*, pp. 177, 479.

34   See Moyal, Ann, *A Bright and Savage Land: Scientists in Colonial Australia*, William Collins, Sydney, 1986, p. 109. Unauthorised appropriation of women's work continued for decades. Professor Radcliffe-Brown plagiarised Daisy Bates' unpublished study and never even returned her original when she requested it. It was published in Bates' own name after her death as *The Native Tribes of Western Australia*. Note also Professor Edgeworth-David's appropriation without permission of the scientific research of Georgiana King. These were not the only cases. Women were banned from membership of most scientific organisations, including London's prestigious Royal Geographical Society which, in the 1870s, turned down applications for membership from Gertrude Bell the archaeologist, and Mary Kingsley the explorer of Africa, only admitting them in the 1880s with reluctance.

CHAPTER 2: THE SPINIFEX PIONEER WHO BECAME THE MOTHER OF THE NORTH-WEST

1   Nancy E. Withnell Taylor's biography of her grandparents, *A Saga of the North West: 'YEERA-MUK-A-DOO'*, Hesperian Press, 2002, provided material for this chapter. Nancy E. Withnell Taylor was the daughter of the late Horace Withnell, one of Emma and John Withnell's twin boys. Information on Emma Withnell comes also from *ADB*, Vol. 6. *op. cit.* Emma's life has also been briefly related by Eve Pownall in *Mary of Maranoa: Tales of Australian Pioneer Women*, F.H. Johnstone, Sydney, 1959. Emma is also mentioned by J.S. Battye & M.J. Fox in *The History of the North-west of Australia*, Jones, Perth, 1915.

2   As well as Emma Withnell, their illustrious descendants would include the famous mining entrepreneur Langley 'Lang' George Hancock.

3   Cited in Taylor, *op. cit.*, p.12.

4   Later the entire area with Roebourne, Cossack and Port Hedland as its main ports would become known as the Pilbara. Nickol Bay was named by Francis Gergory.

5   There is no record as to how many days the Withnells had to remain on the island before the *Sea Ripple* could be refloated.

6   It was usual in Emma Withnell's day for a ship to sound one gunshot on arrival and a second one on landing.

7   The chair is today in the Roebourne Museum.

8   Withnell family records, cited by Taylor, *op. cit.*

9   It must have taken the Withnells years to increase their stock to an economically viable flock by breeding alone. It is likely that they purchased additional sheep, perhaps with some financial assistance from Emma's father, George Hancock.

10   Cited in Taylor, *op. cit.* and Pownall, *op.cit.*

11   Sholl, R.J., Journal 1886, Manuscripts Department, Battye Library, Perth.

12   Vaccinations against smallpox had begun after Edward Jenner developed his cowpox vaccine in 1796.

13   Taylor, *op. cit.*, p. 123.

14   Nancy E. Withnell Taylor describes the friendship between the Withnells and the
      Ngarluma. Emma's son John would write a book about the Aboriginal tribes of the
      north-west of Western Australia and provide Daisy Bates with information for *The
      Native Tribes of Western Australia*, National Library of Australia, Canberra, 1985
      (published posthumously).

15   Emma Withnell renamed Sherlock Station, Brooklyn, but from records it appears that
      Sherlock Station remained the more widely used name.

16   Figures from Taylor, *op. cit.*, p. 230.

17   *Ibid.*, p. 236.

CHAPTER 3: MOTHERING SEVEN LITTLE AUSTRALIANS
AT ALICE SPRINGS

1   Information about life at the telegraph station has been derived largely from the
      memoirs of Atlanta's eldest daughter, Doris Bradshaw (Blackwell), who provided a
      lively account of an intelligent girl growing up in the outback in *Alice on the Line*
      (Doris Blackwell and Douglas Lockwood, Rigby, Adelaide, 1965). Using extracts from
      her father's diary, Doris presented a rather more vivid portrait of him than of Atlanta.
      Additional information about life at the Alice Springs Telegraph Station is contained
      in Francis Gillen's collected letters to Professor Baldwin Spencer, *My Dear Spencer: The
      Letters of F.J. Gillen to Baldwin Spencer*, eds. Mulvaney J., Morphy, H. & Petch, A., Hyland
      House, Melbourne, 1997; Brown, Shirley, *Alec, A Living History of the Telegraph Station*,
      Alice Springs, 2002; and Thomas Bradshaw's photographs on display at the old
      telegraph station, Alice Springs.
          The original Alice Spring rises in a waterhole in the normally dry riverbed of the
      Todd River, named after Alice Todd. The telegraph route through 'Alice Spring' was
      discovered by Scottish-born explorer John Ross, the second man to cross the
      Australian centre after John McDouall Stuart. After the telegraph station and post
      office were moved to Stuart (renamed Alice Springs), the buildings at the old telegraph
      station housed children removed from Aboriginal mothers. It was then known as the
      Half-Castes Home.
          Interestingly, John Ross was the great-grandfather of Alec Ross, a part-Aboriginal
      man who works as a guide at the old telegraph station who was removed from his
      mother when he was sick. 'That's why I was taken from my mother and "removed" to
      the Alice Springs Telegraph Station. If I hadn't been taken away I'd never have enjoyed
      the life I live today. I understand why they took us away and gave us good meals to
      get me back into good health again . . . because my mother lived like her people did
      centuries earlier — a rough kind of life, surrounded by dogs — out in the bush with
      nothing,' Brown, *op. cit.*

2   Thomas Bradshaw seems to have been a distant relative of Aeneas Gunn's cousin Joseph
      Bradshaw, a pioneer of the Kimberleys. Joseph Bradshaw has gone down in history
      because, when searching for new grazing lands for his cattle, he discovered the mysterious
      and elegant cave paintings of the Kimberley region known by Aboriginal people today
      as Gwion-Gwion. A dispute now rages over whether they were painted by Aborigines
      who have lost this particular technique (so different from other Aboriginal art) or were
      painted by people from elsewhere, possibly South-east Asia, or, as researcher and author
      Graham Walsh believes, by a people who predated Aborigines in that area.

3   Stationmaster Stapleton was speared to death by Aborigines at Barrow Creek

Telegraph Station, and the future Superintendent Ernest Flint was also speared and left for dead but later recovered. The death of Stapleton led to a massacre of the local Aborigines by white troops and native police, who on occasions took a very active part in neck-chaining and killing rival Aboriginal tribes.

4   The old Ghan steam train, known as the 'Red Rattler', ran from Adelaide to Oodnadatta; the new Ghan, in 2004 linked to Darwin, does not pass through Oodnadatta. However, the old part of the line is almost as bumpy as the line Atlanta travelled on. The new line between Alice Springs and Darwin is considerably smoother and fulfils the hopes of the pioneers that one day the Australian continent would be traversed by a train.

5   See Hill, Ernestine, *The Territory: A Sprawling Saga of Australia's Tropic North,* Angus & Robertson, Sydney, (1951) 1981, p. 212 for a description.

6   Blackwell & Lockwood, *op. cit.,* p. 38.

7   *Ibid.,* p. 35.

8   See Brown, Shirley, *Alice Springs, Past and Present,* Brown Publishing, Alice Springs, 1993, p. 6.

9   Ownership of the Hermannsburg Mission was handed to the Aboriginal people in 1982.

10   Information about Constable Willshire in Strehlow, T.G.H., *Journey to Horseshoe Bend,* 1969.

11   Spencer and Gillen's *The Native Tribes of Central Australia* influenced contemporary anthropological theory, although some of the authors' social Darwinian assertions about the fossilised society and childlike character of the Arrernte arouse great controversy today. Despite some of his conclusions, Francis Gillen is deemed an important figure in the history of anthropology. Gillen made wax dictaphone recordings of the Arrernte (also known as the Arunta or Aranda) and was allowed to take photographs of secret initiation ceremonies. His diary was published by the South Australian Museum, Adelaide, in 1968; the museum holds the original, along with an important collection of Gillen's photographs of Arrernte ceremonies. Thomas Bradshaw's photographs of his family life and of the local Arrernte are owned by the Northern Territory Department of Primary Industry, Planning and Environment, Arid Research Centre, Alice Springs.

12   According to Stuart Traynor, Senior Interpretive Officer for NT Department of Primary Industry, Planning and Environment, the remaining glass-plate negatives of Thomas Bradshaw's are housed in a safe in the department's office at Alice Springs and a display of prints at the telegraph station. The originals cannot be seen but there is an album of high-quality prints in the department's library. Some glass-plate originals were destroyed by mistake when the Bradshaw family lived in Adelaide.

13   *Naragu* (or namesake relationship), where one person is named after another, is common in Aboriginal society. This seems to have occurred with Tryphena (who appears as Tryff in Thomas Bradshaw's photograph album). She was named after Mrs Tryphena Benstead, wife of Bill Benstead, a pioneer pastoralist who had raised her.

Information about Amelia Pavey from telephone interviews with Rosalie Kunoth-Monks, Amelia's granddaughter, 12 and 18 July 2004, and from NT Primary Industry, Planning and Environment department library, Alice Springs. Jack Pavey appears in the library records as Amelia's father. Kunoth-Monks confirmed that Jack Pavey was Amelia's father and that Amelia was angry and distressed that he had abandoned her. She had no idea what became of Pavey in later life. Kunoth-Monks also said that the 'Bradshaws were wonderful people who taught Amelia never to hate anyone on the basis of colour'. Kunoth-Monks was the star of Charles Chauvel's film *Jedda.* She lives in Alice Springs.

14   Blackwell & Lockwood, *ibid.,* p. 57.

15 *Ibid.*, p. 97.

16 The grave is still there.

17 Shepherd, Shirley, *The Role of White Women in Central Australia Until 1911*, unpublished manuscript, Peter Spillett Library, Northern Territory. Details of Arrernte women's food gathering from *The Native Tribes of Central Australia, op. cit.*, which is still a major source of information about the Arrernte and their traditional practices.

18 Blackwell & Lockwood, *op. cit.*, p. 67.

19 *Ibid.*

20 *Ibid.*, p. 100.

21 *Ibid.*, p. 68.

22 The Strehlows returned to Germany for two years to educate their children but came back to Hermannsburg. Their son T.G.H. (Ted) Strehlow would become a famous anthropologist and linguist and a founding member of the Australian Institute of Aboriginal Studies. He would be given some of the most sacred *tjuringa* (ceremonial carvings) of the Arrernte by the elders and many of these are now stored in the Strehlow Research Centre at Alice Springs.

23 Blackwell & Lockwood, *op. cit.*, p. 108.

24 In her memoir Doris does not elaborate on her mother's gynaecological problems but it appears Atlanta could have had one of several complications — from a prolapsed womb to acute vaginitis, a common enough problem among women in hot climates before the discovery of antibiotics in the 1940s.

25 Blackwell & Lockwood, *op. cit.*, p. 108.

26 *Ibid.*, p. 101.

27 *Ibid.*, p. 200.

28 *Ibid.*, p. 201.

29 *Ibid.*, p. 203.

30 Personal communication, Graeme Shaughnessy, Strehlow Research Centre, Alice Springs.

31 Brown, *op. cit.*

Chapter 4: The Story Behind *We of the Never-Never*

1 For a description of life in the Northern Terriroty and information about the Bradshaws and Aeneas Gunn, see Hill, Ernestine, *The Territory: A Saga of Australia's Tropical North*, Angus & Robertson, 1951 (and subsequent editions), in particular pp. 245–54. Sources for Jeannie Gunn's story are Gunn, Mrs A., *We of the Never-Never*, Hutchinson of Australia Melbourne, (1908) 1982; Gunn, Mrs A., *The Little Black Princess*, A. Moring, London, 1905, reprinted by Angus & Robertson, Sydney, 1982; Gunn Papers 1841–1912, National Library of Australia, Canberra; Nesdale, Ira, *The Little Missus*, Lynton Publications, Blackwood, SA, 1977; *ADB*, Vol. 9, Melbourne University Press, Melbourne, 1983; Linklater, H.T., *Echoes of the Elsey Saga: Research of Pioneers of the Northern Territory in the Epochal Days of the Elsey Station,* self-published, 1980; and Willing, Tim & Keneally, Kevin, *Under a Regent Moon,* Department of Conservation and Land Management, Western Australia, 2002. Also Broadbent, David, 'The Elsey Myth Revealed', *The Age*, 12 May 1979.

2 The *ADB* and Nesdale, *op. cit.*, differ on this point.

3 See Hill, *op. cit.*, pp. 169–70.

4 Jeannie Gunn to Bob Gunn, Gunn Papers, National Library of Australia, Canberra.

5 For the story of Mary Jane (Guy) Bradshaw, see James, Barbara, *No Man's Land: Women of the Northern Territory*, Collins, Sydney, 1989.

6   This reason is mentioned by Jeannie Gunn on p. 4 of the illustrated edition of *We of the Never-Never*, a deluxe edition published by Angus & Robertson in 1987.

7   This aspect of station life is not mentioned in *We of the Never-Never*. The practice of Aboriginal women being used as 'stockmen's gins' occurred on many pastoral stations. It was referred to with indignation by other female authors, such as Jessie Litchfield and Katherine Susannah Prichard. Letters held in the John Oxley Library, Brisbane, dated 1910 and addressed to several Protectors of Aborigines were written by an anonymous writer to complain about the practice of keeping 'stud gins' for the boss's exclusive use, while 'stockmen's gins' were passed from hand to hand.

8   For the following quotes, see *We of the Never-Never, op. cit.*, chapter 2.

9   *Ibid.*, chapter 3.

10   Preludes to *We of the Never-Never*, 1908 edition and others.

11   The following quotes, *We of the Never-Never, op. cit.*, chapter 4.

12   *Ibid.*, chapter 5.

13   For the following quotes, see *We of the Never-Never, op. cit.*, chapter 6.

14   See examples cited in Nesdale, *op. cit.*, and Hill, *op. cit.*

15   Aeneas Gunn to Bob Gunn, February 1902, Gunn Papers, *op. cit.*

16   For the following quotes, see *We of the Never-Never, op. cit.*, chapter 7.

17   For the following quotes, see *ibid.*, chapter 9.

18   For the following quotes, *ibid.*, chapter 10.

19   For the following quotes, *ibid.*, chapter 11.

20   *Ibid.*, chapter 12.

21   The Fizzer drowned trying to cross Cummings Creek. He was buried there and in 1911 reburied at the Elsey Memorial Cemetery, about twenty kilometres south of Mataranka.

22   Jeannie learned that Dolly's (Bett-Bett's) father was Lewis Cummings, a Glaswegian employed by the Overland Telegraph Line, who had left the Roper River camp and gone to work in Adelaide. For almost half a century, possibly to shield Dolly — and other stockmen who had also fathered children — Jeannie kept silent, mentioning only Dolly's mother, Katie Wooloomool, in a newspaper article in *The Age* in 1955.

23   *The Little Black Princess, op. cit.*, p. 156.

24   That Dolly did indeed choose to stay with the Gunns is indicated in a recording made when Dolly was in her nineties as part of a series of oral history recordings about Darwin. A transcript of the interview is in the archives of the Northern Territory in Darwin (NTRS 226). Due to Dolly's advanced age, the interview is rather rambling but the recording is very clear. See also Frizell, Helen, 'Whatever Happened to the People of the Never-Never?', *Sydney Morning Herald*, 3 January 1982; and Linklater, *op. cit.*

25   Gunn, Mrs A., 'Australia's Little Bett-Bett is Now a Grandmother', *The Age*, 15 January 1955.

26   Gunn, A., *Northern Territory Times*, 21 October 1902, cited in Nesdale, *op. cit.*, p. 67.

27   Gunn, A., letter to *Northern Territory Times*, January 1903, cited in Nesdale *op. cit.*, pp. 66–7 and Hill, *op. cit.*, p. 248. Goggle Eye's death is described in chapter 12 of *The Little Black Princess*.

28   *We of the Never-Never, op. cit.*, p. 126.

29   *Ibid.*, p. 177.

30   *Ibid.*, p. 139.

31   For the following quotes, *ibid.*, chapter 16.

32   This was a fairly usual attitude at that time. During World War I, for example, some Anzac soldiers in Egypt and in France (mainly bushmen from Victoria) told their

officers they did not want to be nursed by women; they preferred to be nursed by male orderlies. See the story of Sister Alice Kitchen, p. 415.

33   *We of the Never-Never, op. cit.*, p. 103.

34   Aeneas Gunn to Bob Gunn, 9 October 1902, Gunn Papers, *op. cit.*

35   Jeannie Gunn to Bob and Nellie Gunn, 7 November 1902, Gunn Papers, *op. cit.*

36   *We of the Never-Never, op. cit.*, p. 235.

37   Jeannie Gunn to Nellie Gunn, December 1902, Gunn Papers, *op. cit.*

38   Jeannie Gunn to Bob Gunn, n.d., Gunn Papers, *op. cit.*

39   *We of the Never-Never, op. cit.*, p. 238.

40   Jeannie Gunn's notes and letters to her family and those to the family of her husband are with her personal papers in the Manuscripts Section of the National Library of Australia, Canberra.

41   *We of the Never-Never, op. cit.*, p. 185. These words and many other unrelated passages have been removed from abridged Angus & Robertson editions.

42   See Willing & Kenneally, *op. cit.*

43   See Broadbent, David, 'The Elsey Myth Revealed', *The Age*, 12 May 1979, reporting on the research of Dr Francesca Merlan among the Mangarrayi. See also Merlan, Francesca, *Big River Country: Stories from Elsey Station*, IAD Press, Alice Springs, 1996, pp. x–xvi; and Yunupingu, Galarrwuy, *Our Land is Our Life: Land Rights Past, Present and Future*, University of Queensland Press, St Lucia, 1997.

44   *We of the Never-Never, op. cit.*, p. 68.

45   *Ibid.*, p. 186.

46   *Ibid.*, pp. 185–6.

47   Jock McLennan to Jeannie Gunn, n.d., Gunn Papers, *op. cit.*

48   Jeannie Gunn to Jock McLennan, n.d., Gunn Papers, *op. cit.*

49   McAleer, A.J., 'The Diggers' Heroine of Monbulk', introduction to *My Boys: A Book of Remembrance*, by Mrs Aeneas Gunn, Monbulk RSL, Monbulk, Victoria, 2000.

50   Mrs M. Berry, reminiscences of Mrs Gunn, cited in McAleer, *ibid.*

51   McAleer, *ibid.*

52   Transcript of Dolly Bonson's recorded interview, Northern Territory Archives, Darwin (NTRS 226); also Frizell, *op. cit.*; and Linklater, *op. cit.* Linklater's uncle had known Jeannie at the Elsey.

53   There are no extant letters detailing any contact between Mrs Gunn and Lewis Cummings, or referring to transactions with Dolly's Aunt Judy or her mother. Jeannie mentions in her 1955 article (*op. cit.*) that Dolly had written to her in 1925 saying her mother was with the tribes around old Elsey homestead.

54   Frizell, *op. cit.*

55   According to Jeannie, Dolly told Linklater that she was born in 1892, which would make her fifteen.

56   Gunn, Mrs A., 'Australia's Little Bett-Bett is Now a Grandmother', *op. cit.*

57   In her 1955 article in the Melbourne *Age*, Jeannie gave some of the details of Dolly's early and later life, stating that Dolly was by then a grandmother. She also refers to the 'white strain' in Dolly, which allowed the tribe to give her up and encouraged Europeans to protect her. Copy in State Library of Victoria.

58   Alfred Derham, letter, cited in Nesdale, p. 160.

59   In 1995, management of Elsey pastoral activities was taken up by Max and Mabel Gorringe. The property is today considered one of the best Aboriginal-managed ones in Australia.

CHAPTER 5: AN ENGLISH ROSE IN THE OUTBACK

1   Evelyn Maunsell's story about her engagement and her Cairns wedding were published in a local Limerick newspaper in July 1921 when she was in Ireland. It was based on a journal she kept. Evelyn made several copies of her journal, and gave one to her brothers Tim and Rupert Evans, another to her young sister Ida, one to another brother and one to her parents. Decades later these accounts were used by the late Hector Holthouse, a Queensland sugar chemist and journalist, as the basis for his book *S'pose I Die*, published by Angus & Robertson in 1973 and still in print. Much of the account of her life in this book also relies on this source.

2   Holthouse, *ibid.*, p. 16.

3   *Ibid.*, p. 32.

4   *S'pose I Die*, based on a copy of Evelyn Maunsell's diary and written in an era before political correctness muzzled a lot of statements about the past, recounts (pp. 88–9) how when a Chinese man came to Mount Mulgrave looking for a job, Mary told Evelyn that the Coleman River people preferred to eat white men because the Chinese were 'too salty'. Evelyn noted that 'old-timers' she spoke to told her, on the contrary, 'cannibal blacks preferred Chinese . . . because the whites were too salty'.

5   See Pike, Glenville, *Queensland Frontier*, Rigby, Adelaide, 1978; and Holthouse, *op. cit.* p. 7, where Evelyn Maunsell alludes to Jimmy Collins' reputation.

6   The non-payment of this money is at the time of writing a matter of dispute between Aboriginal groups and the Queensland Government.

7   Information on Paddy Callaghan (whom Evelyn Maunsell refers to as Pat Callaghan) comes from Pike, *op. cit.*, p. 274.

8   Litchfield, Jessie. *Far-North Memories,* Angus & Robertson, Sydney, 1930, p. 56.

9   Her first order included four tons of flour; a ton of coarse salt and a bag of fine salt; twelve seventy-pound bags of sugar, which often arrived in a sticky mass; one bag of brown sugar (for the spiced, salted beef); one case of tea; cases of raisins, currants and sultanas; twenty pounds each of cream of tartar and bicarbonate of soda; two cases of assorted jams; two hundred tins of treacle and golden syrup; six bags of polished rice; three bags of Chinese unpolished rice; one large cask of curry powder; cases of dried apricots, peaches, prunes and apples; a sack each of dried peas, potatoes and onions; a case of Holbrook's dark brown sauce and one of tomato ketchup; bottles of lemon and vanilla essence; hops to brew home-made beer; and Epsom salts (used to cure everything from indigestion to stomach cramps, warts and piles). The order also included two large cases of pipe tobacco, one case each of wooden and clay pipes, and two large cases of matches. See Holthouse, *op. cit.*, pp. 39–40.

10   Holthouse, *op. cit.*, p. 75.

11   This method is not recommended for the treatment of poisonous bites. The pressure immobilisation method followed by prompt medical attention is the recommended treatment today. See Queensland Poisons Information Centre 13 11 26 www.health.qld.gov.au/poisonsinformationcentre

12   Holthouse, *op. cit.*, p. 98.

13   *Ibid.*, p. 100.

14   Evelyn calls it 'beef tea', a term widely used in Evelyn's time but rarely heard today.

15   *Ibid.*, p. 100.

16   *Ibid.*, p. 101.

17   *Ibid.*, p. 115.

18   *Ibid.*, p. 168.

19   Wrotham Park Station is owned by the Australian Agricultural Company and is run by R.M. Williams Holdings. The former Wrotham Park homestead no longer exists but today there are a series of smaller lodges above the river for visitors who wish to experience outback life in comfort.

20   Holthouse, *op. cit.*, p. 176.

21   *Ibid.*, p. 203.

22   *Ibid.*, p. 204.

23   *Ibid.*, p. 206.

24   Evelyn relates that after the partition of Ireland in 1921 and the declaration of the Irish Republic in 1937, Ballybrood (by now crumbling badly) was taken over by the Government of Eire, or Southern Ireland; see Holthouse, *ibid.*, p. 207.

25   Holthouse, *op. cit.*, p. 217.

26   *Ibid.*, p. 221.

CHAPTER 6: ON THE DESERT FRINGE

1   Undated letter, Gunn Papers, National Library of Australia, Canberra.

2   The *ADB*, Vol. 12, *op. cit.*, records in the entry for Myrtle Rose White that her parents' names were Dinah and Mark Kennewell. Information about the life of Myrtle White comes largely from this entry as well as her autobiographical books *No Roads Go By*, Rigby Ltd, Adelaide, (1932) 1962; and *Beyond the Western Rivers*, Angus & Robertson, Sydney, 1955.

3   The deaths of Jane and Henrietta Field were noted in the Adelaide *Advertiser* of 10 February 1862, and mentioned in the introduction to Katie's journal, published in book form by Marcie Muir as *My Bush Book*, Rigby, Adelaide, 1982. Information about the life of Catherine Langloh Parker comes largely from this source.

4   Muir, *ibid.*, p. 46.

5   *Ibid.*, p. 47.

6   *Ibid.*, p. 49.

7   *Ibid.*, p. 58.

8   *Ibid.*, p. 59.

9   *Ibid.*, p. 62.

10   *Ibid.*, p.105.

11   *Ibid.*, p. 147.

12   *Ibid.*, p. 90.

13   The fact that Katie had tried deliberately to create the sentence structures of Yuwaalaraay was pointed out by Henrietta Drake-Brockman in an appendix to the published edition of K. Langloh Parker's *Australian Legendary Tales*, Angus & Robertson, Sydney, 1954, 1955, and other editions.

14   Muir, *op. cit.*, p. 146.

15   *Ibid.*, pp. 115–16.

16   *Ibid.*, pp. 111–12.

17   *Ibid.*, p. 139.

18   Figures taken from the report made by Dalgety's cited in Muir, *ibid.*, pp. 34–6. In 1892 a bore was put down which successfully watered the property. Today Bangate Station is about a quarter of the size it was in Katie and Langloh Parker's day.

19   *Ibid.*, pp. 133 & 138.

20   Myrtle White is very circumspect about her own and her husband's past, living as she did in an era when authors revealed far less than they do today. Myrtle is careful to

refer to family members by aliases in her books; Con is referred to as the 'Boss'; her daughter Doris is 'Little 'un'; son Alan is 'Boy'; and son Garry is 'Little Brother'.

21   Myrtle refers to Lake Elder Station and its depot as Noonameena and Mirrabooka, which style I have followed here.

22   White, *No Roads Go By, op. cit.*, p. 15.

23   *Ibid.*, p. 50.

24   *Ibid.*, pp. 73–4.

25   *Ibid.*, p. 76.

26   See Mary Gilmore in her introduction to *No Roads Go By*, Rigby, Adelaide, 1932, p. 8 where she discusses 'drefting', which also caused sand to bank up against the windows of the homestead.

27   White, *No Roads Go By*, 1962, p. 97.

28   *Ibid.*, p. 134.

29   Myrtle does not say which town she stayed in, referring to it only as 'the city nearest to [the sandhills]', *ibid.*, p. 139. It was presumably Broken Hill.

30   White, *Beyond the Western Rivers, op. cit.*, p. 78.

31   Myrtle does not specify what her illnesses were.

32   White, *Beyond the Western Rivers, op. cit.*, p. 219.

33   *Ibid.*, p. 225.

34   *Ibid.*, p. 229.

35   Her typewriter was bequeathed to the Mortlock Library in Adelaide and her manuscripts are in the Manuscripts Department of the National Library in Canberra.

36   Myrtle White Papers, Manuscripts Department, National Library of Australia, contain references to Myrtle attending an exhibition at the Art Gallery of New South Wales with Miles Franklin as well as meetings of the Fellowship of Australian Writers.

PART 2: HEROIC AUSTRALIAN WOMEN IN WAR

INTRODUCTION

1   Pesman, Ros, in *Duty Free: Australian Women Abroad, Travel and War*, Oxford University Press, Melbourne, 1996, states some sixty Australian nurses sailed for South Africa and the Boer War.

2   Quoted in King, James, *Virginia Woolf*, Penguin, London, 1995, p. 231.

3   Martha Gelhorn, wife of Ernest Hemingway, is credited with this, but Martha's first report was filed in the Spanish Civil War in 1936, twenty-two years after Louise Mack filed hers.

4   Pesman, *op.cit.*, p. 89.

5   Claire Trestrail's contract with the QAIANS is held in the British Public Record Office, Richmond; other details of her work and life were supplied by her son, Peter Trestrail Swan. A Scottish Women's Hospitals doctor gave Claire Trestrail an excellent work reference when she applied for a year's contract with the QAIANS.

6   In order to raise funds for more ambulances and ward staff, John Masefield wrote a book of his war experiences titled *Gallipoli*, published by William Heinemann in 1916 and reprinted four times. He went on to take his book on a fundraising tour of America.

7   Woolf, Virginia, *Mrs Dalloway*, Penguin London, [1950], 1998, p. 71.

8   Adam-Smith, Patsy, *Australian Women at War*, Thomas Nelson, Melbourne, 1984, and Bassett, Jan, *Guns and Brooches: Australian Army Nursing from the Boer War to the Gulf War*, Oxford University Press, Melbourne, 1992, pp. 40–44.

9   Adam-Smith, *ibid.*, p. 195.

10   Cited in Lake, Professor Marilyn (Department of History and Women's Studies, La Trobe University, Melbourne), 'Women Armed for Struggle to Gain Equal Rights', writing in *The Australian* for International Women's Day, May 1997.

11   Adam-Smith, *op. cit.*, p. 377.

12   At St George's, Ascot, Berkshire. Violette attended before World War II; I attended at the end of the war. A book and a film, *Carve Her Name with Pride*, commemorated Violette's heroic death in Ravensbruck.

Chapter 7: Olive May Kelso King

1   Hazel King eventually became senior lecturer in History at the University of Sydney. She edited a collection of Olive's letters under the title *One Woman at War: Letters of Olive King 1915–20*, Melbourne University Press, Melbourne, 1986. The letters present some, but not all, aspects of Olive's life. It is important to realise these letters contain only those facts Olive wanted her father to know and concealed her love affair with a Serb officer. Pages 39–40 of Hazel King's book indicate clearly that Olive and Captain Milan Yovitchitch ('Yovi') were having a passionate affair and that there was considerable gossip about it in Salonika.

2   See entry for Olive King in Volume 9, *Australian Dictionary of Biography*, Melbourne University Press, Melbourne, 1983. See also King, H. ed., *op. cit.*, p. 2, who quotes one of Olive's love poems. Olive refers to her French great-grandmother in a letter dated 6 April 1916.

3   See entry for Sir George Eccles Kelso King, in Volume 5, *Australian Dictionary of Biography, op.cit.*

4   Eliza Hall was co-founder of the internationally famous Walter and Eliza Hall Institute.

5   King, H. ed., *op. cit.*, p. 3.

6   By the time Miles Franklin joined the SWH in 1916 the skirt was shortened to mid-calf length to suit the active lifestyle of the female staff.

7   Letter to Sunny Waring, 14 May 1915, King, H. ed., *op. cit.*

8   The account of Olive's escape from Guevgueli is taken from Hazel King's book, *op. cit.*, pp. 19–20. Interestingly, Hazel bases it on a radio interview Olive gave, and notes that Olive did not give the full details in the letters to her father, hoping he would never learn she had escaped death by a few minutes. Olive King's interview is in ABC Radio archives.

9   It is interesting to compare Olive's enthusiastic account of life in wartime Salonika with the less enthusiastic descriptions provided by Miles Franklin, who served with the SWH at Ostrovo and visited Salonika. See de Vries Susanna, *The Complete Book of Great Australian Women*, HarperCollins, Sydney, 2003, p. 475.

10   Since Greek translations are based on phonetics, this is sometimes written as Mount Hortiach. Accounts of life at this hospital are in Gilchrist, Hugh, *Nightingales in the Mud: Digger Sisters of the Great War*, Allen & Unwin, Sydney, 1989, pp. 85–88, and *Australians and Greeks*, Volume 2, Halstead Press, Sydney, 1997.

11   See King, H. ed., *op. cit.*, pp. 39–40.

12   See references to Olive's diary in King, H.ed, *op. cit.*

13   Olive is not alone in admiring the Serbs greatly. Francesca Wilson, a Quaker aid relief worker with the Serbs, and Muriel Stobart, an SWH nurse who was on the March of Death over the mountains with the Serb Army, also noted the courage and bravery of the Serbs in World War I. J.I. Cudden in *The Companion Guide to Jugoslavia*, describes

the Serbs as courteous, tolerant and good-natured and an exceptionally good-looking race. See also Olive's letters to Kelso King for 1916 in King, H. ed., *op.cit.*

14   See Chapter 2 for description of Dr Agnes Bennett and Dr Lilian Cooper.

15   Mrs Harley's death is recorded in *The Virago Book of Women and the Great War*, Virago, London, 1999.

16   Letter to Kelso King, 18 August 1916, King, H. ed., *op. cit.*

17   Letter to Kelso King, 20 April 1917, *ibid.*

18   Details of the fire of 17 August 1917 from King, H. ed., *op. cit.*, pp 57–60, and from Misha Glenny's *The Balkans 1804–1999: Nationalism, War and the Great Powers*, Granta, London, 1999. Olive's description of the Great Fire in a twenty-two page letter to her father dated 29 August 1917 is, according to Thessaloniki's Byzantine Museums Authority, historically important as it is so detailed.

19   This is the same Jessie McHardy White who left Melbourne on the SS *Benalla* with Alice Kitchen (see Chapter 3).

20   Letter to Kelso King, 12 October 1917, King, H. *op. cit.*

21   See references to Olive's diary in King, H, *op. cit.;* also letters to Sunny Waring for October–November 1917.

22   Interview with Irene Papadopoulos (Thessaloniki, Greece, 1997), who related stories her mother told her about Olive King's life in Salonika and her philanthropic work after the Great Fire.

23   The following description relies on correspondence from early 1918 reprinted in King, H. ed. *op. cit.* The letter in which Olive announces her intentions to marry is missing. Hazel assumes its existence (p. 81) based on Olive's next letter dated 24 April 1918, written from Vodena (Edessa) in northern Greece and referring to a 'shocked and horrified cable' from her father.

24   Interview with Irene Papadopoulos, *op. cit.*

25   Letter to Kelso King, 25 April 1918, King, H. ed., *op. cit.*

26   King, H. ed., *op. cit.*, p. 106; for Sir Charles Wade, see Volume 12, *Australian Dictionary of Biography, op.cit.*

27   Letter to Kelso King, 6 June 1920, King, H. ed. *op. cit.*

28   For years Olive King continued to send money to help the hospital's work with children suffering from cancer and other diseases. When Dr MacPhail retired in 1934, the privately funded children's hospital closed down.

29   Letter to Kelso King, 8 July 1922, King, H. ed., *op. cit.*; likewise quotes and other descriptions about the wedding.

30   It is now generally believed that the assassin was a Macedonian but that the Croatians were involved at long range. The death of King Alexander still arouses great controversy, and there are various Serb and Croatian inspired sites on the Internet speculating over his death or disclaiming responsibility for it.

CHAPTER 8: DR AGNES ELIZABETH LLOYD BENNETT AND DR LILIAN VIOLET COOPER

1   For Hegel's views on women, see *The Philosophy of Right* and *The Phenomendogy of Spirit*, various editions.

2   Curiously, Balls-Headley's *The Evolution of the Diseases of Women*, Smith, Elder, London, 1894, was illustrated by a former female student, Dr Clara Stone.

3   See entry for W.C. Bennett, in Volume 3, *Australian Dictionary of Biography*, Melbourne University Press, Melbourne, 1968.

4   See entry for Agnes Bennett in Volume 7, *Australian Dictionary of Biography,* Melbourne University Press, Melbourne, 1978. Information about Dr Bennett also comes from

her diary and papers held in the Turnbull Library, National Library of New Zealand, ref. 1346/357–8 — the main source for C. Manson and C. Manson's *Dr Agnes Bennett*, Michael Joseph, London, 1966. See also *Dictionary of New Zealand Biography*, www.dnzb.govt.nz/dnzb

5   See entry for Dr Lilian Cooper in Volume 7, *Australian Dictionary of Biography*, *ibid*. See also Morgan, S., *A Short History of Medical Women in Australia*, Rigby, Adelaide, 1970, and Gandevia, B., *An Annotated Bibliography of the History of Medicine in Australia*, Royal Australian College of Physicians, Sydney, 1984.

6   There is, at the time of writing, no extant documentary proof of a lesbian relationship between the two women, although in that era even a hint of lesbianism was shocking.

7   Dr Eleanor Bourne was the first Queensland woman allowed to study medicine but Dr Cooper was the first woman to practise in the state.

8   Williams, Lesley, M., *No Easy Path: The Life and Times of Lilian Violet Cooper*, Amphion Press, Brisbane, 1991.

9   See de Vries, Susanna, *The Complete Book of Great Australian Women*, HarperCollins, Sydney, 2003, pp. 357–377, for the story of Mary McConnel and the Brisbane Children's Hospital.

10   See Lorraine Cazalar's chapter on Dr Lilian Cooper in *Women in History*, Australian Institute for Women's Research and Policy, Griffith University, Brisbane.

11   Dr Bennett's experiences as an Army surgeon in Cairo are related in Volume 2 of Gilchrist, Hugh, *Australians and Greeks*, Halstead Press, Sydney, 1997, p. 132, and are based on her journal in the Turnbull Library, National Library of New Zealand, Auckland. However, the text mistakenly shows Dr Bennett going to Cairo from Paris, while her journal mentions that she disembarked at Alexandria and travelled from there to Cairo.

12   Gilchrist, *ibid.*, pp. 134–135.

13   They would not be released for four months and were treated very badly by their captors.

14   Agnes Bennett papers, *op. cit.*

15   On a visit to northern Greece, I was told how for years afterwards the slopes of the Peak of the Buttercups were littered with skulls and skeletons, guns and equipment; and that walking over them, the fingers of dead men snapped like twigs.

16   Williams, *op. cit.*, has the best description of Dr Cooper's war service of any of the books and articles written about her.

17   Agnes Bennett papers, *op. cit.*

18   Details from the diary of Sister Laura Grubb, attached to BMH Salonika, cited in Jan Bassett's *Guns and Brooches: Australian Army Nursing from the Boer War to the Gulf War*, Oxford University Press, Melbourne, 1992.

19   Manson, C. and Manson, C., *op.cit.*

20   Within a few months, revolution would erupt in Russia and these soldiers would be fighting each other.

21   It is believed that the fact that Dr Mary Garis's fiancé had been killed in action at Gallipoli was what motivated her to enlist with the SWH.

22   Details of Dr Cooper's medals from Werlich, R., *Orders and Decorations of all Nations, Civil and Military*, Quaker Press, London, 1974. Most accounts of Dr Cooper's life mention her Order of St Sava, which was held in far higher esteem than the Russian order, which was given out in fairly large numbers. Werlich refers to more than 5000 Russian decorations awarded by the Tsar in the early years of World War I.

23   For the story of Miles Franklin at Ostrovo see Susanna de Vries, *op. cit.*, pp. 431–506.

Chapter 9: Sister Alice Elizabeth Kitchen

1   Alice Kitchen's journal entries start on 19 October 1914: 'Came on board at 12 noon . . . moved out 2 pm and dropped the pilot outside the heads.' Their convoy had no escort and would not have any protection from cruisers until they reached Albury. Alice's journal was never published but donated anonymously after her death to the State Library of Victoria with no details about her childhood or her life after World War I.

2   The Nominal Shipping Roll for the *Benalla* cites the names of the three nurses who sailed with Alice. Butler, Colonel A.G. in *The Official History of the Australian Army Medical Service in the War 1914–18,* 3 Vols, Australian War Memorial, Melbourne, 1943, and Bassett, Jan in *Guns and Brooches: Australian Army Nursing from the Boer War to the Gulf War*, Oxford University Press, Melbourne, 1992 both comment that the minimum age for a nurse was twenty-five. In World War I, 1947 nurses were between thirty-one and forty, and ninety-one (including Alice and the other senior nurses on the *Benalla*) were over forty. Most returned home in poor health and many experienced financial problems. Due to a clerical error when Alice enlisted, some documents show her age as younger; one gives a date of birth indicating she was in her twenties, although her discharge sheet gives her correct date of birth.

3   Alice only mentions twelve ships sunk in her journal.

4   An identical situation took place in February 2003 when Australian service personnel en route to Iraq refused vaccination against anthrax and were sent home.

5   Braga, Stuart, *Anzac Doctor*, Hale & Iremonger, Sydney, 1999, pp. 123–124.

6   Peter Weir's film *Gallipoli*, although a wonderful evocation of battle scenes, was incorrect in showing nurses with 'bobbed' hair. In 1914–15 nurses were not permitted to bob their hair, which they wore pinned up or plaited and wound round the side of their heads in a style known as 'earphones'. Nor were they permitted to dance in public or wear calf-length skirts until 1916. See the story of Miles Franklin in World War I in de Vries, Susanna, *The Complete Book of Great Australian Women*, HarperCollins, Sydney 2003.

7   A statement in the diary of General Sir Ian Hamilton.

8   See Les Carlyon, *Gallipoli*, Macmillan, Sydney, 2001, pp. 3–53.

9   C.E.W. Bean, in his official history *The Story of Anzac from the Outbreak of War to the End of the First Phase of the Gallipoli Campaign, May 4 1915*, Angus & Robertson, Sydney, 1933, insisted that New Zealanders had started the riot and the Australians joined in.

10 Howitzers fired large shells horizontally at much greater distance than machine guns.

11 Carlyon, *op. cit.*, and Braga, *op. cit.*, pp. 192–194.

12 See entry for Sir Neville Reginald Howse in Volume 9, *Australian Dictionary of Biography*, Melbourne University Press, Melbourne, 1983.

13 Braga, *op. cit.*

14 Young, Margaret, ed., *We are Here Too: Diaries and Letters of Sister Olive L.C. Haynes*, Australian Down Syndrome Association, Adelaide, 1991, confirms Alice's complaints about late pay for nurses as well as soldiers.

15 Austen, Ronald J, *Cobbers in Khaki: The History of 8th Battalion*, Slouch Hat Publications, McCrae, 1997.

16 Alice makes a veiled reference to this woman, who was discharged from the Army in a catatonic state. She is also mentioned in the letters written home by Sister Olive Haynes, quoted in Young, ed., *op. cit.*

17 On supplies, see Goodman, R., *Hospital Ships*, Boolarong Press, Brisbane, 1992.

18 Descriptions of casualties from Masefield, John, *Gallipoli*, William Heinemann, London, 1917, pp. 134–140.

19 Unfortunately Alice's correspondence was not donated to the State Library of Victoria along with her journal. A notice of Major Tubb's death in battle was between the pages

of Alice's diary. Information on Major Frederick Tubb, VC, from Wigmore, Lionel, *They Dared Mightily*, Australian War Memorial, Canberra, 1963.

20 Additional information about Harefield Park Auxiliary Hospital from Butler, *op. cit.*, pp. 269–270. Butler cites twelve doctors and forty-two nurses as working at Harefield. The Nissen huts that housed the hospital staff had been paid for partly by private donors and partly by the Australian government. The Australian War Memorial contains a history of the hospital filed under Document/Harefield Park Hospital.

21 Sisters Kitchen and Elizabeth 'Pearl' Corkhill were recommended for medals but someone, possibly Matron Bessie Pocock, an old enemy of Alice, must have turned down Alice's recommendation because Pearl Corkhill received a medal in September 1918, but Alice did not.

22 The exact number will never be known.

23 These are archived in the State Library of Victoria along with the leather-bound copies of Alice's hand-written journal.

24 The Registry of Births, Deaths and Marriages for the state of Victoria does not hold a birth or death certificate for Alice Elizabeth Kitchen. However, there is an entry for her on the website of the Church of the Latter Day Saints.

CHAPTER 10: JOICE NANKIVELL LOCH

1 Writing Joice Loch's biography, *Blue Ribbons, Bitter Bread,* Hale & Iremonger/Tower Books, Sydney, 2000, I was frequently puzzled as to why accounts by Joice's former housekeeper, Fani Mitropoulou, and her Swiss assistant, Martha Handschin, and others differed from accounts in Joice's autobiography, *A Fringe of Blue,* John Murray, London, 1968.

There were other discrepancies. The dust jacket of Joice's autobiography explained how 'a gift' for narrative journalism took Joice to England in early 1918, where she married Sydney Loch. I was surprised when told by British authorities that they could not find a wedding certificate for Joice. I eventually found one showing Joice and Sydney were married in Melbourne six months later than the date cited in her autobiography. Other aspects of the trip to Cyprus that Joice undertook and described here do not tie in with records or with Sydney Loch's papers.

Joice received a contract from John Murray to write her autobiography only a few months before she fell head-first from a balcony and collapsed onto stone paving. As she was suffering concussion and memory loss, friends of her later years who lived near her in Greece, the well-known archaeologist Dr Philip Sherrard, then compiling of *Athos: The Holy Mountain* (Overlook Press, Woodstock, NY, 1985), and a retired editor, Katherine West, completed Joice's autobiography from the notes and correspondence of Joice and Sydney. Inevitably there were discrepancies which have, in some instances, been hard to sort out.

2 De Loghe [Loch], Sydney, *The Straits Impregnable,* Australasian Author's Agency, Melbourne, 1916.

3 The name of Sydney Loch's contact in the British Secret Service was not revealed by Joice or Sydney in their book *Ireland in Travail,* John Murray, London, 1922, in order to protect him. In *Blue Ribbons, Bitter Bread, op. cit.,* I referred to the secret agent as Major X.

4 Sydney Loch papers and journal, MS 2948, National Library of Australia; letter from Joice Loch to Bob Croker-Poole (cousin), private collection, London.

5 The main source for information about the English community living in Bucharest in World War II (and general conditions there) is Olivia Manning's *Balkan Trilogy*. Filmed as *Fortunes of War* with Kenneth Branagh, the trilogy is regarded as the classic account

of the Balkans from the British point of view. Since 1960, various editions have been published by Random House, London, under different titles. The Bucharest part of Manning's story is called *The Great Fortune* (1960) and documents the period when Olivia, who was press secretary to the British Legation, and Joice saw a great deal of each other.

Additional information comes from Dilks, David ed., *The Diaries of Sir Alexander Cadogan, OM, 1938–45*, Cassell, London, 1971; and Deletant, Professor Dennis, 'A Balancing Act', article on King Carol in *Current History*, Vol. 42, June 1992. Cadogan was head of the Balkan Desk at the Foreign Office under Lord Halifax. The writings of R.D. Smith, British Council lecturer and husband of Olive Manning, famous for putting on performances of Shakespeare in Rumania as the Nazis advanced, also record the period.

6   For an account of the escape of interned Poles in Bucharest, see Olson, Lynne and Cloud, Stanley, *A Question of Honor: The Kosciuszko Squadron*, Alfred Knopf, 2003. This book also mentions two women who supplied the Poles with forged passports. These may have been Joice and Lushya. That Joice supplied the money for the printing press used by the forger to create the passports is confirmed in Sydney Loch's journal but deliberately omitted from the Lochs' reports to the Society of Friends' War Victims Committee in London as the Quakers would have been horrified.

7   See Manning, *op. cit.*, and Deletant, *op. cit.*

8   Paul, Prince of Hohenzollern-Rumania, *King Carol II: A Life of My Grandfather*, Methuen, London, 1988.

9   Like Joice Loch, Francesca Wilson was not a Quaker but a sympathiser and someone with wide humanitarian interests. Francesca saw what the Lochs had been doing and sent back a glowing report to the Society of Friends in London, praising the Lochs for helping the Polish become self-supporting. See Wilson, Francesca, *In the Margins of Chaos*, John Murray, London, 1948, for a description of the Lochs.

10   Russia and Germany had signed a secret pact to carve up Rumania between them, just as they had done with Poland. Bessarabia had been part of Russia until the Brest-Litovsk Treaty following Russia's withdrawal from World War I, which was why the Russians considered the oil was rightfully theirs.

11   Deletant, *op. cit.*

12   Loch, J., *op. cit.* pp.172–173.

13   Deletant, *op. cit.*

14   'Nigel' is the pseudonym given to him by Olivia Manning. He was the spymaster for British Intelligence in Bucharest, an Old Etonian, snobbish, too talkative, disliking women and not liked by Manning.

15   Joice never disclosed the name of the high-ranking German officer or the name of the Jewish scientist for whom she risked her life.

16   Details of this incident come from Joice's letters to Lady Moran, to Gerald Palmer, and to the Croker-Poole family, private collections, London.

17   Loch, J., *op, cit.* Quoted in full in de Vries, Susanna, *Blue Ribbons, Bitter Bread: The Story of Joice NanKivell Loch, op. cit.*

18   Olivia Manning records Nigel's death in *The Great Fortune, op. cit.*

19   This account is reconstructed from Sydney Loch's papers and journal, *op. cit.*, reports he sent to the Society of Friends, Friends House, Euston Road, London, and Joice's (sometimes unreliable) autobiography, *A Fringe of Blue. op.cit.* See also Loch, Joice NanKivell, *The Hopping Ha-penny*, J. Methuen & Son, London, 1956. The story of the Lochs' Operation Pied Piper and their selfless work in refugee camps in Palestine is also related in Greenwood. J. *Quaker Encounters: Friends and Relief*, Vol. 1, William

618 | THE COMPLETE BOOK OF HEROIC AUSTRALIAN WOMEN

618 | THE COMPLETE BOOK OF HEROIC AUSTRALIAN WOMEN

Sessions, York, 1975, and in Wilson, R.C., *Quaker Relief: An Account of the Relief Work of the Society of Friends 1940–1948,* Allen & Unwin, London, 1952.

20   The plot to assassinate Magda Lupescu and King Carol is cited in Paul, *op. cit.* Carol spent the rest of his life in exile in Portugal with Lupescu. The month before he died they married. Their bodies have been recently exhumed and returned to Bucharest for burial in separate plots.

21   Loch, J, 1968*, op. cit.,* p. 185.

22   *Ibid.*

23   For the full story of the Katyn massacre of Polish reserve officers, mostly educated men who would have resisted Polish communism, see Davies, Professor Norman, *Europe: A History,* Pimlico Press, London, 1997, pp. 1004–1005. Only in 1990 did Mikhail Gorbachev finally admit Soviet responsibility for the massacre of Katyn.

24   Cited in Greenwood, *op. cit.*

25   Loch J., 1968, *op. cit.*, p. 210.

CHAPTER 11: SISTERS SYLVIA MUIR, VIVIAN BULLWINKEL, JOYCE TWEDDELL, BETTY JEFFREY AND THE OTHER 'PARADISE ROAD' NURSES

1   Information in this chapter comes largely from interviews with Sylvia Muir in 1998–1999, and Vivian Bullwinkel in 1999; published accounts, including Betty Jeffrey's *White Coolies* (see note 3); Pat (Gunther) Darling's *Portrait of a Nurse,* Don Wall, Mona Vale, 2001; Norman Manners' biography, *Bullwinkel,* Hesperian Press, Carlisle, WA, 2000; and interviews with the nurses' relatives and friends. Also, Sylvia Muir's unpublished journal in the Australian War Memorial, Canberra.

2   From 1975 to 1980, Joyce Tweddell worked in the same Brisbane hospital as my late husband, Dr Larry Evans. Florence Trotter lived near me on the slopes of Brisbane's Mount Coot-tha. I visited Florence's small neat home to take her flowers. Florence was in pain and unable to talk at length. However, I learned how she, Joyce and Sylvia remained close all their lives and how much support the others gave Florence when she became ill.

3   From p. 23 of Betty Jeffrey's memoirs, *White Coolies: A Graphic Record of Survival in World War Two* (1997), one of the first accounts of the Bangka Island Massacre, published in 1954 by Angus & Robertson, Sydney.

4   *Ibid.*

5   The film *Paradise Road* loosely adapted from Betty's book, and directed by Bruce Beresford, opens with a group of attractive Australian nurses enjoying themselves at a dance in the ballroom of Raffles Hotel. Sirens wail as Japanese planes approach. Chandeliers shatter and plaster falls from the ceiling as a bomb explodes and the guests fling themselves on the floor. Sylvia Muir pointed out that this scene was entirely imaginary and created to provide a dramatic opening to the film. In reality, by the time the Japanese started bombing Singapore, the wards were so crowded that AANS staff were working double shifts and matron had issued orders forbidding staff to leave the hospital compound so, even when off duty, they could be summoned to the wards to help out.

6   Jeffrey, *op. cit.,* p. 2.

7   Interviews with Sylvia (Muir) McGregor, at the Wesley Hospital, Brisbane, 1998–1999.

8   On the raft with Matron Olive Paschke were Sisters Annie Trenerry, Gladys McDonald, Hilda Dorsch, Mary Clarke and Caroline Ennis. They may have drowned or landed on some other island and been murdered by Japanese soldiers.

9   Telephone interviews with Vivian (Bullwinkel) Statham, 1999.

10   *Ibid.*

11   *Ibid.* Also Sister Bullwinkel's statement to the International Military Tribunal, 29

October 1945 1010/424 Australia War Memorial, Canberra (Webb War Crimes Commission). In her evidence to the Tribunal, Vivian Bullwinkel stated that she did not hear shots but the Tribunal put this down to her being in a state of shock.

12   Sylvia and Betty called Colonel Yamasaki 'Saki' or 'the Sadist'. Other women's memoirs called him 'Siki'. What Sylvia describes was a traditional Japanese torture.

13   Basset, Jan in *Guns and Brooches*, Oxford University Press, Melbourne, 1992, says 28 nurses attended the club, wearing their ugliest outfits.

14   Manners, *op.cit.*, pp. 118–119 cites Blanche Hempsted and Val Smith, a heavy smoker, as the nurses who pretended to have TB.

15   The Army nurses did not understand the Japanese code of *bushido* or realise what a cultural gulf divided them. For a explanation of *bushido*, see Russell of Liverpool, Baron, *The Knights of Bushido: A History of Japanese War Crimes*, Cassell, London, 1958.

16   Some earlier memoirs do not agree with the franker accounts by Sylvia and Wilma Oram (see note 23). That four nurses did become 'comfort women' to save the rest. Army nurse Jessie Simons in *In Japanese Hands*, Heinemann, Melbourne, 1985, implies that although the women were threatened with starvation, they stood up to their captors and were released. Harassment by Japanese officers is confirmed in Kenny, Catherine, *Australian Army Nurses in Japanese Prison Camps*, University of Queensland Press, Brisbane, 1986. Jan Bassett, *op. cit.*, states that eventually reports of European women being used as 'comfort women' reached higher authorities in Tokyo, who closed the 'social club' down.

17   Jeffrey, *op.cit.*, pp. 148.

18   *Ibid*, p. 149–150.

19   Telephone interviews with Vivian (Bullwinkel), Statham, *op. cit.*

20   The Tribunal that Vivian attended in Tokyo is often referred to as a war crimes tribunal (the title of the Nuremburg Tribunal in Germany). The Tokyo Tribunal's official name was the International Military Tribunal for the Far East, which commenced hearings on 3 May 1946. It was also known as the Webb War Crimes Commission. Proceedings of the Tribunal were published on 20 December 1946 and included Sister Bullwinkel's detailed evidence.

21   Information provided by Mrs J. Griffiths, Joyce Tweddell's niece; information about Joyce in Caloundra provided by Dr Mervyn McNee.

22   Telephone interviews with Vivian (Bullwinkel) Statham *op. cit.*

23   For an account of Wilma Oram's life, see Angell, Barbara, *A Woman's War: The Exceptional Life of Wilma Oram Young*, New Holland Publishers, Sydney, 2002.

24   Information about Betty's life after her return to Australia was supplied by Gwen Friend, who produced a commercial radio drama series with Betty Jeffrey adapted from *White Coolies* in the 1950s, personal communications 4 and 5 December 2003; and Betty Jeffrey's great-niece, Emily Malone, personal communications 6 and 7 December 2003.

25   Jeffrey, *op. cit.*, p.148

26   Sylvia's diary and drawings are also in the Australian War Memorial, along with other nurses' personal items, including the uniform Vivian Bullwinkel was wearing at the Bangka Island Massacre and her medals.

27   Personal communication Emily Malone, *op. cit.*

28   Betty Jeffrey's obituary on the Australian War Memorial web page
www.awm.gov.au/encyclopedia/nurse_survivors

Chapter 12: Mavis Parkinson and Sister May Frances Hayman

1   The story of the Mission and the two women has been told with variations by Hodge, Dr Erroll, *The Seed of the Church*, Anglican Board of Missions, Sydney, 1992; Rowland,

E.C., *Faithful unto Death: The Story of the New Guinea Martyrs*, Anglican Board of Missions, Sydney, 1962; Tomkins, Dorothea and Hughes, Brian, *The Road from Gona*, Angus & Robertson, Sydney, 1969; Benson, James, *Prisoner's Base and Home Again: The Story of a Missionary P.O.W.*, Robert Hale, London, 1957; and *The New Guinea Diaries of Bishop Philip Strong, 1936–45,* ed. David Wetherell, Macmillan, Melbourne, 1981.

2   After the deaths of May and Mavis, as Bishop of Brisbane, Bishop Strong attracted a great deal of criticism for not *insisting* all women serving on missions in Papua return to Australia. From a statement made towards the end of the bishop's life, it seems that the murders of those who stayed at their post preyed on his conscience.

3   For more information, see Paull, Raymond, *Retreat from Kokoda*, Hamilton, London, 1960.

4   Quoted in Tomkins and Hughes, *op. cit.*

5   Benson, *op. cit.*

6   Although it seems unlikely that a broadcast from Papua would have reached as far as Ipswich, various publications by the Anglican Board of Missions suggest it did.

7   Benson, *op. cit.*

8   *Ibid.*

9   *Ibid.*

10   The letter is now in the archives of the Anglican Church in Brisbane and is quoted with the permission of Mavis Mathieson–Frame, niece of Mavis Parkinson.

11   Information supplied by Graeme Barron, Lieutenant Smith's cousin.

12   Benson, *op.cit.*

13   *Ibid.*

14   The International Military Tribunal for the Far East, proceedings published 20 December 1946 (Webb War Crimes Commission) revealed the truth. This was the commission to which Vivian Bullwinkel had given evidence of war crimes.

15   Reports of the behaviour of the Papuan soldiers differ: some accounts credit them with heroic behaviour; others report several soldiers running away when the shots were fired.

16   From the reports of various anthropological expeditions to the remote Upper Dobodura area, it seems that Embogi's grudge against local missionaries was due to the fact they had tried to prevent certain sexual practices, once part of traditional initiation ceremonies. Head hunting, according to anthropologists and ethnographers, had already died out in that particular area.

    For details of feuds between pagan and Christian Papuans and tribal ceremonies and customs in pagan villages at the time of World War II see Sandall, Roger, *The Culture Cult, Designer Tribalism and Other Essays*, Westview Press, Boulder, Col., 2002.

17   Aitere was unclear in his statement to the International Military Tribunal about the exact date. He stated the women were killed between 13 and 16 August 1942.

18   Lieutenant Smith was eventually found by Papuans who handed him over to Embogi. According to Tomkins and Hughes, *op. cit.*, p. 45, a Japanese diary records he was beheaded.

INDEX

A

AANS *see* Australian Army Nursing Service (AANS)
Aberdonian (transport ship), 467–68
Aboriginal legends, 71, 132, 147, 261, 271, 297
    Australian Legendary Tales (book), 267, 296
    The Euahlayi Tribe: A Study of Aboriginal Life in Australia (book), 297–98
    More Australian Legendary Tales (book), 296
    The Native Tribes of Central Australia (book), 132, 135, 147
    Woggheeguy: Australian Aboriginal Legends (book), 298
Aboriginal women
    'black velvet,' 15, 170
    corroboree for, 154–55
    house girls, 134, 135, 153, 186, 267
    rape and violence against, 15, 76, 145, 190, 194, 230
    'station gin' custom, 170
Aborigines
    attacks on Europeans, 156–57, 166–67, 223, 229, 240–42
    Australian Legendary Tales (book), 267, 296
    capabilities, 134–35
    The Euahlayi Tribe: A Study of Aboriginal Life in Australia (book), 297–98
    fire-lighting, 231
    food-collecting and hunting methods, 231
    fostering of children, 15, 162, 228, 241, 265, 271

'going walkabout,' 134, 182, 192, 249
hunting, necessity for, 207
illness and disease, 107–8
inter-tribal conflict, 190, 228
killing of and violence against, 15, 60–62, 71, 76–77, 84, 145, 166, 206–7, 223, 228, 229–30
kinship, 137, 147, 191, 206, 228
legends *see* Aboriginal legends
The Little Black Princess (book), 190, 191, 205, 208–9
medicine man, 146–47
More Australian Legendary Tales (book), 296
The Native Tribes of Central Australia (book), 132, 135, 147
offences and justice, 145
'pointing the bone,' 147, 193–94, 206
rainmakers, 191, 192, 200
rations distributed, 228
relationships with settlers, 15–16, 42–43, 53–54, 60–62, 76, 101–2, 111–12, 131–33
religious instruction of, 148–49
stockmen and drovers, 184, 228
wages, 228
Woggheeguy: Australian Aboriginal Legends (book), 298
women *see* Aboriginal women
see also Arrernte people; Coleman River people; Mangarrayi people; Mitchell River people

(Yir Yoront); Ngarluma people; Noongahburrah people; Palmer River people; Wardandi-Bibbulmun people; Willeroo people; Yangman people; Yuwaalaraay people
Adelphi (Bussell property), 39, 41–42, 50, 52
AFAC *see* Allies Field Ambulance Corps (AFAC)
Africa in World War I, 342
Ah Say, Jimmy, 250
AIF *see* Australian Imperial Force (AIF)
Aitere (Papuan), 593–94
Albania, 336, 341, 363, 380
Alberga Creek (SA), 151
Albert (Aboriginal house man at Mount Mulgrave Station), 16, 227–28, 236–37, 240–42, 244, 256
Alec, A Living History of the Alice Springs Telegraph Station (book), 162
Alexander (Crown Prince of Serbia) (later King of Yugoslavia), 321, 347, 351, 352, 354, 366, 375, 401
    Greater Serbia, 353, 366, 367
    SWH, 401
    Yovitchitch, Captain Milan, ('Yovi'), 347, 352, 360, 374, 375, 383–85, 409
Alexander I (King of Yugoslavia), 321, 382
    assassination in 1934, 384–85
    wedding to Princess Marie, 383–84
    see also Alexander (Crown Prince of Serbia)
Alfred Hospital (Melbourne), 522

Alice Spring (original site), 126
Alice Springs (NT), 5, 122,
    124, 128, 132, 133, 135,
    140, 141, 144, 145, 148,
    154, 156, 159, 161, 175,
    299
    see also Stuart (later Alice
        Springs)
Alice Springs Telegraph
    Station, 14, 120, 121, 128,
    129, 131, 162
    Alec, A Living History of the
        Alice Springs Telegraph
        Station (book), 162
Alice Well Cattle Station (NT),
    127
All Saints Anglican Church
    (Sydney), 349
Allchurch, Atlanta see Bradshaw,
    Atlanta (née Allchurch)
    ('Attie')
Allchurch, Elizabeth (AB's
    sister-in-law), 153
Allchurch, Emily (AB's sister),
    123, 152
Allchurch, Ernest (AB's
    brother), 123, 149, 153,
    158, 159
Allen, Barbara M., 356–58, 360
Allen, Dr Henry, 81
Allies Field Ambulance Corps
    (AFAC), 327–30
Ambrosius, Father, 478, 491,
    508
ambulance drivers
    AFAC, 327–30
    ambulances, 371, 399 see also
        Bridget (ambulance); Ella
        the Elephant (ambulance)
    Australian Field Ambulance,
        453
    Dobraveni dressing station,
        407–8
    field hospitals see field
        hospitals
    massacred at Doiran Lakes,
        337–40
    military hospitals see military
        hospitals
    Ostrovo base hospital, 401,
        404–6
    Salonika, in, 334–36, 341,
        370–71
    Serb Army, 349, 357–58, 371,
        376
    Troyes field hospital, 333–34
    women as, 328, 330, 343
Amelia (Arrernte woman), 135,
    136, 160
American Farm School
    (Thessaloniki), 477, 513,
    514

Anglican church in Australia,
    577–78, 588, 592, 594–95
Antonescu, General Ion, 492
Anzacs
    Anzac Day, 306, 469
    Australian war graves,
        471–72
    Benalla (troopship), 416–19,
        423, 435, 446, 448
    casualties at Gallipoli, 310,
        312, 399–400, 429–35,
        444–45, 458
    Dardanelles plan, 419,
        424–25, 428–30, 451,
        453
    deaths in World War I, 312,
        470, 472
    France, 410–11
    Greece, 507
    No. 1 Anzac Corps, 460
    Salonika, 342
    tented hospitals on Lemnos,
        438–39, 451–52
    Tubb at Lone Pine, 455–57
    venereal diseases, 421, 428
    war injuries see soldiers' war
        injuries
    war veterans, 312, 472, 520
    see also Australian Imperial
        Force (AIF)
Apsley House (London), 85
Arab allies in World War II,
    491, 509
Arltunga goldfields (NT),
    156
Arnissa (Greece) see Ostrovo
    base hospital (Greece)
Arnotts (company), 377
Arrernte people, 129–33,
    134–39, 159
    Amoonguna Settlement,
        162
    Dreamtime spirits and
        totemism, 147
    handouts and rations, 141–42
    hunting and gathering,
        141–42
    kinship rules, 137
    language, 129, 130, 144
    medicine man, 146–47
    women's corroboree, 154–55,
        156
Artsa (Serb mechanic), 343,
    344, 350, 357, 363, 371–77
Ashton, Jean, 551
Asiatic Annie (German-made
    gun), 441
Atherton Tableland (Qld), 244
Atkinson, Magistrate J., 579,
    580, 581–82
Atlanta, SS, 121
atomic bomb, 556, 559

Augusta settlement (WA), 35,
    36–44, 45, 46, 47–48, 52,
    56, 57, 65, 66, 70
    hunting, 39–40
Aunger, Murray, 157–58, 159
Austcare, 515
Australia, maps
    Alice Springs area, 121
    Pilbara coast, 95
    SW of Western Australia, 39
Australian Army Nursing
    Service (AANS)
    Australian General Hospitals,
        522–25
    Bangka Island memorial,
        569–71
    clothes and uniforms see
        clothes and uniforms
        (wartime)
    deaths in World War I, 309,
        450, 462–63
    deaths in World War II, 299,
        527, 534–37, 549–53,
        559, 562–63
    Egypt, 399–400, 432–34
    enlistment, 308, 520–21
    France, 459
    Japanese camps, in, 519,
        539–54, 570
    married women, 311–12
    pay, 421–22, 470, 472
    Royal Medical Corps, 425
    rules and regulations,
        310–11, 417, 467
    Southwell Gardens
        (London), 468
    8th Battalion, 435
    working conditions, 462,
        464–66
Australian engineers in
    Salonika, 335–36
Australian Flying Corps, 373
Australian General Hospitals,
    410, 423–28, 430–35, 458,
    522–25
    see also military hospitals
Australian Imperial Force (AIF)
    Australian war graves,
        471–72
    becomes No. 1 Anzac Corps,
        460
    deaths in World War I, 312
    formed, 306, 326, 423
    France and Belgium, 398–99,
        477
    3rd Division, 375
    rules and regulations, 310–11
    7th Battalion, 455
    8th Battalion, 416–19,
        423–24, 428, 429,
        433–35, 445–46, 449,
        458, 472

11th Battalion, 456
Victoria Cross, 455, 456, 457
see also Anzacs
Australian Inland Mission Aerial Medical Service, 295
Australian Institute of Radiography, 562
Australian Intelligence Officers, 539
Australian Legendary Tales (book), 267, 296, 298
Australian Medical Association, 413
Australian National War Memorial, 564, 567
Australian War Graves Commission, 472
Australian Women's Army Service (AWAS), 313
Australind (WA settlement), 78
Austria in World War I
invasion of Serbia, 325–26, 341, 346, 352–53
Ostrovo base hospital, 410
retreat, 371, 376, 378, 406
Serb Army, 334–36, 400–401, 403
Auteuil (France), 399
Auvergne Station (NT), 185
AWAS *see* Australian Women's Army Service (AWAS)
Awoda, Simon Peter, 575, 584

B
Bakumbari (Papua), 587
Balkan campaign, 334–40, 372, 376, 400–401, 408, 410
Ballarat (hospital ship), 243
Balls-Headley, William, 390
Ballybrood (Maunsell home in Ireland), 253
Bangate Station (NSW), 269
climate, 267
drought, 272–73
garden, 268
location, 264, 265, 266
mortgage, 273
water tanks, 273
Bangka Island (Sumatra)
Bangka Island memorial, 562–63, 569–71
Bangka Strait, 528–31
Japanese prison camp, 531–32, 533, 551–53, 577
Paradise Road (film), 315, 516, 567–68
Radji Beach massacre, 532–39, 554, 558–59, 562, 568, 569–71

Barratt, Lieutenant Rupert, 417, 428, 430, 435, 472
Barrett, Colonel (later Sir James) J.W., 427
Barthou, Louis, 385
Bates, Daisy, 324
Battle of the Coral Sea, 582
Bean, C.E.W., 429
Beard, Alma, 535–36
Bedford, Josephine, 353–54, 396–98, 399, 405–9, 412–13
Beechlands (WA), 84
Belgium in World War I, 311, 326, 353, 399, 472
Belgrade, 306, 341, 373, 376, 378, 379, 382, 384, 409, 497
Bell, Matron Jane, 425–28, 434–36
Benalla (troopship), 416–19, 423, 435, 446, 448, 472
Bennett, Agnes Amelia (AB's mother), 391
Bennett, Bob (AB's brother), 400, 409, 410
Bennett, Dr Agnes Elizabeth Lloyd, 390–413
aviation research, 411–12
awards, 353–54, 389, 409, 411
British Army, 400
brothers, 398–400, 409, 410
clothes and uniforms, 402, 406, 407
contracts malaria, 409–11
death, 412
early years, 391–93
Ostrovo base hospital, 401–4
Royal Infirmary in Glasgow, 411
studies medicine, 390, 393–95
SWH, 307, 335, 399
Bennett, Dr (business partner of AG), 168
Bennett, Sarah (née Darling) (AB's stepmother), 391–93
Bennett, William Christopher (AB's father), 391, 392, 411
Benson, Rev. James, 575, 579–86, 588–91
Bepore (Papua), 575
Beresford, Bruce, 567
beriberi, 543, 551–52, 553, 556, 559, 561
Bertie (Aboriginal stockman on Elsey Station), 184, 189
Beshitch, Mr and Mrs, 367–68
Besley, Elizabeth (GM's sister), 22, 24, 50, 57
Besley, Mr (curate), 24

Bessarabia (Rumania), 483–84, 495
'Bett-Bett' *see* Cummings, Dolly ('Bett-Bett'; 'Little Black Princess')
'Big Charlie' (Yangman rainmaker), 192
Big Wet, 14, 170, 173, 176, 203, 243
Billyard-Leake family, 468
Birdwood, General Sir William, 430
Birrell, Surgeon-General William, 424–25, 451
Bitter Springs (NT), 177
Blackwell, Winifred Doris ('Doris'), 157, 162
see also Bradshaw, Winifred Doris ('Doris') (AB's daughter)
Blackwood River (WA), 40, 41, 43, 45, 48, 69, 70
Blue Ribbons, Bitter Bread (book), 475, 515
Boer War, 305, 444
Bolton, Private Hunter, 417
Bolton, Lieutenant Jack, 417
Bolton, Colonel William ('Bill'), 417, 418, 424, 430, 435
Bonson, Dolly
Darwin during Cyclone Tracey, in, 214–15
death, 215
marriage, 214
recorded interview, 211–15
wartime evacuation to Mildura, 214
see also Cummings, Dolly
Bonson, Joe, 214
Bonson, Matthew, 215
Bonson, William, 213–14
Boronia molloyae (plant), 80
Bosnia, 305, 366
Botanical Register (book), 83
botanical studies and collections *see* Molloy, Georgiana (née Kennedy)
Boulogne (France), 459
Bowen, Stella, 313, 387
Bower, Phoebe, 47, 49, 54, 60, 61
Bowman, Mr (Rutland Plains Station), 226
Boyadine (farm near York, WA), 91
Bradshaw, Atlanta (née Allchurch) ('Attie'), 13, 14, 15, 16, 62, 120–63
Christmas Day cooking, 142–44, 143
correspondence, 148

death, 161
family life, 121
friendship with Amelia
    (Arrernte woman), 135
friendship with Strehlow
    family, 148
health, 150, 160
household work, 125, 130,
    133, 134, 137–39, 141,
    142–44, 149, 153
journey to Alice Springs, 120
medicine chest, 139
music, 144
pregnancy and childbirth,
    140–41, 149, 157
relationship with and care of
    Arrernte people, 134,
    137–38, 146–47
religious instruction to
    Aborigines, 148–49
Bradshaw, Edmund Mortimer
    ('Mort') (AB's son), 122,
    136, 139–40
Bradshaw, Edna (AB's
    daughter), 136, 149
Bradshaw, Eric Ivan ('Jack')
    (AB's son), 122, 136
Bradshaw, Ernie (TB's brother),
    140–41
Bradshaw, Frederick, 166–67
Bradshaw, Joseph, 166–67, 169
Bradshaw, Katherine Constance
    ('Consie') (AB's daughter),
    122
Bradshaw, Mary Jane, 169
Bradshaw, Sheila Pont (AB's
    daughter), 160
Bradshaw, Stuart MacDonnell
    (AB's son), 140–41
Bradshaw, Thomas (AB's
    husband), 120–22, 161
    Arrernte people, relationship
        with and study of, 136,
        144
    death, 161
    friendship with Strehlows,
        148
    magistrate, 144–45
    photography of red centre,
        133, 162
    travel to Alice Springs, 122
Bradshaw, Winifred Doris
    ('Doris') (AB's daughter),
    122, 137, 140, 141, 142,
    144, 153, 156
    see also Blackwell, Winifred
        Doris ('Doris')
Bradshaw family, 150
    amusements and excursions,
        149–50, 158
    education of children, 156,
        159

holiday at Glenelg, 152
home at Halifax St, Adelaide,
    121
move to Adelaide, 159–60
Bradshaw's Run (NT), 167
Breen, Mr (bailiff-caretaker at
    Ballybrood), 253
Brenchley, Sister Margery,
    581–82, 594
Bridges, General Bill, 422–23,
    433
Bridget (ambulance), 351,
    361–67, 369, 377, 379
Brisbane General Hospital
    (later Royal Brisbane
    Hospital), 520, 562
Brisbane (Qld), 396–98,
    412–13, 520–21
Britain in World War I
    air-raids, 469
    Australians and, 421, 436–37,
        462
    British Expeditionary Force,
        460
    British Military Police, 428
    British Official Secrets Act
        1911, 426
    Salonika, 335, 342
Britain in World War II
    British Consulate in Mersin,
        501–3
    British Intelligence, 477,
        485–90, 493
    Bucharest, 485
    Dunkirk, 483, 505
    Radji Beach massacre,
        534–37
    Singapore, 525–26
    War Office, 490–91
British Empire, 16, 210, 306,
    313, 330, 389, 412, 514
Brockman, William, 84
Broken Hill Hospital, 521
Broken Hill (NSW), 132, 260,
    276, 277, 281, 283, 290,
    521
Brooke, Rupert, 432, 434
Brookes, Mrs Charles, 128, 129
Brookes (Constable), 145
Brown, Mr (Lochs' American
    friend), 494–95
Bryant, Colonel, 439
Bryant, Herb ('the Dandy'),
    178, 187, 208
Bryce, Dr Lucy, 313
Bucharest (Rumania) see
    Rumania in World War II
buckboards (wagons), 13, 124,
    125, 129, 150, 151, 152,
    176, 177, 178, 181, 224,
    225, 238, 240, 288
Budapest (Hungary), 489

buggies, 10, 13, 104, 122, 124,
    125, 128, 129, 130, 141,
    149–50, 151, 152, 160,
    161, 167, 179, 220, 224,
    265, 266, 272, 285–86
Bukovina (Rumania), 483, 490
Bulgaria in World War I
    Great Fire of Salonika, 361
    Ostrovo base hospital, 410
    retreat, 406
    Serb Army, 335–41, 375, 403
    Yovi wounded by, 347–48
Bulgarians in World War II,
    485
Bulletin (magazine), 16, 376
bullock wagons, 97, 98, 105,
    106, 113, 172, 184, 185,
    188, 189, 229, 233, 245,
    281, 361
Bullwinkel, Sister Vivian
    ('Bulli'), 517–71
    awards, 516, 517, 564, 569
    Bangka Island memorial,
        562–63
    Japanese prisoner, 550, 551,
        554
    Malacca, 522, 523
    marries Frank Statham,
        569–71
    Radji Beach massacre,
        532–39, 558–59, 562
    state memorial service, 571
    survivor guilt, 519, 537, 563
    This Is Your Life (TV show),
        568
    training, 521
    Vyner Brooke, SS, 315,
        527–29
    White Coolies (book), 566
Buna (Papua), 578, 579, 584,
    585, 589
Bunbury, Lady Richardson, 84
Bunbury, Lt Henry, 61
Bunbury, William, 84
Bush Brotherhood, 577
Bussell, Alfred, 30, 48, 49, 50,
    52, 58, 59, 62, 80
Bussell, Charles, 30, 42, 48, 53,
    56, 57, 62, 84
Bussell, Charlotte Cookworthy,
    14, 71, 72–73, 83, 84
Bussell, Elizabeth ('Bessie'), 14,
    29, 41, 47, 48–50, 52, 54,
    56, 58–60
    see also Ommanney,
        Elizabeth ('Bessie')
Bussell, Frances 'Fanny'
    (daughter), 14, 29, 41, 47,
    48–50, 52, 53, 54, 56, 59,
    74, 75, 84
Bussell, Frances (mother), 29,
    48, 53, 55–57, 59, 72, 74

Bussell, John Garrett, 29–30, 41, 47, 48, 50, 58, 59, 71–72, 84
  Adelphi (property at Blackwood River), 39, 41–42, 50, 52
  Augusta settlement, 41–42
  Cattle Chosen (property at Vasse River), 54–55, 57–59, 73, 84
  Geographe Bay, expedition to, 45
  leaving England, 29–30
Bussell, Lenox, 29, 47, 50, 52, 58, 59, 62, 84
Bussell, Mary, 29, 53, 55–56, 57, 59, 84
Bussell, Rev. William Marchant, 29
Bussell, Vernon, 30, 49, 50, 58, 59
Bussell, William, 29
Bussell family, 14, 35, 36, 40, 41–42, 46–50, 52–53, 54, 56, 75, 84
  Adelphi (property at Blackwood River), 39, 41–42, 50, 52
  Cattle Chosen (property at Vasse River), 54–55, 57–59, 73, 84
  Datchet (house), 40, 53, 54
  farm produce, 60
  GM's relationship with, 42, 45, 49–50, 55, 56, 57, 71, 72–73
  horse breeding, 71
  Vasse River settlement, 45, 46, 50, 54, 55, 56, 57–62, 63, 69, 70–71
  Wardandi-Bibbulmun people, war with, 60–62, 71, 76, 84
Busselton (WA), 84
Bustard, William, 596
Butchers Inlet beach see Nickol Bay (WA)
Byrne, Captain Francis, 28, 89
Byzantine Museums Authority, 515

C
Cairns (Qld), 224, 227, 231, 233, 238, 246, 254, 257
Calgood (Wardandi man), 70
Callaghan, Finlay, 228, 229, 240, 245–46
Callaghan, Paddy, 218, 222, 225, 228, 229–30
Callan Park Hospital for the Insane, 395
Cambridge all-women's

colleges, 330, 335–36
Camden Harbour (WA), 105
camel trains, 123, 124, 133, 141, 144, 146, 154, 277, 278, 281, 283
Canada in World War I, 335
Cape Leeuwin (WA), 35, 36
Cape Town (South Africa), 30, 38, 63
Cape York Peninsula, seasons at, 233
Carol II (King of Rumania), 478–82, 484–85, 490, 492, 496–97, 514
Carter, Capel, 58
Casson, Sister, 535
casualty clearing stations (CCS), 430, 440, 455
Cattle Chosen (Bussell property), 59, 60, 61, 63, 72, 73, 75, 79, 84
CCS see casualty clearing stations (CCS)
Cecilia (hospital ship), 438, 440–42
Chambers, Jim, 298, 300
Chambers, Nora, 549
Champion, Alan, 579
Champion (schooner), 61
Changi, 557
Chapman, Leonard, 61
Charitas nuns, 540, 567
Château de Chanteloup (France), 332–33, 337
Chatham Islands (Australia), 411
Chatsworth (England), 64
Cheon (household manager at Elsey Station), 186, 187, 188, 189, 194, 200, 201–2
childbed (puerperal) fever, 75, 81, 262
China in World War II, 313
cholera, 108, 377, 378, 502
Christmas dinner and preparations, 142–44, 143, 201–2
Churchill, Winston, 424–25, 458, 495
Citadel Hospital (Cairo), 428
Clan McGillivray (troopship), 428
clothes and uniforms (wartime), 307, 311
  AANS, 417, 421–22, 434–36, 447, 458, 459, 472, 521, 527, 546–47
  Agnes Bennett's, 402, 406, 407
  AIF, 417
  Alice Kitchen's, 422, 423, 447

Japanese prisoner of war camps, 530, 541, 545–47, 549, 566–67
Joice NanKivell Loch's, 479
Olive King's, 327, 330–31, 335, 337, 345, 346, 349, 356, 358–59, 384–85
Rouen, 465
Salonika, 341–42
clothing (outback Australia), 104–5, 138–39, 143, 150, 172–73, 183, 188, 191–92, 202, 244
coastal shipping accidents, 108
Cockburn Sound (WA), 31
Coleman River people, 16, 228
Collins, Jimmy ('Terrible Jimmy'), 228
Constantine (King of Greece), 336
Constantza (Rumania), 491, 493, 496–500
convicts/convict labour, 25, 85, 229
Cook, John, 40
Cook, Joseph (Prime Minister), 311
Cookworthy, Charlotte, 71–72
Cooper, Dr Lilian Violet, 390–413
  appearance, 396
  awards, 353–54, 389, 408, 409, 412
  Brisbane practice, 396–98, 412–13
  Czerna River dressing station, 408
  death, 412–13
  Dobraveni dressing station, 407–8
  Ostrovo base hospital, 401, 405–7
  studies medicine, 390, 395–96, 398
  SWH, 307, 399
Corfu (Greece), 366
Corkhill, Sister Pearl, 469
Coulter, Captain Graham, 417, 428, 458
Country Women's Association, 117
Covent Garden (London), 27
Cracknell, Ruth, 567
Crann, Bob, 124, 133
Crawley (WA), 84
Crete in World War II, 506–7
Crick, Billy, 133
Crighton-Barr, Rev. A., 211
Croatia, 367, 371, 383, 403
Crosby Lodge (Scotland), 19
Cumberland (coastal trader ship), 55, 56

Cummangoot (Wardandi girl), 71
Cummings, Dolly ('Bett-Bett'; 'Little Black Princess'), 15–16
early life, 212
found by Gunn expedition, 190
The Little Black Princess (book), 205
nursemaid to governor of Fanny Bay gaol, 212
parents, 190, 212
'promised' to Billy Muck, 191
relationship with and raising by Jeannie Gunn, 191–92, 194, 212, 213
visit to Melbourne, 213
walkabouts, 192
Willeroo tribal attack, 190–91
work at Darwin hospital, 213
work for Ward family, 212–13
see also Bonson, Dolly
Cummings, Lewis, 190, 212
Cunningham, Colonel, 433
Curtin government, 313, 314
Curtis, Sister, 467
cyclones, 109, 110, 214
Cygnet (ship), 47
Cyprus
World War I, 386
World War II, 481, 491–94, 501, 505–8
Czerna River dressing station (Greece), 408
Czernowicz (Rumania), 483–84

D

Daily Mail, 306, 308, 311
Dale, Captain Frank, 417, 428, 435
Dalmatia, 367, 371
Dardanelles plan, 419, 424–25, 428–30, 451, 453
see also Anzacs; Gallipoli (Dardanelles)
Darling, Sarah, 391–93
Darling Downs (Qld), 16
Darling River (NSW), 261–62, 274
Darwin, Cyclone Tracy in (NT), 214
Datchet (Bussell house), 40, 53, 55
Davis, Win, 543, 547
Dawson, Ann, 37, 39, 43, 44
Dawson, Elijah, 28, 37, 39, 42, 43, 44, 53–54

Dawson, Lieutenant Richard, 36, 47, 48
de Crespigny, Colonel, 458
De Grey River plains, 88, 93
De Havilland aircraft, 386
Dean, Mrs, 219–20
dehydration, 430, 446–47
Denison Plains Association, 104
Derham, Alfred, 214
Derham, Dorothy, 214
Derok, Colonel, 350, 353, 367, 370, 374–77, 379, 385
Dickenson, Lieutenant, 586
Dig Down (near Harding River), 98, 99
Dinah (Aboriginal woman at Wrotham Park), 248
disease and illness, 14, 75–82, 107–8, 109–10, 137–38, 139–40, 157, 197–98, 203, 204, 234, 248–49, 288, 291, 404, 477, 505, 542, 545
see also under individual diseases
Dobraveni dressing station (Greece), 407–9
Dobruja (Rumania), 485
Doiran Lakes massacre (Greece), 338–40
Dolly (Arrernte woman at Elsey Station), 129–30, 202
Dreamtime *see* Aboriginal legends
Dresdner Bank, 495
drinking water *see* food and water shortages (overseas during wars)
droughts, 15, 16, 109, 192–93, 199, 200, 272–73
Drummond, James, 80
Drummond, Matron Irene, 521, 522, 525, 527, 528, 534–37, 554, 563, 569, 571
Drury Lane (London), 27
Dry, the *see* droughts
Dryburgh, Margaret, 549, 568
DuCane, Edmund, 84
Duff, Jack, 229–30
Duke of York (Frederick), 21–22
Dunkirk, 483, 505
Dunlop, Helen ('Nellie') *see* Story, Helen ('Nellie')
Dunlop, Maggie, 20, 26, 41, 45–46, 50, 62
Dunlop, Mary, 20, 26, 41, 46
Dunlop family, 4, 20, 23, 44
dunnies *see* lavatories (outback Australia)
Dutton, Harry, 157–58, 159
dysentery, 14, 16, 32, 127, 138,

157, 203, 204, 223, 229, 268, 400, 404, 420, 433, 446–47, 450, 451–52, 453, 454, 502, 503, 548, 552, 556

E

Easom, Bertha, 123, 124, 144, 149
East India Company, 24, 77
Eastern African and Cold Storage Company, 207
Eastern Orthodox Church (Serbian), 305, 335, 349, 352, 358–60, 366, 371, 383
Easter's Billabong (NT), 176
Edinburgh University Medical College, 393
Edwards, Jack, 229
Edwards, Mr (surveyor), 40, 45
Egypt in World War I, 399–400, 410, 419, 428, 430, 454, 457
Ella the Elephant (ambulance), 327, 329–31, 335–37, 339, 343, 350–51, 377
Ellen (colonial schooner), 47, 54, 56
Elsey Station (NT), 16, 168, 172, 179
arrival of stores, 189
cemetery and burials, 198, 204, 216
Christmas dinner and preparations, 201–2
condition of buildings, 170, 175–76, 179–80
homestead, various locations of, 216
improvements to homestead, 184, 185, 187
latrine pit, 180–81
mustering camp, 194–95
replica for *We of the Never-Never* (film), 215
returned to traditional Mangarrayi and Yangman owners, 216
riding tour of property, 184
visitors to, 183–84, 196–97
Embogi (Papuan), 592–93, 594
Emden (warship), 418
Emily Taylor (transport ship), 35–36
Emma (coastal ship), 108
Empire Star, SS, 526
Encounter Bay, 261
England, Maunsells' trip to, 251–52
Erigedung (Wardandi man), 71
Eroro Mission (Papua), 580, 582

Evans, Aubrey (EM's brother)
  ('Tim'), 220, 222, 242, 243
Evans, Evelyn ('Evie') see
  Maunsell, Evelyn (née
  Evans) ('Evie')
Evans, Frank (EM's father),
  219, 251
Evans, Rupert (EM's brother),
  219, 220–21, 223, 242

F
Fairfield Infectious Diseases
  Hospital (Melbourne),
  564, 568–71
Fairlawn (Molloy house), 39,
  70, 74, 77, 80, 81, 82, 83,
  84
Fanning & NanKivell
  (company), 476
Far-North Memories (book), 230
Fellowship of Australian
  Writers, 300
Ferdinand (King of Rumania),
  383
Ferguson, John, 81
Fergusson River (NT), 173–74
Field, Catherine ('Katie') see
  Parker, Catherine Langloh
  (née Field) ('Katie')
Field, Edward (CP's brother),
  262, 263
Field, Henrietta (CP's sister),
  261–62
Field, Henry (CP's father), 261,
  262
Field, Jane (CP's sister), 261–62
Field, Mr (telegraph operator),
  129
Field, Rosa Emily (CP's sister)
  ('Rosina'), 261
Field, Sophy (CP's mother),
  261, 262, 264
field dressings, 443
Field family
  Glenelg, 262
  The Lodge (Adelaide), 262
  Marra Station, 261–62
field hospitals
  ambulance drivers see
    ambulance drivers
  Australian Field Ambulance,
    453
  Auteuil (France), 399
  casualty clearing stations
    (CCS), 430, 440, 455
  Cyprus, 506
  Czerna River dressing
    station, 408
  Dobraveni dressing station,
    407–9
  Guevgueli dressing station,
    337–40, 344, 348, 356

Ostrovo base hospital,
  353–54, 401–7, 410
Rouen Australian Auxiliary
  Hospital, 458, 460–66,
  461
Salonika, 335, 409
Skocivir dressing station, 408
SWH, 307, 330, 399
tented hospitals on Lemnos,
  438–39, 451–52
Troyes field hospital, 332–34
Yellac dressing station, 408–9
Fisher, Andrew, 326
Fisher, Fanny (née Hancock),
  108, 110
Fisher, George, 108, 110
Flinders Bay (WA), 35, 36, 40,
  42, 47, 50, 54, 69
Flint, Ernest, 122, 141
flu epidemic see influenza
Flying Doctor Service, 13,
  295
Flynn, Rev. John, 13, 295
food and cooking (outback
  Australia)
  'bush tucker,' 43, 45, 101,
    231, 236
  Christmas dinner, 142–43,
    201–2
  cooking methods, 33,
    137–38, 182, 231, 244,
    2135
  grown in settlements and
    properties, 45, 53–54,
    133, 234–35, 268
  invalids, for, 196
  Johnnie cakes, 127, 176
  meat killed locally, 281
  outback hotels, 266
  poor quality, 125–26, 137–38
  seeds brought from England,
    39
  transported to remote areas,
    280–81
  vegetables and fruit
    unobtainable, 37, 102,
    275, 282
  war effort, for, 242–43
  see also gardening (outback
    Australia)
food and water shortages
  (overseas during wars),
  381–82, 404, 406–8, 430,
  433, 438, 440, 450, 451,
  461, 502–3, 530, 532,
  541–43, 545
For Those That Love (book), 300
Forsyte Saga (book), 310
Foster, Judge Alfred, 314
fostering of Aboriginal
  children, 15, 162, 228, 241,
  265, 271

see also Bonson, Mrs Dolly;
  Cummings, Dolly
4th Australian Field
  Ambulance, 453
Fowler, Captain John, 417
Fox, Paulina, 218
  see also McManus, Paulina
France in World War I
  Balkan campaign, 335,
    366–67, 400, 403
  Dardanelles, 439
  field hospitals, 332–34, 399,
    403, 460–66, 461
  Germany, 326, 328–30, 353,
    409, 410, 455, 458
  northern France, 465, 470,
    477
  8th Battalion, 458
  war graves, 471
France in World War II
  Consul in Mersin, 502
  resistance, 315–16
  Vichy government, 483
Franklin, Miles, 300, 401, 402,
  409
Franz Ferdinand (Archduke of
  Austria), 305, 325, 385
Franz Josef (Emperor of
  Austria), 335, 371
Frederick (Duke of York), 21–22
free settlers, 25, 40, 85, 89
Freeleagus, Alexander, 515
Freeman, Dot, 543
Fremantle (WA), 31, 32
French, General Sir John, 331
Friend, Captain Matthew, 32
Friend, Gwen, 567
Friend, Mary Anne, 32
Friends war relief organisations
  see Quaker war relief
  organisations
Frizell, Helen, 211
From That Day to This (book),
  300

G
Gage Roads (WA), 31
Gallipoli, 210, 243, 277, 301,
  306, 310, 312, 335, 336,
  342, 399, 400, 401, 411,
  414, 424–25, 428–58, 460,
  477, 483, 513
Gallipoli (book), 310
Gallipoli (Dardanelles)
  Anzac Cove, 429, 434, 435,
    439–50, 453, 454,
    457–58, 460
  Bolton's Ridge, 435
  British troops, 401
  casualties see under Anzacs
  Dardanelles plan, 419, 424–25,
    428–30, 451, 453

despatches, 414, 453
evacuation, 310, 400, 434,
    458, 460, 483
French troops, 335
Ghurkhas and Irish troops,
    456–57
Howse, 428–30
Lemnos Island *see* Lemnos
    Island (Dardanelles)
Lone Pine and Nek, 454–57
map, 451
Suvla Bay, 455–57
Galsworthy, John, 310
Forsyte Saga (book), 310
Gardam, Shirley, 543
gardening (outback Australia),
    38–39, 40, 63, 68, 102,
    108, 133–34, 148, 200,
    233, 248, 268
Garis, Dr Mary, 408
Gartside, Colonel ('Jock'), 417,
    423
Gascon, HMAS *see under*
    hospital ships
Gaywal (Wardandi elder), 76
Geneva Convention, 519, 535,
    536, 594
Geographe Bay, 42, 45, 54, 60,
    79
geological survey party (NT),
    156–57
George, Frederick, 157
George III (King of England),
    22
George VI (King of England),
    469, 566
Germany in World War I, 313,
    326, 329, 334, 335, 340,
    401, 403, 410, 437,
    440–41, 447, 471
Germany in World War II, 471,
    478–90, 500, 502–3, 505,
    508–9
Ghan (train), 123–24
Gillen, Amelia ('Minnie'), 122,
    135
Gillen, Francis, 120, 131–33,
    149
    *The Native Tribes of Central
        Australia* (book), 132,
        135, 147
    photography, 132
    Protector of Aborigines, 131
Girl Guides Association
    (NSW), 383
Gluckstein family, 495–98,
    506–7, 509–10
God-help-us, Billy, 247
God-help-us, Kitty, 247
Goebbels, Dr, 485, 495
gold bullion from Rumania,
    496–500

gold rush in Pilbara (WA), 116,
    156
Gona Anglican Mission
    (Papua), 575–87, 576, 594
gonorrhoea, 421
Gosport (England), 28
Gould, Matron Nellie, 305,
    421–22, 426, 427, 436,
    447
Graham, Tom, 227, 231
Grant, A.C., 246
Grawin South Station (NSW),
    274, 296, 297
Great Depression (1930s), 312
Great War *see* World War I
Greece in World War I, 334–40,
    372, 401
Greece in World War II, 507,
    514
Greek Orthodox refugees, 477
Green, Mr (surgeon), 48, 63,
    75, 80, 81
Gregory, Francis (EW's cousin),
    88, 92, 93, 97
Gregory, Sophia *see* Hancock,
    Sophia (EW's mother)
Grimwood, Reggie, 220, 221
Groppi's Tea Rooms (Cairo),
    423, 453
Grylls, Florence, 401
Guevgueli dressing station
    (Greece), 337–40, 344,
    348, 357
Guildford Castle, HMAS, 429
Gumendjie Bridge (Greece),
    350
Gunn, Aeneas (AG's husband),
    166
    admiration and care for wife,
        181, 196
    assists bushmen, 197, 199
    attacked by Aborigines, 167
    builds bookshelves, 188
    correspondence, 199–200
    death and burial, 204–5, 216
    Elsey Station consortium,
        168
    health, 167, 203–4
    letters to Northern Territory
        Times, 181
    librarian position, 167
    marriage to Jeannie, 167, 203
    meeting and courtship with
        jeannie, 167
    respect for Aborigines, 204
Gunn, Bob (AG's brother), 168,
    199–200, 201
Gunn, Jeannie (née Taylor), 11,
    14, 15, 16, 62, 137,
    166–216, 227, 229, 267
    accused of racism in her
        books, 205–6

arrival at Elsey Station,
    178–79
assistance to Aborigines,
    207–8
childhood in Melbourne,
    167–68, 169
correspondence, 208, 260
death and funeral, 211
education, 168
Fergusson River crossing,
    173–74
flat iron, 175
fundraising for Anzacs, 210
Hawthorn (Vic), 214
health, 196
homestead management
    tasks, 194
hostility of stockmen to, 170
The Little Black Princess
    (book), 190, 205, 208–9
marriage to Aeneas, 167, 203
meeting and courtship with
    Aeneas Gunn, 167
memorial to, 216
'modern' woman, 171
Monbulk (Vic), 209–10
*My Boys: A Book of
    Remembrance* (book),
    210–11
OBE, 210
protection of stockmen's
    reputation, 208
publication of books, 208–9
relationships with Aboriginal
    women, 182, 206
teaching role, 200, 208
travel to Britain and Europe,
    209
We of the Never-Never (book),
    11, 166, 170, 175, 178,
    181, 184, 205, 207, 209,
    215, 229, 267, 300
wedding presents, 169
see also Elsey Station (NT)
Gunn, Nellie, 200, 201
Gunther, Pat, 546
Guthrie, Kirstie, 333
Guthrie (mail steamer), 170

H
Hablett, George, 124
Haifa (Palestine), 495–97,
    508–10
Haig, General Sir Douglas, 460
Hailes, George, 85
Hale, Archdeacon Matthew, 83
Halfpapp, Alby, 244
Hall, Arthur, 220, 222
Hall, Eliza, 324
Hall, Frances (née Maunsell)
    (CM's sister), 220, 222
Hall, Harry, 220

Hall, Maude, 220
Hall, Thomas, 220
Hall, William Shakespeare ('Shaky'), 97–99
Hamill, Jack, 249, 254, 255
Hamilton, General Sir Ian, 425, 428, 430
Hamilton, Private John, 457
Hamilton (Vic), 521
Hampshire, HMS, 460
Hancock, Emma Mary *see* Withnell, Emma Mary (née Hancock)
Hancock, Fanny (EW's sister), 88, 100, 101
see also Fisher, Fanny (née Hancock)
Hancock, George (EW's father), 89, 90, 91, 110
Hancock, John (EW's grandfather), 89
Hancock, John Frederick (EW's brother), 88, 91, 101, 108
Hancock, Sophia (EW's mother), 89, 90
Hancock, Sophia (EW's sister), 109
Harding River (WA), 98, 102, 109, 111
Hardy, Tom, 185
Hardy's Inlet (WA), 70
Harefield Park Hospital (England), 468–71
Harley, Mrs, 331–32, 349, 351, 355
Harper, Iole, 531, 539, 541–42, 551–52
Harrow (school in England), 22
Hay, Isabelle, 325
Hayes, William, 127
Hayman, Sister Frances May ('Merry'), 316, 572, 573–96
escape from Japanese, 584–92
Gona Anglican Mission, 575–84
murder, 593–94
Haynes, Sister Olive, 434
Hayward, Sophie, 29, 30, 59, 71–72
Heavitree Gap (NT), 128
Hébrard (French military architect), 374, 381
Hegel, George, 390
Hempsted, Blanche, 546–47
Hempsted, Pauline, 543
Heppingstone, Charlotte, 66, 78
Heppingstone, Mary, 81, 83
Heppingstone, Robert (father), 28, 40, 43
Heppingstone, Robert (son), 77, 83

Hergott Springs (later Marree), 123
Hermannsburg Mission, 128–29, 130, 153
heroism, 316–17
Herring, John, 36
Hertzegovina, 367
Hewitt, Sergeant, 585
Heysen, Nora, 298, 313
Hillside (farm near York, WA), 91, 92–93
Hiroshima (Japan), 559
Hitler (Adolf), 312, 478, 479, 481, 482, 483, 495, 502, 510, 511
Hivajapa (Papuan), 582, 596
Holland in World War II
Dutch in Sumatra, 532, 540–42, 545, 548, 554, 559
German invasion, 483
Hong Kong, 526
Horn, William, 132
Horty, Admiral, 483
hospital equipment (wartime), 425, 461
hospital ships
Ballarat, 243
British, 399–400
Cecilia, 438, 440–42
Chinese, 526
Gallipoli, 429–30, 432
Galsworthy, John, 310
Gascon, 310, 414, 424, 429, 436–58, 442, 443, 460, 473
Manunda, 558
Neuralia, 453
procedures, 437, 441, 449–50
Red Cross flag, 468
'special' nursing, 449, 457
staff conditions, 447–50, 453–54
Hotel Gazelli (Mersin), 501–2
hotels (outback Australia), 89, 123, 128, 171, 175, 203, 266, 274
House, Charlie, 513
household chores (outback Australia), 43, 44, 49, 50, 59–60, 102, 112, 283
housing (outback Australia), 14, 37, 39, 49, 59, 70, 78–79, 100, 127, 130–31, 176, 179–80, 187, 194–95, 225–26, 279
Howse, Captain Neville, 419, 420
Howse, Col. Neville, 428–29
Howse, Dr Neville, 421, 430
Howse, Major Neville, 423
Howse, Neville, 424

Hugo, Colonel, 438, 448
Hungary in World War II, 483, 485–90
Hutt, Gov. John, 77

I
Ierissos (Greece), 514
Ilias, Major, 438, 448, 454
Imbros Island (Dardanelles), 429, 451
India in World War I, 342, 443, 463
influenza, 148, 248, 249, 293, 296, 371, 470
Ingham (Qld), 476, 515, 520
Inglis, Dr Elsie, 307, 330, 348, 393–94, 399, 401, 403
insects and protection from (outback Australia), 134, 174, 187–88, 201, 234, 283–84
International Red Cross
American Red Cross, 371
awards, 514
Bulgarians, 340
canteens, 358, 380
food parcels, 314, 424, 550, 559
Japanese, 535, 546, 549
Polish refugees, 511
transport ships, 468
volunteers, 308, 423, 431
Ipswich (Qld), 574, 595
IRA (Irish Republican Army), 477
Iran, Shah of, 511
Ireland, Maunsells' trip to, 252–53
Ireland in Travail (book), 477
Ireland in World War I, 469–70
Iron Guard (Rumania), 479, 482, 490–500, 509–10
Irving, Edward, 20–21
Irving, Sister, 524
Isivita (Papua), 586
isolation *see* loneliness (outback Australia)
Istanbul (Turkey), 491, 500–501
Italy, 335, 502

J
Jacobsen, Sister, 463
Jago, Mr (telegraph operator), 129
James, Major-General ('Digger'), 571
James, Nesta, 539, 554, 569
James Pattison (ship), 55–56
Japanese in World War II
Europeans killed in Papua, 594
Pacific campaign, 313

Papua New Guinea, 316, 577–81, 588–94
prisoner of war camps, 539–54, 569, 577, 590
Singapore, 524–32
treatment of women *see under* women in war
see also Bangka Island (Sumatra)
'JDD' (Con White's employer), 276, 290
Jeffrey, Sister Betty ('Bet' or 'Jeff'), 517–71
awards, 517, 564, 567
clothes and uniforms, 566–67
death, 518, 568
early years, 522
Japanese prisoner, 539, 541–42, 552
later career, 564–68
Malacca, 524
Matron Paschke, 531
Nurses' Memorial Centre (Melbourne), 565–66
Singapore, 524–25
This Is Your Life (tv show), 568
Vyner Brooke, SS, 315, 528–29
White Coolies (book), 551, 566–67, 568
Jessie (Aboriginal woman at Wrotham Park), 248
Jessie McPherson Hospital (Melbourne), 521
Jewish persecution in World War II, 482, 497, 499, 500, 509
Jilkminggan (NT), 216
John Murray (publisher), 477
Johnny (carpenter at Elsey Station), 181, 185
Johns Hopkins Hospital (Maryland), 398
Johnston, George, 312
My Brother Jack (book), 312
Jones, Caroline Viera, 305
Josie (Mitchell River Aboriginal woman), 256
Joyce Tweddell Building (Brisbane), 562

K
Kalamaria (Greece), 343
Kanakas (indentured labour), 476
Kanowna (troopship), 472
Kapunda (SA), 521
Karageorge (Serbian royal family), 347, 352, 409

Karratha Station (WA), 115
Katherine (NT), 175
Katherine River (NT), 175, 176
Katie (Arrernte housegirl), 153–54
Kellam, Captain (surveyor), 35, 36, 40
Kellam, Henry, 40
Kelso King, Sir George (OK's father)
death, 386
family life, 322–27
International Save the Serbs Fund, 379
King Alexander's wedding, 383–84
letters to Olive King, 356, 374–75, 382
Olive King's letters, 330, 340, 349, 352–53, 357, 365–66, 370, 374, 377–79, 386
reunion with Olive King, 383
Save Salonika appeal, 366, 373
Serb Comforts Fund, 358
Kennedy, David 'Dalton' (GM's brother), 19–20, 22
Kennedy, David (GM's father), 19, 20
Kennedy, Elizabeth (GM's sister), 22, 24, 50
see also Besley, Elizabeth (GM's sister)
Kennedy, George (GM's brother), 19
Kennedy, Georgiana *see* Molloy, Georgiana (née Kennedy)
Kennedy, Mary (GM's mother), 19, 24, 27, 57
Kennedy, Mary (GM's sister), 20, 22, 24, 57, 74–75, 76
Kennedy, Sister Mary, 311–12
Kennewell, Myrtle Rose *see* White, Myrtle Rose (née Kennewell)
Kennieson, Betty, 554, 568
Keppoch House (Scotland), 20, 21, 23, 41, 44
Kerr, Jenny, 535–36
Kerr, Sister Agnes, 401, 409
Kerwin, Dr, 239
Kidman, Sidney (later Sir), 275, 290, 295
Kimberleys, problems faced by women pioneers in, 180–81
King, Dr Hazel (OK's half-sister), 321, 324–25, 383, 384, 386

King, Georgina (OK's aunt), 323–24
King, Irene Isabella (née Rand) (OK's mother), 322
King, Lady Alicia (née Kirk) ('Belicia') (OK's stepmother), 324–25, 379, 383–84, 386
King, Nicholas (OK's half-brother), 325, 383, 384
King, Olive May Kelso, 319–86
AFAC, 326–30
affair with Artsa, 372, 374–77
affair with Yovi, 343–46, 355–56, 360, 371, 382–85 *see also* Yovitchitch, Captain Milan
ambulances *see Bridget* (ambulance); *Ella the Elephant* (ambulance)
Australia, 382–83, 386
awards, 319, 321, 340, 365–66, 382
chauffeuse, 332, 349, 350
clothes and uniforms *see* clothes and uniforms (wartime)
Corfu, 366–68
Cyprus, 386
death, 321, 386
education, 322–23, 344, 361
France, 329, 332–34, 333
Great Fire of Salonika, 361–66
Guevgueli evacuation, 337–40, 344, 348, 357
health, 355–56, 382
inheritance, 324, 329, 346, 351, 357–58, 369–70
King Alexander's wedding, 383–84
London, 379–80
Salonika, 334–42, 360–61, 373
Save the Serbs canteens, 358, 373, 376, 377, 379–82
Serb Army, in, 346, 348–50, 354, 356, 358–59, 377, 380
Serbia, 377–78, 381, 382
sport, 323, 325, 345
SWH, 307–8, 311, 330
King, Selwyn, 326, 375–76, 377
King, Sir George Kelso *see* Kelso King, Sir George (OK's father)
King, Sunny *see* Waring, Sunny (née King) (OK's sister)
King River (NT), 176
King's School (Sydney), 349

Kingsley, Private Pat, 537–38, 558
Kingston, Const. ('the Wag')
Kintore, Lord, 149
Kirk, Alicia see King, Lady Alicia (née Kirk) ('Belicia') (OK's stepmother)
kitchen, 130
Kitchen, Mary Coliway (AK's mother), 416
Kitchen, Sister Alice Elizabeth, 416–73
  1 AGH Heliopolis, 425–28, 430–35, 458
  Australia, 471–72
  awards, 415, 472
  Benalla (troopship), 417–19
  clothes and uniforms, 422, 423, 447
  Egypt, 423, 452–53
  France, 459–66
  Gascon, HMAS, 310, 414, 436–58, 442, 443
  health, 466–68
  Kanowna (troopship), 472
  letters of condolence, 434, 448, 469
  patients' deaths, 304, 310, 414, 446, 448–50, 453, 455–56
  8th Battalion, 417, 423–24, 428, 458
  Tubb VC, Captain Frederick H, 455–57
Kitchen, William Barratt (AK's father), 416
Kitchener, Lord, 419, 424–25, 460
Kitty (Aboriginal woman at Elsey Station), 194
Kokoda trail (Papua), 578–82, 586, 588
Koningsberg (warship), 418
Kraegen, Carl, 122
Kunoth, Harry, 133, 135, 149, 151
Kyarra, SS, 434

L
Lady Lamington Hospital for Women (Brisbane), 397
Lae (New Guinea), 578
Lake Elder Station see Noonameena Station (SA)
Lake Ostrovo (now Lake Vegoritis), 402, 404
Lakeland, Mrs, 226
land grants (Australia)
  Augusta (WA), 36, 40, 41
  Avon Valley (WA), 89
  Swan River Settlement (WA), 21, 25, 27–28, 31, 32

Larrikin (Aboriginal stockman at Elsey Station), 186
Lashmar, Lilla, 581–82, 594
latrine pits see lavatories (outback Australia)
laundry work (outback Australia), 144, 227
lavatories (outback Australia), 15, 180–81, 219
Layman, George, 40, 76–77, 83
Layman, Mary, 77
  see also Heppingstone, Mary
League of Nations, 313, 384
Lemnos Island (Dardanelles), 428, 429, 438–39, 446, 451, 460
Lempriere, Janey, 416, 418
Leschenault River settlement (WA), 34, 38, 73
Leslie, Tom, 229
Levey, Solomon, 25, 31
Lewis, Dr Sybil, 401
Lilian Cooper Aged Care Centre, 413
Lindley, Prof. John, 82–83
Linklater, H.T., 211
Lister, Joseph, 75
Litchfield, Jessie *(Far-North Memories),* 230
Little, Mr, 175
'Little Black Princess' see Cummings, Dolly ('Bett-Bett'; 'Little Black Princess')
Lloyd, 'Cookie,' 133, 136, 137–38
Loch, Joice NanKivell see NanKivell Loch, Joice
Loch, Sydney (JNL's husband)
  British Army, 510–12
  death, 513
  Joice and, 481, 490
  Operation Swordfish, 491, 493, 496, 501–3, 506, 507
  refugee work, 477–80
Loebok Linggun (Sumatra), 552–53
London, poverty of, 27
London School of Medicine, 396
Lone Pine (Dardanelles), 312, 454–57
loneliness (outback Australia), 10, 14, 50, 63, 72, 101, 102, 161, 170, 188, 231–32, 360
Longreach (Qld), 519
Ludlow, Kitty, 51–52
Lupescu, Magda, 479, 490
Luritja clan, 156–57
Lush, Anna (JG's mother), 168

Lushya, Countess, 478, 480–81, 491, 497–98, 500, 501, 503, 504, 508, 509, 512–13

M
MacArthur, General Douglas, 313, 578
MacAuliffe, Padre, 452
McConnel, Mary, 397
McCrae, John, 472
MacDermott, Ann (née Turner), 75
MacDonnell Ranges, 128, 162–63
Macedonia, 335–37, 341–42, 353, 400–401
McFeat, Mrs, 151
McGregor, Colin, 523–24, 560
McHardy White, Jessie, 364, 416
Mack, Louise, 306, 308, 311, 392
Maclaren King (launch), 580
McLennan, Jock ('Mac'; 'the Sanguine Scot'), 170, 171–73, 184, 189, 203, 206–7, 208, 216, 260
McLeod, Jack ('the Quiet Stockman'), 178, 182, 200–201, 203
McManus, Dick, 224, 233, 239
McManus, Paulina, 239
MacPhail, Dr Katharine, 373, 382, 384
McPhee, Colonel, 417, 446, 451
Maggie (Palmer River Aborigine woman), 225, 226, 228, 240, 248
magistrates (outback Australia), 35, 38, 43, 63, 105, 110, 144–45
mail delivery (outback Australia), 185, 188, 200
Malacca, 522–25
Malanda dairy farm (Qld), 243–46
malaria, 14, 16, 139, 167, 197, 198, 203, 204, 216, 223, 229, 234, 235, 240, 243, 250, 354–55, 357, 378, 404, 405, 409, 410, 452, 514, 545, 551–52 554, 567, 575
Malay pearling workers, 107
Malaya in World War II, 313, 524–25, 528, 535, 539, 564, 577
male-dominated domain of the Never-Never, 170–71

malnutrition and starvation, 33, 272, 371, 381, 477, 511, 538, 542, 545, 550, 554, 556
Malone, Emily, 566, 567
Malta in World War I, 454, 457
Mangarrayi people, 179, 207, 216
Mangles, Captain James, 24, 44, 64–66, 67, 69, 73–74, 75–76, 79, 80, 82, 83
Mangles, Ellen see Stirling, Ellen (née Mangles)
Mangles, James, 24
Manners, Norman, 571
Manning, Olivia, 485
Manunda (hospital ship), 558
Marie (Princess of Rumania), 383–84
Marigui cattle run (WA), 166–67, 169–70
Marigui Station (NT), 167
Marquette, SS, 335
Marra Station (NSW), 261, 262, 265, 267
Mary (Coleman River Aboriginal woman), 228, 244, 256
Mary (Queen of England), 469, 566
Marybrook (WA), 84
Masefield, John, 310, 312
Gallipoli (book), 310
Mater Misericordiae Hospital (Brisbane), 397
Mathieson, Captain Frank, 417, 433
Mathieson Frame, Mavis, 595
Maunsell, Charlie (EM's husband), 16, 218, 251, 255
bushman's skills, 232–33
death, 257
fair treatment of Aboriginal people, 228
fluency in Aboriginal languages, 228
gentleness and consideration, 237
good looks, 221
hard worker, 240
meets and marries Evelyn, 221–24
Mount Mulgrave Station, manager of, 218
quiet manner, 232
Wrotham Park station, manager of, 246–49, 248
Maunsell, Evelyn (née Evans) ('Evie'), 14, 16, 62, 218–57
care of Aboriginal people of station, 233
childhood, 219

Country Women's Association (CWA) work, 257
death, 257
fencing, 245
gardening, 233, 234
household tasks, 233, 255
journal, 233
laundry work, 227
learns from Aboriginal staff, 231
malaria, 235, 240, 243
meets and marries Charlie, 221–24
Mount Mulgrave Station, arrival at, 218, 224–25
parents' home, visit to, 281
pregnancy and childbirth, 235–39, 243, 253, 254
S'pose I Die (book), 228
support for war effort, 242–43
Wrotham Park station, 247, 248
Maunsell, Jane (CM's mother), 220, 223, 238–39
Maunsell, Phoebe (CM's sister), 220, 221
Maunsell, Ron (EM's son), 254, 255, 256, 257
Maunsell family, 222
Ballybrood (home in Ireland), 252–53
holiday to Europe, 249–54
Malanda dairy farm, 243–46, 255
move to Brisbane, 256
Rio Station (Longreach), 256–57
Mayo Clinic (Minnesota), 398
McDermott, Ann, 75
Meares, Emily Ellen, 115
see also Withnell, Emily Ellen (EW's daughter)
Meares, John, 114
medical care (outback Australia), 63, 75, 80–82, 109–10, 122–23, 139–40, 148, 157, 196, 236, 239, 249, 273
see also disease and illness
medical equipment and supplies (wartime), 425, 461, 462, 526, 528–29, 542–43, 552, 554, 559
medical officers and surgeons (wartime), 448, 461–62
medical orderlies (wartime), 399–400, 432, 443, 449
Medical Society of Queensland, 397
Meekin, Joan, 257

Melbourne Herald, 308
Mena House (Cairo), 419, 420, 425
meningitis, 467
Mersin (Turkey), 491, 493, 496, 500–505
Mexico in World War II, 482, 509
Meyer, Annie, 128, 129, 141, 149, 161
Meyer, Charlie, 161
Michael, (Crown Prince of Rumania), 490, 492
Mick (Aboriginal water boy), 137
Middleton, Mr (telegraph operator), 129
Midway Island, 582
military hospitals
AGH see Australian General Hospitals
British, 400, 411, 459
Egypt, 305, 428, 454, 457
Mena House (Cairo), 419, 420, 425
Mount Hortiack British, 342–43, 350, 361, 363–64, 401, 410
Redbank, 521
see also field hospitals
mines, floating, 508, 509, 528
mining (outback Australia), 116, 117, 128, 132, 157, 229, 246, 322
Miola (Aboriginal nursemaid at Marra Station), 261
Mitchell, Sir James, 116
Mitchell, Sir Thomas, 265
Mitchell River people (Yir Yoront), 228, 231, 232, 236–37, 240–42
Mittelheuser, Pearl ('Mitz'), 520–25, 529, 543, 545, 552–54, 563
Molloy, Amelia (GM's daughter), 68–69, 70, 84
Molloy, Captain Jack (GM's husband), 19, 21–24, 34–36, 84–85
medals, 85
meets and marries Georgiana, 19, 21–24, 26
military career, 19, 21–22
reputed royal parentage, 21–22
Resident Magistrate at Augusta, 35, 38, 40, 43, 45, 46, 63, 77
royal parentage reputed, 21–22
Molloy, Elizabeth Mary (GM's daughter), 37

Molloy, Flora (GM's daughter), 75, 79, 84

Molloy, Georgiana (GM's daughter), 80, 83

Molloy, Georgiana (née Kennedy), 14, 19–85
  Augusta settlement, 36–44, 45, 46, 47–48, 50–52, 56, 57, 65, 66, 70
  botanical studies, 20, 44, 50–51, 63, 64–69, 70, 73–74, 75–76, 77, 78, 79–80, 82–83, 85
  childhood and family, 19–20
  correspondence, 31, 32, 38, 41, 45–46, 48, 53, 62, 67–68, 76
  death, 82
  health, 57, 67, 75
  household chores, 43, 44, 49, 50, 59–60, 78–79
  meets and marries Jack, 19, 21–24, 26
  music, 68
  pregnancy and childbirth, 14, 31, 33, 34, 36, 37–38, 40, 41, 42, 43, 44, 51, 57, 63, 64, 67, 68–69, 75, 79, 80–82
  relationship with Bussell family, 42, 45, 49–50, 55, 56, 57, 71, 72–73
  religious beliefs, 20, 21, 23, 30, 57
  Swan River Settlement see also Augusta settlement above
    preparation for, 27–29
    voyage to, 28–32
  Vasse River settlement, 45, 46, 63, 66, 68, 69–71, 74–75, 76–77
  Wardandi-Bibbulmun people, and, 42–43, 53–54, 65, 68, 75

Molloy, John (GM's son), 64, 66–67, 69

Molloy, Mary Dorothea (GM's daughter), 57, 69, 70, 84

Molloy, Sabina Dunlop (GM's daughter), 44, 45, 48, 50, 51, 53, 54, 57, 62, 63, 69, 70, 83

Molloy Island, 45, 51

Monastir (Greece), 350, 357, 377, 403–5

Monbulk RSL, 210–11

Monbulk (Vic), 209–11

Monkey (Willeroo man), 194

Montenegro, 367

Mordern Station (NSW), 291–93

More Australian Legendary Tales (book), 296

Morisset, Lt Col. J.T., 229

Morisset, Rudolph, 219, 229

Mossoul, SS, 335–36

Mould, Emma, 47, 50, 56–57, 61

Mould, Henry John, 57

Mount Fisher Station (WA), 108

Mount Hortiack British military hospital see military hospitals

Mount Kaimaktsalan (Greece), 342–43, 350, 357, 403, 405, 407

Mount Mulgrave Station (Qld), 14, 16
  farewell party, 249–50
  fishing and food-collecting, 231
  garden, 234–35
  homestead and general conditions, 218–19, 224, 225–26
  sale of, 244
  station agent orders, 233
  wet season, 234

Mount Olivet Hospital and Hospice (Brisbane), 413

Mount Welcome Station (WA), 99, 103, 107

Mrs Dalloway (book), 311

Muck, Billy (Yangman rainmaker), 192, 194, 200

Mudros Harbour see Lemnos Island (Dardanelles)

Muir, Sister Sylvia, 517–71
  awards, 517
  Bangka Island memorial, 569–71
  clothes and uniforms, 530, 541, 546, 549
  Japanese prisoner, 518–19, 540–44, 546–48, 552–54
  Malacca, 522–25
  marriage and family, 560–61
  Singapore, 525–27
  survivor guilt, 519
  This Is Your Life (tv show), 568
  Vyner Brooke, SS, 315, 527–29
  youth, 519–21

Mumpaguila (Arrernte child), 135–37

Muncaster, Dr Josephine, 401

Muntok (Sumatra), 531–32, 538–39, 550

Muslims, 335

Mussolini (Benito), 502

My Boys: A Book of Remembrance (book), 210–11

My Brother Jack (book), 312

My Bush Book (book), 267, 298

N

Namatjira, Albert, 163

Nancy (emigrant ship), 90

NanKivell, Geoff (JNL's brother), 477

NanKivell, George (JNL's father), 476

NanKivell, Thomas (JNL's grandfather), 476

NanKivell Loch, Joice, 308, 474, 475–515
  author, 476–77, 487, 511, 513
  awards, 315, 475, 479–80, 514
  birth, 476
  Blue Ribbons, Bitter Bread (biography), 475, 515
  Camp of a Thousand Orphans, 510–12
  clothes and uniforms, 479
  death, 515
  Ierissos earthquake, 514
  Ireland in Travail (book), 477
  medical clinics in Ouranopolis, 513–14
  Operation Pied Piper, 491–511, 514
  Polish refugees, 478–81, 483, 484
  rug-weaving cooperative in Pirgos, 477–78, 513, 514
  The Solitary Pedestrian (book), 477
  spy mission to Hungary, 485–90
  with Sydney Loch, 481 see also Loch, Sydney (JNL's husband)
  Warszawa (troopship), 504–6

Napoleonic Wars, 21, 90

Narran River, 265, 266

National Socialist Party (Germany), 313

Neaves, William Henry, 197–98, 216

Nek (Dardanelles), 312, 454–57

Nellie (Eurasian trader), 554, 568

Neuralia (hospital ship), 453

Never-Never (outback country of northern Australia), 175
  dangers and hardships of, 169, 183–84, 195–96, 196–97
  male-dominated region, 170–71

New Guinea, 578
    see also Papua New Guinea
New Zealand, 395, 411
Newdegate, Sir Francis, 469
Newland, Martha (CP's
    grandmother), 261
Newland, Rev. W.R. (CP's
    grandfather), 261
Newland, Sophy see Field,
    Sophy (CP's mother)
Newman, Father, 580, 581, 582
newspaper reports (wartime),
    306, 308, 311, 453, 557,
    563, 564
Ngarluma people, 101–2,
    107–8, 109, 111–12
Nicholas (Tsar), 352
Nickol Bay (WA), 97, 106, 107
95th Rifle Regiment (British
    Army), 10, 19, 22
No Roads Go By (book),
    294–95, 299, 300
Noonameena Station (SA),
    267, 276, 279, 290
    aridity, 276–77, 280, 282, 291
    cattle carrying capacity, 282
    domestic staff, 284, 286–88
    floods, 291
    homestead, 281
    location, 276
    Mirrabooka outstation,
        277–81
    roads to, 277
    sale to Kidman, 290
    sand surrounding, 280, 284,
        291
    water supply, 280, 291
Noongahburrah people, 267,
    270
    see also Yuwaalaraay language
Northern Territory
    dangers of see Never-Never
        (outback country of
        northern Australia)
    map showing The Elsey and
        Riveren Station, 172
Nungerdie (Ngarluma woman),
    101, 112, 113, 114
Nurses' Memorial Centre
    (Melbourne), 565–66, 571
Nye, Dr Jarvis, 255

O

O'Brien family (owners of
    Mount Mulgrave Station),
    244
O'Harris, Pixie, 300
oil (wartime), 480, 482–84,
    490, 509
Oitanandi (Papua), 588
'Old Goggle Eye,' see
    Wooloomool, King Ebimil

'Old Nellie' (Arrernte woman
    at Elsey Station), 182, 184,
    189, 202
Ommanney, Elizabeth
    ('Bessie'), 73, 75, 84
Ommanney, Henry, 73
Ommanney, Rear-Admiral Sir
    John, 73
Oodnadatta (SA), 124
Oram, Matron Grace, 417,
    436–37
Oram, Wilma, 523, 546, 551,
    565, 568, 569
Orita, Captain, 559, 560
Osmand, J.W., 168
Osmanieh (transport ship), 429
Osterley, SS, 220
Ostrovo base hospital (Greece),
    353–54, 401–7, 409–11
Ottoman Bank (Jerusalem), 512
Ouranoupolis (formerly Pirgos,
    Greece), 477–78, 513, 515
outback Australia
    clothing, 104–5, 138–39,
        143, 150, 172–73, 183,
        188, 191–92, 202, 244
    deaths in, 37–38, 51–52, 57,
        82, 108, 109–10, 147,
        157, 193–94, 197–98,
        203, 273, 282–83
    education of children, 123,
        156
    floods, 111, 151–52, 176, 234
    food see food and cooking
        (outback Australia)
    gardening in, 38–39, 40, 63,
        68, 102, 108, 133–34,
        148, 200, 233, 248, 268
    hazards for cattle, 195–96
    heat in midsummer, 134, 282
    hotels, 89, 123, 128, 171, 175,
        203, 266, 274
    household chores, 43, 44, 49,
        50, 59–60, 78–79, 102,
        112, 283
    housing, 14, 37, 39, 49, 59,
        70, 78–79, 100, 127,
        130–31, 176, 179–80,
        187, 194–95, 225–26,
        279
    insects and protection, 134,
        174, 187–88, 201, 234,
        283–84
    Koolgardie safe, 283
    laundry work, 144, 227
    lavatories, 15, 180–81, 219
    loneliness, 10, 14, 50, 63, 72,
        101, 102, 161, 170, 188,
        231–32, 360
    magistrates, 35, 38, 43, 63,
        105, 110, 144–45
    mail delivery, 185, 188, 200

mateship, 197
medical care, 63, 75, 80–82,
    109–10, 122–23,
    139–40, 148, 157, 196,
    236, 239, 249, 273
medicinal plants, 68
mining, 116, 117, 128, 132,
    157, 229, 246, 322
snakes, 15, 122, 129, 170,
    181, 188, 225, 234, 245,
    291
telegram-sending, 126–27
termite mounds, 180
transport see transport
    (outback Australia)
    see also Never-Never
        (outback country of
        northern Australia)
Overland Telegraph Line, 114,
    120, 133, 199
Oxford University (England),
    22, 29, 32

P
Pacific Islands, 476
Padbury, Walter, 113
Palembang
    Choral Society, 549–50, 568
    prisoner of war camp,
        544–45
Palestine in World War II, 481,
    482, 491, 495, 501, 504,
    507–12
Palm Island reserve, 248
Palmer, Signals Officer, 585
Palmer River people, 226, 228
Panter, J.K., 83
Panton, J.A., 168
Papadopoulos, Mrs, 372
Papua New Guinea, 562, 576,
    594
    see also Gona Anglican
        Mission (Papua)
Papuan Infantry Battalion, 591
Paradise Road (film), 315, 516,
    567–68
Parker, Catherine Langloh (née
    Field) ('Katie'), 14, 15, 16,
    260–74
    accident, 267–68, 269
    assistance to neighbours, 273
    Australian Legendary Tales
        (book), 267, 296, 298
    birth, 260
    death, 298
    domestic skills, 268
    education, 262
    entertaining, 272
    gardening, 268
    gifts from Aboriginal
        women, 270
    Grawin South Station

(NSW), 274, 296, 297
interest in Noongahburrah
people, 270–71
learns Yuwaalaraay language,
270–71
medical assistance to
Noongahburrah people,
271–72
meets and marries Langloh
Parker, 263
More Australian Legendary Tales
(book), 296
My Bush Book (book), 267,
298
pleasures of outback life, 269
pregnancy and childbirth,
264
Randolph Stow, marriage to,
297
*Woggheeguy: Australian
Aboriginal Legends*
(book), 298
see also Bangate Station
(NSW)
Parker, Langloh (CP's husband)
Aboriginal name, 267
background, 263
bankruptcy, 296
death, 297
depression, 297
marriage to Katie, 263
mortgage, 273
see also Bangate Station
(NSW); Grawin South
Station (NSW)
Parkinson, Mavis, 316, 572,
573–96
education, 574–75
escape from Japanese, 584–92
Gona Anglican Mission,
576–84
letter to parents, 584–88
murder, 593–94
Parkinson, Mr (MP's father),
581–82
Paschke, Matron, 525–28, 531,
546, 554, 570
Passchendaele (France), 409,
410
pastoral leases, 92, 102–3
Pavey, Jack, 135
Paxton, Joseph, 64, 74, 83
Pearce, Tom, 175, 216
Pearce (servant), 36, 42, 49, 50
Pearl Harbor, 313, 577
Pearl Shell Fishery Regulation
Act (1873, WA), 112
pearling (northern Australia),
103, 107, 111–12, 116
Peckham, Henry ('the Fizzer'),
185, 188–89, 200, 216, 260
Peel, Sir Robert, 25

Peel, Thomas, 25, 31
Percival, D.K. ('Mimi'), 356,
358, 360
Perth (WA), 33, 34, 35, 42, 43,
44, 45, 47, 54, 55, 56, 57
Peters, Sister ('Pete'), 434, 438,
441
Pikersgill, Irene, 213
Pilbara (WA), 92, 114, 116
Pilsudski (President of Poland),
514
Pink, Olive, 161
Pirgos (now Ouranoupolis,
Greece), 477–78, 513, 515
Plymouth Brethren, 72
Poland in World War I, 477
Poland in World War II, 478,
481, 505–7
Polygon Wood (France), 455,
464
Popescu, Doamna (Madam),
482, 492, 496, 500, 509
Popocatepetl (Mexico), 325
Popondetta (Papua), 590–94,
595
Port Darwin (later Darwin),
120, 123, 140, 159, 169,
170, 171
Port Moresby (Papua New
Guinea), 578, 579, 581,
582, 589
Portugal, 490
Pratt, Sister Rachael, 449, 457
Preiss, Ludwig, 77
press (wartime), 306, 308, 311,
453, 557, 563, 564
Prichard, Katharine Susannah,
308
Prince of Wales, SS, 528, 534–35
Princep, Gavrilo, 305, 306
Prisoner of War Association,
560
Puckapunyal (Vic), 521
puerperal (childbed) fever, 75,
81, 262
Purcell, Tom, 39, 249, 254

Q
Quaker war relief organisations,
373, 377, 380, 477, 478,
483, 485, 489, 491,
493–94, 501–2, 511
Quambi (Woollahra house),
370
Queen Alexandra's Imperial
Army Nursing Service
(QAIANS), 308–9
Queensland, far north, 223, 226
Queensland Meat Preservative
Company, 377
Queensland Medical Women's
Society, 413

Queensland Radium Institute,
562
Quilty, Edna, Nothing Prepared
Me, 180

R
RAAF see Royal Australian Air
Force (RAAF)
Rabaul (New Britain), 577
Radji Beach massacre (Bangka
Island), 532–39, 554,
558–59, 562, 567, 569–71
RAMC see Royal Army
Medical Corps (RAMC)
Rand, Irene Isabella see King,
Irene Isabella (née Rand)
(OK's mother)
rape of women
Aboriginal women see
Aboriginal women
white women, 15, 337, 339,
374, 403, 484, 495, 526,
532, 548, 549, 578, 579,
581
Raymont, Wilhelmina ('Ray'),
543–44, 547, 552, 554
recreation, 144
Red Cross see International
Red Cross
Red Cross Blood Transfusion
Service, 313–14
Redlich, Rev. Vivian, 577,
582–83, 594
refugees (wartime)
Bessarabia, from, 484
Camp of a Thousand
Orphans, 510–12
eastern Poland, 514
Greek Orthodox, 477
Jewish, 478–79, 491–511,
495, 505
Papua New Guinea, 578–79
Polish, 477–81, 483, 484,
491–511, 512
Reid, Caroline, 401
Repatriation General Hospital
(Heidelberg), 563–64
roads (outback), 85, 122, 162,
277–78, 288–89
Robertson, George (publisher),
305
Roebourne (WA), 105–12,
113, 114, 117
Roebuck Bay (WA), 83
Rogers, Sister, 467
Rolleston, Captain, 47
Roper River (NT), 190, 199
Roper River telegraph
linesman's camp, 198
Rosanove, Joan, 308
Rosneath Manse (Scotland),
21, 23, 24, 26, 41, 63

Ross, Robina, 401
Rosy (Arrernte house girl at Elsey Station), 186, 202
Rottnest Island (WA), 31
Rouen (France), 328–30, 458, 460–66, 461
Royal Anthropological Society of Australia, 324
Royal Army Medical Corps (RAMC), 400, 425
Royal Australian Air Force (RAAF), 256
Royal Australian College of Surgeons, 412
Royal Australian Nursing Corps, 564
Royal Botanical Gardens (at Kew, Chelsea in UK), 74
Royal Botanical Gardens (England), 74
Royal Brisbane Hospital see Brisbane General Hospital (later Royal Brisbane Hospital)
Royal College of Surgeons (Edinburgh), 394
Royal Flying Doctor Service, 411
Royal Geographical Society (UK), 44
Royal Horticultural Society (UK), 64, 82
Royal Infirmary in Glasgow, 411
Royal Society (UK), 44
Rugby School (Scotland), 19
Rugby (Scotland), 19, 20, 21, 23, 27
Rumania in World War II, 383, 478–85, 490–500
see also Iron Guard (Rumania)
Rungee (Arrernte woman), 135, 145, 148–49, 154–55, 160
Russia in World War I, 352, 408, 477
see also Soviet Union in World War II
Rutland Plains Station (Qld), 226

S
Sageri (Papua), 587
St Andrew's Cathedral (Sydney), 349
St Demetrios (Salonika), 359–60, 364
St John's Cathedral (Brisbane), 595
St Mary's Anglican Church (Kangaroo Point), 412

Salamaua (New Guinea), 578
Salonika
Great Fire, 360–66, 372
homelessness, 373, 380
later Thessaloniki see Thessaloniki (formerly Salonika)
Mount Hortiack see under military hospitals
Serb Officers' Club, 345, 351, 358, 364–65
Salter, June, 567
Sam (Chinese cook at Elsey Station), 182, 183
Samsing, Sister Hilda
Benalla (troopship), 416–18
in Egypt, 422, 423, 428, 458
in England, 468, 469
in France, 459, 460, 462, 467
HMAS Gascon, 310, 435, 438, 443, 452
returns to Australia, 470–71
Sangara Mission (Papua), 581, 582, 586, 594
Sarajevo, 305, 325, 379
Sarawak, 527
Sarrail, General Maurice, 335, 368
Scandinavia in World War II, 483
Scott, Dr Jessie, 401
Scottish Women's Hospitals (SWH)
Charilaos, 343
establishment, 307, 399
field hospitals see field hospitals
Macedonia, 401–3
Mrs Harley, 349, 351
pay, 402
rules and regulations, 311, 330–31, 343, 345–46, 348, 356, 402
Serb Army, 343
Trestrail, Sister Claire, 309
Sea of Marmara, 430
Sea Ripple (sailing ship), 88–89, 93–97, 94, 154–55, 160
seasons at Cape York Peninsula, 233
Secret Service (British), 477
Seibel, Johnny, 230–31
Seine Bay (WA), 35, 40
Semmelweiss, Dr Ignaz, 75
Semphill, Hamilton, 28, 29
Serb Army
Balkan front, 334–36, 343, 353, 400–401, 408
casualties, 405
Corfu, 366–67
Kelso King's fund, 353, 377

'March of Death,' 306, 336, 346
rules and regulations, 348–49
Serbian Medical Services, 402
SWH, 343
Serbia
Austrian invasion, 305–6, 325–26, 341, 346, 352–53, 371, 378
Greater Serbian plan, 353, 366–68
homelessness, 378
under King Alexander, 383
Macedonia, 401
Servante, Mary, 263
servants and Aboriginal workers, 27–28, 33, 36, 37, 40, 47, 56, 77, 78, 134, 135, 145, 153, 186, 267, 275
Sexton, Dr Helen, 399
Shapovitch, Captain, 364
shipboard conditions, 28–29
shipwrecks, 95–96, 108–9
Sholl, Penelope, 109
Sholl, Robert J. (magistrate), 105, 110
Sholl, Treverton, 108
Sholl family, 105–6
Siai (Papua), 587–88
Siberian labour camps, 511
Sima, Horia, 497
Simmons, Dr Charles, 40
Simons, Jessie, 569
Sin Sin Yu, 231
Singapore, 524–25, 532, 538, 557
Singleton, Irene, 543
63rd Regiment (British Army), 25
Skocivir dressing station (Greece), 408
Slovenia, 371, 383
smallpox, 107–8, 116, 391
Smith, Colonel Ramsay, 425–28, 433
Smith, Lieutenant Arthur, 589–91
Smith, Val, 544, 547, 552
Smithers, Mrs, 278, 279
snakes (outback Australia), 15, 122, 129, 170, 181, 188, 225, 234, 245, 291
soldiers' war injuries
abdominal wounds, 445, 446, 453
amputations, 400, 443–45, 458, 466
blinded by gas, 471
burns, 456–57
cerebro-spinal fever, 466

dehydration, 430, 446–47
dysentery, 400, 420–21, 446–47, 450–52, 454, 502–3, 551–52
enteric fever, 433, 446–47, 454
fear of pity, 468–69
frostbite, 457–58, 465
gangrene, 400, 430, 458
infestations of fleas and lice, 444, 447
patients' deaths, 446, 448–50
plagues, 404–5, 409, 451
septic wounds, 310
shell shock, 433, 444–45, 462, 466
stretcher cases, 442–43
syphilis, 420–21, 427
trench fever, 466
trench foot, 405, 466
trench warfare, 399, 444, 460, 464, 470, 520
typhoid, 400, 418, 433, 447, 454, 502, 506
typhus epidemic, 408
war as mass murder, 308, 310, 414, 432, 456, 470, 472
Solomon and Gluckstein's Bank, 495
Somme (France), 466
South, Vernon, 151
Southwell Gardens (London), 468
Soviet Union in World War II, 483–84, 493, 495, 511
see also Russia in World War I
Spanish influenza *see* influenza
Spencer, Prof. Walter Baldwin, 132, 149
The Native Tribes of Central Australia (book), 132, 135, 147
S'pose I Die (book), 228
squatters, 102
Squire, Mr (telegraph operator), 129
Sri Lanka, 528
Stalin, Josef, 484
Staples, Mr (gardener), 28, 43, 51
Statham, Frank, 569–71
Stirling, Captain James (later Governor), 22–23, 24–25, 32, 34–35, 36, 38, 40, 42, 43–44, 45, 77, 85
see also Swan River Settlement (WA)
Stirling, Ellen (née Mangles), 34, 43–44, 64, 69, 77
Stirling, Mary, 401
Stirling (Scotland), 394–95

stock animals, 27, 60, 88, 95–96, 99, 136, 245
stockmen, 15, 166, 170, 171, 173, 175, 179, 183, 184, 194, 195, 198, 201, 203, 205, 208, 219, 227, 228–29, 240, 249, 264, 283, 421, 1809
Story, Helen ('Nellie'), 20, 21, 23, 26, 30, 31, 38, 41, 46, 53, 57, 62, 63, 67
Story, Rev. Robert, 21, 26, 38
Stow, Randoph Percy, 297
Strehlow, Carl, 129, 147, 148
Strehlow, Frieda, 128, 129, 141, 148, 161
Strehlow Research Centre (Alice Springs), 148
stretcher bearers, 456, 464
Strong, Bishop Philip, 577–80
Stuart, John McDouall, 162
Stuart Highway, 162
Stuart (later Alice Springs), 128
suffragettes, 330, 348
Sulphur (transport ship), 45
Sumatra *see* Bangka Island (Sumatra)
supplies and rations for settlers, 27, 45, 88, 100, 133, 141, 172–73, 185, 187, 233, 245, 247, 281
Sutherland, Henry Charles, 84
Suttee, Dave ('Dan'), 177, 202–3, 208
swagmen, 15, 183
Swan River Association, 24–25, 29, 31
Swan River Settlement (WA), 22–23, 24–26, 84
early days, 32–33
land grants, 25, 26, 27, 31, 32, 35
publication of, 25, 26
Swan River (WA), 22, 24, 25, 31, 32, 34, 35, 36, 60, 66
Sweetman, Thomas, 57
SWH *see* Scottish Women's Hospitals (SWH)
Sydney, HMAS, 418
Sydney Grammar School, 349
Sydney High School for Girls, 391–92
Sydney Morning Herald, 376
Syer, ('Mickey'), 521, 568
Symons, Lieutenant William, 457
syphilis, 420, 421, 427
Szabo, Violette, 315

T
Talbot motor car, 157–58
Tapiedi, Lucian, 582, 594

Taube aircraft, 441
Taylor, Carrie (JG's sister), 168, 205
Taylor, Jeannie *see* Gunn, Jeannie (née Taylor)
Taylor, Mabel, 156
Taylor, Patrick, 55–56
Taylor, Thomas (JG's father), 166, 209
Telegraph, 376
telegraph linesman (outback Australia), 15, 16, 126, 128, 133, 190, 198, 199, 201, 212
Tennant, Kylie, 300
Terrick, John, 209–10
The Euahlayi Tribe: A Study of Aboriginal Life in Australia (book), 297–98
The Floral Calendar (magazine), 76
The Little Black Princess (book), 190, 191, 205, 208–9
The Making of Monbulk (book) *see My Boys: A Book of Remembrance* (book)
The Native Tribes of Central Australia (book), 132, 135, 147
The Solitary Pedestrian (book), 477
therapeutic radiography, 561–62
Thessaloniki (formerly Salonika), 381, 477, 513, 514
see also Salonika
Third Reich, 313
This Is Your Life (TV show), 568
Thoodoo (Ngarluma woman), 101, 112, 113, 114
Throssell, Captain Hugo, 457
'thunder box' *see* lavatories (outback Australia)
Tionda (Papuan), 592–93
Todd, Charles, 157
toilets *see* lavatories (outback Australia)
Tom (Arrernte man), 146–47
Tony (Maunsell family employee), 256
Topkapi Palace (Turkey), 500
Topsy (Aboriginal woman at Wrotham Park), 248
Torres Strait Islands, 562
transport (outback Australia)
buckboards (wagons), 13, 124, 125, 129, 150, 151, 152, 176, 177, 178, 181, 224, 225, 238, 240, 288

buggies, 10, 13, 104, 122, 124, 125, 128, 129, 130, 141, 149–50, 151, 152, 160, 161, 167, 179, 220, 224, 265, 266, 272, 285–86

bullock wagons, 97, 98, 105, 106, 113, 172, 184, 185, 188, 189, 229, 233, 245, 281, 361

camel trains, 123, 124, 133, 141, 144, 146, 154, 277, 278, 281, 283

motor cars, 158–59, 277–78, 291–92

roads, 85, 122, 162, 277–78, 288–89

train, 121, 123–24, 152, 171, 221, 224, 239, 243, 265–66

transport ships *see under individual names*

Transylvania in World War II, 485, 486

Treaty of Versailles, 312–13

Trestrail, Sister Claire, 309

Trotter, Florence ('Flo'), 520–21, 526, 541–42, 569

Troyes field hospital (France), 332–34, 333

Tryphena ('Tryff,' Arrernte woman), 129–30

Tubb VC, Captain Frederick H, 455–57, 464, 472

tuberculosis, 140, 464, 547, 569

Tucker, Ella, 438

Tulcea (Rumania), 498

Turkey in World War I, 429, 435, 440–41, 453, 455, 458

Turkey in World War II, 494, 500

Turner, Ann, 48

Turner, Ethel, 392

Turner, James, 30, 35, 36, 40, 48

Turner family, 35, 36, 48

Tweddell, Sister Joyce ('Tweedie'), 517–71
awards, 517
'comfort women,' 546
death, 518, 562
Japanese prisoner, 532, 548, 552–53, 555–57
Malacca, 522–25
therapeutic radiography, 561–62
training, 520–21
Vyner Brooke, SS, 315, 527, 529

typhoid, 108, 110, 127, 157, 377, 378, 400, 404, 408, 418, 433, 446, 447, 450, 454, 466, 501, 502, 506, 552

Tyson, James ('Jim'), 264, 270–71, 273

U

Underwood, Terry, 9–12

uniforms *see* clothes and uniforms (wartime)

United States in World War II, 482, 494–95, 579, 583, 585, 586

Upper Dobodura (Papua), 591, 593

V

Vasse River settlement (WA), 34, 38, 45, 46, 50, 52, 54, 55, 56, 61, 66, 68, 69–71, 73, 74–75, 76–77, 83

Vasse River (WA), 42, 45, 58, 63

venereal disease, 311, 421, 428

Venizelos, Eleutherios, 336

Vestey Meatworks (Darwin), 214

Victoria Cross (medal), 455, 456, 457

Victoria (Queen of England), 38, 46

Vietnamese orphans, 568

Voluntary Aid Detachment workers (VADs), 307, 326, 334, 336–39, 341, 381, 401–2, 417, 460–62

Vyner Brooke, Sir Charles, 527

Vyner Brooke, SS, 315, 527–29, 532–34, 539, 540, 546, 563, 567, 569

W

WAAF *see* Women's Auxiliary Air Force (WAAF)

Wade, Sir Charles, 380

wages for pastoral workers, 216

Wake, Nancy, 315

Wallace, Abraham, 168

Wanganella, SS, 522–23

war crimes tribunals, 559–60, 592

Ward, Colonel, 264

Wardandi-Bibbulmun people, 40, 41, 42, –43, 44, 45, 53–54, 59, 60–62, 65, 68, 70, 71, 75, 76–77, 81, 84

Ware, Bishop Kallistos, 515

Waring, Harold, 322, 325, 385

Waring, Sunny (née King) (OK's sister), 322, 325, 326, 327, 340, 350–51, 355, 365, 375, 377, 379, 383, 385

Warrior (ship), 28, 29, 30, 31, 89, 104

Warszawa (troopship), 504–6, 508–9

water supply, 127, 130, 138

Waterloo, Battle of, 21

We of the Never-Never (book), 11, 166, 170, 175, 178, 181, 184, 205, 207, 209, 215, 229, 267, 300

We of the Never-Never (film), 215

Webb War Crimes Commission, 592

Wedge, Mr (surveyor), 104

Wedge family, 104–5

Welcome, Mt (WA), 99

Wellard, John, 97, 113

Wellington, Duke of, 85

Wesley Hospital (Brisbane), 518

Westminster Abbey, 594

whalers, 60, 69, 261

wheat cultivation, 50–51

White, Alan (MW's son), 286, 288–90, 299

White, Cornelius (MW's husband) ('Con'), 274
Adelaide houses, 293, 298
death, 298
early life, 274
Ford car, 288–90
health, 275, 290, 296
marriage to Myrtle, 276
Mordern Station, 291–93
see also Noonameena Station (SA)

White, Doris (MW's daughter), 276, 282–83, 298

White, Garry (MW's son), 290, 299

White, Matron Jessie McHardy, 364, 416

White, Myrtle Rose (née Kennewell), 13, 14, 15, 16, 274–300
Adelaide houses, 293, 298
birth, 260
childhood, 274
death, 300
domestic servant, 275
guesthouse, 298, 300
health, 293
meets and marries Con, 275–76
Mordern Station, 291–93
No Roads Go By (book), 294–95, 299, 300
orders supplies, 281
pregnancy and childbirth, 285–86, 288
provides medical assistance, 278–79, 287
From That Day to This (book), 300

For Those That Love (book), 300
travel to Mirrabooka, 277–78
travel to Noonameena, 280
weekly routine, 283
Wonnaminta, 294
see also Noonameena Station (SA)
White Coolies (book), 551, 566–67, 568
Wight, Sister, 535
Wilhelm (Kaiser), 306, 470
Willeroo people, 185, 190, 194
Williams, Elizabeth *see* Allchurch, Elizabeth (AB's sister-in-law)
Wilson, Francesca, 483
Wilson, President Woodrow, 371
Wilton, Sister Mona, 534
Windelup (WA), 59, 61
Winnecke goldfields, 156
Withnell, Emily Ellen (EW's daughter), 108, 110, 115
see also Meares, Emily Ellen
Withnell, Emma Mary (née Hancock), 13, 14, 16, 62, 88–117
achievements, 116
assists Scholl family, 106–7
childhood, 90–92
death, 116
Esselmont at Northam, 115
Karratha Station investment, 115
marriage to John, 91–92
pregnancy and childbirth, 88, 93, 99–100, 109, 112, 113
relationships with Aborigines, 101, 114, 116
Roebourne memorial, 117
sense of humour, 111
teaching children, 112
Withnell, George (EW's son), 115
Withnell, Grace (EW's daughter), 114
Withnell, Herbert (EW's son), 114
Withnell, James (EW's son), 116
Withnell, John (EW's husband), 88–92, 99, 103, 114, 115
Withnell, Lilla (EW's daughter), 114
Withnell, Martha (JW's mother), 90
Withnell, Mary Ann (JW's sister), 90

Withnell, Robert Harding DeWitt (EW's son), 100
Withnell, Robert (JW's brother), 88, 101
Withnell, William (EW's son), 114
Withnell, William (JW's father), 28, 90
Withnell family, 88–117
assists Scholl family, 106–7
butcher's shop, 107, 109
Guildford, 114
Harding River pastoral lease, 102–3
lighter boating business, 107
locations named after family, 116–17
relationships with Aborigines, 101, 114, 116
Sherlock River Station, 102–3, 107, 113–14
shipwreck and financial loss, 108–9
travel to Pilbara, 93–99
Woggheeguy: Australian Aboriginal Legends (book), 298
Wollaston, John (son), 78
Wollaston, Rev. John (father), 77–79, 81
women in war
ambulance drivers, 308, 328, 330, 343
army nurses, status of, 421, 425–28
'comfort women,' 518, 545–49
decoders, 313
employment at home, 308, 313–14
German atrocities, 306
hospital ships, on *see* hospital ships
Japanese treatment of, 518–19, 521, 526, 531–32, 542–45, 553–54, 559–60, 578–79, 581, 582
medicine, in, 308, 390, 393–99, 413
reporters, 306, 308, 311, 392
rules and regulations, 310–11
transport drivers, 313
VADs *see* Voluntary Aid Detachment workers (VADs)
war artists, 313
women (outback Australia)
Aboriginal *see* Aboriginal women
achievements in science, 85
lack of recognition, 82–83

rape *see* rape of women
role of, 78–79, 122, 171
support for one another, 83, 148
Women's Auxiliary Air Force (WAAF), 313
Women's Employment Board, 313–14
Women's Royal Australian Navy Service (WRANS), 313
Wonnaminta Station (NSW), 291, 294
Woodbrook (WA property), 108
Woolf, Virginia, 308, 311, 322
Mrs Dalloway (book), 311
Wooloomool, Katie, 190
Wooloomool, King Ebimil ('Old Goggle Eye') (elder of Yangman people), 190, 191, 192–94
World War I, 84, 161, 242–43, 305, 307, 309, 311, 312, 420
see also under individual countries
World War II, 214, 256, 298–99, 411
see also under individual countries
Worth, Ellen Amelia, 115
WRANS *see* Women's Royal Australian Navy Service (WRANS)
Wrotham Park Station (Qld), 234, 246–49, 250, 254

Y
Yamasaki, Colonel, 519, 542, 544, 547, 550, 554–55, 559–60, 564
Yangman people, 179, 190–94, 202, 205, 207, 216
Yariri, Father John, 587–88
Yeeramukadoo pool (WA), 99, 114
Yellac dressing station (Greece), 408–9
YMCA, 358
Young, Wilma *see* Oram, Wilma
'Young Nellie' (Arrernte woman at Elsey Station), 202
Yovitchitch, Captain Milan ('Yovi')
affair with Olive King, 343–49, 355–56, 360, 371, 382–85
Alexander (Crown Prince of Serbia), 352, 354, 360
career, 366, 368–69, 375, 385
Corfu, 368–69

death, 385
engagement, 347, 351–52,
    374, 375
Greater Serbian plan, 353,
    366–68
Mrs Harley, 351
Ostrovo base hospital, 409
photograph of, 321–22, 347
wounded, 347–48
Ypres (France), 464
Yuwaalaraay language, 265, 267,
    270
Yuwaalaraay people, 261

Z
Zealandia (ship), 522